CREDIT AND COLLECTION
PRINCIPLES AND PRACTICE

Credit and Collection Principles and Practice

ALBERT F. CHAPIN

GEORGE E. HASSETT, Jr.

Professor of Finance
New York University

SEVENTH EDITION

New York   Toronto   London

McGraw-Hill Book Company, Inc.

1960

PREFACE

When Albert Chapin and I undertook the present revision of the sixth edition of "Credit and Collection Principles and Practices" it was, of course, in the expectation of being coauthors throughout the entire work. However, we had arrived only at the formulation of our new definition of credit (which we hoped would prove a positive contribution to the field), and then Professor Chapin was no longer with us. In spite of this great loss, it was decided to proceed with the work, and at length, with the able assistance of many friends, the revision was completed.

About two-thirds of the book was changed in the process. Grouping of chapters was made along functional lines. The four groups are: Fundamentals of Credit, Credit Investigation and Analysis, Financial Analysis, and Protection and Redemption of Credit. Chapters were substantially rewritten and rearranged, particularly those concerning Financial Statement Analysis. Review questions in several chapters were revised.

An expression of appreciation is wholeheartedly given to E. B. Moran, Executive Vice President, National Association of Credit Management, and to his associates W. McAdam and R. Weatherly; to many credit executives including P. Mears of Dun & Bradstreet, Inc.; A. Thevenet of National Credit Office, Inc.; E. Leone of Manufacturers Trust Company; R. Severa of Credit Bureau of Greater New York; L. Sullivan of Lyon Furniture Mercantile Agency; E. C. Braynard of American Credit Indemnity Company; Miss L. Seldo, C.P.C.U. An expression of thanks is given Prof. Herbert Edwards of New York University, who painstakingly read the manuscript and made many valuable suggestions. Finally, thanks to my wife for her continuous assistance.

George E. Hassett, Jr.

CONTENTS

Preface v

PART I. THE FUNDAMENTALS OF CREDIT

1. Credit and Its Functions 3

The Nature of Credit. A Comprehensive Definition. Credit Is Accepted Not Given. The Credit Problem. Credit and Wealth. The Limit of the Credit Economy. Use of Credit. The Abuse of Credit. The Margin between Success and Failure. The Business Cycle. Phases of the Business Cycle. Causes of Business Cycles. Nature of Business Cycles. Indices of Business Conditions. Four Phases of Business Cycles.

2. The Credit Executive 22

Development of Credit Work. The Credit Executive's Position. The Future of the Credit Executive. Qualifications of the Credit Executive. The Educational Qualifications of the Credit Executive. Credit as a Field of Occupation.

3. The Organization and Function of Credit Departments in Business Organizations 32

The Credit Department's Function. Its Place in the Business Organization. Relation to Sales Department. The Independent Credit Department. The Personnel of the Credit Department. Importance of System. Mechanical Aids to Credit Department Efficiency. The Mercantile Credit Department Files. The Customers' Ledger. Importance of Office Mechanism. The Bank Credit Department. The Functions of the Bank Credit Department. Structure of the Bank Credit Department. The Bank Credit Folder. Branch-office Credit Control. Branch-bank Credit Control. Measurement of Credit Department Efficiency.

4. Factors of a Satisfactory Credit Risk 47

The Acceptable Credit Risk. The Four C's of Credit. Acceptability Varies with Policy. Reasons for Varying Policies. Credit Policy and Merchandising Attitude. Analysis of Credit and Analysis of Credit Reputation. Character. Appraising Character. Capacity. Capital. Condition of Business. Comparative Values of Credit Factors.

5. Documents and Records of Credit Transactions. 58

Credit and Documents of Credit. Classes of Documentary Credit. The Book Account. Negotiable Instruments. Essentials of Negotiability. Negotiation. Notice of Protest for Nonpayment. Promissory Notes. Special Forms of Notes. Bonds. Shares of Stock.

6. Documentary Credit 70

Checks. Stopping Payment on Checks. Certified Checks. Cashier's Checks. The "Bad Check" Law. The Bill of Exchange or Draft. The Trade Acceptance. Trade Acceptance Procedure. Bank Acceptances. Travelers' Checks. Warehouse Receipts and Bills of Lading. Letters of Credit. The Trust Receipt. In General.

7. Activities of the National Association of Credit Management 90

The National Association of Credit Management. The Local Associations. Fraud Prevention Department. The Credit Research Foundation. The Graduate School of Credit and Financial Management. The National Institute of Credit. The New York Institute of Credit. Other Activities of the National Association. Publications. Achievements of the National Association. The Robert Morris Associates.

PART II.   CREDIT INVESTIGATION AND ANALYSIS

8. Investigating Credit Factors 103

Points to Be Investigated. In General. Type of Business. Legal Composition. Single Proprietorships. Partnerships. Corporations. Estate Ownership. Trusts, Joint Stock Companies, Cooperative Societies. Location. Record of Concern and Owners. Investigating the Financial Position. Credit in the Industry.

9. Sources of Information 115

Facts and Opinions the Basis of Judgment. Judgment in Selecting Sources. Credit Application. Personal Knowledge. Customer's Record. The Personal Interview. How to Conduct the Interview. Plant Visits. Financial Statements. Correspondence. Indirect Sources. Bank Stories. Trade Stories. The Mercantile Agencies. Prejudices Overcome. Advantages of Cooperation. The Agency and the Law. In General. Attorneys. Public Records, Clippings, and Miscellaneous. Summary.

10. Operation and Services of the Bank Credit Department 127

Credit Classified. Public Credit. Investment Credit. Importance of Investment. A Bank Defined. Banking Credit. Effect of Bank Credit. Bank and Mercantile Credit. Bank Credit Standards. Bank and Client Relationship. Bank Service Charges. Par Payment of Checks. Kinds of Loans. Credits of Persons and Property. Single-name, Double-name, and Accommodation Paper. The Commercial Paper Broker. Reasons for Favor with Banks. The Credit Process in Banks. Type of Work in the Bank Credit Department. Personal Investigations. Qualifications of Investigator. Investigation by Telephone. Information Secured by Investigators. Legal Aspects of Credit Information. Establishing a Credit Line.

Credit Limits. Banks as Sources of Information. Information from Banks. Interpretation of Bank Information. The Bank as Inquirer.

11. Sales Finance and Factoring Companies 152

Origin. Finance Company Operations. Hypothecation of Accounts Receivable. Advances and Charges. Advantages to the Borrower. Disadvantages of Hypothecation. Assignment of Accounts Receivable to Banks. Factors. Factors' Functions. Factors' Capital Funds. Factors' Charges. The Factors' Credit Department. Advantages and Disadvantages of Factors. Legal Aspect of Factoring. Factors' and Finance Companies' Services Compared. Field Warehousing.

12. Trade Credit 165

Trade Credit Defined. Function of Trade Credit. Old and Modern Attitude toward Credit. Trends in Trade Credit. Terms of Sales. The Credit Period. The Practice of Dating. Season Datings. Indirect Datings. Dating for Distant Territory. Competitive Dating. Nomenclature of Terms. C.B.D. Terms. C.O.D. Terms. Cash Terms. E.O.M. and M.O.M. Terms. Proximo Terms. R.O.G. and A.O.G. Terms. Discount Terms. History of the Cash Discount. The Cash Discount Analyzed. Factors Influencing the Cash Discount. The Value of Good Credit. Interpretation of Terms of Sale. Handling the Orders. Analysis of Measure of Risk. Classification of Credit Risk. Credit Limits. Factors of Influence in Placing Merchandise Credit Limits. Methods in Use in Fixing Limits. Revision of Credit "Lines."

13. Retail, Consumer, and Instalment Credit 190

Definitions. Consumer Credit Institutions. Retail and Trade Credit Contrasted. The Trade Credit Manager and Retail Credit. Is Retail (Consumer) Credit Justified? Consumer Loan Credit. Licensed Lenders. Loan Sharks. Costs of Making Small Loans. Credit Unions. Personal Loan Departments of Commercial Banks. Industrial Banks. The Proper Basis for Retail Credit. Credit Application. Sources of Retail Credit Information. Retail Credit and Competition. Retail Credit Terms. Trends in Retail Credit. Instalment Credit. Extent of Instalment Sales. Instalment Terms. Financing Instalment Sales. The Instalment Sale Contract. Instalment-payment Interest Rates. Credit Limits. Use and Abuse of Instalment Credit.

14. The General Agency—Dun & Bradstreet, Inc. 211

Origin and Growth Sketched. Present Extent of Dun & Bradstreet, Inc. Organization of Dun & Bradstreet, Inc. The Reporting and Service Department. Sources of Information. Reporters. Correspondents. Trade Reports. Types of Reports. Interpretation of Reports. Reference Book Department. Interpretations of Dun & Bradstreet Ratings. The Use of the Reference Book. Credit Clearing House, a Division of Dun & Bradstreet. International Division. Municipal Service Division. The Mercantile Claims Division. The Marketing Services Company. Dun & Bradstreet Publications Corporation. Additional Agency Services. Discussion of the Agency Service. Limitations of the Agency.

15. **Special Credit Agencies as a Source of Credit Information** 235

Special Agencies. Advantages and Disadvantages. National Credit Office, Inc. The Bank Service Department. Market Planning Service. Textiles. Credit Reports. C.I.A. Report. Other Departments. Lyon Furniture Mercantile Agency. Method of Operation. Collection Department. Discussion of Agency Service. The Interchange of Credit Experience.

16. **Credit Interchange Service** 250

A Specialized Service. Service without Profit. A Means to Avoid Duplication. Need for National Clearance. Organization of the National Credit Interchange System. Operation of the National Credit Interchange System. Protection against Fraud. Analysis of Interchange Report. Comparison of Reports. In Conclusion. The National Retail Credit Association. Credit Bureau of Greater New York. Services for Members. Automatic Warning Services. Summary. Group Exchanges. Operation of Group Exchanges. Advantages and Disadvantages.

17. **Salesmen, Attorneys, and Miscellaneous Sources of Information** 271

Salesman as Credit Assistant. Salesman's Attitude to the Credit Department. The Salesman's Credit Information. Reliability of Salesman's Information. How to Educate the Salesman. Attorneys as Sources of Information. Type of Attorney Report. How to Use Attorney. Personnel Agencies. The Credit Manager as a Business Builder. The Accountant.

PART III. ANALYSIS OF THE FINANCIAL REPORT

18. **The Financial Report** 287

A Source of Information. Procuring the Statement. Reasons for Submitting Statements. Objections Frequently Encountered. Financial Statement Forms. False Financial Statements. The Continuing and Acceleration Clauses. The Federal Law. New York False Financial Statement Laws.

19. **Financial Statement Interpretation and Asset Analysis** 304

Statement Nomenclature. Purpose of Financial Statement. Authority for Statement Facts. The Accountant's Report. Liability of Accountant. Accountant versus Credit Manager. Methods of Analysis. The Date of the Statement. Classification of Statement Items. Purpose of Analysis. Cash. Accounts Receivable Trade. Discounted Receivables. Pledged Receivables. Notes Receivable. Trade Acceptances. Reserve for Doubtful Accounts. Inventory. Inventory Accuracy. Inventory Valuation. Inventory Analysis. Marketable Securities. Other Current Assets. Miscellaneous Assets. Fixed Assets. Plant, Machinery, and Tools. Furniture and Fixtures. Deferred Assets. Intangible Assets.

20. **Appraisal of Liabilities and Working Capital Analysis** 324

Creditors Classified. Current Liabilities. Accounts Payable. Notes or Bills Payable. Accrued Liabilities. Reserves for Taxes. Deposits. Current Long-term Debt. Long-term Debt. Bonds. Mortgages. Subordinated Debt. Reserves. Capital Stock. Surplus. Capital or Net

Worth. How Much Net Worth? Tangible Net Worth. Contingent Liabilities. Balance-sheet Relationships. The 2 to 1 Current-ratio Fallacy.
Working Capital. Working and Current Assets. The Acid Test. Adequacy of Current Position. Summary of Current Position Analysis.

21. Income Analysis 338

Analyzing the Income Report. Form of Income Statement. The Me-
chanics of Income Account Analysis. Significance of Income Items. Cost
of Goods Sold. Sales: Selling Expense. Sales: Officers' Salaries. Sales:
Net Profit. Analysis of Expense. Net Profit. Reconciliation of the
Surplus Account. Insurance. Fire Insurance. Adequate Fire Insurance.
Coinsurance. The Moral Hazard and Insurance. Liability Insurances.
Life Insurance. The Investigation of Life Insurance. Mandatory In-
surances. Other Insurance. Summary.

22. Ratios, Their Computation and Uses in Financial Analysis 355

The Selection of Ratios. Standard Ratios. Compensating Ratios. Facts
Disclosed by Sales. Sales to Receivables. Sales to Inventory. Sales to
Net Working Capital. Sales to Fixed Assets. Sales and Net Worth. Re-
ceivables to Merchandise. Net Worth to Debt. Net Worth and Fixed
Assets. Net Working Capital to Inventory. Overtrading.

23. Comparative Statement Analysis and Special Analyses 371

Methods of Comparative Analysis. Method of Setting up Statement for
Comparison. The Common-size Statement. "Where-got, Where-gone"
Statements. Comparison by Inspection. Progressive Base Year and Base-
year Trend. Comparative Analysis of Profit and Loss Statement. Source
and Application of Funds. The Trial Balance. Trial Balance Analysis.
Break-even Point Analysis.

PART IV. THE PROTECTION AND REDEMPTION OF CREDIT

24. Collections 391

Collection Problem Varied. Credit Manager Logically in Charge. Importance of the Problem. Reasons for a "Close" Collection Policy. Reasons
for Slow Payments. Types of Debtors. The Marketing Plan and the
Collection Policy. Collection Competition. Necessity of a Systematic Collection System. Follow-up Systems. The Customers' Ledger. The Collection Tickler. Maturity Lists. The Duplicate Invoice System. A
Collection Letter Follow-up.

25. Collection Tools 405

The Invoice. The Statement. The Collection Letter. The Note as a Col-
lection Instrument. Collecting by Draft. The Use of the Telephone. The
Telephone in Long-distance Collections. The Telegram. The Personal
Collector. The Salesman. The Collection Agency. The Local Attorney.

26. Collection Letters 417

Why the Collection Letter Is Used. The Fate of the Collection Letter.
The Writer's Mental Attitude. The Legal Side of Collection Letters. Why

Letters "Pull." Five Types of Appeal. Value of Repetition. Timing the Appeal. Stages to Collection Procedure. Letter Suggestions. What to Avoid in a Letter. The Use of Form Letters. Specimen Letters.

27. **Other Collection Aids and Problems** 435

The Treasurer's Letter. The Salesman's Letter. Collecting Interest on Overdue Accounts. Collecting Unearned Cash Discounts. Purpose of Cash Discount. Why Abuse Is Condoned. Partial Payments. Delinquent Lists. Legal Restrictions of Creditor Agreements. Offering Delinquent Accounts for Sale. The Suit and Judgment. Executing the Judgment. Property Exemptions. Examination in Supplementary Proceedings. Charging Off Bad Debts.

28. **The Creditor's Legal Aids** 450

What Constitutes a Contract. When Does Title Pass? Cancellations and Returns. The Unpaid Seller's Lien. The Right of Stoppage in Transit. Right of Rescission. The Right of Replevin. Legal Procedure. The Right of Attachment. Grounds for Attachment. Enforcement of Rights. Garnishment. The Bulk Sales Law. Variations in the Laws. Interpretation of the Statutes. Creditors' Remedies.

29. **The Insolvent Account** 465

Reasons for Insolvency. Credit Losses. The Meaning of Insolvency. Various Degrees of Insolvency. Rehabilitation and Liquidation. Friendly Adjustments. Extensions. When to Support the Extension Agreement. Legal Aspects of the Extension. Composition Settlements. When Is a Composition Settlement Justified? Assignments. Advantages and Disadvantages of Assignment. Receiverships. Causes for Equity Receiverships. Duties of the Receiver. Creditors' Rights in Equity Receiverships. The Bankruptcy Receivership.

30. **Bankruptcy** 482

The Credit Executive's Interest in Bankruptcy. Bankruptcy Laws of the United States. The "Depression Amendments." Options under the Law. Who May Become Bankrupt. The Acts of Bankruptcy. Trial. Duties of the Bankrupt. Discharge in Bankruptcy. Reasons for the Denial of Discharge. Officers and Their Duties. Provable and Allowable Claims. Filing Proof of Claims. Order of Priority. Dischargeable Debts. Arrangements. Effect of Law on Arrangement. Corporate Reorganizations. Wage Earners' Plans. Agricultural Compositions and Extensions. Other Provisions of the Act. Real Property Arrangements. Protecting the Creditors' Interest. Examination of Debtor. Reclamation Proceedings. Turnover Proceedings. A Few Interesting Facts.

31. **Adjustment Bureaus** 509

Inception of Adjustment Bureaus. Functions of the Adjustment Bureau. Membership Responsibility. Instructions to Creditors' Committees. Origin of Estates. Conduct of Creditors' Meetings. Forms of Control. Friendly Liquidations. Extensions. Compromise Settlements. Receiverships. Bankruptcies. Protection against Unapproved Practices. Field

Men. An Investigation Exemplified. Achievements of the Adjustment Bureau. The Future of Adjustment Bureaus.

32. **Credit Insurance and Guaranties** 520

Credit Insurance. Development of Credit Insurance Companies. Credit Insurance Policies. Classification of Business Lines. Coinsurance. Coverage. Primary Loss. Premium. Insolvency. Claim Settlement. Application for Policy. Credit Insurance Discussed. The Increase of Sales through Credit Insurance. Fire and Credit Insurance. Losses Passed on to the Insured. Who May Become Guarantors. The Form of the Contract of Guaranty.

Appendixes 541

Bibliography 575

Index 577

PART I

THE FUNDAMENTALS OF CREDIT

CHAPTER 1

CREDIT AND ITS FUNCTIONS

The Nature of Credit. Credit so thoroughly pervades the everyday transactions of modern society that the meaning of the word "credit" is generally assumed to be known, and yet no single definition has been found acceptable to a majority of writers. Like many of the terms used in economics, credit has a variety of meanings, evolving from different usages.[1] Thus a working definition of credit is needed.

No consideration of the word "credit" would be complete which did not include its etymology. It is derived from the Latin *credo*, "I believe," and *credo* itself is a combination of two older words—the Sanscrit *crad* meaning "trust" and the Latin *do* meaning "to place." Thus, we have credit as faith or confidence that is engendered between a debtor and creditor which may result in the transfer of value in the present, the payment being deferred to the future.

When an attempt is made to define credit, it is found difficult, unless a concept of potential credit is used, to express in a single definition more than one of several viewpoints. We may place credit definitions in two main classes: those which regard credit as a potentiality and those which regard credit as an actuality. Illustrative of the first class is the definition: "Credit is the power to obtain goods or service by giving a promise to pay money (or goods) on demand or at a specified date in the future" (Joseph French Johnson); while the conception of credit as an actuality is illustrated by the definition: "A credit is the present right to a future payment" (H. D. MacLeod). According to the first definition, credit is regarded as the possession of a power which may or may not have been utilized; while in the second, credit has become debt

---

[1] In the field of accounting, the term "credit" has a specific and technical meaning. The bookkeeper understands the word to denote an entry to record a sale made, or a liability incurred, or an increase in a capital account, or an offset to an asset account. In other words, it is an entry on the right side, in American usage, of an account in a set of bookkeeping records. Entries on the left side of the account are debits. It would appear that the commonly accepted meaning of the word "credit" grew out of this accounting practice.

through the exercise of the power. The definitions cited are also illustrative of credit as defined from the viewpoints of the borrower (debtor) and the lender (creditor), respectively. That there is no real conflict of thought but merely a stressing of different elements by different writers is shown by a few selected definitions which follow:

1. Credit is purchasing power (Mill).
2. The essence of credit is confidence on the part of the creditor in the debtor's willingness and ability to pay his debt (Holdsworth).
3. Credit may be called a "short sale" of money (Johnson).
4. Credit is a "sale on trust."
5. The exchange of an actual reality against a future probability (Levasseur).
6. Credit may be defined as the power to secure commodities or services at the present time in return for some equivalent or services at a future date (Bullock).
7. Credit is the personal reputation a person has, in consequence of which he can buy money, or goods, or labor, by giving in exchange for them, a promise to pay at a future time (MacLeod).
8. The power to secure the present transfer of wealth, measured in dollars or other monetary standard, by a promise to pay at a future time, based on the confidence of the seller in the ability and the willingness of the buyer to meet his obligations (Wall).
9. A credit in law, commerce, and economics is the right which one person, the creditor, has to compel another person, the debtor, to pay or do something (MacLeod).
10. Credit is the power to obtain goods or service by giving a promise to pay money (or goods) on demand or at a specified date in the future (Johnson).
11. A credit is the present right to a future payment (MacLeod).
12. The transfer of something valuable to another, whether money, goods or services, in the confidence that he will be both willing and able, at a future day, to pay its equivalent (Tucker).

Although these definitions may have approximated the idea of credit in its formative years, none of them completely describes credit in its present concept. Thus a comprehensive and positive definition of credit is deemed necessary. In this book we shall adhere to a broad concept of credit as the *measure of the ability of an individual or business enterprise or government authority to obtain present values (money, goods, or services) while deferring payment, usually in the form of money, to a definite future time.*[1]

[1] In business practice any sale or loan resulting from a credit appraisal carries with it the term "credit," i.e., credit sales, transactions, etc.; or, as in accounting practice, a "credit" is made on the books of the purchaser or borrower. Thus the acceptance of credit by the seller leads to a debt or credit on the books of the buyer. Hence the seller frequently states from the accounting point of view, "we have given them a credit." *However, the appraisal was first made.*

This definition includes the actual credit in use as well as the measurement of potential credit. Thus measurement of total ability to buy goods or to borrow money—that is, credit appraisal of a risk—would result in a potential limit of credit at any one time. The amount of credit approved by the appraiser and utilized by the borrower would be actual credit in use. For instance, the ability of a business to buy goods or borrow money may result in the appraisal of $1,000,000 of potential credit; however, if only $700,000 of this amount is used, credit in use, as measured by debt created, is $700,000, and potential unused credit of $300,000 is available. Thus in using the term *credit*, care should be exercised to avoid confusion of these two different concepts of credit as well as the accounting usage.

From the definitions cited, it may be gathered that the most important characteristic of credit is the confidence of the creditor in the potential repayment ability of the borrower. Thus confidence is a requisite ever necessary for a credit transaction because, at best, the future is uncertain.

The measurement of credit is never precise; it is always a measure of probabilities and is as uncertain as the unpredictable future. Since all relevant factors affecting ability to pay can be determined only approximately, the appraisal of credit falls far short of being a science. However, the foregoing example shows that credit appraisal is invariably from the point of view of the creditor.

From the viewpoint of the borrower, credit measures his ability to incur debt or add to existing debt. To the lender, on the other hand, credit represents his measurement of the debtor's ability to borrow money or buy goods up to a specific amount.

Credit Is Accepted Not Given. In business practice, those who authorize a credit transaction, and whom we call "credit executives," "loaning officers," "credit managers," or "credit men," are accustomed to speak of authorization of credit as "giving" or "granting" credit. Is credit a quality bestowed upon the borrower by the lender, or is it the recognition by the lender of a quality or faculty possessed by the borrower? The answer rests upon whether we limit credit to "the present right to future payment" or regard it as a measure of ability which may not have been utilized to its potential limit. If we accept the former view, then the credit of an individual is measured by the amount he currently owes, which, obviously, will not remain constant. Today he may have, let us say, $10,000 borrowed on the basis of credit, because he is owing to others that sum, while tomorrow, having paid his obligations in full, he has no credit whatever and will have to remain without credit until it is "granted" to him by someone willing to accept his promise to pay. The most frequent example of this usage of the term "given or granted credit" is found among banking institutions. Actually, what takes place is an exchange of a lesser credit for a better-known credit. Thus the banker transfers to the borrower a portion of its funds—which is credited to the customer's deposit account—on the basis of the banker's appraisal of the credit offered by its customer. It is apparent, therefore, that the creditworthiness of the borrower first was accepted before the exchange of credit.

It is more reasonable, and also in accord with the more general view, to regard credit as a measurement of power possessed by certain individuals which is not limited to the extent to which it is used. Indeed, we may go a step further and say that credit is possessed by everyone, and it varies among different individuals (and corporations) from indefinitely great to nothing. Credit, therefore, is not a quality bestowed on one by another; it is not "given"; it is not "granted" except in the sense that by "granted" we understand that it is *conceded* to be. It is a quality which we recognize and appraise just as we recognize and appraise, but do not bestow, the quality of beauty. Nor could we say that one was without credit until all appraisers have passed judgment.

The buyer, or seller, or borrower does not really ask for credit; he offers credit, and it is accepted or rejected by the lender according to whether or not the credit is appraised as being acceptable.

The Credit Problem. The study of the credit problem may be divided into three chief phases: (1) the analysis of credit; (2) the measurement and protection of credit; and (3) the effect of credit on business through its influence on prices and values. The problem as outlined embraces not only the credit transactions within this country, but the credit transactions between individuals of this and other countries and the credit transactions between other governments and ours. This is a broad social problem, too great in scope for the limitations of this book. We shall, therefore, confine our study largely to the measurement and protection of business credit. The aim of this book is to give businessmen a practical knowledge and training in judging or determining the status of the credit of a business unit.

Credit and Wealth. The terms credit, wealth, and capital lack precise and fully acceptable definitions among people concerned with either the theory or practice of business. Some regard the terms as synonymous, while others define them in accordance with their varied backgrounds. For instance, capital is assumed to mean net worth (accountants), or productive assets (economists), or total assets (businessmen). Each definition clearly shows that credit and capital are not the same.

Wealth has been defined as any material or physical good that satisfies a human want, provided that good is limited in amount and has value. Or wealth consists of economic goods as contrasted with free goods, such as air and water. Capital goods (fixed assets) consist of economic goods used in the production of wealth. It will readily be seen that credit is none of these, since the use of credit always results in a liability or an equity, not a physical or material good. Wealth may be transferred from one to another, but there is no way by which the man without credit can become possessed of the credit of him who has good credit. One cannot bestow his credit upon another; he can only guarantee or become surety for the other.

That credit is not wealth will readily be seen by examining the statements of both borrower and lender before and after a credit transaction. Let us assume that X has a taxi valued at $2,000 while Y's wealth consists of $800 which he has managed to save. X sells his taxi to Y, taking the $800 in cash, and he accepts Y's credit in the form of a promissory note for the remainder, $1,200. Before the transaction the statements of X and Y will appear as follows:

LENDER X

Assets		Liabilities	
		None	
Taxi	$2,000	Net Worth	$2,000
	$2,000		$2,000

BORROWER Y

Assets		Liabilities	
		None	
Cash	$800	Net worth	$800
	$800		$800

After the transfer has been made the statements will show the following condition:

LENDER X

Assets		Liabilities	
		None	
Cash	$ 800	Net worth	$2,000
Note received	1,200		
	$2,000		$2,000

BORROWER Y

Assets		Liabilities	
Taxi	$2,000	Note payable	$1,200
		Net worth	800
	$2,000		$2,000

The wealth, which consisted of the taxi and the cash before the transaction, is no more and no less after the transaction. Credit has been merely the agency of transfer. It should be pointed out, however, that the use of credit has increased the assets and liabilities of the borrower but that there is no increase in wealth, since claims are not wealth. This function in regard to credit has been aptly stated by John Stuart Mill:[1]

[1] MILL, JOHN STUART, "Principles of Political Economy," p. 309

It seems strange that there should be a need to point out that, credit being only the permission to use the capital of another person, the means of production cannot be increased by it but only transferred; that is, the borrower's means of production are increased by the credit given him, that of the lender are correspondingly diminished, as the same capital cannot be used as such, both by the owner and also the person to whom it is lent.

It should be borne in mind, however, that production *may* be increased as a result of the credit transaction, even though the *means* of production are not increased.

While credit is not wealth when viewed from the standpoint of society at large, since there is, obviously, only a certain amount of wealth in the world at a given time, and it is not increased or diminished by shifting it about through credit transactions, nevertheless, from the standpoint of the individual, the analogy between credit and wealth is close.[1] To the individual or business firm, good credit has great value, and the good credit name or credit reputation should be as carefully guarded as any form of tangible wealth.

The Limit of the Credit Economy. Since credit involves an exchange of values usually represented by a good or money and expressed in terms of money, it will readily be seen that there is an essential relationship between the volume of aggregative goods and the volume of aggregative credit. What the lender really wants in repayment is not goods, as the term is commonly understood, but money. What the borrower promises to pay is money. It may be inferred, therefore, that the ability of the borrower to convert the goods into money within the time limit fixed by the credit transaction is a prime consideration in the measurement of credit. Were it not for this essential of convertibility of goods into money, the theoretic limit of credit at any given moment would be fixed only by the volume of goods subject to exchange. Since the elements of futurity and of convertibility into money enter into the consideration, the theoretic limit of credit of a community is measured at a given time, "not by the community's wealth, but by that plus its power to produce wealth,"[2] while the measurement of the credit of an individual is fixed, at any given level of prices, by his wealth, plus his ability to produce wealth, modified by the extent to which he can convert his wealth into money. As the reader can readily see, the limit of credit of the individual depends upon the flow of goods, which experience has shown is not constant. Goods flow in varying quantities in uncertain periods and at varying price levels, and this movement we have come to know as the "business cycle."

[1] BECKMAN, T. N., and R. BARTELS, "Credits and Collections in Theory and Practice."
[2] JOHNSON, J. F., "Money and Currency," p. 38.

Use of Credit. It has been held by some writers that credit avoids the use of money, by others that it is a substitute for money, while a third class hold that in its relation to money it is merely an option on money. All are agreed that one of the essential services of credit to society is to serve, along with money, as a medium of exchange. Credit, as we have seen, is the agency of transfer which permits the flow of funds to the aid of production. But its use is not limited to its aid to production. It serves, too, to speed up consumption. Credit thus facilitates the production, exchange, and consumption of goods, with the result that a higher standard of living is attained by society.

As a medium of exchange, credit is swifter, safer, and more convenient than money. For instance, a check transferring funds need not be insured; and if it is lost, a new check is easily drawn. But money, being a bearer instrument, once lost is gone.

Credit releases for other useful purposes gold, silver, and other metals which might be selected by a people for use as money.[1] It has been well said that credit, and not money, is the principal medium of exchange. Credit is merely expressed in terms of money, and money serves as an aid to credit in settling the comparatively small balances not canceled by credit itself. Like money, credit is created and retired (in theory at least) as the movement of goods increases and decreases. It thus provides us with an elastic medium of exchange as a claim on money necessary to meet the fluctuation in our business volume.

In addition to its main function as a medium of exchange, credit benefits society at large and the individual in many other ways. Credit permits the concentration of small sums through savings banks, bonds, shares of stock, and the like, making possible the financing of large enterprises whose products are disseminated among the people to the benefit both of society and of the contributors of capital. People are urged to save through the knowledge that every sum, however small, may be employed at a profit to its owner. It thus has a tendency to prevent hoarding, not only making capital useful but removing it from the hazard of theft; and to develop the habit of thrift.

Credit has a tendency to elevate the moral standards of a people, since it is in the interest of each, where credit is universally employed, to prove himself worthy of trust. The interests of a people are bound together through their credit relations, since the welfare of the debtor class is a

---

[1] The use of gold is at present much restricted in the United States, and some other countries, where it formerly was as easily exchanged as any other good. It no longer may be lawfully used as money, and its use in the arts and sciences is under governmental license. It seems probable that gold will not be coined in the future in the United States for use as money. The government instead holds gold bullion and uses it for international settlements and as a basis for the monetary system.

matter of concern to the creditor class and, since practically all are in both classes, the welfare of all is a matter of common interest. Credit not only permits the man with little means of his own to engage in a business enterprise, thereby encouraging production, but it also permits the purchase of all sorts of consumption goods, including, among others, such comparatively more expensive goods as radios, television sets, refrigerators, automobiles, and homes, thus raising the scale of living and adding greatly to the enjoyment of the many.

A general service of credit lies in the assistance which it has given in the development of modern methods of production and distribution. As a result of credit, funds have been placed at the disposal of invention so that large-scale production has been possible, transportation rapid, and communication almost instantaneous. In the present era, manufacture is generally undertaken by minute subdivision of labor so that goods are completed by stages, and in many cases long intervals elapse between the conversion of the material in its raw state and its consumption by consumers. In the handicraft period, this was not so. Goods were largely manufactured for direct consumption. When this country was founded, practically every home was a factory. For instance, sheep were grown by the farmer, who sheared and carded the wool; the wool was spun into yarn and woven into cloth by the female members of the household and dyed and made into clothing for immediate consumption. Today the wool is grown by the sheep rancher, who sells to the broker, who sells to the manufacturer. The material may pass through several processes and ownerships before it is passed on to the wholesaler, thence to the retailer, and finally to the consumer. The significant fact is that credit aids in financing the article in each stage of production and distribution. It is "the instrument which bridges the interval elapsing between the beginning of the process of production to ultimate consumption."[1] Credit is the instrument through which each agent in the process of production is financed, and bank credit, trade credit, consumer credit, and investment credit are the instrumentalities through which credit chiefly works.

The Abuse of Credit. Credit, however, is not entirely a blessing either to society in general or to the individual. Its use may become abuse, and the distinction between the two is not always easy. Its use is attended by some danger. The ease with which one is enabled through credit to use the capital of others for the purposes of either production or consumption may lead to disaster. Optimistic measurement of credit promotes the spirit of adventure. Enterprises are launched which have no economic justification and which could not be undertaken were it not

---

[1] MUNN, G. G., "Bank Credit," p. 4.

for the unwitting generosity of creditors. Other businesses already well established undermine their soundness by overexpansion, with creditors' aid. Profits seem easy and sure, and neither the sincerest debtors nor creditors with the utmost confidence in the credits realize the jeopardy in which they have placed themselves.

A credit, we may say, has been completely justified only when the pledge to pay has been redeemed. One hundred per cent efficiency, however, in credit acceptance and management is not expected, for there will be errors in judging the credit risk, and even the soundest risk may be greatly weakened during the term of the credit by changing conditions or misfortunes over which neither debtor or creditor has the slightest control. But credit is abused when a careful investigation and appraisal of the risk do not reveal a reasonable certainty that the credit can or will be redeemed; and likewise credit in the aggregate is abused when its use permits an excessive flow of goods or services, outstripping the means of repayment. Among the direct dangers of credit is its tendency to encourage overexpansion, overtrading, and speculation, leading to fraud and embezzlement, and the ease with which people may be induced to live more extravagantly than their means warrant.

The use of credit results in a debt which is a lien on future income, and when the production power of the future has been wrongly gauged, the result is at least unpleasant and often disastrous. This is so in the case either of the individual or of the community at large.

The Margin between Success and Failure. The public at large undoubtedly has a wrong impression of the profits of business enterprises. The young particularly should be disillusioned. The success of an individual business is often widely publicized. The public, knowing the success of individual companies, falsely assumes that business in general is reaping inordinate profits. Hundreds of thousands of businesses are struggling to survive and barely avoid losses. This fact receives no wide advertising. Business management has no wide pathway of profit in which to steer its course. Losses, if the safety of creditors is to be secured, cannot be suffered for protracted periods, for losses mean the reduction of capital.

Data from various sources are available to support the statement that the margin of profit taken by business is narrow. A large number of business enterprises are discontinued with losses to creditors or continued under settlements to creditors without going through bankruptcy. In addition to such liquidations, bankruptcies of business concerns for more than three decades between 1920 and 1952 have ranged from a high of over 31,000 in 1932 to a low of approximately 800 in 1945. During the last decade the number of failures has again tended to increase—from about 9,000 in 1949 to 13,700 in 1957. Also, the losses per failure have sharply risen, with total failure liabilities reaching $615,293,000 in 1957. Credit men, therefore, have no easy task in choosing the safe and rejecting the unsafe.

Profit margins for business corporations, measured by return or net worth, are not large. Over a period of 20 years the rate of return on net worth was greater than 10 per cent in only 4 years. In one-half of these years the rate of return on capital was less than 8 per cent. The student should note that, if present value concepts of net worth were used, these returns on net worth would be considerably smaller. Figure 1 represents a comparison on compiled profits of active corporations in the United States. The growth in the economy and in the number of active corporations is also significantly illustrated in this table.

Year	Net worth Jan. 1, millions of dollars	Net compiled profits after taxes, millions of dollars	Rate of return, per cent	Active corporations, number
1937	$133,468	$6,554	4.9	477,838
1938	141,633	3,271	2.3	471,032
1939	137,437	5,946	4.3	469,617
1940	137,864	6,800	4.9	473,042
1941	138,387	9,507	6.8	468,906
1942	142,591	11,132	7.8	442,665
1943	139,629	12,201	8.7	420,521
1944	145,665	11,663	7.9	412,467
1945	150,462	10,551	7.0	421,125
1946	154,565	16,524	10.6	491,152
1947	164,614	20,634	12.5	551,807
1948	180,567	22,668	12.5	594,243
1949	207,220	18,569	8.9	614,842
1950	208,297	25,514	12.2	629,314
1951	223,609	21,717	9.7	652,376
1952	239,038	19,588	8.1	672,071
1953	253,006	19,932	7.8	697,975
1954	265,182	19,800	7.4	722,805
1955	278,498	26,208	9.4	807,303
1956	305,448	26,048	8.5	885,747
1957	327,667	47,413 p*	14.4	960,000 est.

p*—preliminary.

SOURCE: *Statistics of Income*, U.S. Treasury Department.

FIG. 1.   Net profits of corporations in the United States, 1937–1957.

The Business Cycle. That business is always neither in a state of prosperity nor in a state of depression is a fact universally known. It oscillates between prosperity and depression at irregular intervals and with different degrees of intensity. The business economy is made up of many segments, each of which has its own distinct life pattern of growth, stability, and decline. Together they make up the business trend and cycle.

Economists, businessmen, and legislators have given the subject of business cycles much study and have developed many theories as to how the movements can be controlled. It must be said, however, that no effective control theory has yet been demonstrated. The multitude of independent business units, each operating with apparently little correlation, is like a vast uncoordinated machine running at various rates and depending on individual whims and fancies. Naturally it is a matter of chance that it functions smoothly on some occasions. The problem of coordination challenges the ability of the civilized world.

Unless a method of control is demonstrated[1] it will continue to be one of the credit manager's problems to anticipate this business movement trend because he is measuring the solvency of his firm's client at some future date. Solvency, or the ability to meet maturing obligations, is unquestionably affected by financial and industrial conditions. The credit manager is interested not only in the major movements of business as a whole but in the minor movement which may take place within a single industry and run contrary to the trend of business as a whole. There is a third type of movement, the regularly recurring seasonal movement, which may be of considerable importance in certain industries, but which is less difficult of analysis because of its certainty and regularity.

There are, therefore, three types of movement which may have an effect on the solvency of business houses, and which the credit manager must watch: the regularly recurring seasonal movement, the condition of business in general, and the condition of business in the particular industry with which he is concerned.

Phases of the Business Cycle. While it is easier to think of the business cycle as embracing two periods of business—prosperity and depression—there are a number of more or less distinct phases of business within a cycle. We may in a broad way divide the cycle into four per-

---

[1] Great economic, political, and social changes have occurred during the past three decades. Some economists believe the pattern of business cycles has changed and that a severe depression such as occurred in the early 1930's will not recur. That we have learned to eliminate the swings of the business cycle is refuted up to now by the mild recession of 1949, the plight of some of the soft-goods industries in 1951–1952, and the 1957–1958 recession.

iods: (1) prosperity, (2) crisis, (3) depression, and (4) recovery. The division between these periods is usually somewhat uncertain, and they overlap each other. Business gradually passes from one period to the next, and the completion of the cycle may not be clearly discernible. For instance, business may pass through a crisis stage in which there appears to be no depression and recovery because the period is so short. Prosperity appears to follow the slight setback; yet some business units were hurt and possibly liquidated. These movements vary in importance to the credit manager just as they vary among themselves in length and intensity. Indeed, so shadowy sometimes are the lines of division that economists cannot always agree as to just which years or months are prosperous and which are not.

The shorter the time in which there is a complete cycle, and the greater the movement, the greater the significance to the trade credit manager, and, conversely, if the cycle is spread over a long period of time and the movement is not so great, the importance is small. This is so because the trade credit manager will have a great number of credit turnovers in this period. But long-term credit, particularly instalment and investment credit, may be as much affected by a long business cycle as by a short one, or more so.

There are those who argue that, after all, this uncertain movement of business is beneficial to society as a whole. Just as business oscillates between prosperity and depression, so does the benefit oscillate between those whose income is fixed and those whose income depends on profits made. It is held by some that crises and depressions are beneficial to society, as a whole, because they check extravagance and expansion, and that they afford a balance between capital and labor. During the period of prosperity, business enterprises benefit through rising prices and rising profits, but labor suffers because it has to pay the high prices.[1] Conversely, when prices are low during a period of depression, those who have fixed incomes may buy more goods. It is conceded that wages neither rise nor fall so rapidly as prices and that the most sensitive to price fluctuations are wholesale prices, while retail prices both rise and fall more slowly.[2] But a balance of benefit is not effected by the business cycle, because with the period of depression comes diminished production and unemployment, so that the wage earner, instead of being able to take advantage of the lower prices, finds himself out of employment and with no purchasing power whatever.

The severity of the depression of the 'thirties and the suffering caused

[1] The Second World War, the Korean problem, and the threat of a Third World War caused feverish production activity for more than a decade. As of December, 1958, consumer prices had advanced to 123.7 per cent of their 1947–1949 average.

[2] KEMMERER, E. W., "High Prices and Deflation."

by it must have removed from the minds of everyone a belief in its desirability, corrective though the depression might be. A depression lowers a people's standard of living. Society should not and will not long be satisfied with any measures taken either by government or by business which will restrict, as a whole, production, manufacture, and trade. As a people we have enjoyed, prior to the depression and the Second World War, a higher standard of living than ever before known to any country. The Second World War, with its immense waste of human life and material resources, has posed new problems for solution. As an energetic, ambitious, and capable people, we have made further strides toward an even higher standard of living. There is no doubt that our standard of living will continue to improve, but there is also no assurance that at times there will not be periods of lessened activity which will result in temporary setbacks to our economic growth.

Causes of Business Cycles. Economists are not entirely agreed upon the causes of business cycles. Numerous theories have been advanced which seem plausible enough, but the student should be wary of accepting any one theory as the cause of all business oscillations.[1]

Since it is the duty of the credit man to anticipate the different movements of business, it is essential that he have a knowledge of the theories of their cause and the signs of their approach. As we have raised our standard of living, so have we concurrently increased the causes and effects of business fluctuations. Were life confined to the mere necessities of food, shelter, and clothing to be provided by the immediate area in which one lived, fear would be confined to the disastrous effects of floods, drought, insect plagues, and pestilence. In our modern society, in the United States at least, drought, though it may be severe, does not result in famine; for food can be rushed in from those sections where rainfall has been more abundant. In a primitive society the suffering resulting from a severe drought, for instance, would be much more severe in the affected areas, but it would be localized. In our modern society the effect of a disturbance, from whatever cause, spreads. The farmer suffering a crop failure has nothing to exchange for things needed or desired. He must forego the new suit of clothes and his wife the new dress which they otherwise would have purchased. This affects the clothing manufacturer of Rochester and the dress manufacturer of New York. In other words, and more to the point, labor loses the use of the money which it would have received for the production of its manufactured articles. Labor thus may have to curtail its purchases, foregoing luxuries or necessities. Reduced to its simplest terms, an exchange

[1] "He who would understand business cycles must master the workings of an economic system organized largely in a network of free enterprises searching for profit." Mitchell, W. C., "What Happens during Business Cycles."

of food and clothing has not taken place. Were this simple illustration confined to two persons, the effect likewise could be limited. But many persons have a part even in the placing of food in the hands of the consumer, and as many, or more, in the production of clothing.

Goods are no longer exchanged directly for other goods or for services. They are exchanged for money, which is a standard of measure and a medium of exchange. Because we are inclined to see money as the measure of our labor, there is a lack of price flexibility to lubricate the flow of goods. The tendency toward rigidity of prices is fostered by both capital and labor. For instance, the price of capital has a tendency to be fixed by long-term contracts at fixed interest rates while labor, through its unions, fixes a price for its services. Both tendencies hamper the flexibility essential if business is to be kept on an even keel.

Some prices seem to be subject to but slow change, and others constantly appear to be mounting higher, for example, the price of government. Others are obstinately maintained, and still others are the result of the warped judgment of buyers and sellers alike. Examples of the latter are the tulip craze of Holland, the Mississippi Bubble, the Florida land boom, the 1929 stock market crash, and more recently the consumer credit spurt and building boom.[1] The appearance of strength is suddenly lost, production tumbles, and unemployment rises sharply, the effect spreading in all directions.

Human judgment errs when prices fall just as it erred when prices were rising. The effect is cumulative. Overoptimism and fear alternate, both being stimulated by mass psychology. Rising prices stimulate demand as purchasers hasten to buy before prices rise further, and, conversely, falling prices cause purchasers to delay buying in the hope of a cheaper price at a later date. This lessened demand curtails production and so promotes unemployment. Dr. King[2] gives the following description of the tendency of a depression to be self-generating:

As factory production slackens, the factories obviously need less coal. Coal, however, is one of the principal articles of freight carried by the railroads. Curtailment in the demand for coal obviously lessens, therefore, the demand for transportation. As production in manufacturing establishments and on the railroads slackens, fewer employees are needed, hence men are laid off. Those who lose their jobs receive no wages, consequently they are unable to buy their quotas of goods. Shrinkage in their volumes of purchasing diminishes still further the demand for products of factories, farms, and railways, and this shrinkage in demand leads to the discharge of more workers. The fact that charitable or governmental organizations may, at this juncture, step in to grant

[1] See "The Causes of Economic Fluctuations" by Willford I. King for interesting descriptions of these and other booms and crashes.
[2] *Ibid.*, p. 35.

relief to those out of employment alters the picture but little, since contributions for relief come out of the pockets of taxpayers or donors, and hence eventually lessen the buying power of those making the contributions.

As the volume of production declines in the typical factory, mine, or transportation organization, there is no corresponding diminution in overhead cost. The necessary result is that production expense, per unit of output, increases steadily as the volume of business shrinks. Rising expenses narrow the margin of profit on each unit sold. Since the number of units sold has been greatly reduced, and the profit margin per unit has shrunk, net earnings decline greatly. This decline usually necessitates a reduction in dividend payments, and such a reduction curtails the ability of the stockholders to buy luxuries or durable goods. It follows that the decline in net corporate earnings of business concerns generally results in a further slackening of production and in a greater volume of unemployment, and this, in turn, leads to still further declines in wages, dividends, and buying power.

The tendency for a business decline to perpetuate itself is accentuated by the fact that, as corporate earnings fall, stock prices move downward correspondingly.

Still another factor is the measures which may be taken by the government. Governmental actions and laws may influence business movements whether such actions are for the purpose of stimulating business, curbing abuses, raising revenue, or of following regular government routine. The actions of the Board of Governors of the Federal Reserve, the influence of the Secretary of the Treasury, and the attitudes and programs of government departments and bureaus affect business for better or for worse even though the purposes may be benign.

Nature of Business Cycles. Much attention has been given, since the First World War, to these recurring business periods. Economists and businessmen are striving for the more certain forecasting of business trends and in the hope that the violence of the changes may be somewhat lessened. All businessmen would like to avoid the periods of crisis and depression. They would be satisfied with less prosperity, provided they were compensated by less loss during the liquidation period. It is, perhaps, too much to expect that the cycle will ever be done away with entirely, but a keener appreciation of the essential causes of the cycle will enable business to avoid the dangers of inflation, expansion, and maldistribution and thus, in a measure, reduce the extreme fluctuations of the cycle itself.

The most feared period is the crisis, which is usually of very brief duration; if sufficiently violent, it is termed a "panic." A panic is defined as a short-lived, unreasoning fear, but a business panic or crisis is the result of just reasoning on conditions which actually exist, although the panic may be precipitated by some event of comparative minor importance, as the failure of a bank or a business house. When the crisis arrives, businessmen talk prosperity to encourage confidence but act very conservatively in their own business. As Professor Mitchell says, "The volume of business cannot be restored by cheerful conversation." There is not among businessmen real confidence of satisfactory profits and volume of business. Production is halted and workmen are discharged. Being unemployed, or fearing unemployment, they cut expenditures to the lowest possible point. Just when business is most in need of sustained buying, it is conspicuously absent. The causes are cumulative in effect. The less business there is, the less employment; and the less employment, the less business. This might continue until business was at a complete standstill, were it not for the fact that the demand for food and clothing cannot wholly cease. When surplus stocks have been consumed, there comes a demand, gradual at first, for more goods, and thus the same forces work for the recovery of business which brought about the periods of crisis and depression, but in reverse order. Any phase of the circle may be hastened by various causes which operate as potent factors on existing conditions.

The depression of the 'thirties was a period of exhaustion of goods which we were only beginning to replace when we were confronted with the Second World War. For several years all our resources and energy were devoted to that war. When the combat ceased, we had only a few years to replace worn-out clothing, household articles, automobiles, to provide new housing, and to satisfy other demands of the population before a new threat of a major war compelled us to bend all our energies to a preparation for it. Thus a depression which some believed was about to come upon us was pushed further away by the continued prosperity—false prosperity though it might be.

Indices of Business Conditions. The problem for the credit man is to interpret the position of the business cycle, the trend of business, and the period of transition from the present to the next phase of the cycle. This cannot be done by guesswork. Success in interpretation of the business trend is based first upon getting the fullest possible facts concerning business and, second, upon the skill with which those facts are analyzed. If all the significant facts are not taken into consideration, then the conclusions reached may be wrong.

The business forecaster must ever keep in mind that the normal progress of that cycle may be diverted by such unforeseen causes as crop failure, changes in the tariff, inventions, labor troubles, changes in the popular demand, or the sudden opening of new mines. The task of getting business facts is one that is beyond the businessman, so that he will do well to rely upon various business-reporting services, which make a business of interpreting the trend of general business conditions.

In these various services one finds a large amount of data assembled and interpreted for the subscriber. This should be supplemented by one's own observation and judgment, and it is recommended that two or more of these services be used so that one may be compared with another.

Four Phases of Business Cycles. Since each phase of the business cycle recurs at varying intervals, the discussion may be started at any point. Let us assume first a state of prosperity. Upon analysis, it will be found that there is increased buying throughout business, largely on credit. Buying activity "stiffens" prices, or, in other words, prices rise. Rising prices result in larger inventories, again stimulating buying. Sales increase in physical volume but more rapidly in price. The margin of profit widens, since costs lag behind prices. Concerns working near capacity consider the advisability of increasing plant and equipment. Much plant and equipment expansion takes place, financed largely through credit. The result is the expansion of credit reflected in the accounts receivable, the accounts payable which carry the large inventories, and the bonded indebtedness. The large inventory and the added plant and equipment are carried at a high price. Only by increased purchasing by the general public could the business pace and prices be sustained. Sporadic breaks in certain commodities ensue through the attempt to maintain or increase sales. Lagging costs are catching up with the margin of profit. Creditors, especially banks, realize that a large amount of credit is based on prices which may not be sustained. Loans are not renewed, a fact which means that inventories must be liquidated at sacrifice prices. Business has reached a crisis, or if the transition from prosperity to depression is sufficiently spectacular, it is termed a panic.

A panic or crisis is usually short, sharp, and decisive in its results. A depression is a condition which has duration of time attending it.

The transition from prosperity to depression is made with more or less rapidity. As stated above, sporadic breaks occur in certain industries which may cause a general debauch. Prices again become stable, but at a lower level, or decline much more slowly for a time. The weaker enterprises are gradually shaken out by insolvency, while others manage to cling to their business, and still others weather the liquidation process with practically unimpaired credit. All are affected, however, to some extent by the depreciation in value of inventories and less liquidity of receivables; overhead charges are proportionately higher because of decreased business and the difficulty in cutting these costs to meet the changed conditions. There are losses to be taken, and the period of depression is not over until liquidation has been effected.

The transition from depression to recovery is not abrupt, as is the change from prosperity to crisis. Upon analysis it will be noted that all business does not generally recover at one time. Certain industries will show improved conditions while others are still in a state of depression. The first to recover are followed by others, till in more or less time recovery is general. The period of recovery is marked by an increased demand for goods. Inventories begin to move, and that means that the business concern is both buying and selling. Prices begin to stiffen, and there is some margin between costs and sales. Collections improve, and confidence is being restored. The process is cumulative, the revival gradually merges into the stage of general prosperity, and thus the stage is set for another business cycle.

It would be too much to hope, and contrary to past experience, that businessmen in general would not forget a lesson which should have been so well learned. The abnormal conditions caused by the First World War greatly accentuated the movement of the business cycle, and its severe lesson so profoundly impressed upon the businessman has left him cognizant of the danger engendered by the Second World War and the world-wide disturbed conditions which followed it.

TEXT AND RESEARCH QUESTIONS

1. What are the essential elements of credit as defined by Joseph French Johnson?

2. What is the distinction between credit and a credit transaction?

3. How may credit power be developed?

4. A endorses B's note, thereby making it acceptable to C. Has A "given" his credit to B? Explain your answer.

5. To what part of the broad study of credit is this book largely to be confined?

6. If credit has value but cannot be sold, how can one cash in on its value?

7. What effect does the inability of a business to convert wealth rapidly into money have upon its credit?

8. Discuss four uses of credit and four ways in which credit may be abused.

9. What effect does the national manipulation of money and credit have upon the relationship of money and credit and the "flow of goods"?

10. In which of the four phases of the business cycle is business now placed? Why?

11. Name an industry not in accord with the general business cycle.

12. What significance have the years 1932 and 1945 in connection with business failures?

PROBLEMS

1. *a.* Draw up a list of eight indices which in your judgment might be commonly employed to forecast business activities. Briefly explain why you would rely upon each one. What are their shortcomings?

   b. Why would you or why would you not include the index of wholesale commodity prices in this list?

    c. What indices measure credit outstanding? Identify the original source of each index named.

2. *a.* How much gold is there in this country available as a base for money?
   b. How much of this gold is used as a base for money?
   c. How much currency is there in actual circulation?
   d. How does money supply differ from currency? Which is more important?

3. Using the "Survey of Current Business," or any other source, determine for any industry of your choice (*a*) manufacturers' sales, (*b*) inventories, (*c*) back orders, and (*d*) depreciation charges. What significance would these statistics have on your short-range forecast for this industry?

CHAPTER 2

THE CREDIT EXECUTIVE

Development of Credit Work. It may be said with considerable truth that the steam engine, the telegraph, and the telephone, as the principal factors in the development of large-scale business enterprise, are largely responsible for the modern credit department. It might also be said that the traveling salesman has made a credit specialist a necessity. Equal support can be given to the statement that the credit department is merely the inevitable result of our age of specialization. It would be more accurate, however, to conclude that the credit man and the credit department are the result of a combination of these circumstances. This function, together with that of financial control, represents the last phase of business activity to be surrendered or delegated to subordinates by the owner or manager. Thus, it was long regarded as too important a function to be placed in the hands of the bookkeeper or "hired man" and as a result has brought about the development of a credit specialist or executive.

When business was largely under the direction of a sole proprietor, whatever credits were made were approved by the owner. The inventions mentioned above, and others, greatly hastened the development of our country and widened the scope of the businessman's activity. The growth of business units thus aided made it impossible for one man to perform all the functions of production, marketing, and finance. Then, too, credit and merchandise were exchanged largely upon personal acquaintance. It was customary 75 years ago for the buyer to visit the wholesaler once or twice a year and, after several days of entertainment and of inspection of goods, the selection was made. The seller, having sized up his customer, approved the credit. At a later period, the method of purchasing was reversed and the seller, through his representative, the salesman, went to the purchaser. Thus the personal relationship between principals was lost, and in many cases the salesman took over not only the selling but the credit function as well. The credit skill of a salesman largely determined his value. He knew and controlled his trade. To send a new and untried salesman into a territory was hazardous, since it invited the more hazardous and the distinctly dangerous risks. Thus, the responsibility for credits became divided among principals, salesman, and managers. It was but natural that the bookkeeper should be given a part in the approval of credit, since he was in the best position to know how the different customers took care of their credit obligations.

Thus, we find that for some years credit approval was a divided responsibility and a somewhat neglected function. The transition of this function to one-man control was slow but inevitable. The most logical selection for this new position was the bookkeeper who had been assisting in the work. The bookkeeper had no exalted position in the business organization at that time, and consequently, the same individual when he became the credit man—a "glorified bookkeeper" according to someone—still held an inferior position. Neither the credit man nor his employer realized the importance and possibilities of credit department work. It may be said with complete justification that even today credit men have not realized the potentialities of their department.

In bank credit work, recognition of credit responsibilities came earlier. Both loan clerks and credit men processed credit accounts and, if capable, developed into credit officers as business and the need for services expanded.

The date of the establishment of the credit department and the career of the credit man has been fixed as in the early 'nineties. The National Association of Credit Men was established in 1896. This early recognition of the need of association and cooperation among credit men has been a potent factor in the rapid development of the credit man and of the importance of his department. A group of bank credit men formed the Robert Morris Association in 1919. It particularly serves the needs of the commercial banks and is affiliated with the National Association of Credit Management (new name adopted Sept. 1, 1958, see Chapter 7).

The Credit Executive's Position. The material progress accomplished in the last 50 years far outstrips any similar period in history. We have progressed far and fast in means of communication, in inventions and discoveries, in adaptations of power, and in business education. In the development of business, we have attained a remarkable degree of administrative efficiency and tremendous productive capacity through organization and specialization. With all its complexity, business is developing a sense of responsibility and service, of usefulness to society, and a higher standard of ethics and ideals. Here stands the background of the credit executive of today. He is the result of business needs and business experience. Today he is the specialist, the analyst, the business critic who guides and controls over 90 per cent of all transactions involving the transfer of goods. Credit men, through their national association, are assuming responsibilities in the shaping of business ethics. Moreover, as trained observers and thinkers, they are becoming the court of last resort in practical business opinion.

The Future of the Credit Executive. The credit man has progressed far since 1896, but he is still in the process of development. Recognized now as an executive in the financial department of business, he is destined to become in the future an even more significant factor in the science of business. Not only will he be skilled in discovering and interpretating facts in regard to the four C's—Character, Capacity, Capital, and Conditions—but he will become an authority for his concern in the prescribed field of analyzing, interpreting, and forecasting business and business conditions.

Many credit men have not themselves grasped the importance of their work, and some, realizing its importance, have neglected opportunities of selling its importance to other executives in business. The general statement may be made that the office does not make the man important, but that it is the man who makes the office important. When credit men come to a full realization of the potentialities of their place in the business world, and have developed themselves to more completely fulfill their function, the credit department will receive its just recognition.

The student is particularly interested in what opportunities are possible for the future. These opportunities are growing because both business houses and banks, as well as the credit managers themselves, are coming to a fuller realization of the importance and value of a highly developed credit department. The field is ripe for aggressive young men who are prepared by education and general experience and who are adapted to this work.

Qualifications of the Credit Executive. It is important for the good of both the individual and the profession that the young man should not engage in credit work as a career without carefully considering his qualifications and the exacting requirements of the profession. A prime consideration is the interest it will hold for the student. Credit work is devoid of monotony. There are ever-recurring problems, no two exactly alike, which constantly challenge the resourceful and analytical mind of the credit man. It is not true that credit men are born, but, on the other hand, a credit man lacking certain inherent qualities would achieve success only by unnecessarily hard work, likened to forcing a machine to do work for which it was not specially designed, or which is a strain upon its capacity. It is desirable that the credit man should have, or that the credit student should develop, certain qualifications for the work, and in addition, should have a knowledge of certain subjects, the foundation of which can be acquired by education. Granted, then, that there is a natural fitness of the worker to the requirements of his vocation, what other personal qualifications are essential?

The first essential of the good credit man let us call, for the want of a better word, "background," that indefinable quality which is acquired by a liberal education and the successful practice of one's vocation. The student may think it an anachronism to say that one never engaged in a business pursuit should have background, but this is a quality which one begins to develop at a very early age. The student is acquiring it. It grows upon the credit man as he develops in his work and in his preparation for it. Background, akin to, yet differing from, experience, embraces several other qualifications which, although exhibited to some degree as natural tendencies, should be further developed.

An *analytical mind* is an essential for the credit man. He must have the power to resolve problems into their component parts, and to recognize their essential elements. He must have a studious, searching disposition and the patience for a consideration of details. Furthermore, he must have a judicial temperament. The credit man is essentially a judge. He has evidence both accurate and inaccurate and of varying degrees of importance presented to him which he must weigh. His conclusions must be sound and the result of reason. A third major quality without which the credit man's progress is limited is that of *thoroughness*. The credit man's hunger for information should never be appeased. Yet there is efficiency in his thoroughness. Thoroughness consists in going into just sufficient detail to cover the task in hand with completeness and efficiency. Thoroughness is the ability to give the problem the attention which it merits without the waste of time on immaterial points or the duplication of effort. Thoroughness will not leave undone or uninvestigated any important or decisive material factor of the task in hand. Particular emphasis should be given to thoroughness, for there are many errors in the appraisal of credit due to the failure to obtain sufficient information upon which to base a credit decision.

The credit man must constantly be on the watch for out-of-the-ordinary information. He must scrutinize carefully apparently insignificant data. He must be quick to see the significance of chance remarks as applied to his particular problem. This ability may be termed *alertness*. Having an analytical mind, a judicial temper, and thoroughness, coupled with alertness, the credit man should arrive at the right conclusion and make the right decision. He needs then *firmness*, but not obstinacy. Having come to a decision of a proper course to pursue, or having made a yes or no decision, he will adhere to it with the courage of his conviction. With firmness, the successful credit man will be found to possess patience, that is, forbearance, or self-possession under provocation. The credit man "finds on the facts," and though his "findings" run contrary to the wishes or opinion of the customer or salesman, criticism or resentment will not disturb the credit man's sense of balance. Life will be pleasanter and his duties easier if the credit man refuses to be disturbed by the unpleasantness and petty exactions of the credit department in its contact with the policies and personalities of other departments in the business.

He should have the element of resourcefulness and this will cover the quality of *tact*. A quick appraisal of circumstances and the ability to handle them in the most effective manner will enable the credit man to extricate himself from many a misunderstanding. The resourceful credit man will recognize the interests of everyone concerned and give them their proper place without arousing resentment or antagonism. He should possess or develop a good memory. This statement does not imply a paucity of records. These should be complete. There are, however, numberless things which cannot be recorded which the credit man will find of great service if they come to his mind at the proper time.

Paradoxical as it may seem to some, the credit man should be sympathetic to those who may be adversely affected by his decisions. The commercial credit manager, like the banker, is often thought of as a cold emotionless being with no compassion for the misfortunes and adversities of his fellow men. Nothing need be further from the fact. Let the credit manager show a real regard for the interests of his customer, and those of the salesman as well. Such a quality will prove that his attitude is not one of ruthlessness but rather of helpfulness, so far as is consistent with his duty. This attitude may be described as warmth of character or cordiality—the expression of that real friendliness and helpfulness which everyone should feel toward his fellow men.

The final quality required of the credit man is *honesty*, and by honesty is meant more than our ordinary conception of the word, more than an absence of an intent to deceive. The Latin word *honestas* more accurately expresses the quality desired. The credit man should have honor, high moral worth, a nobleness of character. He should strive to fulfill the highest ideals of his profession. It is a fine sense of obligation to others and to himself. As the credit man bases his actions upon confidence, so must the confidence of the entire business world repose in the credit man. His character should be beyond question.

A quality which will prove of inestimable value may be a combined diplomacy and leadership. The author has in mind particularly the necessity of these two qualities in dealing with embarrassed or insolvent accounts. The handling of insolvent accounts calls for united, and not individual, action upon the part of creditors. Having investigated the case and having arrived at a decision of the best plan to adopt, the necessity arises of getting the agreement and cooperation of other creditors. This will require a high degree of diplomacy, for other plans may be formulated by other creditors and tenaciously clung to by them. Diplomacy requires not only the ability to get the cooperation of others, but it requires the ability to yield and to cooperate as well. If the plan advanced cannot be adopted, then the next best plan must be supported. Since cooperation is a prime requisite diplomacy is invaluable in securing it; but obstinacy should have no place in the credit man's make-up.

The Educational Qualifications of the Credit Executive. This is the day of the educated man in business. That which we call business is a system and a science which has been elevated to equality with the learned professions. To be a businessman carries with it the idea, not only of a certain practical shrewdness and capacity, but also of vision in a mastery of its processes, its organization, its specialization, and its complexity. The day of the glorification of the self-made businessman is passing, because trained men are stepping into the responsible positions. In earlier days the young man learned his craft by serving an apprenticeship. If a young man desired to become a lawyer, he "read law" during spare moments while doing odd jobs in a lawyer's office. The businessman started as an office boy, and it was thought until a few years ago that one could become a credit man only by serving a long apprenticeship in a credit department. That method is tedious and narrow, and it does not oftentimes give a breadth of training or a thorough understanding of principles. The student should not get the impression that an apprenticeship can be avoided; but the apprenticeship which must inevitably be served will be greatly shortened by preparation.

The credit man is essentially a student. Education will give him a well-equipped historical background and a technical knowledge, but he must be a student of events and have an alert sense of the significance of business developments. He must develop the ability to see ahead. Credit men, because of their constant study of it, should be able to read the future better than any other group engaged in business enterprises. There must be a greater ability to foresee, and with accurate foresight will come the ability to control.

As a part of his education, the young man, or woman, is advised to identify a few of the clearest thinking minds of his day. To such leaders in economic thought close heed should be paid. Such men not only think clearly but express themselves with convincing force and clearness and, in so doing, help us all to mold a sound economic philosophy. Their utterances should be carefully considered and weighed. Such men aid the student to recognize and understand the political and economic trend of the times. The student will need to exercise care in making his selection among the many books, articles, speeches, and private conversations, as a basis for the development of his ideas. His selection, however, must be broad enough so that he may view questions of public interest in their entirety. The credit man who would rise above the mere routine of his office will wish to direct his attention to the underlying factors which are constantly making future business history.

The student may say that the requirements enumerated call for a superman. Not a superman because there will be in the future many executives who fulfill these qualifications. When we behold what two generations have accomplished in progress, and when we realize that our speed forward is now as rapid as it has ever been, it is realized that only a man with vision can paint a picture of what business will be 30 years hence. More records on a national scale are being kept, and still more will be kept in the future and with greater accuracy. These records must be wisely interpreted to maintain the even flow of the use of credit.

The young man, or woman, who has decided to enter the credit field in business is often confronted with the problem as to how he may best prepare himself for that field. The young man, as well, who is already engaged in credit work wishes to know how he may ensure for himself the most rapid promotion. The answer is to augment the qualifications enumerated in the earlier part of this chapter by a thorough and systematic training. A knowledge of certain subjects may be regarded as essential, while some familiarity with other subjects is highly desirable. This knowledge can be obtained by anyone with a common school education who possesses other requisite qualifications, although in the field of credits as well as in other fields of business, the college-trained man will no doubt be given the preference. Certain it is that familiarity with the debit and credit sides of a ledger account and a knowledge of how to look up a Dun & Bradstreet rating will no longer satisfy an employer as to an applicant's qualifications. Many credit men have found themselves in the credit field by chance, and without any special preparation. Their school has been that of practical experience, and their instructor, or instructors, the man or men with whom they have been associated. The result has been a good, a bad, or an indifferent training. It is an accepted fact that one cannot long closely associate with another without acquiring something of the moral and mental habits of that person. Especially is this true of one at a young and impressionable age. It behooves everyone, therefore, to choose his or her associates in the credit field, or out of it, as carefully as circumstances will permit. Experience is invaluable but progress is much more rapid if supplemented by systematic study.

Credit as a Field of Occupation. The author has some misgiving in attempting to pose as an impartial critic of credit as a field of occupation for young men and women. There is the danger of the presentation of a biased opinion. It is a question whether one so close to an occupation is best qualified to discuss it. There may be a tendency to take too strong a position on one side or the other. One is apt to take too strong a position in thinking that his own field of endeavor is superior or, on the contrary, that pastures are greener in other fields.

The first question to arise is: Who is the credit executive? He is the "specialist, the analyst, the business critic who guides and controls all the transactions of the market place." He controls either goods or money. He will be found in the office of the manufacturer, the wholesaler or jobber, the exporter, the retailer. He is also in the commercial bank, the investment bank, the finance company, and the note-brokerage house. In fact, he will be found in every business except the comparatively few confining themselves to cash sales. He performs a distinct function for which he needs a special though broad training. It is the young man or woman who is ready when the opportunity comes who gets the promotion. As a matter of fact, preparation for credit work is excellent preparation for other lines of endeavor as well. It is true that opportunities are more numerous in some other fields among which may be mentioned selling and accounting, but so are the contestants more numerous, and competition for advancement keener.

A survey of the members of the National Association of Credit Management brought out the information that the credit man holds the title of

Treasurer or secretary in 37.09 per cent of the companies
Auditor or controller in 7.37 per cent of the companies
Vice-president or general manager in 6.91 per cent of the companies
Credit manager (a definite department executive) in 36.06 per cent of the companies
In only 12.57 per cent was the credit man listed as a junior executive

The young man or woman choosing a field of occupation needs to consider whether the advantages are sufficiently attractive or the disadvantages sufficiently unattractive to sway the decision. The credit man finds himself in a generally pleasant environment and with pleasing associations. There is both the opportunity and the need for constant study and improvement. The work is interesting if one is adapted to it, and the credit man may take comfort in the feeling that he is performing a service not only to his house but to society as well. Credit managers are business stabilizers. His work is steady. He is not subject to the violent fluctuations of good and bad business, as some other occupations are. On the other hand, the work is confining in the sense that it is an all-year-round job and an all-year responsibility.

A question which may arise is whether the credit field is oversupplied or undersupplied with personnel. If the question means merely too many or too few credit men, it may be stated that there are neither. Businessmen, however, are looking for young men with tact, adaptability, and good judgment for credit departments. It is, perhaps, harder to break into the credit department because the employment turnover is usually less than in the accounting and sales departments, for example, but, once placed satisfactorily, a pleasant and remunerative career is assured. There is a large chance for improvement in the quality of credit departments' personnel. This is an age of specialization, and it is less than a working lifetime since the credit man was recognized as a specialist in his field. As a result it must be said, in truth, that many are found in credit work with neither aptitude nor training. Credit managers recognize the need and to encourage improvement are actively sponsoring credit education.

The credit manager can hardly complain of his environment. It is true that he is termed an office man, which suggests confinement and is therefore distasteful to some persons. But the credit man is less confined than is the accountant. The best credit men are not tied down to desks. Environment depends largely upon the individual concern. The credit manager is an executive in the financial department of his house. He is on an equal plane with other department heads, and he meets the heads of concerns or the officers of the houses with which he comes into contact. His environment includes his association with other credit men. The promotion of credit standards is attained, in part, through social functions—dinners, conventions, golf tournaments, etc. By education, training, and business standing he is qualified to associate with the best. His business associations will, of course, depend upon the type of men in his business and the type of customers of his business.

TEXT AND RESEARCH QUESTIONS

1. What three principal factors are responsible for the development of modern large-scale business enterprise? How are these same factors related to the development of the modern credit department?

2. Classify the development of American business since colonial times into three principal periods, and indicate the outstanding characteristics of each period as related to the development of credit work.

3. List and briefly explain the essential business qualifications of the credit man.

4. What are the principal educational qualifications in order of their importance?

5. Under what principal division of business is the credit and collection function usually placed? What functions of business are the last ones to be delegated or surrendered by the owner?

6. Summarize the advantages and disadvantages of placing the credit and collection department (*a*) under the supervision of the accounting and treasurer's department; under that of (*b*) the sales department; (*c*) as an independent department.

7. It is frequently said that "the credit manager of today is the treasurer of tomorrow." Why is this so?

8. Should the credit manager avoid routine work so far as it is possible for him to delegate it to others? Why?

PROBLEM

Assume that you are president of a medium-size manufacturing corporation. What are the minimum qualifications you would require of the person who was to be manager of the credit and collection department?

a. In education?

b. In experience?

c. In character and personality?

CHAPTER 3

THE ORGANIZATION AND FUNCTION OF
CREDIT DEPARTMENTS IN BUSINESS ORGANIZATIONS

The Credit Department's Function. The primary function of both bank and trade credit departments is through proper credit analysis and through sound collection methods to reduce business losses to a minimum, thus assisting the company to make a profit. This should be stressed because of the view often taken by those outside the credit department that its work is essentially destructive instead of constructive. It must be confessed, in truth, that this criticism of the operation of certain credit departments is justified because the heads of such departments become unduly obsessed with the importance of avoiding losses. In their zeal to protect their employers from losses, and at the same time to acquire for themselves a reputation for small bad-debt losses, they become overconservative and refuse to accept those credits which seem to have even the slightest hazard in them.

While a credit manager by exercising keen judgment and by adopting a conservative policy may avoid all but a few losses, he will never, except by chance, attain a perfect record. It is obvious that if he errs in accepting some risks, that is, those which prove to be bad, he will also err in rejecting some risks which are good. There is an imaginary line between the good and the bad risks, which, like the division between the true and the false, is no wider than a hair. It is this line of division which the credit man attempts to follow. That is, it is his task to select from the business offered his company that which will result in maximum profits with minimum losses.

A second way in which the credit department can assist in making a profit is through the promotion of a spirit of good will. It is necessary that the credit department should do more than successfully prevent the development of a spirit of dissatisfaction and ill will. The credit department must be a business getter, not in the manner that the sales department is a business getter, nor by employing the sales department tactics, but by its fair action and friendly attitude it paves the way for the sales department. Merchandise, price, and service may be satisfactory to the purchaser, but if the credit relationship, the most delicate of all, be not wisely handled, the business will go elsewhere. The credit manager often is able to cement the friendship of a customer to his house where the sales department has failed. To bind more closely the customers to the institution may be said to be one of the chief functions of the credit department.

The credit department is aided in the accomplishment of maximum profits and minimum losses by its skill in making collections. It is easily comprehensible that the good collector will retrieve some bad credit decisions which, with the poor collector, would result in bad debts. On the other hand, the credit man who is a poor collector not only will lose some collectible credits, but, through delinquent accounts and inefficient collection methods, he makes needless expense for his house.

Another essential in effecting maximum profits and minimum losses is cooperation with other credit departments and other credit men. The day is past when the credit man can function without the assistance of other credit men. He must both impart and receive information. By the very nature of his work, he is dependent upon other credit men for information and for cooperative action in cases of liquidation and bankruptcy. The credit man's individual success is dependent in a measure on the efficiency and the moral plane on which the credit profession stands.

This cooperation is effected by the exchange of credit information through inquiries, personal interviews, trade group meetings, and, indirectly, though by no means of less importance, by furnishing to mercantile agencies and interchange bureaus such information as they may desire regarding credit risks.

Cooperation among credit managers is still far from being complete, although steady progress toward that goal is to be noted. All credit managers are interested in the same goal, namely, to raise the standard of credit and thereby remove as much of the risk from credit as is possible. But some credit managers are unable to adopt a farsighted policy. They refuse to give information freely and fully, and they are suspicious of information given them. They strive for personal advantage and preference with the embarrassed accounts. Such credit managers are not to be trusted, and the man without a high sense of honor and integrity has no place in the ranks of credit men. Improvement in cooperative work has been greatly hastened by the educative measures of the National Association of Credit Management, but much remains to be accomplished.

Its Place in the Business Organization. That this is an age of specialization is just as true of business management as of any other field of human endeavor. A business, before it had grown out of modest proportions, was largely under the control of one man, the owner, who directed the three main activities of business—production, marketing, and financing. With the growth of business units, it became necessary to delegate these functions to others, and then further to subdivide the activities of these divisions. The question, which is not yet entirely settled, is whether the credit department should be an integral part of the financing or marketing branch of a business. It is not only most logical, but also according to the more general practice, to regard the credit department as a part of the financing branch of business activity. Credit is temporarily substituted for money in the sale of merchandise, and the control of this substitute is logically a function of the financing branch of a business. The financing branch of the management is charged with the duty of keeping the business financially sound and with providing funds for the regular activity and special campaigns or ventures of the business. It could hardly be expected to function properly, or be held accountable, if the control of both outgo and income were not in its hands. The company's financial plan and credit policy are bound up in each other.

Relation to Sales Department. It is found that in some houses the credit department is under the influence of the sales manager. In too many others while the credit department is nominally under the control of the treasurer, it is actually under the dominance of the sales manager. Where the credit department is under the control of the sales department, the claim is made that both the selling of merchandise and the gathering of credit data are facilitated, and the sales force cooperates to the greatest degree in following up accounts and making collections. It is claimed that harmony of action is much more certain of attainment where both selling and credit approval are under the approval of one department head. Furthermore, it is contended that, since both departments are working for increased sales, that end will be best attained by having the two departments supervised by one head.

The Independent Credit Department. Many executives are agreed that a concern is best served if its credit department is not subject to dictation from any direction, except that it shall, of course, conform to the policy laid out by the management for it to follow. The credit manager, appreciating fully the function of his department, will serve his house best if his actions are not constricted through the dominance, or the attempt at dominance, by any other department.

A credit manager must make some delicate decisions which command the best efforts of his experienced and specially trained mind. He is a specialist, and, if qualified for the position which he holds, his judgment of a credit risk is superior. He should be, therefore, unhampered by any outside influences in coming to a decision, and, once the decision is made, it should be final. If the credit department works thus independently, its opinions and decisions are based upon actual evidence at hand, unbiased by any outside influences. On the other hand, if the credit manager's decisions are subject to constant review and reversal by a higher authority, the credit manager works under the fear of displeasing a superior officer, or he gets in the habit of evading responsibility by consulting the superior officer or seeking his advice before a decision is made.

From the above discussion, the reader should not draw the conclusion that the credit manager should go about his work with an independent and arbitrary attitude. On the contrary, he needs to keep in constant and closest touch with other departments. Consultations and conferences are vitally essential for the good of the business. These conferences, however, are sought by the credit manager not for assistance in making a decision, but rather for the purpose of getting information upon which to base a decision, or perhaps to impart information in regard to credit department activity. It frequently happens in some concerns that after the credit department has rejected an order the salesman or sales manager attempts to get a reconsideration of it by offering some information having a distinct credit bearing but hitherto thoughtlessly withheld. The proper time to present such information is with the order, and there is a distinct lack of proper coordination between departments where this is not done.

The sales and credit departments sometimes become antagonistic toward each other. The sales department usually measures its results by volume of sales. In attaining volume, it is met by keen competition in price, quality of goods, and service. Where volume of sales, which affects salary and commissions, is at stake, the sales manager is most sensitive. A negative decision by the credit department upon a hard-earned order vexes the salesman and the sales manager. An attempt is made to influence the credit manager to change his decision. This is resented by the credit manager as an interference with his functional prerogative. Thus is friction and antagonism between the two departments engendered.

The remedy is not in uniting the two departments under one head or in making one superior to the other. Balance is more certain of accomplishment if the departments are entirely separate and equal in rank. The real remedy is found in the full realization of the function of each department and a complete and sympathetic appreciation on the part of each department of the difficulties under which the other labors.

To unite the two departments under one head would put an unfair burden upon that head. The sales manager, who works for volume, would find it extremely difficult not to be influenced where volume, commissions, and salaries might be at stake.

The Personnel of the Credit Department. Only a few general statements can be made concerning the personnel of the credit department since the demands made upon different credit departments vary so widely. One small house will have a credit manager acting also as the office manager, and perhaps as the accountant. His assistant or assistants also perform many duties in addition to credit tasks. In another house may be found a credit department with a full complement of workers: credit manager, assistant credit manager, secretary, stenographers, file clerks, adjustment clerk, statistician, collection correspondent, credit editors, reference clerk, investigators, and messengers. Nor is it possible to say how many employees should be required to handle, let us say, 15,000 accounts, or a given volume of business. The size of the department will depend upon the class of customers, that is, upon the amount of investigation that must be made, the amount of oversight and collection work required, the number of orders necessary to make a given volume of sales, as well as the intricacy of the general office system.

The success of the credit department depends first of all upon the department personnel from the credit manager down to the most humble employee and, secondly, upon the organization of the credit department work. The successful executive will select a personnel which can not only accomplish its work in the ordinary line of duty but which can on occasion perform the extraordinary. The following chart, Fig. 2, indi-

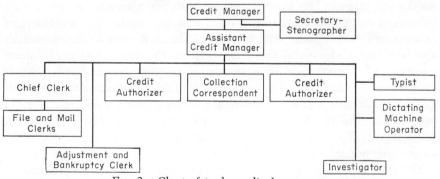

Fig. 2.   Chart of trade credit department.

cates in general the structural organization required to conduct a credit department.

Importance of System. Since the work of the credit department is dependent so largely upon recorded information, there is naturally an abundance of routine and detail work. There must be a system adequate to keeping the records accurate, up to date, and in order, and for the handling of the routine work of the department.

The credit manager's position is executive. He should not permit himself to become hampered by too much detail and routine work. This can be avoided by providing a system which will secure accuracy and accessibility of records and efficiency in handling them. With a competent and well-trained corps of assistants the credit manager is relieved of detail and has an opportunity to do constructive work.

By system is meant method in handling the work of the department and the division of duties among employees so that the functions of the department are accomplished with the greatest efficiency. Too much system resulting in red tape must be avoided. It is suggested that the credit manager will find it of considerable value to himself and to the workers of his department to write a manual covering credit department routine.

Mechanical Aids to Credit Department Efficiency. The credit department cannot attain a maximum degree of efficiency with a lack of system and without adequate mechanical aids. The saving of time is a cardinal principle in office management. In the credit department, this may mean more than the avoiding of unnecessary expense; dispatch may mean the saving of business. The credit executive will not permit his department to be hampered by inferior equipment. Most important among the mechanical aids are the credit files. They must provide accuracy, simplicity, and accessibility, for they are in constant use. The arrangement of the office, comfortable chairs, desks, and light are of no less importance. Dictating machines may add to the dispatch not only of outside correspondence but also to the typing of records and memoranda for internal office use. Billing and posting machines, although usually not under the credit manager's supervision, may greatly facilitate the credit department's work. That the workman is worthy of his tools is nowhere more true than in the credit department.

The Mercantile Credit Department Files. The elaborateness of the credit department files depends largely upon the number and size of the accounts. A large number of accounts will require larger filing space than will a small number, and so will large individual credits usually require more elaborate records than small credits. Every credit department, however, will need a credit information file, a correspondence file, a duplicate invoice file, and a customers' ledger. These files are, of course, subject to additions or variations. For example, some offices might well combine the credit and correspondence files, while others would wish to add an index file. Both files and forms should be adapted to the needs of the business, and the credit manager should consider carefully whether this is accomplished.

The Mercantile Credit Information File. The most advantageous form for this file is the vertical file with folders of letter size. Each account has an individual folder. The folders are of plain manila cardboard with or without a printed form on the cover containing an abstract of the material within. This file is usually on a straight alphabetical basis, though it may be arranged either geographically or numerically. In the latter case an index file is necessary.

The efficiency of this file depends upon its contents and the celerity with which the contents may be examined. Therefore, the method of filing, as well as the selection of material, is important, and the abstract placed on the cover may aid greatly. Within the folder will be found all material pertaining to the subject's credit, such as bank and trade stories, officers' memorandums, important correspondence with the customer, spread forms, financial statements, agency reports, newspaper clippings, and a record of inquiries. In addition, special analyses such as industry comparisons may be included, as well as salesmen's and business development reports. However, letters and papers of merely transitory interest, such as routine letters relating to collections, copies of invoices, and monthly statements, clutter up this file. Such material adds to its bulk and lessens its efficiency.

The Correspondence File. As its name indicates, this file contains the correspondence between the customer and the credit department. It may be run in different ways. Some credit departments keep this file within the credit offices for current correspondence only, sending the correspondence to the general file as fast as the department is through with it. In other offices, there is no separate credit correspondence file, all correspondence being in a general or central file. Here the method should fit the particular business.

The Duplicate-invoice File. The credit department in its various contacts with customers will find it necessary frequently to refer to copies of invoices. They should, consequently, be made available to the credit department. This can be accomplished by having an extra copy of the invoices made at the time of billing, or the general office copies may be made available to the credit department. Filing is primarily by date, and secondarily either geographically or alphabetically.

The Customers' Ledger. The customers' ledger performs a double function in some houses. It is a part of the accounting record and serves as well as an information file for the credit department. As a matter of fact, the customers' ledger is primarily a credit and collection control file, and might well be, as it frequently is, under the supervision of the credit manager. Frequently, objections present themselves to the use of the customers' ledgers by both the ledger clerks and the credit department. In such cases, what is virtually a duplicate customers' ledger is kept by the credit department. But unless certain difficulties present themselves, and where the credit and accounting departments are adjacent, such duplication may be, and obviously should be, avoided.

In commercial banks a daily record of changes in loans is sent to the credit department. This is often a duplicate of data sent to the accounting department.

Importance of Office Mechanism. To describe a credit office system which may be adapted to more than a very small percentage of businesses is clearly impossible. But the importance of system is stressed. This embraces the most efficient mechanical aids, carefully selected and well-trained assistants, and a carefully planned routine. The saving of time is a cardinal principle in credit office management. The true executive does not permit himself to be hampered by inefficient office methods, or by details which can be shifted to an assistant. The executive is constantly alert for improvements in equipment; yet he guards his department against too much system. Red tape has no place whatever in a credit office.

Initial costs for new systems at times appear to be heavy, and yet the most radical installations sometimes will pay for themselves in a short time. The aggressive and successful enterprise does not hesitate to throw out either its machinery or office equipment when either becomes obsolete. Once the question "Will the new equipment save sufficient time, labor, or space to cover the expense of installation?" is answered in the affirmative, the executive can go ahead with confidence.

The Bank Credit Department. It was not until the 'nineties of the last century that the bank credit department came into existence. Even today it is probable that in a majority of the country's banks no credit department will be found. In these banks, credit information is acquired by those officers of a bank who make the loans and is stored in their minds for use as occasion may require. As banks grow and the number of borrowers increases, the necessity for recorded credit data becomes imperative. A second reason for the bank credit department lies in the fact that there has been a considerable development of credit information. Credit is accepted less upon personal acquaintance, recommendations, or references and more upon factual data such as the financial statement, the income account, and the actual experiences of other creditors. The systematic acquisition and recording of such data were a natural sequence. The spread of the corporate form of organization, which facilitated the increased size of the units of business and made their investigation more complicated, was also a contributing factor, forcing them to reach beyond their local boundaries not only for goods and markets but also for financing.

It would be impossible for our larger banks to function without the storehouse of information at their service provided by the credit department.

The Functions of the Bank Credit Department. The bank credit department is a service department. Its value to the bank lies in the accuracy, completeness, and availability of credit information. It serves first of all the loaning officers, who are in fact senior credit executives, and then such other departments of the bank as may have occasion to use it. In a lesser sense, it is a department of service to others than its own organization. To a certain extent its information is available to other banks and to commercial houses which may have an interest in the credit of those whom the bank has investigated. This information is imparted to those customers of the bank who may seek it, to promote good will, and to others on the reciprocal basis under which credit information is generally freely exchanged among business houses.

The work of the credit department may be more clearly exemplified by dividing it into three general parts: (1) investigations, (2) analysis, and (3) filing.

The investigating function includes the assembling of all essential credit information from whatever sources it may be found. This work is largely entrusted to investigators, young men of good appearance and ability, who become skilled not only in locating information but in obtaining it. Officers of the bank, too, assist in the compilation of credit information. This is accomplished through memorandums which are made after customers have consulted various officers of the bank. Such interviews are much more common between bankers and borrowers than between mercantile credit men and customers and provide perhaps the most important sources of information to a bank. Indeed, it may be said that the bank never authorizes a credit without a personal conference except in those cases where the borrower's credit is so well established that the insistence upon an interview would be folly.

The second function, that of analysis, includes the arrangement and interpretation of the credit information. An important part of this division of the credit department's work is the transcription, comparison, and interpretation of financial statements. It should be pointed out, however, that the real or final analysis of credit information is performed by those credit officers whose duty it is to make the final decision as to the approval of credit. For the most part, the credit department puts the information in such form that interpretation is facilitated. A credit analyst usually works with a credit officer.

The third function, filing, may connote to the reader the orderly putting away of information for preservation. Filing in the bank credit department means rather the orderly arrangement of information for reference. The credit files are in constant use. Not only are they constantly referred to by the officers, but they are in constant use for the revision and addition of new information and as the source of information from which answers to credit inquiries are taken. This part of the third function of the department is so important that it might almost be made a separate function by itself, coming under the heading of reporting.

Structure of the Bank Credit Department. In order to cope adequately with each phase of credit department work the personnel is divided into sections, and the work not only of the sections but of individuals becomes quite specialized, particularly in the larger banks. The credit men, however, have an opportunity to become familiar with all the work of the department either through observation or through progressive promotion through the various sections.

The credit department, as a whole, is responsible to the credit manager, and he, in turn, is held responsible for satisfactory service. He occupies the focal position through which the department receives requests for information, and it is through him that information is conveyed to the credit officers. He may or may not be himself a credit officer. He frequently is made a member of the Loan and Discount Committee, sometimes with and sometimes without a vote in its decisions. He must be a man of experience and ability. Though he may have no authority to approve loans, even with the title of credit manager, this fact should not disparage his importance, for it will be noted that banks regard the approval of the larger loans, at least, as too important a matter for the decision of any single officer.

The credit manager in the larger banks has but little time for detail. Much of the actual supervision of the department is left to the assistant credit manager, and he in turn relies upon section heads to see that the work is properly performed.

The Bank Credit Folder. Even a brief survey of the bank credit department would not be complete without mention of the credit folder. Many credit folders are models of what a credit file should contain. Not only is the credit information virtually complete, but it is so classified and arranged that its contents are imparted to the reader in a most orderly manner.

A typical folder may be divided into the following sections:

Front Page or Flyleaf. This page will contain such information for perhaps a 5-year period as balance sheets, net working capital and current ratios, monthly loans and deposit balances, when the account was opened, by whom it was introduced, other bank accounts, credit line, and remarks.

Statement Section. In this section will be filed the original signed financial statements of the customer.

Investigations. This section contains the information obtained by investigators carefully written up, neatly typed, and initialed by the investigator.

Interviews. This section is similar to the above, but consisting of memorandums usually dictated by officers and initialed by them after a conference with the customer.

Analysis. This section comments upon the favorable and unfavorable features of the business or points out the more significant facts developed by the investigation.

Agency Reports. As the title suggests, here will be filed all commercial agency reports obtained on the subject.

Correspondence. This section includes not only correspondence with the subject but also copies of letters in answer to inquiries for credit information.

The folder covers are usually heavy glazed cardboard which stands up well under long and constant use. The various sections may have different-colored paper in addition to the divider sheets to distinguish them easily from each other. The contents of the folder are carefully bound to the cover. Such care in the make-up of the bank credit folder is necessary because of the importance of a credit file to a bank. The mercantile credit department, however, might not be justified in devoting so much time and expense to the preparation of its credit files.

Branch-office Credit Control. Many of the larger corporations have established branches which duplicate the functions of the home office to various degrees. Sometimes these branches perform the order-taking function only. In others an inventory is maintained and selling, shipping, and collecting are accomplished. In still others a plant as well as a selling organization may function. There is, obviously, no one best method for the control of credit in these branches of various types.

The system used may depend on many factors. Among them are the company's product, the size of the orders, the class of customers sold, the proximity to the home office, and the branch-office personnel. Where the branch is large enough to justify a credit department, many companies have found it best to establish such a department with a credit manager answerable only to the general credit executive at the main office. Credit, billing, and collecting functions are all handled at the branch. Whatever the branch credit manager's control, he should, of course, make daily, weekly, or monthly reports to his superior at the main office.

Limitations of various sorts are sometimes placed on the branch credit manager. His authority to approve credit may be limited to a certain amount, larger amounts being referred to the head office, or an account delinquent beyond a certain period may be taken out of his control.

The two chief advantages of the more or less independent branch credit department, other than the dispatch with which orders may be processed, are the proximity to both the customer and the sales department. The customer is thus more than a name to the credit manager and the credit manager is more than a name to the salesmen. The sales and credit departments can confer with each other and on-the-spot decisions can be made.

Where the branch performs merely the order-taking function, the orders are handled the same as those of salesmen reporting direct to the home office. No credit manager is needed. Credit is authorized, the goods are shipped, and billing and collecting are done at the plant. The entire control is centralized there.

Where the branch credit manager is more or less independent, the general credit manager will supervise closely enough so that he will be assured the credit policy of the company is being followed. This may not be so difficult to accomplish since it is probable the branch credit manager was home-office trained. Supervision may be accomplished by inspection of the credit information files, the customers' ledger, and a review of the collection procedure. Files for both rejected and accepted accounts may be reviewed. For the morale of the personnel of the branch credit department, inspection and supervision should not be overdone. As long as results are satisfactory the branch credit manager should not be too circumscribed in his actions.

Branch-bank Credit Control. Banks follow, in general, the methods outlined above in the handling of branch-bank credits. In a bank with many branch offices control by the main office may vary from almost none for some branches to complete for others. Where the functions of a branch are limited to receiving deposits, paying out money, and taking applications for loans, credit investigation, other than that conducted in the personal interview at the branch, and credit approval are functions performed by the main office. Where more or less independence is allowed the branch, the main office must maintain supervision and control. This may be accomplished by forwarding certain credit files to the home office for review. In other banks, experienced credit men are sent from the main office to the branches. They remain at the branch as long as necessary to review the files, to confer with, and to offer suggestions and criticisms to the loaning officers. Whatever the control it must be remembered the bank's board of directors is responsible for all loans.

Measurement of Credit Department Efficiency. At the beginning of the present chapter, it was said that the function of the credit department is to assist in making a profit for the house. The efficiency of the department, therefore, should be measured according to the part it plays in creating a profit. Actually this appraisal of the credit department is extremely difficult because of the intangible factors involved. The good will created or destroyed by the credit department cannot be accurately measured, nor can it be known how many errors are made in rejecting orders which would have resulted in good business and which thus represent lost profit.

It is but natural, therefore, to find that in many cases the credit department is judged almost solely by the tangible factors. Thus a few exceptions taken by customers to the actions of the credit department, and expressed through salesmen or by letter, may weigh heavily against the credit department in the judgment of the management. So, too, is a bad debt a tangible factor which militates against the efficiency record. As a result, many credit men are found who are extremely cautious. Collections are not boldly pressed through fear of offending the customer, and orders with more than a minimum of risk are rejected. Constructive work by the credit department is thus impossible. The efficiency of the credit department should rather be measured by a minimum of good business lost and by the number of doubtful and troublesome accounts which are successfully handled. These conditions together with small bad-debt losses, a minimum amount of capital tied up in accounts receivable, and reasonable credit department expense effect the maximum profit for a house.

The efficiency of a credit department may be supported by records of activities and results, all compared from period to period. Suggested measurement data are (1) volume of work, (2) new business rejected, (3) credit sales as proportion of total sales, (4) collection record, (5) bad debt record, (6) credit department expenses as per cent of sales or outstanding loans.

Volume of Work. In the volume of work, there should be included records of number of orders handled, or if a bank, number of loans made or renewed. The dollar amount in some cases is significant. Important is the number of inquiries handled and how they were processed and answered. For instance, a telephone request for information may be answered without further inquiry, or it may set up a whole chain of additional work activities.

New Business. A comparison of the number of orders or applications received with the number rejected may lead to further analysis, particularly if the proportion appears excessive.

Credit Sales Proportion. Knowing the proportion of cash sales to credit sales is important in evaluating trends in economic conditions. It is also useful in determining the collection period.

Collection Record. An "aging of receivables schedule" and a record of collection activity, particularly the ratio of collections per month to receivables at the beginning of the month, give clear indications of liquidity.

Bad-debt Record. If this record is maintained monthly by number and amount and related to credit sales, it shows the efficiency of the credit processing.

Credit Department Expense Ratio. Allocation of costs could materially affect this ratio of total expenses to sales or outstanding loans. The trend of the ratio is particularly significant when it is decreasing. The criterion of total sales is used because C.O.D. and similar terms are the result of credit department activities.

TEXT AND RESEARCH QUESTIONS

1. State briefly and clearly the primary function of the credit manager and the credit department.

2. Why should a credit department be well systematized? What essential files are to be found in the well-systematized credit department?

3. How would you set about determining or measuring the efficiency of a credit department?

4. Why is just the percentage of bad-debt loss in itself a poor measure of credit department efficiency?

5. "The cost of doing business on credit is the sum of credit and collection department costs and bad-debt losses." Why not abolish the credit department and avoid this expense? What arguments can you advance justifying the credit department?

6. Discuss the differences between trade and bank credit departments.

7. Contrast the data in a trade credit folder with those in a bank credit file.

PROBLEMS

1. In preparing an expense budget for the credit and collection department of a business concern, draw up a list of the items that should be included.

2. A fixes B's credit at $1,250. B now owes $1,125 to A; none past due, and sends in an order amounting to $625. Give three methods of handling the problem. In your opinion which is the best? Why?

3. The Natural and Artificial Stone Manufacturing Company, Inc., quarries and manufactures limestone, marble, and granite and also manufactures artificial stone products. Its products include raw and finished materials for buildings, mausoleums and other cemetery memorials, church altars, fonts, and statuary, etc. Its sales are to building contractors, other manufacturers of stone products, dealers in cemetery memorials, church supply houses, and others. Ten branches are placed in the larger cities throughout the country, each serving an allotted territory. Each branch controls its own credits and collections except contracts of $5,000 or more which are subject to the approval of the home office as to price, content, and credit. There are no organized credit departments, as such, and sales are made to regular accounts

without formal approval as to credits, but the manager is held to a general accountability.   The treasurer exercises a general supervision over credits and collections.   The result is a rather heavy bad-debt loss and a slow turnover of receivables on net 30-day terms.   The company now feels that its credits and collections should be put under a better control with closer supervision by the home office.

Outline a system for handling credits and collections with control centered at the home office.   Cover the delegation of authority and responsibility, and reports to be submitted.   Annual sales by branches range from about $200,000 for the smallest branch to several million dollars.

CHAPTER 4

FACTORS OF A SATISFACTORY CREDIT RISK

The Acceptable Credit Risk. The basis of our entire credit system rests upon the good faith of those who trade upon their credit. The fact that good faith is general rather than exceptional has not reduced necessarily the importance of a close scrutiny of those occasional instances where good faith is lacking. Searching for and avoiding the dishonest debtors is not the creditor's only task. He must also seek to protect the prospective debtor as well as himself from the debtor's imprudence. For it is imprudence on the part of the debtor, no matter how good his intentions, to assume a credit obligation which he will be unable to meet. It may also be stated that, solely from the standpoint of a satisfactory credit risk, the risk is completely and ultimately justified only when it has been canceled by payment. It is, therefore, apparent that the credit investigation is conducted to discover if the prospective debtor is acting in good faith and that he is not misjudging his future financial position in his expectation to have funds available with which to pay. In other words, the creditor wants a reasonably certain affirmative to the queries "Can he pay?" and "Will he pay?"

The Four C's of Credit. The answer to these two questions is sought by considering the risk on the basis of four factors: (1) the intensity of the debtor's desire to pay; (2) his ability to hold or become possessed of funds with which to pay; (3) the extent and form of his present wealth which may be regarded as insuring payment; (4) the extent to which he may be aided or hindered by business conditions in converting his wealth into cash before the maturity of the credit. These four factors of a credit risk have been tersely stated and are known to credit men as the character and the capacity of the debtor or management, the capital investment, and the economic conditions of the industry.

Some analysts have introduced a fifth C, which they title "collateral." As can readily be seen, this C refers to forms of assets which may be pledged to secure the loan. Such assets are accounts receivable, inventories, and marketable securities, which actually represent current

47

capital investments. Long-term capital investments, such as land, buildings, and equipment, are pledged most often in the form of a mortgage.

While these four factors are carefully investigated, the reader will not assume that there is any rigid standard by which to appraise the risk as acceptable or unacceptable. Each analyst fixes his own standard, and the standard of a single concern may be somewhat elastic. Nor should the reader assume that each of the four factors receives undivided attention. All may be appraised at one and the same time. The requirement is that the four factors should measure up to the required standard. To accomplish this, an excess of one factor may offset a deficiency of another. Thus, if a debtor should be somewhat deficient in the amount of capital desired, this deficiency might be more than offset by unusual capacity. However, a deficiency in character or capacity cannot be offset by an excess of capital. Stated in equation form, this would be expressed:

Character + capacity + capital + or − economic conditions = credit risk

Acceptability Varies with Policy. From the above equation it is not to be inferred that a credit risk has a fixed value. Its value depends upon the fineness of character, the amount of capacity, the quantity of capital, and the influence of the prevailing business and economic conditions. These cannot be equal in all risks, and therefore the risk in credit will have wide range. It may be the policy of one house to accept large risks while another concern may be unwilling to accept a credit where any risk can be discovered. If credit risk could be measured as we measure heat, we would find great fluctuations in the measuring fluid when testing various risks. If our graduated scale were marked at a certain point "Bank Credit" many concerns, upon test, would fail to register their credit that high. Many of these concerns would, however, register sufficiently high credit to reach the standards of different commercial houses which would be found at different gradations upon the scale. To continue the simile, the credit man is interested only in his own standard. He applies the test to the applicant's credit to satisfy himself that the measurement is definitely above or below his standard and the risk is accordingly accepted or rejected.

Reasons for Varying Policies. Credit is a vital force in the promotion of industry. It is obvious, however, that, if the losses caused by poor credit judgment exceed the profits resulting from the increased business, the use of credit as a trade builder defeats its end. What then determines the maximum of profit?

Obviously, a first consideration is the margin of profit in the sales. As was pointed out in a previous chapter, the greater the margin of profit, the greater the risks that may be assumed. A liberal credit policy is, therefore, to be expected where the profit margin is large. Conversely, where sales are on a narrow margin of profit, the credit policy must necessarily be strict. A business organized on a basis of large-scale production and requiring a large volume of sales may adopt a liberal policy. Keen competition may force a more liberal credit policy than the house would otherwise desire. In a competitive warfare between two houses selling branded merchandise, sales on inferior credit risks may be made on the theory that the competitor would accept the risk if your house refused it. While the risk may be admittedly distinctly inferior, the action may be justified on the reasoning that the competitor's goods are stifled, and the disadvantage of the greater risk is thus offset. On the other hand, where there is a public demand for a certain branded article, the seller is in a position to enforce strict terms and maintain a high credit standard. Such a monopolistic concern may, however, adopt a very liberal credit policy if it is convinced that greater sales and greater profit will result through the increased volume of production.

While the credit policy of a house cannot be arbitrarily fixed by its credit manager, that policy is without doubt affected by the credit manager's mental attitude. The nature of one credit manager may tend to make him extremely cautious or conservative. Such a credit manager will be inclined to reject greater risks, while another, imbued more with a gambling spirit, will find it difficult to reject any risks except those of the very lowest class. Or one credit manager may have the mistaken idea that a very low percentage of bad-debt losses will rank the efficiency of the credit department as very high, while another may have an equally mistaken idea that somewhat larger losses do not matter, provided a large volume of sales is attained.

Occasionally, a credit manager is encountered who is too greatly influenced by some past personal experience. He may stress, for example, the necessity of capital to the neglect of the other credit factors, or he may be inclined to require more than adequate insurance protection because of an unfortunate experience with a customer who had been inadequately insured. These personal inclinations of the credit manager are to be avoided. They are indications of lack of balance in reasoning power.

Credit Policy and the Merchandising Attitude. It will be found that the credit policies of many houses are elastic. This may be due, not to a lack of policy, but to the necessity of fitting the policy to merchandising needs. This is an age of short-lived merchandise. From manufacturer to consumer, each link in the chain strives for a quick turnover. Sometimes forced liquidation of an inventory is not only desirable, but it may be vital, in order to avoid large losses. Manufacturers and jobbers used to find a market for merchandise which had gone out of style in some rural districts where style was not a particularly important factor. Today, however, not only do styles change more rapidly but they are almost instantly known throughout the country. Goods thus affected have a much wider range of sale than is generally supposed. It may, therefore, become incumbent upon the credit manager for a furniture manufacturer as well as upon the credit manager of the dress house to aid in disposing of an inventory. To meet this or other exigencies, the standard of credit is lowered. On the other hand, when a seller's market prevails, or when the danger of the credit risk is accentuated by adverse business conditions, there is the necessity of raising the credit standard. It is thus apparent that the credit policy and the marketing policy must be coordinated and that the credit manager must have a merchandising as well as a credit point of view.

Analysis of Credit and Analysis of Credit Reputation. In practice it is frequently found that some credit men mistake credit reputation for credit worth. One credit manager regards it as his task to ascertain if the customer has a good credit reputation. He strives to learn how others regard the risk and he acts accordingly. Another credit manager regards as his function the necessity to delve into both the past and present business life, not only to learn the credit reputation of the customer, but to appraise for himself both the willingness and the ability of the customer to pay. It is needless to say that the latter method is superior to the former, provided, of course, that the credit manager is possessed of analytical ability and good judgment, or, in other words, that he correctly appraises the credit worth. The credit manager should not, however, have too great a degree of independence of judgment, unless it be in forming a negative opinion.

By this is meant that, since, with rare exceptions, credit is an essential to the success of a business, a good credit reputation is of extreme importance. While the credit reputation may be good, the risk may actually be poor. This is because the majority of credit men, in appraising the risk, have erred in their appraisal. The credit manager sensing the poor risk would be forced by his judgment to reject it. If the converse were true, and the risk a safe one, though rejected by practically all interested credit men, the credit manager who correctly appraised the risk as a safe one could ill afford to accept the credit, because one creditor would find it very difficult to insure the success of the account, no matter how liberally credit might be accepted. The conclusion to be drawn is that the credit manager may act contrary to the prevailing opinion of creditors when it is his decision that credit should be refused, but that he cannot safely do so when the use of credit is being generally denied to the subject.

Character. There is some significance in the fact that credit men, in naming the factors essential to a satisfactory risk, usually place character first. The assumption is that it is regarded as the most important. This seems logical, for, first of all, there must be not only a willingness to pay, but beyond that, a determination to pay. Determination to pay will be found to vary directly with character. Thus, an entire lack of character may signify not only no determination to pay but even an intention to defraud the creditor. The creditor might, it is true, rely upon the law to exact payment where the capital factor is great, but credit managers frequently have found to their sad experience that the profit in such a case is not worth the trouble and expense.

Never deal with a rascal under the impression you can prevent him from cheating you. The risk in such cases is greater than the profits.[1]

This is sound advice. Matching shrewdness against shrewdness appeals to the speculative instincts of man, but the chances of success are no greater than in shaking loaded dice with a cheat. The speculative tendency in man is hard to resist at times, but it should be remembered that it has no place in conservative credit practice.

Character, however, is not alone sufficient for the approval of credit.[2] Character is merely a moral endowment incapable of doing more than directing the force found in capacity and capital. Yet it is placed first because it may be likened to a switch which throws into operation the dynamo (capacity) which supplies the real power (capital) to redeem a credit.

Character is a difficult quality to appraise. One reason for this is that it possesses no unit of measurement. We can only describe it by adjectives of indeterminate degree such as high, great, low, little, etc. Again, it is an intangible possession, which may be easily simulated. While the credit man seeks accurately to appraise character, what he usually investigates is in reality reputation. The distinction between the two is one of considerable degree. Character is within a man himself, while reputation is in the minds of others. Reputation may or may not be a true appraisal of character. Certainly it is much easier to learn what a man is thought to be than what he actually is. The danger then

[1] Hugh McCullough, First Comptroller of the Currency, *Circular Letter to National Banks,* 1864.

[2] The late J. P. Morgan testifying some years ago in a congressional investigation stated that the basis of credit is character. This statement coming from such an authority made a profound impression upon the business world. Some credit men have regarded the statement as unfortunate in that it gave undue importance to the character factor in a credit risk. J. P. Morgan undoubtedly meant by character the personal element which would obviously include a man's capacity as well as his character, but exclude the capital factor.

is that those who have some acquaintance with a man and who, therefore, are responsible for his reputation, may have erred in their appraisal of him. On the other hand, it may be stated that a man's
character controls his action, and it is from a man's deeds that his reputation is built up.

Character is given a plus or minus rating according to the standard
fixed by the appraiser himself. The standards of business morality will
be found to differ among individuals, but more marked, perhaps, is the
fact that the standards of business morality of some nations differ decidedly from ours. This is a condition that can hardly be ignored in
the appraisal of character where the credit man is dealing with individuals of different nationality.

Appraising Character. The student of credit measurement often finds
an unsatisfactory answer to the question as to how character is to be
appraised. The reason is largely because character is an intangible
quality which can be appraised best through intimate contact. If one
thoroughly knows an individual it is not difficult to weigh his character.
The best advice that can be given, therefore, is to learn everything possible about the past life and record of the prospective customer. Integrity, obedience to law, clean living, and loyalty are qualities of character and should be investigated. Learn, if possible, how good his word
is, his personal habits, his manner of living, his amusements, his environment, and his business code of ethics. Get positive information. Character is frequently misinterpreted because failure to discover unfavorable facts is interpreted as proof of high moral worth. Inaccurate appraisal of character by credit men is probably due more to lack of
information than to a misinterpretation of data. The character factor
must be "plus."

Capacity. In so far as character and capacity are both personal
attributes, they may be said to be correlatives, but here the analogy ends.
High character does not imply great capacity. Nor does great capacity
indicate high character, although the possessor may recognize that "honesty is the best policy." Both factors must be separately appraised,
even though the investigation of both is conducted simultaneously.
Naturally, the investigation of the personal quality of the risk will reveal
both character and capacity attributes.

Capacity, like character, is an intangible possession for which there
is no unit of measurement. Our appraisal of it, therefore, is comparative. The capacity at the disposal of a business may be found solely in
one man, as in the case of a sole proprietorship, or it may be necessary
to appraise the managerial ability of more than one man, as in the case
of a partnership or corporation. In a partnership or a corporation, one
man is often found to be the dominating force. It naturally follows then

that his capacity appraisal will be given the most weight, although those who share with him the managerial function cannot be neglected.

Capacity, to the credit manager, means more than active mental power. The student is apt to think of it merely as mental ability. In a word, it means both physical and mental power, plus the activity with which they are exercised. While mere brawn without brain is practically useless in the management of business, a good physique with a capacity for hard work adds greatly to the capacity factor. The age of management, therefore, has considerable significance. It indicates both physical ability and experience of the managers. Capacity normally increases with experience. Energy, aggressiveness, ambition, shrewdness, and judgment should be taken into consideration. Technical knowledge of the business itself should increase with experience, while a change to a new business may detract considerably from the capacity rating. Other factors to be taken into consideration are executive ability, general education, and training, location of the business with respect to its special advantages and disadvantages, and general business methods.

Two classes of credit applicants are presented with respect to the capacity factor: those who have demonstrated their capacity, or lack of it, and those who are just embarking in business and have yet to reveal their capacity to run a business. Some, in the weighing, will hang in the balance. Although in business for years, they seem to have made no particular headway. Such a risk always in the balance will eventually fall below it, for the inexorable law of nature will compel him to slow up in initiative and energy. On the other hand, a long record of honest and successful business, though without the accumulation of great capital, is strong evidence of the satisfactory capacity of the businessman.

Capacity stands next to character, for the man of character, having a will to pay, and capacity, will find a means to pay. Moreover, a man with high capacity may be relied upon not to obligate himself to such an extent that he cannot find the means to pay.

Capital.[1] In credit practice, it may appear that more attention is given to the analysis of the capital factor than to the character and capacity factors. However, every good credit executive automatically looks for character and capacity before appraising capital. The apparently great importance of the capital factor in the approval of credit is a result of the increasing use of the financial statement as a part of the supporting data.

Capital is a tangible factor and we have a unit of measurement for it—the dollar. Moreover, the businessman has been educated to expose his capital through the medium of the financial statement, and, after all, it

---

[1] Capital and net worth are used interchangeably in this discussion.

must be remembered that it is with the dollar that the loan is to be repaid.

To the credit manager capital means the financial strength of the risk. First of all, it is the amount of money which the subject has at the risk of the business, augmented sometimes by capital which may be invested in or at the risk of other enterprises. Not only is the quantity of capital learned but the nature of the assets in which it is invested and the proportion invested in each.

Capital is the amount which the businessman holds out as a guarantee that a credit transaction entered into can be redeemed. Capital represents the extent to which losses occasioned by errors in business judgment, adverse business conditions, or acts of Providence, such as floods, tornadoes, etc., can be absorbed. The creditor will, naturally, require such a margin of safety, and this margin of safety will necessarily be in proportion to the hazard and to the amount of credit which is used. The creditor will desire to know not only the extent of the capital but also how it was acquired. Whether it is increasing or decreasing, or whether it was acquired by the successful prosecution of the business or by inheritance, will make a vast difference in the final appraisal of the risk. It would be folly to consider the mere financial record as all important; but this record, if honestly compiled, reflects both capacity and character, and is a silent witness to both these intangible qualities.

How to obtain and analyze information on these four factors will be more fully treated in the following chapters.

Condition of Business. In addition to a complete consideration of the three C's—Character, Capacity, and Capital—which may be called internal factors, there are certain external factors over which the credit applicant has little or no control, but which may have a profound influence upon the appraisal of the credit risk. These factors are summarized under the heading Business Conditions—the fourth C of Credit. Most businesses are subject to two types of movement: (1) the regularly recurring seasonal activity and (2) the irregular oscillation of business as a whole. The seasonal activity is expected and can largely be discounted, although the credit manager may not be able accurately to forecast whether the season is to be good or bad. Any number of seasonal industries could be cited. In fact, it would be more difficult to name an industry which is not affected to some extent by seasonal activity. The largest single industry in the country—farming—is distinctly seasonal and casts its influence over industries not even remotely connected with farming. As specific illustrations, toys, paints and varnish, wall paper, and clothing might be cited. The amount of credit which a businessman in a seasonal business may advantageously use, and which, therefore, may be accepted by the creditor with safety, varies with the time of the season. The creditor will take this seasonal variation of credit power carefully into consideration.

When considering the second type of movement, it is necessary, as has been stated in Chapter 1, to consider not only the general movement or trend of business but more particularly to study the status of the particular industry under investigation. This latter movement may be in direct contrast to the larger movement commonly known as the business cycle. Consequently, credit conditions may be found to be generally good in a certain industry while the status of industry, as a whole, may be one of general depression. Business movement has been likened to the ebb and flow of the tide. The businessman, who is ever striving to make progress in one direction, is aided or retarded according to the direction of the tide. When the tide is swiftly against him, the businessman needs staunch character and high capacity reinforced by a comfortable margin of capital. Such a man, a satisfactory risk under adverse conditions, will become an A No. 1 risk when business conditions are better.

Comparative Values of Credit Factors. If a good credit risk has Character, Capacity, and Capital in satisfactory proportions and business conditions are good, success is presumed. From this it may be assumed that the failures in business are lacking in one or more of the credit factors and that a careful study of the histories of business failures would disclose the relative importance of the four factors in the credit risk. Creditors have made such studies. It is unfortunate that the causes of failure of *each* failed concern are not determined and tabulated for the benefit not only of credit managers but of business management itself. The real cause of failure of a business is often difficult to determine, and creditors are loath to finance such studies. Sufficient studies have been made to prove that far more failures are due to a lack of managerial ability[1] than to dishonesty or to insufficient capital, whereas adverse business conditions may have occasioned the failure rather than have caused it. Lack of capital, it is easily demonstrable too, is usually the *occasion* of the failure rather than its *cause.* For instance, let us assume that six men with equal capital engage in business as druggists in the same city and, let it be assumed, with equal opportunity. If one of them should fail, lack of capital could not be the cause, for if it were, since all had equal capital, all would fail. Under the assumption of equal capital, equal opportunity, and honest intent upon the part of all, it is obvious that the first to fail is the man with the least business ability,

[1] Dun & Bradstreet: Successive studies have shown that management failure accounts for more than 70 per cent of all failures in any one year.

or capacity.[1] The next to fail will be he who ranked next in capacity and so down the line until by the removal of competition better business conditions in the retail drug field offsets low business ability in the marginal producer and no more failures occur.

Analyses of business failures have disclosed much dishonesty, but the dishonesty has been largely the *result* of the failure rather than the cause of it. If only a small fraction of those who fail do so because of dishonesty and only a small fraction fail, then it is clear that credit managers need fear only a fraction of a fraction of their potential customers so far as the Character factor is concerned. In spite of this, Character cannot be ignored, for lack of it should definitely remove the man or business from consideration.

Granting, then, that lack of Character is the cause of an insignificant number of failures compared with the total number of businesses, and that poor business conditions and a somewhat inferior capital position may be offset by good managerial ability, it would seem incumbent on credit managers to investigate most thoroughly the Capacity factor. Both its investigation and its appraisal are, however, extremely difficult, for reasons that will readily occur to the thoughtful student. Credit managers in practice, therefore, rely heavily on the insurance feature or guarantee provided by the Capital factor, accepting as satisfactory the Character and Capacity factors with but little real substantiating data. Credit losses would almost vanish were credit managers sufficiently omniscient to put a correct appraisal on managerial ability.

TEXT AND RESEARCH QUESTIONS

1. *a.* What are the two fundamental questions to be answered in every credit risk?
    b. How may these two questions be broken down into four factors, and what in your opinion is the order of their importance?
    c. If an excellent credit risk can be given a value of 100 per cent, criticize the allocation of values, or show the impracticability of attempting to assign definite values to individual factors as in the following equation: Character (25 per cent) + capacity (35 per cent) + capital (40 per cent) = credit risk (100 per cent) when business conditions neither aid nor hinder success.
2. Why does the acceptability of a credit risk vary with the credit policy?
3. In what way may style changes in merchandising affect the credit policy?
4. *a.* How does character differ from reputation?
    b. Do they ever coincide?
    c. In practice do credit men appraise character or reputation? Why?
5. How would you proceed to investigate a debtor's "capacity"?

[1] Cf. Foulke, R. A., and R. V. Prochnow, "Practical Bank Credit," p. 566.

6. How should a credit man keep himself informed as to business conditions?

7. What is the function of the capital factor in a credit risk?

8. Why is the accurate appraisal of the capacity factor difficult?

PROBLEM

Assume that you are credit manager for a concern supplying automobile parts and accessories, chiefly to garages. Your salesman has obtained a first order amounting to $450 on which the customer has asked credit for 30 days. Your salesman has obtained and reports to you the following information in regard to the customer:

R. A. Olson, age 39, married. Investment in business $5,000. Has no other property. Runs a repair garage and filling station. Worked as a carpenter until 1946 when he bought a chicken farm with which he was unsuccessful. For past several years has worked as helper and machinist in various garages. Started present business 5 months ago. Drives a 3-year-old Buick sedan which he bought second-hand for $650. Bank reports he carries a high three-figure checking account. Has never asked for a loan. Aiding in support of a crippled sister. Occupies corner location on main highway. Building is one-story frame construction, somewhat in need of repair. Town has about 12,000 population. Only industry in town is working on half time. Business conditions in town not good. Reported main highway to be relocated four blocks away. Mr. Olson well spoken of by other garage men in town.

a. Classify the above information under the captions Character, Capacity, Capital, and Business Conditions. Include every statement in one (or more) classifications.

b. Summarize the information in brief statements under the above four captions.

c. State whether you would or would not approve the order. Explain your answer.

CHAPTER 5

DOCUMENTS AND RECORDS OF CREDIT TRANSACTIONS

Credit and Documents of Credit. The student who has a clear conception of credit will not confuse credit, which may be an unused power, with credit documents, which are merely the evidence of credit transactions. While credit in its first form was, without doubt, oral credit,[1] we may assume that some evidence of credit was recorded almost as soon as a means of record was devised. Credit documents, or credit instruments, have been developed in such variety that we now have a credit instrument to fit any commercial need. As our credit system develops, certain credit instruments may be discarded or fall into comparative disuse, while new ones may be devised, or old ones adapted to new conditions.

Classes of Documentary Credit. Credit falls into two distinct classes: credit of general acceptability and credit of limited acceptability. Instruments of general acceptability pass freely about the community or state without question and usually at their face value. The only instruments which meet this qualification are certain forms of money. Confidence in all other credit instruments is somewhat limited. They are accepted, or perhaps rejected, only after careful appraisal. While both serve as a medium of exchange, the first class is generally acceptable, while the second class varies from almost general acceptability to virtually no acceptability.

Credit documents, which include records of credit transactions, may also be divided into (1) orders to pay and (2) promises to pay. The document itself reveals in which class it should be placed, but it will be noted that certain documents, in different stages, represent each class. The chief orders to pay are checks, drafts, trade acceptances, bills of exchange, circular letters of credit, money orders, etc., and the chief promises to pay are promissory notes, bank notes, book accounts, bonds, bank deposits, etc. The draft, for example, may be in each class, since it is first an order to pay and also becomes a promise to pay upon its

[1] Often referred to as "jawbone."

58

acceptance. It will be seen that the acceptability of certain orders to pay is greatly enhanced by conversion to promises to pay. The draft, which is again used for illustration, may have no value, since it is an order which the one on whom it is drawn is not obliged to honor. It becomes enforceable when the drawee agrees to pay it, that is to say, when it is accepted.

A further classification might be made according to the use to which the credit documents are put. The open-book account might be classified as commercial, since it is used in commercial business transactions only, while checks, travelers' checks, bank drafts, certificates of deposit, and a number of others might be classified as exclusively banking. Such documents as promissory notes, trade acceptances, drafts, and bills of exchange are both banking and commercial credit documents. Stocks, bonds, mortgages, and debentures are purely documents of investment credit (long-term credit).

We are primarily concerned with the main classification which separates credit money from credit documents of limited acceptability because it is at this line of division that credit caution begins.

Credit money[1] is by no means of minor importance, and the student will find much written upon the subject, but it is not intended to treat of it here. A thorough knowledge, however, of the uses of instruments of credit of limited acceptability is essential to the student of credit.

The Book Account. As stated above, credit was probably first oral, followed at a very early date by some form of written record of the credit transaction. This record was made by the creditor, since it was distinctly to his advantage not to forget a receivable. The development of this primitive record is the book account. Strictly, the book account is not a credit instrument at all, since it is only the memorandum or record of the credit transaction. It must be considered a credit instrument, however, as it is the personal property of the creditor and may be sold by him, the purchaser acquiring the same right of action held by the seller. The most elemental form of book credit is illustrated by the purchase of some article by an individual from a retailer. Nothing may be said about credit or the time of payment. Perhaps even the price is not mentioned. Yet when the sale is made, there are implied all the conditions necessary to an enforceable contract. Confidence is mutual. It is necessary only for the retailer to record the sale, which is an account receivable of the seller and an account payable on the books of the purchaser.

In modern business there have been added many other evidences of debt besides the book entry. The retailer makes use of the sales slip made out in detail and usually in duplicate and often signed by the pur-

[1] See Foster, Bogen, Rodgers, and Nadler, "Money and Banking."

chaser. An identification coin, which serves to establish identity of the purchaser, may be used. There are the records of the shipping and delivery departments. The wholesaler or manufacturer usually has a signed written order which may state the terms and conditions of the contract. The records of the shipping department, the invoice, the bill of lading, the delivery receipt are all evidences of the transaction. In the event of a dispute, the seller might have difficulty in proving the book credit, but he is greatly aided in the proof by this added support.

The open-book account is a quick and easy way of recording a sale on credit. It minimizes the time of both purchaser and seller, and obviates the necessity of carrying large sums of money to make cash payments. Again, it stimulates sales, since it is without doubt true that in some cases the individual would not buy if he had to pay cash, nor would the businessman buy so freely if he were obliged to give a note or trade acceptance. The book account may be sold, though it ranks much lower as a desirable asset than do most of the other credit instruments, and the book accounts of the manufacturer and wholesaler are regarded as much more desirable than are those of the retailer. Banks frequently have book accounts assigned to them as pledges for their loans, and in recent years a large business in discounting book accounts has been developed by finance companies and banks.

One of the weaknesses of the book account as a credit instrument lies in the fact that not in all cases is the maturity of the credit sufficiently definite. No terms may be stated, in which case a "reasonable time" will be understood, or perhaps trade custom will fix the length of terms. Whether the terms are thus fixed by usage or custom, or by contract, payment is made through the voluntary action of the debtor, and there is no effective method of enforcing prompt settlement. The second principal weakness lies in the fact that the book account is not a prima facie evidence of the existence of debt, as are most credit instruments, since it does not contain the buyer's acknowledgment of debt.

Negotiable Instruments. Earlier in this chapter, credit instruments were classified as to general acceptability and limited acceptability and further divided into "orders to pay" and "promises to pay." Credit instruments might also be classified as negotiable and nonnegotiable. The feature of negotiability is most important to the credit machine. Negotiability is the lubricant which has speeded up the credit machine and which has aided it in running so smoothly. While all credit instruments are negotiable in the sense that ownership can be transferred, all are not negotiable under the restricted meaning of the word. Nonnegotiable instruments are governed by the law of ordinary written contracts, while negotiable instruments possess certain added characteristics, which facilitate their transfer and give the holder, provided he is an innocent holder for value, certain special protection. The Negotiable Instruments law[1] which has been adopted in every state and in the District of Columbia is a codification of the law which originated in the custom of merchants and which the law courts have recognized and endeavored to enforce.

Two principal characteristics which serve to distinguish negotiable instruments from ordinary contracts are (1) presumptive consideration and (2) negotiability. If a contract is in the form of a negotiable instrument, it has a presumption of consideration; whereas, in an ordinary contract, one who brings an action upon it must prove that the promise he is seeking to enforce rests upon a consideration. This is an important point, since the first obstacle, the proving of the consideration, is hurdled. The burden of proof that there was no consideration falls upon the maker of the instrument. The second important characteristic is the special feature of negotiability with which the law has endowed certain instruments. Ordinary contracts are often assignable, but the assignee, when he sues, is subject to all the defenses that might have been set up against his assignor. Negotiability carries with it the following results: (*a*) The transferee gets a legal title and can sue in his own name; (*b*) if the transferee is a holder for value and without notice, he is free from the defenses that might have been set up against his transferor, except those which would nullify the contract altogether. This means that the transferee, who is a holder in due course and without notice, by virtue of the law obtains a better title than was held by the original holder. The transferee is not subject to the personal defenses of fraud, duress, want of consideration, lack of title in the transferor, and the like; but he is subject to the defenses of forgery, alteration, infancy of the maker, or any contract void by statute (as a gambling contract). The importance of determining whether or not an instrument is negotiable is based principally upon the fact that the transferees of a negotiable instrument have the added protection which has been described above.

Essentials of Negotiability. In order to be negotiable the instrument must conform to the following express provisions of the act:

1. *It must be in writing and signed by the maker or drawer.* It may be written in ink, pencil, or any other legible manner upon any material strong enough to hold together. Any name by which the signer intends to be bound may be used, including trade names or even initials.

2. *It must contain an unconditional promise, or order, to pay a sum certain in money.* The instrument is not unconditional if it is to be effective only

---

[1] The Uniform Commercial Code, when enacted, will supersede the Negotiable Instruments law. The new Uniform Commercial Code will not only make more uniform the laws of Negotiable Instruments and Sales but will remove the hodge-podge of laws and court decisions relating to credit security devices in the various states.

upon the happening of some contingency. It is not unconditional if payment is to be limited to a certain fund; it must be payable in any event. The unconditional feature is not necessarily lost even though the transaction from which the instrument arises is stated. Acknowledgments of the receipt of money such as "I.O.U.," "received of Smith & Co. $75" are not negotiable. Payment must be in money.[1] No other commodity is recognized by the law.

3. *The time of payment must be fixed or determinable.* By a determinable time is meant on demand, a certain time after demand, date, sight; or a certain time after the happening of some event, provided that event is sure to occur, such as the death of a person. If the date of payment falls upon Sunday or a legal holiday, payment may be deferred to the next business day. The time of payment is further qualified by ordinary and reasonable business and banking hours. The instrument is not invalidated even though it lacks a date. The date when first delivered by the maker or drawer becomes the date of issuance, and this date may be inserted by any holder.

4. *It must be payable to order or to bearer or contain other words of negotiability.* The words "to the order of," "or order," "or bearer" indicate the intent of the maker to permit the negotiation of the instrument.

5. *It must be specific as to parties.* An instrument is negotiable so far as this feature is concerned if it is made payable as designated in the preceding paragraph and, in addition, to one who may not be named but who is so designated that his identity may be ascertained.

6. *It must be delivered.* The instrument is not effective until it has been delivered with the intent to convey title, by the maker or his authorized agent. However, the innocent holder for value can hold the maker even though delivery by the maker was conditional or imperfect. This is one of the protections conferred by the law on the holder in due course.

Negotiation. Negotiation is accomplished by delivery if payable to bearer or by endorsement and delivery if payable to order. Negotiation may or may not be restricted by the endorsement. A blank endorsement is the mere signature of the endorser, and it has the effect of conveying title and adding the endorser's guaranty to the instrument. The endorsement may be a special endorsement, directing the payment to be made to a particular person, or it may be restrictive in its purpose. The restrictive endorsement may forbid the endorsee further to negotiate the instrument, or it may restrict by giving the endorsee title only for a specified purpose, as "pay to A to pay to B" or "for deposit to the credit of C." The endorser may qualify his endorsement by adding the words "without recourse" or any words clearly showing that he does not intend to be liable as endorser. Such an endorser, however, cannot evade the guaranty that the instrument is genuine and that he had title; he merely evades responsibility for the payment of the instrument.

---

[1] The instrument may, however, give the holder the option of selecting another specified commodity.

Presentation and demand for payment must be made on the day the instrument falls due, and in the case of a demand instrument, it must be presented for payment within a reasonable time from the date it is drawn. In determining the due date, the day the instrument is drawn is excluded and the date of payment included. If maturity falls on a Saturday, Sunday, or legal holiday, the instrument is payable on the next succeeding business day. A demand instrument, however, may be presented on a Saturday at the option of the holder.[1]

Notice of Protest for Nonpayment. In the event of dishonor, notice must be given to drawer and endorsers unless that provision has been

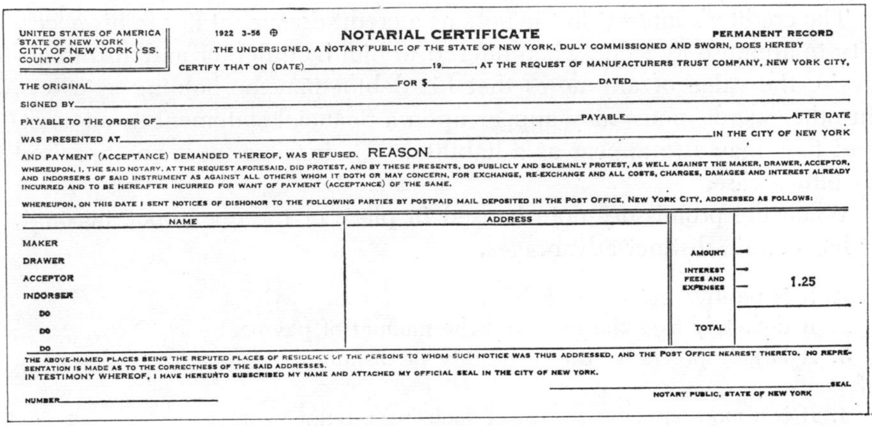

UNITED STATES OF AMERICA
STATE OF NEW YORK
CITY OF NEW YORK } SS.
COUNTY OF

1922 3-56 ⊕ **NOTARIAL CERTIFICATE** PERMANENT RECORD

THE UNDERSIGNED, A NOTARY PUBLIC OF THE STATE OF NEW YORK, DULY COMMISSIONED AND SWORN, DOES HEREBY CERTIFY THAT ON (DATE)______19____, AT THE REQUEST OF MANUFACTURERS TRUST COMPANY, NEW YORK CITY,

THE ORIGINAL______ FOR $______ DATED______

SIGNED BY______

PAYABLE TO THE ORDER OF______ PAYABLE______ AFTER DATE

WAS PRESENTED AT______ IN THE CITY OF NEW YORK

AND PAYMENT (ACCEPTANCE) DEMANDED THEREOF, WAS REFUSED. REASON______

WHEREUPON, I, THE SAID NOTARY, AT THE REQUEST AFORESAID, DID PROTEST, AND BY THESE PRESENTS, DO PUBLICLY AND SOLEMNLY PROTEST, AS WELL AGAINST THE MAKER, DRAWER, ACCEPTOR, AND INDORSERS OF SAID INSTRUMENT AS AGAINST ALL OTHERS WHOM IT DOTH OR MAY CONCERN, FOR EXCHANGE, RE-EXCHANGE AND ALL COSTS, CHARGES, DAMAGES AND INTEREST ALREADY INCURRED AND TO BE HEREAFTER INCURRED FOR WANT OF PAYMENT (ACCEPTANCE) OF THE SAME.

WHEREUPON, ON THIS DATE I SENT NOTICES OF DISHONOR TO THE FOLLOWING PARTIES BY POSTPAID MAIL DEPOSITED IN THE POST OFFICE, NEW YORK CITY, ADDRESSED AS FOLLOWS:

NAME	ADDRESS		
MAKER			
DRAWER		AMOUNT	—
ACCEPTOR		INTEREST	—
INDORSER		FEES AND EXPENSES	— 1.25
DO			
DO		TOTAL	
DO			

THE ABOVE-NAMED PLACES BEING THE REPUTED PLACES OF RESIDENCE OF THE PERSONS TO WHOM SUCH NOTICE WAS THUS ADDRESSED, AND THE POST OFFICE NEAREST THERETO. NO REPRESENTATION IS MADE AS TO THE CORRECTNESS OF THE SAID ADDRESSES.
IN TESTIMONY WHEREOF, I HAVE HEREUNTO SUBSCRIBED MY NAME AND ATTACHED MY OFFICIAL SEAL IN THE CITY OF NEW YORK.

______ SEAL
NOTARY PUBLIC, STATE OF NEW YORK

NUMBER______

FIG. 3. Certificate of protest.

waived. Failure to give notice may act to discharge the liability of the endorser. The holder should, therefore, notify all parties in order to hold his full rights. Notice of dishonor is usually given by formal protest by a Notary Public although this is not essential. The law requires that a foreign bill of exchange, that is, one drawn by a person in one of the United States or in a foreign country, upon another person residing in another of the United States or in another country, shall be protested (see Fig. 3). It is well to note in passing that this provision as to protest does not include promissory notes.[2]

Promissory Notes. "A promissory note is an unconditional promise, in writing, signed by the maker, to pay, in the United States, at a fixed or determinable future time, a sum certain in dollars to order or to bearer."[3]

[1] A few states, *viz.*, Arizona, Kentucky, and Wisconsin, have omitted this Saturday provision. It is also omitted in Vermont except as to the optional clause.

[2] The student is recommended to a more complete study of the Negotiable Instruments law, if he is not already familiar with it. A very good digest of it will be found in the "Credit Manual of Commercial Laws."

[3] Federal Reserve Board, Regulation A, Series of 1920.

The promissory note is both a commercial and a banking credit instrument, and its use is common by both. It is a more advanced form of credit instrument than the open-book account, since it is a positive and unconditional promise in writing, and, if drawn to order or to bearer, it acquires the privileges and protection afforded by the Negotiable Instruments law. The significance of the promissory note lies in the purpose for which it is used, that is, to evidence indebtedness incurred through the purchase of goods, or it may cover the advance of capital. In this latter sense, the note may be given for an outright loan of money or for a loan of capital in the form of an extension of the time of payment of a credit already due.

The creditor's interest in the note as a credit document lies in his necessity to appraise its value when offered to him by a debtor and also to appraise the value of any notes that his debtor may be holding as assets. In other words, notes may appear upon a financial statement as an asset, and they may also appear as a liability. Their value must be appraised in either case.

When the promissory note is used in place of the open-book account, it has certain distinct advantages.

1. It is positive evidence of debt.
2. It definitely fixes the time and the amount of payment.
3. It largely precludes the possibility of dispute as to quantity and quality of goods.
4. It is a more effective means of securing prompt payment.
5. It has a higher value as a salable asset than the open account.

On the other hand, the advantages of the open-book account seem to outweigh those of the promissory note, since the great preponderance of business is transacted through the open-book account. Notes are extensively employed in but a few industries. Rarely does the consumer give a note unless he is purchasing on the instalment plan. Comparatively rarely, also, does the manufacturer require a note from the wholesaler or retailer, or the wholesaler from the retailer, unless the retailer be regarded as an inferior credit risk, or to evidence a debt already due on which an extension of time is granted.[1]

It is the inflexibility of the promissory note in addition to the simplicity and minimum accounting in the use of the open-book account which makes the latter so greatly preferred. The open-book account is adapted to the cash-discount system while the promissory note is not. The buyer may exercise either the option to pay cash or to take the full time allowed by the net terms if the account is in the open-book form, but there is not this flexibility when a note is given.

---

[1] Exceptions are presented by certain industries, such as jewelry, lumber, etc.

However, while the use of the promissory note given in exchange for merchandise has greatly decreased, the promissory note given in exchange for loans of money by banks is in common usage.

Special Forms of Notes. Notes may be drawn so that they are payable in instalments or the amount to be paid may be covered by a series of notes usually of equal amounts and with maturity dates equally spaced. When either of these forms of notes is used, there is added usually the provision that upon default in payment of any of the instalments or any of a series of notes, as the case may be, all subsequent instalments or notes shall at once become due and payable at the option of the legal holder thereof. The effect of such a provision is to convert notes with stated maturities into demand instruments, thus enabling the holder to take appropriate action at once upon the entire indebtedness, instead of separate actions as the instalments or notes become due, or an action delayed until the final payment became due.

Certain other stipulations placed on the face of the note are legal in various states. In all states the payment of interest may be stipulated, provided the rate of interest is not illegal. In some states there may be included in a negotiable instrument a stipulation for the payment of an attorney's fee or the cost of collection, if the instrument is not paid at maturity. These stipulations may be for the "cost of collection" or for a "reasonable fee" or for the addition of a stated percentage of the face of the note. The reader should realize, however, that, while "a reasonable fee" might not invalidate the instrument, a stated percentage would if it were so high that the court might not regard it as reasonable or legal.

Another form of note, which may be used in some states, is the judgment note. Its purpose is to avoid the delay and expense of a court trial, and at the same time increase the probability that the note will be paid at maturity. For, obviously, a debtor, knowing a judgment may be promptly recorded against him if he defaults, will try strenuously to avoid default.

Before accepting instruments providing for the collection of costs or for taking a judgment without trial, the creditor should ascertain whether he could enforce such provisions in the courts of the state where such actions would necessarily be brought.

Bonds. A bond is a written promise, under seal, to pay a specific sum of money at a fixed time in the future. Several other characteristics are usually found in the bond contract. The face of the bond is usually $100, $500, $1,000, or in multiples of $1,000; the time of payment is usually 10 years or more after the bond is drawn; and it is usually one of a series of similar bonds all carrying a fixed rate of interest. The bond differs from the promissory note in that it is a more formal instrument, is under seal, and is one of a series all alike. Also, all the bonds of an issue are usually covered by a trust indenture or deed of trust made out to a trustee whose duty it is to take remedial action for the benefit of all the bondholders upon violation of the terms of the indenture or pertinent statutes. It may be classified as follows:

Character of Obligor. The two main types under this classification are civil bonds and corporation bonds. Under the first classification are found government, state, and municipal bonds, while under the second are industrial, public utility, and railroad bonds.

Purpose of Issue. Among the purpose of issue might be mentioned equipment bonds, school bonds, refunding bonds, building, etc.

Character of Security. Bonds may be unsecured, such as civil bonds and corporate debenture bonds, or secured by personal guaranty or lien security. Under lien security will be found, among others, first-mortgage bonds, general-mortgage bonds, and collateral-trust bonds.

Terms of Payment of Principal. Bonds thus classified are called straight-maturity bonds, callable bonds, perpetual bonds, serial bonds, and sinking-fund bonds.

Form. Bonds may take the form of coupon bonds, registered bonds, or registered coupon bonds. Certain bonds are negotiable. To be negotiable, it is necessary only that the bond fulfill the requirements of the Negotiable Instruments law.

A bond is purely an instrument of investment credit, and it is as a liability of a prospective or actual customer that the credit man must usually appraise it, although it must also frequently be appraised as an asset. While usually the duration of mercantile or bank credit falls within the period of credit of the bond, and, therefore, has precedence over the bond, it is well to remember that under certain conditions the bond issue may become due almost overnight. The interest on the bond is, of course, a current obligation.

The credit man in appraising the bond as a liability will be interested in the purpose of issue, the authorized amount of the issue, the amount actually issued, the interest rate, the maturity date, and the method of retirement. A further analysis of the bond will be made in a later chapter.

Shares of Stock. While shares of stock, strictly speaking, are neither orders to pay nor promises to pay, they may, nevertheless, be treated as credit instruments. A share of stock represents a fraction of ownership in a corporation, and the certificate of fractional ownership may be transferred from one to another, with certain restrictions, as are other credit instruments.

The holders of shares of stocks in many cases, while they are part owners of a corporation, take no part in the management of it but stand, rather, in the position of a creditor who has loaned money to an enterprise in the hope of sharing in the profit made, either through the declaration of dividends or through an increase in the value of the stock itself. From another viewpoint, that of the corporation, shares of stock are a means of obtaining permanent capital, and it is not a strain on reason to consider the corporation, because of its accountability, as debtor to its stockholders. It is well to point out, however, that the rights of all other creditors of a corporation are superior to the owner-creditor rights of the stockholders.

On the other hand, the stockholder has not the usual rights of a creditor. There is no stipulated maturity, no promise for repayment, nor can the corporation be in a default to its owners. There may be no specified rate of return. The owner-creditor cannot compel the corporation to repay. He can only transfer his right or property in the corporation to another. Since the stockholders in the aggregate are the owners of a corporation, it is incongruous to think that ownership has any credit obligation to itself. It appears, therefore, that, while it may be agreed that shares of stock are merely certificates of ownership, involving no obligation to pay, they may well be regarded and included as credit instruments.

The two main classifications of stock are "common" and "preferred." Common stock represents ownership in a corporation and carries with it the common rights of a stockholder but no special privileges. Preferred stock may not carry with it some of the rights and privileges of common stock, but it may have certain more or less valuable preferences. It may be preferred as to assets or as to dividends or both, while, on the other hand, it is usually nonvoting and its dividends are limited.

There are many variations of both common and preferred stocks, especially the preferred, affecting the control, income, or risk of the stockholders. For example, stock may be participating or nonparticipating, cumulative or noncumulative, redeemable or convertible.[1] Assuming for the moment the position taken in a preceding paragraph that the stockholders are creditors, it will be seen that while the stockholders' rights are inferior to the rights of all other creditors, the creditor rights of the common stockholders may be inferior to the creditor rights of the preferred stockholders.

The student of credit will be interested in certain other characteristics of stock. He will need to be able to differentiate authorized stock and issued stock, unissued stock and treasury stock, par value and nonpar value stock. He will also need to appraise shares of stock which may be held as an asset, as well as to consider their relation to the assets and liabilities of a business when representing capital of that business.

[1] For a more complete discussion of capital stock, see Bonneville, Dewey, and Kelly, "Organizing and Financing Business."

TEXT AND RESEARCH QUESTIONS

1. How may credit instruments be classified?

2. What instrument of credit is assumed to be the oldest credit instrument?

3. List the reasons for the popularity of the book account.

4. Why are the book accounts of the retailer generally subject to a greater discount than those of the manufacturer and wholesaler?

5. What are two chief weaknesses of the book account?

6. What effect has the Negotiable Instruments law had upon the use of credit?

7. What is meant by an "innocent holder for value"?

8. How is the position of the transferee of a negotiable instrument strengthened by that law?

9. What are the six essentials of negotiability?

10. How is title to a negotiable instrument transferred?

11. On what days do not negotiable instruments fall due?

12. Why is it always advisable to protest indorsed instruments for nonpayment?

13. What are five advantages of the promissory note?

14. Why is the open account generally preferred over the note as a commercial credit instrument?

15. Define a collateral note.

16. What is a judgment note?

17. How do bonds differ from notes?

18. Why should a credit manager have a knowledge of the use of bonds?

19. What points should be considered in appraising the bond (*a*) as an asset and (*b*) as a liability?

20. How do bonds differ from shares of stock?

21. Why should shares of stock be included in a discussion of credit instruments?

PROBLEMS

1. *a.* Draw a promissory note. Underneath the note list in abbreviated form the essentials of a negotiable instrument. Draw a straight line from each of the essentials to the corresponding part of the note.

   b. List three nonessentials of a negotiable instrument.

2. Mr. Alden and Mr. Baldwin, as accommodation endorsers, endorsed a note for Mr. X payable to Mr. Conover. Mr. Conover sold the note to Mr. Douglas who resold it to Mr. Eldred. Mr. Eldred, under the belief Mr. X would default, has transferred the note to Mr. Froberg for two-thirds of its face value and has endorsed it without recourse. Assuming Mr. X will default, state the rights and obligations of each of the endorsers. What action would you have taken were you in Mr. Eldred's place? Why?

3. Describe three different cases in which the "without recourse" endorsement would be the proper form of endorsement.

4. Mr. A. E. Jones owes Mr. R. A. Brown the sum of $1,000 and agrees to

give Mr. Brown a promissory note in that sum with interest due 90 days from date. Draw this note for Mr. Jones.

Mr. Brown endorses the note to Mr. G. E. Green by a special endorsement; Mr. Green endorses it by a blank endorsement and delivers it to Mr. W. A. White; Mr. White transfers it to Mr. R. U. Blue by a conditional endorsement (conditioned upon completion of a contract between them) and Mr. Blue endorses to Mr. James Black by a qualified endorsement. Mr. Black endorses to Mr. B. E. Smart, his attorney, by a restrictive endorsement. Prepare each endorsement.

CHAPTER 6

DOCUMENTARY CREDIT

Checks. It has been held that the check fails to qualify as a credit instrument, since, in theory, it is an order to a bank to pay instantaneously a certain sum of money which the bank is holding for that very purpose. Practically, however, instantaneous presentation and payment is impossible; hence the check, through the element of futurity and the confidence of the payee that money will be exchanged for the check, which, after all, is tinged with some uncertainty, partakes of the nature of a credit instrument. Whatever argument the theorist may advance, one should never forget that credit caution is essential before the acceptance of any check. Because the use of checks is so general in this country, some persons overlook the fact that they are essentially credit instruments and of but limited acceptability. There is some risk involved, and before the payee assumes that risk he should satisfy himself on three points, namely, that it is the order of the person whose name appears as the drawer, that the drawer has a claim on a previously established quantity of credit with the bank on which it is drawn, and that the bank will be able to meet the demand made upon it.[1]

The check has become the most generally used medium of exchange in this country, but it is well to point out in passing that, while it gives the holder the right to immediate payment in money, the chief use of the check is to transfer credit.[2] The bank or banking system merely transfers the credit of the drawer to the payee and pays out comparatively little money over the counter.

In the use of checks, a certain amount of care is necessary. The check is a negotiable instrument and hence is easily transferred. Before it is

[1] The danger that the bank would be unable to meet its check demands became real during the bank crisis of 1932 and 1933. Businessmen in many instances refused to accept checks in exchange for merchandise. During the greatest alarm, when checks were received they were rushed to the bank for deposit or to be cashed. Deposits are now fully insured up to $10,000 in all national banks and in those state banks which have qualified for deposit insurance.

[2] A credit on the books of the bank from one account to another, or others.

presented to the bank on which it is drawn, it may pass from hand to hand canceling many debts, thus avoiding the use of money, but such use of a check is attended with some danger, since failure to present the check for payment within a reasonable time will discharge the drawer from liability thereon to the extent of his loss occasioned by the delay. Forwarding a check to the bank on which it is drawn by a circuitous route may, as a general rule, be said to constitute negligence, if delay is occasioned thereby. In the event of the failure of a bank, the loss on outstanding checks will be divided between payees and depositors, the payees bearing the loss on any checks which they have failed to present "within a reasonable time," subject, of course, to deposit insurance.

The bank is under no obligation to the holder of a check until it accepts or certifies the check. The holder of a check can only present it for payment promptly and, in case it is dishonored, give the drawer due notice and thereafter sue the drawer. The drawer, however, if his credit has been damaged by the wrongful dishonor of his check by a bank, can recover whatever sum is fixed by the discretion of a jury.

It is also well to bring to the attention of the student of credit practice that the payee who holds a check marked "in full of account" when, as a matter of fact, the check is not in full of account, may accept the check and move to collect the balance. Though this has been changed by statute in some states[1] the general rule is as follows:

If the claim is liquidated and there is absolutely no question as to the amount due, a check for a lesser amount than the claim, even though marked "In full of account," does not settle the account, and the creditor may keep the check and sue for the balance.[2]

The creditor, however, may not accept a check sent in full of account and then sue for the balance if there is a dispute over the amount due. In that event, he may return the check and sue for the amount claimed by him, or he may accept the check in full payment of the claim which it covers.

Stopping Payment on Checks. The bank is the depositor's debtor and at the same time it acts as his agent. The depositor can order the bank, by means of a check, to pay, and he has equal authority to order it not to pay, but the order to pay cannot be revoked after the check has been paid, accepted, or certified. Since stop payment orders are somewhat troublesome to a bank and may easily be overlooked, banks customarily ask a depositor who wishes to stop payment of a check to sign its Stop Payment Request form. This form usually includes a statement that the depositor will not hold the bank liable if the check should be paid con-

[1] Among them are Alabama, California, Georgia, New York, North Carolina, and Virginia.

[2] "Credit Manual of Commercial Laws," p. 335, 1952.

trary to the request through inadvertence or oversight. In the absence of a statute there is no required form for the notice to stop payment. Even an oral order has been held effective. But when the form mentioned above has been signed, it has been held valid and enforcible in some jurisdictions while others[1] have set it aside as contrary to public policy.

Certified Checks. Ordinary checks, frequently termed "personal" checks, vary greatly in their acceptability. The seller may be unwilling to accept the buyer's check or, having accepted it, feel uncertain as to its payment. The drawer, who has directed the bank to pay, may also direct the bank to stop payment of the check. The risk attendant upon an unpaid check is largely overcome if the bank certifies the check. This is accomplished by having the bank stamp the word "certified"

Fig. 4.   Check showing bank certification stamp.

upon the face of the instrument and having the cashier or bank teller initial the certification (see Fig. 4). At the same time, the amount of the check is deducted from the depositor's balance, and the instrument has become the bank's acceptance. The drawer, the payee, or other holder of the check may request certification.

The bank is under no obligation to certify checks, but it is done as an accommodation or as a service to its depositors. The value of certification lies in the fact that the promise of the drawer has been changed for the promise of the bank. Payment is thus virtually ensured, although the drawer may, for valid reasons and with the consent of the bank, delay or stop payment altogether. Payment is virtually certain if the bank remains solvent. Should a bank that is not a member of the Federal Deposit Insurance Corporation fail, the question as to who would bear the loss depends largely upon at whose request certification was made.

[1] See *Speroff v. First Central Trust Co.*, 149 Ohio St., 415.

Cashier's Checks. A cashier's check is a bank's order to pay drawn upon itself. It is called a "cashier's check" because the cashier is usually the officer who authorizes the payment. This instrument is ordinarily used by a bank to pay its own obligations, but a cashier's check may be purchased by a customer or an outsider for a small fee. As a credit instrument, the cashier's check ranks with the certified check.

The "Bad Check" Law. Just as the Negotiable Instruments law was intended to facilitate and make safe the use of credit instruments, the Bad Check laws are intended to protect the seller or creditor who accepts checks in lieu of money. The effect of the law is to facilitate trade by promoting the use of checks. The laws in general provide that a maker who issues and the holder who negotiates a check, knowing that there are insufficient funds or credit to meet it, are guilty of a crime. The strength of the law lies in the provision in most of the statutes that proof that a "check, draft, or order was made, drawn, uttered, or delivered" and payment was refused by the drawee because of lack of funds or credit establishes a prima facie case of intent to defraud and of knowledge of insufficient funds in, or credit with, the bank. The result is a shifting of the burden of evidence from the prosecution to the defendant. Under the general laws relating to the intent to defraud, it was next to impossible to prove that the giving of a worthless check was with the intent to defraud. Under the present laws, it is incumbent on the defendant to prove that it was *not* given with intent to defraud.

In many of the states, the giver of a "not-good" check is given a definite time, varying in the different states from 2 to 10 days, in which to make the check good and thus remove the presumption that it was given with fraudulent intent. Such an act merely removes the not-good check as prima facie evidence and shifts the burden of proof back to the prosecution in the event it is desired to prosecute for intent to defraud.

Prosecution in some of the states may not be started until this time allowance has elapsed, and in other states shall be abated if payment is made within the limit specified.

Whether the law includes a check given for a preexisting debt is a point not yet settled for all states. It is held that the law applies to the giving of value in exchange for the check and that the creditor, when he accepts a check, is not deprived of anything of value, nor has the giver of the check secured anything of value from his creditor. The recipient of the check had a creditor's right the status of which has not been changed merely by the receipt of the check. Such a check may have been given with no intent to defraud but to escape the harassment of an importunate creditor. On the other hand, it has been held that in such a case the check is given because the giver expects to gain an advantage thereby. He expects to deceive persons who are pressing for payment; he expects them to think a debt paid when it, in fact, is not paid. The position is taken that by the issuance of such a check a prima facie case is established which may be rebutted in trial, and then the intent to defraud and the insufficiency of funds become a matter of fact for a jury to determine.

If the check be postdated, another factor is brought in for consideration. The weight of authority is to the effect that one who accepts a postdated check cannot resort to the Bad Check law if the check is dishonored because of lack of funds or credit. But to this also exceptions must be noted because of different state court decisions. The reasoning in regard to postdated checks is clearly set forth in the following decision of the highest court of New Jersey:

The giving of a check presently payable is an implied representation by the drawer that he then has funds on deposit in the bank upon which it is drawn sufficient to meet it upon its presentation for payment. The giving of a postdated check carries with it no such implication, but rather the contrary. It is a mere promise to discharge a present obligation on a future day. And the fact of its non-payment when the due date arrives—without more—is no more evidence that it was given with fraudulent intent than is the permitting of a promissory note to go to protest proof of such intent or the failure to pay the purchase price of goods sold on credit standing alone evidence of fraud in the making of the contract. Fraud is never presumed, but must always be proved, and an intent to defraud cannot be predicted solely upon the mere non-performance of a future promise. The citation of authority in support of such proposition is unnecessary.[1]

The New York Bad Check law, essentially the same in principle as the laws of other states, is quoted in full. This law, it will be noted, makes the offense a misdemeanor or larceny according to the circumstances attending the giving of the check.

§ 1292-a. **Issuing fraudulent check, draft or order; how punished.** Any person who, with intent to defraud, shall make or draw or utter or deliver any check, draft or order for the payment of money either in his own behalf or in behalf of any other person, or as an agent or representative of another or as an officer or agent of a corporation or purporting to be such agent, representative or officer, upon any bank or other depositary, knowing at the time of such making, drawing, uttering or delivering that the maker or drawer has not sufficient funds in or credit with such bank or other depositary for the payment of such check, although no express representation is made in reference thereto, shall be guilty of a misdemeanor; and if money or property is obtained from another thereby is guilty of larceny and punishable accordingly. In any prosecution under this section as against the maker or drawer thereof, the making, drawing, uttering or delivering of a check, draft or order, payment

[1] *State v. Barone*, 98 N.J.L. 9, 118 Atl. 779.

of which is refused by the drawee because of lack of funds or credit, shall be prima facie evidence of intent to defraud and of knowledge of insufficient funds in or credit with such bank or other depositary. Where such check, draft or order has been protested, the notice of protest thereof shall be admissible as proof of such presentation, non-payment and protest, and shall be presumptive evidence that there was a lack of funds in or with such bank or other depositary. Where such check, draft or order has not been protested, a certificate under oath of the cashier of such bank or other depositary that there was a lack of funds in or with such bank or other depositary shall be admissible as proof and shall be presumptive evidence of such lack of funds. The word credit as used herein shall be construed to mean an arrangement or understanding with the bank or depositary for the payment of such check, draft or order.

§ 2. This act shall take effect September first, nineteen hundred thirty-three.

Court decisions have shown in how many ways an issuer of a bad check can be exonerated. Bad Check laws have not stopped the issuance of bad checks. Indeed the number of worthless checks being presented to banks is probably higher now than ever before. In recent years banks have reached into every strata of our society for checking accounts. The use of checks has become common and somewhat careless, and it is small wonder that so many are returned, marked "n.s.f."

The laws of all the states, except Vermont,[1] define the act as a misdemeanor or felony, but many of them permit the criminal to expiate his crime by making the check good within the maximum time accorded by the law. Fortunately, in the majority of cases all that is necessary is to notify the drawer of the check that it has been returned because of insufficient funds, and the drawer in question makes good without further action. Since the laws, except those of Vermont, require criminal action, the layman should be cautioned against threatening his debtor with the Bad Check law. In doing so he might lay himself open to a charge of committing a penal offense, or he may be charged with resorting to blackmail or extortion.

The Bill of Exchange or Draft. The bill of exchange or draft is a written order signed by the giver or drawer ordering the person to whom it is addressed to pay a definite sum of money at a definite or determinable time to the order of a third person or to bearer (see Fig. 5). The third person or payee is frequently the same as the drawer. It will be noted that this credit instrument arises out of the initiative of the creditor. It is his demand rather than the debtor's promise to pay. Since there is not general confidence that the draft will be accepted and, if accepted,

---

[1] There is no criminal liability in Vermont covering bad checks and no presumption of intent to defraud, but provision is made for civil arrest.

paid, the instrument has very little value until the drawee has signified his intention to honor it by writing the word "accepted" across its face and then signing it. Upon this act, it becomes the drawee's promise to pay or "acceptance." In domestic commerce, the instrument described above is usually called a "draft," whereas the term "bill of exchange" is generally used in foreign transactions. Drafts are usually classified according to their time of payment. Thus we have sight, or demand, drafts; time drafts, payable at a fixed future date; and arrival drafts (*i.e.*, payable upon arrival of goods, at their destination).

Drafts have largely disappeared as credit instruments embodying the credit arising out of the sale of goods (although certain industries

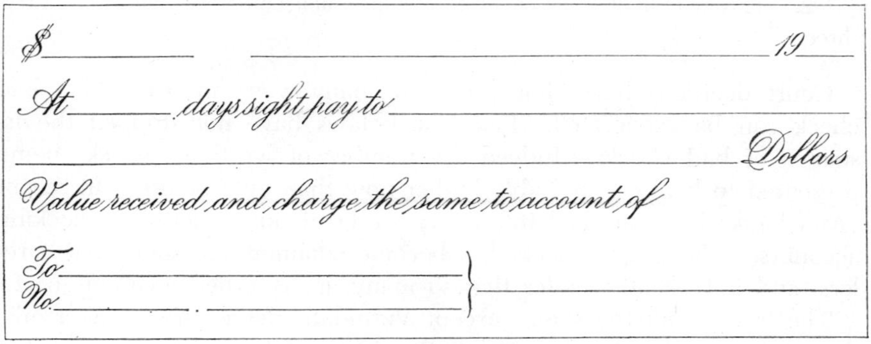

FIG. 5. Form of draft.

present exceptions), but the draft is a collection instrument of great favor with some credit men. A modified form of the draft, however, is in considerable use in the form of the trade acceptance, which will be discussed in the following section.

The Trade Acceptance. The Federal Reserve Board has defined a trade acceptance as a "draft or bill of exchange, drawn by the seller on the purchaser of goods sold, and accepted by such purchaser." From this definition it will be seen that a trade acceptance is a credit instrument properly used only by the seller and the buyer of goods where a sale of goods is involved. In fact, as will be seen in the illustrated form (Fig. 6) of the trade acceptance, it specifically states: "The transaction which gives rise to this instrument is the purchase of goods by the acceptor from the drawer." Thus, the trade acceptance in its proper usage has, as the cause of its origin, the sale of merchandise, which itself may be the source of the funds which will redeem the acceptance at the proper time. Thus we say the paper is self-liquidating in character and, for that reason, finds more ready acceptance if the holder wishes to discount it at his bank.

The trade acceptance is not a new credit instrument, as it was in general use prior to the Civil War. Subsequently, it was displaced in the favor of businessmen by the open-book account, which, as we have seen, is more adaptable to the cash-discount system. The Federal Reserve Act fosters the use of the trade acceptance, and an intensive campaign for its use was instituted both by banks and by the National Association of Credit Men. The campaign was only partially successful. Industry has not to any considerable degree embraced the use of the trade acceptance, although it is in general use in certain industries and sporadically used in others.

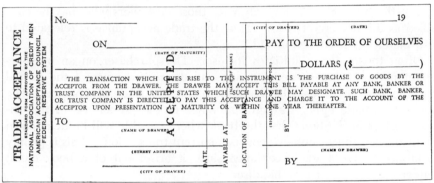

FIG. 6. Trade acceptance.

Trade Acceptance Procedure. The trade acceptance is designed to supplant in its use both the open credit of the book account and the check in payment of it. In practice, the trade acceptance is handled as follows: The seller of merchandise accompanies the goods or the invoice with a trade acceptance form, often in duplicate to enable the buyer to retain a copy for his files. The buyer accepts the document by signing his name across its face, dating it, and designating the bank where it is payable. It is returned to the seller, who may discount it at his bank or hold it in his safe until it matures. At its maturity it is treated exactly like a check by the holder, the payee bank, and in fact any bank which may negotiate it.[1]

This is accomplished through the fact that the Negotiable Instruments Act provides that an instrument payable at a bank is equivalent to an order to the bank to pay for the account of the debtor. The trade acceptance does not nullify the cash discount option, if there be one, for the purchaser may, of course, return a check in immediate payment in-

[1] A few states provide exceptions. For instance, Missouri, Montana, and New Jersey limit the bank's liability to the day of maturity if the acceptance has a fixed or determinable date of maturity.

stead of the acceptance, but the claim is made by some that the trade
acceptance suggests that the longer term of credit be taken. Whether
or not this is a disadvantage to the seller depends upon the worth of the
money, the possibility of collection expense, and the greater risk resultant from the longer credit period. It was the expectation of the
sponsors of the trade acceptance that its use would enhance the credit
standing of the acceptor, since he would show his willingness to bind
himself to payment, and by honoring his acceptances he would establish his ability to pay. That this is not entirely the result may be
ascribed to the abuses of the trade acceptance.

Abuse of the Trade Acceptance. Some credit managers attempt the
use of the trade acceptance only with those customers who may be classified as inferior credit risks. Thus the trade acceptance is relegated to
use merely as a collection aid.

Often the customer initiates its use. The purchaser on an open-account basis, having an account due and desiring the use of the capital
for a longer period, asks his creditor to accept a trade acceptance. The
request is made either through ignorance of the proper use of that instrument or in the hope that the bank where payable will be deluded in
thinking that the acceptance covers a current transaction. This is plainly
a misuse of the trade acceptance since it arises out of a book credit
rather than a sale of merchandise.

Bank credit men must be on the alert for the fraudulent use of the
trade acceptance. Unable to borrow on their own notes, two businessmen merely exchange trade acceptances where no sale of merchandise
is involved. Now fortified with two-name paper, apparently covering
a bona fide sale, each may be able to induce his bank to discount the
spurious paper which he holds.

Any use of the trade acceptance other than to cover a bona fide sale
of merchandise is an abuse. It is many times improperly substituted
for the promissory note or the draft, neither of which is limited, as is the
trade acceptance, to merchandise transactions.

Advantages of the Trade Acceptance. The seller has a formal acknowledgment of the obligation. This may be more theoretical than
real. Businessmen do not deny their obligations, and percentagewise
cases of this nature are infinitesimal.

Liquid commercial paper is substituted for the book account. Financing either through the sale of customers' accounts or using them
as collateral in borrowing has greatly increased in the past score of
years. The vendor of limited capital who finds it necessary to hypothe-
cate his receivables might well press the use of the trade acceptance,
since he will finance himself with more ease and at less cost than through
the hypothecation of accounts receivable.

Another advantage relates to collections. Payments, especially from nondiscounting customers, are much more apt to be according to terms, and the costs of collections considerably reduced.

There are advantages, too, to the buyer. If his credit standing is at all in question, he finds it improved by giving, and, of course, meeting, his trade acceptances.

The use of trade acceptances tends to check overbuying, one of the most common causes of financial difficulty, and it also has the tendency to promote closer collections on his part. Here is a real advantage to many a businessman, though many would be loath to admit it.

Since the buyer would be in a better competitive position with cash buyers the use of the trade acceptance might result in some instances in a lower price.

Reasons for Nonuse of the Trade Acceptances. The disadvantages of the trade acceptance seem to outweigh the advantages. It is obvious that it requires more accounting than does the book account; although this advantage is somewhat offset by smaller collection costs.

The trade acceptance is not well adapted to small purchases or to short terms. This is true both from the accounting and financing viewpoints.

It is not well adapted to cash-discount terms. The buyer may not presently know whether he can avail himself of the cash-discount privilege so he may delay signing the acceptance till the discount period has elapsed. The seller in the meantime is deprived of paper which he might wish to discount.

The trade acceptance tends to lengthen terms, since the buyer is less inclined to discount if he has signed an acceptance and the seller, on his part, is willing to grant longer terms because he gets a document he can turn into cash.

If the trade acceptance came into general use, doing away with book accounts, the bad-debt losses of banks and finance companies might be lessened, while the bad-debt losses of business houses might increase. This would result from the fact that bank and finance company creditors would have recourse to the bankrupt's customers while this valuable asset would be removed from the reach of business creditors.

One of the reasons why sellers refuse to urge its use is the sales resistance it engenders, while buyers' sales resistance is fostered by its too rigid time of payment.

The student has gathered that a main reason for the trade acceptance was an aid in financing. It was to furnish an easy means of financing to the business concern and a safe one for the banks. It has not exactly worked out that way. The businessman, even though he might have acceptances available, has preferred to fight for his own credit.

Or the banker, partly to flatter the good borrower, has suggested if he needs funds his own name on a note is sufficient.

Bank Acceptances.   By virtue of an amendment to the Federal Reserve Act it became lawful for banks to give domestic acceptances. Through this instrument, bank credit is substituted for the purchaser's credit.   The seller may be unwilling to accept the buyer's credit, but he would have no hesitancy in making shipment upon the strength of a bank's acceptance.   Let us assume that A, in New York, wishes to purchase from B, in Birmingham, Ala., a quantity of cotton.   B is uncertain as to A's credit, and furthermore he would like to sell for cash.   A therefore arranges with a New York bank to accept B's draft drawn at 90 days from sight.   B sells the bank's acceptance to a bank in Birmingham, which may, in the event that it needs funds, resell or, as it is termed, "rediscount" it.   Thus it will be seen that neither the buyer nor the seller has funds tied up in the transaction, nor has the issuing bank during the duration of the draft. The transaction is financed entirely by credit, the funds actually being supplied by the purchasing bank in Birmingham. A may have sufficient credit with his bank so that the acceptance is obtained at a small cost, or the bank may require him to turn over to it collateral as surety that when the acceptance becomes due, he will have the funds to meet it.

The bank acceptance also affords the holder of a warehouse receipt a means of transferring the money invested in the commodity to a bank. The bank exchanges its acceptance for the warehouse receipt, and the acceptance is then sold in the open market for the highest price or, in other words, at the lowest discount.   A typical Acceptance Agreement is given in Appendix A.

Travelers' Checks.   A traveler's check is, in effect, a promise to pay given by a bank, express company, or tourist agency, payable to the order of the purchaser as payee.   These checks are easily obtainable, since they are furnished by almost every bank and the large express companies and for convenience are usually furnished in denominations of $10, $20, $50, and $100.   Their superiority to the personal check for one traveling is obvious, when it is understood that they are generally accepted by hotels, tourist agencies, railroads, the larger stores, and banks.   The ability of the drawer to pay is unquestioned.   When the traveler's check is presented, the points for consideration are the validity of the instrument, that is, whether it is what it purports to be or a forgery, and the identity of the payee.   This latter is determined through the signature of the payee.   When the traveler's check is purchased, the payee signs in the presence of the issuing bank and signs again in the presence of the paying officer, who satisfies himself that both signatures were made by the same person.   These checks are payable at par in the United States and at the current rate of exchange in other countries, thus permitting the traveler to obtain the currency of the country in which he may be traveling.

These convenient credit instruments are considerably used by others than travelers, as a substitute for the personal checking account as they find a more ready acceptability, on the one hand, and are safer than carrying an equivalent amount of cash, on the other. The cost is small. They may be purchased for their face value plus a commission of ¾ per cent.

Warehouse Receipts and Bills of Lading. The warehouse receipt and the bill of lading are both documents which, technically speaking, are not credit instruments. They are, rather, documents of title; but, although there is no direct promise to pay in them, there is the surrender of possession and the implied promise to deliver the merchandise. They may, therefore, be treated as credit instruments.

The warehouse receipt is an acknowledgment of the warehouseman that he has received for storage certain goods which will be delivered on demand, provided the terms of the receipt are complied with.[1]

The warehouseman or company, usually abbreviated to just the warehouse, agrees to the safe custody and the redelivery of the goods described by the receipts upon payment of warehouse charges. The warehouse receipt may be negotiable or nonnegotiable, the distinction being that under the nonnegotiable form the goods will be delivered only to the depositor, or one named specifically in the receipt, while the negotiable form permits the goods to be delivered to the bearer or a specified person or on his order. Warehouse receipts are frequently employed as collateral for bank and finance company loans. They provide desirable collateral provided the merchandise is not subject to rapid physical deterioration or to excessive market depreciation.

A field warehouse receipt is an acknowledgment that goods are stored on the premises of the owner, but under the custody of an independent warehouseman.

A bill of lading is a document issued by a common carrier to a shipper which serves as a receipt for goods, a contract to deliver the goods, and a document of title.

Bills of lading are of two kinds, the straight and the order bills of lading. The straight bill of lading is nonnegotiable and is prominently so marked, while the order bill of lading is negotiable. The carrier acts as bailee while the goods are in his possession. Bills of lading are an important form of collateral available to banks as security for loans, particularly the order bill of lading. Under the straight bill of lading, the

---

[1] "Warehouse Receipts as Collateral," pp. 3–6.

nonnegotiable form, title to the goods rests with the consignee, while under the order bill of lading title is retained by the person to whose order the bill of lading is made out, usually the shipper himself, until the bill of lading is endorsed and delivered to another by which act title to the shipment is conveyed. The carrier, not knowing who may have title, will deliver the shipment only upon surrender of the bill of lading properly endorsed. The order bill of lading in the hands of a bank is, therefore, equivalent to possession of the shipment and consequently excellent security for any loan, provided the shipment is not of a perishable nature, has a ready market, and is not subject to much depreciation in price. The straight bill of lading does not offer the same protection to the bank, since delivery may be made by the carrier to the consignee without the surrender of the bill of lading.

The order form of bill of lading permits the shipper to make what is equivalent to a C.O.D. freight shipment. The order bill of lading properly endorsed and accompanied by an "upon arrival of goods" draft is forwarded to a bank in the consignee's city. Upon arrival of goods the buyer goes to the bank, pays the draft, and obtains the bill of lading, which will enable him to get possession of the shipment.

Letters of Credit. Letters of credit are divided into two classes: traveler's letters of credit issued for the purpose of providing the traveler with funds, and commercial letters of credit issued for the purpose of overcoming the obvious difficulties arising between foreign buyers and sellers in arranging for trade and credit terms and means of collection.[1] Letters of credit of both classes accomplish their purpose by substituting the credit of the bank for that of the individual, firm, or corporation.

A traveler's letter of credit is a letter from a bank addressed to one or more of its correspondents stating that drafts not to exceed a specified sum drawn by the beneficiary will be honored by the bank. When the letter is addressed to only one correspondent, it is said to be a specially advised form, while if addressed to a number of correspondents it is called a circular letter of credit.

The traveler, in purchasing a traveler's letter of credit, usually pays the full amount of the credit to the bank plus a fee of about 1 per cent, although in some cases it may be arranged that payment will be made to the bank only as drafts are drawn upon it. The purchaser receives from the bank not only the letter itself but a complete list of correspondents which will honor the letter, a letter of indication (or identification) introducing the traveler to the correspondent and bearing the traveler's signature, and also a telegraphic code by means of which the traveler may communicate with his bank. The signature of the traveler,

---

[1] MUNN, G. G., "Bank Credit," p. 33.

a specimen of which is found in both the letter of credit and the letter of indication, is his means of identification. The traveler, desiring funds, presents the letter of credit to a correspondent, who in turn draws a draft on the issuing bank which the beneficiary must sign. Payment when made by the correspondent to the beneficiary is recorded by the correspondent upon the back of the letter of credit. Each correspondent to whom the letter is presented is thus informed as to how much credit is still unused. When the credit has been exhausted, the bank making the last payment retains the letter of credit, which, with its draft, is forwarded to the issuing bank.

The commercial letter of credit, while the same in principle, is usually more complicated than the traveler's letter of credit. The commercial letter of credit is the means by which the bank substitutes its credit for that of the individual, firm, or corporation, for the purpose of facilitating trade, particularly foreign trade. It has been specifically defined as

> . . . an instrument drawn by a bank, known as the "credit-issuing bank" (and eventually the "drawee bank"), in behalf of one of its customers (or in behalf of a customer of one of its domestic correspondents), known as the "principal" (who guarantees payment to the credit-issuing bank), authorizing another bank at home or abroad, known as the "credit-notifying or negotiating bank" (and usually the "payee bank"), to make payments or accept drafts drawn by a fourth party, known as the "beneficiary," when such beneficiary has complied with the stipulations contained in the letter.[1]

The stipulations may be many and varied. The purpose and manner of using the letter of credit are easily comprehended when illustrated.

The Import Company of New York wishes to purchase a quantity of Irish linen from The Export Company of London. The latter company, unwilling to take the credit risk of The Import Company, has stipulated that shipment will be made upon bankers' credit. The Import Company applies to its bank for a letter of credit (Fig. 7) which, after careful credit investigation, is furnished by the bank. One of the stipulations is that The Import Company shall pledge the goods as security. Upon receipt of the letter of credit The Export Company proceeds to ship the goods, forwarding the bill of lading together with its draft to a London bank. The London bank, presumably the credit-notifying bank, notes that all the stipulations of the letter of credit have been observed, and pays the draft, thus closing the transaction so far as The Export Company is concerned. The negotiating bank, in turn, charges the credit-issuing bank and forwards both draft and documents to the credit-issuing bank. The latter bank surrenders the documents to The Import Company upon receipt of funds from that company, or, perhaps, the

---

[1] *Ibid.*, "Bank Credit," p. 34.

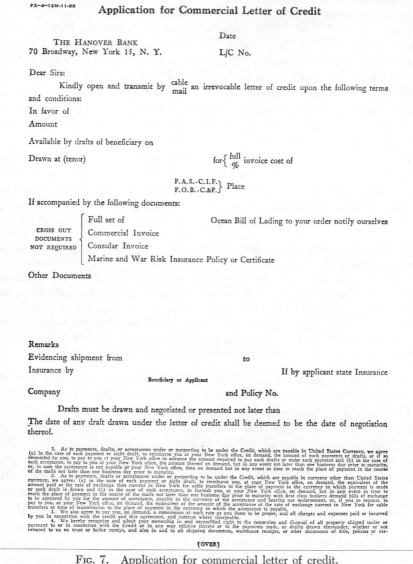

FIG. 7. Application for commercial letter of credit.

shipping documents are surrendered by the bank in exchange for a trust receipt.

There are a number of variations of the letter of credit. It may, for example, be an export, import, or domestic letter of credit. It may be supported by a bill of lading and relative papers, in which case it is called "documentary," or it may be "clean," that is, relying upon gen-

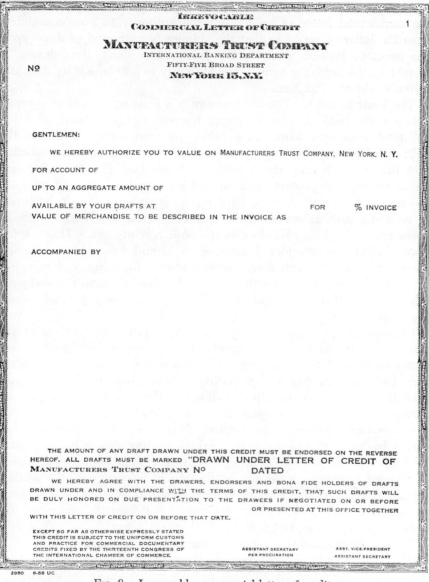

IRREVOCABLE
COMMERCIAL LETTER OF CREDIT

MANUFACTURERS TRUST COMPANY
INTERNATIONAL BANKING DEPARTMENT
FIFTY-FIVE BROAD STREET
NEW YORK 15, N.Y.

№

1

GENTLEMEN:

WE HEREBY AUTHORIZE YOU TO VALUE ON MANUFACTURERS TRUST COMPANY, NEW YORK, N. Y.

FOR ACCOUNT OF

UP TO AN AGGREGATE AMOUNT OF

AVAILABLE BY YOUR DRAFTS AT   FOR   % INVOICE
VALUE OF MERCHANDISE TO BE DESCRIBED IN THE INVOICE AS

ACCOMPANIED BY

THE AMOUNT OF ANY DRAFT DRAWN UNDER THIS CREDIT MUST BE ENDORSED ON THE REVERSE
HEREOF. ALL DRAFTS MUST BE MARKED "DRAWN UNDER LETTER OF CREDIT OF
MANUFACTURERS TRUST COMPANY N⁰   DATED

WE HEREBY AGREE WITH THE DRAWERS, ENDORSERS AND BONA FIDE HOLDERS OF DRAFTS
DRAWN UNDER AND IN COMPLIANCE WITH THE TERMS OF THIS CREDIT, THAT SUCH DRAFTS WILL
BE DULY HONORED ON DUE PRESENTATION TO THE DRAWEES IF NEGOTIATED ON OR BEFORE
                                        OR PRESENTED AT THIS OFFICE TOGETHER
WITH THIS LETTER OF CREDIT ON OR BEFORE THAT DATE.

EXCEPT SO FAR AS OTHERWISE EXPRESSLY STATED
THIS CREDIT IS SUBJECT TO THE UNIFORM CUSTOMS
AND PRACTICE FOR COMMERCIAL DOCUMENTARY
CREDITS FIXED BY THE THIRTEENTH CONGRESS OF   ASSISTANT SECRETARY   ASST. VICE-PRESIDENT
THE INTERNATIONAL CHAMBER OF COMMERCE.   PER PROCURATION   ASSISTANT SECRETARY

2980   9-58 UC

FIG. 8.   Irrevocable commercial letter of credit.

eral credit alone. It may be in dollars, sterling, or other currency. It
may be revocable, irrevocable (Fig. 8) and unconfirmed, or irrevocable
and confirmed. The latter is the safest for exporter and importer, since
the issuing bank cannot withdraw its credit, and the credit-notifying
bank has added its unqualified assurance that the obligation will be performed.

An "authority to purchase" may sometimes perform the function of the commercial letter of credit, but the authority to purchase differs from the letter of credit in that the shipper is instructed to draw upon the importer instead of upon the bank. The draft, thus drawn, is bought by the notifying bank. The authority to purchase is used mainly in trade with the Far East.

The Trust Receipt. The trust receipt is a trust agreement or contract between the bank and its borrower temporarily substituted for other collateral securing a loan. In general, the trust receipt evidences the delivery of certain property by the bank to the customer and specifies that title to such property is with the bank (see Fig. 9). The customer receives the property in trust and is accountable to the bank until the total debt is settled. The trust receipt may be used in substitution of collateral such as securities, acceptances, notes, merchandise, etc., or in exchange for bills of lading, warehouse receipts, etc. Thus an importer buying goods under a letter of credit and wishing to warehouse them gives the bank a trust receipt in exchange for shipping documents. These enable him to obtain the goods and place them in a warehouse, whereupon the bank takes the warehouse receipt as collateral and cancels the trust receipt.

In domestic trade, trust receipts are used principally to aid in the purchase of automobiles and household equipment by dealers from the manufacturers of those articles. The buyer places his order with the manufacturer who ships the goods to the buyer, but usually, if the trust receipt is to be used, the bill of lading or other documents of titles are forwarded to the finance company or other lending agency which pays the manufacturer the purchase price. Now the seller is paid, the purchaser has possession of the goods, and the lending agency has possession of the documents of title. Through the trust receipt the buyer (trustee) is allowed to retain possession of the goods belonging to the lending agency (entruster) and may be commissioned to sell them. The agreement also usually provides that the trustee will hold the goods, not use them or pledge them, but will return them on demand, and, when sold, will keep the proceeds in a separate account clearly marked.

The trust receipt has certain weaknesses. For instance, the bank might find it exceedingly difficult to take possession of goods covered by the trust receipt because of difficulty in identifying them. Then again, the trust receipt partakes of the nature of a secret lien, and by some courts has been so held, and consequently, may be unenforcible as against third parties unless the transaction has been recorded. It has also been held to be a chattel mortgage and a conditional sale.

The lender seeks to strengthen the creditor-debtor relationship by

TRUST RECEIPT

Place...

Date...

The undersigned (hereinafter called the "Trustee") hereby acknowledges receipt from **MANUFACTURERS TRUST COMPANY**, New York, (hereinafter called the "Entruster") of the documents listed below representing the goods therein specified, a security interest in both said documents and said goods remaining in or hereby passing to the Entruster.

In consideration of such receipt and other valuable considerations, The Trustee agrees to hold said documents and goods in trust for the Entruster and subject to its security interest, to be used promptly by the Trustee without expense to the Entruster for the following purpose(s) checked below but for no other purpose(s) and without liberty to pledge the same, or, unless hereafter expressly provided to sell the same:-

- ☐ 1. To transfer to carrier (land, water or air).
- ☐ 2. To transfer to warehouse.
- ☐ 3. To deliver said goods to...who
  have/has agreed to purchase the same for $......................................payable in............................
- ☐ 4. To sell said goods.
- ☐ 5. To manufacture and sell said goods, manufactured or unmanufactured.

The Trustee agrees to account by delivering to the Entruster immediately upon the receipt thereof by the Trustee, any one of the following, according to the purposes for which the goods are withdrawn as indicated above:-

1. Proper and sufficient negotiable bills of lading to the order of the Entruster.

2. Proper and sufficient negotiable warehouse receipts to the order of the Entruster.

3, 4 and 5. Proceeds of the sale of such goods in whatever form received, to be applied by the Entruster under the terms of its Credit No............................, issued for the Trustee's account and/or to the payment of any obligations for which said goods and documents are security or were security before this transaction and of any obligations arising as part of this transaction and of any renewals of such obligations. If such proceeds be notes, bills receivable, acceptances or in any form other than cash, they shall not be so applied by the Entruster until paid; the Entruster, however, to have the option at any time to sell or discount such items and so apply, conditionally upon final payment of such items, the net proceeds thereof.

The Trustee agrees to pay all charges in connection with said goods, documents and any proceeds thereof, and will at all times hold said goods, documents and proceeds separate and apart from the property of the Trustee and will definitely show such separation in all its records and entries.

The Trustee will at all times keep said goods fully insured at the Trustee's expense in favor of, and to the satisfaction of the Entruster against loss by fire, theft and any other risk to which said goods may be subject. In the event for any reason the Trustee fails to make the loss payable under any of said policies, to the Entruster, the Trustee hereby assigns to said Entruster, all the avails or proceeds of any and all of said policies and agrees to accept said avails or proceeds in trust for the Entruster, and to forthwith deliver the same to said Entruster in the exact form received (with the indorsement of the Trustee where necessary). Manufacturers Trust Company or any of its officers is hereby irrevocably empowered, with power of substitution and revocation, to endorse any such check in the name of the Trustee. The Trustee will deposit the insurance policies with the Entruster upon its demand.

The Entruster may at any time terminate this trust and bailment and the Trustee agrees forthwith upon demand to deliver said documents and goods to the Entruster. The Entruster may enter into any place where such property is kept and stored, without notice or demand, and without legal process, (and I/we waive all claims for damages caused thereby) and take possession of said goods, manufactured or unmanufactured, and any documents representing the same (until delivery of said goods and documents to the purchaser(s) pursuant to a sale hereby authorized and the receipt by the Trustee of the proceeds of such sale) and the proceeds of any sale, wherever said goods, manufactured or unmanufactured, documents or proceeds may then be found. As to articles manufactured by style or model, the Trustee's interest therein may be forfeited, at the election of the Entruster, in the event of any default on the part of the Trustee, against cancellation to the extent and as provided by law of the Trustee's then remaining indebtedness with respect to such articles.

The Trustee agrees that the Entruster assumes no responsibility for the correctness, validity or genuineness of the documents released to the Trustee hereunder or for the existence, character, quantity, quality, condition, value or delivery of any goods purported to be represented by any of such documents.

The rights of the Entruster as specified herein or in any relative agreement between the Entruster and the Trustee, shall include any and all rights to which the Entruster is or may be entitled under the provisions of the Uniform Trust Receipts Act of the State of New York, as amended from time to time, and/or under any other applicable statute or law now or hereafter existing at any time or times.

No waiver of any rights or powers of the Entruster or consent by it shall be valid unless in writing signed by it. The rights and powers herein given the Entruster are in addition to those otherwise created.

Credit No..   ....Trustee

Amount...   By...
                                                      (OFFICIAL SIGNATURE)

Maturity...   Business Address...

2288 12-57

FIG. 9. Trust receipt.

adding to it that of entruster-trustee, so that not only does he have a lien on the goods but when the goods are sold the lien follows on the proceeds of sale. The lien will not hold unless there is a compliance with the laws of the state in which the transaction takes place. In those states where the trust receipt has been held to be, in effect, a chattel mortgage or conditional sale, the laws pertaining to those instruments must be complied with. In those states where the Uniform Trust Receipts Act has been adopted,[1] each transaction need not be recorded or filed, but before engaging in trust receipt transactions the entruster must file a statement, signed by entruster and trustee, with the Secretary of State setting forth that the entruster is engaged in or about to engage in trust-receipt transactions and a description of the goods to be acquired by the trustee. Filing is effective for a year and renewable for like periods. Otherwise the lien is lost when and if the goods reach the hands of a bona fide purchaser.

In General. The merchant's advantage in the business world is in knowing the most modern way of financing his business requirements, and, whenever it is appropriate, he should not hesitate to make use of an instrument of credit even though its use may be new to him. He will find, as stated at the beginning of Chapter 5, an instrument of credit to fit every necessity, instruments designed to promote the use of credit to make its use safer for both debtor and creditor. The credit man must, of course, be thoroughly conversant with the documents of credit, since they are the instruments with which he must daily deal.

TEXT AND RESEARCH QUESTIONS

1. What three questions may be raised in considering the risk in accepting a check? Which question is of the least importance?

2. Why may not a creditor accept a check marked "in full of account" for a disputed account and sue for the balance?

3. What distinction, if any, is there in the acceptability of certified checks and cashier's checks?

4. What evil was the Bad Check law designed to remedy?

5. What is the purpose of making a bad check prima facie evidence of intent to defraud?

6. Why do not postdated checks and checks given for the redemption of credit come within the Bad Check laws of most states?

7. What is the distinction between the draft and the trade acceptance?

8. Why has not business more generally adopted the use of the trade acceptance?

9. What is the practice of "kiting" checks and trade acceptances?

10. In what respects are bank acceptances and commercial letters of credit alike, and in what respects do they differ?

[1] The Uniform Trust Receipts Act has been adopted by Alabama, Arizona, California, Connecticut, Delaware, Idaho, Illinois, Indiana, Maryland, Massachusetts, Minnesota, Mississippi, Montana, Nebraska, Nevada, New Hampshire, New Jersey, New Mexico, New York, North Dakota, Oregon, Pennsylvania, South Dakota, Tennessee, Utah, Virginia, Washington, and Wyoming.

PROBLEMS

1. *a.* A dealer in cotton has a cash capital of $50,000 which he invests in cotton and places in a warehouse. The warehouse receipt he offers his bank as collateral in order to borrow money to buy more cotton. If the bank requires a margin of 25 per cent, show how much cotton may be purchased with the cash capital if the dealer repeats the operation three times, making four purchases including the original purchase.

   b. How much did the bank loan and what is the value of its collateral?

   c. Assuming that the above operation has taken place, explain the use of the trust receipt in the sale of the cotton.

2. An insolvent business presents the following Statement of Affairs.

Cash....................	$ 2,942.12	Notes Payable to Bank....	$ 30,000.00
Accounts Receivable.......	32,128.67	Accounts Payable.........	148,742.56
Inventory...............	41,000.00	Accrued Wages and	
Furniture and Fixtures....	1,200.00	Social Security Taxes...	832.40
Deficit..................	102,304.17		
	$179,574.96		$179,574.96

The assets have "expected to realize" values. All creditors are unsecured. Set up a new Statement of Affairs with Accounts Receivable converted to Trade Acceptances Receivable, and Notes Payable to Bank converted to Trade Acceptances Discounted. Compute the percentage each class of creditors will realize on their claims under each Statement of Affairs.

3. An importer of coffee in New York purchases a quantity of coffee from a shipper in Rio de Janeiro, Brazil, under an irrevocable and confirmed letter of credit. Diagram the movement of the letter of credit and the shipping documents between the principal, the issuing bank, the negotiating bank, and the beneficiary.

4. An automobile dealer carries his inventory of cars by means of what is known as "floor plan financing." He has just ordered fifteen new cars from the manufacturer. Explain just how the trust receipt is used in this method of financing.

CHAPTER 7

ACTIVITIES OF THE NATIONAL ASSOCIATION OF CREDIT MANAGEMENT

In no department of business is cooperation recognized as of greater essential importance than in credit work. The credit man realizes that his measure of success is dependent to a large extent upon the success of other credit men operating in the same industry; and, since there is an interlocking of industries through the fact that single concerns buy in different industries and likewise sell to different industries, there is, consequently, a common interest among all credit men. The standard of credit within an industry cannot be raised to any extent by a single credit man. All, however, working together can impose the desired standard upon the buyers of the industry. Thus the credit man is dependent upon other credit men not only for credit information but for help in maintaining or raising the credit standard.

Another phase of credit work in which cooperation is essential is in insolvency, as has been shown in the chapters dealing with that subject. Under our theory of insolvency legislation, an insolvent business belongs to the creditors. In such cases, the creditors have a position akin to partnership where cooperation is most essential. To organize for cooperation was a most logical sequence. It was realized that the function of the credit men of the country was not merely to choose good accounts but to develop good ones. The result was the organization of credit men on no less than a nationwide scale to promote both the spirit and the means of cooperation.

The National Association of Credit Management. This is the professional and service organization of the commercial and financial credit interests of the United States. It was organized in 1896, when businessmen with vision came to realize that the credit structure of the country required as definite organization as any other phase of business in order to meet the growing demands for credit and to handle this demand efficiently. The primary purpose of forming this organization was to protect business against credit loss and abuse, to maintain a sound and economic credit technique, and to promote all possible developments of

90

sound credit business. From a membership of less than 600 it now has more than 36,000 of the leading manufacturers, wholesalers, and financial institutions of the country.

The governing power of the national organization is vested in the president, three vice-presidents, and a nationwide board of directors consisting of thirty-one members. The officers and directors, who serve without pay, are executives of nationally known business houses. As a nonprofit cooperative association, owned and controlled by its membership, much of the work is done through committees of representative members. However, the national association and its local affiliated offices now employ a paid personnel of more than 1,700 persons. In addition to the adjustment bureaus and interchange bureaus, the association has a wide scope of activities which are briefly described in this chapter.

The Local Associations. The national association is made up of 140 local affiliated credit associations in all the major business centers of the country. Each local association is a self-contained, self-supporting unit, functioning under the supervision of a local board of directors and managed by a secretary. All members of local associations are members of the national organization. In joining a local association, the national association is also joined automatically, since the membership fee includes the dues in both bodies.

The purpose of these many local units of the national association is to provide a nationwide coverage to meet the credit service needs of business. In addition to the close contact between credit executives made possible by these local associations, the actual credit services built by this organization are made highly efficient and effective by having this nationwide service network through the local associations. There is not only personal value to the credit manager through close contact with fellow executives but actual service value to any firm belonging to the National Association of Credit Management.

Fraud Prevention Department. The object of this department is to safeguard credit extended by its subscribers through the medium of investigation and prosecution of all violators of the penal laws covering commercial fraud. The services of the Fraud Prevention Department are available to all commercial firms, banking institutions, etc., which, under special arrangement, are entitled to call for investigation in any matter which they believe to be of a nature that might later warrant the attention of the official prosecutors.

The Fraud Prevention Department was inaugurated on June 1, 1925, and from that date to January, 1959, convictions numbered 1,753 individuals.

The department works in close cooperation with the federal, state, and municipal authorities in the prosecution of all offenses defined by the National Bankruptcy Act and Postal laws (pertaining to the use of the mails in a scheme to defraud); and the various penal laws of the states covering the obtaining of monies, property, or credit through the issuance of a false financial statement; conspiracy to defraud; and in general all punishable fraud.

Probably the most outstanding success of this department is its activity in eliminating from the business world various groups of individuals whose business while conducted outwardly in a legitimate manner is merely a cloak to defraud creditors of amounts estimated in millions of dollars.

These groups, operating in large centers, resort to various schemes in order to obtain merchandise, merchandise which on its receipt is quickly turned into cash through its disposal at prices far below the market value. Not alone, therefore, do these groups defraud their creditors and fail to make any payment for the shipments received, but they also destroy the shipper's market through their underselling of his product.

With the cooperation of the federal and state authorities many of these schemes have been frustrated by the fraud prevention department with the support of its subscribers. The benefits accorded creditors through this medium cannot be determined in dollars and cents.

The Fraud Prevention Department does not function in any matters of a civil nature, nor does it participate in adjustments or collections.

The personnel of this department is composed chiefly of former experienced government investigators who are fully acquainted with the phases of commercial fraud and whose activities during the past 34 years have caused the sum of approximately $2,500,000 to be returned to estates which they have investigated.

The Credit Research Foundation. This Foundation, which is affiliated with the National Association of Credit Management, was chartered as a separate organization under the laws of the state of Delaware on Jan. 3, 1949. It is governed by a board of 15 Trustees elected by members at the annual meeting held in May in conjunction with the annual Credit Congress of the National Association of Credit Management. Membership in the National Association of Credit Management is a requirement for membership in the Foundation.

The purposes of the Foundation are to promote and direct research and education with a view to improvement of credit and financial administration. These purposes seek to improve credit techniques, to survey and analyze credit department operations and functions, to provide a clearinghouse for credit ideas and problems, and to promote a better understanding of the relationship of credit to other departmental activities in business and in government. The Foundation also seeks to foster higher professional standards by providing educational programs for credit executives and to stimulate interest in the development of more competent executives to fill important positions in credit management.

The Board of Directors of the National Association of Credit Management in its annual meeting in Chicago in November, 1951, delegated to the Foundation the responsibility for the direction and management of all educational activities of the Association. Under this action the Foundation gives general oversight to the activities of the National Institute of Credit and the Graduate School of Credit and Financial Management, but each of these educational organizations retains its original identity and continues to report directly to the Board of Directors of the National Association of Credit Management as heretofore.

The research projects of the Foundation completed and published since its establishment include studies on the following topics: Credit Department Expenses, Field Warehousing for the Credit Executive, Training for Credit Management, Analysis and Evaluation of Credit Management Functions, Measurement of Credit Department Effectiveness, Quarterly Survey on the Status of Accounts Receivable, Foundation Report on Credit Department Organization, Methods of Calculating Reserves for Doubtful Accounts, Credit Orientation and Training for Salesmen, Punched Card Accounting and the Credit Department, and an 800-page "Credit Management Handbook."

Many other valuable studies and survey reports are released periodically by the Foundation to assist credit and financial executives in their jobs of efficient credit administration. Future plans include reports on Analysis and Rehabilitation of Financially Distressed Debtors, a Foundation report on the Small Business Investment Act of 1958, and a report on the Organization of a Credit Department for the Small Business. The Foundation also is working with a number of industry groups and with local credit associations on special problems of specific interest to those groups. As the educational and research arm of the National Association of Credit Management, the Credit Research Foundation renders a valuable service to the credit profession generally and to its members in particular.

The Graduate School of Credit and Financial Management. The basic aim of this School is to prepare executives for the assumption of additional managerial and administrative responsibilities in the field of Credit and Financial Management. A planned training program is provided for a period of three summers with attendance of 2 weeks each summer. The program seeks to help executives become more competent, to improve their thinking processes and analytical abilities, and to facilitate the exchange of experiences and ideas with other seasoned executives from widely diversified businesses.

The School is sponsored by the National Association of Credit Management, the Credit Research Foundation, the Amos Tuck School of Business Administration of Dartmouth College, and the Graduate School of Business of Stanford University. One session is conducted at Stanford University in July, and another session is held at Dartmouth College in August.

Only mature, experienced executives are eligible for attendance and must be recommended by the management of the firms they represent. The average age of those in attendance is forty years. About one-half are credit executives and the other half are treasurers, controllers, financial, and other general administrative officers. On the average these executives have spent 10 years in credit work and are responsible for the direct supervision of 17 persons. More than 40 per cent are college graduates and an additional 30 per cent have attended college 1 year or more but have not graduated.

By the use of carefully selected cases and problems a broad view of management and of national and international business situations is maintained in the instructional process. While the more specialized operations are being examined and discussed, constant emphasis in instruction is placed upon the values to be derived from the development of the individual's skills and understandings that are commonly characteristic of competent executives.

The areas of instruction include Problems of Credit and Financial Management, Management Policies and Functions, Development of Executive Abilities, Economics of Money and Credit, Current Trends in Marketing, Economic and Business Conditions, Financial Management Policies, and the Development of Executive Leadership. Problem Seminars in Credit Management, a Problem Analysis test, special reading and study assignments to be completed between the summer sessions, and the preparation of a Management Study Report constitute additional work required of each member. Those completing the 3-year program to the satisfaction of the Faculty are awarded a diploma.

The National Institute of Credit. In the adoption of a constitution the National Association of Credit Management had a vision which is now being realized. That vision called for a membership composed of men educated and trained for the important functions in Credit Management. Article II of the Constitution laid the foundation for this achievement in the following words: "To encourage training for credit work through departments of colleges and universities, by correspondence courses, and the grouping together of the younger men and students in an Institute of Credit." Accordingly, there was founded in 1918 the National Institute of Credit which 6 years later was incorporated as a nonprofit institution under the educational laws of the State of New

York. The Institute functions through chapters organized in cities where there are local Associations, and where there are no local Associations the students' studies are supervised by correspondence from the office of the Institute in New York City. The work of the student is recognized by course certificates as he progresses. Awards are based upon the satisfactory completion of prescribed courses of study and practical laboratory work experience. More than 1,800 men and women have qualified for the Associate Award and over 1,100 have received the Fellow Award since the Institute was established. Its programs are offered in cooperation with more than 65 colleges and universities throughout the United States.

To qualify for the Associate Award, a candidate must have completed the following courses in a chartered chapter of the Institute or in an approved college or university:

Accounting........................... Full year (4 to 6 semester hours)
Economics............................ Full year (4 to 6 semester hours)
Credit and Collection Principles......... Half year (2 to 3 semester hours)
Advanced Credits..................... Half year (2 to 3 semester hours)
Business Correspondence............... Half year (2 to 3 semester hours)

In addition to the above a candidate must present evidence of at least 3 years of business experience in Credit or related work.

The Fellow Award is available to those who have qualified for the Associate Award and who, in addition, complete the following courses in a chartered chapter of the Institute or an approved college or university:

Business Law......................... Full year (4 to 6 semester hours)
Public Speaking...................... Half year (2 to 3 semester hours)
Salesmanship or Marketing............. Half year (2 to 3 semester hours)
Credit Management Problems.......... Half year (2 to 3 semester hours)
Financial Statement Analysis........... Half year (2 to 3 semester hours)
Applied or Industrial Psychology....... Half year (2 to 3 semester hours)
Techniques of Supervision............. Half year (2 to 3 semester hours)
Elective courses................................(4 to 6 semester hours)

These elective courses are to be chosen by the candidate with the purpose of furthering his major interest and should be selected from the fields of Finance, Accounting, Marketing, Management, Advanced Economics, Communication, or Foreign Trade.

In addition to the above requirements a candidate must present evidence of at least 6 years' business experience in Credit or related work of which 3 years may have been offered for the Associate Award. He must also pass a comprehensive Fellow Award examination which is given in June of each year in three parts, namely: Part I, Legal Aspects of Credit; Part II, Credit Management Problems; Part III, Human Relations in Credit.

Those who have had 10 or more years of Credit Department experience of a supervisory or managerial nature and who are thirty or more years of age may qualify for the Fellow Award by passing the comprehensive Fellow Award examination without having completed all the course requirements prescribed for the Associate Award and the Fellow Award.

The classroom work in the courses prescribed by the Institute program may be taken through three mediums: first, the classes conducted directly by local associations; second, classes conducted in recognized colleges and universities where arrangements have been made for such conduct or cooperation between the local association and university authorities; third, transfer credit for work previously completed in recognized colleges and universities upon presentation of an official transcript of record even though no preliminary arrangements may have been made between the local association and the university.

Wherever local chapters have been organized, the members hold regular meetings throughout the school year for the discussion of pertinent subjects. These meetings are not only educational but also widen the credit man's acquaintance and enable him to form contacts and friendships which are so valuable to everyone in this field of endeavor. Chapters are governed by the members themselves under the supervision of a Board of Directors selected by the members.[1]

The New York Institute of Credit. Successor to the National Institute of Credit, New York Chapter, it has been organized as an educational corporation and operates under a charter granted by the Board of Regents of the State of New York. As stated in the charter: "The purposes for which the corporation is formed are to establish, maintain and conduct a school offering post-secondary courses in credit and related financial subjects." The New York Institute of Credit is the New York Chapter of the National Institute of Credit, and offers the programs of courses that cover the requirements for the Associate Award and the Fellow Award of the National Institute of Credit. In addition, the curriculum of the New York Institute of Credit has been expanded to embrace a program of courses which covers the equivalent of a 2-year college course of study.

Other Activities of the National Association. *Foreign Department and Foreign Credit Interchange Bureau.* In an effort to be of assistance to association members engaged in foreign trade, in 1919 the Foreign Department and the Foreign Credit Interchange Bureau were established. Comprehensive and authentic ledger experience reports on foreign buyers are supplied to subscribers to this particular phase of

---

[1] Those interested in further information concerning the National Institute of Credit and its program should direct a request to the Director of Education, National Institute of Credit, 229 Fourth Avenue, New York 3, N.Y.

N.A.C.M. activity. The paying records of over 350,000 foreign buyers located in all parts of the world are on file. The *Weekly Bulletin* to members gives up-to-date comments on current foreign credit, collection and exchange problems, and special surveys are made on behalf of the membership at various intervals. One of the main activities of the Foreign Department and the Foreign Credit Interchange Bureau has been the monthly Round Table Conferences on Foreign Credit, Collection, and Exchange Problems. Minutes are taken of these general discussion meetings and are available at a nominal cost to interested exporting manufacturers throughout the United States. Moral suasion letter service is available to members on past-due and delinquent accounts abroad. Special foreign trade groups in several industries are regularly in operation. The activities of the Foreign Department and of the Foreign Credit Interchange Bureau, which is owned by its members, are under the direction and supervision of experienced export executives.

Industry Credit Group Department. Upward of 400 credit groups have been established within industries for the purpose of intimate discussion, deliberation, and action on the part of mutually interested creditors in their industry credit problems. Specialized industrial service is a valuable supplement to the general services and has produced decreased receivables and valuable standardization of industry credit practices. Coordination through interchange of the Industry group activities removes the danger of industry isolation and affords cooperation between industries in matters of common credit interest.

Adjustment Bureaus. These bureaus, sponsored by the National Association of Credit Management, are organized to aid and protect creditors in both voluntary and involuntary liquidations. They are located in the principal cities throughout the United States. The functions and method of operation of these bureaus are fully described in a later chapter.

Collection Departments. More than sixty of the local Associations presently offer collection facilities for the processing of delinquent accounts on behalf of members. In some instances, the Collection Department (also variously known as Commercial Claims Division, Collection Committee, Credit Managers Collection Bureau, etc.) functions separately; in others, collections are handled personally by the Secretary-Manager of the Association or by the Adjustment Bureau.

Business Service Department. This supplies intimate study and inspection of specific credit situations, with the main purpose of rehabilitation of a deserving business or early liquidation of undeserving business at a time when reasonable returns can be made to creditors. All such service is performed on request of, and is supervised by, the interested creditors.

Washington Service Bureau. The increasing complexity of business and the increasing influence of government over business have emphasized governmental developments, policies and regulations. The Association's Washington Service Bureau provides information on these developments as well as on government contracts, payments on government claims, surety bonds and similar matters that do not require action as a manufacturer's agent or attorney.

Credit Standards and Ethics. Since its inception, the association has promoted and advanced high standards for commercial credit practice and continues to maintain and promote a definite platform of business ethics.

Legislation. The correction, modification, or enactment of pertinent laws has been one of the continuing purposes of this association. Its effectiveness is evident by its success in having been largely instrumental in the passage of legislation, a portion of which is cited in a subsequent section.

Publications. *Credit and Financial Management,* the official publication of the Association, has nationwide monthly circulation. It acts as a clearinghouse for successful credit methods and includes pertinent articles on credit and financial matters, business reports, and analyses; also included are particular articles concerning new developments on credit departmental operation. An "Insurance Issue" is published annually in October, and the November edition is devoted to "Office Equipment and Management."

The Monthly Business Letter. From his extensive and intimate contacts with credit and financial matters, the Executive Manager reports monthly his interpretations of the major economic developments as they apply particularly to the credit and financial field.

Credit Manual of Commercial Laws. A legal digest of the laws affecting every phase of credit and sales procedure, revised yearly to include all new enactments or changes in existing laws. It is generally accepted as the most practical and comprehensive guide to protective action.

The Credit Management Handbook. This practical handbook presents the principles, methods, procedures, and techniques of effective credit management. It serves as a guide and reference volume for every phase of credit activity.

Credit and Financial Department Forms. Many important forms used in credit department work are offered by the association. These include several varieties of financial statement forms, insurance statement forms, and collection enclosures. Because of their standardization and uniformity, considerable savings are effected by their general usage by credit approvers.

Achievements of the National Association. Each year has seen constructive action undertaken. As early as 1897, the organization started a nationwide movement against the secret sale of stock of goods in bulk and out of the regular course of business, resulting in statutes in practically all of the states at the present time. It has taken leadership in framing and securing passage of the National Bankruptcy Act in 1898 and has been influential in, though not approving all, the amending legislation since enacted. It sponsored the adoption of fictitious-name laws and improved false financial statement legislation. It took an active part in securing the passage of the Federal Reserve Act and entered the congressional fight to help secure the par payment check system under the Federal Reserve Act. It has been estimated that par payments have saved business more than $160,000,000 annually. With the expansion of instalment selling, it sponsored the revision of the Conditional Sales laws.

In 1920, it founded the National Institute of Credit. It has developed a nationwide system of adjustment bureaus for the elimination of waste in liquidation and has sponsored legislation providing for arbitration of commercial disputes which has been put on the statute books in several states. It has raised more than $2,000,000 as a fraud prevention fund and secured more than 1,700 convictions. In the flood of debtor relief legislation of the past few years, it has worked to safeguard creditor interests. Its more recent activities include cooperation with the federal government in national bankruptcy investigation and participation in writing the credit provisions in industry codes.

The Robert Morris Associates. Bank credit men formed in 1919 an organization known as the Robert Morris Associates, which is closely affiliated with the National Association of Credit Management both in the letter of its by-laws and in the spirit of its membership. As expressed in its by-laws, the purpose of the Robert Morris Associates

. . . shall be to encourage and protect trade and commerce and to combine the influence of its members for more effective cooperation in carrying out the objects and plans of the National Association of Credit Management; to promote friendship and understanding among the bank credit men of the national association; to bring about a closer relation between mercantile and financial credit men; and to improve methods of gathering, compiling, analyzing, and disseminating credit data.

Headquarters are maintained at Philadelphia, Pa., where a monthly bulletin bearing the name of the organization is prepared and mailed to its members. The publication provides a valuable medium for the expression of opinion on bank credit practice, data, and articles of interest.

TEXT AND RESEARCH QUESTIONS

1. Why is cooperation among credit men a prime necessity?
2. *a.* When was the National Association of Credit Men (now Management) formed, and what is its present approximate membership?

b. Why would you advise a credit man to join the local association of credit men?

3. What is the purpose of the credit protection department of the National Association of Credit Management?

4. Why is prosecution of fraud more efficiently handled by the credit protection department than by creditors' committees?

5. Of what service to business is the department of research?

6. *a.* What four subjects of study are regarded as essential for the young credit man? What are the next four in importance?

    b. Why should every young credit man join the National Institute of Credit?

    c. Would you advise the young man intending to go into credit work to work for the Associate Award and the Fellow Award of the National Institute of Credit? Why?

7. *a.* Who are the Robert Morris Associates?

    b. What, in brief, is its purpose?

8. In what important legislation has the National Association of Credit Management taken an active part?

9. What is the "Credit Manual of Commercial Laws"? The Foreign Credit Interchange Bureau? *Credit and Financial Management?*

PROBLEM

Develop a 4-year program of college courses from the catalogue of your university or college which you feel would effectively fulfill the educational qualifications of a prospective credit executive.

PART II

CREDIT INVESTIGATION AND ANALYSIS

CHAPTER 8

INVESTIGATING CREDIT FACTORS

The second phase of credit study embraces investigation and appraisal of credit risks. This discussion is carried on through the several chapters of this section. Of immediate interest to the credit analyst, however, is a brief survey of the principal information sources essential to proper credit analysis, including a review of the leading types of business entities.

Points to Be Investigated. The success of credit risk appraisal depends primarily upon getting the essential credit facts. The credit man may err in drawing his conclusions when in possession of a certain set of facts, but he surely cannot be accurate in his judgment when points which would have an influence upon his credit judgment are unknown to him. In the author's opinion, the causes of errors by credit men are about evenly divided between improper interpretation of credit data and the lack of sufficient information prior to the credit decision. The reader will not, however, overlook the fact that the time and cost of investigation are subject to such controlling factors, among others, as the size of the order, the amount of profit in it, and the risk involved in selling to that particular class of trade.

The purpose of the investigation will also have its influence upon the time involved and the method to be pursued. The trade credit department instigates an investigation in practically all cases for one of three reasons. Either a new or prospective account is to be investigated, or an old account is being periodically revised, or some special circumstance calls for the revision of the account. Investigations by banks are made for the same reasons, with the added one that the investigation may be made at the request of one of its customers or by another bank. Just what sort of information, or what points to cover, where to go, and how to get the information desired will be treated in this and following chapters.

In General. Every factor relating to a credit risk has some bearing upon the credit decision and should, therefore, have some weight either for or against the acceptance of the credit risk. When favorable and unfavorable factors disclosed by the investigation are intermingled in the information and seem to be about evenly divided, a decision is hard to reach. While the factors of a satisfactory risk have been discussed in a previous chapter under the headings of Character, Capacity, Capital, and Condition of Business, the investigation of these different factors is usually regrouped under General Information or Antecedents, the Financial Position, and the Credit Hazard in the Industry.

The different effects of some of the information to be found under these headings will be discussed in subsequent paragraphs. Mainly to be considered under General Information or Antecedents are the type of business, its legal composition, its location, and a complete record of the concern and its owners. The significance of the antecedents can hardly be overestimated in the appraisal of a credit risk. Too many times, however, the credit manager in actual practice fails to obtain a complete record of the concern, its owners, and its management.

Investigation of the financial position will include its past financial record, as well as a thorough analysis of its present position, its trading record, by which is meant its reputation, and its record and method for taking care of its credit obligations. Still another factor which will have its influence and must not be overlooked in the general investigation, though it may be kept somewhat in the background, is the credit hazard in the industry.

Type of Business. It is essential that the credit manager should know and properly appraise the factors which are peculiar to the different types of business within an industry. After having considered the name, which may in itself have some significance, the kind of business conducted will have first attention. While there are many special types of business, two general divisions may be made of all, namely, manufacturers—those who produce or assist in the production of goods—and merchants—those who sell the article without changing its form in any way. There are, for example, in the textile field four general types of business, the manufacturer, the contractor, the jobber, and the retailer. Each presents a credit hazard peculiar to itself because of the type of business which it conducts. While various types cannot be treated specifically, what it is desired to bring out may be accomplished by stating that in many instances, though by no means in all, retailing is the simplest form of business, while in many instances jobbing demands a considerably broader knowledge of the general market and trading conditions as well as a larger capital. Manufacturing requires not only a broad knowledge of markets and marketing conditions but manufacturing ability and experience as well, together with a large capital. Each type of business presents its own peculiar credit hazard.

Furthermore, the hazards in each type of business may be peculiar to each different industry. The manufacturer, for instance, may produce an article highly seasonable, or subject to the whims of fashion, or a specialty. The creditor has a very different group of credit factors to consider from those of the manufacturer of a product of steady demand.

Legal Composition. While the credit hazards of different types of business are the result of economic conditions, the hazards resulting from the form of the business ownership and control are fixed by law. These hazards of business form vary but little, consequently, in different industries and in different types of the same industry. Both the rights of the owner and the rights of the creditor are fully defined. While there are various types of ownership, the three most important are the single proprietorship, the partnership, and the corporation. Other forms occasionally encountered are estate ownerships, trusteeships, business trusts, cooperative societies, joint stock companies, etc. The credit factors peculiar to the more common of these legal forms of business will be set forth.

Single Proprietorships. Single proprietorships are the most numerous form under which business is conducted. The single proprietorship is also the simplest form of a business entity. There are, in fact, no legal restrictions which the creditor should guard against except to be sure that the business conducted be a legal one, that the owner be neither a minor nor insane, and, if the owner is a married woman, that she has the legal right to transact business.

In a single proprietorship, the owner's total personal wealth, except for certain property exempted by various state laws, is at the risk of the business. The proprietor is free to operate the business according to his own judgment and without interference or restraint. There is, therefore, great flexibility in the management. When the proprietor is a man of sound judgment and all-around ability, with experience and sufficient capital, he presents a very desirable risk. These are points in favor of this form of business control.

There are, however, some disadvantageous points which the creditor should take into consideration. There may be ostensibly a sufficient personal estate to ensure the goodness of the credit risk. The thorough credit manager will be certain that the title to such property is not in the name of his wife, nor that there is joint ownership of husband and wife. In either case, such property is removed from the reach of creditors. If a woman appears as the owner of a business, it should be ascertained that she is not a "dummy" for the real owner, her husband or other relative who for legal or other reasons may not be able to hold property. In some lines for which a woman is peculiarly adapted, she presents a better risk than would a man. The woman in business, however, is apt to show less tenacity than a man. She becomes more easily discouraged when confronted with adversity and, abandoning the enterprise, finds a refuge with some relative or friend.

Capacity is often a factor which should be carefully investigated in a single proprietorship. It is rarely that one finds production, marketing, and financing ability highly developed in one man. Conducting all departments of a business of any size imposes a severe strain. Considerable hazard is involved in the health of the owner. If he becomes ill, the business may be badly conducted. In the event of death, the creditors' money may be tied up for some time, even though the estate is amply solvent. Some added protection is given when the proprietor carries life insurance for the benefit of the estate or for his creditors.

An analysis of business failures would no doubt show a larger percentage of failures in single proprietorships than in partnerships or corporations. This is due in a large measure to the ease with which an individual may engage in business, with the result that many an enterprise is ill advised in its inception. In the new enterprise capacity and capital will require particular attention.

Partnerships. This form of business ownership presents some individual characteristics with which every credit man should be familiar. The first fact to be ascertained is: Is it a general or limited partnership? This information is easily obtained, since a limited partner must plainly set forth that his liability is limited. Otherwise, he may be made a general partner. This question is of importance to the creditor because in a general partnership each partner is liable for all the debts of the firm while the special, or limited, partner is not liable beyond his investment in the business. It is therefore important to know the sum contributed by the limited partner, or partners, and the date of the termination of the agreement. While in a general partnership the partners are individually and collectively responsible to their creditors and to each other for their acts, and the property of each, both in and out of business, is available for the payment of the debts of the business, there is not a parity among all the creditors. Business and personal creditors have not an equal claim upon all the assets. This fact becomes of importance only upon the insolvency of the partnership or of any partner. If the partnership becomes bankrupt, the general creditors of the partnership have a prior claim to the firm's assets over the creditors of the individual partners. Likewise, the personal creditors have a prior claim to the personal assets of the individual partner. If, however, a creditor has the endorsement of a partner, the effect is to make him both a business and personal creditor.

Unless there is an agreement to the contrary, the death of a partner terminates the partnership, or a partner may withdraw at will. The estate of a partner cannot be held liable for any debts incurred subsequent to his demise, nor is a partner liable for any debts incurred subsequent to his withdrawal. Withdrawal or death will not, of course, release an individual or an estate from liabilities incurred while a member of a partnership. Upon the death or withdrawal of a partner the creditor should either revise his credit file or proceed as though he were investigating a new account.

Among the advantages of the partnership from the creditor's point of view is the fact that partnerships, on the average, require and control a larger capital than do individual proprietors. An advantage over the corporation is the fact that each general partner is responsible for the acts of all partners, and it affords a simple, compact form of organization. It permits of the use of diversified abilities, and when well balanced presents an extremely desirable business unit. The real strength of a partnership lies in the joining of the diversified abilities and the capital of the individuals.

Its greatest disadvantage lies in its lack of stability. It is subject to dissolution without warning. The creditor must particularly guard against dissension among the partners, or complications arising from the personal obligations of the several partners, as well as complications arising from the termination of the partnership which, as has been stated, is so easily accomplished.

The ideal combination in a partnership with moderate capital consists of three persons, one an experienced marketing man or distributor, the second experienced and successful as a buyer or manufacturer, and the third with ability as a financier, each in charge of his branch of the business and working in harmony with each other.

Corporations. While the corporation is the most complicated form of business organization under discussion, it has certain features which give it a preference over the proprietorship and partnership as a business risk. The complications arise out of the legal requirements of the several states and the variations of the legal requirements in different states. The laws are, however, fundamentally alike, the most important differing features to the credit man being the laws relating to exemptions from levy on certain corporation assets, and the limitations of the business which may be carried on. In general, the interests of creditors are well protected by the various state laws: there are but few laws prejudiced to their interests.

A favorite definition of a corporation was framed by Chief Justice Marshall in the famous Dartmouth College case, as follows: "A corporation is an artificial being, invisible, intangible, and existing only in contemplation of law." Since a corporation

. . . exists only in contemplation of law and by force of law, and when that law ceases to operate, and it is no longer obligatory, the corporation can have no existence. It must dwell in the place of its creation, and cannot migrate to another sovereignty.[1]

If authorized by its charter it may do business outside the state of its creation where the laws permit a foreign corporation to do business within their borders, but each state has the power and privilege of prescribing the terms upon which it will allow foreign corporations to transact business within its borders. The question arises as to what is transacting business within a foreign state. The reader may also query how this matter may involve the credit department. While a discussion would be too lengthy for this chapter, and it is not primarily the function of the credit manager employed by a corporation to see that his company observes all the requirements of the law, the question is of direct interest to the credit department since its ability to enforce its contracts in a foreign state may be involved.[2]

The foregoing paragraph refers to the creditor corporation's authority to transact business. The credit manager is primarily interested in the credit factors presented by customers having this form of business organization. Perhaps the most emphasized fact is the limited liability of the ownership. Although stockholders usually have no liability once their stock is fully paid, they may, in some states, be held jointly and severally liable for unpaid wages and fringe benefits in the event the corporation becomes bankrupt. A second fact, which may, upon occasion, be called an advantage or a disadvantage, is that it possesses only those powers granted to it by law. It therefore lacks something of the flexibility possessed by the single proprietorship and the partnership. This may restrain it from plunging into wild adventures. That it permits hidden identity and hidden responsibility may also at times be regarded as a disadvantage.

In spite of the legal intricacies of the corporation and other disadvantages, it is nevertheless a favorite form of business organization with the credit manager. Some of the reasons follow: Usually the business is not terminated by death nor is its routine affected. This is particularly true of the larger corporations. An individual usually represents only a fraction in the ownership and management of a corporation and the wound in the corporation caused by his passing is quickly healed unless it be a large one. While limited liability is listed as a disadvantage, on the other hand the personal creditors of the owners cannot touch the assets of the corporation. The corporation easily per-

---

[1] Chief Justice Taney, *Bank of Augusta v. Earle,* 13 Pet. 519, 558.
[2] See "Credit Manual of Commercial Laws," 1959.

mits of an expansion of capital. Thus large amounts of capital from many sources are brought together in a single enterprise. It is an ideal unit for large-scale production with diversified ownership and management. Its existence may be perpetual. It must be remembered, nevertheless, that a business corporation is no better than the individuals who manage it.

Estate Ownership. Estate ownerships are briefly treated here since death so frequently forces the credit manager to deal with them. In the majority of instances estate ownerships are of brief duration, operating only until the business can be sold or liquidated. It is seldom that great success attends them and frequently they are unsuccessful. They are subject to the disagreements and dissensions of the heirs of the estate, and, in addition, those in the active management of the business may not be sufficiently capable or experienced.

In selling to this form of business organization, it is essential to know that all the legal requirements are being observed both by the creditor and by those in charge of the business. The management of the estate is vested in one or more executors or administrators. The executor or executors are appointed by the will of the decedent to carry out the provisions of the will. Since their powers are clearly defined, or, let us say, limited, by the terms of the will, the creditor should obtain a copy of the probated will or otherwise satisfy himself of their power to act. Administrators are appointed by the court, usually for the purpose of liquidating the business. They may, however, in some cases be empowered to continue it. In the event the estate is managed either by executors or administrators, it is essential to know whether they have properly qualified and are under bond.

Upon the death of a customer, the style under which the account has been carried by the creditor should be changed to indicate estate control. For example, the correct style might be illustrated as follows: "The Acme Hardware Co., Estate of G. A. Hardwick, Proprietor." If at the time of the customer's demise there are any bills outstanding, the creditor should know how long a period he has in which to file his claim with the executors or administrators in order to share in the distribution of the estate. The creditor should also know how long a time is given before the administrator or executor can be compelled to settle claims. These periods of time vary in different states and the laws of the state in which the estate is located should be consulted.

Trusts, Joint Stock Companies, Cooperative Societies. These are forms of business organizations which most credit men will rarely encounter. When they do, the paramount question to be determined is where the liability lies. In joint stock companies and cooperative societies usually there is unlimited joint and several liability for all debts contracted while the individual was a member. There may be, however, state legislation to modify this general statement.

The so-called Massachusetts Trust, or the Business Trust, or Common Law Trust, is an attempt to obtain

. . . the advantages belonging to corporations without the authority of any legislative act, and with freedom from the restrictions and regulations imposed by law upon corporations.[1]

Whether such an organization may be regarded as a quasi corporation or as a form of partnership depends upon the declaration of trust. The trustees may themselves avoid personal liability on any contract entered into by them by express provision to that effect. Likewise, the articles of association may be so drawn that any debt incurred by the trustees for the association may be a lien upon the trust property, but that the trustees have no power to bind the shareholders personally. Furthermore, action against common law trusts for the recovery of a debt must be in the nature of an action in equity to subject the trust property to the payment of the indebtedness. Altogether this form of business organization detracts from the desirability of the credit risk rather than otherwise, and causes the credit manager to view it with some suspicion.

Location. A few brief remarks upon the location of a business as a credit factor would seem unnecessary because of the simplicity of the principles involved, and yet how often is failure encountered because of an unwise selection of a location. The location of a business must be logical. A vacant, deserted, grocery store in a new and sparsely settled community is mute testimony to the error of judgment of the proprietor in selecting a location. The retail store should be conveniently placed. This usually means upon the ground floor with a sufficient population near to afford it patronage or upon a public thoroughfare where the public daily passes. A trade center gradually moving to a new center is an unfavorable factor. Furthermore, a business should not be subjected to too great competition. When there are more retail stores than a community can support, it is a survival of the fittest. The proprietors that fail usually have some bad debts for creditors to absorb, and during an intense struggle for survival even those who win may be slow to pay and scarcely desirable as customers.

The jobber may operate out of the high rent area but he should be in a jobbing center. That is, he should have a natural territory readily accessible to his salesmen and to his goods, and not within too great a radius. Most jobbers, like the retailer, supply local needs, the locality merely being enlarged to a radius of two or three hundred miles.

[1] *Hussey v. Arnold*, 185 Mass. 202.

An adequate supply of labor, power supply, transportation facilities, reasonable rent, and to a lesser degree nearness of raw materials, enter into the location problem of the manufacturer. How long established in the present location is a question that should be given consideration in each type of business. A new location must be tried out, and until the business has been established at an address for some time success is usually uncertain. Frequent moving from place to place is a distinctly unfavorable sign.

Record of Concern and Owners. The record of a concern and its owners are often inseparable, and then again the owners frequently have a history quite apart from that of the concern. These records may best be treated separately. The credit analyst will be favorably or unfavorably impressed by the record of the concern and its principals. As was remarked in the discussion of character, the reputation of the principal or principals will have great weight. A favorable impression is obtained when those in executive positions are regarded in their community as thrifty, energetic, capable, and with good habits. Beware of the concern one or more of whose members are lazy, gamblers, dissipators, or who are "crooked." Derogatory information of this nature, however, is extremely difficult to obtain. The businessman with a clear record decidedly impairs his credit standing when he associates with him in any executive capacity a man with a bad record. Failures in business, on the other hand, sometimes occur solely through moral and mental shortcomings of business associates, or through outside conditions of business which could neither be foreseen nor guarded against. In every case the conditions surrounding the cause of failure should be carefully examined, and where a man has shown a proper sense of responsibility to his creditors, failure should not subsequently preclude him as a credit risk. The relation between fires and credit will be discussed in a future chapter, but it may be stated here that the record of fires, as well as of burglaries and lawsuits, distinctly impairs the desirability of the risk. Fires and burglaries point distinctly at dishonesty, while lawsuits, whether won or lost, indicate the truculence of the concern. A quarrelsome customer is hard to do business with. A feature which may detract from the desirability of the credit risk is an interest divided between two or more businesses. The chances of success are brighter if all one's energy is devoted to a single enterprise.

Two other points are of particular importance. If the business is a partnership or corporation, those in control should operate harmoniously together. Finally, the man who has demonstrated his capacity while in another's employ is not always successful when managing his own business.

While the record of the concern is interwoven with the records of its owners and officers, a few points should be separately considered. A most important factor is the length of time a concern has successfully operated. The critical period of a business in most industries is its youth. If a business has demonstrated over a number of years its ability to function, that fact must weigh heavily in the credit measurement. This statement, however, is true only where the management is still virile. An enterprise often suffers from "dry rot," an expression used by businessmen to signify antiquated methods and management senility. The personnel should be properly balanced. In a partnership or corporation there should be two or more active in the operation of the business, and a proper mixture of youth and age is desirable. Young men are energetic and enthusiastic and while they are more adaptable to modern business methods and changes than older persons, they are inclined toward overoptimism and overtrading. Men of advanced years, on the other hand, lack the resiliency necessary to enable them to recoup losses or to recover from a decline in business. A good combination is often the young man with a man of middle age. The energy and overenthusiasm of youth are balanced by the fine judgment and experience of middle age.

Just as it is said that a man may inherit a business, so may it be said sometimes a business inherits a man. Corporations, sometimes designated family corporations because of their ownership, may find themselves burdened with the sons or grandsons of the founder or founders of the business. Executive positions, for which these heirs may not be qualified, must be made for them. The business may ill afford the salary withdrawals when these executives contribute so little in return. It is well to give extra attention to the management factor in those family corporations which may have reached the third or fourth generation.

If there is one bit of advice in regard to antecedents more important than any other, it is the necessity of a complete record. The antecedents should show no breaks or gaps in the record of either the concern or its managers. If such a gap appears, be suspicious of it. Be sure that it does not conceal some very unfavorable feature. To be sure, the record may be "padded," but one's business life is a matter of record and with the proper amount of investigation that record can be uncovered.

Investigating the Financial Position. A more thorough treatment of the financial position will be given in subsequent chapters devoted to the analysis of the financial statement. It is sufficient here merely to repeat the statement made in a previous chapter under the caption Capital to the effect that since credit is redeemed with capital, and there is a definite measurement of it, capital receives among all credit factors the greatest attention. In the investigation of the financial position a search is made not only into the financial position but also into the trading record. The first assumes a study of successive financial statements, while by the latter is meant an analysis of the manner in which the subject has redeemed its credit. In the investigation of the financial position, as in the antecedents, the greatest benefit is obtained when the investigation is complete.

Credit in the Industry. Without a thorough knowledge of the general setup of the industry to which he sells, no credit manager can be said to be master of his position. Such questions as the location of the industry, the successive steps in the production of the commodity, the method of distribution by manufacturer, jobber, and retailer, the general financial strength of those engaged in the industry, the terms of sale and the general observance of those terms, and the general credit hazard of the industry as determined by the financial strength and moral stamina of both sellers and buyers are matters of which the credit manager should have an intimate knowledge. In a word, the credit manager is advised to *know* his industry. The work of the credit manager has developed beyond mere skill in appraising an individual risk. He is responsible for the large funds of his concern loaned to customers, and this large and important position calls for a mastery of the industry and the business unit as a whole, as well as a mastery of the details of his own department.

TEXT AND RESEARCH QUESTIONS

1. For what different purposes are credit investigations made by mercantile houses? By banks?

2. Why is a consideration of the "credit hazard in the industry" necessary?

3. Why should a credit manager investigate thoroughly a risk's "antecedents"?

4. List (*a*) the advantages; (*b*) the disadvantages of the single proprietorship form of business.

5. What are the reasons for the popularity of the corporation as a form of business organization?

6. How would you proceed to investigate the "character" factor of a corporation?

7. What advantages may a partnership have over a single proprietorship?

8. What investigation should be made when credit sales are made to an estate ownership?

9. What is the first point to be determined when selling on credit to trusts, joint stock companies, or cooperative societies?

10. Why is not the successful operation of a business for a period of years proof of credit stability?

PROBLEM

Prepare a chart contrasting forms of business organizations, namely, sole proprietorship, general partnership, limited partnership, and corporation. As a basis of your contrast, use

a. Ease of formation.

b. Possible aggregate amount of capitalization.

c. Liability of owners.

d. Flexibility of management.

e. Reports to governmental agencies.

CHAPTER 9

SOURCES OF INFORMATION

Investigation, analysis, and appraisal of the credit risk include how and where to obtain pertinent information and how it is used by the credit appraisers of banks, trade houses, retailers, and numerous related agencies. Sources of information are vast and range from those commonly used to those disclosed only by the credit man's resourcefulness in seeking out unusual sources which may be productive of information. Obviously, only those sources which are somewhat commonly used can be treated here.

Facts and Opinions the Basis of Judgment. If all the facts having a bearing upon a credit risk could be placed before the credit analyst, and if those facts were accurately interpreted by him, the only remaining uncertainty would be due to unforeseen events caused by the element of futurity. These would be relatively few. Unfortunately, the credit man very rarely has before him all the facts bearing upon a risk. How often, on the other hand, he may fail to get facts which would have modified his judgment or reversed his decision is a question which it is not safe to attempt to answer. The aim of all credit men is to have sufficient and reliable data. Without it no confidence can be placed in the accuracy of the credit judgment. The first requisite, then, is to know how and where to get sufficient data upon which to make an accurate credit decision.

Facts will be supplemented by opinions. The credit manager seeks information from those who have previously formed an opinion of the subject as a credit risk, and, obviously, his own judgment will be influenced by the conclusions which others have reached. In his reliance upon the opinions of others, the credit manager should be careful not to let this type of information carry too much weight, and he should carefully choose those whose opinions he takes.

Judgment in Selecting Sources. To know where information is to be had and how it may be obtained are usually not the only requisites. The credit manager must gather his facts expeditiously and, at the same time, bear in mind the element of cost. The problem, then, resolves itself into a question of knowing where certain types of information can be obtained and how to obtain that information most expeditiously and economically. This requires a knowledge upon the part of the credit manager of all the sources which may be drawn upon to supply information in his industry and the types of information to be obtained from each. It would be difficult, if not indeed impossible, to enumerate all the sources which might be tapped, but the more common are known to all credit men. As has been hinted in a previous paragraph, however, comparatively few of even the common sources are ordinarily used by some credit departments.

The more common sources of information may be classified as follows:

1. Direct
   a. Application for credit
   b. Credit executive's personal knowledge
   c. Customer's record (filed data)
   d. Personal interview
      (1) By credit officer
      (2) By credit officer's representative
      (3) By salesmen or business solicitors
   e. Survey of plant or business
   f. Financial statements
   g. Correspondence with customer and other inquirers
2. Indirect
   a. Bank "stories"—by investigator and by letter
   b. Trade "stories"—by investigator and by letter
   c. Agencies (including Investment Manuals)
      (1) General
      (2) Special
      (3) Interchange bureaus
   d. Attorneys
   e. Public records
   f. Clippings (news and trade papers)
   g. Miscellaneous

For the guidance of the reader, a brief explanation of these sources of information is given here. However, their use in credit analysis is more fully discussed and illustrated in the chapters pertaining to the several different uses of credit and credit information.

Credit Application. The application for credit is a most fruitful source of data, particularly for trade houses, retailers, and dealers in consumer credit. In most cases it initiates the relationship between the borrower and the lender. In form, it ranges from a single one-page statement to a complicated form of four to six pages. The general credit application is filed only once as a basis of initiating the relationship;

but in instalment credit transactions a new application is filed for each purchase. Samples of credit application forms are found in the Appendix.

Personal Knowledge. Personal knowledge of the principals particularly refers to what the credit executive knows about their character and capacity. It is sometimes referred to as "knowing your account." It is highly intangible, often being expressed as a "feeling" or "impression."

Customer's Record. The customer's record furnishes important antecedent information. It gives the inquirer an idea of the amount of credit previously used and of how the customer handled it, with particular reference to his ability to discount bills, or whether he was prompt or slow in payment. It shows whether extensions have been necessary and gives the reasons for such requests for additional time. It also shows the extent of current indebtedness.

Information concerning affiliated business of the customer, particularly subsidiary companies, companies with similar directorates, and family relationships, may prove equally important as the customer's direct business. For example, insufficient balances in a bank account may be offset by related business.

The Personal Interview. That the personal interview is a valuable source of information has been overlooked in the past by many credit managers. Increasing use by credit officers of the personal interview, both with management and with others interested in the proper performance of contracts, is evidenced by the presence in the credit files of the growing number of officers' memorandums of personal calls. These reports record the discussions with the customer concerning business trends and how his company is doing. "Personal interview" also refers to bank, trade, and agency "stories," although they may in practice often be obtained by telephone or through correspondence. In some cases the personal interview is a "top-level" contact, and the information received may be quite confidential.

Personal interviews, however small in number and percentage of customers, have lost nothing of their importance even though the participants in the interview may not be both principals. In a word, the importance of the personal interview can be summed up in the statement that it affords both parties, the seller and the buyer, an opportunity to sell themselves to each other.

Credit managers are too prone to regard the interview merely as an opportunity to cross-examine the customer in regard to his business and credit. They forget that customers as well as they themselves are receiving impressions. The best chance which the credit department has to promote good will, and even sales, is thus lost. The credit manager will not, of course, forget that it is his first duty to safeguard his house against imprudent credits and that sales can be bolstered only where the credit is justified. But, whether the applicant is worthy of a large credit or any at all, the credit manager should strive to leave the impression of a policy of fair and considerate treatment for all customers.

With some customers, whose good credit is almost a matter of public record, the interview would be wasted time if it were devoted to establishing credit (which is already established) rather than to developing mutual good will. However cold and calculating men may try to be, business cannot entirely remove the human element. It is increased or it is retarded by the impression made upon the mutual parties by the interview. The result of the successful interview may be to cement the friendship of the customer to the house. Whenever an order is to be placed, other things being equal, it is the house regarded as friendly to the purchaser which will get his order.

How to Conduct the Interview. The credit manager will have occasion to converse with old customers and with new. The personal interview is most frequent at the opening of new accounts. It is desirable that the credit department should have made some preliminary investigation, whenever possible, before the interview is held. The interview thus affords an opportunity to clear up any questions raised in the course of the investigation. The course the interview will take will depend upon the particular situation. While the customer may evidence great haste and show by his attitude that he is ready to answer all questions and be away, usually the conversational form of interview, although somewhat longer, is preferable. The credit manager should prove a good listener, interjecting only remarks and questions enough to steer the conversation and keep the potential customer talking about himself and his business. The businessman is interested in his own problems, and an attitude of friendliness and intelligent understanding on the part of the credit manager will induce the applicant to talk freely. The interview directed toward bringing out facts pertaining to capital strength, organization, present conditions, and future outlook will enable the interviewer, at the same time, to form his opinion of character and ability.

The man just engaging in business with a limited capital has an opportunity to convince the credit manager that he possesses honesty and determination, together with native ability and a knowledge of the business undertaken. The established concern in good standing may wish fully to acquaint the credit manager with its condition, so that the latter may be able the better to answer inquiries from other credit departments, where the account is less well known. Or an opportunity is thus provided a customer to explain any condition known to exist and seemingly damaging to his credit. Many times the credit manager is in a position to offer good advice, and frequently the customer seeks it. A word of warning, however, should be here injected. Advice too freely volunteered is often resented as presumptuous. Nevertheless, the young man about to engage in business could adopt no better plan than to choose a good banker and a mercantile credit manager with recognized judgment who, as his credit partners, should also act as his business advisers.

The personal relationship established by the interview may stand both parties in good stead in their future dealings. It is well, however, to keep the relationship a business one. Credit men who have become very friendly with some of their customers have found it very difficult, subsequently, to refuse a favor though their best judgment told them the request was not for the best interests of their employer.

Personal interviews by the credit analyst with other creditors, bank or trade of the account, give both an opportunity to exchange ideas and opinions. Particularly does this afford the budding credit executive the opportunity to learn the fine points of his job while still under the benevolent guidance of a supervisor.

The substance of a personal interview is written up, usually in memorandum form, for the credit folder. Before it is filed it is usually routed through other personnel interested in that account.

Naturally, salesmen and bank business development men have first-hand contact with, and impressions of, a customer. Their interviews should be recorded and forwarded to the office as soon as practicable.

Plant Visits. In spite of the complexity of modern business plants, the credit executive, like the security analyst, finds it highly desirable to interview the customer in his own environment. The customer is at ease. Looking over the factory, retail shop, or farm gives the credit man a first-hand impression of character and capacity. However, he should not be misled by an imposing office, but should get out into the plant and, if possible, talk with the employees. Naturally, a written record of all such interviews and impressions should be made as soon as practicable after the visit. Memories tend to become hazy even after a short time interval.

Financial Statements. Since there are several chapters on financial statements, it would seem necessary to say here only that they are an important part of each credit situation. A financial report may be received by hand delivery—particularly if the customer is proud of it— or sent through the mail. On the other hand, they may be obtained in the form of stockholder reports, or from S.E.C. libraries (if a security is listed), or from the libraries of stock exchanges. Various credit reporting agencies and leading manual services such as Standard &

Poor's, or Moody's Manuals, or Fitch's, or Best's insurance reports may also be a source of financial statements.

Correspondence. Where casual personal calls are not practicable, valuable information can be elicted by interchange of correspondence regarding the status of the account, progress reports, and conditions in the industry.

Indirect Sources. A great deal of credit information, if not indeed the greatest part, is obtained from indirect credit sources. Probably most small businesses obtain credit data this way for the reason that indirect sources are probably the least expensive. There is no one best source of credit information, and it would be difficult to say that bank information is better than trade stories. However, there is a tendency for large commercial banks to have more, if not better, information. Other large financial houses such as factors and finance companies also have substantial credit folders on their customers. Industrial corporations selling in large volume to individual accounts have credit folders similar to those of banks.

Bank Stories. Bank stories are of several types, the details of which are covered under the appropriate chapter. For the present, bank stories are understood to be a record of personal interviews concerning the customer or "name" obtained from a bank credit executive by a representative of another bank, or by a trade supplier, or by an agency. Even though the bank may not have a particular account, it will, for a good customer, investigate a name and pass along relevant information received.

Trade Stories. Similarly, a trade story is a record of a personal interview concerning a customer or "name" obtained from a trade supplier or retailer by a representative of a bank, another trade house, or an agency. Opinions concerning noncustomers, but who are houses in the industry, are also sought as trade information.

The Mercantile Agencies. A classification of all the sources of credit information might be made by dividing the sources into those which are free, the idea being one of reciprocity, and those for which a charge is made. Most prominent in this latter class are the mercantile agencies.

For the name, which is hardly explanatory of the function of these institutions, we are indebted to the founder of R. G. Dun & Co. That institution was launched under the name The Mercantile Agency, Lewis Tappan & Co., Proprietors. Subsequently, all agencies engaged solely in supplying credit data came to be known as mercantile agencies, though the name primarily applies to the institution known as Dun & Bradstreet, Inc.

Mercantile agencies are divided into two classes, general and special, the division referring to the kind of business reported on rather than the type of information. There is, however, considerable dissimilarity in the type of information furnished by different agencies.

Agencies prepare reports and may rate the names. The reports cover the four C's of credit, leaving to the subscriber in most cases the decision of selling or loaning. The decision is always with the creditor. Most large creditors use the agency report as basic information for starting a credit folder.

The more important agencies are Dun & Bradstreet, Inc., National Credit Office, Inc., Lyon Furniture Mercantile Agency, Credit Interchange Bureau, National Retail Credit Bureau; various specialized associations, such as National Jewelers Board of Trade, Better Business Bureaus and, for individual specialized reports, Bishop's Agency, Inc., and Proudfoot's Commercial Agency, Inc. In addition, such agencies as Standard & Poor's, Moody's, Fitch, and Best's all publish manuals which are of value to the credit analyst.

Of all the agencies engaged in the occupation of furnishing credit information, only Dun & Bradstreet, Inc., qualifies as a general agency, since it is the only agency which undertakes to supply credit information on any businessman or business house which is buying or borrowing on credit. This agency, a combination of R. G. Dun & Co. and the Bradstreet Company, is both the oldest and the largest of mercantile agencies. It does not, however, enjoy a monopoly of supplying credit information, since it has keen competitors in some of the special agencies.

Prejudices Overcome. While, in the early days of the agencies, business houses as creditors were glad to avail themselves of all the information possible in regard to their customers, these very houses resented, as debtors, any attempt on the part of the agencies to obtain information in regard to their—the debtors'—own standing. Business houses that were accustomed to give references could not accept the idea that the gathering of information, as a business, should meet with anything except opposition. It was felt that matters regarded as strictly private were being pried into and that that very fact impugned their credit. The work of the agencies, it was felt, involved no less a matter than trafficking in the financial reputation of merchants. An attitude of considerable hostility on the part of the business public was thus fostered.

The agencies, on their part, feared litigation and punishment under the general rules of law in respect to the publication of libels. The one sure defense to suits for libelous statements was the truth of those statements, and this, coming from so many sources and through so many employees, the agencies did not feel that they could guarantee. During their existence, the responsibility of a mercantile agency for its statements has been clearly defined by litigation. Liberal interpretation of the law by many American courts has given the mercantile agencies considerable freedom in gathering and reporting credit information to their subscribers.

Between the hostility of businessmen, coupled with their reluctance to give the agency any cooperation, and the constant fear the agencies were under in giving out credit reports, it would seem that the new enterprise could hardly survive. On the other hand, the agencies were greatly aided by a real need for their services. Unlike old European business houses, with long-established reputations for good credit, the United States presented a young and rapidly growing country with new enterprises of unknown credit constantly springing up or moving to new locations. The Civil War, which like all such conflicts entailed widespread economic and financial disturbance, gave a new impetus to the work of the agencies.

Advantages of Cooperation. On their part, the mercantile public began to see the advantage of cooperating with the agencies. The good businessman realized that here was an excellent way to advertise his good credit standing. The man well rated, whose credit had been hitherto limited to a few houses with which he had formed a business relationship, now found his business solicited by the best houses available to him. The result was a wider selection of goods and better prices.

Perhaps it may be said that one of the great accomplishments of mercantile agencies has been the wide advertising of the credit of the American businessman. The frankness with which the businessman imparts information about his financial condition and credit worth has greatly developed since Lewis Tappan first undertook to supply credit information to the subscribing public, and the development is still going on. While there are still some businessmen who hinder the work of the agencies, most houses receive the agency reporters as a matter of course and willingly impart to them the information they seek. Our larger concerns, in fact, volunteer information in regard to any changes in their organizations or policy that might be of interest to creditors, and their financial statements are forwarded as rapidly as they are compiled.

Cooperation, however, between the agency, the subject of inquiry, and the subscriber has not yet reached the ideal state. It is the view of some that the agency on its part does not cultivate with sufficient intensity the good will of its subscribers and subjects of inquiry, while its subscribers do not realize that the agency, as their employee, is due every aid and assistance that the employer can give to make the service of the employee most efficient and that businessmen, as subjects of inquiry, forget that their own safety as creditors depends upon the promotion of the reciprocal basis upon which credit measurement rests.

The Agency and the Law. In the earlier stages of the agency, its work was considerably restricted through its fear of court action. The danger feared was a suit for libel as the result of publishing, through error, in some report false defamatory words. Such a publication is prima facie a libel and implies malice in its publication.[1] Through a wise and liberal interpretation of the law, United States courts have generally followed the reasoning of an English judge who said:

If a person who is thinking of dealing with another, in any matter of business, asks a question about his character of someone who has means of knowledge, it is for the interests of society that the question should be answered; and if answered in good faith and without malice the answer is a privileged communication.[2]

That an individual may fall back upon the defense of a privileged communication has been well established. Contrary to English interpretation of law, the courts of the United States have generally extended the same privilege to mercantile agencies. Our courts have held, however, that the mercantile agency

. . . can shelter itself behind the privilege of which we have spoken, only in case the false defamatory matter was communicated to particular subscribers in response to particular inquiries, but not in case such false defamatory charges are contributed generally to its subscribers, many of whom would have no personal interest in the particular disclosures made.[3]

From the above it will be deduced that it is dangerous, not only for the agency but for the individual as well, to give derogatory or defamatory information to one who has made no inquiry or who may have no direct interest in such information.

Another feature to be considered in avoiding liability is the prudence, skill, and diligence with which the agency must act in carrying out its contract to furnish credit information to its subscriber. There is no doubt that the agency is liable, in the absence of an express contract to the contrary, for the *negligent* performance of that contract. The agencies, therefore, stipulate in the contract with the subscriber that they shall not be responsible for any loss occasioned by the neglect, unfaithfulness, or misconduct of anyone on whom they rely for information, and neither the correctness nor the truth of the information is in any way guaranteed. That this feature of the contract will protect the agency, in the case of gross negligence, cannot be positively stated. A New York court has held that

[1] "Credit Manual of Commercial Laws," p. 200, 1933.
[2] *Ibid.*, p. 201.
[3] *Ibid.*, p. 202.

A contract between a commercial agency and its subscriber does not release the agency from gross negligence in falsely representing that it had investigated a prospective customer upon the subscriber's request.[1]

In connection with the reliability of the information furnished by the agency, it is well to point out that the subscriber cannot recover from the agency for any damages that he may have received through relying on an agency report, whether the agency was grossly negligent or not, if the report at the time was so old that it could not justifiably be relied on. In one such case, brought into court, it was held that a statemen made 60 days previously could not justifiably be relied on. With the marked development in the efficiency of agency service, and in view of the rapid changes in business conditions, the tendency of the law seems to be to restrict the length of time during which such statements may be relied and acted upon by creditors with legal protection.[2]

Still a third point which involves the agency is whether a creditor may bring an action against a debtor for statements made to an agency. Court decisions have developed the general doctrine that

. . . a statement made to one person with the expectation that it be communicated to, and acted upon, by another is the same as if made directly to the latter.[3]

But

. . . if the statement made by the merchant to the agency is changed by the latter, the merchant is not liable.[4]

In General. The general agencies number among their subscribers every kind of industry, financial institution, and profession which is an acceptor of credit. All do not use the services of the agency in the same way, but all find the agency indispensable. Banks, for instance, find the reference book among other uses an aid in determining whose business it is advisable to solicit. The special reports are used to obtain the record of the concern, to supply leads to other important information, and to corroborate information received from other sources. Small mercantile houses in their credit practice frequently rely almost wholly upon the ratings. That the agency is both efficient and reliable is proved by its growth. Two potent forces compel it to maintain its efficiency—the subscriber and the subject of inquiry. A maximum of efficiency will naturally result from the full cooperation of both with the agency.

[1] *Munro v. Bradstreet,* 155 N.Y. Supp. 833.
[2] BREWSTER, "Legal Aspects of Credit," p. 107.
[3] *Bradley v. Bradley,* 165 N.Y. 183.
[4] *Wachsmuth v. Martini,* 154 Ill. 515.

It would be exceedingly difficult to determine the influence which the mercantile agency has had upon business in this country. Not only has the agency classified and catalogued the credit of business houses, but it has advertised that credit upon a nationwide scale. Through the use of the services of the agency, the businessman finds it almost as safe to sell the customer in the remotest part of the country as he does to sell the similarly rated one in the next township.

It should be borne in mind, however, that the mercantile agency, whether general or special, is but one source of information, and its work is far from infallible. While it is entirely logical for creditors to employ such a specialized service to provide them with credit information, credit managers as a whole do not rely solely upon agencies and particularly not upon any one agency. Other sources of information will be utilized not only to augment the information with which to work but to provide a "cross check" upon data supplied by the agency.

Attorneys. In out-of-the-way localities and small communities, the attorney can be a satisfactory source of credit information (see Chapter 17).

Public Records, Clippings, and Miscellaneous. In following customer accounts, credit analysts must keep constantly on the alert for fire records and bankruptcies. Information of this type is either clipped from newspapers, or trade papers, or obtained from litigation records.

Although this list of credit sources is fairly comprehensive, it by no means exhausts the possibilities of the field. For instance, friends of the customer, business acquaintances, and other references such as building superintendents, neighbors, ministers, etc., may all be sources of information which may be important for the credit folder.

Summary. Naturally, the gathering of credit information entails a relatively greater or lesser expense. The amount of business offered and the presumptive margin of profit will be the best guides as to what cost is justifiable in building up a particular credit folder.

TEXT AND RESEARCH QUESTIONS

1. What are the two most important considerations in the investigation and analysis of credit risks?

2. What part do the following considerations play in the assembly and interpretation of credit information? Give illustrations where possible:
   a. Cost.
   b. Accuracy.
   c. Availability.
   d. Judgment.
   e. Purpose and relation to risk.

3. Discuss direct sources of credit information, indicating their importance.

4. Why is the personal interview a good source of information?

5. What is meant by bank stories?   Trade stories?

6. Of what use are public records?

7. Why is it important to design a good credit application form?

8. Outline briefly the historic development of Dun & Bradstreet, Inc.

9. What economic factors associated with development of our country account for the growth of this agency?

10. Discuss briefly the legal status of the mercantile agency in the United States as to liability for (a) negligence; (b) libel.

11. What is the essential difference between the legal status of the English and American agencies?

CHAPTER 10

OPERATION AND SERVICES OF THE
BANK CREDIT DEPARTMENT

Credit Classified. As we have seen in a previous chapter, credit, when reduced to documentary form, may be classified according to its acceptability. It might also be classified according to (1) the use of the funds or wealth exchanged, as in productive or consumptive credit; (2) the form of the borrower's responsibility, as in public or private credit; (3) corporate credit; (4) personal credit. If it is desired to classify credit for the purpose of its study, the most logical method is to classify it according to the nature of its uses. Thus we have five broad classes of credit: public, consumer and instalment (including retail), investment, banking, and trade (manufacturing and wholesale). The line of demarcation between these five classes is by no means distinct, and the question arises as to whether or not other classifications of the uses of credit should not be considered as, for example, agricultural credit, which seems to partake of some of the features of several of the other classes of credit, and yet is sufficiently different from each almost to warrant separate classification. Also, instalment credit overlaps in investment, banking, and trade credit.

Public Credit—the power of the government or a political subdivision of the government to borrow—is of the greatest importance to all—business concerns and individuals alike. Closely coupled with it, of course, is the subject of taxes. The subject is too vast for treatment in this volume.

Investment Credit. The term "investment" has several different meanings in common usage. We treat of it here as the placement of funds in productive assets to earn a profit. Thus a credit instrument such as a bond or stock may be issued. The institutions through which investment funds are mainly placed with business enterprises are known as investment banks or, as more commonly referred to, investment bankers. The investment banker is the intermediary between the business desiring funds and the investing public. Unfortunately for the small business

127

unit, the services of the investment banker can be utilized only by the bigger businesses.

The function of the investment banker is to market the securities of the issuer and to do this he usually underwrites, that is, guarantees, the sale of the issue. The marketing function should not be confused with that of the security exchanges. An investment banker originates an issue of securities and sells it to the investing public while the security exchanges provide a market for the resale of securities. As with public credit, long-term investment credit is handled by specialists. This is the job of the security analyst.

Importance of Investments. A knowledge of investments is particularly important to those who have funds to invest and to those who wish to employ those funds. The latter will wish to know the sources of investment credit and the forms in which it clothes itself, while the former will wish to have expert ability in appraising the contemplated credit. Each is in itself a separate study.

COMMERCIAL BANKING CREDIT

A Bank Defined. A great many people think of a bank as a storehouse for money. While a certain minimum amount of money is essential to a bank, it does not traffic in money; it is rather "an institution which deals in credit."[1] Since credit is measured in terms of money and involves a promise to pay money, a sufficient amount of currency must be kept on hand to meet such demands. The relative amount of actual money on hand to the total demands that may be made for money has been determined by experience.

A broad division of banks could be made between commercial, savings, and investment banks. These different banks often overlap in their activities, and we may find each one performing to some extent the function of another. It is the commercial or business bank, which is engaged in receiving deposits, making loans, and making collections on commercial paper, which should be held in mind in this discussion.

Banking Credit. In a bank credit transaction, the bank gives its promise to pay money on demand or at a definite future date and receives in return the borrower's promise to pay at a definite date in the future. It is merely an exchange of rights—an immediate right given to the borrower to the use of money against a future right given to the bank to demand money. The borrower may not immediately exercise his right to demand currency (in the great majority of instances he does not) in which case the bank "deposits" it to his credit, while the promise to pay

[1] JOHNSON, J. F., "Money and Currency," p. 44.

received by the bank, which may be in the form of a promissory note, becomes a part of its "loans and discounts." In this way may be created two very important items appearing in every bank statement, the asset "loans and discounts" and the corresponding liability "deposits."[1] Commercial bank credit may, then, be defined as the power of a bank to create credit[2] in return for a promise to pay on demand or at some future time.

Effect of Bank Credit. The service of a bank to a community provides not only a source of money, or, more properly, purchasing power, to those whose credit is acceptable, but it also serves as an agency for the transfer of credit. The former is accomplished through loans of various sorts, as a result of which the borrower may either demand money, or, by means of a check, transfer to another the right to demand money. As a matter of fact, in the majority of cases, the option to demand money is not exercised either by the borrower or the one to whom the option is transferred. Instead, the right is again transferred (by endorsement) to another individual, or more probably to some bank. The latter finds that the demands which it may make upon others are very nearly offset by the demands of other banks upon it, the difference being adjusted by the actual payment or receipt, as the case may be, of a small amount of money, or by giving or receiving the right to receive or pay money. Thus, banks serve as the medium through which credit freely passes.

It will be seen that this service of the banks greatly aids the exchangeability of credit and thus increases the acceptability of certain credit instruments. Checks, for example, are a common medium of transferring credit, because of the accessibility of banks and the efficiency of banking machinery. Whenever a bank guarantees or insures credit, as by the use of the bank acceptance or certification of a check, the effect is to enable such credit to be used in any direction almost without the necessity of stopping to consider values. Credit is thus made much more effective because of its close approach to general acceptability.

Credit centralizes in the banking system. In its broader phases the study of the effect of bank credit is an attempt to determine its influence upon prices, values, business conditions, etc. This branch of credit study is recommended to the student, but it is far too large a subject to treat of it here.

Bank and Mercantile Credit. If we examine the nature of a bank's work, the very close analogy of bank and mercantile credit will be quite apparent. The purpose of both is to foster production and trade. Fur-

---

[1] Deposits, as described above, are loans of money by the bank to a borrower. Deposits are also created in another manner. "Cash," in the form of money or checks, may be deposited with the bank, making the bank the debtor to the depositor.

[2] A loan deposited to a customer's account is credited to his account.

thermore, in general, the clients of the bank are the customers of the mercantile house. Both deal in short-term credit, and both measure the acceptability of a credit risk by a consideration of his personal qualifications, his financial condition, and the activity of his business. The same sources of information are available to both and utilized by both. The essential difference lies in the fact that the value extended by the mercantile creditor is goods or services, while the bank creditor loans money or the right to demand money. Both kinds of credit are essentially commercial in their nature.

A second important difference lies in the standard of credit, or the degree of risk acceptable to the two institutions.

Bank Credit Standards. It is freely stated that the standard of bank credit is higher than that of mercantile credit. This simply means that, in general, the bank requires greater certainty of payment than does the mercantile house. Chief among the reasons for this difference in standards are the following: The bank must always be able to pay its obligations upon demand or as fast as they mature. Borrowers must, therefore, return funds to the bank according to the schedule of maturities. In bank credit, terms are definite. Banks, sometimes of necessity, grant renewals to borrowers who find it inconvenient to pay at maturity; but these cases must be comparatively limited lest the banks' liquidity be impaired. Banks can in turn preserve their liquidity by rediscounting some of their "paper" with the Federal Reserve or other banks. In general, however, it may be said that the liquidity of banks depends largely upon the liquidity of their customers. On the other hand, the mercantile creditor, in some lines at least, can permit a certain delinquency among his customers because he, in turn, can default to his creditors for a short period of time without a serious reflection on his credit standing.[1]

Liquidity, or the ability to meet maturing obligations, is greatly aided by loaning money for short periods only and only when there is reasonable certainty that the loan will be repaid when due. The reader can readily understand, however, that the question of a bank's liquidity involves more than the question of short loans which will be met at maturity. The study of a bank's liquidity embraces the entire distribution of its resources and obligations.

The bank is custodian of the funds of the community. It accepts a delicate trust in caring for the funds of the depositor. The bank, which is acting in the nature of a semipublic servant, must see to it that no

---

[1] Deposit insurance, which now covers each individual account up to $10,000, was enacted by the federal government in 1933. This is intended to insure the confidence of depositors in their banks and thus prevent the runs which caused the banking crisis and panic of 1932–1933.

undue risks are taken. The mercantile house, on the other hand, is not so dependent on the good will of the public and hence has more freedom in its activity.

Then, again, the bank's margin of profit is smaller than the average mercantile margin of profit. It is obvious that with the larger profit the mercantile house can afford to take a larger risk. Banks, too, are usually found to be a debtor's largest single creditor, and ordinarily the bank's credit period is longer than the terms of sale on merchandise. These two facts would tend to make banks more cautious. Finally, banks are under the supervision of state or federal authorities and have to conform to strict laws, whereas mercantile houses are relatively unrestricted in their business activities.

Bank and Client Relationship. A businessman may use his bank as a borrower or merely as a depository for funds and as an agent for the collection of checks or other commercial paper. In either case, as has been shown, a deposit is created. Businessmen should be cognizant of the great service rendered to the credit system by banks through their collection of checks and to the individual concern which uses the bank merely as a collection agent and as a depository for funds subject to the depositor's order. When this latter service is a gratuitous one, the bank finds its recompense in the use of the funds left in its care. It is for this reason that the bank will usually require that a firm using the bank solely as a checking account shall maintain an average balance of a certain amount, or be subject to a service charge. It will readily be seen that considerable bookkeeping work is attached to handling the checks deposited for collection and those drawn upon the bank. The bank when it loans money, therefore, will exact not only interest on the amount loaned (discount) but will also expect the borrower to leave on deposit an average balance of about 20 per cent.[1] This is called a compensating balance.

It is apparent that the borrower is paying a higher rate of interest than the discount rate on the money that he uses. Thus it would seem that the bank is getting a higher rate of interest than the regular quotations. From the above it might seem that a businessman who wished to use, let us say, $8,000 would need to borrow $10,000, since 20 per cent of the loan must needs be left in the bank. But it may be assumed that the borrower has used the bank as a checking account for some time previous and that his balances have averaged between $1,500 and $2,000. Thus

---

[1] The size of the average balance left on deposit by the borrower will be found to vary in different places. The usual range is between 15 and 25 per cent. At the present time, an average balance of 20 per cent seems generally satisfactory to New York banks. F. Paschal Gallot, *Why Compensating Balances? Credit Executive,* August–September, 1958.

it will be seen that when the conditions are as has been assumed above, the full amount borrowed may be used.

Banks may also advance the argument that borrowers increase the bank's operating costs, increased costs which the borrowers should pay. This is accomplished by the 20 per cent average balance requirement. That there is nothing singular in this practice will be seen when it is remembered that the interest charge rarely represents the whole cost of borrowing from whatever source. This is exemplified by real estate loans when costs of investigation, furnished abstract of title, and recording of mortgage must be borne by the borrower; and most commonly exemplified in the purchase of an automobile on the instalment plan where payments include not only interest on the money borrowed but an added sum to cover the costs of credit investigation, supervision of the loan, and collection of the payments.

Then the bank may advance in justification that it is required to keep a certain reserve and that this is a method of passing the reserve requirement along to its borrowers. Thus both the bank and the customer are kept in a good current position. And then, too, the application of the 20 per cent rule may be regarded as a premium which the borrower pays to insure a line of credit.

Once a bank establishes a credit line for a borrowing customer it morally binds itself to place at the disposal of its customer a credit force equal to the line granted. . . . This, perhaps, is the most important benefit derived by a commercial borrower in return for the 20 per cent requirement.[1]

Whether the relationship between the businessman and his bank is merely that of depositor and depository or borrower and lender, the mutual dependence of banks and business is apparent. As in all business relationships, transactions should result in benefit and profit to both. The businessman on his part will find his interests best served by the bank if he frankly supplies it with as much information as it may desire about his business and if he maintains not only a good liquid position but also carries sufficient balance to make his account a desirable one at his bank. On the other hand, the businessman expects his bank to collect his checks for him and pay out his deposit as ordered. He expects, too, that his bank will maintain a sufficiently liquid position so that he may draw upon it for credit at any time up to the amount to which he is entitled.

Bank Service Charges. The alternative to a balance, the earnings from which are sufficient to cover the bank's expense in serving its client, is a service charge. It is largely since 1930 that banks have adopted the practice of analyzing individual accounts to determine

[1] Munn, G. G., "Bank Credit," p. 227.

whether they are profitable. Cost analysis has been forced upon banking institutions by lowered interest rates, by smaller rates of return from their various revenue producing assets, and by higher expenses.

Losses may occur not only in small accounts but also in large ones where the activity is great. Cost analysis reveals the loss which may be recoverable by a service charge or may be eliminated by increased balances. Many banks have a published schedule showing the average balance required for a given number of monthly deposits and checks. Some institutions are now soliciting business on a no-balance service charge basis, deposits being made only as checks are drawn. But these features of bank service are utilized by personal as contrasted to business depositors. It is the relationship between the bank and its business client with which we are chiefly concerned.

Par Payment of Checks. Some banks, comparatively few in number, levy a service charge through the payment of checks at less than their face value. The service charge is thus imposed, not on the depositor, but on the depositor's creditors. Because the discount is not large, the practice has not met with the opposition that it deserves. All national banks and all other banks that are members of the Federal Reserve System must pay checks at par. The practice of nonpar payment, therefore, is limited to those state banks which are not members of the Federal Reserve System and do not maintain a clearing account with the Federal Reserve.[1]

Kinds of Loans. The credit transaction between the bank and its client is evidenced by some form of credit instrument. The various credit instruments which are the concrete evidences of the extension of credit have already been discussed. These various forms of loans may be further classified in a number of different ways, as, for example, according to maturity, according to purpose, according to security. Since liquidity is a first requirement of a bank, the maturity of its loans is important. The bank would consider the relative amounts in short-term, intermediate-term, long-term, and demand or call loans. The purpose of the loan or the use of the funds borrowed may be described as commercial, agricultural, investment, speculation, consumption, etc. Perhaps the most important classification from the credit man's and borrower's standpoint is according to security. Here the two main classifications are, obviously, secured and unsecured. A secured loan is one made by a bank which not only relies upon a promise to pay but is insured against loss by a lien upon specific property. This form of security may take the form of mortgage security, but in commercial loans

---

[1] A recent survey disclosed 12,746 banks that clear their checks at par and 1,728 banks that do not. The trend is toward a reduction in the number of nonpar payment banks.

it more often takes the form of collateral. Security offered may consist of stocks, bonds, warehouse receipts, bills of lading, merchandise, book accounts, life insurance, notes, acceptances, etc. Collateral of known value and easily convertible into cash is preferred. Government bonds, for example, furnish the highest type of collateral.

Unsecured loans are distinguished from secured loans by the absence of specific property pledged to the payment of the loan. The former is based solely on the credit of the makers or the makers and endorsers, while the latter have the added security of the pledge of specific property. The borrower's promissory note is most commonly used in the unsecured loan. Unsecured loans are also referred to as "single-name" or "double-name" paper, depending upon whether or not the "paper" bears the endorsement, and thus the guarantee of a second party. While loans on "two-name" paper are classified as unsecured, it will be understood that there may be considerable added security by the addition of a strong second name.

Credit of Persons and of Property. It is well to point out at this time the difference between the credit of a person or persons and the credit of property. While property cannot, of course, give a promise to pay, since it is inanimate, it can, nevertheless, furnish the means of payment. The distinction is apparent in the contrast of single-name paper and the loan secured by collateral. In the first instance, the lender relies upon the borrower's general credit standing and financial ability to pay, while in the second instance, the reliance in whole or in part is in the ability of the collateral to liquidate the indebtedness. The student will be careful, therefore, not to impute to a person the credit which is really the result of property. This distinction is found in the mechanic's lien laws which stipulate that the labor or materials must have been furnished upon the credit of the building and not only upon the general credit of the owner or contractor. Likewise, a loan may be extended to the owner of real estate based not upon the credit of the borrower but upon the credit or the means to liquidate found in the real estate itself.

Single-name, Double-name, and Accommodation Paper. Bankers and businessmen have come to speak of commercial credit instruments as "commercial paper" or more briefly as just "paper." Promissory notes bearing the promise to pay of a single person are thus spoken of as own note and, if unsecured, straight note. A considerable proportion of commercial paper is of this class. The retailer, who buys goods and gives his vendor his written promise to pay or who gives his note to secure a prolongation of credit when an open-book account is due, gives his single-name paper. The businessman who goes to his bank and borrows by giving his promissory note is likewise giving single-name paper. In the first instance, if the vendor should sell the right which he holds to his bank, it would be necessary for him to endorse the note in order to convey title, and by endorsing it he also guarantees payment. The note thus becomes two-name or double-name paper. The risk which the bank has assumed is greatly lessened by the vendor's guarantee.

It is obviously much less probable that both should be unable to pay than that one should default. But the strength of the credit is not necessarily doubled or, in other words, the risk halved by the addition of the second name. It depends largely upon the relative credit strength of the two names. A note with one good name and one doubtful one may be preferable to a bank to a note bearing two mediocre names.

Double-name paper arises usually from an actual commercial transaction involving a sale of goods, and, consequently, there is actual value behind the note which will furnish the means to liquidate it. But, as a matter of fact, the strong business house does not need to bolster up its credit in this way. Its bank, aware of its strong solvent position, is ready to discount its note without the evidence of any single mercantile transaction to back it up. Nevertheless, a careful distinction should be drawn between double-name paper based upon a commercial transaction, or, as it is said, which is self-liquidating, and paper which has been signed by an endorser who has not received value. Such an endorser loans his credit as an accommodation to his friend. The purpose is to augment the credit strength of the instrument by loaning a name, but he who thus lends his name becomes liable for payment whether that possibility was contemplated or not. One who is thus confronted with the necessity of making good is quite inclined to evade, if he can, the collection of the note. It is a somewhat common though reprehensible practice for businessmen to exchange notes and then to present them properly endorsed for discount at their respective banks. The notes have the semblance of added strength, but in reality no strength is added. Disaster to either may be disastrous to the other. Both being in a weakened position and leaning upon each other, they do not halve the risk; they double it.

Another method of bolstering the strength of a credit instrument is by securing it by the pledge of property in payment of the debt. The promise to pay may carry with it collateral security such as stocks, bonds, bills of lading, warehouse receipts, etc., or mortgage security, either real estate or chattel mortgage, or personal security, which is exemplified in two-or more name paper. Where security is given, the credit may be based in whole or in part upon the property pledged, as brought out in a preceding paragraph.

The Commercial Paper Broker. Acting as a specialized intermediary institution between the borrower and the lender, the commercial paper broker is sometimes found. It is the function of the broker, or the commercial paper house, as his organization is called, to sell the note or notes of his client principally to banks and, to a much lesser extent, to other investors such as insurance companies, business houses, and wealthy individuals.

The growth and decline of the commercial paper system provide another illustration of the transition to which our entire credit system is constantly subject. Seventy-five years ago, the established practice of financing was to discount customers' notes or to offer the bank the borrower's own note with one or more accommodation endorsers. This did not prove ideal to either party. Subsequent to the Civil War, because of the unsettled conditions, the credit risk increased, and the uncertain value of the currency made long-term credit undesirable. To induce a cash settlement, wholesalers of merchandise began to offer liberal cash discounts to their purchasers. This resulted in the substitution of the open-book account for the promissory note and necessitated new credit lines and new methods of borrowing. The lusty growth, too, of many businesses rendered it impossible for local banks to take care of their credit requirements. The borrower felt, in some instances, that he was too much dependent on the local bank and hence too much under its control. To meet these changed conditions, there came into being the broker who took the borrower's notes and sold them not to the borrower's own bank but to any other bank which could be induced to buy. When the notes were sold a day, a week, or a month later, the proceeds, less the discount and the broker's commission, were forwarded to the borrower.

Trend of Note Brokerage Business. Reaching a peak of $1,296,000,000 in January, 1920, the amount of outstanding paper declined steadily until May, 1933, when only $60,000,000 was reported outstanding. Most of this paper was sold through regular brokers. However, about 1935, sales finance companies tapped this market in the form of direct sales. Their paper found a ready market. About two-thirds of the currently outstanding commercial paper of $3,294,000,000 in October, 1958, represents finance companies' liabilities.

That this type of paper has had a ready market with banks and industrial firms is apparent from the substantial recovery since the 'thirties.

Reasons for Favor with Banks. Chief among the reasons for the popularity of commercial paper with banks are the following:

1. It has proved eminently safe. The highest percentage of loss to sales in recent years was reported as 0.043 per cent for 1924, while no losses whatsoever were reported for the years 1928 and 1933.[1]

2. It provides a self-liquidating medium of short-term investment when the bank has idle funds to invest.

[1] Bank Service Department, National Credit Office, New York.

3. The bank is under no pressure to renew loans, and greater diversification of both type of industry and geographical location is possible.

4. Commercial paper is invariably paid at maturity.

On the other hand, a bank may lose the opportunity to loan a desirable customer sizable sums if the customer is using the open paper market. In this event, the bank may be compensated for the loss of business, in part at least, by the customer's deposit balances the use of which the bank enjoys.

The Credit Process in Banks. Through their deposit and loan relationships banks accumulate and constantly revise credit information concerning the affairs not only of their customers but of other businesses and persons in whom their customers are interested. Even on personal loans where a deposit account is not a prerequisite, a wealth of data may be accumulated from information detailed in the loan application.[1]

In a commercial bank the credit or loaning officer is primarily responsible for the type and extent of information desired for analysis. As will be shown, direct customer contact is through the officers, while indirect information is gathered mainly by the Credit Department.

Type of Work in Bank Credit Department. In general, bank accounts are classified as borrowing or nonborrowing. Usually the credit department maintains a complete card record of average balances of all deposit accounts. Thus past deposit relationships are immediately available, even on nonborrowing accounts. It is the usual practice, too, for the Credit Department to record borrowing data on the average-balance card. Also, in many banks each credit officer maintains in his own files the record of the accounts with whose supervision he is charged so that he may have an immediate reference. Most of the Credit Department's work, however, is concerned with borrowing accounts.

The work of the Credit Department may be broken down into the following activities:

Account Correspondence with Customer. This activity is concerned with such information as the day-to-day happenings pertaining to the progress of the company, discussions concerning financial statements, borrowing relationship, and the condition of the deposit account.

Keeping the File Up to Date. Periodically the credit supervisor has a "checking" made with other banks of account and trade suppliers to find out their impression of the account. This process is called revising the file. In addition, agency reports are currently obtained and various periodicals upon issue are scanned for news releases.

Answering Inquiries Regarding the Account. There are two types of inquiries. Other customers of the bank may inquire concerning the account, or noncustomers who are vendors to the subject may inquire.

[1] A form of consumer credit.

Inquiries by the Account. Here again there are two types of inquiries. The customer, himself, may want information regarding other accounts of the bank or he may ask the Credit Department to obtain information from another bank concerning one of his customers.

Statement Analysis. This consists of a careful study of the subject's financial position. Financial statements are sought and obtained. The Credit Department "spreads" them on the bank's statement forms for comparative study and analysis, and points out any significant facts revealed. The simplified forms, to which all are accustomed, enable either Credit Department or loaning officers to make a rapid review of the subject's financial position.

Personal Investigations. Banks, manufacturers, and wholesalers located in the larger business centers avail themselves of the opportunity to call upon each other personally through their credit departments for credit information. The business house which is somewhat isolated does not have the same opportunity. When a credit department finds other vendors, within reasonable proximity, selling to its customers, a personal interchange of credit information often produces valuable information. It has several advantages over any other method of exchange of information. Foremost, among these advantages, is the speed with which the information can be compiled.

Speed, as has previously been emphasized, is an absolute essential in the modern credit department. By a personal investigation only as much time is required to permit one or more investigators to call upon or to telephone the references available, or to "take the name through the market."[1]

A second advantage is the superior type of information obtained. The efficient investigator will learn more, as a general thing, through a personal interview with a creditor than would be obtained by correspondence. This is so because personal acquaintance begets confidence, and also because the creditor will say more than he might be willing to commit to paper or more than he would take the time to write. A third advantage is that the investigator receives up-to-the-minute information. This is of considerable importance in any industry where the credit condition can change almost overnight. Credit men sometimes hesitate to give certain information of a derogatory nature to agencies to be broadcast, but the same information might be freely imparted to an individual creditor to whom the exact condition could be carefully explained.

This method of credit investigation is largely employed by banking

---

[1] This is a common expression in large cities. It means calling upon all, or practically all, of the available sources of supply for credit information. Thus the consensus of opinion of credit men in the industry is obtained. Opinions are thus obtained, not only from references given but from creditors whose names may not be given, and from credit men who may have rejected the account as well.

houses in all centers where there are enough bank or mercantile creditors to make the method feasible.

Qualifications of Investigator. Credit managers seem to have very different views of the qualifications necessary for an investigator. At least, investigators are encountered in credit work with widely divergent qualifications and abilities. In the writer's opinion those who call at credit departments for credit information might well be classified as investigators and messengers. The latter have no real idea of their task or how to go about it. They may have a few set routine questions which are asked but these might as well be asked by mail. Such an investigator elicits no more information than would a written inquiry. In fact, he merely replaces a postage stamp. His superiority over that means of communication lies merely in his ability to bring in a return a little more promptly.

The true investigator is a valuable assistant to the credit department. He is a reporter with some of the instincts of a detective. In addition to natural ability and aptitude for the work of an investigator, he needs training for and training in the work. To elaborate somewhat upon his qualifications, the credit investigator, usually a young man, should have a pleasing personality with some aggressiveness or, let us say, pertinacity coupled with a large amount of tact. His training will have given him a knowledge of the fundamentals of credit department work and a knowledge of the setup of the industry with which he is connected, together with its market. The true investigator will have some ability in the analysis of a financial statement. He will study the market to know where information may be obtained and the quality of that information. The investigator who knows where to go and how to get information receives a ready hearing at credit departments. The one who asks every distributor on every name gets scant consideration and less information. The few who stand out among the hundreds of mediocre investigators will be the outstanding credit men of the future. The investigator who asks unnecessary questions and is tactless may become no less than a pest in credit departments, and is treated accordingly.

The efficient investigator will carefully inform himself of the status of the account in his own office, whether it be a new account or one under revision. The investigator who asks information should be in a position to give some information.[1] Even if the account is new, that

---

[1] Bank investigators will rarely give credit information. This is not because banks are unwilling to cooperate. In most instances the investigator is not sufficiently familiar with an account to reflect accurately the bank's attitude toward it. The investigator, therefore, is instructed tactfully to refer to his bank such requests for information as he may receive.

fact and the size of the order should be known. Rumor mongers and talebearers, however, soon become known as such and, consequently, they are not intrusted by credit departments with the more confidential and, at the same time, more valuable credit information.

While it is not the function of the investigator to make the credit decision, his advice and counsel are often sought. He may thus indirectly influence the credit decision. Through his closer contact with the market he more closely senses the attitude of the market toward the risk. He receives impressions which it may be hard to convey in the cold facts of his report. Altogether, the qualified investigator is a most valuable assistant in a credit department.

Investigation by Telephone. The oral investigation is conducted, to some extent, by telephone as well as by personal interview. Some houses, however, refuse to give any information by telephone, both because the identity of the inquirer cannot be definitely determined, and because the telephone makes an arbitrary demand upon the time of the one furnishing the information. Where the voice of the inquirer is unknown, the first disadvantage is often overcome by the dispenser of information promising to call back in a few minutes with the information. The information is thus sure to reach the house from which the call is purported to come.

The use of the telephone, as a means of exchanging credit information, seems to be increasing. While it should be used with discretion, the telephone is too valuable an instrument to be discarded altogether for this purpose.

Information Secured by Investigators. Ever since credit has been used in business, purchasers have been educated to submit to prospective vendors the names of those who could testify as to the buyers' credit worth. These references usually form the nucleus from which the investigator works. While too much importance should not be placed upon information received from these "hand-picked" references, they are often valuable in supplying other leads to the investigator. More valuable results are usually obtained by taking a name through the market, as explained in a previous paragraph. The methods of conducting the investigation will naturally differ according to the preliminary knowledge of the name under investigation. In most industries there will be found a few large distributors from at least one of whom a reference upon almost any name can be obtained. These large distributors are valuable not only as a starting point but because their credit managers are considered excellent judges of credit and in close touch with the affairs of their customers and conditions in the industry. The credit man making an investigation should be cautioned against placing too much importance upon the paying experience of these large distributors. Weakness may be discovered through the experience of a smaller vendor whose standard of credit may not be so high as that of the larger house. The small vendor often is not in a position to force as prompt payments as the larger distributors do.

The investigator should usually confine himself to questions relating to the ledger experience of the vendor and to the vendor's attitude toward the account. Frequently, the one answering the inquiry will anticipate the questions of the investigator by giving a complete and concise statement covering the case. When this is done, the interview should not be prolonged by nonessential questions, or questions asked just from habit. The types of questions to be asked both of the mercantile house and the bank have been discussed in previous sections and do not need repetition.

The investigator should be sure that he understands the significance of the information given. In the New York market, for example, there are found certain common expressions more or less ambiguous and subject to misinterpretation. A few of them follow:

1. "They pay promptly."

   Payments reported as prompt by one seller might be reported as 2 weeks slow by another.

2. "They discount."

   By another house the same payment might be described as anticipation. Either description might properly be applied to a 10-day payment on terms such as 2/10 net 60. What does the statement mean when the terms are, for example, 6/10/60 extra? Does it mean payment in 70 days or at some previous date?

3. "Our limit is $1,000."

   Do they buy the limit, or only a hundred dollars or so?

4. "They are slow."

   This may mean to one credit man 5 days and to another 60 days.

5. "They anticipate."

   Do they anticipate voluntarily or by request?

6. "We turned it down."

   For what reason?

7. "The account is satisfactory."

   It may be slow and yet satisfactory to some houses. The word "satisfactory" is too indefinite.

8. "It is a small account."

   Does the selling house discourage the buyer or is it small of its own volition?

The above are merely samples of representative statements, and the comments, while not complete, are suggestive of the ambiguities that may exist in credit references.

To sum up, the concern which presents a good credit risk will be found through the trade investigation to pay promptly, to buy in logical markets from logical sources of supply, to trade fairly, and not to confine its sales to too few customers. In addition, it will be conservative or at least not speculative; it will confine its purchases to a reasonable number of vendors, and will devote its interest, energy, and capital to its own business.

Legal Aspects of Credit Information. In the exchange of credit information it must be remembered there are three parties involved: the one who seeks information, the one who gives it, and the subject of the inquiry. The relationship between the investigator, the dispenser of information, and the subject is rather delicate. Each has his rights, legal or moral, and inquirer and dispenser have obligations to each other and to the subject. The credit manager should be aware of the legalities involved and those of his staff charged with investigating and giving credit information should be informed.

The subject has the right to have the truth, or what is believed to be the truth, told about him. Credit information should be given with considerable caution. If the subject is unduly praised as a credit risk and the statements are made as of a matter of fact and not of belief, the inquirer, if he relied upon the information to his injury, may recover damages. On the other hand, statements implying the subject's insolvency, or want of veracity and the like, may be held to be libelous per se, thus giving the subject a right of action.

One who gives credit information need have no fear, provided he takes a little precaution. If he speaks or writes disparagingly, his statement should be made in good faith, that is, not maliciously, and he should have reasonable grounds for his opinion. Suits for libel in the credit field are rare. Should they occur, the defendant has two defenses, either of which will generally avail. One defense is the truth of the statement and the other is that the communication was privileged. In general it may be said a statement is privileged if it is made without malice, in the belief it is true and to one or to those who have a mutual interest in the information. If the publication of derogatory statements is so made that it is available to those who have no interest in it, the statement is not privileged. It is an invasion of the right of privacy.

Credit information might be classified as fact or opinion. One who gives information should be careful to differentiate between the two. Banks, and many other business concerns, usually include in their letters answering inquiries a statement to the effect that information given is an opinion only and that neither the bank nor any of its officers assumes any liability for it, and that it is given in confidence. Such a statement, however, furnishes no protection if the information is known by the one who gives it to be false, or the opinion is given with such reckless disregard of its accuracy as to amount to a fraud.

When credit information is exchanged, it is implicitly understood that it shall be held confidential. The breach of such a confidence is a serious offense in credit circles. Yet such breaches do occur and are a potent reason for the reluctance on the part of some creditors to give their experience and opinion as creditors.[1]

Establishing a Credit Line. Probably the clearest way to illustrate the procedure of establishing a credit line in a commercial bank is to sketch a sample case. Assume that Mr. Bayles, president of Corporation X, wishes to establish an unsecured bank line of credit of $100,000 to finance seasonal peak inventory. Traditionally banks expect a new customer to be introduced by someone to the bank. It may be a mutual acquaintance, one of the bank's representatives who has solicited the account, or the account may approach the bank of its own volition. Banks do not refuse accounts merely because they are not introduced. Let us assume that Mr. Walker, a friend of Mr. Bayles and whose company is a depositor of the bank, arranges for an interview with the vice-president of the bank, Mr. Smith.

Mr. Bayles, familiar with bank requirements, will approach the interview fortified with the proof of his power to act for his corporation. This will consist of a copy, attested by the corporation secretary, of the board of directors' resolution authorizing the borrowing and empowering Mr. Bayles to act. He will also present to Mr. Smith detailed financial statements for the past 3 to 5 years.

The interviewing officer will obtain personal data, and after Mr. Bayles has left, he will probably write a memorandum covering the interview. In his memorandum he details such information as why the corporation needs funds, when the funds will be needed, for how long they will be used, what other banks have the account, and perhaps several trade references.

While Mr. Bayles does not expect an answer immediately, he would like to know shortly what funds will be available. Consequently the credit officer and credit department must work expeditiously so that the loan committee may properly pass on the risk. The bank officer, therefore, prepares a Request for Information sheet and sends it to either the Credit Manager or to the Divisional Supervisor in the Credit De-

---

[1] A Statement of Principles in the exchange of credit information between banks and mercantile creditors has been designed by the National Association of Credit Management and Robert Morris Associates. It is reproduced in Appendix B.

partment. The credit files will first be checked since the prospective customer might have been under solicitation. It will further be necessary to check with other banks of account and, since it is a new account, trade experiences and opinions may be obtained. Agency reports will be ordered, public records checked, and, if a large corporation, investment manuals consulted. The actual work, which may include the "spreading" of the statements, falls to the lot of the Credit Investigating Division. If additional references are uncovered, it is the duty of the Credit Department to get the information from them. If there are few references obtained, the bank may inquire of the general or special agencies for the names of interested subscribers. In the event that there is some doubt about the management, such special agencies as Bishop's[1] may be utilized to obtain individual reports.

The bank's own records are searched for affiliated or related business. This information is then summarized in a History of Account sheet, which may be used as a flyleaf of the credit folder.

When the investigation is finished, the completed stories are first reviewed by the Supervisor of the Investigators and then the folder including the spread statements is returned to the Divisional Supervisor who checks the information carefully and who may summarize the salient points for ready reference by the credit officer.

The credit officer now is in a position to make a decision based on all the facts presented. In some cases, the approval of a loaning committee is also required. This is particularly true in the larger risks. When this is necessary, the credit folder circulates among the members of the loaning committee so that each may study the data and form an opinion of the acceptability of the account. Thus a credit folder is established for a borrowing account. It now falls to the lot of the divisional credit man to keep the file up to date.

When other qualified persons inquire about the account, the divisional credit man most frequently answers the inquiry. It must be remembered, however, that the bank's relationship with its customer is semiconfidential; consequently great care must be exercised in giving information to others. As a matter of fact, a record of inquiries is usually maintained in the credit folder along with the reason for the inquiry. Where the information is imparted by letter, copies of the responses made are also retained.

It is quite clear, from the foregoing description, that banks attempt to make a thorough investigation before accepting the credit. Consequently their collection problem is confined to a very small fraction of the total loans handled.

[1] Bishop's Service, Inc., New York, N.Y., an agency reporting on corporations and individuals which emphasizes the personal factors in its reports.

Credit Limits. Lines of credit are based on facts obtained, analysis of the facts, the use the customer will make of funds, experience with the account, and what other creditors are doing on the particular account. If the bank is the sole appraiser of the credit, probably a straight note line of no more than 50 per cent of the tangible net worth is indicated, provided that all other factors are satisfactory.[1] Where more than one bank is servicing the customer, this 50 per cent is distributed among the participating institutions. Here banks must make sure that the customer is not obtaining permanent capital by rotating his borrowings among banks. The guiding principle is that the banks should not have a greater interest in the business than the owner has.

Banks as Sources of Information. Banks are valuable sources of reliable credit information, particularly in regard to borrowers of the bank. While this statement hardly needs any elaboration, it may be well to point out that banks usually make a very careful and thorough investigation before an unsecured loan is made, and, in addition, if the bank has had the account for any length of time, the facts of the investigation are supplemented by the bank's experience. As the general standard of bank credit is high, it is reasonable to assume that the borrowing customer enjoys a comparatively good credit standing. Unless, then, the bank loan is based upon collateral, or some other form of security, it may be assumed that the bank has a thorough knowledge of its borrowing customers.

In addition to its borrowing accounts, the bank usually has information on two other classes of accounts, namely, its checking accounts and business investigated in the course of its new business activities or as a result of credit investigations arising from a customer's or other bank's inquiries. The bank's knowledge of the checking account may be limited to its observation of deposits, balances, and checks which pass through its hands. On the other hand, the bank may have a credit file, as a result either of an investigation or of information which may have come to it without solicitation. As one of its services to another bank or to a customer, a bank will frequently have occasion to investigate an account with which it may have had no direct contact, the thoroughness of this investigation naturally varying with the circumstances. The conclusion to be drawn is, that while banks, like most sources of information, vary in the quality and the quantity of information that they possess, as a class they are in possession of much credit information. Furthermore, since the statement, oft made, that credit centralizes in the banks is no doubt true, they ought to be a potent force in controlling the volume and standard of credit not only through

[1] If the loan is to be secured, the possible amount of borrowing may actually exceed tangible net worth.

their own loans, but also through the influence of their recommendations to others as well.

Although often possessing the information desired, banks are not always productive of as much valuable credit information as might be expected. This fact is worthy of some discussion. The discussion should be prefaced, however, with the statement that the causes of this condition are only partly the fault of the banks, and that these causes are constantly being corrected. Some credit men have a prejudice against the bank report because they doubt the reliability of the information given. Indeed, they go so far as to say that occasionally a bank will make a favorable report upon a borrowing customer because, if an unfavorable report is given, mercantile credit will be denied to the bank's customer and, without merchandise, funds cannot be raised to repay the bank loan. This thought can be generally denied. Banks have too much integrity to resort to such practices. A much more probable cause for dissatisfaction upon the part of the mercantile credit manager with bank information is due to a lack of understanding between the mercantile inquirer and the bank dispenser of information. The mercantile credit manager complains that the bank does not respond with the frank and detailed information with which the mercantile credit manager greets the inquiries of the bank. This statement is frequently true and the reasons are several. Some of these are cited.

1. Banks feel that merchandise creditors do not require or in some cases deserve as much detailed information as banks possess because, in the bank's opinion:
   a. Merchandise creditors accept a lower standard of credit and have a wider margin of profit.
   b. The danger resulting to the merchandise creditor from a "leak" is less because he may be one of many while the bank may be, in its class, the sole bank of account.
   c. The bank is the largest creditor, hence the risk is greater.
   d. The bank because of its semipublic position must exercise more care and caution in getting complete data, and, as a result, is charged with a greater responsibility in keeping it confidential.

2. Banks have invited—and their standard of credit compels—the borrower to disclose the most confidential information. This confidence the bank does not feel at liberty to violate.

3. Through experience banks have learned that mercantile credit men do not always recognize the confidential nature of information imparted to them by banks. Information thus gained has been repeated by the mercantile credit man to the subject to the detriment of the bank's standing with its customer.

4. The bank may fear its attitude toward its customer will be misinterpreted if exact details are divulged. A conservative policy adopted by its board of directors, or its by-laws, for instance, might require loans to be made by the

bank only upon collateral or endorsement. This fact might also explain lack of detailed information in the bank's possession.

Information from Banks. Information is sought through a bank to obtain either what the bank has learned through its investigation, or the experience of the bank with its customer, or both. It will be clear to the reader that the bank is under a greater obligation to disclose its own experience than it is to pass along information which it is assumed the inquirer could get through some other source. Yet the division between the two types of information is somewhat finely drawn. There should be, however, in the above remarks, a hint to the investigator to confine his inquiry to proper as well as reasonably legitimate questions. The questions which may arise in connection with banking investigations may include the following:

1. How long have you had the account?

This question will reveal not only how well the bank may know the account but it may also indicate the subject's tendency to change his banking connections, usually an unfavorable sign in itself.

2. What is the subject's line of credit and is it granted on an unsecured or secured basis? If accommodation is extended on a secured promissory note, information should be given, at least in a general way, as to amount and frequency of loans extended.

These are fair questions to ask because the aim is to bring out the extent of the subject's indebtedness and also to ascertain how much credit is still available to him at the bank.

3. Are balances commensurate with the line of credit extended?

It is usually expected that an average balance of 20 per cent of the loan will be maintained. If so, balances are considered commensurate. If commensurate or more than commensurate balances are maintained, the bank is usually glad to say so, and this information is ordinarily sufficient for either bank or mercantile credit purposes. Where the bank intimates that balances are at an unsatisfactory level, the question may be properly opened as to the amounts, and if this situation is a recent state of affairs or chronic with the account. Generally speaking, banks are very reluctant to disclose exact figures, especially of their good accounts, and it is not necessary that they do so. On the other hand, both bank and mercantile credit men are often doubly interested in the house which gives evidence of having funds incommensurate with its business needs and this bond tends to facilitate interchange of more specific information than usual. In the latter instance, asking for the average balance is not an impertinent procedure.

4. Does the borrower clean up loans periodically?

Normally, if this answer is in the affirmative, it is an indication of the liquidity of the account and that it is regarded by the bank as a desirable account. Policies of larger banks differ widely and the banking conditions in the large city financial institutions differ noticeably from those of the out-of-town or country banks.

A large commercial bank interested in all the commercial business it can obtain will frequently have highly desirable borrowing accounts against full security consisting of such raw materials as grain, cotton, rubber, etc., which may run continuously considerable periods on a renewal basis. Out-of-town or country banks will generally have a number of good and highly desirable, but slow, borrowing accounts.

Periodic liquidation of borrowing, however, is excellent proof of a liquid position.

5. What is the bank's opinion of the subject and its attitude toward it?

This question may disclose some significant facts not brought out by the previous specific questions.

The questions given above are not intended to serve as a fixed set of questions to be asked in all cases, but are rather intended to show the general type of information which may be sought. The investigator may desire answers to special questions in certain cases, and if the questions are proper, there is no reason why they should not be asked. He may, for instance, wish to verify the "cash in bank" item as submitted by the financial statement. This item on the financial statement will seldom agree exactly with the figures of the bank, because of the outstanding checks. But the bank's figure should always be at least the amount claimed. A serious discrepancy should excite suspicion and call for an investigation.

In analyzing the relations between the bank and its customer, the credit man should consider whether the subject is receiving a bank line of credit commensurate with his business capacity. If the subject does not have adequate banking facilities, the question arises as to his ability to pay promptly. Failing to get bank credit there may be the resort to hypothecation or to finance itself through some other indirect and more expensive means. Another question to be considered may be called the timeliness of the loan. A loan negotiated during the subject's dull season should arouse suspicion. A second feature in regard to timeliness is whether the maturity of the bank loan will conflict with the liquidation of other maturities. Usually, the purpose of a bank loan is to tide over the heavy expenses incident to the peak in seasonal operations. In other words, the bank loan is for the purpose of bridging the gap between the maturities of the payables and the receivables.

Interpretation of Bank Information. In the interpretation of information imparted by a bank it should be remembered that banks are, as a rule, conservative and cautious. The terminology used in bank reports, which may seem to the uninitiated rather vague, arises through the bank's caution lest it be directly quoted. It is sometimes necessary to read between the lines of a bank report to discover what the bank may be trying to convey or, on the contrary, to conceal. The size and location of the bank and the class of customers it serves should be taken into account. The same words uttered by a large city bank and a small country bank might have a vastly different meaning. For instance, "we have a satisfactory account" reported by a small country bank and also by a large city bank might mean in the one case balances of a few hundred dollars, while in the other, it might indicate balances of several thousand dollars.

The Bank as Inquirer. Our previous discussion has been based upon the bank as the dispenser and the mercantile house as the seeker of information. Banks ask for information as often as they are called upon to furnish it. Where one bank is the inquirer, and a second bank the dispenser of information, the type of information sought is along the same general lines already discussed. The investigation may frequently be carried further, for the bank, as already explained, may be willing to impart information of a more confidential nature to another bank than to a mercantile house, especially in the case of a mutual borrowing account where the necessity for self-protection outweighs any tendency to be reticent. The subject's statement and standing may be discussed in detail by the bank, and the investigator may be given the names of both mercantile men and other banks in close touch with the subject, from whom information might be obtained.

When the bank is making a trade investigation, the information which it seeks is often of a different type from any hitherto discussed. The bank is, of course, interested in how the subject takes care of his obligations, but this information, if the subject be a customer, is often available to the bank in the vouchers which pass through its hands. Canceled checks also furnish the names of the subject's creditors. While the investigator will bring in some ledger facts, the heart of his report—if there may be any heart in it—will consist of what he has learned about general conditions in the subject's industry, and how the subject is regarded by those who have constant dealings with him. The good bank investigator, therefore, instead of confining himself to ledger details, seeks to get in touch with the credit manager or some other executive of the house who can tell him just what the attitude of the house is toward the account. The bank and mercantile houses are partner-creditors, and, as such, their interests are bound together. It is most logical that, where their interests are so interrelated, they should aid each other and strive to appreciate each other's attitude.

TEXT AND RESEARCH QUESTIONS

1. What services does the investment banker perform for business?

2. Why are the services of the investment banker not available to the small business?

3. What are the chief sources, other than individuals, of investment funds?

4. What credit instruments are customarily used in investment credit?

5. Banks as a credit function are sometimes said to substitute their "better-known" credit for the businessman's "lesser-known" credit. Explain and illustrate this statement.

6. How does bank credit differ from mercantile credit? Explain and illustrate.

7. What does the businessman expect of his bank with respect to credit, and what does the banker expect of the businessman?

8. What constitutes single-name paper, and what constitutes double-name paper?

9. What are the principal tests of satisfactory collateral for security for a loan?

10. Discuss the function of compensating balances.

11. What is commercial paper?

12. What do you understand a personal investigation to embrace?

13. What are the advantages and limitations of a personal investigation?

14. What is the distinction between an investigator and a messenger?

15. Why is a careful interpretation of information necessary?

16. Since it is generally conceded that banks possess much credit information, why are they not a more satisfactory source of information?

17. State a common attitude assumed by a bank toward a mercantile investigator.

18. Your customer has a highly seasonal business. He is a borrower from his bank. Make up a list of questions and answers to fit this hypothetical case.

19. Of what service can a businessman's own bank be to him in making investigations? What caution should be observed in this connection?

20. List the questions that a bank investigator might ask of a mercantile creditor.

21. Why do banks exchange information more freely with each other than with mercantile creditors?

22. What are a creditor's obligations in giving credit information?

23. Why are telephone investigations frequently unsatisfactory?

24. What is a bank "line of credit"? How is it obtained, and how can it be retained?

25. Why was it necessary to have "guides" for exchanging credit information?

PROBLEM

Assume that the time is January, 1946, shortly after the end of the Second World War. One of your prospective accounts has referred you to its bank.

The credit officer of the bank has made the following statement in regard to the bank's account: "This company was organized in November, 1943. The officers are Thomas B. Pitman, president and treasurer, and Isaac Grossman, vice-president and secretary. Mr. Pitman is the principal at interest. This company is a contractor and manufacturer of machine parts and tools and their main item at present is manufacturing tire-repair equipment for garages. They have a complete machine shop. During the war they did 100 per cent government work. Just recently they purchased a plant in Paterson, N.J., which is equipped, and I understand they are operating almost entirely from there. They have a lease still on the 38th Street location and have their office there yet.

"The account opened with us in March, 1945, and balances have averaged from low to moderate four figures. We have established a line of credit for them of $80,000 on a secured basis against assigned A/Rs, and at present there is $26,000 owing on this basis. We have a margin, of course, but we do not care to discuss this phase. We have not seen a later financial statement than that of Feb. 28, 1945, although we believe we may receive a current one shortly. That statement showed a net worth of about five high figures, including monies due Mr. Pitman. However, they have been doing quite well in the past months, and from conversations we have had with Mr. Pitman we learn the company earned $60,000 more. We have not checked the name in the trade, but according to a Dun report of April, 1945, the company has been extended credit up to $4,300 and payments have been prompt to slow 60 days. The $4,300 high credit was paid promptly, while in several instances bills of $900 or so have been paid slow as much as 60 days. Our experience with the account has been satisfactory. As far as we know, we are the only bank of account."

Analyze the above statement. Consider these questions: Is it a blanket recommendation? Is it a common practice for banks to say whatever they can that is favorable or nice about their customers? What can you read between the lines in this statement?

If you had a $5,000 order, would you be favorably or unfavorably impressed by the above statement? What would your action be? Why?

CHAPTER 11

SALES FINANCE AND FACTORING COMPANIES

Origin. Although they do not function as commercial banks under either the state[1] or national banking laws, both sales finance and factoring companies are specialized lending institutions which do diversified financing, including industrial and consumer financing. A good part of the funds supplied to business, and to individuals, are comparatively short-term loans. Sales finance companies were originally referred to as discount companies, or as commercial credit companies.

In their early history, which lies wholly within this century, sales finance companies financed only producers and manufacturers; today financing includes consumers. In contrast, factors were the early American commission merchants who handled goods on consignment. Subsequently they assumed the role of sales agents and, in addition, took on the responsibility of checking and cashing sales.

Transactions accomplished by either sales finance companies or factors are inevitably of a secured type, which is most frequently receivables.

When the original discount companies began to operate, bank loans were on "own paper," collateral loans, or guaranteed through the endorsement of responsible persons. The automobile industry was just starting, and the banks were reluctant to finance it. While the distribution of automobiles has very largely been financed by finance companies, these institutions have broadened their fields of financing to include the financing of sales and inventories in virtually all the fields of industry. In the last 30 years their growth has been rapid.[2] The remarkable increase in volume of business financed is reflected in the summary amounts of outstanding consumer credit (see Fig. 11, Chapter 13).

Although the sales finance companies pioneered this growth development in the use of industrial and consumer credit, practically all types of

[1] Textile Banking Co., Inc., operates under the supervision of the New York State Banking Department.
[2] In 1929 Roy A. Foulke, vice-president of Dun & Bradstreet, Inc., estimated the total capital of the entire specialized finance industry as less than $1/2 billion.

financing institutions participate in buying consumer instalment paper. Thus, both business companies and individuals appear to sanction this medium of specialized financing as economically justified.[1]

Some confusion is engendered through the fact that many finance companies refer to themselves as factors though their method of operation differs materially from that of factoring companies. These older companies have come to be known as old-line factors, and their method of operation will be described separately from that of finance companies.

Finance Company Operations. That the term "diversified financing" is fully justified is shown by the classification of receivables outstanding of one of the larger finance companies.[2] The classification includes instalment receivables, "personal loan" receivables, wholesale notes and advances, open accounts and notes receivable, factoring receivables, loans on inventories, loans to dealers, distributors, and customers (secured), and temporary advances to customers (unsecured). Of the divisions in the classification we are mainly interested in factoring and financing through open accounts receivable and inventory.

Almost any form of borrowing may be, of course, for the purpose of financing inventory. In the sense in which the term is used here, inventory financing means the use of the inventory itself as security for the lender. The most notable media for securing some measure of protection for the lender in inventory financing are warehouse receipts, trust receipts, and factor's liens. Warehouse receipts and trust receipts have already been described. It is with the discounting of accounts receivable that the credit manager is most concerned and with which the remainder of this section will deal.

Hypothecation of Accounts Receivable. The finance company usually operates by one of two methods. One method is to make a direct assignment or sale of the receivables by the borrower to the finance company, while the second method is to assign the receivables to the finance company as collateral for loans. This distinction of methods is of but little interest to the creditor who is analyzing a risk. In either case, there is an assignment of a more or less valuable asset. In either method, the credit of the assignor may be, and often is, secondary to that of his vendee. Hence, an ample amount of receivables will be required to protect any sum that may be advanced.

Assignment may be either covertly or openly done. Under the latter method, known as the notification plan, the debtor is advised (perhaps upon the original invoice) that his account has been sold or assigned and that he is to make payment to the finance company. Under the covert method, known as the non-notification plan and used in the

---

[1] See Chapter 13, Retail, Consumer, and Instalment Credit.
[2] Several large finance companies control factoring companies.

majority of instances, the debtor knows nothing of the assignment and consequently remits direct to his vendor. To safeguard the finance company under the non-notification plan,[1] a contract is signed by the parties which provides among other things: (1) the finance company's advances and charges; (2) that the assignor is made the company's agent in receiving collections; (3) that the assignor permit the company's auditors to call at their pleasure to inspect his books and records; (4) that the assignor transmit on the day of receipt all original checks, drafts, etc., received on any assigned accounts; (5) that the assignor guarantee payment of assigned accounts; and (6) that the assignor give the company power of attorney to transact any business relating to the assigned receivables, including the endorsement of credit instruments with the assignor's name. To the copy of an invoice to be discounted the borrower attaches the original shipping documents, bill of lading, trucker's receipt, postal slip, or other evidence of delivery. Occasionally, the assignor is required to file an application for fidelity bond, together with his financial statement, with the finance company. Commercial banks are now active participants in this method of financing.

Advances and Charges. Advances made at the time of assignment will usually range between 70 and 90 per cent of the face value of the accounts. The remainder is paid the borrower as the accounts are liquidated. Not all the receivables may be acceptable to the finance company. In that event, the better rated accounts may be hypothecated, while those of inferior rating will remain the property of the borrower

---

[1] In a United States Supreme Court decision (*Corn Exchange National Bank, etc., et al, v. Klander,* 63 Sup. Ct. 679) it was held the assignee under the non-notification plan had not *perfected* his lien. The court said "if there are any means under the applicable State Law by which . . . a hypothetical subsequent assignee can defeat the prior assignee, then the trustee defeats the prior assignee. If the assignment is not so perfected according to the State Law as to be absolutely invulnerable to attack, it takes effect only as of the date on which the bankruptcy petition is filed, the bankrupt's debt which is secured thereby is deemed to be an antecedent obligation and the assignment is a preference within the terms of Section 60-a of the Bankruptcy Act." The court held that the assignment was not so "perfected" since in Pennsylvania at the time when the assignment was made a second assignee who had given notice (by notifying the debtor of the assignment) took priority over the first assignee who had not. This decision made clear that assignments must conform to the applicable state law in order to be valid.

By amendment of Section 60-a of the Bankruptcy Act, Mar. 18, 1950, a transfer wholly or in part for a new and contemporaneous consideration may not be attacked by the trustee (at least to the extent of such consideration) unless required by state law to be perfected by recording, delivery or otherwise, and the transferee failed to so perfect his title within the time prescribed by state law, but in any event, within 21 days of the transfer. A transfer to secure a future loan actually made, or which becomes security for a future loan, is treated the same as a transfer for contemporaneous new consideration.

until eventually liquidated. Even if all receivables may be acceptable to the finance company, it is apparent that the hypothecator can raise on them only about three-fourths of their face value.

While the charges of the various finance companies vary somewhat, they are in the aggregate fairly uniform. A popular charge seems to be $\frac{1}{25}$ of 1 per cent a day, not upon the amount advanced but upon the net face amount of receivables, plus a service charge upon a certain minimum quantity of receivables discounted. The monetary expense amounts roughly to from 10 to 18 per cent.

The agreements between the two parties almost invariably require the borrower to guarantee the collection of the accounts which he hypothecates. The usual practice is for the discount company to hold an overdue account for a certain number of days and then require a settlement on it. Since the borrower is rarely in a position to return the cash advanced on the account, the finance company accepts other collateral in the form of fresh accounts receivable, not yet due, and believed to be good.

Advantages to the Borrower. A system which has gained such wide prevalence must present some distinct advantages to those who use it. Its purpose is to provide a method whereby capital tied up in financing customers' purchases can be released for use by the seller. This would seem to be a very distinct advantage unless disadvantages are discovered to outweigh the advantages. Those who advocate hypothecation point out that the discounting of receivables in the form of notes and trade acceptances is not condemned and that therefore the discounting of receivables in the form of book accounts should not be disapproved.

The claim is also advanced that instead of adversely affecting the liquidity of the borrower, the money advanced is used to pay off merchandise and bank creditors and that through more prompt payment his credit standing should be enhanced.

To the argument sometimes advanced that the borrower would be tempted to overbuy or overtrade, the response is made that it is no more probable than with those concerns which discount notes and trade acceptances or sell for cash.

Another advantage claimed is that this method of financing offsets the cash discount. That is, it enables the borrower to take advantage of discounts offered, thereby saving a financing charge greater than that of the discount companies.[1] Again, since it is merely a method of cashing receivables, it makes no difference to the seller whether the cost is remitted to the customer in the form of a cash discount or it is a financing charge remitted to the discount company. In this connection it is to be

[1] See Chapter 12.

noted, however, that when receivables are cashed by discounting customers no further expense is entailed, whereas the seller still has bad-debt and collection costs to meet from the nondiscounting class.

A final argument is presented that hypothecation of book accounts provides a means of raising additional cash in the event of an emergency.

Disadvantages of Hypothecation. Hypothecation was vigorously opposed in the past by both bank and trade credit men. In its early days, as the lending proved safe and profitable to the lenders, there arose groups of opportunists to prey upon the unfortunate's need for funds. Businessmen and banks came to look upon these as vultures who robbed unsecured creditors of access to the choicest assets, the accounts receivable, just prior to bankruptcy. It has taken years to rectify the ill will thus engendered, and unsecured creditors, though not fully approving, realize this type of financing will have to be taken into consideration in credit investigation and analysis.

Foremost among the numerous reasons advanced for opposition are the following:

1. The cost to the borrower. It is agreed that the business house with good credit does not need to resort to this method of financing, and, it is argued, the financially weak cannot afford it. Financing at 18 per cent, for instance, cannot easily survive the competition of 6 per cent, or less, financing.

2. The lender is secured. This deprives the unsecured creditors from participating in the accounts receivable, one of the most valuable assets, in the event of liquidation.

3. The secrecy of the relationship is condemned. Since the usual method of borrowing is under the non-notification plan, creditors are deprived of their fair right to judge the debtor's financial condition and his managerial activity. Unscrupulous and dishonest debtors may easily deceive their creditors. Secret liens of some kinds are ineffective as against creditors. It is argued that, like the chattel mortgage and the conditional sale, the assignment of accounts should also be recorded in order to secure the assignee.[1]

4. It affords an opportunity for the dangerous practice of overtrading and speculation.

5. It is held to be strong evidence of a weakened financial position. This is a somewhat logical deduction; for this method of financing is not cheap financing. It is often the only available, or last resort, financing.

The two main objections are undoubtedly secrecy and cost. Indeed it may be said that, if the feature of secrecy could be removed, all the other objections would become mere factors in the risk.

---

[1] The following states have recording statutes: Alabama, Arizona, California, Colorado, Florida, Georgia, Idaho, Louisiana, Missouri, North Carolina, Ohio, Oklahoma, South Carolina, Texas, Utah, and Washington.

Assignment of Accounts Receivable to Banks.   Banks, and to a lesser extent commercial houses, have always utilized the assignment of accounts receivable as a means of protection of an existing credit, or, if the assignment and loan were concurrent operations, the arrangement was entered because the bank felt an obligation to support its customer but did not feel warranted in doing so unless its loan was protected by collateral.   Such loans were usually made at bank rates and not at the considerably higher cost described in a previous section.

The increasingly active participation of banks in this method of financing is an interesting development.   Commercial banks have become aware of the profit possibilities in loaning against the pledge of accounts receivable and are competing more actively with finance companies for this business.   Formerly the business house would have obtained funds principally from short-term bank loans.   Now, banks with a plethora of loanable funds are employing some of their funds in this type of financing and finding it profitable.

Banks generally make loans of this nature at legal rates of interest, but frequently with an added flat service charge, which may vary from $\frac{1}{2}$ of 1 per cent to 2 per cent.   The actual cost of financing thus depends upon the service charge and the average length of this type of loan.

Factors.   Factoring is usually associated with the textile industry because it provides a continuous flow of working funds to the manufacturer in the amounts which the highly seasonal character of his business makes necessary.   While concentrated chiefly in the textile industry, factors also extend their services to such varied lines as coal, glass, lumber, paper, petroleum products, etc.   Originally, a factor was one who sold merchandise or other property entrusted to him for that purpose, and, in fact, this continued as one of the functions until about the present century.   The terms "factors" and "commission houses" were often coupled.   Today factors are frequently spoken of as old-line factors, as already stated, to distinguish them from finance companies, which have attempted to usurp the term.

Factors' Functions.   The main functions of the factor follow.

Purchasing Accounts Receivable.   The factor discounts the net amount of the client's receivables, provided such sales have been submitted to and approved by the factor as to the customer's credit before shipment and that invoices and shipping documents are delivered to the factor.

Guaranteeing the Seller against Customer Insolvency.   Thus the factor, through cashing the sale, is responsible for payment by approved customers, but only if there is unconditional acceptance of the merchandise by the customer.   If the factor has discounted a sale and the merchandise is subsequently returned to the client, the factor may, at its option, charge the amount back to the client, and, if requested, the returned merchandise is to be set aside and pledged to the factor for his further protection. The factor usually retains enough margin, varying from 10 to 15 per cent, to protect him against any returns and disputes between the client and his customers.

Billing, Ledgering, and Collecting the Receivables. The client may elect to do his own billing. If so, he tabulates his sales daily on a Sales Assignment Sheet and sends it to the factor together with duplicate invoices and shipping documents. The factor must, of course, ledger these accounts and follow them up for collection.

Financing Clients' Operations. This the factor does through the purchasing and discounting of receivables and by making loans on the security of the client's inventory.

This statement of the main functions of the factor gives only a slight idea of the size and complexity of his operations.

Factors' Capital Funds. The capital funds of factors seem small as compared with the finance companies. But the latter, it must be remembered, include the automobile industry in their financing, and many, too, include some old-line factoring in their operations. Eighteen of the old-line factors, each with capital funds of more than $1,000,000, have aggregate funds of more than $83,200,000, while the three largest finance companies alone have aggregate capital funds in excess of $738,813,311.[1] Both types of institutions borrow large amounts from the banks and through the investment market.

Factors' Charges. Factors' charges can be treated only in a general way. The interest rate covering the factors' advances is usually fixed at 6 per cent per annum pro and con. The factor may remit to the client any amount due as per Account Sales standing to the client's credit and the client may at any time pay any balance owing in whole or in part. The factor has the contractual right to hold a sufficient number of assigned invoices, against which he does not advance, to protect him against returns of merchandise or otherwise. But, with unquestioned accounts, the factor often discounts sales in their entirety as promptly as is possible and even permits overdrawals.

In addition to the charge for money advanced, the factor also charges a commission on the net amount of the client's sales. The rate differs according to the desirability of the client from the factor's viewpoint, his type of product, terms of sales, size of average invoice, the kind of trade he sells, and volume of business to be offered to the factor. This charge

---

[1] The three largest finance companies reported capital funds at the close of 1957 as follows: General Motors Acceptance Corporation, $273,831,963; C.I.T. Financial Corp., $249,426,098; and Commercial Credit Corporation, $215,555,250. It is interesting to note that the latter company also reported aggregate bank credit lines in excess of $585,000,000, more than twice its own capital funds.

ranges from slightly under 1 per cent to 2 per cent. In addition, the client may be charged with certain expenses, such as postage for mailing out invoices, etc.

The Factor's Credit Department. The most important department of the factor's organization is the credit department. It has to investigate and appraise the credit of thousands of businesses and many millions of dollars of sales pass under its scrutiny annually. The department must be both large and efficient since the factor operates on a narrow margin of profit and must depend on volume for an adequate income. Factors exchange credit information freely among themselves and with banks. Taken as a class, factors' credit departments rank almost on a par in efficiency and thoroughness with those of commercial banks.

Advantages and Disadvantages of Factors. Two advantages to the client are obvious. He has additional funds approximately equivalent to the amount that otherwise would be tied up in accounts receivable, or more if he borrows on the security of his inventory. Second, he has no credit and collection costs as such and no bad-debt losses. In other words, he has no uncertainty about these costs. He knows they will amount to no more than 1 to 2 per cent commission which he pays.

There are other advantages to the client. In a sense the client provides his own short-term financing. As he makes sales, he has funds; and if a huge inventory or long processing period necessitates more funds, the factor may furnish as much as two-thirds of the inventory value.

The factored account does not have to seek credit lines and keep them renewed. The source of financing is established and continues as long as the relationship is mutually satisfactory. If a business borrowed from a bank, it would be difficult to time its borrowing so closely to its needs. From the bank the business would borrow an amount all of which it might not immediately need, and as the loan approached its due date the business would have to build up its balance to meet it. Thus the business is paying interest on what is, from its viewpoint, idle money. At all times a client is expected to maintain a compensating balance. On the other hand, the client does customarily maintain with the factor a reserve of 10 or 15 per cent of receivables not discounted.

Larger sales may be made to certain customers because the factor may take a larger risk because of his greater capital and because he may control the account through other clients who sell the same account. Another advantage is that no current liability is incurred unless borrowing on the security of the inventory is also practiced.

The client may save in credit department and accounting expense a sum larger than the commission he pays the factor for these services. The larger funds obtained through the factor mean the client is not so restricted in his operations. He should be able to take the cash discounts on his purchases and he may make more advantageous purchases of raw material or install more efficient machinery.   Having provided for necessary financing, the client can concentrate on production and selling.

The client can go to his factor for advice.   The factor, because of his many contacts, has a much broader survey of the market than does a single client and may be much more sensitive to economic changes.

From the client's viewpoint there may be several disadvantages.   One of those most often voiced by critics is that the factor is too strict on credit.   The client feels the factor has too great a regard for safety and too little for sales.   However, the factoring contract usually permits the client to make a sale, at his own risk, which the factor has disapproved. Such risks are undoubtedly inferior as a class, and the client feels he should not have to assume them while the factor restricts himself to the superior risks.   A second disadvantage may be the cost.   It is undoubtedly true that many businesses can handle their own credits and collections and borrow necessary funds at a lesser cost than through the factoring system.

There is not the same closeness to customers because, making no credit investigation and establishing no contact through collections, the vendor has contact with his customer only through his selling department.

Many feel that to resort to factoring is a reflection on credit and financial standing.   It is true that factoring may be a lifesaver for a weak concern.   On the other hand, many a concern in the soundest credit position continues the factoring relationship.   Factoring is not done in secrecy.   The alert vendor can accurately appraise his risk in selling a factored account.

Legal Aspect of Factoring.   A distinction has been drawn between the methods utilized by the factor and the finance company.   The one *lends,* taking an assignment of accounts as security; the other *buys* accounts outright, with no recourse to the client.   The assigned invoice customarily bears a legend, imprinted either by the factor or his client, substantially as follows:[1]

> For Value Received This Account Is Assigned to,
> Owned by, and Payable Only to
> James Talcott, Inc.
> 225 Fourth Avenue
> New York 3, N.Y.

Thus is notice given to the purchaser.   Should he ignore this notice and remit direct to his vendor, the factoring contract stipulates the vendor

[1] "Law and Contemporary Problems," p. 606, School of Law, Duke University, 1948.

receives the check as the factor's agent and must as such remit the original check to the factor. If there are merchandise loans, the client's creditors and others are warned of the possibility of prior liens in those states having factor's lien laws, either by filing or posting, or both. All states having laws bearing on the subject require either filing or recording the notice of lien in the town or county clerk's office where the borrower, or the merchandise, or the factor, or some combination of them, is located. All, however, do not require posting. Where there are posting requirements, they are generally similar to those of New York. These require the factor to maintain, on the door or other conspicuous place at the main entrance of premises where goods are stored, a sign which gives in legible English the name of the factor and designation as factor.

Most states having factors' lien laws provide that the lien shall extend to all goods; that is, "all goods and merchandise from time to time consigned to or pledged with" the factor. When the goods are sold, the lien does not follow the goods but switches automatically to any proceeds of the sale. Of course, to establish a lien, whatever the law of the state, it must be complied with.

Factors' and Finance Companies' Services Compared. The factor and the finance company are alike in that both render financial aid through inventory and receivables. How they differ may best be shown by summarizing some of the facts already related.

The old-line factor purchases receivables outright without recourse for nonpayment, while the finance company generally acquires a security title in receivables pledged as security for a loan with recourse to the pledger for receivables not paid.

The factor notifies the customer of the assignment and collects in his own name. The finance company generally does not notify. The customer is ignorant of the assignment and thus remits to his vendor, who receives the payment as a trustee for the finance company.

The factor posts a detailed Accounts Receivables Ledger and often prepares and mails customers' invoices. The finance company may ledger the assigned accounts or keep only a summary receivables control account to indicate changes in loan balances. It does not prepare invoices.

The factor's advances are based on receivables and inventory. He may also make loans on own paper and other collateral. The finance company also does not restrict itself solely to receivables and merchandise.

The factor often advises with the client on selling policy and selling agents. The finance company is generally not closely enough associated with the client to render this service.

The factor occasionally provides "house" space and facilities for storage and display of merchandise and a selling office. This is a service which the finance company does not render.

Field Warehousing. Under the part of the factoring agreement relating to loans upon merchandise, it was seen that the lender acquired security by virtue of his title to, and possession of, merchandise obtained by the consignment of the merchandise and a lease of the premises where it was stored. Financing through Field Warehousing follows the same general plan except that commodities are held in the custody of an independent third party. Field Warehousing is the establishment of a warehouse through which warehouse receipts are issued to cover raw materials or finished products held in storage on the owner's premises, but actually and legally under the custodianship of a bona fide public warehouseman. The warehouse receipts furnish acceptable collateral for loans from banks, factors, or finance companies, provided, of course, the inventory itself meets the requirements of satisfactory collateral.[1]

This method of warehousing generally includes the following:

1. The leasing, and the recording of leases, of premises used for storage.
2. Placing of sufficient signs to give proper notice of possession.
3. Placing of locks upon leased premises where commodities are stored, or the employment, day and night, of bonded watchmen in the event of open yard storage.
4. Compliance with all provisions of the Uniform Warehouse Receipts Act and the laws and regulations of the state.
5. Employment of a warehouse manager by the field warehouse company at each branch warehouse location operated, and the bonding of all such warehouse employees.
6. Periodic inspections of the warehouse premises and the commodities stored therein by the warehouse company's own traveling examiners.

Protection through insurance against losses by fire and lightning, burglary, and other hazards is provided by Insured Warehouse Receipts which can be obtained from some of the larger nationally recognized warehouse companies.

When this method of financing is utilized, the borrower's financial statement will, of course, reveal his obligation to the lender, but the statement may not reveal the fact that the lending agency is secured or

---

[1] In many industries the inventories at some time during the year rise to comparatively high peaks. To carry such inventories, financial assistance may be required. Canned goods, clothing, flour, fuel oil, grain, groceries, lumber, meat packing, oil petroleum, and tobacco are representative of the scores of commodities which may be financed through this method. It is utilized largely by manufacturers, jobbers, and distributors. It is obvious that the inventory to be warehoused must be of sufficient size and value to make the method economically advantageous.

the nature of that security. It is not, however, a method of secret financing since the notices placed upon the premises indicate the establishment of a bailment.

TEXT AND RESEARCH QUESTIONS

1. How does a sales finance company differ from a commercial bank?

2. Discuss hypothecation of receivables. How does it differ from discounting receivables?

3. Why is only 80 to 90 per cent of the face value of the receivables advanced?

4. Why is non-notification justified?

5. How does the finance company attempt to protect its risk in non-notification financing?

6. Why should general creditors object to the non-notification method of hypothecation of receivables.

7. What are the pros and cons for financing a business through selling receivables?

8. What media are used to give the lender security in inventory financing?

9. Why do finance companies utilize the chattel mortgage in inventory financing?

10. What are the factor's main functions?

11. When is factoring practicable?

12. Discuss "cashing sales."

13. How are factors and finance companies alike, and how do they differ?

14. Contrast general warehousing with field warehousing.

15. What is the purpose of field warehouses?

PROBLEMS

1. Mr. Hans Jacobsen is a wholesaler and retailer of leather. His principal sales are to manufacturers of shoes and other leather goods. Terms of sale are 2 per cent 10 days, net 30 days, and 2 per cent 10 days, net 60 days. The retail business is relatively unimportant. He owns and occupies a two-story brick building, on which there is a first and second mortgage, in the outskirts of a large Middle Western city, where his business is conducted. He has a $40,000 bank loan, on own paper, due next month. Relations with the bank recently have not been smooth. Mr. Jacobsen would like the bank to increase the loan to $60,000, while the bank has indicated it would prefer to have the loan paid at maturity. At the present time Mr. Jacobsen has, in round numbers, Cash, $7,500, Accounts Receivable, $70,000, and Inventory, $95,000. At times Mr. Jacobsen stocks a considerable quantity of leather, taking advantage of price fluctuations.

How do you suggest that Mr. Jacobsen should finance his business? Give reasons.

2. The Tasterite Frozen Food Company finds that because of the seasonal nature of its business its inventory is as follows:

January.............	$ 800,000
February...........	600,000
March.............	500,000
April..............	500,000
May...............	400,000
June...............	300,000
July...............	1,800,000
August.............	2,000,000
September..........	1,980,000
October............	1,950,000
November..........	1,800,000
December...........	1,200,000

a. Suggest a means of financing this heavy inventory.

b. Explain in detail how the method you choose operates.

CHAPTER 12

TRADE CREDIT

Trade Credit Defined.[1] Since our classification of credit developed according to its uses, the reader will readily assume that trade or mercantile credit arises from a sale of goods by a manufacturer or by a distributor to another manufacturer or a retailer. In accordance with our earlier definition of credit, trade credit is the measure of the ability of the trade house to secure goods (economic goods, including labor) to be used commercially in exchange for a promise to pay at some specific future time.

This ability is measured both as potential credit and credit in use, and together they constitute a line of credit used for the purpose of buying goods. Thus one of the characteristics of trade credit is that the thing exchanged is goods, distinguishing that form of credit from banking credit, which, as we have seen, is an exchange of credit for money, or credit for credit. To draw a clear line of division between the domain of bank credit and trade credit is very difficult, since in both cases the credit is facilitating in type, and should be to a large degree self-liquidating.

Function of Trade Credit. While investment and banking credit aid in the production and distribution of goods, these forms of credit are not limited to goods or merchandise as is trade credit. While investment credit may provide the capital for the plant and equipment, or even the capital which makes trade credit possible, the latter is used solely to promote production and exchange of merchandise.

This is an age of specialization in which goods pass through many hands before they finally reach the consumer. Trade credit assists in virtually all steps of production and distribution. When the article reaches the consumer, it may have passed through the hands of a dozen or more owners, and it is safe to assume that trade credit was utilized by each. But in the hands of these different producers, the operations were not entirely financed by mercantile credit.

Any link in the production chain may be taken for illustration. As-

[1] The terms "trade" and "mercantile" are used interchangeably.

sume that the dress manufacturer buys a quantity of material to be made into dresses. Mercantile credit should assist in the financing only to the extent of the cost of the material. Labor, printing, stationary, advertising, and other costs must be financed either by the capital of the manufacturer, or by other forms of credit, or by both. When, however, the manufacturer passes along the manufactured dress to the retailer, on a credit basis, the credit has increased from the cost of the material to the selling price of the finished article.

A fundamental in regard to trade credit, which it is well to bring out at this time, is that the credit period should not exceed the buyer's interest in the article which is the basis of a credit. In other words, the credit should not outlive the transaction. If a retailer buys an article on 60-day credit terms, and in 20 days sells the article for cash, the need for credit terminated at 20 days, and after that period the manufacturer is aiding in financing not his own merchandise but some other part of the business.

Old and Modern Attitude toward Credit. A study of the history of credit and credit practice would be both interesting and enlightening. The attitude of the community today toward credit has undergone a marked change when compared with the attitude of the community of a few centuries ago. Rigid were the laws and harsh the attitude toward the delinquent debtor of a few centuries ago. The real risk was not upon the lender but upon the borrower. Well might a man hesitate to incur a credit obligation when he considered the penalties which hung over his head if he failed to fulfill it. Imprisonment, enslavement, and even death were among the punishments found in history for failure to pay debts. It is comparatively late in the history of civilization that we find imprisonment for debt done away with. The rigorous and relentless attitude of a few centuries ago toward the delinquent debtor would not be tolerated in this age of industrialism. Honest misfortune is not so punished even by him who suffers from it. It is only when credit is used to defraud that our laws become punitive, and then in no spirit of vengeance nor hope of redress, but as a deterrent to others. Debtor and creditor are today in a sense partners. The credit relationship is entered into in the hope of mutual profit. It is recognized that a man in business has placed his capital at some risk, and the creditor recognizes not only his own risk, but that of the debtor as well. As has been stated, they are in a sense partners since both have risked capital in the same enterprise.

Trends in Trade Credit. It is the period since the Civil War which has wrought the greatest development in our credit system. This development has been merely adaptation of the credit system to environmental change. Since the Civil War, transportation facilities have greatly improved, and such inventions as the telegraph, telephone, and automobile have been brought into full use, while the radio and aviation, although up to the present time greatly developed, hold still more in store for us. Added to these inventions, which are at the disposal of all industries, are the countless industrial inventions and the genius of American management. It was inevitable that the growth of the country and changing conditions should develop credit into an intricate and sensitive system.

Business practices are never static for long periods. The pilgrimages of the retailer to the market gave way in the 'eighties of the last century to the traveling salesman who sold by sample. Growth of transportation and communication facilities has been the cause, in part, of smaller and more frequent orders placed directly with the manufacturer. The part played by the traveling salesman, though still important, has been lessened. Now the larger retailer is again visiting the market in the persons of his buyers. Thus to some extent the traveling salesman has been supplanted by the traveling buyer. Resident buyers also serve as shoppers on a large scale for a clientele scattered throughout the country. Manufacturers, too, have largely taken over the function formerly performed exclusively by the wholesaler or jobber. While it is impossible to predict accurately what the future trends will be, the credit executive knows changes in methods will take place in business which may alter the risk in mercantile credit, raising or lowering it, and which may have an influence on terms, shortening or lengthening them.

Terms of Sale. The credit relationship between buyer and seller is usually established upon a definite basis expressed in the terms of sale. The time and general conditions of payment are specified by the terms of sale, or, more properly but less commonly used, the terms of credit. Although it has been held that the "terms of sale" refers properly to the time limit of the credit period, and has nothing to do with the cash-discount option, nevertheless, we have come to regard the terms as covering all the conditions of payment.

The Credit Period. A very wide divergence is found in the length of the credit period under which goods are sold. In spite of the tendency to shorten terms we find credit terms extending 6 months or 1 year and in some instances for an even longer period, but with the most common terms ranging from 30 to 90 days.[1] Terms are commonly referred to by

---

[1] The reader should remember that there is no such thing as uniformity of terms in many industries, nor, oftentimes, within a single business. It is clearly the function of the seller to fix the terms as well as the price, but either may be changed by agreement between buyer and seller. Alluring terms are thus held out to the buyer as an inducement often to the detriment of the credit relationship between buyer and seller.

credit men as *regular* or *special,* meaning that the terms are those customarily found within the industry, or regularly granted by the concern itself, or, if special, are by agreement between buyer and seller different from the regular terms. Frequently, credit men will describe terms by referring to them as *recommended,* that is, terms recommended by a trade association for adoption by the industry.

When all the different terms of sale are hastily considered, it would seem that they are the result of chance, or were fixed in a haphazard manner as dictated by the sellers' fancy, or necessity. A close study of terms will, on the contrary, disclose that they are fixed by conditions which are current, or which did exist at some time in the past. Among these factors having an influence on terms of credit a few will be mentioned without any attempt to arrange them according to their importance:

The Purpose to Which the Goods Will Be Put. It has already been stated that the upper limit of credit is fixed by the length of time that the owner is interested in the goods or that they remain in one phase of production. This is true of consumptive goods only. Goods which are sometimes distinguished as capital goods, as, for example, machinery, do not come within that generalization for two very good reasons. First, they do not themselves provide the means of payment since they are not sold, but usually are "worn out." Hence the buyer's interest in them extends over a much longer period than could be covered by short-term credit. Second, it is generally considered desirable that the fixed capital should be owned outright by the business, although there may be some exceptions to this statement. The buyer should, therefore, either pay cash or buy upon long terms, involving the use of instalment and investment credit in contrast to trade credit.

The Nature of the Article Has Its Influence upon Terms. If it involves a small amount, the tendency will be toward short terms. The same is true of articles which are perishable. Obviously, the credit should not outlive the article itself. Standardized merchandise usually is sold upon short terms because of the ease in replacing it, and its consequent short marketing period. On the other hand, goods of a seasonal nature will be sold on terms to correspond with the season of use, and will involve the use of "season dating" terms of sale.

The Buyer's Ability to Pay May Be Instrumental in Fixing Terms. It is customary in selling farm machinery to make the date of payment agree with the sale of the farmer's crops. Under this heading comes also what are known as payday terms. Dates of payment are made to correspond with the paydays of the industrial workers of the town.[1]

The Location of Customers May Have Its Effect upon Terms. More distant customers may get longer terms than near customers, so that

[1] STEINER, W. H., "The Mechanism of Commercial Credit."

the additional time in transit is borne by the seller and not by the buyer. It is quite common for some eastern houses to grant an extra 30 days to all customers west of the Rocky Mountains.

Competitive Conditions May Fix Terms. It is sometimes as necessary for the manufacturer to compete in terms as it is for him to compete in price, quality of goods, or service. Competition may force the seller to grant terms that he can ill afford to make.

The Degree of Risk in the Credit of the Buyer Will Be Considered. The greater the risk, the less willing is the seller to take that risk for any length of time. For example, in the textile field, the good credit risk is sold upon "regular" terms, that is, 6 per cent discount at 70 days, with possibly extra dating as a concession by the seller, while the buyer who is an inferior credit risk may be forced to buy on 30 days, or 10 days, or perhaps for cash.

Terms Have a Tendency to Shorten and Lengthen with Changes in the Business Cycle. This can be very briefly explained in this way.[1] The period of prosperity is a period of expansion in which it is profitable to borrow money, and, it would seem, desirable to still further stimulate sales by granting longer terms. Goods are in good demand, therefore, and sales are easily made. In fact, a seller's market may exist. The seller thus is in a position to dictate terms, and furthermore, he may be impelled by necessity to keep down his investment in receivables in order to finance his own expanded operations. Hence, both credit and terms will be conservative as long as buying is stimulated. When buying slackens, the seller is under the necessity of acting to keep up the volume of sales and, consequently, terms of credit may lengthen. During the period of depression the tendency is distinctly toward longer terms, since it now has become a buyer's market, and the need for business forces the seller to terms concessions. The longer terms continue until the cycle has moved well into the recovery stage, when terms again begin to contract.

The reader will not, of course, assume that these changes in the length of terms are general, or that they take place simultaneously in different industries. The student will, however, observe the tendency to shorten or lengthen terms according to the condition of business. The situation is difficult to analyze because of its complexity.

The Practice of Dating. By the term "dating" is meant the placing of an arbitrary date upon the invoice from which date the terms begin to apply. Although there are several kinds of datings, the purpose of all is to defer the due date of the bill. The dating may be expressed in several ways; it may appear as a part of the terms, or it may be expressed by giving the invoice an arbitrary date after the true date. Datings are of several kinds, although, in the last analysis, their purpose

[1] *Ibid.,* Chap. VI.

is either to adjust the time of payment to the marketing period or to meet competitive conditions. W. H. Steiner names four types of datings: (1) season datings, (2) indirect datings, (3) datings on shipments to distant territories, and (4) competitive, or extra, datings. These types will be briefly discussed.

Season Datings. The manufacturer takes upon himself the function of assisting the retailer in financing such goods as may be purchased from the manufacturer. As we have seen, there is some relationship between the credit period and the buyer's selling season. The season dating is recognition on the part of the seller of the buyer's marketing period. Some industries are highly seasonal, as, for example, the straw-hat industry or the doll and toy industries. Clothing adapted to each of the four different seasons falls within the same category.

Season datings apply on season purchases, that is, upon a stock of merchandise that is purchased for a subsequent selling season. The season dating should not be granted when dealers place small orders, evidently for immediate consumption, for this would be contrary to the principle that the marketing period should mark the outside limit of the credit term.

Certain distinct advantages of this method of marketing accrue to the seller. The manufacturer is relieved of the speculative element in the manufacture of his goods. Instead, he manufactures upon orders, thus transferring to the buyer the task of forecasting his market. Since he manufactures upon orders, he is relieved of the uncertainties of the market and can devote all his attention to manufacturing costs and spread his manufacturing over a much longer period. This enables him to keep his plant running during the off season and to avoid congestion in the plant during the busy months. The manufacturer is relieved to some extent of the necessity of providing warehousing space and insurance, and he is relieved of congestion in his shipping department through being able to distribute shipments over a much longer period.

The advantages to the buyer are that he is pretty sure to have his stock on hand when the active selling season begins, and he may make some sales from it long before the date of the invoice. Another advantage often received is a lower price than is quoted just prior to the active selling season. It is quite customary in some industries for the manufacturer to protect the buyer against a decline in price. This is done by a provision in the contract of sale to the effect that in the event of a decline in price the manufacturer will credit the customer with the difference between the contract price and the price at the date of dating. This gives the merchant confidence to buy. In the event of rising prices, the contract price prevails.

It will be noted that the credit risk is somewhat increased because of the longer credit period. Naturally, goods bearing season dating are shipped only to those buyers whose credit meets the required standard of the seller. A disadvantage to the buyer attached to the preseason shipment is the necessity to cover the goods with insurance and to provide storage space. These particular disadvantages are avoided by the buyer in what is really a form of season dating, the indirect dating.

Indirect Datings. This form of dating provides a means of deferring payment by deferring shipment to a certain date. No dating appears on the invoice, and, while some of the benefits of season dating are received by the buyer, the arrangement is classified as "indirect dating." It is the practice among the manufacturers of silk thread, embroidery silk, and other small silk goods to solicit orders during the latter part of July and the month of August, for the fall trade. These orders may bear shipping dates of Sept. 20 or Oct. 1 or according to the volition of the buyer. The order is manufactured, packed, and labeled with the buyer's name and address and awaits only invoicing and releasing on the specified date. The advantages of this method to both buyer and seller are quite apparent.

Dating for Distant Territory. This is, in reality, a form of competitive dating, since it is granted by the distant seller so that he may be on an equal footing with the nearby seller. In a number of different industries, it is the practice of the eastern seller to give the Pacific Coast buyer 30 days extra or to increase the regular net terms. The same result may be obtained by applying the terms to the date of arrival instead of to the date of shipment. This kind of dating is recognition on the part of the seller of the cost, in the form of extra time, of the long-distance shipment.

Competitive Dating. Whenever the dating does not fall within one of the three classifications, already given, it may be regarded as "competitive," or "extra," dating. This form of dating gives the buyer extra time without any apparent reason other than as a concession to the buyer as an inducement to buy. Manufacturers of dress materials, for example, usually sell under terms of 6 per cent, 10 days, 60 days extra dating, commonly expressed 6/10/60. This extra dating is not occasional but is usual and is now regarded as an integral part of the terms, and, hence, such terms are regular. To understand thoroughly the reason for such terms, a history of the industry would be essential. Probably, in most instances, such terms are forced upon the seller both by competitive conditions and by insistence on the part of the buyer that he should receive terms somewhat commensurate with his marketing period.

Nomenclature of Terms.[1] It has already been stated that there is

[1] These definitions conform to those reported in "Credit Manual of Commercial Laws," 1959.

often no such thing as uniformity of terms within an industry, and it may as truly be stated that the same terms are sometimes differently interpreted. There are a number of abbreviations in more or less common use which are fixed in their interpretation. These will be briefly explained in the following paragraphs.

C.B.D. Terms. These letters are an abbreviation of cash before delivery. They cannot properly be referred to as credit terms, since, whenever they are employed, there is an absence of credit altogether. No harsher conditions can be imposed by the seller, unless a distinction is made between cash before delivery and cash with order (C.W.O.) terms. The latter means that the seller not only will not deliver the goods but that he will not even select them for the purchaser until paid for.

C.O.D. Terms. Cash on delivery terms are slightly less harsh than C.B.D. terms. While it is true that the purchaser must pay before he receives the goods, nevertheless some measure of credit is approved indirectly. The seller must have a certain amount of confidence in the buyer to go to the trouble of having the goods manufactured and packed and to take the risk that they will be accepted. If not accepted, carrying charges both ways must be paid by the shipper, the cost of packing and unpacking must be borne, in addition to which there is the danger of damage to the goods while in transit or of depreciation in value. Frequently, the purchaser is required to place a deposit before a C.O.D. shipment is made as a guarantee that the shipment will be accepted. This is particularly true where the goods have to be made to order.

The substitute for the C.O.D. terms when shipment is made by freight is "S.D./B.L." or sight draft with bill of lading attached. This credit instrument has already been explained (see p. 75).

Cash Terms. Cash terms should not be confused with C.B.D. or C.O.D. terms. Under the latter, possession is not surrendered until payment is made. Under "cash" terms, it is. Contradictory as it may seem, cash terms are credit terms. The period of credit, however, is no longer than the buyer may reasonably require to examine the goods before acceptance and payment. Unless fixed by court decision or "custom of the trade," if a case were brought to court it would be incumbent upon the court to fix the limit of credit. By custom cash terms have come to be generally regarded as 10 days. When merchandise is sold on a cash basis it is usually quoted "net"; that is, since there is no option as to time of payment, there is no discount quoted.

E.O.M. and M.O.M. Terms. In reality, both E.O.M. (end of month) and M.O.M. (middle of month) terms grant dating additional to the credit period of the terms proper. Unlike other forms of dating, however, their use is not ostensibly based upon the need or desire for more time. Usually these terms are requested and granted under the guise of an accommodation. A buyer who may have several or many purchases during the month, in order to avoid trouble and expense in making several payments, requests the privilege of grouping all the month's purchases together and regarding the date as end of month. It will be noted that if purchases are evenly distributed throughout the month, the average date of purchase will fall at the middle of the month. The seller is, therefore, granting 15 days dating. This may not seriously inconvenience him, and there is some advantage in handling the payment in one check instead of several.

E.O.M. terms are subject to serious abuse. A buyer, having obtained this concession, next requests that all purchases of the twenty-fifth, or after, bear dating as of the first of the following month, under the plea that the late purchases cannot be audited and included in the month's payment. This concession also being granted, the tendency of the buyer is to postpone purchases, whenever possible, until the twenty-fifth of the month, thus obtaining a maximum of 35 days over the original terms. It is, of course, the seller's privilege to resist these encroachments upon the credit terms, and he should be alert to see that his legitimate profit is not thus invaded.

M.O.M. terms are much less common than E.O.M. terms but are treated in the same way. Usually they are used in conjunction with E.O.M. terms. A seller may be unwilling to postpone the purchases of a month until the end of the month, but he may be willing to permit the buyer to make two payments, the first half month's purchases being dated the fifteenth, and the last half, the end of the month.

Proximo Terms. The word "proximo" indicates that the date of payment falls within the following month. Terms of 2/10 prox. in reality are no different from 2/10 E.O.M. E.O.M. is used as the designation of such terms in the textile industry, while proximo is more generally used in the wholesale grocery line and in the sale of automobile tires.

R.O.G. and A.O.G. Terms. Abbreviations of "receipt of goods" and "arrival of goods" are sometimes used to indicate that the terms date from the arrival of goods at destination instead of from the date of shipment, as is more usual. These terms are, in reality, a form of competitive dating, the shipper thus placing all purchases upon the same basis regardless of their distance from the point of shipment. The privilege of dating the terms from the date of their receipt is often limited to the discount option. If that option is not exercised, the net portion of the terms dates from the date of shipment.

R.O.G. terms present an unsatisfactory aspect to the shipper in that he does not know the date of arrival of the shipment and therefore does not know when the discount option expires. He may, therefore, easily be imposed upon by the none too scrupulous buyer who may find it to his convenience to stretch the discount period a few days. This objection to these terms can be overcome by the seller requiring proof of the delivery, as, for example, the freight receipt, but he is often loath to exact such proof.

Discount Terms. It is the usual practice for the seller to quote two or more options involving the time and amount of payment. One quotation (the terms part) covers a portion, at least, of the buyer's marketing period and thus aids him in financing his business, while the lesser price and the earlier payment option are for the benefit of him who does not need the seller's financing assistance. This latter option, which is commonly called the "cash discount," should not be confused with the trade discount or the quantity discount[1] by the reader. The cash and trade discounts are entirely different in their nature, although some discount terms partake of the characteristics of both and are hard to classify. The basic difference between them is that the cash discount provides an option of lesser price for earlier payment, while the trade discount is not affected by the time of payment. The trade discount has been aptly called "a cumbersome price adjustment."

The trade discount provides a convenient method of concealing from the public the price obtained by the seller, and it provides the means to concerns publishing catalogues of changing quotations by changing the trade discounts without the necessity of publishing a new catalogue. Another instance of the use of the trade discount is to permit a price adjustment to a certain class of buyer, as a differentiation is sometimes made between the jobber and the retailer, without changing the basic quotation. Other trade discounts are encountered which have no obvious justification. These may be regarded as historical or the result of trade custom.

History of the Cash Discount. The reader has already been informed that the promissory note together with the trade acceptance formed the basis of our credit system prior to the Civil War. That great struggle, like all great conflicts between two peoples, had its marked influence upon the commercial developments of the combatants. There followed a period of reconstruction during which banking facilities were inadequate, and specie payment was suspended. The excessive issue of greenbacks, in which the public did not have full confidence, made the value of credit instruments uncertain. With the better transportation facilities afforded by the great expansion of the railway system, it was inevitable that sellers of merchandise should reach out for wider markets. The nation was gradually changing from an agricultural to an industrial people. But the per capita wealth was small, and new merchants had to be financed. It was essential that the seller should greatly assist the

[1] Quantity discounts may violate the Robinson-Patman Act.

bank in financing trade. Hence terms of 4, 6, or more months were common. When the buyer had largely ceased to visit the market and, instead, was called upon by the "runner" or "drummer" of the seller who sold from sample, the personal contact between seller and buyer was lost. It was but natural that the seller should have less confidence in the buyer whom he had never seen and should consequently attempt to sell him on shorter terms.

All of these factors tended to make the switch from the note-and-acceptance method to the open-account and cash-discount system a logical and natural one. The seller had two chief reasons for offering the cash discount. If he could sell for cash, he could avoid bad-debt losses, and he could have the use of the money for the taking of discounts offered him or for the expansion of his own business. It became quite common for the seller who had been accustomed to sell on 4 or 6 months' credit to offer 8 per cent or even larger discounts for payment within 10 days. Today, terms are shorter, and discounts smaller. Merchandise which used to be sold on terms of 6 months or 6 per cent cash is now sold on such terms as 2 per cent cash net 60 days. The contraction of terms and discounts is due to several causes. Banking facilities have increased, thus removing much of the necessity for financing assistance upon the part of the seller. Then, too, business is now carried on at long range under highly competitive conditions, resulting in a narrower margin of profit. The credit risk has improved; buyers can more easily finance themselves or secure bank aid, so that so great a difference between the cash price and the credit price is not a necessity. In other words, the seller does not have to offer so large a discount to attract a cash payment. The tendency of the times seems to point to a slow yet rather certain narrowing margin between the cash and the time price and also to a contraction of the credit term or time limit of payment. What, however, may be the vogue some years hence cannot be foretold.[1]

The Cash Discount Analyzed. Merchandise is commonly quoted at a definite price, which curiously enough, is not the cash price but the price to be paid at some future time or the credit price. A buyer of hardware, for example, receives a quotation of, let us say, $100 for certain hardware with terms of 2 per cent discount if paid within 10 days or due net in 60 days, customarily written as 2/10 net 60. Through these terms the seller makes two distinct offers of the same merchandise, each equally valid:

$98 payment due in 10 days
$100 payment due in 60 days

[1] An exception is to be noted in the development on a large scale of the instalment sale.

The buyer has the option of accepting either offer and the right to delay his decision, for 10 days, as to which offer he will accept. At which price should he be billed? Since the credit price was already in use when the so-called "cash discount" became an integral part of the terms of business, it was but natural to continue its use in billing. It was logical too, because of the uncertainty, to charge the customer with the larger amount and make an adjustment if he chose the alternative quotation. The practice of invoicing and ledger posting the larger amount has helped to fix that in the minds of businessmen as the price and the corresponding terms as the due date. Actually in the above quotation there are two due dates, again each equally valid. Payment at a certain price is due in 10 days; payment at a different, but certain, price is due in 60 days.

The cash discount—in this instance, $2—is regarded by many as the premium allowed by the seller for advance payment of a bill not due. The buyer, if he is financially in a position to exercise the option of earlier payment at a lesser price, is commonly accustomed to regard the discount taken as a financing profit, while if he neglects or is unable to exercise the earlier option, his thought is that he is obliged to forego this additional profit. The discount is regarded as a part of the seller's profit which is transferred to the buyer. Although this is the common viewpoint, it is a delusory one.

The true price of merchandise is often camouflaged by the manner of quotation. In the illustration used above, the hardware is worth not $100 but $98. In other words, the seller is willing to take $98 for his merchandise, but he requires $2 extra to reimburse him for the use of $98 for 50 days and for the credit risk which he is accepting. This difference of 2 per cent is not therefore a premium or a financing profit obtained by the buyer in a position to take it. On the other hand, if the buyer fails to exercise the earlier option, the "discount" of $2 is the price he pays for borrowing $98 from the vendor for 50 days. That is, the buyer is being financed at a cost of 14.89 per cent.[1] Assuming the worth of money to be 6 per cent, the buyer is paying 8.89 per cent above the value of the money for the privilege of being financed by his vendor.

This 8.89 per cent, however, does not represent profit to the seller, since he has costs in connection with the credit customer from which he is freed by the cash customer. Among those who fail to take discounts will be found those who run over the net period of 60 days and from whom it will be difficult and expensive to collect.

---

[1] This is explained as follows: The buyer has the use of $98 for 50 days. Since it costs him $2, he is paying at the rate of 2.04 per cent ($2 ÷ 98). As he uses the money for only 50 days at a cost of 2.04 per cent, if he used it for a full year it would cost 14.89 per cent (2.04 ÷ 50/365).

Bad-debt losses will also occur among this class. The difference of 2 per cent in the quotations, instead of being a premium for advance payment, is, rather, a premium paid by the buyer to the seller to insure him against loss for (1) the use of the money for the time involved, (2) the expenses of carrying the account and making the collection, and (3) the losses by bad debts.

The so-called cash discount marks the division of buyers into two classes, those of superior and those of inferior credit. Those with superior credit either have the funds themselves or can borrow them from the bank in order to pay the cash price. Those of inferior credit cannot borrow from the bank, since the bank is unwilling to take an inferior risk, and must therefore pay the higher price for financing to their merchandise creditors. The buyer who aligns himself with the inferior credit class must not only pay for his own credit risk, but his payment is based upon the average risk of the entire class. The buyer in this class helps to pay the bad-debt losses caused by others as well as the costs of collection for the entire class.

The reader will, of course, understand that this premium is not accurately fixed according to the financing costs mentioned. The premium paid may more than cover the value of the money, the collection costs, and the bad-debt losses, in which case the net terms prove to be more profitable than the cash terms. On the other hand, the premium may be too low to cover such costs. In this case, the cash customers are aiding in financing the credit customers.

Factors Influencing the Cash Discount. From the preceding discussion, it would seem that the discount should be determined by such factors as the length of time required by the buyer, the cost of carrying and collecting the account, and the credit risk representing the danger of bad debts. Other factors must also be considered. It is self-evident that the discount rate must exceed the current rate of interest; otherwise there is no incentive to borrow from the banks in order to pay cash. Furthermore, the maximum size of the cash discount is also limited. If too great, it fails in its function to divide the cash and time customer, since the time customer will strenuously attempt to force the discount rather than be penalized by an exorbitant financing charge. The value of the money to the seller may be a factor. If the seller has not sufficient credit to enable him to borrow from a bank, he may offer a larger discount to attract payment if the size of the profit permits it.

Rate of turnover of merchandise seems at times to influence the rate of discount, the slower moving articles generally calling forth a higher rate of discount. The old policy of "charging what the traffic will bear" may affect the discount. A class of trade may be sold whose risk is small; yet the discount (or financing charge) may be high. As a general rule, the poorer the risk, the greater the discount, or, conversely stated, the poorer the risk, the higher the financing charge. Competition may fix or raise the discount rate. A vendor is in competition with other vendors for the customer's money. Unless the discount rate is equal to that of other vendors, the discount will be ineffective, provided the buyer cannot discount all bills. Again, the seller's margin of profit will affect the discount. The narrower the margin of profit the less the risk which may be taken, and, consequently, the less the need for a high financing charge.

Still another factor is the condition of business. When business is good, there is a tendency both to shorten terms and to lessen the cash discount, while the reverse is true when business is bad. Then the seller is willing to sacrifice both terms and discount in order to stimulate sales.

The Value of Good Credit. As stated above, cash discount divides buyers into two classes: the discounters possessing superior, and the nondiscounters inferior, credit. The discounters are, naturally, heavy borrowers from the banks, while the nondiscounters, having inferior credit, are unable to borrow and must of necessity seek the aid of their merchandise creditors. Thus it is said that the banks measure the credit of the better accounts, while the merchandise creditors measure the credit of the poorer risks.

The cash discount marks a division between customers, eliminating practically the entire credit risk on the better class and enabling the credit man to concentrate on the poorer class.

That good credit has real value to the possessor is apparent when the value of the cash discount is computed. For example, terms of 2/10 net 30 are equivalent to 36 per cent per annum. This computation is made in this way. The bill being due in 30 days may be paid 20 days earlier, or in 10 days, with a saving of 2 per cent. If 2 per cent is the value of 20 days, then 36 per cent is the value of 360 days. A table is given for the convenience of the reader showing the percentage per annum gained by paying the cash price under some of the more common terms.

Per cent	Days	Net	Per cent per annum
1	10	30	18
2	10	30	36
2	10	60	14
3	10	30	54
3	10	60	22
4	10	60	29

If money itself may be said to be worth 6 per cent, the value of credit under terms 2/10 net 30 is 30 per cent. The supposition here is that the buyer will be able to keep a given sum constantly employed, that is, that he will be able to save 2 per cent eighteen times per year. This, in actual practice, would hardly be possible. It should be noted that the buyer cannot save in a year a greater sum than is offered to him in discounts. If, for example, a merchant's purchases are $40,000 per year under terms of 2/10 net 30, the discount is $800. Let us also assume that $8,000 capital is required if discounts are not taken. Furthermore, let us assume that $4,000 more is required to carry the inventory on a cash rather than on a time basis. It is apparent that if the $4,000 must be borrowed at a cost of 6 per cent, or $240, the sum saved is $560, or 7 per cent. Conversely stated, and this is the more important viewpoint, the merchant who fails to take his discounts under these hypothetical conditions pays the additional sum of $560 because of his inferior credit.

Interpretation of Terms of Sale. The reader will find some seemingly peculiar interpretations of terms. It will be well to remember that frequently there is neither uniformity in terms nor uniformity in their interpretation.[1] It is necessary, therefore, to conform to the custom of the industry or to the interpretation of the seller in many instances. For example, the regular terms of the manufacturers of certain textiles are 6 per cent in 10 days, with 60 days dating, commonly written 6/10/60. Such a bill is due 70 days from its date, less a discount of 6 per cent. Thus, a bill for $1,000 dated Oct. 10 would become due Dec. 20 (allowing 30 days for a month as is a general practice). The amount due on that day is $940. No option is given the buyer by the terms, nor do they authorize any penalty. In general practice, however, several options may be allowed. The buyer may be allowed, if he wishes, to convert the terms to 7 per cent discount if paid in 10 days, written as 7/10. By exercising this option he chooses to "anticipate" the full 60 days, and he is permitted to take one discount of 7 per cent instead of taking two discounts—first 6 per cent and then 1 per cent. Logically the latter method should prevail for the bill is due in 70 days in the amount of $940. By paying in 10 days he advances or loans $940 to the seller for 60 days.

Assuming an interest rate of 6 per cent per annum, the "anticipation" would amount to $9.40 for the 60 days ($940 × 0.01 = $9.40) or a total discount of $69.40. Thus, by making one deduction of 7 per cent instead

---

[1] The seller must be careful not to run afoul of the Robinson-Patman Act designed to prevent unfair trade discrimination. Different discounts to customers of the same class, or, allowing some customers to take the cash discount after the discount period had elapsed, particularly if the customer was a habitual offender, would seem to be a violation of the law.

of two deductions, 6 per cent and 1 per cent, the buyer is the gainer in the amount of $0.60. With the exception just described, all payments are based on the amount of $940 and the due date of Dec. 20.

Money is assumed to be worth 6 per cent, or some other agreed upon rate, per annum, and the seller acquires a right to payment on Dec. 20. If the buyer does not pay on that date, he is "borrowing" the creditor's money and should pay for the "loan." If, on the other hand, he pays on Nov. 20 he is "loaning" to the creditor for 30 days and the creditor pays. Thus, a payment on Jan. 20 would amount to $944.70 ($940 plus interest on that amount for 1 month at 6 per cent, $4.70) while a payment made on Nov. 20 would be in the amount of $935.30 ($940 less interest on that amount for 1 month at 6 per cent, $4.70).

To charge interest on delinquent payments and allow interest for anticipation seems the fairest alternative for a deviation from the terms of sale. But slow payments and anticipation are not a right; they are a privilege, which may be granted or withheld at will by the seller. The fact that the seller may be powerless to prevent his customer from borrowing does not alter this statement.

The courts, however, in decisions involving this type of terms, have held the buyer has lost his right to the discount if he does not pay by the date stated. The seller may insist not only upon the payment of the gross amount of the bill but he is legally entitled to interest at the legal rate from the date of maturity to the date of payment. In practice, however, this right is exercised only when friendly relations with the customer have been severed or when the purchaser has become insolvent. The seller deals more rationally with the purchaser whose good will he desires to retain. To revert to the illustration given above, if the seller insisted upon, and could obtain, the full amount of $1,000 on the seventy-first day, the customer would be paying, and the seller collecting, at an annual rate of more than 2,190 (365 × 6) per cent. If the $1,000 payment were made on the thirtieth day after maturity the annual rate of interest would still exceed 72 per cent. Obviously, if the purchaser must pay $60 for the use of $940 he will retain the money as long as possible, and on his next purchase he would seek a vendor who would treat him more fairly.

Handling the Orders. Understanding the terms of sale is essential to the trade credit department's operation; processing the order promptly is equally important. Since almost no two offices handle the details in the same way, to describe the method pursued by any one would accomplish no definite result. In a general way, however, the routine may be given. In most cases there is a necessity for dispatch in getting the credit approved. Consequently, the orders take precedence over any other activities of the department. The first step taken is to determine whether the account is new or one that has been sold before. If the latter, the task is usually much simplified. It is only necessary to refer to the credit department record to see if the account is in good standing, and that the order will not bring the account above the credit limit set. If, however, it proves to be a new account, the office mechanism is quickly set in motion to procure information upon which to judge the credit risk. This will include first of all a search for ratings in whatever credit agency books the concern has subscribed for. In some credit departments, if the rating proves to be a satisfactory one, the investigation may proceed no further. Others, however, will wish to make a thorough investigation. The credit manager, or his assistant, will denote either upon the order, or upon a "rider" attached to the order, the information it is desired to have. This may include credit agency reports, trade reports, bank information, a financial statement, etc.

Procuring this information is delegated to a clerk, as is also the task of following up the order to see that final action is not long delayed. As soon as adequate information is available, the credit manager acts upon it and, if the account is accepted, fixes a credit limit upon it. The salesman or sales department and other interested departments as well are notified of the action taken. The necessary credit department records are made, a folder for the customer in the credit information file is started, and the account becomes one of the many already "on the books" of the concern. This, however, does not terminate the credit department's interest in the particular account. Not until the credit is redeemed by the payment of the customer may the credit department relax its vigil, and regard the credit as proved to be justified.

Before the credit is redeemed, various things may occur which will occupy the credit department's attention. The debtor may move his place of business, which will entail a change of records throughout the seller's organization, or the buyer may suffer a fire or other catastrophe which may jeopardize the credit, or the personnel or organization may be revised. Of those accounts which call for positive action the most common cause is failure to pay at maturity, necessitating some degree of suasion. This will be more fully covered under the chapters on collections.

Analysis of Measure of Risk. The expression "maximum sales and minimum losses," so commonly used, does not quite express the end to be desired by the credit department. This is so, because the expression implies that there is one standard for all businesses, while, as a matter of fact, both the sales and losses will vary owing to such causes as margin of profit, need for volume of business, or the necessity of moving the inventory or a portion of it because of such reasons as obsolescence or rapidly declining prices. The margin of profit will prove a large factor.

If, for example, the net profit of sales is 2 per cent and a bad debt of $1,000 is incurred, sales to the amount of $50,000 will be required to offset that loss, while if the profit were 5 per cent, sales of only $20,000 would balance the same loss. In fixing a credit standard or policy, a concern will naturally take this factor into consideration. In order to determine that credit measurement is in accord with the credit policy, a credit analysis of both sales and bad-debt losses should be made.

Classification of Credit Risks. Such an analysis of sales as suggested above might be based upon agency ratings, or preferably, the credit manager would divide all accepted risks into four or five classes according to his estimate of the probability of failure. The following analysis of a hypothetical case will illustrate.

ANALYSIS OF SALES OF COMPANY FROM STANDPOINT OF CREDIT RISK
(Sales $1,000,000 per annum. Net profit on sales exclusive of bad debts, 2.5 per cent.)

	Class 1	Class 2	Class 3
Sales..................	$150,000	$300,000	$350,000
2.5 per cent profit........	3,750	7,500	8,750
Bad debts...............	None	600	1,167.34
Bad debts, per cent.......	None	0.2	0.33⅓
Net profit..............	3,750	6,900	7,582.66
Per cent net profit........	2.5	2.3	2.16⅔

	Class 4	Class 5		Total
Sales..................	$125,000		$75,000	$1,000,000
2.5 per cent profit........	3,125		1,875	25,000
Bad debts...............	833.34		2,399.32	5,000
Bad debts, per cent.......	0.66⅔		3.2	0.5
Net profit..............	2,291.66	Loss	524.32	20,000
Per cent net profit........	1.83⅓	Loss	0.7	2.0

FIG. 10.   Classification of risks.

The above analysis (Fig. 10), it will be noted, shows a very satisfactory profit for the first four classes while the bad-debt losses of Class 5 exceeded the total profit. Furthermore, this analysis is solely a failure analysis. A similar study of the cost of obtaining the business and handling it through the order, shipping, and accounting departments would, in most cases, disclose greater than average costs among the poorer risks and therefore less than the 2.5 per cent profit assumed above. Certainly, more than average cost would be discovered in the collection department, for it is the poorest risk which must be watched most closely and from which it is most expensive to collect. The conclusion to be drawn, if there are no other factors to be considered, is that in so far as this fifth-class risk can be determined in advance, the sales department should be instructed not to solicit it.

There are, as a matter of fact, other factors involved in considering the cost of selling the less desirable, though not poor, risk. The policy of the house in regard to the distribution of its merchandise may affect the degree of risk that will be acceptable. A house, for instance, is introducing its goods to a certain territory and may be willing to forego profit to that end. Then there is the cost of covering a territory in the selling effort and the absorption of overhead expenses. There may arise other factors in certain cases which must be considered. The study presented above, the reader should understand, is not presented as offering a solution, but rather as presenting one of the factors involved in determining the selling policy.

Credit Limits. One of the most baffling problems to confront the young credit analyst is to determine how much credit may reasonably be accepted. The analyst may feel assured an applicant is worthy of credit, but he realizes at the same time that it would be unwise to approve of unlimited credit. Yet this question is often raised: If a customer's credit is good for $1,000 in merchandise, why is it not good for $2,000? If a bank will lend a businessman $10,000, why will it not lend him $20,000? It has been said that the creditor may prudently lend what the debtor may prudently borrow. While this epigrammatic statement is largely true, it is not entirely so, for it assumes that all creditors of the same debtor should have like limits.

A distinction should be drawn between credit limits that are, in fact, merely warning posts in the approval of credit and limits that represent the credit manager's final judgment. The former are fixed well within what is regarded as the limit of safety. Their purpose is to make the approval of credit within the limit more or less a routine matter, obviating the necessity of a review of the customer's credit each time an order is received. The practice of assigning such a limit to an account is to be commended. It should give the management of the business as well as the credit manager a feeling of confidence that the acceptance of credit is under control. Since limits thus fixed are found ample in practice for the majority of customers, only a few customers will require the credit manager to fix the ultimate amount of expansion of their credit. But these few will tax the credit manager's utmost skill and best judgment.

Factors of Influence in Placing Merchandise Credit Limits. This section will deal with the factors that may require inclusion in the arrival at a limit of credit. The factors involved might be divided into two groups: those pertaining to the debtor and those pertaining to the creditor. No attempt to allocate them, however, will be made, nor will they be evaluated, since factors will assume different proportions of value in different cases.

Size of the Creditor Concern. A risk that might logically be taken by a large concern might be far too great a risk for a small creditor. The capital of the large concern would hardly feel a loss that might be fatal to a small concern.

Principle of Diversification. This factor is quite similar to the one mentioned above. It is a well-established principle that the risk is lessened by having it spread. It is as important to the short-term creditor as it is to the investor. Not to permit too much credit to one debtor is to follow the old adage, not to put too many eggs in one basket.

Hazards of the Debtor's Business. The risk is obviously increased if the debtor is in a business of great risk. There is risk in all business, but when there are added risks due to violent price fluctuations, rapid style changes, fickle demand, and the like, it is apparent that the credit risk is increased.

The Percentage of Profit. The lower the margin of profit on sales, the higher the credit standard. This is a rule with very few variations. One might readily understand that a risk might be taken for $100 profit which would not be taken for $10 profit. Where the profit is small, many more dollars of sales are required to wipe out a loss than where the profit is large.

Terms of Credit. A creditor might have complete confidence in a risk, provided he could be assured the risk would not be increased during the term of the credit. The shorter the time, the less, the creditor feels, will the risk change.

Business Conditions. If business is excellent, the risk is lessened because of the greater gross income of the debtor. On the other hand, curtailed sales may mean that the debtor has insufficient left after paying his expenses to pay his creditors. Obviously, too, the debtor's seasonal cycle must be considered. A risk reasonable enough at the beginning of the debtor's active selling season might be unjustified at its close.

Creditor's Merchandising Policy. Emphasis is placed upon merchandising policy rather than upon credit policy. If the policy of the creditor is to achieve a wide distribution of its goods and a certain volume of sales, the tendency will be to place liberal limits. Then, too, in those numerous cases where merchandising policy changes with business conditions, credit limits will likewise change.

Use of Credit by Borrower. The merchandise creditor knows the general use that will be made of the credit. Its purpose is, of course, to finance the creditor's goods. To banks this is a question of prime importance.

The Need of the Debtor. This factor has a close analogy to the one given in the preceding paragraph. It is a consideration of the amount of credit from the debtor's viewpoint. How much credit the debtor can most profitably use obviously should be considered in every instance.

The Management Factor. This factor can hardly be overemphasized. The importance of management has elsewhere been stressed as a credit factor. The credit manager's faith in the management oftentimes determines not only whether or not credit shall be accepted, but also how much. This factor *may* be considered to the virtual exclusion of all others.

Competition. In fixing credit limits, a credit manager may be swayed by the practices of his concern's competitors. He may find it extremely difficult to keep limits within the bounds of safety according to his own judgment if the customers are granted much larger limits by competitors. A credit manager may be confronted with credit extended by competitors without proper investigation and analysis. He may also be confronted with limits based upon ultimate payment rather than upon debtor's ability to comply with terms of sale.

The Aggregate Credit. The amount of credit a single creditor will be willing to accept will be greatly influenced by the aggregate amount of debt outstanding or the extent to which the debtor uses credit to finance his business. This information is usually obtained through his financial statement, in the analysis of which the credit manager will appraise the debtor's use of the entire creditor capital as well as owner capital. Assuming that all capital is satisfactorily employed, the credit manager may well consider the proportion of creditor capital to owner capital. The greater the owner capital in relation to the creditor capital, the less the risk. It is obvious, therefore, that the less the aggregate credit, the more of that credit a single creditor may be willing to assume. Perhaps no feature of a credit problem is of greater importance or needs more careful scrutiny than a debtor's aggregate credit. A credit manager before he can fix a limit as between his concern and the debtor must fix a limit for the combined creditors. The credit limit of a single creditor may rise and fall as the total credit used by the debtor falls and rises. The student should realize that this section covers merely a phase of this problem. It is intended here merely to stress the aggregate credit as a factor in fixing a single unit of that credit.

Methods in Use in Fixing Limits. Commercial credit managers have adopted many different methods of fixing customers' credit limits that have proved satisfactory, no doubt, for the warning-post type of credit limit. There is, however, no substitute for the good credit manager's expert judgment and experience in determining a customer's ultimate credit. The methods more commonly used will be briefly described. The reader should consider them with a critical mind.

One of the most common practices is for the credit manager to *gauge his credit by the amounts of credit accepted by other creditors.* Some carry this practice so far as to strike an average of the "high credits" of a trade report or of personal trade references. Limits thus placed, it might be argued, are the composite judgment of the creditors. But this assumes that the other creditors, unlike the one who utilizes this method, have used their best judgments in determining their high credits. As a matter of fact, trade reports or trade references do not disclose how much credit creditors might be willing to accept, but rather how much they have accepted.

A practice is sometimes made of *shipping a first order of a nominal amount and gradually increasing* the customer's limit if invoices are satisfactorily paid. It is obvious that by this method a customer's credit might be unnecessarily restricted initially, while, if not curbed, it might eventually reach an unjustified amount.

Many credit managers have worked out a *schedule of limits based on credit-agency ratings.* Many concerns, for various reasons, rely almost solely on credit-agency ratings in the acceptance of credit. In those concerns, consistency requires limits to be carefully graduated according to the ratings. Obviously in such a schedule every limit might be criticized as too high or too low, or the limits in the lower brackets might be too high while those in the upper brackets might be low, or vice versa. Consistency, however, would be maintained in that customers with like ratings would have the same limits. This is essentially one of the methods used by credit insurance companies in fixing credit insurance coverage limits.

Another method that some credit men feel keeps the credit within a safe limit is to *hold it to a certain percentage of the customer's net worth or of his net working capital.* This method assumes that all businesses with a like net worth or a like net working capital are entitled to the same credit. Obviously this method lacks flexibility. Two customers with the same capital would enjoy the same credit, though one used his capital most efficiently while the other did not.

A method that has much to recommend it, though certain important factors are ignored, is *to gauge the customer's credit according to his need of the creditor's merchandise.* This method may include a consideration of the customer's seasonal needs, the turnover period of the merchandise, and the number of vendors supplying the same kind of merchandise. This method approaches the concept that what the debtor may prudently use the creditor may prudently extend, but it obviously does not cover the problem of how the financing of the merchandise is to be divided between purchaser and vendor. The creditor might find himself doing a disproportionate share of the financing resulting in slow and unsatisfactory collections. Two customers might need equal quantities of a seller's goods, and yet if one were threatened with bankruptcy while the other maintained an excellent financial position, like limits would hardly seem justified.

Another practice is to *place no limit as long as the customer discounts his invoices or pays them promptly.* Here, obviously, the customer's orders must not appear unreasonable at first. Later, as confidence is engendered by prompt payments, any amount the customer may order may be checked without question. This practice may be fraught with danger. With no other information to guide him, the credit manager, when it is too late, may discover the credit accepted to be far beyond the realms of prudence.

The foregoing might be classified as rule-of-thumb methods of placing credit limits. While some of them might serve satisfactorily in fixing the warning-post type of limit, there is, as stated before, no substitute for the good credit manager's judgment based on all the pertinent factors in a given case. It is not possible to devise any formula by which limits may be calculated mathematically and on a scientific basis. Such a scheme would lack the flexibility necessary to achieve maximum sales and minimum credit losses.

The use of mechanical formulas, unless they are understood, is fraught with danger. Nevertheless, the student could use the formula of purchaser's sales reduced to cost of sales divided by the number of suppliers and by the number of credit periods. The result would be an approximate amount for a probable credit limit. This presupposes that the business is relatively small, that the financial statement is good, and that business conditions in the future will be similar to those in the past.

At the best, lines of credit are based on assumptions, experiences, estimates, and forecasts, all of which permit only an approximately accurate appraisal, and they are established with the full acknowledgment that some estimates will prove to be poor and will result in losses.

Revision of Credit "Lines." Credit "lines" or "limits" may not remain fixed. That is, the credit manager must not regard them as correct for more than a comparatively short time after the "lines" or "limits" are placed. This is so, because the standing of businessmen is constantly undergoing change, which is the result of the business acumen of the customer, or the lack of it, or because of variations in local conditions or general oscillations of the business cycle. In order, therefore, to keep the credit of customers correctly appraised, it is necessary to supplement the original investigation with new data concerning the credit risk. Some credit departments review the credit information periodically, for example, every 6 months, while others make such revision of the credit lines as may be deemed necessary. With many concerns the receipt of a new rating book is made the occasion for a review of the credit information files and a revision of the credit limits. It is obvious to the student that the efficiency of the credit information files is dependent upon their being kept up to date.

TEXT AND RESEARCH QUESTIONS

1. Summarize briefly four distinguishing characteristics of trade credit.
2. What is the modern attitude toward credit as contrasted with the attitude 50 years ago?
3. List as many reasons as you can why terms in business are not uniform.
4. Would or would not uniform terms be desirable? Why?
5. How may cash discounts be distinguished from trade discounts?
6. In what ways does the cash discount measure a good credit?
7. What are the advantages to seasonal dating? (*a*) To the seller? (*b*) To the buyer?
8. What effect might the prospects of rising prices have upon the buyer and seller customarily using seasonal datings?
9. An invoice for $2,000, dated Sept. 5, bears terms of 1/10 prox. What amount should the debtor pay if he delays payment until Oct. 25? What is the "net" date?
10. Why is speed essential in handling the order?
11. What are credit limits? Discuss fully.
12. Why are credit limits used?
13. What influences the ability of a business to establish credit limits?
14. Evaluate methods used in fixing credit limits. Is there a relationship between method used and credit losses?

PROBLEMS

1. *a.* Assuming that unsatisfactory conditions in the textile field cause a net profit of only 1½ per cent on net sales, reproduce the schedule, Fig. 10, showing the profit or loss derived from each of the five classes.

   b. Under what circumstances, if any, would sales to Class 5 be justified?
2. Hays & Company have annual sales of $1,000,000 on terms of 2/10 net 30. One-half of the sales are discounted. The other half are paid on an average of 70 days from date. If an interest rate of 6 per cent, bad debts of $5,000, and collection expenses of $3,000 are assumed, from which half of the sales does Hays & Company derive the greater profit, and how much?
3. A merchant has five invoices, each for $300 bearing terms of 1/10 net 30, 1/10 E.O.M., net 30, 2/10 net 60, and 6/10/60 extra. The net 30 invoice is due today, and each of the others is dated 1 week ago. He has only $900 to meet these bills. Which should he pay? Why? What factors other than the size of the discount might be involved?
4. *a.* Arthur Hays, a retailer, has a net worth of $10,000. He purchases during the year $50,000 of goods under terms of 2/10 net 30. He

finds it impossible to take his discounts, paying instead on an average of 50 days. By borrowing $5,000, which he is able to do at 6 per cent, all discounts can be taken. What percentage of additional profit on his net worth will be earned by taking the discount?

b. In the above problem what capital would Mr. Hays require to "earn 36 per cent per annum on terms of 2/10 net 30"?

5. Assume a group of 10 invoices, each in the amount of $946.80, and each dated Nov. 1. The various terms of sales are as follows: C.O.D., 2/10 net 30, 2/10 net 60, C.B.D., 6/10/60 extra, cash terms, 1/10 proximo, 2/10 net 30 E.O.M., 8/10 E.O.M., and 3/10 net 60 as of Dec. 31. Draw up a payment schedule listing the invoices, according to their payment dates, to take advantage of all discounts offered. Show the alternative due date, if any, under "Net, date due."

Amount of invoice	Terms	Less discount		Net, date due
		Due date	Amount	

6. Refer to Problem 5. Compute the per annum interest rate of those invoices which allow cash discounts.

CHAPTER 13

RETAIL, CONSUMER, AND INSTALMENT CREDIT

Definitions. In contrast to bank and trade credit, which has the function of oiling the wheels of the productive economy, retail, consumer, and instalment credit have the function of procuring for an individual, or through him for his family, money, goods, and services for use. Consumer credit, personal credit, and retail credit are frequently used synonymously, and all refer to the credit of the individual. Through consumer credit the individual exchanges his credit for money, goods, or services.

Instalment credit, however, may be broader than consumer credit in that it covers both individual and industry term credit and merges into long-term financing (over 5 years). However, instalment credit, as here discussed, includes all forms of partial-payment plans used by individuals in acquiring consumer goods. Thus the figures on instalment credit are reported by type of merchandise or asset acquired as well as by type of holder.

Consumer Credit Institutions. Money is exchanged for consumer credit by various institutions, the principal of which include (1) small loan companies or personal finance companies; (2) commercial banks,[1] through personal loan departments; (3) finance companies; (4) industrial banks; (5) industrial loan companies; and (6) credit unions. Goods are obtained through retail stores or outlets among which must also be included retailers of automobiles, boats, airplanes, and houses. Physicians, dentists, lawyers, laundries, garages, among others, exchange their services for the consumer's credit. A broad knowledge of consumer credit in its different classifications is of importance to all because all at some time use it. Some of the subdivisions of consumer credit will be discussed in subsequent sections of this chapter.

Retail and Trade Credit Contrasted. It is not intended in this chapter to give the reader instruction upon the management of a retail

---

[1] 97 per cent of all commercial banks are engaged in consumer lending. "Consumer Instalment Credit," Board of Governors of the Federal Reserve System, 1957.

credit office. The purpose is rather to survey the retail credit field, and to discover the alliance between the different fields of credit, and the influence retail credit has particularly upon trade credit appraisal.

While basically the purposes of trade and retail credit are alike, namely, to promote trade, this is accomplished by trade credit aiding or promoting production, while retail credit has as its ultimate aim the destruction of utility or the consumption of goods. The safety of trade credit is partially assured by the fact that the goods which pass from seller to buyer will eventually be sold by the buyer and thus assure the receipt of a sufficient sum to redeem the credit. No such sum is provided as a result of a retail credit transaction. The purchaser proceeds to consume the article purchased and he must provide the means to pay for it from some other source.

Another difference is found in the cash discount usually allowed in trade credit. The customer who can pay cash gets the benefit of the cash discount. In retail credit very rarely is any distinction made in the price between the charge and the cash customer. The cash customer receives no preference. Indeed, the rather common impression prevails that consideration is extended to the credit customer which the cash customer does not generally receive.

A difference is also found in the attitude of retail and trade customers toward credit. The latter, as a class, disclose their basis for credit much more freely than do the former. The businessman often regards his business as apart from himself, and if his business happens to be incorporated, the separation is still further removed. He gives information more or less freely. The same man may resent the retail credit manager's attempt to learn something of his personal income and his personal habits and character. Another difference lies in the fact that in retail credit the credit manager is always dealing with the debtor himself or his spouse while the trade credit manager often arranges the credit and secures the collections through an employee of the customer. Thus it will be seen that the retail-credit manager has an extremely delicate task not only in maintaining, but in promoting, the good will of credit customers.

The Trade Credit Manager and Retail Credit. Although the retailer is directly and primarily interested in this type of credit, yet jobbers, functional middlemen, and manufacturers are less directly, though not less fundamentally, concerned with it.[1] The ability of the manufacturer to meet his obligations depends in part upon the promptness with which the jobber and the retailer to whom he sells pay him. The jobber, like-

---

[1] BECKMAN, T. N., and R. BARTELS, "Credits and Collections in Theory and Practice."

wise, is dependent upon the retailer and the retailer, in turn, upon the consumer. Thus it may be seen that the whole credit system is affected by the consumer's ability to pay. While the manufacturer may be more directly concerned with the jobber's and retailer's ability to pay, after all the ultimate purpose of the manufacture of goods is to have them consumed. Businessmen are, therefore, vitally interested in the consumer's well-being and his ability to buy and pay for a large quantity of goods.

The good trade credit manager, therefore, appraises the retailer's community's ability to pay, and also the discretion which the retailer uses in selecting his credit customers. Given a prosperous community and a merchant with good credit judgment, the trade creditor or the bank has a favorable factor toward a satisfactory credit risk. On the other hand, a farming community suffering from a partial crop failure, or too low prices, or an industrial community suffering from the stagnation of its industry, strikes, and the like, adds to the hazard of the credit risk of the retailer.

Another factor which the trade creditor may well give some attention is the competition to which the retailer may be subjected. The retailer may be forced to accept credit in larger amounts and for a longer period than his good business judgment decides is warranted. He must meet competition in this form, and to do so requires a larger capital to carry his accounts receivable. Often it is found upon analysis that this extra capital is furnished by the retailer's merchandise creditors.

It is obvious from the foregoing that our entire business prosperity has as its foundation the prosperity of the individual or the consumer, and that personal credit likewise may be said to be the foundation upon which our entire credit system rests. While it is true that, in theory, retail credit could be abolished without abolishing other forms of credit, to shatter or seriously weaken this foundation of credit would cause the whole credit structure to totter. The growth of instalment credit strengthens this opinion (see Fig. 11).

Is Retail (Consumer) Credit Justified? The early English laws gave some relief to the unfortunate or incompetent businessman who had become insolvent, but no relief whatever was given to the poor debtor who used his credit for his personal, instead of his business, needs. It was felt the use of credit was justified only for the purpose of facilitating trade and this did not extend to the consumer. The old theory of the legitimate use of credit held that its purpose was to finance the production of goods from the sale of which funds would accrue to retire the loan. But production of goods will avail society but little unless with production there goes distribution. Distribution of goods and not the production of them is the modern economic problem. Any type of credit is economically justified whenever it aids distribution; for distribution

(Estimated amounts of short- and intermediate-term credit outstanding, in millions of dollars)

End of year or month	Total	Instalment credit					Noninstalment credit			
		Total	Automobile paper[a]	Other consumer goods paper[a]	Repair and modernization loans[b]	Personal loans	Total	Single-payment loans	Charge accounts	Service credit
1939	$ 7,222	$ 4,503	$ 1,497	$1,620	$ 298	$1,088	$ 2,719	$ 787	$1,414	$ 518
1941	9,172	6,085	2,458	1,929	376	1,322	3,087	845	1,645	597
1945	5,665	2,462	455	816	182	1,009	3,203	746	1,612	845
1950	21,395	14,703	6,074	4,799	1,016	2,814	6,692	1,821	3,291	1,580
1951	22,617	15,294	5,972	4,880	1,085	3,357	7,323	1,934	3,605	1,784
1952	27,401	19,403	7,733	6,174	1,385	4,111	7,998	2,120	4,011	1,867
1953	31,243	23,005	9,835	6,779	1,610	4,781	8,238	2,187	4,124	1,927
1954	32,292	23,568	9,809	6,751	1,616	5,392	8,724	2,408	4,308	2,008
1955	38,670	28,958	13,472	7,634	1,689	6,163	9,712	3,002	4,579	2,131
1956	42,097	31,827	14,459	8,510	1,895	6,963	10,270	3,253	4,735	2,282
1957	44,776	34,105	15,496	8,687	1,984	7,938	10,671	3,502	4,760	2,409
1958	45,065	33,865	14,131	9,007	2,145	8,582	11,200	3,543	5,018	2,639

[a] Represents all consumer instalment credit extended for the purpose of purchasing automobiles and other consumer goods, whether held by retail outlets or financial institutions. Includes credit on purchases by individuals of automobiles or other consumer goods that may be used in part for business.

[b] Represents repair and modernization loans held by financial institutions; holdings of retail outlets are included in other consumer goods paper.

Source: *Federal Reserve Bulletin.*

Fig. 11. Consumer credit outstanding.

193

means the greatest quantity of goods to the greatest number of people. As society achieves better distribution the result is a higher and higher standard of living.

Nevertheless, it is still the opinion of many people that all goods bought for consumption should be paid for in cash. Obviously, there is no economic reason for compelling the man or woman who has an abundance of money to pay cash for each purchase, and it is hardly possible for anyone to set himself up as an authority as to who ought to pay cash and who need not. However, the retail discount houses, through shaving prices and services, do an increasing amount of cash business. The use of one's credit should be left to individual freedom of decision, the merchant deciding not whether the buyer should use his credit, but rather, whether he, the merchant, is justified in accepting it. The individual's decision to buy upon a credit basis is frequently an unwise one; nevertheless, it is one form of personal freedom which we all enjoy.

After all, what is the distinction between buying for one's personal needs and for business needs? The purchasing agent for the household, usually the wife or mother, is conducting a domestic business. Even the individual who buys solely for himself or herself is usually a producer and, as such, as much entitled to operate on a credit basis as is any merchant. Then, too, it may be said that the individual who buys on credit is merely balancing the credit which he must accept. A man, for instance, who receives his pay monthly is accepting his employer's credit. The employee, deprived for the time being of what he has earned, substitutes his credit as buying power. Moreover, the fact that he has accepted his employer's credit supplies the means of redeeming his own credit, just as in trade credit it is expected that the goods which are the basis of credit will supply the means of redeeming the credit.

In the largest sense, retail credit has justified itself. From the viewpoint of both the retailer and the consumer there is a proper and an improper basis for retail credit, and a very careful discrimination between them is required. It is not the use of retail credit, but its abuse by either merchant or customer, which is to be criticized.

Consumer Loan Credit. Mention must be made of that type of consumer credit which takes the form of small personal loans made to individuals many of whom not only cannot offer any security in the form of property but have little or no capital which the lender can rely upon to safeguard the risk. Very few people have a realization of either the extent of such borrowing or its cost to the borrower.

It has been estimated that the small-loan institutions advance more than $4,000,000,000 a year to the American people in cash. Less than one-quarter of the families of the United States have been able, or willing, to lay anything by for emergencies. Among the institutions extending small loans are included small-loan companies, credit unions, industrial banks, remedial loan societies, personal loan departments of commercial banks, savings banks, employer loan services, pawnbrokers, and a group of illegal lenders commonly referred to as "loan sharks." Some of these institutions are to a degree charitable; some are organized not for profit but for mutual help; others render a service commensurate with their charges.

Licensed Lenders. Consumer loans by licensed lenders are made for many purposes, but more than half of all such loans are for consolidation of bills; doctor, hospital and medical expenses; and clothing, food, and rent.[1] An analysis reveals that 25.4 per cent of all loans granted were for the consolidation of bills and another 17.5 per cent were for doctor, hospital, and medical purposes. Clothing, food, and rent accounted for 11.5 per cent. Other purposes of borrowings include travel expenses, business needs, assistance of relatives, home furnishings, repairs, taxes, fuel, automobile expense, mortgages and interest, moving expense, insurance, education, and funeral expenses.

Small-loan laws have been enacted in forty-three states and the District of Columbia.[2]

Most of the laws are applicable to loans up to $500, though a few states name a higher limit. The maximum rates of the various states range from 2½ to 3½ per cent per month on the unpaid balance. Illustrative of the rates are New York with 2½ per cent per month on the first $100, and 2 per cent per month on the next $200, and ½ per cent to $500; and Ohio with 3 per cent to $150, 2 per cent to $300, and ⅔ of 1 per cent to $1,000.

Loan Sharks. The loan sharks having no legal status prey upon the unfortunate who gets into their clutches and often compel him to pay the amount borrowed several times over before being released. These illegal lenders, it is estimated, defraud borrowers every year out of more than $100,000,000. They operate in every state, though they find operation more difficult in the thirty-one states that have effective forms of the Uniform Small Loan law. In the four states that have no protective laws and in the eight states and the District of Columbia where the laws are largely inoperative, they flourish. The interest rates vary. Probably 240 per cent (per annum) is a representative though by no means maximum rate. Rates of more than five times that amount have been

---

[1] The New York State Consumer Finance Association, "A Look at the Consumer Finance Business in New York State," 1950.

[2] Kansas, Montana, North Dakota, and South Carolina have no small-loan laws. In several states the laws are practically inoperative.

uncovered. Their victims must be classified as ignorant, unfortunate, improvident, or dishonest.

Costs of Making Small Loans. It has been noted that maximum interest rates vary from 30 to 42 per cent per annum. These rates may seem exorbitant when compared with interest rates currently paid by many business borrowers. The small-loan rates are high because the costs, per unit of dollar lent are high. Compare what we might term "overhead" costs on loaning $100,000 to one corporation and loaning $100,000 to more than 333 personal borrowers.

In the State of New York the 4-year (1941–1945) average operating expense of representative companies was 14.69 per cent of average outstanding loans exclusive of a loss experience ratio of 2.02 per cent or a total expenses and losses of 16.71 per cent. Interest collected on loans was at the rate of 26.49 per cent. Thus it will be seen that the net return on loans averaged 9.78 per cent of the loans. The return on equity capital after taxes averaged 8.96 per cent. For the years 1943 and 1944 the returns were 6.74 and 6.76 per cent, repectively.[1] These figures seem to justify the interest rate collected, namely, 26.49 per cent.

Bad-debt losses do not seem to cut extravagantly into income. In the year 1929, the personal finance companies of the United States lost in bad debts and uncollected charges 1.96 per cent of the volume of loans made. The percentage rose to 7.80 for the year 1933, a year of severe depression, but had returned to 1.89 per cent for the year 1937. Thus the normal bad-debt loss would appear to be approximately 2 per cent of loans. The cost of investigation to determine Character, however, is heavy, and following up the loans to see that payments are made on their instalment dates accounts for much of the cost. Expense is relatively heavy because small loan companies conduct a strictly retail business.

Credit Unions. A credit union is a cooperative association organized to promote thrift among its members and to create a source of credit for useful purposes. The object is not profit but service to its members. It provides its members with a place to put their savings in very small amounts and also a source of borrowing in time of need.

The successful credit unions are generally composed of at least 100 persons who have a common bond of occupation, residence, or association. Many credit unions are formed within the employees of a company, the membership of a church, or the residents of a small community. Credit unions may be organized under either state or federal law. Federal credit unions are chartered by the Federal Deposit Insurance Corporation. Funds to lend are accumulated through shares taken out

[1] *Special Report of the Superintendent of Banks on Licensed Lenders,* State of New York Banking Department, 1946, p. 14.

by the members. Members are elected by a board of directors and pay a membership fee of 25 cents. Shares are $5 each, and a member must agree to pay at least 25 cents a month toward the purchase of at least one share. Dividends on shares are limited to 6 per cent annually. Dividends voted by the membership may be declared and paid only if all expenses are paid and a required reserve for bad loans is set up.

Service on the borrowing side is confined to members who may borrow for provident or production purposes on a secured or unsecured basis within certain restrictions. The interest charge may not exceed 1 per cent per month on unpaid monthly balances. Funds not loaned are largely invested in government bonds.

Credit unions owe their success to several factors. Among these are a bond of fellowship among its members and their active interest in the credit union. They govern themselves and manage their own loans and investments at very small expense. Often the employer furnishes the office space; and the board of directors and the membership, the credit, and the auditing committees serve without pay. Some of the larger credit unions employ a paid manager and the necessary clerical force but expense is held to a minimum.

At the end of 1957 there were 18,433[1] credit unions operating in the United States. The reported membership was 10,081,113 persons, and assets of the credit unions totaled $4,093,710,089. Membership grew threefold during the last 10 years and paced the growth in consumer credit.

Personal Loan Departments of Commercial Banks. Many of the commercial banks of the country are now engaged in making personal instalment loans. Most of the larger banks have opened separate personal loan departments for that purpose. Many loans are made, to selected risks, without comaker, endorser, or collateral, but the signatures of comakers are a favorite form of protection. For its partial protection on unsecured loans, banks frequently require the borrower to take out a special life insurance policy in favor of the bank and for the amount of the loan. The policy expires after the maturity of the loan. Any form of satisfactory collateral, such as stocks and bonds, savings bank deposit books, life insurance policies, chattel mortgages, etc., will be accepted. Banks offer practically the same service in regard to loans as do the other moneylending institutions, except pawnbrokers, in the consumer credit field. They offer the other lending agencies keen competition.

Industrial Banks. Industrial or Morris Plan banks had their origin in Virginia in 1910. Arthur Morris had a note copyrighted on which the borrower secured the signature of two or more persons as comakers.

[1] "The Credit Union Yearbook," 1958.

An investigational charge was made and that and the discount deducted from the amount of the note. The note was paid off by the monthly purchase of "investment certificates." Maximum loans for personal or small business purposes range in the various states from $1,000 to $5,000. Penalties are levied for late payments and other contract infractions. In the matter of interest rates they are confronted with the competition of commercial banks, finance companies, and other lending agencies. This type of bank has come to operate much like commercial banks.

The Proper Basis for Retail Credit. That there is immense potential credit power in the consumer class will not be denied. But evidences of group eligibility do not mean that careful discrimination is not necessary. Some will be encountered entirely lacking in character. Others buy unwisely. Some are dishonest; others merely extravagant. The retail credit man should satisfy himself that his prospective customer can and will pay. He also wants to know *when* he will pay and if he can be *made* to pay. Character is a fundamental upon which all legitimate business dealings are based. Bad-debt losses would have a strong foe and the credit manager a powerful ally if he could know that a staunch character was behind each account receivable. But the person with character may buy unwisely or carelessly. Hence, the retailer must be careful to see that the customer does not buy beyond his ability to pay.[1] (All financing institutions must observe this precaution.)

The wealth or capital of the customer should not receive too great consideration. Reliance on this factor alone often involves the retailer in expensive methods of collection. The expense of collecting and the time required to make the collection would hardly warrant granting credit to one who is slow and negligent even though wealthy and who, therefore, could be made to pay.

Credit Application. The application for credit is the basis for either the consumer credit folder or a charge account. As most forms are similar, the one used for instalment credit is illustrated.[2] It may be adapted for special circumstances. The acceptance of a credit depends basically on the analysis of the four C's—Character, Capacity, Capital, and Conditions. Character must be satisfactory; capacity is assessed on the type of job, family, and salary; the capital factor is measured against the amount owed to others; and the evaluation of business conditions is predicted on the probability of continued employment. Any good budget schedule will then indicate the limit of debt at any one time. For example, if the applicant's budget permits, per month, 15 per cent for clothing, 10 per cent for household equipment, 12 per cent for

---

[1] NEIFELD, M. R., "Personal Finance Comes of Age," p. 179.
[2] See Appendix K for Credit Application form.

mortgage payments, it is quite simple to compute the limit for the amount of monthly payments.

Sources of Retail Credit Information. The retailer endeavors to determine the applicant's responsibility by his general position or status in life and by the actual experience of stores or other institutions. The applicant's status, as confirmed by his employer, will indicate how desirable he should be as a credit customer, while actual experience of other stores with him will verify or modify the conclusion drawn. Where it is indicated that the line of credit is to be small, the investigation for purely economic reasons may be limited to the experience of other stores or other credit institutions. When a more thorough investigation is to be made, there are usually five important sources of credit information, namely, the applicant whose statements are to be verified, the trade, credit association, or credit agency reports, the bank, and the employer.

In using these sources of information, the retail credit man will verify the statements of the applicant and learn from the trade such facts as how many accounts are carried, the highest credit extended, whether overbuying is indicated by large amounts owing, if bills are paid according to terms, and whether the account is active enough so that trade information can be relied upon. Bank information is usually confined to statements as to whether balances are high, low, or medium; whether the bank has ever extended the customer any accommodation; and the like. Credit agency reports strive to give the antecedents and history including the steadiness of residence, business, employment, etc. The employer will usually confirm the data given by the applicant. Personal references are regarded as of little value unless, as is rarely the case, they may disclose something detrimental. Personal references, however, are sometimes the only source available to the credit man in locating "skips."

It may be said, in conclusion, that there is a proper basis for retail credit from the creditor's standpoint when the investigation has disclosed a satisfactory record, when the buyer's financial integrity and resources seem to conform to his mode of living, and when his history or record has disclosed his intentions and habits of meeting his obligations.

The sources of information enumerated in this section, however, are not utilized by all retailers who may sell on a credit basis. The merchant in the small town, for example, frequently does not look for information beyond that obtained from the applicant himself. The "trade" is eliminated because the customer may not have other charge accounts; the local bank either has no information or does not wish to divulge it; credit agencies, the merchant feels, perhaps mistakenly, are too expensive; and trade associations or local chambers of commerce are either lacking or not organized for full cooperation among merchants.

The small-town merchant has these sources of information often-times indirectly available to him in the form of the local credit *reputation* of the customer. The merchant also has the advantage of a personal acquaintance with the customer. He knows where the customer is employed, approximately what he earns, the size of his family, and other information which would aid him in appraising the subject as a credit risk. If the customer is a farmer, the size and productivity of the farm, the farmer's ability as a manager, his industriousness, and his reputation for meeting his obligations are probably known to the local merchant. Personal acquaintance is an excellent substitute for organized service.

The small merchant, whether he may be in the large city or a small village, has a credit service available though he may not use it. Many successful merchants in small towns are staunch supporters of their local Credit Bureaus. The Associated Credit Bureaus of America cover every city, town, village, and crossroads in the United States and Canada; and other agencies mentioned elsewhere also stand ready to offer their services. Individuals, the less as well as the more affluent, are classified as to credit in the files of automobile finance companies, the chain stores such as Sears, Roebuck and Co., Montgomery Ward, the banks, and personal finance companies.

Withal many a small merchant elects to play a lone hand in credit.

It is a well-substantiated fact that nonusers of credit bureaus have much heavier credit losses than users. It is another well-known fact that when a slow payer gets an account with a merchant because the Credit Bureau was not consulted he buys twice as much as the average customer. In other words, when he finds a victim he loads up. Consequently, when a merchant elects to play a lone hand in credit, the cards are stacked against him.

Retail Credit and Competition. Theoretically, to sell strictly for cash is the ideal business. Cash in hand, in exchange for merchandise, is certainly preferable to a charge slip. But through the acceptance of credit, the retailer can increase his sales and presumably his profit. Credit is a means of increasing sales, first, by increasing the number of sales and, second, by increasing the size of the average sale. Cash buyers shop around for the best bargains, while a credit customer becomes identified with a store. The credit customer feels that he is receiving a more personal service than is extended to the cash buyer. A credit clientele is not a shifting clientele as is a cash trade.

Furthermore, the credit customer will buy more. It is easier to surrender one's credit than cash for goods. The prospect of increased volume of sales is very alluring to the retailer. There may be for him fifteen times the net profit in a $60,000 volume, one-third credit that there would be in a $40,000 volume, all cash. In fact, the retailer may have no choice. A large section of the public, demanding credit, would go to other stores, and the all-cash retailer would be destroyed by lack of volume and, consequently, a disproportionate overhead.

Retail credit is one of the services which the retailer can offer to customers. Competition forces the retailer to offer that service. Even the cash-and carry stores of the chain systems are recognizing that fact, and supply Credit Bureau service to the managers of their stores in credit-granting districts. Thus they have replaced with sound credit the managers' gambling on their own unofficial responsibility.

Retail Credit Terms. Competition also has its effect upon terms. Merchants too often compete with each other through liberality of terms. This competitive condition benefits no one and makes efficient credit control more difficult for all. That terms are abused is patent to all who have any knowledge of them. A wide divergence exists between *granted* credit terms and *enforced* credit terms. The stated 30-day terms of innumerable merchants, in practice, average 60- to 100-day terms. Naturally, the retailer would prefer shorter terms, but he is hampered in enforcing them by his own past experience, by local traditions, by competitive credit practice, and by the necessity to hold his trade in competition with other stores.

Another reason for the abuse of terms, as the author sees it, is the failure to make the terms definite and the failure to come to an understanding with the customer with reference to them. The customer too often gets the impression that his agreement, if indeed there is one, such as "to pay early in the month for all purchases of the preceding month" can be disregarded. The very indefiniteness of the pay date and slow collection practices encourage procrastination.

Rarely is the retail credit customer given any monetary incentive to pay promptly. In mercantile credit terms, the buyer is often encouraged to make prompt payment by the offer of a cash discount. But the retailer makes no distinction so far as price is concerned between the cash customer, the prompt-paying customer, and the slow-paying credit customer.

The average individual is honest, and he pays promptly. Furthermore, he knows that, if he does not pay promptly, his credit privilege will be impaired and may well be denied him. The inherent honesty of people plus the system whereby merchants and businessmen report all slow accounts to a bureau, where the record becomes available to all, has resulted in a promptness of payment which is gratifying and a low bad-debt loss that can be termed as astonishing.

Trends in Retail Credit. The trade and bank creditor will find that different retailers present very different problems for analysis.

With the larger concerns there will frequently be found extensive investigations, audits, careful analyses; in fact, everywhere are order and system. With the smaller retailer, the credit risk can be accurately appraised only by getting to know the merchant himself, his habits, his location, and the competition and other obstacles which confront him. Those who run their business in an orderly and systematic way and have an intelligent grasp of its details as to overhead cost, merchandising, etc., present a desirable risk, provided they are not confronted with a competition which they cannot meet.

Methods of distribution are constantly changing. Merchants must be alert to meet the new conditions resulting from change. Within a single lifetime such changes have occurred as house-to-house selling, mail-order sales, the trend toward the larger cities and declines in the populations of country villages. Automobiles and good roads have enabled the consumer to reach the larger centers, passing by the local storekeeper. The parcel post has greatly aided selling by mail, but only the mail-order houses and the larger department stores can use it. The development of the chain store, which first moved into the area of the independent merchant but has now in the form of self-service supermarkets withdrawn to more widely scattered locations, has caused the voluntary or involuntary retirement of many a merchant.

Consumer credit itself has shown a trend toward expansion. Not only has credit selling been embraced by a larger proportion of the retailers, but there has been a widespread trend to permit credit in larger amounts and to include credit in moderate amounts to persons formerly denied its use because of limited income.

These changes, obviously, have affected retailers, hence, their credit. Is the change for the better or for the worse? Many a small retailer has been driven out of business by the competition of the chain store. The small merchant often is unable successfully to cope with the superiority which comes from organization, volume, buying ability, modern merchandising methods, progressiveness, and adequate capital.

In the analysis of retail risks, these conditions should, therefore, be given prime consideration. The retailer who fails to see and meet the new conditions in merchandising is already beaten. Many have seen it and have striven desperately to meet it. Some have succeeded, others have failed. The advantage is not all with the large combination. Many independent stores have joined in buying syndicates and have found other means of meeting competition.

Each individual risk must, of course, be judged separately. But these trends are brought to the reader's attention because the trade and bank creditor have to pay more than usual attention to these questions: What is the retailer's ability? What competition must be met? And what, finally, are his chances of success?

Instalment Credit. The origin of instalment credit is uncertain, but it is believed to have had its inception, in so far as this country is concerned, in New York City about a century ago when a furniture store first made use of this type of credit terms. Its popularity, however, is confined to the period of last few decades. The rapid growth of instalment credit began after the First World War.[1] At that time it broke through the restrictions under which it had hitherto been held and became popular with both buyers and sellers in many lines.

Extent of Instalment Sales. For a long time the instalment sale was largely confined to the impecunious among purchasers, and the public generally regarded merchandise, purchaser, and seller as all belonging to the poorer class. Today it is not regarded as a means of purchase forced upon the improvident as a last resort but as a more desirable means of purchase to be utilized in various instances by all classes of society. Like the regular charge account it is a convenient method of buying even for those who are able to pay outright. It is a type of credit, however, which frequently is quite expensive.

Not only the consumer purchases upon the instalment payment plan. There is a vast amount of instalment credit used in the business field for the purchase of industrial machinery and equipment[2] as well as for goods and services.

The growth and distribution of instalment credit is illustrated in Fig. 12.

Instalment Terms. The tendency in normal times of instalment sales terms of retail stores seems to be a moderate down payment and a length of time to pay conforming in some degree to the life of the article sold. Typical terms range from a down payment of 10 per cent and maximum terms of 36 months for refrigerators to a down payment of 20 per cent and maximum terms of 3 months for children's dresses.

Instalment terms are also found which have no relationship to the article sold. Many stores feature a 6 months' account, under which the customer may buy up to a fixed limit and pay the account in six monthly instalments, repurchasing up to the limit each time a payment is made. Leading men's clothing stores in New York feature the 90-day account, under which one-third of any month's purchases are paid in each of the three following months. For example, a customer purchasing $30 in June and $60 in July pays the $90 in the following instalments: July $10, August $30, September $30, and October $20. Under the so-called "revolving credit plan"[3] a customer may purchase up to a fixed

---

[1] All writers point out that to date the largest single factor in consumer instalment credit is automobile financing.

[2] Such purchases are not included in consumer instalment credit.

[3] In some of these cases, banks finance the retailer, and the purchaser pays the bank.

(Estimated amounts outstanding, in millions of dollars)

End of year or month	Total instalment credit	Financial institutions						Retail outlets					
		Total	Commercial banks	Sales finance companies	Credit unions	Consumer finance companies[a]	Other[a]	Total	Department stores[b]	Furniture stores	Household appliance stores	Automobile dealers[c]	Other
1939	$ 4,503	$ 3,065	$ 1,079	$1,197	132	......	657	$1,438	$ 354	$ 439	$ 183	$123	$ 339
1941	6,085	4,480	1,726	1,797	198	......	759	1,605	320	496	206	188	395
1945	2,462	1,776	745	300	102	......	629	686	131	240	17	28	270
1950	14,703	11,805	5,798	3,711	590	$1,286	420	2,898	746	827	267	287	771
1951	15,294	12,124	5,771	3,654	635	1,555	509	3,170	924	810	243	290	903
1952	19,403	15,581	7,524	4,711	837	1,866	643	3,822	1,107	943	301	389	1,082
1953	23,005	18,963	8,998	5,927	1,124	2,137	777	4,042	1,064	1,004	377	527	1,070
1954	23,568	19,450	8,796	6,144	1,342	2,257	911	4,118	1,242	984	377	463	1,052
1955	28,958	24,450	10,601	8,443	1,678	2,656	1,072	4,508	1,511	1,044	365	487	1,101
1956	31,827	27,084	11,707	9,100	2,014	3,056	1,207	4,743	1,408	1,187	377	502	1,269
1957	34,105	29,375	12,714	9,573	2,472	3,332	1,284	4,730	1,393	1,146	374	529	1,288
1958	33,864	28,943	12,730	8,740	2,664	3,381	1,428	4,922	1,702	1,220	360	425	1,215

[a] Consumer finance companies included with "other" financial institutions until September 1950.
[b] Includes mail-order houses.
[c] Represents automobile paper only; other instalment credit held by automobile dealers is included with "other" retail outlets.
SOURCE: *Federal Reserve Bulletins.*

FIG. 12. Instalment credit, by Holder.

amount which he agrees to repay in four monthly instalments. No down payment is required, and, as fast as payments are made, the customer may repurchase.[1]

Gaining considerable vogue are credit coupon books. These books are sold on an instalment payment plan, the coupons being accepted in the store as cash for purchases. A large New York City department store offers a $25 coupon book for a down payment of the service charge of approximately 6 per cent. The coupon book is paid for in five monthly payments.

The terms cited are illustrative of the many variations under which merchandise can be obtained by the consumer with consumer credit.

Financing Instalment Sales. There is not the difference between the outstanding credit periods of open credit and the instalment plan which is commonly supposed. Many retail stores' accounts will average from 70 to 100 days or even more.

Instalment credit, nevertheless, has high capital requirements. The ability of a retailer who has adopted the instalment plan to finance himself is often a matter of considerable concern to his mercantile creditor. Many merchants have come to grief because they have discovered too late that neither their capital nor their credit could stand the expansion which the plan required.

The strain upon working capital is readily made apparent in contrasting instalment sales and open-account sales. A retail store with annual charge sales of $120,000, whose collection period averaged 60 days, would require an average capital of $20,000, to be invested in accounts receivable. A business of the same annual sales volume, $120,000, with a 10 per cent down payment, and a 12 monthly payment plan for the balance, would find its accounts receivable averaging $58,500, necessitating a greater capital of $38,500 to be furnished by owner or creditors or shared between them.

The practice is very common among instalment sellers of discounting customers' instalment notes with banks and finance companies or placing the notes as collateral for bank loans. But customers' notes are not always attractive to these financial institutions. This may be due to the kind of articles sold, the type of purchaser, or the size and terms of the individual transaction. Small stores, forced into credit sales through the competition of larger stores, have found the problem of financing particularly troublesome. To meet this problem, certain finance com-

---

[1] The three sets of terms set forth in this paragraph are equivalent to open charge accounts paid in 3⅓ months, 2 months, and 2½ months, respectively. Since open charge-account payments in many stores average over 2 months, the instalment terms do not impose so heavy a carrying charge upon the seller as might at first be inferred.

panies have undertaken to guarantee and to discount the retailers' credit sales. This has necessitated placing a credit representative of the finance company in the retail store, sometimes resulting in friction between that representative and the store's sales force. As yet this plan of financing has achieved no widespread popularity or success.[1]

The Instalment Sale Contract. The instalment contract itself commonly takes the form of conditional sale, chattel mortgage, or bailment lease, the choice depending largely upon state laws. The privileges of the seller and buyer are much the same under each type of contract.

Since the contract is written by the seller, it is natural that his protection is stressed. A typical contract permits the seller to use the following remedies at his discretion:

1. If the buyer violates any provision of the contract, the seller may declare all remaining payments due and/or repossess the goods.

2. After repossession, the seller is given the widest control of the resale and the resale price.

3. If the resale fails to satisfy the seller's claim, he can sue the buyer for the residual amount.

4. Only the written provisions bind the seller, the contract specifically excluding all oral agreements.

5. The buyer may sign away homestead rights, privilege of notice of repossession, etc.

What is omitted from a contract may be as significant as what is included. In the event of trouble, the buyer may find that the following items are omitted:

1. Penalties imposed on the buyer for legal fees may not be adequately stated.

2. The right to redeem repossessed goods may not be given.

3. Specific monetary terms and charges are not given in detail.

The buyer may also become aware for the first time of the following:

1. Unconditional promise of payment has been made, regardless of the quality or performance of the merchandise, even when guaranteed. Here the buyer's only remedy, often precluded because of ignorance or expense, is to go to court where this feature of the contract will not be upheld.

2. Violation of the contract is treated identically, regardless of whether it is caused by fraud or otherwise.

3. The contract may be assigned to a disinterested and unscrupulous holder who can enforce all its terms upon the buyer.

The buyer, too, is often woefully ignorant of another feature of the instalment sale. This is the rate of interest the buyer may pay for this type of credit.

[1] A revolving credit account through a bank is another means of achieving this end.

Instalment-payment Interest Rates.   Present low interest rates in practically all financing, keen competition, and government regulation have
effected a considerable reduction in rates of instalment financing.   For
instance, automobiles may now be purchased with a financing charge
at the rate of 6 per cent per annum on the original unpaid balance.   Thus,
if the amount to be amortized by twelve monthly payments is $1,400,
the finance charge, exclusive of fire and theft insurance, may be $84.
But this is not a rate of 6 per cent annum on the monthly amounts
borrowed, nor are the finance companies permitted to thus advertise it.
In this instance, the computation is simple.   The simple interest rate is
6 per cent, and the amount owing over the 12-month period is equivalent
to $1,400 borrowed for 6½ months.   The true rate of interest is then
$$\frac{12}{6\frac{1}{2}} \times 6 \text{ per cent} = 11.076 \text{ per cent.}$$

Another illustration of interest rate computation follows.   A finance
company offers a loan of $100 to be repaid in eight monthly payments
of $14.25 each.   The amount repaid is $14 more than the amount received or 14 per cent.   Since the loan period is only two-thirds of a year,
converted to an annual basis the interest rate becomes 21 per cent on
the amount originally borrowed.   The full amount, however, is borrowed
for only 1 month, and the loan is retired at the rate of one-eighth of the
principal per month.   The average length of time the full loan is outstanding is, therefore, the sum of the series of numbers 1 to 8 divided
by the number 8 or 4½ months.   A loan thus amortized is equivalent
to a loan not amortized but paid in full in 4½ months.   The actual rate
of interest thus becomes the simple rate of interest, 21, times the number of payments, 8, divided by the average length of time the loan is
outstanding, 4½ months.   Simplified, the actual rate $= \dfrac{21 \times 8}{4\frac{1}{2}} = 37\frac{1}{3}$
per cent.[1]

Credit Limits.   Although it is difficult to set precise rules for approving consumer and instalment credit limits, we start with the analysis of
the four C's of credit, and we may further be guided by the three "safety
principles" as stated by Milan V. Ayres, a much-quoted economist.   They
are: (1) down payment should be sufficient to give the purchaser a sense
of ownership; (2) at no time should the unpaid balance be more than the

---

[1] This can be stated as the following formula:

$$AR = \frac{N \times SR}{(N+1) \div 2} \text{ or } \frac{2N \times SR}{N+1}$$

when *AR* is the actual rate of interest, *N* the number of instalment payments, and
SR the rate of simple interest.   This formula is applicable when the instalment
payments are in like amounts, as is usually the case.

resale value of the goods; (3) payment should be complete before sufficient time has elapsed to permit the buyer to feel that his purchase is obsolete. A fourth rule is that the periodic payment should not exceed the budgetary limit prescribed by sound management of the individual's income.

As for the total extent of instalment credit, the limit is indefinite but may expand with capacity. Thus as long as there is growth in the economy, consumer and instalment credit may grow.

Use and Abuse of Instalment Credit. The danger from instalment credit, like any other credit, comes not from its use but from its abuse. Both buyers and sellers have learned through experience their particular problems in the use of the instalment sale. The consumer, on his part, has learned that he must not obligate himself beyond his ability to meet his payments and that he must budget his income according to his necessities, while the creditor has learned that the safety in instalment credit is more dependent upon the credit of the purchaser than it is upon the lien which may be retained upon the article sold.

The principal credit abuse condoned by both the buyer and seller is "overbuying," as based on present and expected income. The tendency seems to be to rely upon the same factors in the approval of instalment credit as in the regular charge account, treating the instalment terms merely as a more convenient method of payment. Less and less reliance is placed upon such conditions as retention of title and right of repossession.

The profit in instalment sales, it must be remembered, is really in the final payment or payments. If the collections are not made according to schedule, are effected at too great a cost, or perhaps are not completed, the effect on profit is readily seen. Repossessions, too, while they may offer protection are both undesirable and expensive, and, if too numerous, they may be disastrous.

TEXT AND RESEARCH QUESTIONS

1. Why should banks, manufacturers, and wholesalers have an interest in the proper use of retail credit?

2. Should or should not credit be used for consumptive purposes? Explain your answer.

3. List as many classes of creditors as you can who commonly accept personal credit in addition to retailers?

4. What are the two principal purposes of consumer borrowing?

5. What is the justification of an annual interest rate of 30 per cent on small personal loans?

6. To what principal factors do credit unions owe their success?

7. Refer to the trade clearance report shown in Fig. 27, page 264. State why you would or would not open an account for Mr. Doe.

8. As credit manager of a city retail store how would you proceed to investigate the credit of a prospective customer?

9. Why is the retailer often compelled to accept credit rather than to sell strictly for cash?

10. What would be the effect, if any, of a higher standard of living for the public upon the extension of retail credit?

11. In what respect does instalment credit differ from the open charge account?

12. What major changes have taken place since the beginning of the century which have affected the distribution of goods?

13. What sources of credit are available to people who desire or are forced by necessity to borrow money?

14. Why must such borrowers usually pay a higher rate of interest?

PROBLEMS

1. List the favorable and the unfavorable factors disclosed in the report on John Q. Public in Appendix F. Would you recommend credit and if so, what limit would you suggest? How did you derive the limit?

2. Mr. R. A. Smith signs a note for $300 and agrees to pay that amount in 10 monthly instalments of $30 each. The lender deducts "interest" at 6 per cent of $300 or $18 and an investigation fee of $3. What is the true annual interest rate, without compounding, paid by the borrower?

3. Mr. Munson buys an automobile which has a cash price of $1,650 and also insurance of $80. He makes a down payment of $630 and wishes to finance the remainder, $1,100. The seller adds a finance charge at the rate of 6 per cent per annum or $99 and Mr. Munson signs a note for $1,199 payable in 18 equal monthly instalments of $66.61. Compute the true interest rate, without compounding, which Mr. Munson pays.

4. A diamond ring is advertised for $190, $10 down and 18 weekly payments of $10 each with "no carrying charge." The same ring may be purchased for $170 cash.

    a. What interest rate, per annum, without compounding, would be paid by the purchaser on credit?

    b. If the cash necessary to buy the ring, $170, could be borrowed for 6 per cent and repaid in 17 weekly payments how much would be saved from the advertised price?

5. You are an interviewer and credit authorizer in a department store in a medium-size city. You have just interviewed Mrs. James A. Smathers, 231 Hyde Street, your city, who wishes to open an account in her husband's name. You have learned that Mr. Smathers for the past 7 months has been working as a carpenter on various outside construction jobs. His earnings have averaged $465 per month. Previous to that he was drawing unemployment compensation. They have four children ranging from 2 to 10 years. Mr. Smathers is 34 years old, his wife is 30. They pay $80 per month rent.

At present he has a savings account with $66 in it. It is now September, and Mrs. Smathers says she wishes to buy some shoes and clothing for the children and herself. She has some money for the purchases but, she thinks, not enough and she would like to complete her purchases on credit. She says her husband is aware of her trip and agrees to the credit purchases. They have no bank account and no charge accounts. You have recognized the address as in the section of the city where the families with the smallest incomes live.

a. Do you recommend that the account be opened? On a charge-account basis? On an instalment basis?

b. If so, what limit would you place on the account? Give your reasons.

CHAPTER 14

THE GENERAL AGENCY—DUN & BRADSTREET, INC.

As indicated in Chapter 9, Sources of Information, there is only one general agency providing credit reports or ratings on all types of industry and trade. The consolidated Dun & Bradstreet, Inc., has operated as the general agency since 1933.

Origin and Growth Sketched. To understand the occasion which made the agency a possibility, it is necessary to review the conditions of industry in the United States which led to and culminated in the panic of 1837. The 18 preceding years may be described as an era of internal improvement. The Erie Canal was opened in 1825, and many others were in operation or in various stages of completion. Railway building was begun in 1828. Immigration was started of a considerable magnitude, and there was a constant movement westward, which resulted in the settlement of large tracts of land in Ohio and further west, bringing about a large increase in agricultural production. Foreign loans on a large scale were negotiated. Most conspicuous of all was the development of transportation facilities, which assumed an exceptional importance in the large area and vast, though widely scattered, resources of the United States. With this unequaled industrial and commercial growth came the usual excesses. There were a multitude of enterprises in advance of the demand, while others were useless and most foolishly undertaken. Speculative operations became excessive. Withal, financial and political influences aggravated the situation. The placing of public deposits with state banks, through the refusal to renew the charter of the United States Bank and its consequent withdrawal from business, increased the opportunities of these local banks for extending credit. The launching of injudicious enterprises was thus fostered. Transportation facilities opened up new possibilities and new values for land. The latter became highly speculative.

Instances are not lacking in which lots in cities and farms were quoted, and even sold, at higher prices than have been realized for them from that day to this.[1]

[1] BURTON, T. E., "Crises and Depressions," p. 282.

Cincinnati was the metropolis of the West, St. Louis merely a small trading post, and Chicago only a thriving village.

This period of expansion and inflation, which culminated in a crisis, was followed by a period of depression and liquidation. Mercantile failures in proportion to the number of firms in business surpassed anything hitherto reported. Not until the summer of 1843 may the end of the depression be said to have been reached. During this period occurred the failure of Arthur Tappan & Co., wholesale and retail distributors of silk. With Arthur Tappan was associated his brother Lewis, who had gained a wide reputation as an excellent judge of the credit risk of the firm's customers. The extent to which his advice in credit matters was sought by other merchants suggested to him the idea of organizing a credit-reporting bureau devoted to collecting and disseminating credit information. He accordingly, on Aug. 1, 1841, opened the first commercial rating agency under the name of The Mercantile Agency, Lewis Tappan & Co., Proprietors.

The Bradstreet Company, likewise, owed its origin to a commercial failure. In 1848, John M. Bradstreet, a lawyer of Cincinnati, Ohio, was made assignee of a large insolvent estate. While engaged in this capacity, he acquired considerable information concerning both the debtors and the creditors of this estate, and he conceived the idea of selling this information to a number of New York concerns. So successful was this venture that, in 1849, he founded Bradstreet's Improved Commercial Agency. In 1876, this institution was incorporated under the name The Bradstreet Company.

While The Bradstreet Company took its name from its founder, John M. Bradstreet, R. G. Dun & Co. was successively known as The Mercantile Agency, Lewis Tappan & Co., Proprietors; Tappan & Douglass; and B. Douglass & Co. before it took its final name. As the reader might surmise, Mr. Douglass first became associated with Mr. Tappan and then succeeded to his interests. He took into partnership with him his brother-in-law, Robert Graham Dun, who bought Mr. Douglass' interest in 1859 and who continued as the active head of the business until his death in 1900.

The latest major change occurred in March, 1933, when R. G. Dun & Co. acquired the interests of The Bradstreet Company and have since operated as a single agency under the name of Dun & Bradstreet, Inc. By this move the competition between the two agencies was removed, some economies of operations were possible, and duplication of information asked of creditors and of businesses being investigated was discontinued. The logical result of the elimination of one of the agencies is better service for subscribers. This agency, however, is still subjected to keen competition. There are a large number of special agencies each of which serves one or more industries and some of which have built up a reputation and prestige which enable them virtually to dominate the use of credit in their particular industry. None of the special agencies, however, enjoys so wide a reputation as this oldest and largest of all credit agencies.

Present Extent of Dun & Bradstreet, Inc. A recent directory of Dun & Bradstreet, Inc., lists 142 branch offices in the United States and 18 in Canada. The Canadian offices are under the ownership of Dun & Bradstreet of Canada, Ltd., while the foreign offices in other countries are conducted by subsidiaries or affiliates of Dun & Bradstreet, Inc. Through this world-wide system, offices are maintained in Argentina, Australia, Belgium, Brazil, Chile, Cuba, France, Germany, Great Britain, Holland, Mexico, New Zealand, Portugal, Puerto Rico, Southern Rhodesia, Spain, Switzerland, the Union of South Africa, Venezuela, and Uruguay. In other countries correspondents are used.

While only 160 offices are listed in the United States and Canada, there are approximately 75,000 cities, towns, and hamlets, all of which are covered by representatives in person or by correspondents. Thousands of correspondents, and representatives throughout the United States and Canada are busily engaged every business day in gathering and disseminating credit information.

Organization of Dun & Bradstreet, Inc. The activities of Dun & Bradstreet, Inc., which are world-wide in scope, are divided into eight principal departments or divisions. These eight departments or divisions are as follows:

Reporting and Service Department
Reference Book Department
Credit Clearing House, a Division of Dun & Bradstreet
International Division
Municipal Service Division
Mercantile Claims Division
Marketing Services Company
Dun & Bradstreet Publications Corporation

Each of the departments or divisions of the business is engaged in some aspect of the gathering, preparation, analysis, or dissemination of information pertaining to business and business enterprises. A description of the specialized activities of these eight divisions of the business is given in later paragraphs.

To expedite the preparation and distribution of the various types of reports issued by Dun & Bradstreet, Inc., the United States has been divided into twelve regions, roughly similar to the twelve Federal Reserve districts. These twelve regions, in turn, have been divided into forty-two reporting districts. Under the supervision of the districts are the suboffices and reporting stations, which are located in the larger business centers of each district. It is through this network of offices that the investigations of several million business enterprises in the United States are made.

The Reporting and Service Department. This department is by far the most important division in relation to its value to business. It is the reporting department that prepares and edits the credit report and assigns the credit rating on the hundreds of thousands of business enterprises in the United States.

Sources of Information. The information included in credit reports on the various types of business enterprises consists generally of data obtained by direct interview with the management of the business under investigation, supplemented by information obtained from banks and trade, including the tremendous files and records of the agency. In every investigation, the management of the business is afforded an opportunity to furnish information that would aid in analyzing the over-all condition of the enterprise and in determining the rating. Federal, state, county, and municipal records and newspapers and other publications such as trade magazines are important sources of information. The information is then studied by highly trained reporters who analyze the data as a basis for the rating. As the work of the reporting department has become specialized, so has the work of the reporter, who now is classified either as an Analytical Reporter, City Reporter, Resident Reporter, or Traveling Reporter.

Reporters. An Analytical Reporter is a thoroughly trained investigator and analyst who prepares and edits analytical reports on the principal manufacturers and wholesalers and on the larger retailers located in the territory covered by the district or suboffice. The work of these reporters is sometimes further specialized in that they generally investigate only those companies engaged in a particular industry such as drugs, chemicals, and food. Consequently, they become specialists in their field, having gained a wide knowledge of the industry, its peculiarities and problems, and conditions affecting the industry.

The City Reporter handles investigations of all other business enterprises located within the city limits. His work usually is centered in a specified area within the city, and thereby he becomes thoroughly familiar with all businesses, business conditions, and sources of information located within the territory that he covers.

The Resident Reporter usually resides and works in the larger outlying communities in each district. The work of the resident reporter is comparable in all respects to that of the city reporter with one general exception. The resident reporter, unlike the analytical reporter and city reporter, does not edit the credit report but mails the information obtained through his investigation to the district or suboffice. This information together with information obtained direct by the office from other sources is then incorporated into a report by specially trained report writers.

The work of the Traveling Reporter, while basically of the same nature as that of the other three classes of reporters, in some respects differs widely. In contrast to the other reporters, the traveling reporter usually does not make investigations in answer to specific inquiries. Instead, once each year he calls at and investigates business enterprises located in his assigned territory, comprised principally of suburban and country towns. Like the resident reporter, the traveling reporter does not edit reports but sends the results of his investigations to the district or suboffice where they are treated in the same manner as information sent in by the resident reporter.

In the larger offices such as New York and Chicago, Dun & Bradstreet, Inc., also employs reporters who are engaged solely in obtaining information from federal, state, county, and municipal records. Included in the information thus obtained are suits and judgments, deeds, mortgages, corporate charters, business names, and all other data that may have an effect on the financial condition and rating of a business enterprise.

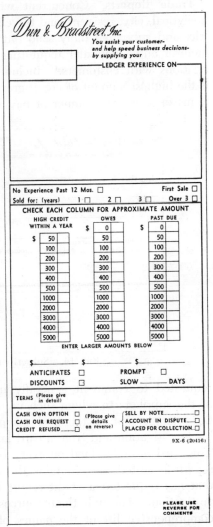

Fig. 13. Request for credit experience.

Correspondents. Dun & Bradstreet, Inc., also maintains representation in nearly every small town or village in the country. This representative is known as a correspondent. The correspondent is the best man available locally and may be an attorney, banker, or businessman. The principal value of the correspondent to the agency lies in his ability to answer inquiries immediately. Although these representatives, in general, are not trained to the high degree of efficiency attained by the reporter, their familiarity with local conditions and local businessmen is an offsetting factor.

Trade Reports. Concurrent with the investigations made by the analytical, city, resident, and traveling reporters and correspondents, district and suboffices daily send out thousands of inquiries to the manufacturer and wholesaler requesting information regarding their business relations with customers.[1] Included among the information requested is the highest amount of credit granted, amount owing, amount past due, terms of sale, and manner of payment. Merchandise suppliers also are

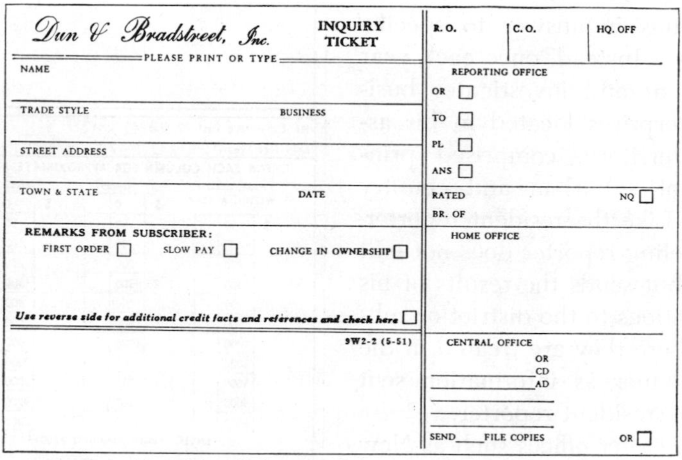

Dun & Bradstreet, Inc.
INQUIRY TICKET
R. O. | C. O. | HQ. OFF
PLEASE PRINT OR TYPE
NAME
REPORTING OFFICE
OR ☐
TRADE STYLE
BUSINESS
TO ☐
STREET ADDRESS
PL ☐
ANS ☐
TOWN & STATE
DATE
RATED
NQ ☐
BR. OF
REMARKS FROM SUBSCRIBER:
FIRST ORDER ☐ SLOW PAY ☐ CHANGE IN OWNERSHIP ☐
HOME OFFICE
Use reverse side for additional credit facts and references and check here ☐
9W2-2 (5-51)
CENTRAL OFFICE
OR
CD
AD
SEND____FILE COPIES
OR ☐

FIG. 14. Subscriber's request for report.

requested to comment generally upon such transactions. The names of the suppliers to whom such inquiries are directed are obtained from the management of the business primarily by the reporter as part of his investigation and from a card known as an Interested Number Card. This card is maintained on every business enterprise on which a credit report is edited and contains the subscriber number of each concern that has requested a credit report on the business enterprise under investigation. Through these sources, Dun & Bradstreet, Inc., obtains a comprehensive list of the names of concerns from whom merchandise is purchased and also assures that the data given under the Payments caption in the credit report does not consist solely of information made available by suppliers named by the concern under investigation. A subscriber obtains a report by either telephoning the agency and giving its subscription number or files an inquiry ticket (see Fig. 14).

[1] See Fig. 13, Request for Credit Experience.

Types of Reports. The reporting department prepares and edits two types of commercial credit reports, namely, the Analytical Report, and the Regular Report.[1]

Analytical Reports are edited by trained specialized reporters on the larger and more complicated business enterprises. These reports are featured by complete method of operation information and by comparative detailed financial statements. They include an analysis of the business based upon these comparative figures in the light of method of operation characteristics, financing methods, and other supplementary data.

The information in the Analytical Report is presented in nine parts, namely, Officers and Directors, Rating, Summary, History, Operation-Location, Subsidiaries (where applicable), Financial Information and Analysis, Trade Investigation, and Banking Relations. Each report indicates whether or not the rating has changed and lists the current rating.

Under the Summary caption appear the salient points of the report in short, decisive sentences (see Figs. 15a, 15b, 15c).

Following the Summary is the History section, which reports on the original inception of the business to the present time. Each change which has had an important effect on the business is outlined. Also included in this section is a brief description of the background and business career of each officer or partner and the capacity in which he serves the business.

The nature and scope of operations are comprehensively covered under the caption Operation-Location. The products sold or manufactured, the trade to which distribution is made, sales territory, number of accounts, selling terms, number of salesmen, seasonal aspects of the business, number of employees, facilities, and location are all reported under this caption.

The Subsidiary caption is one of the outstanding features of the Analytical Report. Under this caption, the name and location of each subsidiary and the percentage of stock ownership by the parent concern are given. A brief description of each subsidiary is also given, including details of financial condition, nature of operations, and comprehensive coverage of intercompany relations, such as merchandise transactions, loans, advances, endorsements, and guarantees with the parent company and with other related concerns.

Financial Information presents the comparative financial statements for 3 years, including operating details such as net sales, net profits, and dividends or withdrawals. Under the analysis portion of Financial Information, the trend of operations and financial position of the busi-

[1] See Appendix C1 for sample of Regular Report.

ness is carefully reviewed in the light of the operational characteristics of the business.

Under the caption Trade Investigation, the paying record of the business is reflected by a tabulation of ledger experiences. The Banking Relations section of the Analytical Report outlines the nature and scope of the relations of the business with its depositories.

Regular Reports[1] are written on all concerns not covered by Analytical Reports. The outstanding feature of this type of report is the Summary section, which gives the reader, right at the start, a brief synopsis of the high lights of the case. The lead-off caption further indicates the age, size, background, financial condition, paying habits, and rating of the business. Captions used to identify the remaining sections of these reports are History, Operation-Location, Financial Information, and Payments.

Each of the two types of commercial credit reports is designed to give the reader a clear and concise picture of the over-all condition of the business and its management. Each commercial credit report, of course, carries a rating which reflects the financial strength and the composite credit appraisal, or a symbol which reflects only the estimated annual sales of the business. Financial information such as balance sheets and related financial statements are issued immediately upon receipt, as is all other current information which may have an important effect upon the business.

In addition to the two types of commercial credit reports, the reporting department also investigates and produces Key Account and Special Purpose (Cost Plus) reports. These reports provide a "made-to-order" reporting service designed to answer specific questions by subscribers about "key" customers whose orders are large or whose sales, collection, or inventory problems are unusual. This special and expanding service includes personal supervision by a staff analyst at frequent intervals and always keeps in mind the specific problem of the subscriber.

Interpretation of Reports. In a previous chapter it was stated that credit risk could be measured by appraising the factors of Character, Capacity, Capital, and Conditions of Business. These factors may be revealed by the answers to six questions which the credit manager poses about every credit risk. These questions are (1) Who are they? (2) What have they done? (3) What are they doing now? (4) In which direction are they going? (5) What is their financial position? (6) How are they meeting their obligations? Let credit managers have sound and satisfactory answers to these questions and business will have sound and satisfactory credits. The questions as stated assume the subject is either a partnership or a corporation in which there are several

[1] Illustrated in Appendix C2.

executives composing the management. The questions would apply equally to a single proprietorship.

Regardless of the type of Dun & Bradstreet report, answers to these questions are given, in so far as the information is available.

Who Are They? This introduces the subject of the report and establishes the type of legal entity. The name or names of the principals, the trade style, and the corporate name are not without significance. Particularly significant may be changes in the trade style, names under which the principal or principals have operated in the past, or the corporate names through which they have conducted business. An imposing name will not mislead the credit manager though it may mislead customers. Corporate or trade names closely simulating well-known businesses should be carefully scrutinized. Trading on another's fame is all too common. If a name, be it a corporate, trade, or family name, is changed, why was the change made? With some credit managers all nationalities do not rank alike. Consequently the impression made by a name may be favorable, neutral, or unfavorable, and, whichever it is, the impression may not be confirmed unless it is accentuated by other information in the report. A flashy or imposing trade or corporate name will not conceal, but will emphasize, a bad record.

What Have They Done? A brief sketch highlights the accomplishments of the principal or principals. How old are they? Does their previous record indicate ability and reliability? Have they been successful in the past? In what fields are they experienced? Is anyone in an executive position tainted with an unsavory reputation? Do any of the principals have other business interests, and, if so, is this good or bad? The report gives factual information; the credit analyst must appraise it. There must be no lapses; continuity is essential in the historical development.

What Are They Doing Now? The agency answers this question under the heading Operation-Location. This question is of major importance, for what the business is currently doing plays a very influential part in determining the safety and elasticity of the risk. Unfortunately, the credit manager cannot get as close to the business as he might desire through the information imparted by this section. It may not disclose, for example, at what percentage of capacity the business is operating, the relation of costs to gross profit, the backlog of orders, etc. But the credit manager may learn from it whether the location, or, if the business has branches, the locations are desirable or not. He may need, too, to take note of the state in which the business is located because of the less favorable laws, from a creditor viewpoint, in some of the states. He may be informed of such facts as the size and appearance of the premises occupied, the number of employees, the classification of its

ANALYTICAL REPORT
RATING CHANGE

D U N & B R A D S T R E E T, I N C.

2071   (A) CD 4 AUGUST 18 195—
BRISTOL CANDY CORP   MFG   BRISTOL 3 PA
BUCKS COUNTY
100 EDGELY ROAD

Chester G. Hoover   – President   F. Charles Young   – Vice President
Henry T. Conroy   – Secretary & Treasurer

DIRECTORS: The officers and Mrs. Mary S. Lawrence

RATING: B 1 to B+ 1

STARTED: 1916 (Present Control 1946)   PAYMENTS: Discount
NET WORTH: $312,817   SALES: $1,106,165
SUMMARY
LAST MARCH THE PLANT WAS EXPANDED GREATLY TO INCREASE PRODUCTION AND LOWER
COSTS. CURRENT FIGURES SHOW THE INITIAL RESULTS. SALES ARE UP ABOUT 40%
AND EARNINGS ARE UP EVEN MORE. THE FINANCIAL POSITION CONTINUES STRONG.

HISTORY
STARTED: October, 1916 by F. Bradford Lawrence, who died in March, 1946. Under
the provisions of his will, the three key employees were bequeathed a 50% interest
in the business and the subject corporation was formed to carry out this provision.

INCORPORATED: June 29, 1946 under Pennsylvania laws.
Authorized Capital Stock: 250,000 shares Common $1.00 par value.
Outstanding Capital Stock: 150,000 shares.

MANAGEMENT & CONTROL: Mary S. Lawrence, the widow of F. Bradford Lawrence, the
founder, owns 50% of the outstanding capital stock. The remainder is owned by
Chester G. Hoover (25%), Henry T. Conroy (15%), and F. Charles Young (10%). Life
insurance of $25,000 is carried on each officer with the corporation as beneficiary.

Chester G. Hoover, born 1886, married. Employed sales department, Federal Biscuit
Company, Philadelphia, 1913–1923. Since associated with this business as General
Sales Manager to June, 1946 when he was elected President and General Manager.

Henry T. Conroy, born 1903, married. Cashier of Fidelity Trust Company, Baltimore
1924–1931. Then employed as Office Manager of this business to 1946 when he was
elected Secretary and Treasurer.

F. Charles Young, born 1898, married, was employed in the plant from 1923 to 1935
when he became Plant Superintendent. Elected Vice President in June, 1946.

Mrs. Mary S. Lawrence takes no active part in the management.

OPERATION-LOCATION
Products: Manufactures packaged confections, including chocolates, hard candies,
and novelty sweets, (U.S. SIC #2071). Seventy-five percent of the volume is in
chocolates which retail from $1.25 to $2.50 a pound. Brand Name: "Honey Crunch".

Distribution: To retail candy (35%), chain (25%), drug (20%), grocery (10%) and
department stores (10%).
Number of Accounts: 2,000 active.
Terms of Sales: 2%-15-Net 30.
Territory: The Eastern Seaboard from Maine to Florida.
Seasons: Sales are highest in November and December (40%).
Salesmen: 10 on salary and commission.
Employees: 125.

Production Facilities: Owns and fully occupies a three-story brick building,
sprinkler equipped, comprising 50,000 square feet of floor space. Also an adjacent
two-story brick building which formerly housed the plant but is now used for warehousing. The buildings, machinery and equipment are in excellent condition.
(CONTINUED)

PLEASE NOTE WHETHER NAME, BUSINESS AND STREET ADDRESS CORRESPOND WITH YOUR INQUIRY.
The foregoing report is furnished, at your request, under your Subscription Contract, in STRICT CONFIDENCE, by DUN & BRADSTREET, Inc. as your agents and
employees, for your exclusive use as an aid in determining the advisability of granting credit or insurance, and for no other purpose. 9R4-3 (33053)

Fig. 15a. Analytical Report.

products and how they are divided in its market, the terms under which
it sells, and its seasons. The credit manager needs to remember that
the reporter is repeating, for the most part, what he is told by the subject, and some of the unfavorable features of the operation, if there are
any, may be suppressed. The credit manager, from his knowledge of
the industry, will form his own opinion of the soundness of the method
of operation or of any hazards there may be in it.

ANALYTICAL REPORT
RATING CHANGE

D U N & B R A D S T R E E T , I N C.

BRISTOL CANDY CORP
Page 2 (A)

BRISTOL 3 PA
AUGUST 18 195-

COMPARATIVE FINANCIAL STATEMENTS

	Jun 30 195-	Jun 30 195-	Jun 30 195-
Cash	$ 78,171	$ 72,913	$ 87,486
U.S. Govt Bonds	36,710	70,126	---
Accounts Receivable	38,040	29,584	68,640
Inventory	58,053	71,874	138,442
TOTAL CURRENT ASSETS	210,975	244,499	294,570
Fixed Assets	31,232	28,549	253,755
Cash Value Life Insurance	4,154	5,047	6,416
Prepaid Expense	2,036	1,947	6,496
TOTAL ASSETS	248,398	280,043	561,237
Due Banks	---	---	25,000
Accounts Payable	20,179	9,802	10,654
Federal Income Taxes	30,395	38,712	79,131
Accruals	18,049	12,816	8,635
TOTAL CURRENT LIABILITIES	68,624	61,331	123,420
Due Bank-Deferred	---	---	125,000
Common Stock	150,000	150,000	150,000
Earned Surplus	29,774	68,712	162,817
TOTAL LIABILITIES	248,398	280,043	561,237
NET WORKING CAPITAL	142,350	183,168	171,150
CURRENT RATIO	3.07	3.98	2.38
TANGIBLE NET WORTH	179,774	218,712	312,817
Net Sales	735,198	771,035	1,106,165
Net Profit	54,774	68,938	124,105
Dividends	15,000	30,000	30,000

CENTS OMITTED. The foregoing figures were prepared from annual financial reports of
the auditors, James Wheaton & Co., C.P.A.'s, Philadelphia, Pa. Statements were received by mail accompanied by transmittal letters signed by Henry T. Conroy, Treasurer. At the last statement date, Accounts Receivable were net of a reserve for bad
debts of $3,106. Fixed Assets were net of reserves for depreciation of $31,612.
Inventory consisting of finished goods $44,106, in process $14,719 and raw materials
$79,612, valued at the lower of cost or market under the "Lifo" method. Fire
Insurance: Inventory - maximum coverage $200,000 under a monthly reporting policy;
Fixtures and Equipment - $75,000; Buildings - $200,000. Contingent Debt: None

(CONTINUED)

FIG. 15b. Analytical Report, p. 2.

In Which Direction Are They Going? The answer to this question,
if it can be found, may be decisive, particularly in what credit managers
are wont to call borderline cases. This question may not be directly
answered in the report, but progression or regression, or the lack of
either, may be indicated by the general tenor of the report. Oftentimes the answer is illusive, and the management itself may not be sure
of its direction until it has proceeded some distance on the way.

What Is the Financial Position? This is revealed by the financial statement and supporting information, or, in the absence of a statement, by such financial information as the reporter is able directly or indirectly to obtain. The subject's banking relations are included as a part of this section, or separately, in the analytical report. The subject's financial position is most important, for it reveals his resources and the demand on those resources. In the analytical-type reports an analysis of the financial statement by the reporter is included. These analyses are valuable, for they often contain explanatory statements supplied by the subject and not available elsewhere. The analysis given in the report may, of course, be augmented by the credit manager's own deductions from the statement.

How Is the Subject Meeting His Obligations? The answer to this question is found, with more or less accuracy and completeness, in the Payments or Trade Investigation section. This section reveals, subject to the reservations above, not only how obligations are met, but several other inferences may be drawn. These may be covered in such mental questions as: Are there sufficient creditors reporting to give a cross section of all the subject's creditors or were the references "hand-picked" by the subject? Is the report sufficiently recent to be of full value? Does the high credit (HC) reported indicate the subject is generally well regarded by his creditors? Does the length of time sold reported by the creditors indicate lack of sufficient experience as to pay habits to be reliable, or is the subject's tendency to shift to new sources of supply indicated? Does the payment record harmonize with the balance of the report, particularly the indicated liquidity? Are there indications certain creditors are favored in payments? If so, why?

Banking Relations are given in a section bearing that heading in the analytical report and are included in all reports if the relation with the bank is of any importance creditwise. Often the bank is the principal creditor and a statement by it may reflect its confidence in the account as well as the subject's dependence upon the bank for aid.

From the contents of the report, a rating is assigned and a summary formulated. The rating and the summary, which are in the first part of the report, reflect as accurately as possible the facts and the analysis of the facts given in the report. The summary is an attempt to highlight in a few lines the more important facts stated in the report.

Reference Book Department. This department publishes a volume bimonthly known as the *Reference Book* which lists commercial enterprises—manufacturers, wholesalers, retailers, and other businesses in the United States and Canada, generally those buying regularly on credit— on which credit reports have been written. The *Reference Book* does not, however, include some service and professional establishments, such

ANALYTICAL REPORT

RATING CHANGE

D U N & B R A D S T R E E T , I N C .

BRISTOL CANDY CORP
PAGE 3 (A)

BRISTOL 3 PA
AUGUST 18 195-

ANALYSIS

Annual sales volume has been at a high level since formation of this corporation. Net profits were correspondingly high and, except for moderate dividends, were retained and invested in Government bonds to finance a plan of plant modernization and expansion. Construction under this plan of fixed asset expansion was started early in the last fiscal year and completed in March. The cost of approximately $250,000 was financed with an unsecured term bank loan of $150,000 and liquidation of Government bonds. The term bank loan is payable $12,500 semi-annually for six years.

Net sales were 43% larger in the last fiscal year. This increase in the dollar volume resulted from both a 25% price increase in August, following a rise in raw material and labor costs, and increased unit sales subsequent to March. Net profit also was higher as a result of the sales expansion and lower unit production costs subsequent to March, when the plant and manufacturing improvements were completed.

In prior years, seasonal use was made of unsecured bank loans up to $100,000. There has been no recourse to this type of financing during the last three years as inventories were turned rapidly and the collection experience was excellent. Financial position at the last fiscal closing was sound. Compared to net sales of that period inventory comprised primarily of raw materials was equivalent to 45 days sales while accounts receivable were equivalent to 22 days sales.

TRADE INVESTIGATION

Sugar, the basic raw material used, is purchased on a sight draft basis under annual contract with one broker. Such drafts have been honored on presentation. Other raw materials, such as cocoa, flavorings, nut meats, and packaging materials are purchased from seven suppliers. Recent experience of the principal suppliers are included in the following results of a trade survey completed August 12, 195-

	HIGH CREDIT	OWE	PAST DUE	TERMS OF SALE	PAYMENTS
1.	$ 30,000	3,450	-0-	2-10-30	Discount
2.	25,000	-0-	----	2-10-30	Discount
3.	5,555	-0-	----	2-10	Discount
4.	5,399	----	----	2-10-31	Discount
5.	5,000	----	----	2-10	Discount
6.	4,939	264	----	2-10-30	Discount
7.	3,000	----	----	2-10-30	Discount
8.	658	----	----	2-10	Discount
9.	Requirements	----	----	Sight Draft	Prompt

BANKING RELATIONS

An account is maintained at a local bank. Balances average in medium to high five figures. In 195-, a five-year, unsecured, term loan of $150,000 was granted. Other details of this loan are outlined under "Analysis". A low six-figure line of short term, unsecured, bank credit which is available has not been used in recent years.

8-18-5 (803 1 29)

FIG. 15c. Analytical Report, p. 3. Source: Dun & Bradstreet, Inc.

as real estate brokers, barber and beauty shops, and stockbrokers, even though credit reports may have been written on these businesses. All *Reference Book* listings are compiled from information in the complete credit report. In addition to the name of the concern and its business, a financial and credit rating is given in most instances. A four-digit U.S. Standard Industrial Classification Number appearing before the name classifies the business completely and precisely. Whenever a "C" precedes the code number, the rating on the business has been changed in that particular edition of the *Reference Book*, and whenever an "A" precedes the code number, the name is a new one and has been added. A numeral shown immediately preceding the rating represents the last digit of the year the business was started or came under its present ownership within the past 10 years. The ratings in the *Reference Book* are designed to express, within the limitations imposed by the use of symbols, an appraisal of the information and comments assembled by the agency from the concerns listed, from references, and from other sources. Examples of typical listings in the *Reference Book* are contained in Fig. 16.

The *Reference Book* also contains supplementary information which is of considerable value to the sales and shipping departments as well as to the credit department. Included are the names of more than 20,000 banks and the population of each city, town, and village which are listed alphabetically according to state. Small or state editions of the *Reference Book*, designed primarily for the use of salesmen, are also published twice a year, in January and July, by the Reference Book Department.

Ratings. Probably the most important feature of the *Reference Book*, and the one for which it is universally known and used, is the rating of the commercial enterprises listed. A rating consists of two elements, namely, estimated financial strength and composite credit appraisal. The Key to Ratings shown in detail as Fig. 17 gives the symbols used to reflect the estimated financial strength, the composite credit appraisal, and the indeterminate listings as to the combined estimated financial strength and credit appraisal; an explanation of the symbol used to indicate the absence of a rating is also shown in the Key to Ratings.

```
STEDMAN FALLS  ▲  Wolfe  42
1st NAT BK OF STEDMAN FALLS......$220M
Y I Masten Pr T H Tarrington Cas
  61 47 Beckdorff Joseph.......Pwnbkr     3
C 57 12 Borden Carl Inc...........Frn   B 1½
        (Also Cedar Rapids Iowa)
  50 52 Caffrey James & Bros...Darpdt   C 1½
  59 LA Caffrey Sirman E & Son...Toys 7   —
  54 41 Chandler Fred...........Cnf 7   G 3½
  59 42 Charlie's News Stand......Bks   E 2½
A 50 52 Cooper F B Jr & Co....Darpdt 8  G 3½
  17 21 Crandall Louis........Pprhg 4   H 3½
  52 11 Cruger Samuel...........Lbr     E 2½
  59 12 Dalzell Howard J Jr......Drg    F 3
  59 12 DesJardins Henry......Drg 4     E 2½
  59 83 Economy Oil Co Inc.....Petrpdt   2
  59 52 Emory Benson Sales Co...Spgg 7  G 3½
  52 62 Erlich Henry J.......Agimpt     F 3
  53 31 Fink's 5c to $1 Store........3   F 3
  50xRA Fox Tobacco & Candy Co Inc....  C 1½
  24 21 Franklin Worth C......Sawmll    G 3½
  50 42 Gage S A & Son............Gr    C+1½
  59 21 Globe Wine & Liquor Shoppe*..   F 3
  50x73 H & A Tool & Model Co Inc...3   F 3
  20 82 H & H Brewing Co*..........      2
  27 41 Sheffield Publishing Co Inc....  C 2
  57 23 Spencer William E......Radios   C 1½
  53 92 Spitzer Maude G (Mrs S H)..Dg   F 3

STILLWELL   1,125   Polk  81
POLK COUNTY TR CO.................$48M
Aubrey C Bird Pr Arthur Thomas Cas
  43 11 Cedar Street Transit Co*..Buses A▲ A1
  76 74 Ceruzzi Armature Service......  H 3½
A 14 22 E & B Stone Works..........8    H 3½
  73 42 E E D Termite Control Co......2 H 3½
  17 11 Faber & Bell.........PlbgCntr   G 3½
  54 13 Llewellen Edward......GrMt      E 2½
  73 11 Lloyd Lindsey & Co....AdvgAgcy  A▲ A1
  56 21 Lohman Louis........Wnwr 5       3
  58 13 M & E Food Shop........Tav      F 3
C 54x13 McGraw Bessie E (Mrs Wm E)..3  G 3½
                          GrMtSstn
  52 12 McGuire James J.......Bldmtl    G 3½
  53 93 Mayfield Enos..........Gs 2     F 3
  56 21 Mlle Shop.............Wnwr      F 3
  57 12 Morton R Glen & Co Inc.....Frn  Inv
  45 82 Novak Aviation Service......7    3
  39 81 Novak Fred L Co Inc.....Brooms  E 2½
  52 11 Oberg Olaf A NR.........Lbr     H 3½
  52 12 O'Brien Building Material Inc... C 2
  54 13 O'Connor's Foods Inc.....GrMt   F 3
  42 12 )2                    Trkg
  59 12 Paley Morris..........Drg       G 3½
C 55 21 Palumbo & Co.........UAts        2
  56 21 Power's Shop..........Wnwr      C 2
```

FIG. 16. Reference Book excerpt. Source: Dun & Bradstreet, Inc.

Interpretations of Dun & Bradstreet Ratings. When a rating is assigned to a business enterprise, the rating is shown on the report and in the *Reference Book.* When no rating is assigned to a concern listed, the dash (—) is shown on the report and in the *Reference Book.*

A rating is a symbol which summarizes and classifies relatively the elements of character, capacity, and capital of business enterprise and the trend of its current position. A rating reflects, as accurately as possible, the facts and the analysis of the facts given in the credit report. The letter portion of the rating indicates the estimated financial strength, and the numerical portion of the rating reflects the composite credit appraisal where the letter and numeral are used together. In practice the most commonly used measure for estimated financial strength is the tangible net worth of the business. In some instances, however, the tangible net worth of a business is not the same as the net worth shown by the financial statement because of the elimination of intangible items such as good will, patents, and the like. The estimated financial-strength portion of the rating is not intended to indicate the liquidating value of a business, but rather its fair, going concern value. There are four degrees of composite credit appraisal, namely, high, good, fair, and limited.

KEY TO RATINGS						
ESTIMATED FINANCIAL STRENGTH			**COMPOSITE CREDIT APPRAISAL**			
			HIGH	GOOD	FAIR	LIMITED
Aa	Over	$1,000,000	A1	1	1½	2
A+	Over	750,000	A1	1	1½	2
A	$500,000 to	750,000	A1	1	1½	2
B+	300,000 to	500,000	1	1½	2	2½
B	200,000 to	300,000	1	1½	2	2½
C+	125,000 to	200,000	1	1½	2	2½
C	75,000 to	125,000	1½	2	2½	3
D+	50,000 to	75,000	1½	2	2½	3
D	35,000 to	50,000	1½	2	2½	3
E	20,000 to	35,000	2	2½	3	3½
F	10,000 to	20,000	2½	3	3½	4
G	5,000 to	10,000	3	3½	4	4½
H	3,000 to	5,000	3	3½	4	4½
J	2,000 to	3,000	3	3½	4	4½
K	1,000 to	2,000	3	3½	4	4½
L	Up to	1,000	3½	4	4½	5

CLASSIFICATION AS TO BOTH ESTIMATED FINANCIAL STRENGTH AND CREDIT APPRAISAL

FINANCIAL STRENGTH BRACKET			EXPLANATION
1	$125,000 to	$1,000,000 and Over	When only the numeral (1, 2, 3, or 4) appears, it is an indication that the estimated financial strength, while not definitely classified, is presumed to be within the range of the ($) figures in the corresponding bracket and that a condition is believed to exist which warrants credit in keeping with that assumption.
2	20,000 to	125,000	
3	2,000 to	20,000	
4	Up to	2,000	

NOT CLASSIFIED OR ABSENCE OF RATING

The absence of a rating, expressed by the dash (—), is not to be construed as unfavorable but signifies circumstances difficult to classify within condensed rating symbols and should suggest to the subscriber the advisability of obtaining additional information.

INVESTIGATING

"Inv." in place of the rating is an abbreviation of "investigating." It signifies nothing more than that a pending investigation was incomplete when the book in which it appears went to press.

DUN & BRADSTREET, INC.

Fig. 17. Key to Ratings, Dun & Bradstreet, Inc.

A "high" composite credit appraisal invariably applies in connection with any of the estimated financial strength symbols when the following eight primary conditions are met: (1) sound legal constituency, (2) the concern has been in business for 1 year and preferably 3 years or more, (3) experienced, well-balanced management with no gap in antecedents, (4) no criticized failures or criticized fires, (5) financial statements regularly submitted or made available on request for use in the report, (6) financial affairs in healthy condition, (7) trend points to a continued healthy condition, and (8) obligations retired according to agreement. Each and every one of these eight conditions is weighed and a conclusion is reached on a relative basis. In exceptional instances a "high" credit rating may be assigned where one or more of these conditions are not apparent if the deficiency is offset by other conditions which are exceptionally favorable.

A "good" composite credit appraisal applies when all or practically all the conditions outlined for a "high" credit rating are met but to a somewhat less although still satisfactory degree.

The same standard of relativity applies in the "fair" credit case. For example, a "fair" composite credit appraisal may reflect a top-heavy but still not a dangerously top-heavy financial condition. "Fair" credit simply means a third-degree credit position reflecting a continued though reduced status of business stability compared with the "good" credit risk.

The "limited" or fourth-grade credit rating rarely applies with estimated financial strength ratings in the higher ranges, as businesses of that size, warranting no better than a limited rating, are usually in such a position that a nonclassification symbol is more applicable.

The blank (—) symbol is assigned when no other symbol applies to the circumstances and is used regardless of the size of the subject. The blank (—) symbol informs the credit man that circumstances exist which make it difficult to classify the account within condensed rating symbols and, as brought out in the Key to Ratings, suggests to the subscriber of the agency the advisability of obtaining additional information.

Dun & Bradstreet, Inc., has an indeterminate classification for subjects of reports, namely, the numerical classification. An explanation of this classification and the four brackets or ranges which it covers are shown in Fig. 17, the Key to Ratings.

A rating, or the absence of a rating, or any concern listed is not intended to be more, nor should it be inferred to be more, than a reflection of the tenor of the information assembled, nor should it be construed as suggesting or intimating that credit be restricted, or withheld, or accepted.

The Use of the Reference Book. Dun & Bradstreet's *Reference Books* are very valuable books to any credit department. Most credit men regard them as indispensable. Yet the well-trained credit man will use them with caution. The credit student has probably already become impressed with the necessity of verifying credit information whenever possible. While the credit man is not of a suspicious nature, neither does he have a childlike credulity. Therefore, he does not believe that the agency ratings are infallible. In the first place, the rating may have been based upon insufficient information. Reporters sometimes fail to discover all the pertinent facts. Moreover, the facts may have been misinterpreted and a wrong rating assigned. The books contain over 2,950,000 names. Obviously, there must be errors. Add to the possibilities of error mentioned above the fact that there are approximately

5,331 changes in the *Reference Book* each business day, and it will be seen that between the printing of one edition and of the next, the changes run into the hundred thousands.[1]

These changes, however, are usually not radical. A concern's condition usually changes gradually, so that a change in the rating may as often mean a better rating as a poorer one, and in either event it may be a change to the next higher or lower credit or capital rating, a change which might not materially affect the creditor's confidence in the account. Obviously, it is difficult to express in one symbol the relative credit rating, particularly when it is based on a report which contains mixed information, including both favorable and adverse facts. In all cases where an amount of any consequence is involved, the credit man prefers to analyze the report and arrive at his own conclusion. If the rating is distinctly inferior, credit may be at once refused. On the other hand, if the rating indicates that the risk is doubtful, that fact points to the necessity of making a further investigation before accepting or rejecting the risk.

The *Reference Book* is much used in revising the credit files. It is a common practice, and one to be commended, to check the credit files with each new *Reference Book.* Either a downward or an upward change in rating may indicate the necessity for a new investigation. If the rating is upward, revision may mean the possibility of a larger line of credit and, consequently, more business from the customer. The *Reference Book* also has utility as a guide to the sales department. It aids in locating those who may become customers and indicates which may prove to be the more desirable from the standpoints of both credit and volume.

Banks use the *Reference Book* to learn the ratings of unknown names appearing on the "paper" presented to them by their customers for discount.

Credit Clearing House, a Division of Dun & Bradstreet. This division is actively engaged in furnishing information to the apparel trades and allied lines. It is a centralized division which through subscribers' inquiries records the subject's buying activity and amounts of the orders

[1] For the year 1957, the agency's statistics show the following *Reference Book* changes for the United States and Canada:

Names added	Names obliterated	Rating changes	Total changes	Average for each business day	Names in January, 1958, issue
466,588	432,775	721,380	1,620,743	5,331	2,953,659

of the inquirers. Inquirers are nationwide and they enable a running record of normal and abnormal purchases to be maintained on well over 100,000 active accounts. Credit opinions are supplied on each transaction recorded. The Credit Clearing House is divided into two departments, Male Apparel and Women's Wear, each staffed with thoroughly trained credit analysts who are familiar with the buying habits, trade customs, and seasonal factors peculiar to the two industries. Every 3 months, to coincide with the four retail sales seasons, the *Apparel Trades Book* is published by the Credit Clearing House. This volume contains the name of each retailer of men's and women's wear in the United States, lists trade styles and branches through cross references, and through symbols denotes the type of merchandise sold and the credit rating based on a specialized key to ratings.

International Division. Dun & Bradstreet has foreign branches, affiliates, and correspondents in important trade centers of the world. Foreign-trade analysts familiar with the business customs, language, and local selling conditions in the countries they cover conduct on-the-spot investigations of local exporters, importers, and other commercial enterprises. These investigations are reflected to a great extent in the more than 250,000 reports on file at New York on leading foreign customers for American goods and services. This department annually publishes the *Latin American Sales Index*, which contains the listings with a trade code key of over 180,000 industrial, commercial, and professional enterprises in Latin America.

Municipal Service Division. This department prepares comprehensive financial surveys of states, counties, cities, and districts. These surveys are prepared from information obtained through personal interview, study, and extensive investigation made by analysts who are thoroughly trained in municipal finance. Such surveys contain a detailed analysis of the economic and social characteristics, management, debt, and current operations of the governmental unit under study. They are designed to furnish investors such as bond dealers, banks and trust companies, and insurance companies with complete information regarding bonds issued by such governmental units as a basis for investment.

The Mercantile Claims Division. This division dates back to 1857 and was organized to assist in the collection of past due amounts resulting from merchandise sales on credit terms. As an aid to the collection of delinquent accounts, subscribers to this service are furnished with two types of gummed labels to be attached to invoices and reminder letters. The first of these labels notifies the debtor that collection of past due amounts are made through Dun & Bradstreet, Inc., and the second label notifies the debtor that the account, if not paid within a specified period of time, will be turned over to this division of Dun &

Bradstreet, Inc., for collection. Then follow a series of letters and personal calls each designed to obtain payment. Finally, if none of these steps has resulted in payment of the account, it then is turned over to an attorney for collection.

The Marketing Services Company. The Marketing Services Company was organized in 1935 to carry on and expand various types of studies in economics and business statistics which Dun & Bradstreet, Inc., has made for more than 80 years. This division, through the facilities of the organization as a whole and the skilled analysts in its employ, is engaged in the preparation of surveys on a wide range of subjects, such as the sale and distribution of consumer goods and commodities, sales and operating trends, and other subjects of importance to business and to others having a need for such specialized information. These surveys are based on information obtained through personal interview with the farmer, mechanic, housewife, clerk, banker, or business executive by the trained reporter, correspondent, and analyst, supplemented by data obtained from other authoritative sources.

Dun & Bradstreet Publications Corporation. This corporation publishes *Dun's Review and Modern Industry, Dun's Statistical Review, Compass Points of Business, The Weekly Trade Review,* and statements about business conditions. Its business conditions staff handles inquiries about business conditions and related statistical data; compiles indexes and barometers; prepares information, tables, and charts about trade, industrial, and economic activity for various company uses. *Dun's Review and Modern Industry* each month places before approximately 115,000 heads of American businesses information about the effects on business of significant influences and developments, principally (1) summaries of important economic studies, (2) frank statements of opinion on important and often controversial questions by national leaders, and (3) reports of industrial and trade activity and other similar material. *Dun's Review and Modern Industry* is mailed to the president or other active executive head of each subscriber concern in the United States as a part of its regular agency service.

Additional Agency Services. The agency furnishes letters of introduction to its subscribers, upon request, to enable the subscribers' representatives, when traveling, to inquire for information at any of the agency's branch offices. The *Reference Book* may be consulted, or a full report read. There is no extra charge for this service.

When a subscriber inquires about a name, the agency supplies, in addition to the report then in its files, or the report prepared as the result of the inquiry, continuous service on the name for a period of a year. This continuous service includes all new and additional information obtained during the year of service. When a new report is issued after the year of continuous service, a renewal notice is sent to the subscriber stating that the year of service has been completed and that a new report has been prepared and may be obtained by returning the renewal notice.

During 1950, the position of Consulting Reporter was created. These reporters, who are top reporters in the business, and who are "professional" consultative reporters, work very much on their own responsibility, and work closely with subjects of reports, their banks, and trade suppliers in handling the more complex credit problems and credit reporting situations.

During 1951, Service Consultants were set up in the offices of Dun & Bradstreet, Inc., for the purpose of effecting a broadened and more personalized relationship with subscribers to the service. The objective of the Service Consultant is to make certain that each subscriber receives the maximum value from his relationship with the agency and makes the fullest possible use of the various agency services.

Also during 1951, the Building Trades Division was formed with its broad purpose to develop a service to meet the unique requirements of suppliers in the building industry. Two initial steps were taken: (1) the publishing of the Consolidated Ledger Abstract which is an interchange of ledger experiences of trade suppliers in a particular local area and (2) the selection and appointment of Building Trades Specialists in each office active in this field to become the authority on the construction and allied trades in their respective offices, and to supervise the writing of reports in the industry.

The Business Library has facilities for the use of service subscribers, business executives, trade associations, banks, and others of the business world in locating published information. A competent staff handles inquiries by telephone and by mail; there is an attractive reference room for those who visit the library. The Business Library collection of standard business and economic literature is supplemented by up-to-date books, pamphlets, releases, reports, and clippings on subjects of special and timely interest. For interest, data are available on various aspects of business management, credit, commodities, industries, prices, statistics, and the like. The library maintains files of trade journals, newspapers, and government releases, as well as collections of current business and trade directories, biographical directories, business histories, operating and financial ratios. The library resources include about 15,000 volumes, 15,000 pamphlets, 200 periodicals, and 200 drawers of vertical files.

Dun & Bradstreet, Inc., also sponsors educational films which may be obtained for a nominal rental fee.

Discussion of the Agency Service. The purpose of the somewhat extended discussion of the agency and description of its methods has been to enable the reader to determine for himself the scope of the information furnished and the speed and reliability of its service. As has been brought out, the relation between the subscriber and the agency is that of principal and agent. Naturally, a criticism of the work of the agent will raise the question of cooperation on the part of the principal. The agency no doubt has cause to criticize the aid given by the subscriber, but as a matter of policy, criticism is not expressed. The subscriber, on the other hand, has no such reticence. He feels free to criticize the agency and its finished product.

Some credit managers feel that the reports do not always contain complete or satisfactory antecedent information in the history section of the report. This particular feature of a mercantile agency report is of paramount importance. Herein the agency can render a service that it is not possible for other reporting media to supply. Antecedent information is regarded as a very useful guide, and therefore this feature cannot be too strongly emphasized for the mercantile agencies to conserve and develop. Because of the age of the mercantile agency under discussion, its files should contain almost a century record of business.

Agencies sometimes fail to procure and incorporate in their reports satisfactory financial information. In too many reports, either there is no financial statement or there is the complaint that much of its value is lost through the fact that it is plainly not based on books of account or accurate records but is merely approximated or represents an estimate. In connection with this criticism, it is pertinent to remark that a greater insistence on the part of credit men on financial statements, both directly in their dealings with customers and through the agencies, would result in an improvement in this feature of the service.

Many credit managers regard the payment section as of little value. Their criticism is that this section is too brief, as it often gives the ledger experience of too small a portion of the subject's total creditors. Furthermore, it is claimed that the data are too old to indicate present paying ability and too often obtained from "hand-picked" references provided by the subject of inquiry. An additional reason for lack of confidence in this section is the fact that the credit manager sometimes hesitates to give the agency derogatory facts for indiscriminate distribution among its subscribers. Also, in too many instances, the information is furnished the agency in a loose and haphazard fashion. Unless ledger information is accurate, it is dangerous. While this is a criticism of the agency report, the criticism is directly chargeable to the credit manager himself.

Another criticism is the age of some of the reports when received. The agency strives to revise reports every 6 months. It fails, however, fully to follow this program. Too often it attempts a revision after the subscriber has requested the report. The practice, in such a case, is to send the old report on file stamped "will revise" or "will send later information." The revised report may reach the subscriber too late to be of any value to him.

Credit men feel that their requests for reports are not promptly filled. No doubt such delays are exaggerated in their minds. It is but human to remember one delayed report and to forget the nine received promptly. The agencies claim that their prompt service is in just about that proportion, that is, that 90 per cent of the requests for reports are filled within the space of one working day.

Finally, the quality of the reports is sometimes criticized. It is felt that the service would be much improved by a better type of reporter— more experienced and better paid—working on a quality basis rather than on quantity production. Some excellent reports are obtained by the credit man—reports which at once stamp the reporter as highly qualified for his position, but the proportion of quality reports is felt to be too small.

Dun & Bradstreet makes a consistent effort to utilize the most modern methods of speeding service. In some offices a taped answering service logs requests for reports and passes along to the subscriber the fact that there is a report, and its date. A clerk subsequently transcribes the request and mails the report to the subscriber.

The newest service, installed in January, 1959, is called "Priority Service." It is particularly useful in giving out-of-town inquiries preferred attention. Through this service, the report will be mailed either the same day or, if it is a "two-way priority," a summarized reply will be telegraphed.

Limitations of the Agency. Obviously, from the very nature of its service the agency cannot always give up-to-the-minute service. Those creditors who wish information brought completely up to date must cover the space intervening since the latest special report in some other manner, usually through their own investigation.

Another limitation is found in the general exclusion of information which it might be difficult to substantiate. Its reports are largely factual. While the reader has been cautioned to differentiate between facts and opinions, oftentimes opinions and mental convictions are of great value even though the evidence on which they are based is elusive. The reader will realize that sometimes the inside story cannot be published.

The agency is limited in that it cannot fit its service to the needs of each individual subscriber. On the other hand, each subscriber must accept the same standard of service. Agency service is gauged to meet the requirements of the greatest number or, let us say, the average requirement in quality and completeness of its reports. The price that the average subscriber is willing to pay puts a limit on the quality of the report. The creditor, however, who wants a "made-to-order" report may always ask for Key Account and Special Purpose (Cost Plus) reports.

The agency is under some restraint, as compared with individual creditors, in the circulation of derogatory information. It must be reserved or conservative in the inclusion of this type of information for publication.

Unfortunately, credit information is not always truthful. The agency can hardly be censured if it fails to detect dishonesty. Misleading or false information may be, and no doubt frequently is, given by the subject, and not only are trade creditors themselves guilty of the failure to give information, but what they give is also sometimes misleading or even false.

TEXT AND RESEARCH QUESTIONS

1. Account for the growth of the general agency.
2. What is the extent of Dun & Bradstreet, Inc., mercantile agency service?
3. List all the sources of information through which the agency obtains its information.
4. What type of information is supplied the agency by the local correspondent?
5. How does the agency train its full-time reporters?
6. What qualifications must a subject have in order to be assigned a high credit rating?
7. Without looking at the summary, carefully read the report on Bristol Candy Corp., Figs. 15a, 15b, and 15c; then write the summary and assign a rating. Compare your summary and rating with that of the agency.
8. What are the uses for the *Reference Book?*
9. Why are there variations in ratings for a "high" credit?

PROBLEMS

1. Refer to the town of Stillwell, Fig. 16. State in essay form what is revealed in regard to the following names: E and B Stone Works, Faber & Bell, and Palumbo & Co.
2. Refer to the report in Appendix C1 of Penn Pines Pharmacy, Miles Gross, owner. List the statements in the report that reveal the "capacity" factor. Is Mr. Gross's success due to his "capacity" or to the favorable business conditions? Why?
3. You are the assistant credit manager of the Ajax Fixture Mfg. Co., Inc., one of whose customers is Adamson Hardware Co. Your credit department

has just received a Dun & Bradstreet report on this company (in Appendix C2), and your credit manager has asked you to analyze the report and make a recommendation.   Your company's ledger experience is listed on the fourth line of the Payments section of the report.   Today, Oct. 10, 1959, the account owes your company $10,070, of which $5,875 is past due up to 6 months. Your problem is to determine your future attitude and course of action with the account.   Your written recommendation must be backed by precise and logical reasons for your action.   Discuss fully.

CHAPTER 15

SPECIAL CREDIT AGENCIES
AS A SOURCE OF CREDIT INFORMATION

Special Agencies. In addition to the older general agency, creditors have available the services of a number of special agencies often referred to as trade agencies. These special agencies offer services sometimes along lines similar to Dun & Bradstreet's agency, and sometimes along quite different lines. They differ from the general agency in that they confine their activities to a special industry or to a few allied industries. Among the larger of such special agencies are the Lyon Furniture Mercantile Agency, the National Jewelers Board of Trade, and the National Credit Office, Inc. These agencies receive the more or less active support of their various industries. The special agencies, to some extent, duplicate the work of the general agencies, and in a sense they may be said to be complementary to the general agencies. Many well-appointed credit offices will be found to be subscribers to the general agency as well as to the special agency catering to its own industry. So far as the agencies themselves are concerned, they regard each other as competitors.

Advantages and Disadvantages. The advantages and disadvantages of the special agencies cannot be treated satisfactorily in one discussion, since there is great divergence among the special agencies themselves. Some of their general features and problems, however, can be contrasted with those of the general agencies. One advantage of the general agency is that it embraces all lines. Thus, only one service may be required, whereas, if several different lines were sold by one house, the services of several special agencies would be required to cover them. Then, too, the general agencies claim that their greater prestige gives them an entree where it would not be accorded to the special agency, and thus a greater amount of credit information is made available to them. This point is undoubtedly true where the special agencies have not gained a substantial foothold, but it would hardly apply where the special agency has made itself a powerful factor in its industry.

235

The special agency lays claim to superiority mainly through its specialization and concentration. It claims to know the problems of its industry thoroughly. It knows the larger houses, where to get information, the manner of doing business, and the economic condition within the industry. Because of its restricted size, it claims, also, to be able to give a more prompt and a more personal service. Some special agencies, because of the power that they have developed in the industry and the extent to which they are relied upon by their subscribers, claim that they can command far more detailed information than is usually imparted to the general agencies. It is a fact that some special agencies seem to secure greater cooperation from their subscribers than do the general agencies. This is probably due, in part, to the fact that the customer's cooperation is more carefully cultivated by the agency and, in part, to the fact that the agency seems to a greater extent to be in and of the trade itself. Some of the special agencies are very small, and, where the industry is small or concentrated within narrow territorial limits, an intimate contact between the management of the agency and the industry itself is afforded. Other special agencies, while falling far below the general agencies in size, are, nevertheless, large organizations oftentimes maintaining numerous branches and hundreds of employees.

The advantages and disadvantages or, in other words, the efficiency of the special agencies cannot be covered in one generalization. They differ too greatly in purpose and method of operation. The merits of each special agency should be carefully considered. The points involved are, as in the case of the general agencies, the scope, the speed, and the reliability of their service. Each credit man should, of course, familiarize himself with the service of any agency which is operating within his own industry. A few of the larger special agencies will be discussed as sources of credit information.

National Credit Office, Inc. In the list of the larger credit agencies is included the National Credit Office, Inc., with headquarters in New York City. Since 1931 it has been a subsidiary of Dun & Bradstreet, Inc. Branches are located in Atlanta, Boston, Cleveland, Chicago, Detroit, Philadelphia, and Los Angeles.

Organized in 1900, it has grown from a comparatively inconspicuous start to a credit agency now comprehensively serving several major industries and the financial institutions closely associated with those industries. Originally, the principal activity was the furnishing of credit information on the various divisions of the cutting-up trades of the textile industry. Today, distinct departments, each under a manager, are operated covering industries grouped as follows:

T<small>EXTILES</small>

Menswear

Manufacturers of men's and boys' tailored clothing, jackets, slacks, and casual wear
Manufacturers of men's and boys' shirts, pajamas, underwear, robes, and sportswear
Manufacturers of work clothing, uniforms, and rainwear
Manufacturers of men's and boys' fabric hats and caps
Jobbers of menswear fabrics and trimmings

Dress and Sportswear

Manufacturers of dresses, blouses, skirts, sportswear, bathing suits, infants and childrens wear, housecoats, aprons, nurses' and maids' uniforms

Coat, suit, and intimate apparel

Manufacturers of coats, suits, sportswear, skirts, rainwear, children's coats and snow suits
Manufacturers of lingerie, negligees, corsets, brassieres, bed jackets, and robes
Manufacturers of neckwear, laces, and embroideries
Jobbers of womenswear fabrics

Textile mills

Dealers, processors, and jobbers of yarns and raw materials
Weavers and knitters of woolens, worsteds, and felts
Manufacturers of synthetic, cotton, and blended fabrics
Knitters of hosiery, underwear, and outerwear
Manufacturers of laces, veilings, braids, and rugs
Dyers, bleachers, finishers, and printers of textiles

Converting and household goods

Converters of cotton, synthetic, silk and other fabrics
Manufacturers of curtains, bedspreads, drapes, tufted products, sheets, pillowcases, quilted products, handkerchiefs, work gloves, seat covers, bags, and bias bindings
Manufacturers of upholstered furniture, mattresses and jobbers of upholstery fabrics

Wholesale and retail

Jobbers of hosiery, underwear, knit goods, and dry goods
Jobbers and exporters of cotton, rayon, and synthetic fabrics
Department stores, chain stores, and other retailers handling piece goods, dry goods, knit goods, and floor coverings

M<small>ETALS AND</small> E<small>LECTRONICS</small>

Aeronautical

Manufacturers of airplanes, engines, parts, and equipment. Airlines, Aero distributors

Appliances

Manufacturers of domestic, office, and industrial appliances; heating, ventilating, refrigeration, and air-conditioning equipment

Automotive

Manufacturers of motor vehicles, trailers, bodies, engines, accessories, and parts

Electronics

Manufacturers of radio and television sets, components, electrical, electronic, and nucleonic equipment
Distributors of electronic parts

Machinery
   Manufacturers of farming, road building, construction, electrical, metalworking, textile, and other machinery
Metal products
   Manufacturers of castings, forgings, stampings, and screw machine products
   Shipbuilding

CHEMICALS

Paints
   Manufacturers of paints, varnishes, enamels, and lacquers
Inks
   Manufacturers of printing inks
Rubber
   Manufacturers of tires, tubes, mechanical goods, and rubber products

AUTOMOTIVE CREDIT SERVICE

This division of N.C.O., with headquarters in Detroit, provides an integrated credit service on the wheel goods industry. A.C.S. issues specialized reports on all manufacturers of automobiles, trucks, tractors, buses, truck trailers, and mobile homes. It is used by the industry's leading suppliers, including steel mills, parts, and tire manufacturers.

At the start of 1957, A.C.S. enlarged its activities through the acquisition of *Mobile Homes Credit Guide*. The Guide is a bimonthly clearance service for banks, finance companies, manufacturers, and other suppliers of the *mobile home dealers*.

LEATHER AND COATED PRODUCTS

Footwear
   Manufacturers of all types of shoes and slippers
Handbags
   Manufacturers of handbags and purses
Luggage
   Manufacturers of trunks, suitcases, and briefcases
Accessories
   Manufacturers of leather garments and gloves, belts, wallets, key cases, and similar products

Distinctive features of National Credit Office service include credit advice and flexible methods of obtaining and distributing late information following the writing of a report.

The C.I.A. report (discussed later), introduced in 1954, is an example of the development of a short, concise report. Whether it is a short report or a full report, each one carries the suggestion of a definite line of credit or a summary classifying the account from a credit standing. This line or classification is changed by some form of special notice or "additional" to the base report as additional facts may warrant.

The Bank Service Department. Thus in the Bank Department, covering concerns selling paper on the open market, the notes of each com-

pany reported upon are classified in one of the following categories:
Prime, Desirable, Satisfactory, Fair, or Not Recommended. This department's report is of particular value to the banker who may never
have had the opportunity, in the course of usual business, of inquiring
into the affairs of a concern functioning in some particular industry.
Thus a banker in the wheat belt, desiring to purchase the note of a
lumber or steel company, finds it highly desirable to have a comprehensive report edited by one who has had the opportunity of surveying
the financial affairs of all the lumber or steel companies using the open
market. Among this number, of course, would be others functioning in
the same competitive sphere as the concern under question.

Reports on all concerns offering their commercial paper in the open
market—including about 100 of the largest commercial receivable,
small-loan, and sales finance companies—are written in the Bank Service
Department. They lend themselves to exceptionally thorough and
comprehensive treatment, since for several reasons access to more than
the usual amount of information is offered the analyst. If operating
details, such as bad-debt losses, profits, dividends, etc., are not submitted
by the company for publication, they are sometimes given in confidence
to the agency to assist in analysis and proper classification. A report
based upon three comparative financial statements is edited. An analysis
is made of the statements to disclose any distortion in its financial position such as top-heaviness with inventory, receivables, fixed assets, and
debts. Next follow a record of the officers and the business itself; a
description of the concern's operating methods, the names of any subsidiary or affiliated concerns; and an explanation of intercompany loans
and sales. Wherever possible an official of the concern and one of the
commercial paper broker who handles the notes are interviewed at the
time a report is being revised. Trade checkings are made by mail;
bank checkings, by personal call or, where necessary, by letter.

Market Planning Service. For those selling the apparel manufacturing trades, the converting industry, and the electronic parts distributors,
the Marketing Planning Service furnishes aid in the planning of sales and
production. The annual story of each trade, its current conditions, its
major markets, and the factors which influence its sales potential are
given in trade and market surveys. Subscribers are told what customers
and prospects sell, how much they sell, and what they buy. Biweekly
and monthly reports point up those changes—markets, products, purchases, and distribution.

Textiles. All phases of textile manufacturing are included in this
division, the oldest in the company. Thus a discussion of its operation
and reports will serve to illustrate how the several divisions of National Credit Office, Inc., operate. Of particular interest is the cut-up

trade-manufacturers of men's and women's wear. This division of the textile industry presents a greater credit problem than perhaps other lines of trade for the reason that a style element predominates and is a direct influence in the success or failure of a concern. Manufacturers of apparel have highly seasonal operations with spring and fall peaks. A manufacturer of popular price women's wear, for example, may have no liabilities on June 30 and Dec. 31, the dates that would probably be selected for financial statements.

Three months later at the peak of manufacturing operations, however, liabilities might be several times as large as net worth. Concerns in the cutting-up trade operate upon a small margin of profit and aim at large sales volume. Where liabilities are at times great as compared to tangible net worth, a concern, if it misses the current styles or fails to market its output rapidly enough to meet maturing obligations, must sell its accumulated inventories at a loss, which frequently wipes out the owner's meager capital and necessitates voluntary bankruptcy or liquidation. This hazardous field is divided by the agency into thirteen divisions under the direction of six managers, who are responsible for the quality, speed, and thoroughness of the reports prepared in their respective divisions.

No reference book is published and no ratings are used. Each report, whether a full or short one, contains a summary in which a specific line of credit such as $1,000, $1,500, $5,000, requirements, or no line, is definitely suggested. The amount of the suggested line of credit in theory is determined by dividing the normal seasonal purchase requirements of the concern by the number of its merchandise suppliers. Thus, a concern which would normally purchase $60,000 of goods as its requirements for each season and would make these purchases from 30 distributors would receive a recommended line of $2,000. When a subscriber supplies an account with the larger part of his requirements, the agency may recommend a special credit line in proportion to the subscriber's importance as a supplier.

Subscribers to the Textile Department furnish well over 90 per cent of the piece goods requirements to the various divisions of the cutting-up trade. Banks which may have accounts in that industry are also daily users of the service. Out-of-town members are actively served by teletype or telegraph.

Credit Reports. By means of a tickler system reports are revised automatically, two or four times a year, depending upon the degree of risk, with special revision whenever need for special revision is indicated. A master card for each concern is maintained. When an inquiry is received, a file copy of the report is immediately mailed to the inquiring subscriber and the number of the subscriber and the date recorded on

NCO *Specialized Service*   **CURRENT INFORMATION**

```
TAILORED APPAREL CO.    MFRS. MEN'S SUITS
FZ:HL-111-A             SPORT COATS & SLACKS   PHILADELPHIA 47, PA.
                        APRIL 18,              245 N. Spring St.
```

ANTECEDENT COMMENT - Records clear. Established 1940. Various
changes since. John Phillips dominant factor. Amply experienced
and well regarded personally. Successful. Also an officer of
affiliated contracting unit Vance Clothing Co. Inc. and Vice-
Pres. of Summer Wear Co. Inc. (separately reported by NCO) since
inception in 1950. Subject specializes in woolen and worsted
clothing while Summer Wear Co. Inc. manufacture suits of
synthetic fabrics only. Subject manufacturers medium price line.

CONDITION AND TREND -	11/30	11/30	11/30
Cash	32,000	$ 29,000	$ 49,000
Receivables	210,000	313,000	480,000
Merchandise	59,000	348,000	240,000
Due from Affil.	-	59,000	6,000
Current Assets	301,000	749,000	775,000
Current Debts	130,000	580,000	540,000
Working Capital	171,000	169,000	235,000
Net Worth	208,000	293,000	357,000
Sales	1,802,000	2,310,000	3,016,000

Auditor: Dennis & Kaufman, C.P.A.

TRADE - GOOD

	HIGH CREDIT	OWING	PAST DUE	TERMS	PAYMENTS
	$33,000	33,000	0	60/60	ppt
	30,000	25,000	0	60	ppt
Over	25,000	15,000	0	60/60	ppt-ant
	29,000	19,000	0	60	ppt-ant
	25,000	2,000	0	60	ppt
	23,000	23,000	0	60	ppt
Over	10,000	1,200	0	60	ppt
	10,000	1,800	0	60/60	ppt

Since inception in 1940 payments usually prompt or better with purchases generally in 60 or 70 days. Occasionally extended 60 plus
60 terms.   -continued-

FIG. 18. National Credit Office, Inc., credit report.

the master card. Through this record, subscribers are furnished revised reports and current financial statements for a year after making
an inquiry. When the year is up, the subscriber is given an opportunity
to renew the service if he is still interested in the account.

A typical full report is partly reproduced in Fig. 18. The first page, it
will be noted, gives the concern's name and address and the names of

the officers or the principals at interest. Then follow a brief synopsis giving the high points of the record of the principals; trend of the business; its summarized current financial position and trend; a current trade investigation; names of the important sources of supply; analysis of the record and financial condition; ending with the suggested definite line of credit. The full report which expands the business record of the principals and of the business as well as the method of operation, and the name of the bank or banks is reproduced in Appendix D. The agency reproduces the latest financial balance sheet, generally on the agency's standardized form, by means of a photographic copy.

C.I.A. Report. In contrast to the detailed antecedent report (C1), all departments except Bank Service use a concise report (C.I.A.), particularly for smaller companies. The antecedent information is brief, new information is highlighted, financial data are summarized, and repetition is avoided. Thus both the subscriber and reporter may each save time in the need to scan or prepare a one-page report. On the other hand, when necessary because of the growth of a business and greater subscriber interest in the company, the C.I.A. report is expanded to the more detailed report. An example of the C.I.A. report is shown in Fig. 19.

Other Departments. Service given to subscribers in other departments is, in the main, similar to that given in the Textile Department. The primary function of the National Credit Office, Inc., is the thorough periodic investigation, analysis, and editing of comprehensive credit reports by trained specialists and the extending of credit advice to its subscribers in the lines of industry and commerce which have been enumerated. The one fundamental difference in the operation of all departments is found in the Metals and Electronic and the Automotive Credit Service Departments, where reference books are published bi-monthly. Also, a monthly list is released showing all changes of credit suggestion either favorable or unfavorable.

Group Meetings. The National Credit Office conducts or participates in fifteen credit discussion groups in the textile, metals, leather, and paint fields. The group members constitute the principal suppliers to the particular industries. They meet periodically, usually monthly, to discuss companies that are credit problems, conditions in the industry, and new government regulations. These meetings also afford an opportunity for credit men to become better acquainted with others in their field and thus lay a basis for personal exchange of information.

Credit News. A weekly *N.C.O. Credit News* is issued by the major departments of the National Credit Office. This includes a list of all significant credit changes such as financial embarrassments, revision in credit suggestions, new financing, and changes in trade payment record or

```
                        SAMPLE          C.I.A.REPORT


BROWN CO., Inc., GEORGE D.    ELECTRONIC PARTS      LANCASTER, PA.
WAD:MM-19-B                       JOBBER            200 Delaware Ave.
                             Sept. 24, 19---

George D. Brown, Pres.-Treas.-Dir.        Carl W. Brown, Vice-Pres.-Dir.
Mrs. Florence R. Smith, Sec.-Dir.         C. A. Strauss, Dir.

NEW INFORMATION - For the first seven months of 19-- sales declined 10%
largely the result of industrial conditions in the coal and nylon hoisery
industries. Operations claimed to be profitable.

BACKGROUND - Record clear. Established 1934. Incorporated 1946. George
D. Brown the founder and controlling stockholder. Born 1886. Carl W.
Brown, son of the Pres. Born 1914. Active many years here. Charge of
purchases. Management has shown ability.

NATURE OF BUSINESS - Sells primarily to dealers and service men. Branch
Pottstown, Pa.   Employs 40.

FINANCIAL            12/31/--      12/31/--       12/31/--

Cash             $   13,000    $  39,200     $  25,200
Receivables         134,000       168,100       185,300
Merchandise         217,000       195,200       199,700

Current Assets      364,000       402,500       410,200
Current Debts       154,000       187,900       109,400
Working Capital     210,000       214,600       219,800

Net Worth           238,000       246,600       271,200

Accountant:  Marks Trade

TRADE - EXCELLENT
          HIGH CREDIT    OWING      PAST DUE      TERMS        PAYMENTS
       $    15,600      7,400          0       2/10th prox       dis
            2,300        300           0       prox              dis
            2,000         0            0       2/10th prox       dis
            1,900        400           0       2/10/30           dis
            1,800        800           0       2/10/25           dis
            1,700        300           0       10/25             dis
            1,500         0            0       2/10th prox       dis
SUPPLIERS
Precision Apparatus              RCA-Victor
Allianco Mfg. Co.                J.F.D. Manufacturing Co.

BANK   Seventh National Bank, Lancaster, Pa.

ANALYSIS - Steady progressive trend over long period of years. Inves-
ment strengthened considerably through the retention of earnings. During
the last year part of the working funds went towards a $20,000 expansion
in fixed assets.

Sound financial condition maintained right along. Company has never had
difficulty in handling trade bills.

Satisfactory non-borrowing bank account.

CREDIT SUGGESTION - AVERAGE LINE  $5,000.            March 195_
```

FIG. 19.   C.I.A. Report, National Credit Office, Inc.

management. Also comments are included on industry conditions and major credit facts.

Independently of these surveys, reports are also edited by reporting department heads on market-wide developments and situations in their respective lines. These reports, issued at irregular intervals or as the situation demands, are called *Current Comments.*

Lyon Furniture Mercantile Agency.   This is one of the older mercantile agencies.   It is a special trade agency, which started business in 1876, since which time it has published semiannual books of ratings covering furniture, floor covering, upholstering, bedding, interior decorating, undertaking, and kindred lines of industry in the United States. It had a competitor in the Furniture Commercial Agency Company from 1890 until 1917, when the two agencies merged and continued with the present name.   The agency has attained a position of high importance as a credit authority in the lines of industry covered.   Its executive office is in New York City with seven branch offices located in important trade centers throughout the country.

Its membership, according to its statement, numbers about 95 per cent of all manufacturers and wholesalers selling in the lines of trade that it covers.   With so large a percentage of the industries as subscribers it is obvious that the agency wields a considerable influence.

Method of Operation.   This is one of the agencies which operates quite similarly to Dun & Bradstreet, Inc., with the exception that its activities are confined exclusively to the special lines of industry mentioned above.   An outline of its service to its subscribers includes reference books issued semiannually in the months of January and July, with weekly reports and supplements.   The latter give records of changes in ratings, new businesses, dissolutions, successions, assignments, receiverships, trusteeships, failures, bankruptcy petitions, current business changes, and accounts placed for collection.   The current reference book is thus augmented by a continuous supplement.

The reference book, known as the *Lyon-Red Book*, through its ratings gives the subscriber credit conditions and capital and pay ratings. Traveler's editions in pocket size are available for any state or group of states.   In addition to names and data in reference to subject, the book includes under each city and town the name of a bank or banker and the population. (For ratings see Fig. 20.)

All Lyon's subscribers are given a weekly publication which records changes in ratings, new businesses, successions, fires, failures, suits, judgments, and claims.   The customer thus receives the changes as they occur and is able to take prompt action.

Trade experience of subscribers is obtained by means of a weekly "tracer sheet" which lists subjects throughout the country selected for that week's trade investigation.   When the "tracer sheets" are in, and the trade experience has been tabulated, a "result" sheet is mailed to those subscribers who have cooperated by submitting their experiences with the various names listed (see Fig. 21).

The agency furnishes its subscribers with credit reports based on careful investigation, furnishing information under the following head-

Form 93

LYON RED BOOK — CREDIT KEY

CAPITAL RATINGS	PAY RATINGS
Estimated Financial Worth	Based on suppliers' reports

A		$1,000,000	or over
B		500,000	to $1,000,000
C		300,000	to 500,000
D		200,000	to 300,000
E		100,000	to 200,000
G		75,000	to 100,000
H		50,000	to 75,000
J		40,000	to 50,000
K		30,000	to 40,000
L		20,000	to 30,000
M		15,000	to 20,000
N		10,000	to 15,000
O		7,000	to 10,000
Q		5,000	to 7,000
R		3,000	to 5,000
S		2,000	to 3,000
T		1,000	to 2,000
U		500	to 1,000
V		100	to 500

Z—No financial basis for credit reported.

INDEFINITE RATINGS

F—Estimated financial responsibility not definitely determined, presumed high.

P—Estimated financial responsibility not definitely determined, presumed moderate.

W—Estimated financial responsibility not definitely determined, presumed small.

Y—Estimated financial responsibility not definitely determined, presumed very limited.

The omission of a rating is not unfavorable, but indicates that sufficient information is not at hand on which to base rating.

1—Discount.
2—Prompt.
3—Medium.
4—Variable, prompt to slow
5—Slow.
6—Very slow.
7—C. O. D. or C. B. D.

8—Pay rating not established, but information favorable.
9—Claims to buy always for cash.

SPECIAL CONDITIONS

12—Business recently commenced.
13—Inquire for report.
21—Buys small, usually pays cash.
23—Sells on commission.
24—Name listed for convenience only.
29—Rating undetermined.
31—Financial statement declined, or repeatedly requested and not received.

SYMBOL INTERPRETATION

● or 12 — Business recently commenced.
✦ or 116 —New statement recently received.
▲—Indicates information of unusual importance.
⊙—Sells on installment plan.
(?)—Sells from residence, office or catalogue.

CREDIT GRANTORS—NOTE

No system of ratings can ALWAYS convey an accurate summarization of existing conditions. Book ratings reflect conditions believed to exist when assigned, and are based upon information obtained from financial statements, from the trade, special reporters, correspondents, financial institutions and other sources deemed reliable, but the correctness thereof is in no way guaranteed.

Conditions are constantly changing, and changes as made are shown in the "LYON Weekly Supplement and Report", and in Lyon Credit Reports.

Should any error, or inaccuracy in rating be noted, it should be reported only to the Agency, in order that correction may be made.

Inquire for Detailed Credit Report on all NEW ACCOUNTS, and make inquiry at least once a year on old accounts or when change in rating is indicated in the "LYON Weekly Supplement and Report".

(OVER)

FIG. 20a. Lyon-Red Book—key to rating.

ings: Antecedents; General Information; Financial Information; Summarized and Current Financial Statements; Analyses; Bank and Trade Investigations; Lyon Weekly Interchange of Trade Experience Results; Collection Records; and Summary. In so far as possible, the agency endeavors to anticipate failures, and through its system subscribers are kept posted on weak, questionable, or failing customers.

Collection Department. Apart from its service in supplying credit information, a main function is the collection of delinquent accounts.

SPECIAL RATINGS

Key Numbers interpreting Credit Items and
Business Conditions; as appear in

LYON WEEKLY SUPPLEMENT AND REPORT

12 or ●—Business recently commenced.

13—Inquire for report.

21—Buys small, usually pays cash.

23—Sells on commission.

24—Name listed for convenience only.

29—Rating undetermined.

30—Rating in abeyance, pending later information.

31—Financial statement declined, or repeatedly requested and not received.

47—New ownership or change in ownership.

49—Dissolved.

50—Succeeded by —

51—Rating raised to —

52—Rating lowered to —

54—Rating suspended.

55—Given bill of sale, or notice thereof.

56—Reported selling out, or discontinuing.

57—Have sold out.

58—Sold out at auction.

59—Damaged by water.

60—Damaged by flood or storm.

61—Damaged by fire.

62—Burned out.

63—Partially insured.

64—Fully insured.

65—Inventory not insured.

66—No insurance.

67—Will continue.

68—Deceased.

69—Estate continues.

70—Claim placed for collection with Lyon Agency.

75—Suit reported.

76—Execution issued.

77—Judgment reported.

78—Attachment proceedings reported.

79—Closed by Sheriff or Marshal.

80—Sold out by Sheriff or Marshal.

81—Chattel mortgage.

82—Chattel mortgage foreclosed.

83—Deed of trust for benefit of creditors.

85—Real estate mortgage foreclosed.

87—Assignment for benefit of creditors.

88—Petition for Receiver filed.

89—Temporary Receiver appointed.

90—Receiver appointed.

91—In hands of Receiver.

92—Voluntary petition in bankruptcy.

93—Involuntary petition in bankruptcy.

94—Petition for arrangement, reorganization extension or composition.

95—In bankruptcy.

96—Inquire for important new report.

98—Trustee appointed.

99—In liquidation to discontinue business.

100—First dividend paid.

101—Second dividend paid.

102—Final dividend paid.

103—Asking extension.

104—Called meeting of creditors.

105—Offering to compromise.

106—Unable to locate.

107—Discontinued or out of business.

108—Claims should be given immediate attention.

109—Settled and resumed.

110—Settlement paid.

111—Removed to —

113—Capital stock increased to —

114—Name changed to —

115—Cannot report definitely as yet.

116 or ✚—New statement recently received.

117—Received discharge in bankruptcy.

118—Discharge in bankruptcy denied.

119—Not for book listing.

120—Discontinue book listing.

(OVER)

FIG. 20*b*.   Lyon-Red Book—key to rating.   (*Continued.*)

The collection department is also a valuable source of information for its credit-reporting division. Through the close cooperation between the credit and collection departments the agency is in a position to advise subscribers promptly when a subject begins to run slow in payments. The subjects themselves are aware of the authority that the agency wields, and this has a tendency to induce them to pay as promptly as they are able or as promptly as the standard terms of the industry may require.

In addition to the services already described, the agency endeavors to maintain a close supervision over all subjects reported. Inquiries of subscribers are closely watched, and through these and trade investigations any sudden increase disclosed in the purchases of a subject is noted, and an explanation requested. Overbuying with or without fraudulent intention is often detected, and subscribers warned.

Discussion of Agency Service. A question may arise as to whether it is the proper function of an agency to serve the credit manager only in

LYON WEEKLY INTERCHANGE OF TRADE EXPERIENCE
"RESULT" of "TRACER" No. 35
CONDUCTED BY
LYON FURNITURE MERCANTILE AGENCY

Sent only to subscribers who *co-operate*, and give the ledger and paying record of their customers.

EXPLANATION.— The numbers in first column denote the number of houses reporting. The 1-2-3-5-6-7 at head of next columns are Lyon Red Book "Pay Ratings," and numbers under them denote number of houses reporting on each condition.
A number in parenthesis in the "Amount Reported Owing" or "Amount Reported Past Due" column indicates the number of houses reporting.

This information is strictly confidential for your exclusive use as an aid in granting credit. Any disclosure to the parties whose names appear is a violation of the terms of your contract with the Lyon Furniture Mercantile Agency.

Result of Tracer No. 35 | ISSUED ONLY TO THOSE WHO ANSWER THE "TRACER" | OCTOBER 24.

■ Funeral Director exclusively.

No. of Houses Reporting	1	2	3	5	6	7	AMOUNT REPORTED OWING	AMOUNT REPORTED PAST DUE
14	11	1	1			1	(7) 7510	(1) 160
5	5						(2) 5546	
7	1	3	2	1			(1) 200	
10	2	4	3	1			(4) 860	
10	2	1	2	1	1	3	(5) 423	(2) 74
5	4	1					(1) 50	
10		1	5	2	2	1	)6) 3397	(2) 1261
10	5	3	2				(4) 817	(1) 274
4	4						(2) 1047	
11	2	3	2	2	1		(6) 764	
9	3	1	1	1	1	2	(4) 11373	(1) 2500
10	1	3	2	2	1	1	(2) 454	(1) 75
4	3		1					
5	3	2					(1) 278	
3	1	1	1				(2) 5027	
3	2	1					(2) 512	
16	3		2	6	4	1	(8) 2651	(5) 1384
8	1	2	3	1			(3) 714	(1) 157
6	5	1					(2) 760	
2	2							
13	3	5	3	2			(6) 1459	(1) 475
7	6	1						
4	1	2	1				(1) 207	
14	12	2					(4) 3199	
8	7	1					(1) 177	
13	10	2	1				(1) 39	
6	5	1					(2) 372	
4	4						(2) 523	
10	2	3	1	2	1		(2) 639	
4	2						(1) 152	

■ Funeral Director exclusively.

No. of Houses Reporting	1	2	3	5	6	7	AMOUNT REPORTED OWING	AMOUNT REPORTED PAST DUE
7	2	3	2					
4	3	1						
16	13	3					(1) 120	
15	10	4	1				(3) 776	(1) 177
4	3	1						
6	1	1	2	1			(2) 1332	(2) 1197
2	2							
9	6	2	1				(2) 1387	(1) 194
6	1	1	1	1	2		(2) 907	(2) 907
35	30	5					(12) 10663	
16	12	4					(6) 13994	
25	13	7	3	2			(7) 2755	(1) 135
14	5	3	5		1		(5) 910	(1) 21
10	2		4	1	3		(4) 1215	(2) 524
6		2		2	1	1	(1) 550	(1) 120
23	20	3					(5) 1697	
11	7	3	1				(2) 943	(1) 79
10	7	2	1				(3) 492	
10	3	3	2	1	1		(5) 5798	(2) 4927
9	1			1	2	5	(2) 2038	(2) 1374
11	9	2					(1) 73	
13	8	3	1	1			(1) 45	
17	15	1	1				(1) 898	
8	2	1		3	2		(5) 708	(3) 333
18	7	6	3	2			(8) 4078	(3) 245
12	3	3	4	2			(5) 1392	
26	15	7	3				(6) 4393	
8	4	2	1		1		(1) 94	
7	2	2		3			(2) 136	
5	2	2	1				(1) 1176	
4						4	(2) 421	(1) 299
3	3		2	2			(2) 2030	(1) 758
6	4	2						
4	4						(1) 141	
4	3	1					(1) 160	

(OVER)

FIG. 21. Lyon Weekly Interchange "result."

gathering credit information or if it should add to that function the interpretation of the information and the conclusion as to the desirability of credit. Many agencies combine the two functions, and they do so because, obviously, they have a demand for both types of service. Rating books provide a service which, in a sense, stands halfway between a conclusion as to credit and credit data. When an agency supplies credit data, the value of its service depends upon the completeness and accuracy of those data. Assuming both completeness and accuracy of the information, the credit manager has before him all the factors necessary to be considered. The adaptation of the risk to his concern's credit policy is possible.

When an agency undertakes a checking service, several questions may arise in the credit manager's mind. If the agency relies largely upon trade experience, it should be at least representative. The credit manager will sometimes wonder if a debtor's creditors are fully represented on the agency's records. The subscriber may raise a doubt, too, concerning the ability of the agency representative to interpret correctly the data at hand; he may hesitate to accept the judgment of one whom he does not know and has never seen. And, too, there is much rigidity in the recommendations made. In a recommendation to ship, the risk may be too great for the subscriber who must necessarily demand a high standard of credit, while, in another case, a refusal to recommend might preclude a risk that another subscriber would be entirely willing to accept.

To concerns whose volume of business does not warrant the employment of a credit manager the service may be of much value. It may be used, also, to confirm the credit manager's decision, based on information received from other sources, or the recommendation may be used in those cases where an immediate decision is urgently demanded.

Another angle is to be considered. The agency through its recommendation, provided its subscribers are complete enough and follow its recommendations, controls the credit of the purchaser. A question seriously to be pondered is whether or not it is for the public good that an agency should have the power and responsibility of determining the businessman's destiny through the use of his credit. This question may be raised in connection with all agencies which undertake to control their subscriber's decisions.

The Interchange of Credit Experience. It may be stated that complete information, correctly interpreted, concerning a credit applicant's character, capacity, capital, and the condition of business will establish very exactly his credit power. The credit analyst may thus appraise the applicant's willingness and ability to pay, but the analysis of the risk may be verified or proved wrong by ascertaining how he does actually take care of his credit obligations. The two methods are complementary to each other, and both are used by nearly all credit men in the analysis of each risk.

The debtor's record is written in the ledgers of his creditors. To obtain ledger experience, which is complete and reliable, with the least expense and duplication of effort has long been a problem of credit men. The mercantile agencies, commendable as may be their services in other respects, have failed to furnish reports with complete and up-to-date ledger information. Direct interchange is somewhat expensive and may be far from complete, although it is not intended to suggest that direct communication among credit men in regard to their mutual customers should be supplanted.

The following chapter shows how credit clearing and related activities assist in credit evaluation.

TEXT AND RESEARCH QUESTIONS

1. Contrast the methods of operation of the National Credit Office and the Lyon Furniture Mercantile Agency.

2. List and briefly explain four weak points in the value of commercial ratings.

3. Of what value are commercial paper reports of the National Credit Office?

4. Why does the C.I.A. report appeal to subscribers?

5. What is the weakness in the plan of those agencies which furnish only derogatory information to subscribers?

6. The *Lyon-Red Book* rates a business N 5 75. What does this mean?

7. Compare the strong and weak points of the general agency with those of special agencies.

8. How do you account for the fact that the National Credit Office does not issue a rating book in its textile division?

9. What are the weaknesses of the method of the interchange of information?

10. Should a credit manager utilize the services of both Dun & Bradstreet, Inc., and a special agency? Why?

PROBLEMS

1. Your credit manager has just referred to you an order amounting to $649 for a number of pieces of casual furniture. You do not find the name in your files but you do find it in the *Lyon-Red Book* rated M 5 116. What does this tell you about the account? How will you handle the order?

2. Refer to the report on Tailored Apparel Co., in Appendix D. Write a full report on the

(a) Character, (b) Capacity, (c) Capital, and
(d) Business Conditions factors of the risk.
(e) Would you sell Tailored Apparel Co. on open account? Discuss.

CHAPTER 16

CREDIT INTERCHANGE SERVICE

If an examination were made of the files of creditors, it would be found that the contents of those files could be divided into three general classifications. One of these would cover the subject's record, or, in the credit manager's parlance, antecedent information. A second would deal with financial structure information, while the third would cover more or less completely the "ledger experience" of other creditors. It is with the last type of credit information that this chapter deals.

A Specialized Service. Ledger experience, or the record of how a debtor pays his bills, is an outgrowth of the recommendation, or "reference," with which businessmen a century ago used to fortify themselves when seeking new creditors. The new creditor eventually came to seek ledger experience direct from the old. To facilitate the exchange of ledger experience, the first Credit Interchange Bureau was established about the first of the present century. Various other bureaus soon followed, and in 1912 a Central Bureau was opened in St. Louis to enable the various local bureaus to exchange information, thus widen their sources of information, and so increase the value of their service. In 1919, the National Association of Credit Men took over the Central Bureau at St. Louis and have operated it ever since under the Credit Interchange Bureau Department of the National Association of Credit Management. While there are competing services, some of which will be referred to later, this section refers principally to the two largest clearance groups, which are the Credit Interchange Bureaus (trade credit) and National Retail Credit Association (consumer credit). The latter group, in addition, clear reports on delinquents.

That there is full justification for such a service is at once apparent. Since antecedent information varies but little during the course of a year and, in fact, may not change at all, and since new financial information is generally available only once a year, the question arises as to why ledger experience, which is an everyday record, should be shackled to the more slowly changing parts of the usual credit report. Either the creditor must pay for and read the same antecedent and capital structure information each time that he wishes to revise his credit information, or he must forego the benefit derived from following from time to time his customer's paying ability.

Service without Profit. The Credit Interchange Bureau is a medium only for the assembling and distributing of ledger facts. It has studiously avoided the offering of any recommendations or opinions, leaving to the individual credit man the task of determining whether each individual order and risk would properly match up. It strives to give ledger facts on a national scale. It is under the control of creditors themselves, but no creditor or group of creditors is in a position to dominate the bureau to their own selfish ends. Owned and operated by creditors themselves and for service to themselves, subscribers pay only the cost of operation. Credit experience belongs to creditors, and, always ready to exchange it with each other, they have provided their own medium for doing so.

A Means to Avoid Duplication. Credit experience was at first interchanged directly between creditors. Assuming 20 creditors of a single debtor, each of whom sought the experience of all the others, each would answer 19 inquiries on the same name, or 380 altogether, where 20 would have sufficed had there been a medium to circulate them among all. Privately owned agencies might also have interrogated the 20 creditors in our imaginary case, thus swelling the duplication of expense and effort and adding to the confusion that now abounds in this feature of credit work. The Credit Interchange Bureau offers a medium for cutting out at least most of the direct interchange—a job similar to that handled by the Federal Reserve in clearing checks. Whether credit men should take a bold position and insist that all ledger experience, except direct communication between creditors, should be cleared through one source is a question which lies somewhat in the future. It would reduce fraud, and possibly overbuying.

Need for National Clearance. Ledger experience, for the most part, has been available to credit men only on a restricted basis. Debtors have volunteered as references only those supply houses certain to give favorable information, and it has been difficult to get the names of other creditors through other sources. Creditors have formed trade groups, which will be further described in a subsequent section, for the purpose of exchanging credit experiences. These have not proved entirely satisfactory, for these groups are local and not national, and frequently a customer either buys from only one house in an industry or buys from only one house in an industry in a locality. The trade group therefore finds among its members only one creditor interested in the name and possessing information on it.

The only practical basis of effecting cooperation between creditors is to accept the customer himself as the basis for that cooperation. The aim is to bring the creditors of that customer together regardless of the lines of business in which they may be engaged, their locations, or the customer's location. A further purpose is that all creditors should have available to them a single medium through which a customer's buying and paying habits would be set forth.

Organization of the National Credit Interchange System. Fifty-seven bureaus, covering major and minor markets of the country, plus a co-ordinating unit, the Central Credit Interchange Bureau located in St. Louis, Mo., now constitute the National Credit Interchange System.

NAME...

TRADE STYLE...

STREET ADDRESS..

CITY.. STATE.......................................

·REPORT PROMPTLY ALL NEW AND RE-OPENED ACCOUNTS

This is important.   Your Bureau can serve you and other members better when its files are up-to-date.

CREDIT INTERCHANGE BUREAUS
NATIONAL ASSOCIATION OF CREDIT MEN   No.
F-9

FIG. 22.   Reporting new accounts.

The members of each local bureau own and operate the bureau under the supervision of a Local Association, or, in some instances, under the supervision of the National Association of Credit Management. The principle of member direction and control and service at cost prevails in all instances. These Credit Interchange Bureaus operate particularly in the trade area of credit, although there is some overlapping in smaller areas with retail clearing.

Operation of the National Credit Interchange System. Each participant in the service supplies the local bureau with a list of the accounts on his ledgers and supplements that list with new accounts as they are opened after the original list is filed. The form used for reporting new and reopened accounts is illustrated in Fig. 22. Bureaus further increase their sources of information by having members, at the time of making inquiry, supply the names of all other known creditors of the subject.

Each local bureau operates on a zone of operation basis, which is the normal trade territory of the market served by the bureau. Each bureau reports the names of all its members' customers outside its zone of operation to the bureaus in whose zone of operation the customers are located. Thus, the files of the local bureau on all subjects in its zone of operation constitute a record of all creditors selling a customer, as well as all markets in which he is buying. When a clearance is made, members of all bureaus selling the customer under investigation are canvassed for information without regard to industry or location.

MEMBER INQUIRY

Credit Interchange Bureaus

229 Fourth Ave. NEW YORK 3 · 1218 Chestnut St. PHILADELPHIA 7

PRO. NO.

SEND US REPORT ON: DATE..........................

NAME..........................

TRADE STYLE..........................

STREET ADDRESS..........................

TOWN.......................... STATE..........................

TYPE BUSINESS.......................... UNFILLED ORDER: $..........................

CHECK FOR AUTOMATIC REVISION:
☐ 4 MONTHS
☐

☐ SEND PRELIMINARY REPORT
☐ SEND ONLY THE COMPLETED REPORT

OUR EXPERIENCE: (REPORT DOLLARS ONLY)

HOW LONG SOLD	DATE OF LAST SALE	HIGH CREDIT	OWING (INCLUDE NOTES)	PAST DUE (INCLUDE NOTES)	TERMS OF SALE	MANNER OF PAYMENT
						☐ DISCOUNTS ☐ PAYS WHEN DUE .... DAYS SLOW

IMPORTANT LIST KNOWN SOURCES OF SUPPLY BELOW. THE BUREAU WILL MAKE EVERY EFFORT TO OBTAIN THEIR INFORMATION AND INCLUDE IT IN THE REPORT.

NAME ADDRESS

....
....
....
....
....
....

BANKS WITH..........................

MEMBER

F-1

FIG. 23. Inquiry and reporting form.

The zone of operation bureau is responsible for the compiling and writing of all reports on subjects in its territory. When a member makes an inquiry on a customer located in the zone of operation of the bureau receiving the inquiry, the files of the bureau will disclose the identity of creditors in the local market, as well as the identity of other markets throughout the country where the customer is buying. On advice from the zone of operation bureau, these markets accumulate information from interested creditors which is forwarded to the zone of operation bureau making the request, where the completed report is written. On request, copies of the report are placed in all markets in which the customer is buying merchandise. If, on the other hand, an inquiry is received by a bureau on a subject located in another bureau's zone of operation, the bureau receiving the inquiry canvasses its local members for information and immediately forwards the inquiry on to the zone of operation bureau in which the subject is located so a national clearance can be instituted.

An inquiring member receives, first, a copy of any report, or reports, less than 1 year old[1] at the time his inquiry is received; second, one or more preliminary reports containing revised information from local and nearby markets as it is available; third, and finally, a report containing information from all known creditors and references supplied by him and other members. This report thus becomes an up-to-date review of the buying and paying habits of the customers with all creditors whose interest it has been possible to discover.

Protection against Fraud. One of the commonest forms of commercial fraud is facilitated through the abuse of credit. In the credit man's parlance this is called buying for a "bust." A standard pattern is usually followed. Orders are broadcast in nominal amounts to every wholesaler and manufacturer whose name and location the "crook" can discover or whose salesmen call upon him. The one known method of combating this type of activity is to have some central reporting point to which all suppliers may transmit information on the orders received. First orders, unsolicited orders, or requests for samples, quotations, and catalogues when they are out of relation to the subject's reasonable activity, are very definite warnings to creditors. It is for that reason that Member Inquiry and Reporting Form (Fig. 23) covers these points.[2]

To revise its file or to make a new inquiry, the Bureau sends out a form to its members and possible suppliers requesting specific credit data. Thus a complete survey is obtained, including not only names supplied, which are generally the "good" suppliers, but also others who may have had difficulty with the account.

Analysis of Interchange Report. The tabulating of the reports received becomes the interchange report. Thus a Credit Interchange Report contains a veritable mine of information to those who analyze it carefully. Beginning with the left-hand column—Business Classification—the analyst has the opportunity of discovering the various types of

[1] Reports over 120 days old are revised, and a new report is sent to the inquiring member.

[2] Note that the inquiry is for others to give their data and at the same time report the inquirer's own experience.

merchandise handled by his customers and the number of individual concerns in each industry from whom this merchandise is purchased. A careful analysis of this column will often disclose that a customer's purchases of a given line of merchandise are being too greatly scattered among too many creditors and particularly among too many markets. When a customer is discovered to be buying certain types of merchandise from distant markets wherein it is known that cost of transportation is an important factor, it is generally found that there are reasons for it. It may indicate inability to maintain necessary credit requirements in the local market because of faulty paying habits. Very often it indicates inexperience and lack of business ability on the part of the customer. In some lines, it is a warning that the customer is attempting to carry too many varieties of merchandise. This is an important factor because it may indicate lack of organization or selling ability and an effort to maintain in stock every article of merchandise for which customers may ask. Unless the customer is operating a large establishment well financed and having a substantial volume of trade, this is always a potential source of difficulty for him. Similarly, in the event of liquidation, it means a badly broken-up stock not readily salable and generally composed of odd lots of merchandise for which there is no market.

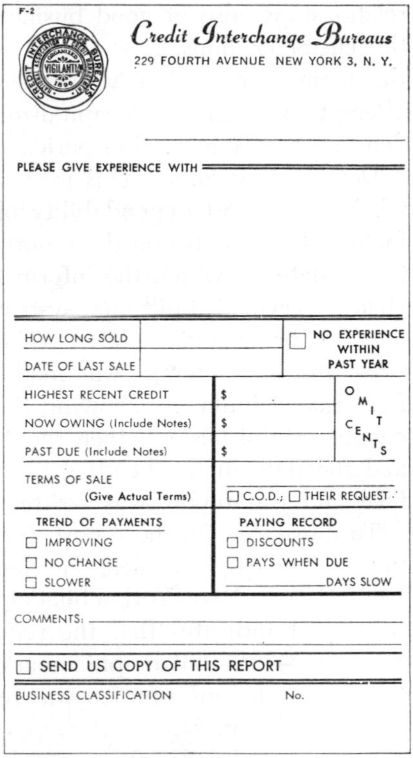
F-2

Credit Interchange Bureaus
229 FOURTH AVENUE NEW YORK 3, N. Y.

PLEASE GIVE EXPERIENCE WITH

HOW LONG SOLD
DATE OF LAST SALE
☐ NO EXPERIENCE WITHIN PAST YEAR
HIGHEST RECENT CREDIT $
NOW OWING (Include Notes) $
PAST DUE (Include Notes) $
OMIT CENTS
TERMS OF SALE (Give Actual Terms)
☐ C.O.D.; ☐ THEIR REQUEST
TREND OF PAYMENTS
☐ IMPROVING
☐ NO CHANGE
☐ SLOWER
PAYING RECORD
☐ DISCOUNTS
☐ PAYS WHEN DUE
______DAYS SLOW
COMMENTS:
☐ SEND US COPY OF THIS REPORT
BUSINESS CLASSIFICATION No.

FIG. 24. Form for reporting member's experience.

How Long Sold. This information does not usually indicate with any degree of accuracy the length of time in which the customer has been engaged in business. Because of present-day bookkeeping records it is difficult for creditors to establish accurately the date of their first sales to a given customer. The information, however, is important in determining the degree of confidence which creditors seem to place in the account. It is particularly important in checking against possibility of fraud, since, unless a concern is just beginning in business, a large number of comments showing that the account has just recently been opened is an indication of difficulty or impending trouble. It may mean that the customer is obliged to shift his source of supply because of unsatisfactory credit relationships, or it may mean that he is either deliberately or unwisely accumulating unreasonably large amounts of merchandise. Information that a substantial number of creditors have been selling an account for a considerable period of time is an indicator of satisfactory relationships, also of good business ability and judgment on the part of the customer himself, showing as it does due regard for obligations; the maintenance of a well-ordered, carefully selected stock; and an attempt continuously to capitalize on the advertising which he may have done over a considerable period of time.

Date of Last Sale. This is an important column on the report. The whole value and dependability of the report are dependent upon this factor. Other dates on the report may or may not have any relationship to the date on which the information was gathered. The Credit Interchange Service is built on a system which guarantees the impossibility of juggling or changing dates. The series of dates on the report show when the first attempt was made to gather information. The Date of Last Sale column, by showing the date of the last sale of the creditor, clearly establishes whether the information is reasonably up to date, and the date in the heading of the report indicates that on which the final and full report was written.

To illustrate: On the report shown in Fig. 25, in the left-hand column, under Business Classification, New York–Philadelphia is shown a number 921–50. New York–Philadelphia being the first market shown on the report indicates that the request for the information originated in the New York–Philadelphia market, and the figure 921 indicates that the request for information was received by the New York–Philadelphia Bureau on Sept. 21.

In the left-hand column, under the Baltimore market appears the number 923-1104, indicating that the request originating in Baltimore was received in the Baltimore bureau on Sept. 23 and that members of that bureau were canvassed for information as of that date.

The Date of Last Sale. This column is the acid test of the information, since it at all times shows whether the experience indicated covers recent transactions or is generally out of date. Compared with How Long Sold, Date of Last Sale is an important factor in determining the degree of confidence placed in the customer by the creditors.

One of the definite and certain ways by which creditors can avoid some bad-debt loss is for them to make it a general practice to check carefully all of the dates given in connection with ledger experience information accumulated from any source and particularly dates of last sale

FORM 6

NATIONAL ASSOCIATION of CREDIT MEN

Credit Interchange Report

Guarding the Nation's Profits

OFFICES IN PRINCIPAL CITIES

---------------------- & CO   --------------NEW JERSEY   OCTOBER 7, 19__
                                   -------------COUNTY

The accuracy of this Report is not guaranteed. Its contents are gathered in good faith from members and sent to you by this Bureau without liability for negligence in procuring, collecting, communicating or failing to communicate the information so gathered.

BUSINESS CLASSIFICATION	HOW LONG SOLD	DATE OF LAST SALE	HIGHEST RECENT CREDIT	NOW OWING INCLUDING NOTES	PAST DUE	TERMS OF SALE	PAYING RECORD			COMMENTS
							DIS-COUNTS	PAYS WHEN DUE	DAYS SLOW	
NEW YORK PHILADELPHIA 921-50										
Elec	2yrs	9-5_	1854	1500	644	10px		x	30-60	
Drg	yrs	9-5_	1263	201		30		x		
Pvl	2-43	9-5_	3867	316		30		x		
Mtr	1944	8-5_	2044	2044	1218	30			60	Slower
Ppr	4-48	9-5_	422	422	422	2-10n30			60-90	
Ppr	yrs	9-5_	320	320	320	1-10	x			
Inds	6-46	8-5_	569			Net 30		x		
Hfgs	yrs	8-5_	141			2-10-30				Has cr. bal. returned mdse was 30-90 days slow.
WESTERN PA 923-519										
Fdp	yrs	9-5_	1657			2-10			30	
Chem	2-49	9-5_	3109	1215	438	30		x	45	Slower
NEW ENGLAND 923-103										
Chem	yrs	8-5_	10508	1975	328	1-10-30		x	20	
BALTIMORE 923-1104										
Fdp	4-44	9-5_	6672	530		Spec.		x		
Hdwe	yrs	9-5_.	1210	900		2-10-30	x		30	
NOR. WISC. MICHIGAN 923-501										
Ppr	6yrs	9-5_	880			2-10-30	x			
CLEVELAND 923-456										
GenM	yrs	9-5_	14304	1988	1040	1-10-30		x	10	
Inds	yrs	9-5_	9800	8040	8040	1-10-30			45	
Bu 77 ms										

FIG. 25. Credit interchange report.

as shown by creditors contributing information. Ledger experience is a most valuable type of information provided the date of accumulation is known. That information lacking, it can come to be a most dangerous type of information, as is indicated by the way in which fraud promoters sometimes utilize ratings based on ledger experience information for the promotion of their schemes.

Highest Recent Credit. This column is not intended to show the greatest amount of credit which would be allowed the customer. It is very frequently helpful, however, particularly in the case of concerns slow in payment, as a comparative figure against amount owing, a comparison which will show whether the customer is continuing his indebtedness at the highest mark established or is being successful in gradually reducing it. Generally speaking, when the total amount owing is equal to the total amount of high credit, it is a good indicator that the customer is at the maximum of his business difficulties, and it frequently presages difficulty.

Of course, this does not apply during periods when business is steadily improving and the customer's purchases increasing as a consequence. That sort of situation, however, is readily checked by reference to the manner of payment.

There is one exception to this, and that again is in the case of fraud. The professional fraud promoter always makes it a point to have his bills paid promptly up to the time he begins the promotion of his scheme. But some check against fraud has already been established, and some comments on it will be made later under other headings.

Amount Owing. Contrary to somewhat common belief, the Credit Interchange Service does not claim that the amount shown as owing on a report is representative of the total indebtedness of the customer. It varies quite materially from time to time according to seasons in various industries. Nevertheless, knowledge of the business in which the customer is engaged will enable the analyst to make comparisons of reports issued over a period of time which will be very helpful in determining the general trend of the customer's affairs.

Amount Past Due. This column needs little explanation. Generally speaking, it is the first indicator of difficulty on a report. When amounts owing are generally past due in total, a serious situation of affairs is indicated. At the same time, this column is a good barometer of improved conditions, as is illustrated on the report (Fig. 25) where the past-due amounts are generally less than the amount owing, and this information taken in connection with the date of last sale clearly indicates that here is an instance where creditors are working with a customer in an effort to overcome his difficulties. The sample reports in Appendix E indicate a worsening situation.

Terms of Sale. In itself, the information in this column is particularly valuable at times in analyzing manner of payment when it is indicated that there is a variation between the treatment of various creditors. Quite often, discounts of varying sizes result in the prompt attention to some accounts, while others offering no discount are permitted to run slow. The creditor, too, has the opportunity of determining the basis on which other creditors are selling the customer. It is often noted in slow-pay accounts that the terms are generally C.O.D., cash in advance, or sight draft bill of lading, which is in itself an indicator that other creditors have discontinued credit accommodations because of previous experience with the customer.

This is not to be taken literally, since there are many classifications of business where usual terms are C.O.D. or S.D./B.L., or these terms may be requested by the customer. Business classifications should always be checked carefully before arriving at any final conclusion with reference to these terms.

Manner of Payment. In the main, this is merely a summary of the experience of the creditors as indicated by the preceding columns on the report. In effect, it is the summary of the experience in convenient form for quick, ready reference. It must be remembered, however, that the acid test of credit responsibility is not to be found merely in whether a customer discounts, pays when due, or permits his account to run slow. There are many other important contributory factors outlined in the other phases of the report which must be carefully studied if a clear and accurate analysis of the account is to be made. It must be remembered that there are many lines of industry in which terms are such as to make it almost essential that a customer discount his bills if he is to continue his credit accommodations.

Particular care should be exercised in analyzing the affairs of those customers where the manner of payment information is contradictory. Generally, there are good and sufficient reasons for variations. Terms, discounts, personal acquaintanceship, policies in an industry, or a market —all have a bearing on manner of payment.

Similarly, here again is a point where date of last sales is of vital importance, since in many instances where manner of payment seems to be contradictory, an investigation will disclose that the variation is due largely to the time element; that is, a customer may have been slow on purchases made 6 months ago but be discounting his accounts with those who have sold him recently, thus clearly indicating that he is making progress. When the reverse is true, it is likewise an indication that the customer is losing ground.

It is unfortunate but true that in many instances the only analysis made of credit interchange report is a casual glance at the manner of payment. Excepting only for those accounts which are very good or very unsatisfactory, this method of analysis can be both erroneous and costly. No single column or phase of the report can stand alone. The report represents an accumulation of those facts which experienced credit executives have determined are essential to an accurate appraisal of a customer's standing. Manner of payment alone is not satisfactory.

It must be analyzed only in the light of the important facts which appear elsewhere on the report.

Comments. In general, comments are only an elaboration on facts stated elsewhere on the report. They are particularly valuable, however, in the case of those customers who make it a general practice to take unearned discounts, make unauthorized returns of merchandise, and do those other things which are generally considered as unethical practices. Conversely, they are often helpful as a delineator of the progress being made by a customer.

Comparison of Reports.[1] As indicated elsewhere, when a member makes a request for a credit interchange report, the general practice is immediately to send him a copy of any previous clearance in the files of the bureau. Oftentimes this information is more up to date than the member can secure through any other source. In every instance, it is valuable for comparative purposes.

All the facts are disclosed by that comparison. Not only is the improvement in the paying record shown, but in analysis of such columns as High Credit, Amount Owing, Amount Past Due, etc., those columns are generally very clear indices of progress or lack of progress. This is not only with reference to the general standing of the customer but also it indicates whether he is conducting his business in accord with the general trend of affairs, whether his purchases are being reduced when business is slacking up, whether they are increased when business is improving, and whether he is either reducing or increasing his inventory as business justifies. A little study and analysis of comparisons will quickly enable the credit manager to develop a vast fund of vital and valuable information from these comparisons.

In Conclusion. A credit interchange report is a clear, well-arranged, and organized statement of facts. Information of a personal nature is never permitted to enter into it. The personal opinion of individual creditors is not incorporated. Contributors to the report are permitted to make a clear, frank statement of their experience with the customer and nothing more. The credit interchange bureaus make no attempt at recommendations. Many believe that much of the harm which has resulted from unwise credit in the past has come about through heads of business retaining and continuing credit departments as underpaid, underrated, unimportant adjuncts of the business; that this opinion of credit departments generally has as its foundation the belief that the credit manager is not obligated to use his own experience, knowledge, and judgment; that he can depend entirely upon ratings, recommendations, and conclusions prepared by and offered to him by outsiders. Operating on that basis, the credit manager becomes not an executive but merely a clerk.

[1] See Appendix E for a comparison of an eventual bankrupt.

The National Association of Credit Management recognizes that any improvement in the mercantile credits of the nation can be brought about only by gaining greater recognition from the heads of business of the importance of their credit departments and of the vital part that the credit manager plays in the welfare of the business. It is on this premise that the credit interchange bureaus have adopted the policy of confining their activities to the accumulating and distributing of facts—and facts only—placing these facts before the credit manager with the belief that he, because of his knowledge, experience, and ability, is in a much better position to analyze them than any outsider.

To illustrate this: The credit manager has before him two orders: one for merchandise on which there is a large profit; the other for items which are carried for accommodation of customers and generally sold at no profit or perhaps a slight loss. No outside organization, it is held, can make intelligent recommendations to govern under such circumstances. It must remain for the credit manager to secure the facts for himself and then be guided strictly by his own judgment and in the light of his experience and acquired knowledge of the business which he is serving.

What the Credit Interchange Bureaus do for trade creditors in specialized clearing service is similarly accomplished by the National Retail Credit Association for the retail merchants, bankers, and others, who finance consumer and instalment credit of individuals in the purchase of goods. In addition, this Association reports delinquencies.

The National Retail Credit Association. Few retailers of any size who accept consumer (retail) credit today function without the aid of organized credit interchange bureaus. The exceptions will be found principally among the many smaller neighborhood stores where local residents buy on credit in limited amounts on the basis of personal acquaintance with the proprietor. Remarkable progress has been made in the growth of cooperation among retailers in credit methods and techniques since the turn of the century.

In 1912 a National Association of Retail Credit Men was formed, and today is known as the National Retail Credit Association. It has a membership of over 46,000 retail establishments. These are served by more than 1,880 local credit bureaus, known as the Associated Credit Bureaus of America, through which members clear new applications for credit. These members furnish the paying habits of their customers upon request and report daily those accounts which have become delinquent. All bureaus operate more or less on the same plan.

These service bureaus cover every city, town, village, and crossroads in the United States and Canada. No agency has greater power for efficient credit control than these retail credit bureaus. Even small towns supporting only the local grocer, butcher, baker, etc., could profitably maintain a local credit bureau for the clearance of local names. A description of the operation of the Credit Bureau of Greater New York presents a clear view of the kinds of services rendered.

Credit Bureau of Greater New York. This bureau, one of the largest of the local bureaus, but typical of other bureaus in its operations, has a membership of over 1,200, which includes department stores, specialty shops, banks, hotels, finance companies, brokerage houses, real estate firms, automobile dealers, coal and oil companies, public utility concerns, credit card companies—nearly 100 classifications of business in all.   The bureau has on file the credit records of more than 6,500,000 individuals who have charge accounts in the territory known as Greater New York.

Members are registered by code numbers, which are assigned to each new member. The bureau makes one card for each customer of a reporting retailer and records the individual's name and address and the code number of all concerns which have reported that name. When the member desires information, he files a "Request," as shown in Fig. 26.

Services for Members. The bureau serves its members with two main types of credit reports. The trade clearance (Fig. 27) discloses the record of purchases and payments; and the special report, reproduced in Appendix F, is a combination of both personal and business history and paying habits. A number of types of short-form reports designed for special purposes, such as verification of business connections or residence of the customer, are also supplied to members. The bureau has for a number of years operated what it terms a Locate Department whose function it is to try to locate for members their missing debtors. Other reports furnished by the Locate Department include one giving details concerning ownership of real property and a real estate report which provides specialized rental information of interest to real estate management credit men. The bureau is equipped to supply subscribers with a private investigation report at a somewhat higher cost. This report is compiled from a comprehensive investigation of the subject's personal and business record, character, habits, associations, social background, health, morals, and financial condition. A sample employment-check report is reproduced in Appendix F. Through a separate corporation, a collection service is provided. Any member has available to him, through the credit bureau, reports on any account located within the United States or Canada. The bureau does not publish a rating book, as its files are changing daily, a rating might be obsolete before it could be published.

Trade clearance reports are designed to show how the subject pays his bills. The inference is correctly drawn that as he pays others so will he pay the inquirer. When a trade clearance is requested, the bureau immediately sends the inquirer a copy of the information on

F1

| FLEASE MAKE ALL INQUIRIES IN DUPLICATE | CREDIT BUREAU OF GREATER NEW YORK, INC. | FURNISH FULL NAMES AND ADDRESSES |

853 BROADWAY, NEW YORK 3, N. Y.

Reports - SPring 7-3900
Executive - SPring 7-9500

| PULLER | IN | S | C | NC. | OUT |
| | | J | Q | | |

MEMBER'S NAME
BLANK & COMPANY

ATTENTION OF
Mr. White

| CODE NUMBER | YOUR ACCT. NO. | DATE |
| 9000 | | 10/22 |

LAST NAME	FIRST NAME	MIDDLE NAME	HUSBAND'S NAME
Doe	John	J.	Mary
			WIFE'S NAME

PRESENT ADDRESS   CITY
21 Meadowbrook Drive, New York 23, N.Y.

FORMER ADDRESS   CITY
76 Eastside Drive, New York 33, N.Y.

| AGE | NEW ACCOUNT | REVISION | SOLICITED | DELINQUENT | INACTIVE |

OCCUPATION (HUSBAND)   TITLE   DEPARTMENT
Attorney

NAME OF BUSINESS   ADDRESS OF BUSINESS   CITY
Doe, Doe & Doe, 405 Lexington Ave., New York City

OCCUPATION (WIFE)   TITLE   DEPARTMENT

NAME OF BUSINESS   ADDRESS OF BUSINESS   CITY

BANK OF REFERENCE   BRANCH OR ADDRESS   SPECIAL CHECKING ☐
Manhattan Bank & Trust Co. - Midtown   REG.—CHECKING ☒

STORE OR BUSINESS REFERENCES   ADDRESSES   CITY
Smith & Jones

Lord & Brown

Black & Taylor

SPECIAL INSTRUCTIONS

CHECK TYPE OF SERVICE DESIRED—SEE PRICE LIST

LOCAL TRADE	S	OUT-OF-TOWN TRADE	SPECIAL	RUSH
CLEARANCE ☐	S S	CLEARANCE ☐	REPORT ☒	SPECIAL ☐
IN-FILE	INSTALLMENT	SPECIAL HANDLING	RESIDENCE ☐	PRIVATE
TRADE ☐	CLEARANCE ☐ ☐	REPORT ☐	BUSINESS CHECK ☐	INVESTI-GATION ☐

☐ IF NO TRADE IN FILE, CHANGE TO SPECIAL REPORT

FILL IN ON THIS LINE NAME OF
OTHER TYPE REPORT DESIRED

Fig. 26. Request for Credit Clearance Report.

file and then "clears" all local trade references given on the inquiry. When no references are given and the previous report is more than 1 year old, three members are cleared and their experiences are sent to the inquiring subscriber upon receipt. Any suits or judgments on record are included in the trade clearance report but are not checked up to date. Members can secure a code list which will acquaint them with the concerns reporting the various experiences. Trade clearances are both requested and issued by mail, by messenger, by telephone, teletypewriter, and telautograph.

DOE, JOHN J. (MARY)　　　　　REC'D 10/20　　WRITTEN 10/22　　FOR: #9000

NAME
　　21 Meadowbrook Drive, New York 23, N.Y.　OCCUPATION　Attorney

RESIDENCE

FORMER
RESIDENCES } 76 Eastside Drive, New York 33, N.Y.　FIRM NAME　Doe, Doe & Doe

　　　　　　　　　　　　　　　　　　　ADDRESS　　405 Lexington Ave., New York City

DATE CLEARED	MEMBER	SELLING SINCE	HIGH CREDIT	PAYS	REMARKS
10/21/58	2N	old	$97.59	30	l.s. 9/58
	315	11/50	78.50	30-60	l.s. 8/58
9/3/58	104	old	200.00	30-60	owes $97. for 8/58
7/6/58	19	old	inactive		
6/29/58	1447	10/50	50.00	30	

special report in file for #104 dated 6/26/54

TRADE CLEARANCE REPORT　　　　　　　　　　T-6

CREDIT REPORTS　　**CREDIT BUREAU OF GREATER NEW YORK, Inc.**　　EXECUTIVE OFFICES
SPring 7-3900　　　　　853 BROADWAY, NEW YORK 3, N. Y.　　　　　SPring 7-9500

FIG. 27.　Trade clearance.

The *special report* furnishes the most complete information available through outside investigation concerning the age, marital status, residential and business history, bank experience, bill-paying record, and suit and judgment record of the subject.

Personal investigation is made at the business address. Quite often the report will disclose whether the position is permanent or temporary and whether the subject is working on a salary or commission basis. It also describes the size or stability of the employing firm, length of time applicant has been employed, and other information necessary to establish a basis for credit acceptance. An endeavor is made to cover the period of employment for at least 3 years.

Bank references, when given, are cleared, and complete details contained in the report. When no bank is given, effort is made to locate a bank account, and the data included.

Speed of Service. The retail credit department must act with speed both in the opening of new accounts and in the revision of old ones. The bureau consequently must be organized for the fastest practical service. Reference has previously been made to messengers, telephone, and mail. In addition to these three means of communication, some of the larger members of the bureau have telautograph and others telephone-typewriter connections with the bureau. Members, of course,

Name	BLANK	JOHN	L.	MARY
	LAST NAME	FIRST NAME	INITIAL	WIFE'S NAME

Address   18 Wesley Road, New York 33, N.Y.

Former Address 51 Seton Blvd., New York 26, N.Y.

Occupation Salesman

Business   Doe & Co., 4th Avenue & 12th Street, New York City

	OWING NOW		FOR MONTHS OF
	$269.80		March-June, 1958

ATT'Y	SLOW PAY	DECLIN'D	N.G.CK.	UNSAT.	P.&L.	LOAD UP	SKIP	DEC'SED
XXXX								

REMARKS

Date 10/22/58   Member No. 9000

Report Every Account the Day It Becomes Unsatisfactory — Mail Immediately to the

CREDIT BUREAU OF GREATER NEW YORK, INC.

853 Broadway, New York 3, N. Y.

IMPORTANT—Give all the information you have, such as the full name, present and former residence and business addresses. The greater the amount of information the more quickly we can identify the proper master card. These reports are immediately placed in the files; members having accounts with the debtor are notified and the information published in the Bulletin when sufficiently derogatory.

DEROGATORY REPORT BLANK

Fig. 28. Derogatory report.

are expected to cooperate with the bureau by answering promptly requests for their ledger experience. In fact when they become members, they bind themselves to clear requests within 24 hours.

Automatic Warning Services. One of the most important functions of the Credit Bureau is to record daily the delinquent accounts, bad checks, impostor operations, and other derogatory information reported by members. These reports are usually received on the special derogatory report form illustrated in Fig. 28, but notices of bad-check and impostor operations are telephoned in to the bureau immediately by members as they occur. Upon receipt of such derogatory information, the staff bureau searches the files for a previous record on the customer and enters the unfavorable information on the file card. The code numbers of all members who have previously made inquiries on the name are then entered on the form, and a notice is prepared for each, warning them of the newly reported derogatory information. Thus all members are able to control further credit to the customers reported, until the account of the reporting member is paid or adjusted. This procedure is not followed in disputed cases, because of the possibility that the customer may have a legitimate reason for nonpayment of the account.

Summary. It is apparent that the retail credit bureaus are more than clearinghouses for trade experiences with customers. They are centrally located depositories for information gathered in many ways. Some data are obtained by personal investigations; other material is secured by ledger interchange; court records are combed for listings of suits, judgments, bankruptcies, and tax liens; newspapers are culled for information regarding criminal arrests, social marriages, money inheritances, and business achievements. In short, anything that may affect an individual's credit position either favorably or unfavorably is recorded. Where domestic troubles exist between husband and wife, the credit bureau usually will receive from the husband, or his lawyer, a statement of nonresponsibility, which is processed in the same manner as derogatory information. The modern retailer or banker can ill afford to forego the regular use of the services of these local credit bureaus. However, various estimates indicate that less than one-third of persons buying on credit terms are reported by the retail credit bureaus.

Either because of habit or because of the feeling that their interests may be better served, local businessmen often form their own independent exchange groups.

Group Exchanges. What may, for want of a better term, be classified as group exchanges takes a variety of forms. Sometimes a few concerns in a given line in a single market join together in exchanging information. In other instances, exchanges of information are promoted through a given industry, either through its trade association or otherwise; or single markets or locations join together in an exchange of information. There are, too, a wide variety and number of privately owned or pseudo-cooperatively owned organizations operating as mediums for the exchange of information in an industry or in two or three industries or in sections or otherwise. Some group exchanges have been organized and operated under the Credit Interchange System.

Operation of Group Exchanges. As great a variety is found in the methods of operation of group exchanges as in their forms. Some, within their restricted fields, duplicate the activities of credit interchange. Others report the members' code numbers and furnish subscribers with a key to code numbers so that the identity of reporting creditors can be determined. Others merely list their customers with a central office. A card index is then made of all customers bearing the code numbers of each member selling the individual customer. The service consists in advising members, upon inquiry, of the names of other members selling the account. Communication is then direct with each creditor.

This method of operation has its distinct advantages. It is particularly adaptable to a small trade group. It is comparatively inexpensive to operate, since it is necessary to have only a clerk to keep the file up to date and to answer the inquiries of the members. The inquiring member can adjust his speed in clearing the information to the urgency of the occasion. A marked advantage may lie in the fact that the inquirer, by knowing whence the information comes, can weigh its value and can, if the occasion requires it, obtain more than the usual ledger experience. It will be noted that the actual expense of getting the information is borne by the inquiring member.

One method of operation, usually restricted to small groups, is to list the names to be cleared on a sheet, a copy of which is sent to each member. Information is filled in, and, when all have reported, the data are tabulated and sent to the inquiring member. Usually, each contributing member may have a free copy of the report if he wishes it.

A common method of conducting these group activities is by periodical meetings attended in person by the members. These frequently take the form of luncheon engagements, which may account, in some degree, for the success of the method. Lists of debtors are usually prepared in advance and circulated among the members so that each member may be prepared to disclose the experience of his house. Discussion, which may be both particular and general, follows the luncheon.

Advantages and Disadvantages. The value of interchange and credit groups is unquestioned. If they did nothing more than promote the proper spirit of friendship and fellowship among those in an industry, they would be well worth while. However, they can go much farther than that. Properly organized and operated they can be made to serve as an extremely valuable medium for keeping customers out of the bankruptcy court, by rehabilitating them before their affairs reach the hopeless stage. They can do much toward the elimination of unfair and unethical business practices. They can contribute largely to the elimination of the price cutter, for, after all, terms and discounts are a component part of price, and competition in credit is just another species of price cutting and perhaps after all the most damaging and difficult to control. Best results to creditors are visualized when all industries are organized into groups nationally or locally, as may be required for cooperation in matters of credit.

Specific advantages of interchange of credit information are briefly summarized here. Among its desirable features is the fact that ledger experience is both sought and obtained without the necessity of a multitude of checkings.

Total clearances are cut down. In cases where this is not true, its corollary is: For the same number of inquiries, a greater number of experiences are available.

Customers of the bureau, as well as noncustomers, are circulated. Thus it is a method which locates other creditors for the subscriber.

It is termed up-to-date information, and, as has been shown, its reports will range, in fact, from current to 90 days, with the average probably actually under 45 days.

It gives the subscriber facts, and not opinions, upon which to base his decision. It should be particularly valuable on the smaller accounts where greater reliance is ordinarily put on the man and his management than on financial structure.

It discloses favoritism, that is, prompt payment to some creditors while others are allowed to wait.

Finally, the information can in general be relied upon, for it comes from reliable houses.

Opposed to these statements advancing the favorable features of interchange, some credit managers offer certain objections.

Interchange tends to supplant direct communication between creditors. When direct communication is limited, as is so often the case, to ledger experience only, the weight of this complaint is greatly lessened. Fuller discussion between credit men of a mutual account is not stopped by interchange. It is significant that the National Association of Credit Management, realizing that much direct interchange is merely a routine of supplying ledger experience, is discouraging direct interchange.

Another complaint is that the membership is not sufficiently great to include more than a fraction of the creditors of the country. Hence reports may not include the experience of all creditors.

Credit managers assert that it accentuates a bad situation where a debtor is in financial embarrassment. The report, it should be remembered, can also disclose the cooperation of the creditors and their confidence in a debtor who is in difficulty.

Then, too, there are those who complain that answering inquiries is too burdensome.

Other say that it takes too long to get a complete clearance, though they may admit that a fresh clearance cannot be made more quickly by any other method.

Finally, members often fail to report new or reopened accounts. However, the system does pick them up when the name is circularized on a member's inquiry, or when an account becomes delinquent.

With regard to credit groups particularly, there may occur other disadvantages. Occasionally, an exchange agency will be found, privately owned or with an unscrupulous management not thoroughly supervised, which uses the information obtained as bait for collection and liquidation business. In other instances, the service is offered as a means of bolstering up trade associates which find it difficult to maintain their membership.

In a sense, these groups may be discriminating against other creditors. Assume a business which makes its purchases from members served by two different groups. Each creditor must confine his information to that to be secured from his own group only. Carrying the assumption farther, we may easily conceive of two or three creditors precluded from any information, since they might not logically belong to any group.

It is asserted that credit-group activity, while essential and important, should at all times be predicated upon an exchange of information covering all the creditors of a customer—in other words, that there should be a single medium through which all would exchange their ledger experience information.

TEXT AND RESEARCH QUESTIONS

1. Why should ledger experience be divorced from antecedent and financial information?
2. *a.* What reasons are there for exchanging ledger data direct between creditors?
   b. What reasons can you advance against the direct exchange of ledger data between creditors?
   c. What information other than ledger data is possible of exchange only by direct communication between creditors?
3. Estimate the length of time that it would probably take to get a national clearance from bureaus in Chicago, Philadelphia, Milwaukee, Boston, and central New York. The inquiry originated in Philadelphia.
4. Would a report from another trade agency be made any faster?
5. Interchange depends upon cooperation of its subscribers. Is this a strength or weakness of interchange? Why?
6. How could nationwide clearance be accomplished? How expensive would it be? What other problems are involved?
7. Contrast the work of the Credit Interchange Bureau with that of the National Retail Credit Association.
8. Under what conditions do local credit groups assist each other?

PROBLEMS

1. Study the report in Fig. 25, and answer the following question, stating the reasons for your conclusions:
   a. In what line of business is the subject engaged?
   b. Is it a large, medium, or small business?

    c. Is it a new or long-established business?

    d. Is its credit restricted, or is it able to buy freely on credit?

    e. Are creditors fully satisfied with the account?

2. Assume that you are credit manager for one of nine concerns in your city manufacturing men's shirts, collars, hats, and hosiery. All sell about the same trade. Three companies have a net worth of at least $1,000,000 each, two have a net worth of about $35,000 each, and the others have net worth of $5,000 to $20,000. Your concern is one of the largest. How would you suggest that the group should exchange credit experience?

3. Assume you are chairman of a credit group composed of fifteen members who meet periodically for the purpose of exchanging credit information and promoting greater cooperation within the group. Two of the members attend the meetings only occasionally and there are usually two or three other absentees. You have found the following types of credit managers within the group:

    a. One who listens but very rarely contributes any information.

    b. One, a regular attendant, who wants to talk all the time.

    c. One who is suspected of "leaking" information to his sales department.

    d. One who ventures no opinion because of his fear of the management of his company.

    e. One who opposes every new suggestion.

Analyze this problem stating the best method of attaining regular and full attendance, and harmonious cooperation.

CHAPTER 17

SALESMEN, ATTORNEYS, AND
MISCELLANEOUS SOURCES OF INFORMATION

Salesman as Credit Assistant. For the most part, the credit manager of modern business must rely upon the many sources of credit information available to him for facts upon which to base the credit decision. That the credit manager should turn to a member of his own organization who is in a position to interview the customer and inspect his business would seem most natural. Such a medium is the salesman. Yet the extent to which the salesman should be used as a credit assistant is a matter of considerable disagreement among credit men. Practically all are agreed that the salesman is in an excellent position to act as a credit investigator, but his ability and willingness to act are less certain.

The extent to which the salesman may be used as a credit reporter to the advantage of his concern depends upon a number of conditions. Chief among them are the ability and the training of the salesman and the class of customers upon whom he calls. The young salesman, untrained in credit and financial matters and without experience, will fail to distinguish between desirable and undesirable credit factors, or, indeed, to know whether or not a certain condition may have any bearing at all upon the credit risk. On the other hand, though of excellent judgment, he may be unwilling either to take the time necessary to make a few inquiries and issue his report, or he is unwilling to give any information, especially of a derogatory nature.

The true salesman is the representative not merely of the sales department, but of the whole house. Indeed, as has been truly said, to many a customer the salesman *is* the house. The customer's impression of the house with which he deals is gained largely through the salesman. As the representative of the house, he is a representative of its credit department. Furthermore, it is not only the salesman's duty to his house but it is to his individual interest to cooperate with the credit department.

The salesman's worth to his house is based not upon the volume of orders he books, but upon the net profit produced over a period of time.

This result depends not only upon his ability to sell the merchandise in which there is the most profit, but to customers where bad-debt losses will not be incurred and collections will be effected promptly. It is natural that the salesman's first thought is to make a sale, but he must remember that there is no profit in a sale, nor is it a complete sale, until the payment for the material has been received. If, therefore, the salesman is remunerated according to the profit he produces, as he ought to be, a farsighted policy will compel him to strive for profit and not merely for volume in sales.

Salesman's Attitude to the Credit Department. The salesman's main function is to get his customers' orders, and the larger part of his energy will be devoted to that result. Nor can he fail to attempt to sell a customer whose credit may be in some doubt. It is not the salesman's prerogative to make the credit decisions, but merely to report the facts and the conditions, as he sees them, to the credit department.[1] The wise salesman will not, of course, waste his time on a prospective customer who clearly would not be accepted by the credit department.

The salesman, unless he has been made familiar with his company's credit practice and policy, may become antagonistic to the credit department, through some unfavorable credit decision which has caused him to lose a customer's business. Such an attitude should not be permitted to exist. The wise credit manager will exhibit considerable patience in explaining the credit policy and the reason for credit decisions, especially to new salesmen. Assuming that the credit decision when made is the right decision and that the credit man always exhibits an attitude of absolute fairness and impartiality to all salesmen, he will rarely fail to gain not only the salesman's respect but his cooperation as well. The credit department can hardly expect cooperation on the part of the salesmen unless the credit department gives full cooperation on its part.

Frequently, salesmen are encountered who prefer to adopt a hands-off policy. If, in their relations with the customer, they touch upon no credit or collection matter, they feel they are in a better position to soothe little irritations. While the good salesman will not agree or sympathize with the customer but will, on the other hand, back up the house, nevertheless, the customer has an opportunity to air his grievance before an apparently neutral salesman, and having thus put himself on record feels mollified toward the house. This attitude on the part of the salesman does not prevent him from being on the alert for credit indications both good and bad.

[1] A study concerning salesmen indicated that "of 157 replies about salesmen activities, about 37% indicated that salesmen were at least moderately active in credit function." "Credit Orientation and Training for Salesmen," Credit Research Foundation, New York, 1948, p. 2.

The Salesman's Credit Information. To be of value to the credit department, the salesman uses good judgment in distinguishing what may be credit factors from those that have no effect on the credit risk. To tell the credit manager that a customer is "as good as gold" is useless, for it indicates a biased opinion loosely given. To bring in credit data which proves that the customer has A1 credit is to render valuable assistance not only to the credit department, but also himself and to his house. Usually the salesman's credit data, far from being complete, will be confined to information that can be gained with comparatively little trouble on the salesman's part. It is a mistaken idea, however, for the salesman to slight this part of his work. If he spends an hour selling a man, it is certainly worth 10 minutes more to make sure that there will be no hitch at the credit end.

The salesman, always functioning as a credit assistant as well, should ever be on the alert for information concerning his customers. He is not confined to the customer himself for information, for he will gather it in conversation with other customers of the same town, at the hotel, and, particularly, from other salesmen whose acquaintance is made while traveling. The thorough salesman and credit assistant desiring to ascertain for himself the credit standing of a customer has another valuable source of information in his customer's local bank, where significant information may sometimes be obtained.

It is a fact, however, that a salesman usually reports only the result of his observations and the answers to a few routine questions asked of the customer. His observations may include the following points:

Location. The salesman should observe the location of the store in arrangement, and its condition and its value, the window and store display, and the efficiency of the clerks are included under the caption.

Location. The salesman should observe the location of the store in its relation to the business or shopping center, transportation and parking facilities, the side of the street, whether shady or sunny during shopping hours, the number and character of the passers-by, and the like.

Local Conditions. This has to do with the local activity of business. If local industry is active and if the crops are good, it adds to the safety of the credit while, on the other hand, such a condition as a temporarily torn-up street passing the customer's place of business might seriously affect his ability to pay.

Personal Factors. The salesman is in a position, through his personal interview with the customer, to form an opinion as to his character and his ability. By a few discreet inquiries in the town, the salesman may also learn the customer's reputation as to these factors.

General Information. Information of a general nature, such as how long in business, the business organization, the names of the partners, if

SALESMAN'S REPORT
Attach to First Order

```
                                                        yes or no
         Mr. ..................................... (age about .... md .....) Date .........
Business
in name  Mrs. ..................................... (age about .... md .....)
of:
         Inc. ........................................ Post Office ........................
Have you asked for signed statement? ..........................................................
Have you left statement blank in subject's hand? ..............................................
Did subject decline to give signed statement? ...............................................
Did subject promise to fill in, sign, and mail statement? .....................................
Credit is based in numerical order in the following:  Answer to best of your ability.
```

1	Honesty	?	....
2	Ability	?	....
3	Net Worth	?	....
4	Prospects	?	....

```
Is Location Good? ............... Does subject, relative or clerk manage business? ..........
Is subject attentive? ................................. Former occupation ...................
Principal occupation of nearby populace ......................................................
How much credit will subject need? ...........................................................
How is subject reported to pay? ..............................................................
How does subject propose to pay us? ..........................................................
Does subject carry insurance? ......... Mdse. $..... Store Bldg. $..... Homestead $..........
Name of subject's bank: ......................................................................
Estimated value of stock: ....................................................................
Does subject seem economical? ................................................................
Is this subject's first experience in business? .............................................
Commenced new? ................................. Succeeding whom? .............................
On what basis was purchase made? .............................................................
Did purchaser assume debts of business he succeeded? .........................................
REMARKS:
.........................................................................Salesman sign here.
I have filled in this report to the best of my ability...........................,Salesman.
     REFERENCES.                        Salesman must not use colums below.
```

Give names only.	H. C.	Owes	Due	Past Due	Notes	Method
1						
2						
3						
4						
5						

REMARKS:						
1						
2						
3						
4						
5						

```
Asked Reports ............................... Order Passed ...........................
Asked Clearance ......................................................................
Asked References .....................................................................
```

FIG. 29. Detailed salesman's report.

a partnership, or directors, if a corporation, may be ascertained in the course of the conversation.

Capital Resources. The credit manager should carefully consider whether or not it is advisable for the salesman to attempt to get financial information. Often the businessman is reluctant to discuss his financial affairs with a salesman, and, in many cases, his financial statement is on file at the agencies. Having made it thus available to the creditor, the customer should not be requested to duplicate it by every salesman calling upon him.

References. The businessman has been educated to give references, and though one may be frequently encountered who is reluctant to give other information, the salesman will rarely encounter one who will hesitate to give references. The value of such names, however, as sources of information, may not be very great. Naturally, in giving the names of business houses those will be selected which can make the best report. Their experiences will not be typical. More valuable as references are the names which the salesman may get in some other manner. He observes the brands of merchandise carried, or possibly the names of shippers on unopened packages, or invoices lying upon the customer's desk. He meets salesmen from other houses calling upon the same customer. Such references when they can be obtained may disclose the buyer's real paying habits.

The salesman may also be of material assistance to the credit department by fully discussing terms with the customer. Many controversies over cash discounts, and many difficulties in making collections promptly, are due to false impressions left by the salesman, or, perhaps, even insinuations that terms can be infringed upon with impunity. The salesman should be impressed with the fact that terms are as vital a part of the contract as is the price and that he has no more authority to change the one than the other, either by direct statement or by implication.

In still another way can the salesman be of assistance to the credit department. The credit man is receptive to credit information not only while he is opening the account but as long as the account is an active one with the house. The salesman should be the eyes and ears of the credit department in that respect. As the representative on location, he should keep himself informed of the progress of his customers, and not fail to pass along to the credit department credit factors as they develop. Much unpleasantness to the house, to the customer, and to the salesman himself may thus be avoided. It has been found a wise plan for the credit manager to hold periodic conferences with each salesman, during which the status of each account is freely discussed. At these conferences it may be well to have a stenographer present so that comments of importance may be recorded for the files.

Through these conferences, misunderstandings, if any exist between salesman and credit manager, are banished. The salesman is kept informed of the policy of the house and the attitude of the credit man toward the accounts. The credit manager, on his part, is getting significant and intimate details in regard to customers and territory from one who, as an eyewitness, is best able to observe them. A salesman traveling over the same territory for a number of years, if trained to be credit-minded, can hardly fail to be a most valuable credit assistant.

Reliability of Salesman's Information. A discussion of the salesman as a credit assistant would not be complete if it did not include the motives which make the salesman's report so often doubted. Credit managers abound who regard any salesman's report with considerable suspicion. Whenever such a credit manager is encountered, there is a justifiable inference that the failure of salesman and credit manager to work together is largely, or at least partly, the fault of the credit manager. All credit managers, however, recognize the tendency on the part of salesmen to regard all credit risks optimistically. The salesman develops an optimistic attitude. Having worked hard and enthusiastically to secure an order, it is most natural for the salesman to continue his efforts to break down any opposition that he may encounter. Therefore, having sold the customer he proceeds to attempt to sell the credit department.

Happily, this attitude on the part of the salesman, which was general not so many years ago, is disappearing as a result of the education of both sales and credit managers. Some salesmen, however, whose income is a commission on their net sales, adopt a shortsighted policy and a selfish attitude. Under their contract, commissions are based upon the amount of sales collected. If a given sale results in a bad-debt loss, the only loss to the salesman is the loss of his commission, while the house loses the rest. Even though the salesman has but little confidence in his customer, he labors to get the order approved by the credit department, because he is gambling only on his commission. In fact, he reasons that he stands to lose nothing more than he has already lost, for he has already invested his time and labor in procuring the order. Some credit managers argue from this that if the salesman will spend his time in selling an account, he hardly would supply any credit information detrimental to his interest.

How to Educate the Salesman. Only a few suggestions can be given here as to how to educate the salesman for his role of credit assistant. That education should begin when the salesman first assumes his duties. He is introduced to the credit manager presumably by the sales manager and informed by the latter that he is expected to aid and cooperate with the credit department. Thereupon the credit manager may explain the credit policy, discuss the use of forms and records which concern the salesman, illustrate how the salesman can act as the eyes and ears of the credit department, and how the credit department can aid the salesman in his work by keeping him informed of the exact status of his territory.

Make the salesman feel that he shares the responsibility of bad-debt losses in his territory. Let him know that the credit department is relying upon him for reports as to the credit worth of his customers, and that as he proves his ability as an interpreter of credit risk, his information is given weight, and his judgment respected. Question and discuss with him the reports which he submits. If he reports, for instance, that the customer's location is excellent, and that he is not subject to keen competition, further questioning may bring out contradictory facts which the salesman either did not sense or which he chose not to disclose to the credit department. If the salesman finds that it is both difficult and undesirable to "put one over on" the credit department, he will soon cease to try.

Attorneys as Sources of Information. Attorneys have long been used as a source of credit information with varying success. A survey of

Answering an inquiry from a New York concern, as to the credit standing of one of his neighbors, Lincoln, before his election to the Presidency, wrote the following letter:

Yours of the 10th received. First of all, he has a wife and baby; together they ought to be worth $500,000 to any man. Secondly, he has an office in which there is a table worth $1.50 and three corner chairs worth, say, $1. Last of all, there is in one corner a large rathole, which will bear some looking into.

Respectfully,

A. Lincoln.

FIG. 30.   A. Lincoln—on credit reporting.

credit departments will disclose that some credit men rarely, if ever, use the services of an attorney in making a credit investigation, while others will be found who will warmly support the claim that the attorney is an excellent source of information. There may be various reasons for the success of one credit man and the failure of another in the use of the attorney's services. Satisfaction may depend upon such factors as the class of trade sold, the type of information expected, and the use to be made of this information.

The attorney is generally regarded only as a supplementary source of information. He is a local man and, supposedly, can furnish information based upon personal knowledge, or personal investigation. He is favorably situated for this purpose. He may know the subject of inquiry personally and be well acquainted with his inside affairs. From the nature of the attorney's work it is presumed that he has a large circle of friends and acquaintances among whom is the subject, or at least someone close enough to the subject's affairs to supply the attorney with information. Furthermore, it is assumed that his training will qualify him as a reporter. On the other hand, some credit men are suspicious of an attorney's report because it is feared that the subject may be the friend of the attorney, or perhaps a relative. Sometimes it is felt, too, that the attorney is inclined to give a favorable report because the subject is a local man and the inquirer an outsider and a stranger.

The value of the attorney as a credit reporter depends upon his ability to judge credit factors, and the fidelity with which he conducts the investigation and renders the report. One point distinctly in favor of the attorney's report is that it is up to date. On the other hand, the reply to an inquiry may not be promptly given. Frequently, the attorney feels that he is not sufficiently well paid to spend the necessary time in getting the information, or the inquiry may be turned over to his secretary to answer. A chance for dissatisfaction lies in the possibility of misunderstanding of credit standards. For example, good credit may mean prompt pay to the credit man, whereas to the attorney who reports it, the words mean merely that the subject is financially able to pay, has no judgments against him, and is suffering no curtailment of his credit, although payments are rarely, if ever, made according to terms.

Type of Attorney Report. Since the attorney is a local man, he is best qualified to give information along the lines of his own observation and the subject's local reputation. Thus, we find attorneys giving information on the following factors affecting the credit risk:

1. How long in business
2. Habits and business ability
3. Estimated value of stock
4. Local reputation
5. Value of real estate (net)
6. Net worth
7. Claims and lawsuits
8. Progress

How Long in Business? The attorney is usually in a position to give this information, at least approximately. A long business experience, provided the management has not lost its aggressiveness and the balance of the report is favorable, lends much weight to a favorable credit decision.

Habits and Business Ability. While the attorney may not be business trained, and, therefore, unable to judge at first hand the business acts of the subject, the businessman will soon establish a reputation for good, fair, or poor ability and it is this reputation which is transferred to the report.   The attorney can, of course, judge between good and bad habits.

Estimated Value of Stock.   Unless the attorney is familiar with the inside affairs of the merchant, the answer to this question will be entirely a matter of opinion.   It may be the attorney's opinion or the opinion of others.   In any event, the accuracy of the answer is not assured.   The answer does, however, give the credit man a general idea of the value of the stock carried, or gives him a figure to compare with the salesman's or other estimate.

Local Reputation.   In the smaller communities, the attorney will be thoroughly familiar with the subject's local reputation, and in the larger communities, it will not be difficult for him to obtain it.   This section of the report may be very significant.

Value of Real Estate.   The attorney is often familiar with any parcels of real estate which the subject may own.   Furthermore, he is often a very good judge of real estate values.   The encumbrances which the subject has placed upon his real estate are either known to the attorney or are easily attainable, since they are matters of record.

Net Worth.   This is usually a matter of hearsay, or even rumor.   In most instances it is at best merely an opinion.   In many cases, however, it will be approximately correct.

Claims and Lawsuits.   This question lies right in the attorney's own field of activity.   The legal troubles besetting the local merchant come directly under the purview of the local attorney, or, by keeping conversant with the activities of the local courts, he has knowledge of the suits instituted, and of the progress and outcome of those suits.

Progress.   This, again, may be a matter of opinion or reputation. However, the answer in the majority of cases will be correct.   The merchant's friends, neighbors, and business competitors soon form a rather accurate opinion of the progress of each merchant.   It is this general opinion which is usually transmitted to the creditors.

How to Use Attorney.   Many concerns make it a practice to use the attorney as a source of information only in towns of less than, let us say, 12,000 where his acquaintanceship might cover most of the businessmen of the town or enable him to get the desired information with but little time and trouble.   On the other hand, some firms of attorneys in larger cities have found this source of revenue sufficiently great to warrant opening up a commercial department to specialize in collecting and disseminating credit information and in handling credit departments. Naturally, not all attorneys who may be approached for information will furnish the same quality of report.   Some credit men restrict their inquiries to the small merchant in the small town where it is felt that accurate and quick information may be obtained through the medium of the local reporter, while other credit men report some attorneys of certain of the larger cities as a superior source of information through the fact that they have amassed credit information superior in quality and in quantity to that possessed by the mercantile agencies for that locality.

Not all attorneys are willing to serve commercial houses as credit reporters. How, then, to obtain the names of attorneys who will perform this service? The answer may be found in a number of published attorney's lists. The house publishing the list assembles the names, charging each attorney a small fee for listing his name, and then sells or presents the complete list to credit men. The attorneys are carefully investigated and selected for their integrity, ability, and responsibility. The publishers keep the list up to date by the issuance of monthly and quarterly supplements, thus keeping the list free of all but reputable attorneys.

The cost of this service is limited to the fee paid to the attorney for his report, except in those cases where an initial charge is made for the attorneys' list. If there is a charge for the attorneys' list, it is usually in compensation of some service or protection given to the creditor aside from names and addresses of attorneys. If more than the usual investigation is desired, the attorney should be so advised and the fee increased. Some attorneys' lists specify just how much the attorney is entitled to receive, the amount depending upon the size of the city in which he is operating. It is reasonably held that the investigation can be conducted with the least expense in the smaller communities, where the fee is consequently less.

Personnel Agencies. Both Bishop's Agency, Inc., and Proudfoot's Commercial Agency, Inc., investigate individuals and business enterprises not only for credit purposes but for a host of other reasons. Their reports are of excellent reliability and are available usually on a contract basis.

The Credit Manager as a Business Builder. As has been shown in the preceding sections, the personal interview may be productive of the most beneficial results. The regret of most credit managers is that such interviews are not more numerous. Since there is so much difficulty in persuading customers to visit the credit department and particularly those customers the credit man would most like to see, the thought naturally presents itself that the credit man would overcome this difficulty by a visit to the customer. This is a growing practice and one which should be further developed.

The peculiar advantage accruing to such an interview results from the fact that the credit manager is enabled to make an inspection of the business itself and that his customer, as host, will more thoroughly acquaint the credit man with details than he otherwise would. The scope of the inquiry is governed by the circumstances in each case. The purpose of such interviews is always twofold—to obtain credit information and to develop good will—but the ratio between those two objectives will vary greatly. In one instance the credit of the customer is but little questioned, while it may be very desirable to promote good will. In another instance the risk the seller is asked to take is great and calls forth a very inquisitorial attitude upon the part of the credit manager.

When engaged in these interviews, the interviewer must exercise all his resourcefulness and tact. In the first place, his trip is carefully planned. He decides whom he wishes to interview, and posts himself thoroughly by obtaining all the information possible through the usual channels. The purpose of his visit to one customer may be merely to leave with the customer the feeling of the friendliness of the house. Or, with another, the credit manager may wish to protect a credit already allowed where a serious weakness seems to have developed. In such an event, the credit manager may feel warranted in examining the books and the condition of the business, the plans, and outlook for the future. Weaknesses in the organization or leaks in the business may be apparent though unseen by the proprietor. In view of his broad experience the credit manager may offer many useful suggestions. If the interview is tactfully conducted in a spirit of helpfulness, the confidence of the customer will be gained and the suggestions welcomed and seriously considered. It is, of course, assumed that the credit manager is qualified for his role by ability, by education, and by experience.

Here, too, may be an opportunity to observe the *esprit de corps* of the whole organization. This has become highly desirable. Management often publicly testifies that its most valuable asset is its personnel. Yet often, too, management does little to secure the wholehearted allegiance and support of this asset. Where a sizable credit is involved, the creditor may do well to observe, or inquire into, the general attitude of the employees—from top management down through the junior executives and the working force—to the company. A happy, contented personnel is a more productive personnel and assures a better credit risk.

The net result of such a promotion and protection trip is a better understanding between customer and house, the protection or retrenchment where weak risks are concerned, and credit limits increased and larger orders encouraged where conditions warrant.

In conclusion, one instance may be cited of the result of a call upon a customer. The customer conducted a small department store in a city of 40,000 population. Because of slow pay, his line of credit was restricted to $400 although the salesman reported he could easily sell him more if it would be accepted by the house. Annual purchases amounted to about $1,200. The credit manager called upon the customer, gained his confidence, discussed his business with him, and then interviewed his banker. As a result, some suggestions as to financing and cutting down of inventory in certain departments were made. The customer was shown how he could pay his bills according to terms, and an offer was made to double his line of credit as long as he met the seller's regular terms. The offer was accepted, and the customer's purchases for the past several years have averaged about $2,500 per annum. The net result of that one visit has thus far been about $5,000 of increased business.

The Accountant. It is becoming increasingly common for creditors not only to insist upon a financial statement but to insist that the statement be compiled by a competent and disinterested accountant. Obviously, the accountant, who makes a thorough audit of a concern's business, is in an excellent position to give credit information, and it is but natural for the creditor to wish to question the accountant concerning the debtor's affairs. While the accountant is in a position to give valuable information, he cannot be said to be a very productive source of information. In the first place, he is employed by the debtor in a strictly confidential capacity. The accountant is not at liberty to give information, whether it be favorable or unfavorable, unless authorized to do so by his principal. Then, too, if he is authorized to disclose the financial statement, he may not care to discuss it with the creditor, either because he does not wish to take the time to do so or for some other reason.

An objection to the accountant as a source of credit information is sometimes made because he often attempts to pose as the credit authority instead of credit consultant. That is, he often wishes merely to recommend his client without discussing his client's position. The credit manager, on the other hand, is seeking to add to his store of facts upon which to base his decision. The accountant, while he may go thoroughly into the financial position, may not have other pertinent facts which are in the hands of the credit manager. Nor is he in many cases as capable a judge of credit as is the credit manager.

The fact that a reputable accountant has compiled the financial statement is important, and sometimes he may have his client's permission to expand upon the information disclosed by the statement. But the credit manager should have a full appreciation of the confidential nature of the accountant's information and not be too critical if the accountant refuses information.

TEXT AND RESEARCH QUESTIONS

1. To what extent can the salesman be used as a source of credit information? List briefly those points of information which he can obtain to advantage.

2. Upon what factors does the value of a salesman's report primarily rest?

3. What should be the proper attitude of the salesman toward the credit department?

4. In what ways can the credit department be of help to the salesman?

5. *a.* Criticize briefly the reliability of salesmen's credit information.

   b. How would it be possible effectively to hold the salesman responsible for losses on bad debts and inferior credit risks?

6. How would you go about educating a new salesman in such a way as to obtain a maximum degree of cooperation with the credit department? Outline briefly the progressive steps that you would take.

7. List the points on which the attorney's report is (*a*) inferior to the salesman's report; (*b*) superior to it.

8. Summarize briefly in numerical order the various factors on which credit information can be obtained from attorneys.

9. *a.* Name and briefly explain three ways in which attorneys may be compensated for requests for credit information.

   b. Which of these methods is most satisfactory?

PROBLEM

Design a form of salesman's report for use by a wholesaler of coal.

PART III

ANALYSIS OF THE FINANCIAL REPORT

CHAPTER 18

THE FINANCIAL REPORT

A Source of Information. The financial report is a very important source of credit information. Its value, however, in appraising the credit power of the debtor or credit applicant should not be overestimated.

A good financial report is composed of four parts. Part one is the balance sheet, which is a listing of assets, liabilities, and net worth accounts, all purporting[1] to indicate certain values for a particular date; part two is the schedule of income and expense accounts, both often estimated, for a specific period of time; part three consists of a discussion of business activities and various schedules supporting the balance sheet and income statement; and part four is the accountant's certificate. In the absence of such certification, the report will be signed by responsible management officials. To place too much reliance upon the debtor's financial statement, while other sources of information are slighted, is a mistake frequently made by credit managers. Indeed, there are those who seem inclined to regard a financial statement almost as a guarantee of the debtor's good credit. Such an attitude is indicative (1) of too much credulity on the part of the credit manager, that is, he does not sufficiently consider the possibility of falsity or error; or (2) the credit manager relies upon the statement because he has not interpreted it correctly; or (3) he has placed too great a reliance upon the laws enacted to prevent the issuance of false statements. A financial report is only as reliable as the persons responsible for it.

The thorough student of credit analysis will avoid these errors. He will attempt to evaluate the financial statement in each case as merely one of the sources of information yielding credit data. He will realize that its importance varies according to circumstances, or, in other words, that it does not carry the same weight in all cases. He will carefully

[1] For a discussion concerning the reason why balance sheets only appear to balance, see R. A. Foulke, "Practical Financial Statement Analysis."

avoid a subordination of data gathered through other sources to conclusions which might be drawn from the financial statement.

The sound credit manager, on the other hand, will not underestimate the financial statement as a source of information. It furnishes, in many cases and in fact most cases, all the information available in regard to the capital factor, and this factor, as has been pointed out in a previous chapter, is regarded by some credit managers as being the most important of all. It undoubtedly receives the most attention in actual practice. The reasons for this will be readily understood. Capital has a definite unit of measurement in terms of dollars, while character and capacity are intangible factors, and the financial statement, therefore, furnishes a more or less accurate medium for recording the capital factor. A further reason for the time devoted to the financial statement is the difficulty frequently encountered in correctly interpreting it. These two facts, together with the importance of the capital factor, account for the credit manager's interest in the financial statement and the time he devotes to its analysis.

The consideration of the financial statement, as a source of credit information, may be divided into three parts: procuring the statement, the interpretation of it, and financial statement legislation. These three phases of financial statement use will be considered in this and succeeding chapters.

Procuring the Statement. Many business houses are still encountered who are reluctant to furnish their creditors with financial statements. This reluctance may be explained, in part by the fact that the use of credit preceded the use of accurate records, or, indeed, in many cases, any records at all. Credit was based upon confidence engendered by appearances, and personal acquaintance with the risk, while, today, the seller's close personal contact with the credit risk has, to a large extent, disappeared and there is, consequently, a greater reliance upon recorded facts. There also appears to be reasonable excuses, in some instances, for not making a financial statement to creditors. Some of the arguments in favor of the financial statement and the objections encountered will be considered in the following paragraphs.

The debtor has open to him two methods of placing his financial statement in the hands of his creditors or prospective creditors and he may use either, or both. He may place his statement in the hands of one or more mercantile agencies for distribution, or he may give his financial statement to each or to some of his creditors. The former method is termed the "indirect method," and the latter the "direct method."

The Indirect Method. While the greatest number of financial statements are received through the commercial agencies, credit managers are often dissatisfied with financial statements thus obtained. Often such statements are too old to be relied upon, or they are not sufficiently complete. Moreover, inaccuracies are apt to creep in through transscribing them several times. Statements are frequently given orally to the reporter, and are not taken from books of account. Such statements are obviously of but little value. These objections to the indirect method of obtaining financial statements, however, are not sufficient to discourage their use. The wise credit manager will use discretion in insisting that a financial statement be given direct. The circumstances in the case often will not warrant such a demand. The credit reputation of the debtor, the quality of other credit information available, and the relative size of the order involved might make the direct request for a financial statement nonessential, and irritating to the customer.

The Direct Method. Just as there are cases when the indirect statement is satisfactory, so are there cases when only a financial statement received direct from the customer will suffice. The financial statement received direct from the debtor is less apt to be inaccurate, it is more apt to be the latest statement compiled, and given in more detail or with more subsidiary information than the statement submitted through the mercantile agency. Often the use of the creditor's own financial statement form can be obtained and thus just the information particularly desired is furnished. The debtor knows just who is in possession of his statement, and who is relying upon it. This in itself has a salutary effect upon the maker. And then, too, the aid of the false financial statement laws can be more easily invoked when a statement is placed directly in the hands of the creditor. It is pertinent to note that banks almost invariably demand a financial statement direct from a customer before a loan is granted. Any creditor, whether bank or mercantile, is justified in insisting upon a direct financial statement when the credit information available does not warrant the acceptance of the risk. Indeed, the creditor need not stop there in his search for information. The investigation should be continued until the credit manager feels justified either in rejecting or accepting the risk.

Reasons for Submitting Statements. Resistance frequently will be encountered in the attempt to obtain financial statements. Such resistance the credit man will attempt to overcome by persuasive and convincing reasons for submitting statements. Among some of the reasons which may be advanced by a creditor, and with which the credit manager should be familiar, are the following:

1. Blind faith is not a basis for credit. When the customer refuses to disclose his financial position, he is asking that his credit be accepted on faith alone. The debtor should be willing to prove his credit worth.

2. Creditor and debtor relationship is, in a sense, akin to a partnership. Both are investing capital in the same enterprise and both are dependent

upon that enterprise for the safety of their investment. The investor has a right to complete information, a fact the government has recognized in a law administered by the Securities and Exchange Commission prescribing the information that shall be made available before the larger concerns may offer their securities to the public.

3. The financial statement aids in fixing the amount of credit. The financial statement affords the best basis for gauging the amount of debt that the debtor can prudently incur.

4. With a financial statement in his possession, the creditor proceeds with more confidence. Likewise, the debtor may act with more confidence because he has established his right to do business on his credit.

5. Since confidence is engendered by the possession of a statement, the natural result is increased service on the part of the creditor.

6. The debtor may receive valuable and constructive criticism. Every business house will find among its creditors a few credit men with superior astuteness and experience. The advice of such men may be invaluable.

7. The debtor's moral fiber is strengthened by the knowledge that he has placed himself on record. He has set a standard which he feels he must improve or at least maintain. Having put himself on record, he may hesitate to engage in any speculative enterprise or to falsify his financial standing.

8. The financial statement tends to stamp out the incompetent businessmen, and those who cannot hope to succeed because of lack of sufficient capital. The good businessman should realize that the general practice of giving statements should help to remove the unfair competition that incompetency permits. In the long run only the successful business is good business.

9. The general practice of giving statements compels practice of keeping adequate books of account. This is a distinct aid to competency and therefore a benefit to business in general.

10. Finally, the giving of financial statements is a general practice in some industries and is fast becoming so in others. The time is ripe for all businessmen to aid in this practice which tends toward the proper safeguarding of credit and, through credit, business in general.

Objections Frequently Encountered. In the previous paragraphs, reasons were advanced favoring the submission of statements. The credit manager will have to meet and overcome various objections advanced by reluctant customers. In this he will not always be successful, but the following statements and answers might be of some use in this problem:

1. The statement is made by the debtor that he is obtaining all the credit needed and, therefore, does not have to submit a statement.

This argument is one of those most frequently voiced and it is also one of the most difficult to answer. In the first place, the remark of the debtor should be verified. Oftentimes the remark is not justified by the facts, or, if the credit is used, it has been secured by collateral or guarantees. Furthermore, the debtor may be limiting himself to his present sources of supply. This would be particularly disadvantageous in the event that he should suddenly need to place an order outside of his regular sources of supply. Then, too, in the event of a rumor reflecting upon his credit all of his creditors, operating somewhat in the dark, might curtail his credit, or take some other action embarrassing to him. Financial statements distributed among his creditors would allay any fears and have a steadying influence upon the credit relationship. Constant pressure and a degree of insistence upon statements will eventually overcome this objection.

2. The customer does not want his statement to reach his competitors' hands.

Very often this is an excuse, rather than a reason, for not giving a financial statement. The chances are remote that any information imparted to a well-organized and a well-conducted credit department would get into the hands of a competitor. The entire department is trained to guard all credit information against misuse. Such an argument imputes carelessness or lack of integrity to the credit department and its representatives. The customer's fear may be dispelled by an explanation in detail of the methods used to safeguard credit information in the credit department.

3. Statements are given to Dun & Bradstreet, Inc., or other agencies and are thus available to all creditors.

Oftentimes, the request for a statement is withdrawn upon the debtor's assurance that the agencies have his latest statement. Obviously, there is no logic in credit managers insisting upon the inclusion of financial statements in agency reports if each credit man requires that a financial statement be submitted direct to him. Reasons for a direct statement have been given in a previous paragraph. The statement is too old; it obviously may contain errors; it does not give the information called for by the creditor's own form; or, it may not be signed. The creditor may also suggest that his customer show his good faith by sending him a signed statement through the mail. This latter request should not be made too bluntly, since it carries the implication that the creditor doubts the truth of the statement. While, on the other hand, if he has reason to doubt the truth of the statement he may, with considerable bluntness, request that a signed statement be mailed to his house.

4. The customer refers to his existing creditors.

Information thus received, while invaluable, is not alone sufficient for a basis of credit. Since it has been the customer's practice not to submit financial details, such information can cover only the experience of creditors with the subject of investigation. Furthermore, such information often is not given with sufficient detail or accuracy upon which to base a reliable conclusion. If the customer's bank be specifically referred to, it can be pointed out that banks, as a rule, do not give out detailed information. In many instances, merely an expression of opinion is given by the bank's credit department and, furthermore, the credit manager does not know how much information the bank may have upon which to form an opinion.

5. The customer states that he either discounts or pays promptly.

This fact, in itself, does not ensure prompt payment or discounts for the future. Cases have been frequent where payments have been prompt almost to the day of bankruptcy. When a debtor takes this position, he is attempting to force the acceptance of his credit on blind faith. The debtor would see the unreasonableness of this procedure, if the attempt were made by any one other than himself.

6. The customer states that he fears that income-tax authorities will get possession of the statement and assess a large tax.

This is sometimes given as a reason, whereas it is in reality an excuse. In many such cases there would be no cause for a larger tax assessment, as the subject very well knows. The statement is made as an excuse for not revealing the true financial position, and to impress the creditor. In other cases it may be a true reason. In such a case it is an admission of discrepancy between the details submitted to the government and those submitted to creditors. One or the other must be false. The answer to this argument, whenever it is advanced, is that the creditor wants the statement solely for his own guidance and that he agrees to hold it as strictly confidential. As a matter of fact, a customer who offers this excuse prejudices his position. If he indicates that his tax return is false he destroys the basis for confidence and should be dealt with accordingly.

7. Occasionally the claim is made that statements are valueless, since there is no assurance that they are correct.

If the credit manager can place no reliance upon the statement then he cannot rely upon any information given by the subject. If this is admitted to be so, then all business transacted upon a credit basis is a gamble. Actually, the credit manager has faith in the integrity of businessmen in general and justifiably so. Furthermore, it may be pointed out that there are both state and federal laws which provide for punishment of those who obtain the acceptance of their credit by the means of a false financial statement. These laws tend to reinforce the moral fiber of any who may be tempted to issue false financial statement. Faith in a financial statement is measured by faith in the man who issues it. Every credit manager knows that many false financial statements are issued. Many are proved to be false, and probably many more are issued which escape the detection of credit men. Elsewhere, the author warns against too implicit faith in the financial statement.

8. The customer believes in maintaining complete secrecy concerning his business affairs.

Such a customer is asking his vendors to accept his credit on blind faith. But few businessmen today fail to see the unreasonableness of this position. Some may, however, indicate this as their reason for refusal to give a financial statement when as a matter of fact they are merely attempting to force an acceptance of their credit without disclosing their financial position. This attiude will prevail so long as a sufficient number of creditors are found who are weak enough to yield to the buyer's attitude. Happily, credit managers are asking for statements with increasing insistence and, consequently, the number of businessmen who find it possible to maintain the ready acceptability of their credit without disclosing full information is decreasing.

Financial Statement Forms. It is usual for credit departments to furnish to their customers blank forms of financial statements. This practice greatly facilitates the procuring of statements and provides the credit manager with an opportunity to get before the purchaser just the questions he particularly desires answered. Considerable care, therefore, should be taken in drafting a form or forms to be submitted to the customer. Standardization is desirable, so far as possible, because the purchaser becomes familiar with the standard form and has less hesitation in filling it out. A standard form, however, would hardly be the best form for every type of business. It is suggested that any drafted form should conform as nearly as possible to those blanks which are in most common use. Excellent guides can be found in the forms recommended by the National Association of Credit Management and those used by our commercial banks, illustrations of which will be found in Appendix G.

Although some business firms may design a form for each type of legal business entity as well as for special types of business activities, it seems to the author that only two types are necessary: the long form for large business units and the short form for smaller business units.

Elaborate forms requiring much detailed information may not, in use, prove successful with the small businessman. He may not have at his command records in sufficient detail to fill out the more intricate form, and the apparent task of answering so many questions may discourage him entirely from the attempt. On the other hand, the larger houses, with complete accounting systems, will have readily available all the information that a creditor may reasonably require.

ACCOUNTANT'S SUPPLEMENTARY INFORMATION

Relating to the attached financial statement as of_____(date)

Issued by_____Address_____

A. Do the figures on this statement agree with the figures in your report: Yes___ No___
Exceptions_____

B. Did you confirm the following items by direct correspondence:
1. Cash _____Yes___ No___   4. Due from Contractors___Yes___ No___   7. Due to Contractors___Yes___ No___
2. Accounts Receivable _____Yes___ No___   5. Accounts Payable ___Yes___ No___   8. Others (describe) ___Yes___ No___
3. Customers Notes and Acceptances___Yes___ No___   6. Notes Payable _____Yes___ No___
Describe any other method used and relate to the item affected:_____

C. ACCOUNTS RECEIVABLE
1. Does aging agree with your report? Yes___ No___. If not, give aging below for merchandise shipped to customers:
Months   _____ $_____
of   _____ $_____
shipment: _____ $_____
     Prior Months_____ $_____
        Total $_____
2. In your opinion, is provision for bad debts adequate: Yes___ No___ If no opinion, explain:_____
3. In your opinion, is reserve for discounts adequate: Yes___ No___ If no opinion, explain:_____
4. To your knowledge, have any receivables been sold, pledged or assigned during the year immediately preceding the statement date: Yes___ No___
If yes, explain:_____
5. To your knowledge, do Accounts Receivable include any amounts due from subsidiary or affiliated concerns: Yes___ No___
Do Accounts Receivable include any individual accounts owing in excess of 25% of the net worth shown on attached financial statement: Yes___ No___
If yes, state amount $_____ and number_____

D. MERCHANDISE INVENTORY
1. Did you observe and test the count of the physical inventory quantities: Yes___ No___
If no, state how verified_____
2. If not verified, was detailed listing of inventory submitted to you: Yes___ No___   Is copy of original inventory listing in your possession: Yes___ No___
3. How was the inventory priced?_____
4. Did you test the inventory as to prices: Yes___ No___; Arithmetical Accuracy: Yes___ No___
5. To your knowledge, has any merchandise been pledged as collateral during the year immediately preceding statement date: Yes___ No___
If yes, explain:_____

E. INVESTMENTS — Describe_____

F. GENERAL
1. Are you a Certified Public Accountant: Yes___ No___ What State_____ How often do you audit the books?_____
2. Have all expenses and tax liabilities known to you been accrued: Yes___ No___
3. Does the statement include all assets and liabilities known to you: Yes___ No___ Exceptions:_____
Explain_____
4. Do you know of any material contingent liabilities: Yes___ No___ Explain:_____
5. Tax closing date:_____ Last taxable year examined by Internal Revenue Service:_____
6. If client is not incorporated, state amount you believe will be withdrawn for personal income taxes of principal or partners on income earned to statement
date and not shown in statement: $_____
7. Other comments, if any_____

TO NATIONAL CREDIT OFFICE, INC.

The above information is in answer to your inquiry regarding the attached financial statement of my/our client as of the date shown.

⌐   ¬   _____
                                        (Firm Name of Accountant)

                                       _____
                                  (Signature of Individual Authorized to Sign)

L   ⌟   Dated_____

ST 18-57   NATIONAL CREDIT OFFICE, INC. • TWO PARK AVE., NEW YORK 16, N. Y.

Fig. 31. Accountant's supplementary information.

False Financial Statements. The credit manager's appraisal of a risk is based upon the information he has gained bearing upon that risk. The possibility of misinformation should in all cases be considered. The probability of serious error in information received through indirect sources is not great because there is usually no motive in misleading the creditor. Information directly received, however, should be more carefully scrutinized because of the presence of a motive to deceive. The financial statement offers to the dishonest businessman a most excellent opportunity to present false information. This is so because of the great reliance placed upon the capital factor by many credit men, and because of the difficulty in detecting any falsity in the financial statement. To discourage this practice of issuing false statements, both federal and state laws have been passed to punish those who are proved guilty. The practice still persists to some extent; hence the caution to all credit men to give weight to the financial statement according to the appraisal of the character of the man who makes the statement.

The False Statement laws usually provide that one making a false statement for the purpose of using his credit and with the intent that the statement shall be relied upon is guilty of a misdemeanor punishable by fine and imprisonment. In several states, however, a crime is committed, according to the state law, only when property is obtained upon the strength of the statement. Two points stand out as necessities in establishing guilt under the law. It must be proved, first, that the statement is *materially* false and, second, that it was made with the *intent* that it be relied upon. A statement, to be materially false, must so misrepresent an item or items that if the true facts were shown, an ordinarily cautious man would not have accepted credit upon the strength of it, whereas, as falsified, credit would have been accepted. Minor misrepresentations not affecting the general financial standing of the subject are insufficient upon which to base an action. Intent that the statement should be relied upon must also be proved. This may be proved either by showing that the statement was forwarded to a mercantile agency for general distribution among its subscribers or that it was presented to an individual concern from whom the maker of the statement was seeking to obtain goods on credit. The laws of most states cover not only the exchange of credit for goods, but the exchange of credit for more time in which to pay (in the words of the statute "the extension of a credit") as well.

Furthermore, the proof which is required for the conviction of a crime must be "beyond a reasonable doubt." It is not sufficient that the complaining creditor shall himself be convinced of the guilt of the maker of the statement. The complainant must be ready to prove that a certain item or items in the statement render it materially false. This is most easy of accomplishment through those items which are statements of more ascertainable fact, such as *cash*, the *receivables*, or the *liabilities*, as distinguished from those items which are more generally estimates or statements of opinion, such as *merchandise, machinery* and *fixtures*, and *real estate*.

The prosecuting attorney will likewise be very reluctant to undertake a prosecution if the falsity of the statement is plainly apparent. For example, a statement given entirely in round numbers[1] is plainly lacking in accuracy. The courts take the position, and justly so, that no ordinarily cautious man would rely upon such a statement and that when a creditor in possession of such a statement sells upon credit, then the basis for the credit cannot reasonably be the financial statement.

In summary, then, the complaining credit man must be ready to submit facts to prove beyond a reasonable doubt the following:

1. That the defendant made the statement.
2. That the statement is materially false.
3. That the statement was made for the purpose of obtaining goods on credit or the extension of a credit.
4. That the statement was made with the intent that it be relied upon.
5. Practically, too, it may be necessary to prove the statement was relied upon to the creditor's loss. Otherwise the prosecuting attorney and the court may be very reluctant to try the case.

The Continuing and Acceleration Clauses. Financial statement forms almost invariably contain a clause stating that the statement may be relied upon not only when submitted but the creditor may continue to rely upon it until it is withdrawn by the maker. The statement found in Fig. 32 is typical: "There has been no material unfavorable change in my financial condition, and if any such change takes place I will give you notice. Until such notice is given, you are to regard this as a continuing statement." Were it not for such a clause the creditor could rely upon financial data only if the debtor reaffirmed the statement for each credit approved.

Notice of withdrawal of a statement is usually given in practice by the submission of a new statement. Statements may also be implicitly withdrawn; for instance, by refusal to issue a new statement or reutter the old. Were a debtor to withdraw his statements by formal notice to his creditors, prompt and complete curtailment of his credit would undoubtedly result. In any event, a creditor may rely upon a financial statement for only a reasonable time, according to court decisions. Financial statements should be obtained at least annually, and since it is a customary practice for business concerns to issue statements annually, it would seem of doubtful wisdom for a credit manager to rely on statements for a longer period.

The acceleration clause is often employed in bank loans. The purpose of this clause is to enable the bank to advance the due date of the

---

[1] For instance, in even thousands. Statements rounded off to even dollars would be accurate enough for most purposes.

loan if, in its opinion, the safety of the loan is jeopardized. It gives a bank a right which it rarely needs to exercise, but its existence may have a salutary effect upon the borrower. An illustration of the acceleration clause will be found in Appendix H. In general, it may be said the clause gives the bank the option of calling the loan "if there be such a change in the condition or affairs (financial or otherwise) of borrower as in the opinion of bank to increase its credit risk."

The Federal Law. Attempts to enact a federal law, designed solely for the prosecution of makers of false financial statements, have thus far failed. There is, however, a federal law under which prosecution may be brought when the United States mails are used to transmit the false statement. This is Section 215 of the United States Criminal Code, commonly known as the federal law to prevent the use of the mails to defraud. Federal authorities have always vigorously attempted to keep the mails clean and free from aiding in any scheme to defraud. The law provides:

Whoever, having devised or intending to devise any scheme or article to defraud, or for obtaining money or property by means of false or fraudulent pretenses, representations, or promises, etc., . . . shall place or cause to be placed any writing in the mails shall be fined not more than one thousand dollars, or imprisoned not more than five years, or both.

Under this law it is sometimes easier to secure conviction than it is under a state law and in a state court. An advantage under this law is that prosecution can be brought either in the district in which the statement was mailed or in the district in which it was received. To convict the maker of the statement, the complainant must be ready to prove the first four points as set forth in the previous paragraph and, in addition, that the statement was sent through the mail.

The envelope bearing the post-office cancellation stamp presents incontrovertible proof of the use of the mails, provided the statement can be definitely linked up with the envelope. In order to remove any uncertainty concerning the proof of this point, many houses are using the envelope-statement form illustrated in Fig. 32. When both the statement and the post-office cancellation stamp are on the same sheet, proof is self-evident. When the statement is separate from its container, more caution in the handling of both is necessary. The envelope containing a financial statement should be dated and signed and permanently attached to the statement by the person who opens it. Subsequently, if it is necessary to prosecute, the testimony of the clerk who received the statement will have weight in court.

New York False Financial Statement Laws. In 1912, New York enacted a false financial statement law which has often been referred

Form 6W

FINANCIAL STATEMENT OF_____   Date_____ _19____

Kind of Business_____   Address _____

At Close of Business on_____19___ City_____   State_____
ISSUED TO_____   ←{ Name of firm asking for statement

[THIS FORM APPROVED AND PUBLISHED BY NATIONAL ASSOCIATION OF CREDIT MANAGEMENT]

For the purpose of obtaining merchandise from you on credit, or for the extension of credit, we make the following statement in writing, intending that you should rely thereon respecting our exact financial condition.
[PLEASE ANSWER ALL QUESTIONS. WHEN NO FIGURES ARE INSERTED, WRITE WORD "NONE"]

ASSETS	Dollars	Cents	LIABILITIES	Dollars	Cents
Cash In Bank			Accounts Payable (for Merchandise)		
On Hand			Notes & Acceptances Payable for Merchandise		
Accounts Receivable			Owe to_____ Bank		
(Amt. 60 Days Past Due $._____)			(When Due_____Secured) (Unsecured)		
(Amt. Sold or Pledged $ _____)			Income Taxes, Accrued		
Notes and Trade Acceptances Receivable			Other Taxes, Including Sales Taxes, Accrued		
(Amt. Sold or Pledged $._____)			Interest, Accrued		
Merchandise Inventory. Not on Consignment or			Rental, Payrolls, etc., Accrued		
Conditional Sale, at Cost or Market whichever is lower.			Payables to Partners, Relatives.		
(Amount Pledged $_____)			Other Current Liabilities (Describe)		
Other Current Assets (Describe)					
			TOTAL CURRENT LIABILITIES		
TOTAL CURRENT ASSETS			Mortgage on Land and Buildings		
Land and Buildings (Depreciated Value)			Chattel Mortgage on Mdse. or Equipment		
Machinery, Fixtures and Equipment (Depreciated Value)			Liens on Mdse. or Equipment		
			Other Liabilities. No Current (Describe)		
Due from Officers or Non-Customers					
Other Assets (Describe)			TOTAL LIABILITIES		
			Net Worth or {Capital $ {Surplus $		
TOTAL ASSETS			TOTAL NET WORTH AND LIABILITIES		

BE SURE TO ANSWER ALL THESE QUESTIONS

ANNUAL NET SALES	COST OF GOODS SOLD	GROSS PROFIT	OPERATING EXPENSE	NET PROFIT FOR YEAR (Before Federal Taxes)

Amount you are liable for as endorser, guarantor, surety $

Amount of delinquent taxes:
Sales tax $____Income tax $____
Property tax $____Other taxes $____

Amount of merchandise held on consignment $

Amount of machinery or equipment held under lease $

Amount of machinery or equipment under conditional sale $

Amount you pay per month on lease or conditional sale contract $

What books of Account do you keep?

Date of latest inventory

Date of latest audit

Title to business premises is in name of

If premises leased state annual rental

Name of your bank(s)

INSURANCE CARRIED

Fire
Merchandise $
Furn. & Fixt. $
Building $
Extended Coverage $
U & O $

Liability
General $
Auto & Truck $
Burglary $

Life for Benefit of Business $

SCHEDULE OF REAL ESTATE	TITLE IN WHOSE NAME	APPRAISED VALUE

BUY PRINCIPALLY FROM THE FOLLOWING FIRMS:

NAMES	ADDRESSES	AMOUNT OWING

The statement above and on the back of this form has been carefully read by the undersigned (both the printed and written matter), and is, to my knowledge, in all respects complete, accurate and truthful. It discloses to you the true state of my (our) financial condition on the. _____day of _____ 19____. Since that time there has been no material unfavorable change in my (our) financial condition, and if any such change takes place I (we) will give you notice. Until such notice is given, you are to regard this as a continuing statement. The figures submitted are not estimated. They have been taken from my (our) books and physical inventory taken as on date shown.

Name of Individual or Firm_____
If Partnership. Name Partners}_____
If Corporation. Name Officers}_____
How long established_____Previous business experience_____
_____Where_____

Date of Signing Statement_____Street _____City_____State_____

Witness_____   Signed by_____
Residence Address
of Witness_____   Title_____
50M-8-54

FIG. 32a. Envelope financial statement.

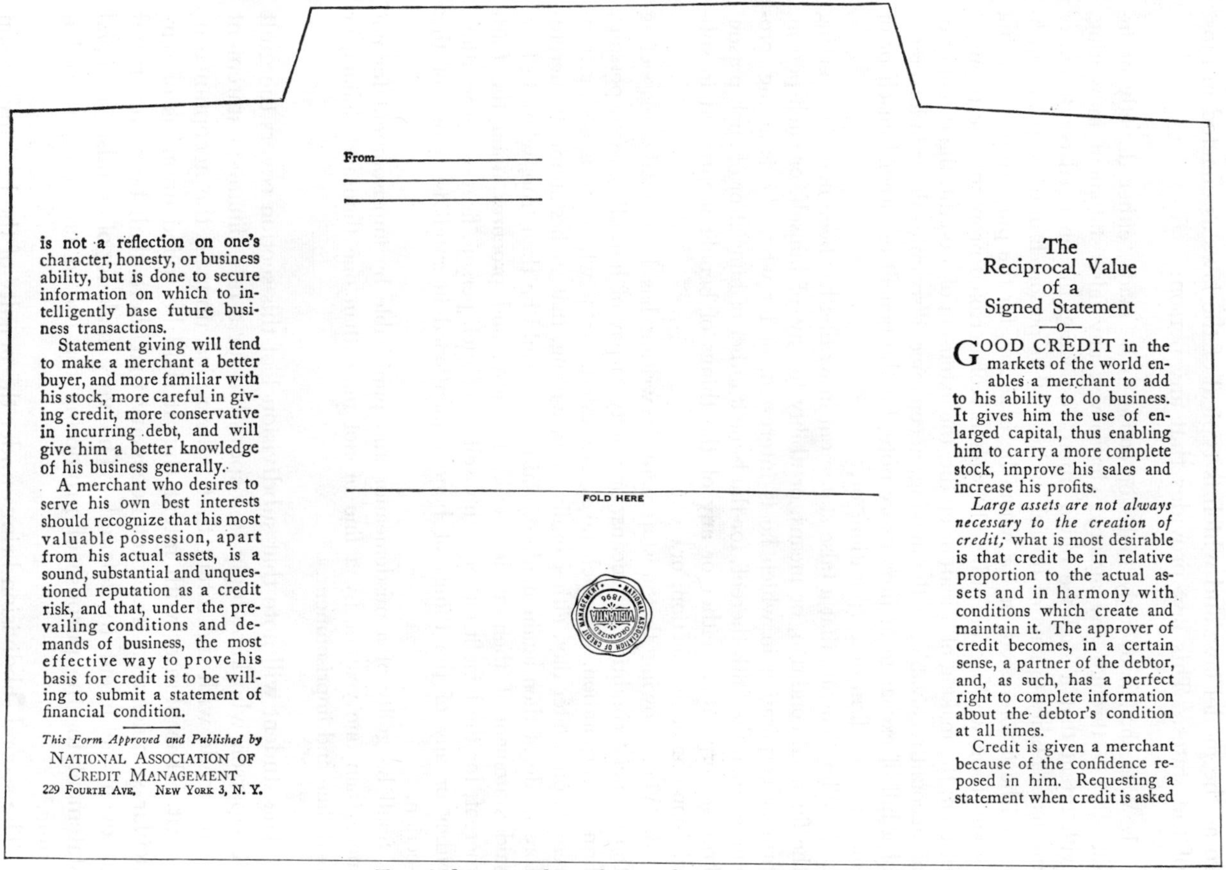

The Reciprocal Value
of a
Signed Statement

GOOD CREDIT in the markets of the world enables a merchant to add to his ability to do business. It gives him the use of enlarged capital, thus enabling him to carry a more complete stock, improve his sales and increase his profits.

Large assets are not always necessary to the creation of credit; what is most desirable is that credit be in relative proportion to the actual assets and in harmony with conditions which create and maintain it. The approver of credit becomes, in a certain sense, a partner of the debtor, and, as such, has a perfect right to complete information about the debtor's condition at all times.

Credit is given a merchant because of the confidence reposed in him. Requesting a statement when credit is asked is not a reflection on one's character, honesty, or business ability, but is done to secure information on which to intelligently base future business transactions.

Statement giving will tend to make a merchant a better buyer, and more familiar with his stock, more careful in giving credit, more conservative in incurring debt, and will give him a better knowledge of his business generally.

A merchant who desires to serve his own best interests should recognize that his most valuable possession, apart from his actual assets, is a sound, substantial and unquestioned reputation as a credit risk, and that, under the prevailing conditions and demands of business, the most effective way to prove his basis for credit is to be willing to submit a statement of financial condition.

This Form Approved and Published by
NATIONAL ASSOCIATION OF
CREDIT MANAGEMENT
229 Fourth Ave., New York 3, N. Y.

From

FOLD HERE

FIG. 32b. Envelope financial statement-cover.

to as the model law, and which is typical of the laws as enacted in most of the states. This law provides that any person:

1. Who shall knowingly make or cause to be made, either directly or indirectly, or through any agency whatsoever, any false statement in writing, with intent that it shall be relied upon, respecting the financial condition, or means or ability to pay, of himself, or any other person, firm or corporation, in whom he is interested, or for whom he is acting, for the purpose of procuring in any form whatsoever, either the delivery of personal property, the payment of cash, the making of a loan or credit, the extension of a credit, the discount of an account receivable, or the making, acceptance, discount, sale or indorsement of a bill of exchange or promissory note, for the benefit of either himself or of such person, firm or corporation; or,

2. Who, knowing that a false statement in writing has been made, respecting the financial condition, or means, or ability to pay, of himself, or such person, firm or corporation in which he is interested, or for whom he is acting, procures, upon the faith thereof, for the benefit either of himself or of such person, firm or corporation, either or any of the things of benefit mentioned in subdivision one of this section; or,

3. Who, knowing that a statement in writing has been made, respecting the financial condition, or means, or ability to pay of himself or such persons, firm or corporation, in which he is interested, or for whom he is acting, represents on a later day, either orally or in writing, that such statements theretofore made, if then again made on said day, would be then true, when in fact, said statement if then made would be false, and procures upon the faith thereof, for the benefit either of himself or of such person, firm or corporation, either or any of the things of benefit mentioned in subdivision one of this section,

Shall be guilty of a misdemeanor and punishable by imprisonment for not more than one year or by a fine of not more than one thousand dollars, or both fine and imprisonment.

The student will note that subdivision 1 of this section covers the guilt of a person who knowingly is responsible for a false financial statement being made with the intent that it be relied upon in the acceptance of credit. The phrase "with intent that it shall be relied upon" is of particular significance. It is not necessary that there shall be actual fraud or even the intent to defraud. The very making of a false financial statement for the purpose of promoting the use of credit is in itself a crime.[1]

The second subdivision brings under the penalty of the law any person who, knowing that a financial statement is false, uses it either for his own benefit or for the benefit "of such person, firm, or corporation in

---

[1] As a practical matter, if the issuance of a false statement proves to be merely an abortive attempt to procure credit, it is unlikely, unless the case be unusual, that a prosecution would be undertaken.

which he is interested or for whom he is acting." The question is frequently raised as to whether this law does not make guilty an employee who is directed to make a statement which he knows is false. Under the words of the statute, the employee to be guilty must either be interested in the concern or acting for it. The employee who is merely carrying out orders in the regular routine of his employment cannot be made responsible. To do so would be eminently unfair, since, in such a case, the employee would be either in fear of losing his position if he refused to obey orders or in fear of the law if the orders were obeyed. Rightly, the party who gives the orders is made the guilty party.

The third subdivision is also of particular benefit to creditors. It is noted that, while the statement originally must have been made in writing, and while it may have been a true statement at the time it was made, if, at a later date, the statement is said, either in writing or orally, to represent at that time the true condition, when, in fact, the statement does not represent the true condition, the person so reuttering the statement is made guilty.

In addition to the above law, New York has enacted another law relating to false financial statements. This is Section 442 of the Penal Law, reading as follows:

Where property is purchased by aid of a duly signed financial statement and in said statement the buyer shall state that he conducts a specified kind of business and keeps books of account of said business, upon failure to pay for such property at maturity of the account, the seller may, at any time within ninety days thereafter, request the buyer to produce his said books of account within ten days after such request. The buyer shall then permit the seller to fully examine such books of account and to make copies of any part thereof. Failure to so produce the books is presumptive evidence that each and every pretense relating to the purchaser's means or ability to pay, in said statement contained, was false when made and known to the buyer to be false.

To use this law several points must be covered. First, the creditor must have a duly signed financial statement; second, the statement must specify that books of account are kept; third, the seller must act within 90 days after the maturity date of the credit; fourth, if the creditor is permitted to examine the books, he may discover falsity in the statement, or he may satisfy himself of the solvency of his debtor; and, fifth, if the debtor refuses to show his books, then the creditor may bring an action against the debtor for issuing a false financial statement, and the burden of proof is on the debtor to prove that the statement that he issued was not false.

It will be seen that this is a law to which the creditor might resort if he has lost confidence in the debtor during the period of the credit, provided, of course, that the credit was based upon a financial statement in which books of account are specified. The effect of this action probably would be to induce the debtor to pay if he were able to do so. Naturally, the creditor would not resort to action under this law so long as he wished to retain the good will of the customer, but every credit man is confronted with circumstances under which he feels it much more important to collect what is due him than to retain the customer's good will.

TEXT AND RESEARCH QUESTIONS

1. Why is not the financial statement alone sufficient as a basis for credit approval?

2. Why is there a greater need of financial statements today than there was 50 or 75 years ago?

3. What are the advantages of the "direct" statement over the "indirect" statement?

4. What reasons do businessmen give for not submitting financial statements to creditors?

5. In drafting a financial statement form to be submitted to customers, what points should be carefully considered?

6. Why is a certain degree of standardization of forms desirable?

7. When is the falsity of financial statements most apt to be discovered?

8. What is the motive which actuates a businessman in making false statements?

9. How would you proceed to judge the truth and accuracy of a statement?

10. Why should all statement forms include phrases similar to "This statement is made with the intent it be relied upon to obtain credit" and "You are to regard this as a continuing statement"?

11. Why is it desirable that the applicant specify the books of account which he keeps?

12. What are the advantages, if any, of the federal law relating to the use of the mails over state laws?

13. When is a statement materially false?

14. What is the motive of credit managers in prosecuting those who give false statements?

15. What is the purpose of the "acceleration clause"? Does a bank, in its dealings with borrowers, frequently resort to it?

PROBLEMS

1. The Ajax Hardware Co., not incorporated, have dealt with you for 3 years, the highest credit being $167. Payments have been from a few days to 2 months slow. A mercantile agency report does not contain a financial statement, and trade reports indicate that payments are from prompt to 70 days slow, with the highest credit reported by any creditor $600. You have received an order for about $900. Write a letter requesting a financial statement.

2. Refer to Problem 1. Assume that you have received an answer to your request for a financial statement in which your customer refers you to the mercantile agencies and further states that he cannot understand why after several years of dealings you should ask for a statement. He states that no other creditors have made the same request. Write the customer a second letter.

3. Refer to Appendix H. Quote the clause or clauses:

    a. That make the representations of the financial statement a part of the contract between the creditor and debtor.

    b. That tie in the financial statement with the false financial statement laws.

    c. That reissue the financial statement every time a new credit is sought.

CHAPTER 19

FINANCIAL STATEMENT INTERPRETATION
AND ASSET ANALYSIS

Statement Nomenclature. The term "financial statement," or just "statement," is loosely used whether the document is properly termed a financial statement or whether it might more properly be called a balance sheet, a statement of assets and liabilities, a statement of conditions, a statement of affairs, or given some other name. When the credit man speaks of a financial statement, he usually has in mind a balance sheet supplemented by other pertinent financial facts, including the income or profit and loss statement when it can be obtained. Stated in other terms, the common conception of the financial statement is a formal document containing the balance sheet, supplementary facts, and operating details.

Purpose of Financial Statement. Many financial statements are made for the express purpose either of furnishing financial information to the stockholders of a corporation or to attract investors into the corporation through the purchase of bonds or stock. Another very large number of financial statements is made for the purpose of interesting prospective bank and mercantile creditors in the acceptance of credit or reassuring those who are already creditors. These statements may serve as well for the information and guidance of the management, and for filing with federal and state income-tax authorities. It is from the viewpoint primarily of management, bank, and mercantile creditors that our investigation of the financial statement, as a source of credit information, is to be made.

At some long-ago period, traders, no doubt, found it necessary to record business happenings, or keep a diary of business transactions for their own information. This simple method of compiling a cumbersome record for the owner of a business has long since given way to an intricate, carefully built accounting system which is becoming more and more standardized, but which is still merely a written record of business activities. The growth of modern business enterprises has made necessary not only standardization of factory and office routine, but also that executives and their subordinates should have available reliable data regarding the activities of their organization.

Records were first compiled for the information of the owner. It was a natural sequence for the businessman to offer this record, or for those secondarily interested to demand it as a proof of his financial soundness. As a consequence, we find the use of the financial statement as a source of credit information steadily increasing.

Authority for Statement Facts. Prior to the investigation of the statement itself the analyst will do well to ascertain, if he can, by whom the statement has been compiled, because faith in the correctness of the various items will vary with the reliance which may be placed upon the ability and the integrity of him who made it. It is well to consider more than the signature of the official appended to the statement, or in many cases—perhaps most—that official is merely relying upon someone else for the accuracy of the facts presented. The statement should be interpreted in the light of the general record and the reputation of the concern which makes it. That no statement is more reliable than the man behind it is an axiom generally accepted by credit managers.

The above remarks apply particularly to that class of statements which are referred to as unaudited. When a statement bears an auditor's report, as well as the signature of an official of the company, a greater dependence is placed upon the report of the accountant than upon the signature of the company's official. There are three reasons for this attitude. First, the fact that the statement was compiled by one who is assumed, whether rightly or not, to be an accounting expert; second, that the statement was compiled by one who had no direct interest in the impression that the statement would make, whether good or bad; third, that the accountant has his professional standing to maintain, and, furthermore, that he is subject to certain disciplinary measures either at the hands of the state under which his charter may have been granted, or at the hands of a society of accountants to which he may belong.

Creditors have found, unfortunately, that the mere fact that a statement was prepared under the supervision of a firm of public accountants is not proof of the truth and accuracy of the statement. There are two points to be investigated even in the certified statement. The first question to be answered is who are the accountants? Can they be relied upon? Are they competent? Are they trustworthy? The competency of the certified public accountant can generally be assumed but it must be remembered that much of the actual work, oftentimes, is in the hands of junior accountants in the employ of the public accountants. It must be said in truth, however, that incompetency on the part of accountants gives the credit manager but little cause to worry. Nor should the reader infer that the author is raising the question of the general trustworthiness of public accountants. Their ethical code and integrity are, as a class, undoubtedly high. There will be found, however, unworthy representatives in all the professions. It is for the unscrupulous accountant that the credit manager should be on the alert. As a matter of fact, bank loaning officers and mercantile credit managers are not only insisting upon a greater number of audited statements, but are, in many instances, insisting upon the privilege of approving or rejecting the firm of accountants selected by the prospective debtor to make the audit. The accountant with high integrity will attach his name only to the statement which discloses *all* the liabilities and which shows the assets, according to his opinion, at their true worth.[1] He will not, in exchange for a fee, prepare a favorable report when the true report would be unfavorable. Businessmen are more and more recognizing the distinction between the true auditor and the charlatan.

The Accountant's Report. The second point, perhaps the more important of the two, is the extent of the auditor's investigation. The most competent and the most trustworthy auditor may be limited in the scope of his investigation. The auditor's report or certificate, if carefully read, will disclose his limitation, if there has been any. For example, the certification which follows may be termed an unqualified certificate because no reservation or qualification whatever has been made:

I have audited the accounts of the John Doe Manufacturing Co. for the year ended Dec. 31, 19—, and I certify that the above balance sheet is, in my opinion, a true statement of the financial condition of the John Doe Manufacturing Co. at Dec. 31, 19—.

(Signed)   Richard Roe,
Certified Public Accountant

In contrast to the certificate above, by which it is seen that, in a sense, Richard Roe stakes his reputation as an accountant upon the accurateness of the balance sheet, is shown the following certificate which is decidedly qualified:

The balance sheet herewith presented is a true copy of the assets and liabilities as shown on the books of the company.

(Signed)   Richard Roe,
Certified Public Accountant

The accountant's statement in this case is almost worthless to the creditor. It proves no more than that the books of the company are in

[1] Some credit agencies, on receiving a financial report, ask the accountant to complete the supplemental data. The type of questions asked are shown in the National Credit Office, Inc., Accountant's Supplementary Information, Fig. 31.

balance. The creditor can assume no more than the certificate states. Put in a negative sense, he must assume that the cash has not been verified, the accounts receivable not tested, the inventory not checked, or any other action taken which naturally falls within the scope of an investigation. If the analyst would avoid trouble, he should understand that the accountant's certificate must be strictly interpreted.

A third illustration of an accountant's certification is given.

We hereby certify that we have audited the books and accounts of . . . . for the year ended Dec. 31, 19—, that the above balance sheet is in agreement with the books and in our opinion fairly presents, subject to the comments in our complete report, the financial position of the company as at Dec. 31, 19—.

(Signed) Roe, Doe, & Co.,
Certified Public Accountants

There is no objection to this form of certification, provided the complete report accompanies every balance sheet put into the hands of creditors. It rarely does. In its absence, credit managers are prone to overlook the qualifying phrase or to assume that the comments, if known, would have an insignificant value in interpreting the subject's financial position. In some cases, nothing could be further from the truth.

The terms "report" or "opinion" are now preferred by accountants to the term "certificate," and the former will undoubtedly gradually supersede the latter in general use. A typical form of audit report, known as the Short Form of Report and presently in general use, states:

We have examined the balance sheet of the XYZ Company as of ———— and the statements of income and surplus for the fiscal year then ended, have reviewed the system of internal control and the accounting procedures of the company and, without making a detailed audit of the transactions, have examined or tested accounting records of the company and other supporting evidence, by methods and to the extent we deemed appropriate.

In our opinion, the accompanying balance sheet and related statements of income and surplus present fairly the position of the XYZ Company at ———— and the results of its operations for the fiscal year, in conformity with generally accepted accounting principles applied on a basis consistent with that of the preceding year.

This form, it will be noted, is more specific in explaining the scope of the audit, thus defining and limiting the auditor's responsibility.

Liability of Accountant. The accountant owes much of his employment to creditors. Many concerns regularly employing outside auditors would not do so if it were not for the insistent demand of creditors for certified statements. The question, then, may rightly be asked: For whom are accountants employed? Though paid by the concerns which they are auditing, they are, in many instances, really issuing the statement for the creditors. Yet creditors, who have suffered losses through certified false financial statements upon which they have relied, have had no redress against the accountants except for fraud. The courts for a long time held it to be unreasonable to hold the accountant liable to any other than his employer. Court decisions in more recent cases,[1] however, have taken a broadened viewpoint of fraud so that it may include gross negligence on the part of the accountant in making the audit.

If the accountant intentionally certifies to a false statement and so becomes a conspirator in a scheme to defraud, he may rightly be held liable. The later reasoning of the courts imposes upon him the duty to be not only honest but diligent in the performance of his work. Creditors will take a reasonable view of the accountant's liability. They do not wish to make him assume the position of a guarantor, nor do they wish to hold him to any liability for errors of judgment honestly made. They do expect of him honesty, expertness, and a reasonable degree of thoroughness.

Accountant versus Credit Manager. A balance sheet is nothing more than a condensed inventory of assets, liabilities, and capital shown in terms of money on a given date. In this inventory, only the cash and the liabilities are fixed in their valuation. "Cash" has reached its final form, and from both the owner's and the creditor's standpoint the liabilities are subject to neither increase nor decrease. Aside from the items of cash, the balance sheet presents assets of some uncertainty as to their value. For example, accounts receivable, although they represent ascertainable facts, may be to some extent uncollectible, while such items as merchandise, machinery, real estate, etc., are shown at a value which can be no more than an estimate or opinion.

It has been said the financial statement is the result of facts, accounting convention, and personal judgments.[2] In the preparation of the financial statement, it is the function of the accountant to ascertain the facts, to follow accounting convention in the valuation of certain items, and to use conservative and expert judgment in fixing the value of these items which are, to a certain extent, valued by appraisal. In this, the accountant is greatly aided by having available all the records and data and usually the opportunity of physical inspection. He appraises, combines, classifies, and the result is the condensed inventory of assets and liabilities which we call the balance sheet.

The task of the credit manager is, to some extent, the reverse of this

[1] *Ultramares Corp. v. Touche Niven,* 255 N.Y. 570. *State Street Trust Co. v. Ernst et al.,* 278 N.Y. 104, 15 N.E. (2d) 416.

[2] Examination of Financial Statements by Independent Public Accountants, *Bulletin of the American Institute of Accountants,* 1936, p. 1.

process. He receives the condensed inventory and considers it, item by item, in an attempt to fathom any hidden significance that there may be in the item. He compares various items with each other to discover any disproportion among them. He attempts to get behind the bare statement of values to discover the processes by which those values were determined.

Methods of Analysis. The analysis of a financial statement, if it is to be a thorough analysis, may be divided into three parts: internal analysis, comparative analysis, and sales analysis. The internal analysis treats each item in a statement according to its own value and its relation to every other item. It is the first step to be taken in every analysis, and in the absence of comparative statements and the sales figure it is the only step that can be taken. Comparative analysis is the method by which two or more statements of different dates are compared with each other. In this method, similar items of different statements are compared with each other to discover distortions or trends. Sales analysis covers the important question of "turnover." It is the method by which probable profits or losses are forecast for the future. In this method of analysis, the sales volume is compared with certain of the more important items of the balance sheet. Ratios, to be explained later, may be used in each of these analyses.

The Date of the Statement. The date of the statement should be taken into careful consideration for two major reasons. No business remains in a static condition. Kaleidoscopic changes are constantly taking place. Usually, too, the business from a capital and credit standpoint is going either forward or backward. The date of the statement or, let us say, its age warns the analyst of the progression or regression that may have taken place. The second reason for the careful consideration of the date of the statement is to compare the position of the business at the date of the statement with changes in condition which may result from seasonal activity, from the condition of the industry itself, and from the condition of business in general.

The creditor, unfortunately, has not reached the point where he can command financial statements from his customers at frequent intervals. The prevailing practice of concerns, from which statements can be obtained at all, is to issue them once a year, although banks are to some extent both demanding and obtaining semiannual and even quarterly statements. A concern should normally issue a financial statement at least once a year, and it will be found that this will be done either at the end of the calendar year or the end of its natural business year. While either date may be accepted as satisfactory, from the credit manager's standpoint, a statement made when the business is as its peak would be most desirable, since it would show the condition of the concern when it is most extended. Some credit managers are encountered, however, who prefer the statement made at the end of the concern's natural business year, since such a statement discloses the customer's ability to liquidate his short-term indebtedness.

The natural business year end of any business is the time when its operations come to a temporary close, or there is at least a seasonal lull in its activity. December 31, which is the closing date of perhaps three-fourths of all business, is a highly inconvenient closing date for those concerns which find themselves in the middle of a busy business season at that time. More than a third of businesses which now take inventories on Dec. 31 could change to some other date, and savings amounting to millions in inventory takings could thus be effected. Not only would management and stockholders benefit, but accounting firms would be greatly relieved of the rush to make audits following the end of the year. Both clients and creditors could be better served by the accounting profession because audits could be made more promptly following the taking of inventory and under less pressure than now prevails.[1]

The selection of the natural business year end as the statement date would also aid credit agencies which now are under the necessity of incorporating the new statements in credit reports, revising ratings, and making such changes as the new factual information may require. Against these advantages is the reluctance of business to change a practice and the obvious reason that a change in the statement date would make more difficult comparisons with previous years.

Whatever may be the date of the statement, the analyst will do well to assume that the statement presents the best possible condition that could be presented as of that date. Furthermore, if the statement is old, that is, if the regular date for the issuance of a statement has been permitted to lapse, the reasonable assumption is that the credit position has become less favorable, for the concern presumably would make a later statement if it could show an improved condition.

Classification of Statement Items. The financial statement, as previously stated, is a condensed inventory of assets and liabilities. Condensed as it is, its items are frequently further combined into a few groups, according to the manner in which they function within the enterprise. While the division is an arbitrary one, it is also a more or less natural one. In order to classify the items for the purpose of our discussion, the assets will be divided into four groups: current assets, miscellaneous assets, fixed assets, and deferred assets, including intangibles.

---

[1] The National Business Year Council was created in 1935 by the National Association of Credit Management, the Robert Morris Associates, the National Association of Cost Accountants, and the American Institute of Accountants to study seasonal operations and to aid businesses in selecting the most logical date.

A similar division is made of the liabilities[1] into current liabilities (with frequently a subdivision of accrued liabilities), long-term liabilities, and net worth. Each of these groups will be briefly explained.

1. *Current assets*, as the name implies, comprise those properties which, in the normal course of business, usually 1 year, are readily converted into cash which may be used for payment of debts. Current assets are also frequently described as "quick" assets, and certain of the current assets are further classified as "quick current" or "slow current." Cash and cash equivalents plus current receivables are classified as "quick current" assets. Subgroups of current assets may also be made of working assets and other convertible assets. Under this subdivision, working assets would include only the cash, the receivables resulting from the sale of merchandise or services, and the inventory, while other convertible assets might include good marketable securities or other very liquid temporary investments. If there is a doubt about the convertibility of an asset, it is not a current asset.

2. *Miscellaneous or other assets* are those assets about which there is an uncertainty as to their collectibility or convertibility into cash during the current year, or those assets which the management has no intention of converting into cash in the normal course of business. The following are some examples of miscellaneous assets: (a) receivables which are collectible after 1 year, or which are doubtful of collection; (b) miscellaneous current assets, so classified by the accountant. A conservative analyst treats miscellaneous current assets as a doubtful current asset.

3. *Fixed assets* are those assets used in the production of goods or services. There is no intention of converting these assets to cash except in final liquidation or for their scrap value. As their name implies, they are more or less permanent assets, such as furniture or fixtures, machinery and real estate, etc.

4. *Deferred charges, or deferred assets*, frequently also titled "prepaid charges," consist of payments which have been made, the benefit of which will fall in subsequent accounting periods. This group of accounts may be illustrated by such items as insurance premiums, prepaid interest, prepaid taxes, or discount on bonds sold.

Grouped with deferred and prepaid accounts would be intangibles such as good will, patents, etc. These deferred expenses and intangibles frequently have little value in liquidation. Although the prepaid accounts may tend to lessen the demand on cash during their life, they contribute nothing to cash, which may be used to pay current or even long-term debt.

[1] Liabilities are discussed in detail in Chapter 20.

The Securities and Exchange Commission classification of assets for industrial and commercial corporations includes: Current Assets, Investments, Fixed Assets, Intangible Assets, Deferred Charges, and Other Assets. The student will note that this classification segregates investments from the miscellaneous "other" assets and subdivides the deferred group.

Liabilities are classed as either current or long-term, including in each group specific reserves.

1. *Current liabilities* are those which are payable within the current year from statement date, and payment of which is usually made from the proceeds of the current assets. The most common items in the current liability group are the accounts payable, the notes payable, and current sinking fund requirements or maturities of long-term debt. There may be other current liabilities which, though neither entered in the books not yet due, are, nevertheless, actual and should be shown. These consist of such items as wages, rent, taxes, or interest, the payment of which will fall at some later period. This subgroup is called "accrued liabilities."

2. The usual practice is to classify any liability which becomes due or is payable after 1 year from the date of the statement as a *long-term liability*. This class includes usually all long-term notes, bonded indebtedness, real and chattel mortgages, all net of current payments, and certain liability reserve (i.e., Reserve for Pensions).

3. *Net worth*, which is ownership capital, or equity, includes capital stock, various types of surplus, and contingency, or special reserves. The several types of reserves are discussed more fully later.

Purpose of Analysis. When the credit man has the final statement of a debtor placed before him for his consideration, he studies it from three standpoints. (1) He makes a judgment upon the reliability of the report, based upon the first C of credit analysis—Character. (2) He appraises what credit men are wont to call the liquidity of the business, by which is meant the degree of the sufficiency of cash[1] to meet the obligations of the business at all times. This feature of liquidity is approved according to the standards or requirements of the creditor house and, accordingly, accepted or rejected. Thus a seller who is willing to wait for his pay for some time after the maturity date of the debt may be willing to accept a risk somewhat deficient in this quality of liquidity, while a second creditor might refuse to sell a concern whose statement indicated, in any degree, slowness of payments. (3) The

---

[1] The phrase "sufficiency of cash" does not imply a large quantity of cash but rather the flow of cash into the business resulting from the sale of its products, or the ability to provide cash through short-term borrowing from banks or other financing institutions.

analyst must consider the ability of the risk, either partially or completely, to liquidate. By this is meant the ability to reduce appreciably the liabilities by a forced or sacrifice sale of a portion of the assets or to meet all the liabilities by the quick sale of all assets. The purpose of financial statement analysis might be stated in another way. It is to determine whether the funds used in the business are most ideally invested in the various assets of the business, whether the sources of those funds are ideally proportional between creditors and owners to give the creditors adequate safety and the owners satisfactory income, and whether the sales and profits indicate that the capital is being used with maximum efficiency. Disproportionate investment in the assets[1] means that some of the capital is idle capital, while disproportionate investment of capital[2] by creditors and owners results in a lack of safety for the creditors or in a curtailment of income for the owners.

Cash. According to Webster, "cash" means money at hand or readily available. This definition of cash is fair enough from the credit man's standpoint as long as the cash is not assigned. Under it may be included ready money in drawer or safe, bank deposits payable on demand, checks, money orders, or other instruments, received as money, which, in the ordinary course of business, will be received by a bank as a cash deposit. Under this definition there cannot properly be included postdated checks, I.O.U.'s, receipts for expenditures, or other memorandums which may be held in the cash drawer. If correctly stated, cash may be accepted at its face value.

The creditor usually asks that cash be segregated as follows:

1. Cash on hand
2. Cash in bank

This segregation is important, for there are a number of reasons for considering the terms separately. Cash on hand is usually of the lesser importance, because, under normal conditions, it should be relatively small. The item "cash in bank" is subject to verification. While it is usually impossible to obtain from a bank the exact amount of any of its customer's balances, the bank will usually verify a balance given on a balance sheet, particularly if the bank is named therein. The reader will, of course, realize that the books of the bank and its depositors may not agree, owing to checks drawn and in transit or deposit items in transit. Ordinarily, however, the bank's balance should be equal to or exceed that of the customer. A statement of the cash balance may also enable the investigator to draw from the bank information as to whether the balance is an average balance or inflated for the occasion.

[1] Idle plant.
[2] Creditor's contribution equal or greater than owner's interest.

The average balance maintained, when learned by the investigator, enables him to judge whether or not the account may be a desirable one to the bank. Particularly is this true if the customer be a borrower from the bank. In the latter event, a commensurate balance, usually 20 per cent, must be maintained. Another point worthy of consideration is that the bank has a lien upon the cash balance, if the bank is a creditor.

How much cash a concern should carry cannot be covered in a general statement. The amount varies with different businesses and at different seasons. The creditor should judge as accurately as he can the cash requirements, and, if cash appears to be ample, he will be satisfied with this item of the statement. A customer would be well advised to hold a minimum amount of cash since, as cash, it is nonproductive. Many large corporations make a daily record of their receipts and expected payments and invest any excess cash in short-term government securities.

Accounts Receivable-Trade. The "accounts receivable" item is, or should be, the sum total of "accounts owing by customers, good and collectible, not pledged or sold." In order to verify this item as an asset and to appraise its liquidity, the credit man would like to examine the customer's accounts receivable ledger in detail, and, indeed, this is frequently done by bank and other credit men when a thorough investigation is being made. Ordinarily, however, such a detailed consideration of accounts receivable is hardly possible, and the analyst has to be content with the consideration of certain points which would influence his appraisal of this item.

The credit man would like to have an "aging" of the receivables, in other words, a schedule which divides the accounts into those which are not due and "ages" those past due according to how long past due— for instance, 30, 60, 90, 120 days, or more. If large amounts of receivables are over 6 months past due, the analyst may desire further explanation and certainly should place the excessive past due accounts in miscellaneous assets. He should know the subject's usual terms of sale and discounts offered under them, since terms may aid in determining the number of days required in collecting the receivables, and the discount shows the amount that will be deducted by the accounts when making payment. He would like to know whether the receivables have been full depreciated for bad debts, a point sometimes, but not always, covered by showing in the statement a reserve for bad debts. He would like to know, too, the location of the accounts, since bad industrial conditions in certain sections might render them slow of collection. Sales to subsidiaries or to affiliated companies, or disproportionately large sales to one or a few accounts, may present an element of danger. The success of parent, subsidiary, and affiliated companies is apt to be bound together closely, so that, when support is needed, it is most likely to be lacking, while the loss of a large customer, or more particularly its bankruptcy, might be disastrous.[1]

Instalment receivables should be segregated and those due after 1 year classified in the miscellaneous group as not current. For analysis purposes, a separate aging schedule should be obtained.

Discounted Receivables. If the receivables have been sold on a recourse basis, the analyst might consider working out an alternate comparison. In the new comparison, the discounted receivables would be classified as both current assets and current liabilities. In this way, his statement comparisons from time to time on this company, and with other companies in the industry, will be validated. The reader should note that a net position of receivables sold destroys the possibility of any effective computation of collection periods and current ratios.

Pledged Receivables. Receivables may be pledged to secure debt. For adequate protection to the loan, the borrower is required to pledge his best accounts, and in amounts greater than the value of the loan. This difference is called the "margin." An analyst may need to ascertain his protection by working out a current position excluding both the pledged receivables and secured debt. Frequently the margin for general creditors proves to be scanty.

The relation of the date of the statement to the seasonal activity of the business should not be neglected. Other points to be considered are the relation of the accounts receivable to other items, particularly the sales and inventory. This relationship is discussed in a subsequent chapter.

Finally, emphasis is placed upon the limitation of the item given in the first sentence of this section. The accounts receivable included in the statement should be good and not questionable; they should be collectible according to terms or with reasonable promptness; and they should be the property of the maker of the statement. If there are any liens upon them held by another, they should be shown. When the accounts receivable conform to the principles here laid down, they form an asset in which the creditor may place much confidence.

Notes Receivable. Like accounts receivable, this item may sometimes represent obligations of others than customers. For example, partners, officers, or employees may have given notes for sums advanced to them. When such is the case, these miscellaneous notes should be segregated

---

[1] Note: Receivables due from subsidiaries or affiliated companies are "controlled," and collection may be postponed if convenient in times of stress. A conservative analyst may prefer to carry these receivables in the miscellaneous group rather than among the current assets.

from customer's notes so that the former may be separately appraised as an asset. Whether these miscellaneous notes are good current assets or not must be determined by the analyst.

Notes receivable, since they are a written promise to pay a certain amount on a definite date, are superior to accounts receivable, as an asset, *provided* they are obligations of a class of customers with a credit standing not inferior to the accounts-receivable customers as a class. It should be remembered in this connection, however, that in comparatively few industries is it customary to give notes for goods. If it is not the general practice, then the reason for substituting the note for the book account must be sought. It will be found, in such cases, either that the notes represent accounts which have become due and are settled by note rather than by check or that the creditor has insisted upon a note under the impression that it would, to some degree, lessen the risk. Such notes are obviously inferior to good accounts receivable. The superiority of the credit instrument cannot overcome the inferiority of the obligor. Hence, the analyst may find himself obliged to regard notes receivable as a somewhat frozen instead of a very liquid asset, and he may even deem it necessary to scale down the item, to cover possible bad debts.

Aside from the warning given above, the interpretation of notes receivable is quite similar to that of accounts receivable. The analyst should be on the alert to discover whether any notes shown as assets may have been discounted and yet carried at their face value or a contingent liability may have been created by such discounts without being shown upon the financial statement.

Trade Acceptances. While trade acceptances might be included under the caption Notes and Bills Receivable, it is better to have them segregated to facilitate analysis. If trade acceptances are customarily taken in payment of goods, they represent a very liquid asset. The rapidity with which they convert into cash depends upon the terms under which they are drawn. A knowledge of the terms is therefore important. The analyst will, of course, wish also to consider the general credit standing of the acceptors to enable him to judge the delinquencies and the bad debts arising from this class of customers.

Reserve for Doubtful Accounts. This is a valuation reserve, since it in effect writes down accounts receivable to a probable liquidating value. Whether the reserve is adequate is a matter of judgment. The conservative analyst would expect it to be in line with the average in the industry.

Inventory. Merchandise or inventory is always an item of great interest to the credit analyst, and it should be subjected to the closest scrutiny. Often it is a mystery item whose true appraisal is difficult. Even the principals in a business do not always have implicit confidence in the accuracy of the merchandise inventory, as disclosed by the statement.

The term "inventory," as used in its general sense, refers to any goods in whatever stage of completion together with the necessary supplies, which in the normal course of business is sold as merchandise or stock in trade. By "necessary supplies" is meant any packing materials, crating, wrapping paper, boxes, etc.

In retailing and wholesaling companies, inventory represents stock to be sold, usually without further processing. In a manufacturing company, inventory consists of raw material, work-in-process, and finished goods.

A number of questions arise in the analysis of inventory. The more important ones are reviewed here.

Inventory Accuracy. Can the creditor rely upon the accuracy of the inventory? Does it include any goods held on consignment or subject to a lien of any sort? How was the quantity and value arrived at? The approved method is the physical inventory. Worthy of less reliance is the perpetual inventory system, while the inventory that is a mere guess has almost no value in aiding the credit man to appraise the credit risk.

A growing practice, which should be ardently fostered by all credit men, is to have the certified accountant assume responsibility, within his limitations, for the accuracy of the inventory. This the accountant does by having the inventory taken under his supervision, thereby making it possible for him to verify the physical quantity and, with perhaps somewhat less accuracy, the value of it.

In a great many financial statements, the inventory represents fully 50 per cent of the total assets. Where the accountant has verified the other items in the statement and has accepted the inventory "as submitted," the verification cannot be regarded as complete. If it is good practice to verify all other items on the statement, why is it not just as reasonable to verify the inventory? Of what value is a certification which does not include verification or definite tests of the inventory by the accountant?

Certification of inventories is the next forward step in the accounting profession. Accountants would do well to encourage its practice. It is an inevitable development, and we believe that the accountants recognize this opportunity for service. In this undertaking they can most certainly rely on cooperation from credit grantors and merchants.[1]

Inventory Valuation. How is the merchandise valued? The business public is becoming educated to the accepted practice, which is to compute the value of merchandise at the cost price or the present market price, whichever is lower, in the instance of each item. The credit man

[1] From an unpublished pamphlet of the Uptown Credit Group of the Textile Industry, New York, 1934, Samuel Bertcher, chairman.

can hardly assume, however, that the proper practice has been invariably followed, for *either* cost or market price may have been wrongly used, or even selling price *may* be used in the computation. To show the inventory at selling price, while it must be said that it is rarely done, is distinctly bad practice, for it records a profit that has not been earned without taking into account the expense that must be undergone in selling the merchandise. Furthermore, if the profit should subsequently be earned, it belongs to a subsequent accounting period.

It is likewise improper to value the inventory at the present market price when that exceeds the cost price on the principle that profit must not be recorded until the goods are sold. On the other hand, if the market price is lower, it must be used because the replacement price or present price determines the ultimate price at which goods are sold. To follow the rule of cost or market, whichever is lower, is extremely important in those industries in which prices may fluctuate widely. An inventory at cost might grossly exaggerate the actual income that might be derived from the sale of the merchandise. An inventory taken at market value might also indicate a false profit if there has been a further decline in price between the time the goods were inventoried and their sale.

The "last in–first out" method of inventory valuation has gained favor with businessmen, particularly since 1939[1] and the advent of high tax rates. The "lifo" method is based on the assumption that the latest units of inventory purchased are the first ones sold and the price paid for these units is the price used in computing the cost of the articles sold. Thus the profit is determined by using the actual cost of all the goods sold. The motive of this method is to nullify gains or losses resulting from "the cost or market—whichever is lower" basis of inventory valuation in a rising or falling price level. Since taxes are paid on current profits, which may be lower because of the use of this inventory method, "lifo" inventory valuation has aroused considerable interest.

Under this method the inventory shown on the balance sheet may or may not have a close relationship to its present market value. For example, a concern with an inventory of 1,000 units valued at $10,000 would, if its inventory never was less than 1,000 units, always carry that quantity of its inventory at the same price. Recent cost or present market might be far above or far below that value.

This method, unless there were an explanatory statement showing the relation of the stated value of the inventory to its present market value, would add to the analyst's difficulty in determining whether the inventory is in proper relation to sales and current assets, as well as in determining its liquidating value.

[1] Approved for Income Tax purposes.

Other methods of inventory valuation are frequently encountered such as the "base-stock" method, "average-cost" method, and "inventory-reserve" method. The base-stock method is quite similar in its effect to the "lifo" method, since under this method a certain quantity of inventory is carried at the same value year after year, regardless of its cost or market value.

The inventory reserve is used to accomplish the same purpose as the "lifo" and base-stock methods of valuation. Inventories, however, are valued on the customary basis of cost or market, whichever is lower, and, during a period of rising prices, a reserve is provided on the liability side of the balance sheet for the net book gain on the base stock. During falling prices, losses in inventory value are charged against the inventory reserve. Thus the profit shown is not affected by either rising or declining prices.

Regardless of the method of inventory valuation, the aggregate net profit would vary but little over a sufficiently long period of time, but the net profit of the respective years within the period might vary considerably, depending upon which method was used. It will at once be seen that, since income-tax rates are not stationary and net losses cannot be carried forward and backward intact, the selection of an inventory method of valuation is of supreme practical importance.

Inventory Analysis. Of what does the inventory consist? The nature of the business will answer the question in part. It will not, however, disclose the condition of the stock. If the subject be a manufacturing concern, it is desirable to have the inventory segregated into raw goods, goods in process, finished goods, and supplies. This enables the credit man to judge whether or not the customer is presenting a balanced inventory and, also, to appraise more correctly the value of the inventory in the event of forced liquidation. Some kinds of merchandise are subject to much greater depreciation than others when thrown on the market. Every credit man should acquaint himself with the depreciation that is usual in his own industry. As a general rule, it may be said that the raw material will suffer the least depreciation because of its availability to other manufacturers. Contrasted to the raw material, goods in process may require considerable depreciation, for much time and labor must be spent to put them in salable condition. The finished product may more readily be sold but at a larger discount from the replacement value than in the case of raw material. The condition of the inventory involves also freshness, salability, and style. In some industries, there are rapid changes of style and fashions, and for these and other reasons merchandise may rapidly deteriorate in value.

The ultimate objective in the analysis of merchandise is to determine whether or not the stock is normal for the time of year at which the inventory is taken. Usually, the statement will be issued at the end of the season when the stock is low. The analyst should guard against the possibility that merchandise for the new season has been taken in but omitted, together with the corresponding liabilities, from the balance sheet. This practice, while absolutely wrong, is sometimes countenanced even by accountants.

It is, in fact, impossible to warn the reader of all the evil practices and, as well, honest errors in judgment that may be encountered in the inventory. While pleading guilty to reiteration, the author can give no better advice than to have in mind largely the character and the capacity of the owner of the business when putting an appraisal upon the inventory item of his financial statement.

Marketable Securities. At statement date, because it may be at a time of the seasonal lull in a company's activity, the business may have surplus funds. The problem is: Should a favorable cash position be shown, or would good business judgment dictate the placing of surplus funds in short-term investments? The author would not criticize management if it did the latter, thus maximizing the use of its capital. However, to make sure that the funds are available when needed, the analyst should question any investment except short-term government bonds.[1] Management should attend to the activities of producing and selling goods and should not be "playing the market." Businessmen have a tendency to hold on to investments, other than short-term government bonds, even though the funds invested may be needed to pay creditors. Soon conducting a business becomes a secondary activity in favor of investment, which at best is only prudent speculation. Some creditors, particularly commercial banks, will require the borrower to dispose of marketable securities as a prerequisite to borrowing.

As a general rule, marketable securities may be considered as current assets if they represent good liquid values. Otherwise, they should be classed below the line as miscellaneous assets.

Because investments usually are carried at cost, the analyst must ascertain their current market value. The possible profit on an investment is a "hidden asset," but a loss is actual at statement date, whether taken or not. Consequently it will be necessary to reflect losses in preparing the spread. This is best done by reducing the cost to current market values and carrying this amount as a current asset or—if one is inclined to be conservative—as a miscellaneous asset. The difference, in either case, would be treated as an intangible account titled "Excess Cost over Market." Thus surplus is not disturbed; the balance sheet still balances, and there is only adjustment to be made in a source and application of funds statement (discussed in Chapter 24).

[1] Includes certificates and notes.

Other Current Assets. These accounts bear close attention. Only if the analyst is sure that an account is properly so classified will he treat it as a current asset. He must assume nothing.

Miscellaneous Assets. Investments, advances to subsidiary companies, and even receivables from controlled or affiliated companies should be grouped in this part of the analysis. Any type of asset that is doubtful of collection, or even of long-term collection, is not a current asset.

The credit or financial analyst must watch this group of assets for potential losses. He should also make sure that the total amount for this group is not out of proportion to the total current and fixed assets.

Fixed Assets. As credit terms have increased in length and instalment terms have become a permanent feature of the credit economy, the credit executive has found that an analysis of the current position alone is insufficient. He consequently has to consider more fully all parts of the financial report. Does a business concern own or lease its facilities? Does it adequately depreciate its plant? What prices were paid for the plant? Was it paid for in stock or cash? What insurance is carried? These are a few of the questions he must consider.

Plant, Machinery, and Tools. Other questions raised in the analyst's mind in the consideration of this item are chiefly these: Are the physical size of the plant and the quantity of the machinery and tools commensurate with the volume of business attained? Are they properly valued and properly depreciated? In the event of liquidation, what may be realized upon them? How modern is the plant, and is the machinery to any degree obsolete? While these are a part of the fixed assets and therefore contribute very little, directly, to the payment of current obligations, nevertheless they are essential to the business and are the means of production of the current assets upon which constant liquidation of the liabilities depends. Therefore, their efficiency and value are of considerable interest to the creditor.

The credit manager should always bear in mind that the usual practice is to carry fixed assets such as real estate and machinery at their cost value, subject, of course, to depreciation charges. The value thus shown may be considerably misleading since the asset may have been acquired when prices were either much higher or much lower than at the time the analyst is weighing the statement.

Furniture and Fixtures. This item is usually of minor importance in the analysis of financial statement. The analyst should consider whether the amount invested in furniture and fixtures is commensurate with the size and nature of the business and whether the proper procedure with reference to depreciation is being carried out.

Deferred Assets. There may appear on the balance sheet items called "deferred assets," "deferred charges," or "suspense debits." All may mean virtually the same thing. Under such a caption are included such items as insurance premiums paid, interest, taxes, rent, stationery and supplies, and other sundry expenses paid, a part of which, ascertained by calculation, justly belongs as a charge to the period following the date of the statement. These items are usually disregarded by the analyst when he is appraising the liquidating value of the assets, because, with comparatively rare exceptions, nothing can be recovered from them. Nevertheless, they are rightly included in the balance sheet, for, if permitted to remain in the expense account, the income account would not show the true results of the operation for the period, nor would the surplus account reflect the true condition of the business. The presence of such items in the balance sheet is an indication of proper accounting methods and, therefore, creates a favorable impression.

The trend toward placing some of these accounts among current assets on the theory that they lessen the drain on cash during future operating periods is generally deplored by credit men. To them it would appear to be a step toward the rationalization that all assets are current. The analyst should have no confusion if he will correctly define current assets.

Intangible Assets. Under this heading may be grouped such items as copyrights, patents, good will, trade marks, formulas, and processes. The proof of the value of these items is usually found in the measure of the success attained by the business. If the business is unsuccessful and under the necessity of liquidation, it may be found that the intangibles have been greatly overvalued upon the balance sheet. It is significant that the tendency among conservative concerns is to carry the intangible assets at a nominal figure. Some of these assets, however, as, for instance, a nationally and favorably known trade mark or trade name, may virtually ensure the continuance of a concern in business, for new capital and new management will always be ready to step in and utilize the distinct advantage given by a trade mark or trade name already favorably known to the general public. A careful consideration of both the liquidating value and the earning power of all intangibles should be made. In addition, a point that may have some significance is the proportion of the capital stock that may be represented by the intangible assets.

In the author's opinion, both deferred and intangible accounts may be grouped together as proper deductions from net worth to obtain tangible net worth. In most cases this total is not a significant factor affecting net worth, but if it is, the analyst should look into it with care.

TEXT AND RESEARCH QUESTIONS

1. What is the distinction between balance sheet, financial statement, statement of assets and liabilities, and statement of affairs?

2. Give four different purposes for which financial statements are made.

3. How much reliance is to be placed in statements certified by a certified public accountant?

4. Why should the accountant's certification be carefully studied?

5. How would you define a financial statement?

6. How does the date of a statement assist in its interpretation?

7. What advantages would result to credit men and accountants in having all statements presented as of the end of the concern's natural business year?

8. What three questions must the analysis answer affirmatively in order to have a satisfactory risk?

9. By what three methods are financial statement values determined?

10. Define current assets.

11. Compare quick current assets with current assets. Is the difference significant?

12. Why should "cash in bank" be segregated from "cash on hand"?

13. Of what value is an aging of receivables schedule?

14. Discuss methods of valuing inventory.

15. Which method of valuing inventory do you recommend for your line of business? Why? Discuss fully.

16. Discuss the treatment of marketable securities in credit analysis.

17. What are some of the problems incurred in the analysis of fixed assets?

18. What is the justification, if any, of setting up as assets expenses that have been paid?

19. When is "good will" justified as an asset upon a financial statement?

PROBLEMS

1. List the questions that the credit analyst would like answered in a thorough consideration of the inventory of (a) manufacturer and (b) retailer.

2. Refer to the balance sheet of a dress manufacturer for this year shown in Fig. 35. Submit an analysis of the assets confining the analysis to comments on the various items together with questions which you would raise and which you would like to have answered for a more thorough analysis, for example:

Cash

Would like to know

    Cash on hand

    Cash in bank

    Name of bank or banks of deposit

    If balance is demand or time deposit, etc.

CHAPTER 20

APPRAISAL OF LIABILITIES
AND WORKING CAPITAL ANALYSIS

Creditors Classified. All creditors fall within three classes: secured, preferred, or general. The secured creditors hold a lien on specific property to which they may resort according to the terms of their various contracts. Sometimes the property itself is in the possession of the creditor, as in the case of merchandise held in the custody of the lender or securities held by a bank. Or the property utilized to afford creditor security is left in the possession and use of the debtor as in mortgages on real property, machinery, furniture and fixtures, and equipment. If the security, upon the enforcement of the lien, is found insufficient to cover the debt, the creditor assumes the status of a general creditor for the unpaid portion.

Preferred creditors are those whose claims, within limits set by law, take precedence over the general claims. Wages of employees and unpaid taxes are in this category. Indeed, certain claims may be said to be both preferred and secured. Unpaid real property taxes are a lien upon the property and tax lien sales are by no means uncommon.

The general creditors are given no special protection by law, nor can they, in a liquidation proceeding, resort to any property to the exclusion of any other creditors. The general creditors share proportionately in the residual property after the preferred and secured creditors have been paid in accordance with their respective rights.

As long as the debtor remains solvent and meets his obligations, this classification of claims is of minor importance, but it assumes importance just as soon as there is a probability of liquidation. Hence, in the analysis of the liabilities the classification of creditors should be carefully considered.

Current Liabilities. All liabilities that are payable within 1 year from statement date are current. If there is any doubt about when the account is to be paid, a conservative credit analyst will group it among current liabilities. Also, the practice of netting liabilities as offsetting tax anticipation notes against accruals of taxes invalidates comparisons of current positions with that of other companies. It also fails to show the actual tax liability that must be paid. The offsetting asset should be restored to its proper group. The more important current liabilities are Accounts and Notes Payable, Accruals, Current amounts of long-term debt, and sometimes subordinated debt.[1]

Accounts Payable. This item should represent the amount owed to creditors upon open account for merchandise and supplies. The amount will not be overstated but it is possible that, through faulty bookkeeping methods, carelessness, or intent, not all the accounts payable may be included. Some bookkeepers, for example, file miscellaneous bills and enter them under expense accounts when paid. Such items are truly obligations and should appear upon the balance sheet. If the statement is made purely for creditors, a segregation may be made of accounts due and accounts not due, or, of accounts still subject to discount, and accounts past due for discount. Such a segregation is very desirable. Obligations on open accounts incurred for anything except goods or supplies should be placed in a separate account. Such an account might include unpaid salaries or bonuses, in which event the creditor will, no doubt, regard such claims as preferred. The management of a concern owing its inside people a considerable amount of money would be quite inclined to take care of them first.

Notes or Bills Payable. Under this heading may be included the following items:

1. Notes given for merchandise purchased
2. Trade acceptances
3. Notes payable to banks for money borrowed
4. Notes payable to individuals or concerns other than banking institutions
5. Other notes, such as notes given for advances either against merchandise or outstanding accounts as collateral, or purchase money notes given for unpaid balances on machinery or equipment

While all notes payable may be grouped under the one head, the item is, obviously, much more understandable if the notes payable are segregated as indicated above. A general observation may be made to the effect that when there is no segregation, if the item ends in round numbers the indication is that the item represents notes payable to banks or others for money borrowed, while an item ending in odd amounts probably covers notes given for merchandise or equipment purchases, or, possibly, customers' notes discounted at the bank although included in the assets. Notes of reasonable amount payable to banks

---

[1] The amount of lease payment should be reviewed when considering current liabilities.

are regarded with favor by the mercantile creditor, while too large an amount may indicate that receivables have been pledged as security or that other collateral has been given. On the other hand, too small an item may indicate the subject's inability to get the banking accommodation which he needs.

Notes and trade acceptances may be looked upon with favor or disfavor according to whether or not it is customary in the industry to close purchases of merchandise by these instruments. Where it is not customary, the obvious assumption is that these credit instruments are demanded by creditors because of the inferior credit position of the purchaser.

An item indicating that notes have been given to individuals or other than banking institutions is usually frowned upon by mercantile creditors. The item may indicate that the subject is not in good banking credit, or, having borrowed the limit fixed by sound banking practice, additional funds have been secured elsewhere, frequently from relatives or friends. Aside from the fact that it may be unwise for the borrower to extend his current liabilities beyond the limit fixed by bank and mercantile credit men, there is added the fear that this class of creditors will be treated by the debtor as preferred creditors in the event of threatened financial embarrassment. Such loans are often obtained upon the distinct, though secret, understanding that the lender will be taken care of before the final crash, and, besides, it is but natural for relatives and friends to receive more consideration than mercantile or bank creditors. When such an item appears upon the balance sheet it is well to inquire who the creditor is, the security given, the date of maturity, and the cost of the loan.[1]

The fifth class, or miscellaneous group of notes payable, will have to be interpreted according to the circumstances attending their issuance. Notes secured by collateral may indicate some deficiency in borrowing power. At best, the general creditor is at a distinct disadvantage, as compared with the secured creditor. Such notes as purchase-money notes, although they may be forced by the necessities of the business, may be a severe though temporary strain on the current assets.

A careful consideration of the notes payable, and of the accounts payable as well, is suggested, for these items disclose the care and ability of the management in financing current assets. A careful investigation of these items will also disclose how much credit support may be expected of these two classes of creditors.

Accrued Liabilities. In addition to liabilities incurred for money borrowed or purchases made, there may be other items, usually expenses, which, though not matured, belong to the accounting period covered by the statement.

[1] Debt of this type is often subordinated, but the question is "to what"?

Such items include salaries and wages, insurance, rent, taxes, and interest. The presence of an item of accrued liabilities indicates that the balance sheet has been thoughtfully prepared. The absence of such an item may not be serious, but in many cases, accruals, not considered in making up the statement, would throw quite a different light on the business, especially when such items are large and paid at infrequent intervals.

How should accruals be treated in analyzing the financial position of a concern? This question is quite easy to answer. It is to be assumed that the accruals are constantly ripening into maturity. At best, the date of payment is not far removed. They must, therefore, be regarded as current obligations and not merely as current obligations but as obligations which will take precedence over both bank and mercantile creditors. As a matter of fact, some of the creditors represented by accruals, for example, employees and the government, are actually preferred creditors in the event of liquidation.

Reserves for Taxes. Reserves are defined and classified in a later section. The Reserve for Taxes is mentioned here because the tax liability of many concerns is no longer insignificant. The item may include a definite amount for social security taxes and estimated amounts for property, income, and other taxes. Moreover, the analyst should remember that taxes are a preferred liability. He will not be able, in most cases, to verify the adequacy of the reserve, but its adequacy or inadequacy may be apparent. He will accept the accuracy of the item according to his faith in the statement as a whole.

Deposits. Whenever the item "deposits" appears as a liability upon a balance sheet there may be uncertainty whether the concern is a debtor to the depositors or a trustee of their funds. Often the item represents money deposited for safekeeping or in trust for special purposes, such as deposits of employees' Christmas or savings funds. The item may not be large enough to have much bearing on the risk, but, in the absence of a clear explanation of it, bank and mercantile creditors will be inclined to regard it as a preferred claim whether or not it be legally one.

Current Long-term Debt. In most cases the accountant will include among current liabilities any sinking-fund payment or current maturity of a serial nature. However, some treasurers, incorrectly believing that a sinking fund (since it may be contingent on earnings) need not be included as current, fail to show it at all. Consequently, it is necessary for the analyst to determine the amount of such funds and list them among the current liabilities. Of course, care must be exercised to deduct the current sinking fund from the long-term liabilities.

Long-term Debt. Included in this category would be bonds, mortgages, subordinated debt, and certain reserves. In general, accounts payable due after 1 year are also included in this part of the analysis.

Bonds. This item indicates the subject's obligation for money borrowed upon a promise to pay at a definite future date, often with real or personal property mortgaged as collateral security. Since the bondholders may be secured creditors, there may be but little or nothing left for general creditors in a forced liquidation. While bonds are frequently disregarded by the credit man because they are regarded as a fixed or long-term liability, it should be borne in mind that, in some instances, as, for example, a default on interest payments, they may become due and payable almost overnight. Thus if a firm shares only as a general creditor, the credit analyst who has looked only at the current position is in for a rude shock when he learns what is left after secured claims have been liquidated. A careful consideration of this item should include the amount of bonds authorized and issued, the purpose of the issue, the security, the interest rate, the maturity, and the method of retirement. The interest accrued on bonds is, of course, a current liability, as well as the portion of the bonds, if any, maturing within 1 year.

Contrary to the original use of the term, a sinking fund is not an accumulation but is, in most cases, a current payment in cash or bonds to a trustee who uses the funds to retire debt during the current period. It is a method of periodic debt reduction over the life of the debt. A good analyst will always work out a sinking-fund schedule as part of his analysis of a bond indenture. Such a schedule lists the payments to be made over the life of the long-term debt issue.

Mortgages. Mortgages are divided into two classes, namely, real estate mortgages and chattel mortgages. Through custom, when the word "mortgage" only is used, it usually means a real estate mortgage. When personal property, such as goods, machinery, or equipment, is mortgaged, the term "chattel mortgage" is used to distinguish such mortgage from a real estate mortgage.

How the analyst will regard the mortgage as affecting the financial risk will depend largely upon the circumstances. A real estate mortgage, in some instances, may be looked upon with considerable favor, since it releases, for use in the business at a reasonable cost, capital which otherwise would be tied up in real estate. Chattel mortgages also need not be always condemned. A mortgage given to secure the payment of the purchase price of machinery or equipment may be justified, but any lien upon any of the trading assets of the concern is very damaging to its credit.

The facts concerning the mortgage should be learned and used in the appraisal of the effect of the mortgage upon the credit risk.

Subordinated Debt. Mainly because of high tax rates, it is cheaper for a business to borrow than to sell equity capital. In recent years the practice of using subordinated long-term debt has grown, but it is necessary for the analyst to find out to what it is subordinated. In most cases only bank and other long-term creditors have claims senior to subordinated debt. Subordinated debt is a subdivision of long-term debt.[1]

Reserves. The reserves constitute a class of items most frequently misused and more than ordinarily difficult for the analyst to interpret unless the purpose of the reserve is clearly set forth on the balance sheet. The term itself is confusing. By the uninformed a reserve might be mistaken for an asset. Accountants are frequently substituting for "reserve" the words "allowance" or "provision" as in the expressions "allowance for bad debts" and "provision for depreciation." While placed among the liabilities, the reserves represent merely bookkeeping entries of amounts set aside from the surplus or net-worth accounts for specific purposes. This item on the balance sheet can be understood only when the purpose of the reservation is disclosed.

Upon analysis, reserves will be found to fall naturally into four groups, and such a grouping aids greatly in the understanding of the significance of the item. The four groups are: valuation, current liability, long-term liability, and contingency reserves.

Reserves to Meet Real or Expected Shrinkage in the Value of Certain Assets. These are termed valuation reserves and may be illustrated by such entries as reserve for bad debts, reserves for depreciation of plant, machinery, equipment, etc. While in accounting reserves appear on the liability side, when a balance sheet is drawn off, it is quite a common practice to show this type of reserve not as a liability but as a deduction from the asset with which it is associated. Such reserves may aid in placing an estimate upon the liquidating value of the asset and, when the reserve applies to a fixed asset, may also aid in judging how soon it may be necessary to replace it.

Reserves to Cover Operating Expenses Known to Have Accrued but Uncertain as to Amount or Not Yet Matured. Illustrative of this class of reserves are reserves set up for taxes, rent, etc. Reserves of this nature are hardly distinguishable from accruals, and they are, indeed, to be treated as such by the analyst. They are often termed liability reserves.

Long-term Reserves. Such reserves for pensions, fire protection, deferred income, etc., are grouped in this area of liabilities. In some cases deferred income should be carried as a current liability. For instance, a warranty contract fee might involve mainly expense rather than income during the succeeding period. If the reserve expense will amount to more than 70 per cent during the current year, the author recommends treating the account as a current liability.

[1] In rare cases it may be included with current debt.

Reserves to Meet Any Possible Contingency Which May Arise. Such a reserve is, in fact, merely a segregated portion of the surplus. How the item will be regarded will depend somewhat upon whether or not the analyst can discover whether the "contingency" is near or remote. The contingency might represent a lawsuit actually brought against the concern or imminent, and the concern might provide against its unfavorable outcome by removing a certain sum from its surplus. The purpose of this type of reserve may be to serve as a warning either that the surplus would otherwise be overstated or that it will be lessened if the "contingency" becomes real. An analysis of the reserve, therefore, is necessary to determine its placement in the analysis. Only if it is a true segregation of surplus should it be retained as part of net worth.

Capital Stock. Capital stock is placed among the liabilities of a corporation, because, as a legal entity, the corporation upon liquidation or dissolution would owe to the stockholders whatever might remain after *all* other obligations have been met. Since the stockholders are the last to share in the assets of the business, the creditors may not be keenly interested in this item. A study of it may, however, aid in a better understanding of the business. For this purpose it is desirable to know the different classes of stock, the amount authorized, the amount issued and fully paid, and the dividend requirements of the preferred stock. The stringent protective provisions of this latter class of stock may cause serious difficulty for the corporation if dividends are not paid for any protracted time. If there is no preferred stock, book value of common stock is determined by dividing net worth by the number of shares outstanding. Some analysts use this value for comparison purposes.

Surplus. This is an item too often misunderstood and neglected by credit men in the analysis of a balance sheet. An analysis of the item might, in some instances, throw considerable light not only upon the earnings of the company but upon the character and capacity of its management as well. The surplus account has been termed the shock absorber of the business, since any change in the value of the assets, either upward or downward, will change the amount of this item. Surplus is merely the difference between the book value of the assets and the reported liabilities including the outstanding stock.

Too often the creditor assumes that the surplus account represents profits earned by the business. While this is commonly so it is by no means generally true. Surplus may arise in several ways among which the most common are:

1. Accumulation of profits through the normal trading or manufacturing activity of the business.

2. Through the sale of new securities at a premium.

3. The "paid-in" surplus, created by having a premium paid in on capital stock.

4. Donated surplus, consisting of any donation of value, most commonly in the form of stock.

5. Reappraisal at higher value of such assets as plant and property, intangibles, and even investments and securities.

6. Sale of capital assets at more than their book value.

The true significance of any changes in the surplus account cannot be ascertained unless it is known how the change was accomplished. For this purpose a study of the income account is essential.

What constitutes a good ratio as between capital stock and surplus? Credit analysts feel that the surplus account should be neither too great nor too small, but they are inclined to be very indefinite when pressed to be more specific. The surplus account, it is felt, should be large enough to absorb any ordinary losses that might befall the company without an impairment of the capital stock itself. Stockholders often watch the surplus account with greedy eyes. As that account increases, there is temptation, augmented perhaps by pressure of stockholders, to declare a cash dividend. Cash dividends represent a withdrawal of a current asset which the company may ill afford at the time. If, however, the dividend is declared in stock, it represents an expansion of capital, which is usually very favorably regarded by the creditor, with no attendant strain upon the current position of the company.

Capital or Net Worth. In the balance sheet of the individual or the partnership, the term "net worth" is used to show the book net worth or equity of the owners in the business. The terms "capital and surplus" express the same thing for the corporation. Net worth is a differential amount calculated by deducting from the total of the assets the total liabilities, including any liability reserves. It measures the amount that assets may shrink, while still leaving creditors protected.

How Much Net Worth? A frequently asked question is: Does the business have sufficient net worth? There is no definite answer to this query. Only after a thorough analysis by competent analysts can an *approximate* estimate of net worth be obtained. Such factors as type of industry, industry trend, owning or leasing facilities, amount of inventories needed, credit policies, stability of earnings, amount of current assets, debt proportion, and other measurements all affect the final judgment as to adequacy of net worth. Debt should not be excessive, and earnings must be sufficient to pay interest costs, provide an adequate return to the owners, and build reasonable reserves for contingencies and expansion. If the analysis casts doubt upon too many of these criteria, net worth is probably inadequate.

Tangible Net Worth. Tangible net worth is determined by deducting from net worth all deferred and prepaid expenses and intangibles. This group of accounts has significance when as a total they are an unusual proportion of the total assets. However, the student is cautioned to attribute no definite value to tangible net worth, since there are so many variables to consider. At best it represents merely a differential account.

Contingent Liabilities. While the balance sheet itself may not customarily show contingent liabilities, no discussion of the financial statement should fail to include them. Many a creditor has suffered a loss through his failure to discover the existence of contingent liabilities. A contingent liability may be defined as an existing condition which may become an obligation dependent upon the happening of a certain event. Such a possible obligation may assume many different guises, among which the most common are:

1. Discounted accounts, notes, or trade acceptances receivable
2. Commitments or contracts for merchandise or services
3. Endorsements and guarantees
4. Pending lawsuits

As a matter of fact, the good credit analyst never limits his investigation to a consideration of actual liabilites. He proceeds to discover, if he can, how the subject may have involved himself with contingencies which may produce obligations. These contingent liabilities—and the four classes mentioned above are representative—the author terms "created contingent liabilities." The credit analyst goes further and considers the ability of the subject to absorb any shock which may be suffered through contingencies which are less apparent but which may befall any business. Such a consideration includes the conditions in the trade, the possibility of the cancellation of contracts and the return of goods, advances in industrial technology, litigation in connection with patents, and the like. Possibilities of this sort are more remote and, obviously, cannot be listed upon the financial statement. The created contingent liabilities, however, are ascertainable and should be disclosed. There are five ways by which the accountant can show contingent liabilities upon the balance sheet, as follows:

1. The contingent liability is shown as a contra item to the contingent asset.
2. Where receivables have been discounted, the full amount of receivables is shown with the amount discounted deducted, the net amount of the receivables being included as an asset in the balance sheet.
3. The item discounted is not shown among the assets, but the amount discounted is written short upon the liability side to indicate that the amount is not included in the total.
4. The nature of the contingent liability is explained by a footnote.
5. A reserve may be set up to meet the contingency.

A full discussion of all the occurrences which may result in actual liabilities is impractical here. It is enough to warn the analyst that he needs carefully to consider first the probability of the creation of a liability and, second, the effect that the actual obligation would have upon the credit standing of the subject.

In discussing the relationships of the various parts of financial reports, the author has grouped them according to balance-sheet relationships, income relationships, and mixed relationships, i.e., between balance sheet and income statement.

Balance-sheet Relationships. There are within the balance sheet itself a number of relationships which command the analyst's attention. There should exist within a business a certain proportion in the different classes of assets and liabilities, which may be studied through the balance sheet. The purpose of the analysis is to determine whether the management has preserved a wise balance or proportion in the business, or whether the credit position may be damaged through distortion.

Among the first of such relationships to receive serious consideration by credit managers was the relationship of current assets and current liabilities. It was but natural that the current assets should have commanded the first attention of the creditor since they are the assets which in the normal course of business operations are converted into cash. The current liabilities are of equal importance since they provide a constant demand upon that cash. Many credit managers, who for years had only balance sheets to scan, in fact, give but scant attention to any other items when reading a financial statement. The reader should not gather from this statement that the current assets and current liabilities so far overshadow all other items as to make them unworthy of study, but that there has been a lack of thoroughness on the part of credit managers in general in making a complete analysis of the subject's financial position.

Another criticism may be added. Credit managers have been prone to summarize the relationship between the current assets and the current liabilities and to express the result as a ratio commonly known as the "current ratio." For this ratio many have erroneously accepted as a standard $2 of current assets for each dollar of current liabilities known among credit managers as the 2 to 1 current ratio. Actually, the "old timers" had the "feel" of the account and automatically gave weight to variations.

The Current Position. To understand a concern's current position involves much more than a consideration of the totals of the current assets and the current liabilities. Since it is but a quantity measure, the quality of each account must also be proved good; otherwise the quantity is deficient.

In a study of the current position then, there should be included a consideration or appraisal of each individual item and such relationships as cash to current liabilities, cash to notes payable, or bank loans, quick current assets to current liabilities, accounts payable to bills payable, receivables to merchandise, sales to receivables, sales to merchandise, and sales to net working capital. It is only when the current position is so studied that the totals of the current assets and current liabilities expressed as a ratio can disclose their fullest significance to the credit manager.

The 2 to 1 Current-ratio Fallacy. The first attempt, no doubt, on the part of credit men to reduce balance-sheet appraisal to any law or standard resulted in the 2 to 1 current ratio. This was because only scanty balance sheets were supplied and this relationship undoubtedly did apply to the greatest number of businesses, but the error was in the assumption that it applied to all. Assets may shrink in value, and, in the event of liquidation, the cost of liquidation must be borne by the assets themselves. Credit men felt that there was a reasonable factor of safety in allowing 50 per cent for shrinkage and liquidation. Obviously, shrinkage in value and liquidation costs will vary in different industries, in different locations, and even in different seasons of the year.

It is the qualitative analysis which is of the utmost importance. This fact can be most easily illustrated by citing two kinds of businesses offering considerable contrast in their inventory items, the jobber of groceries handling principally canned goods and the manufacturer of millinery. In the first, shrinkage and liquidation costs would be small, while in the latter the value of the inventory is subject, in view of style changes, to sudden and great deterioration in value.

If, then, the 2 to 1 ratio must be rejected, the question arises as to what does constitute a satisfactory current position. The answer is that the current position is satisfactory from the creditors' standpoint when there are sufficient assets of sufficient liquidity to meet the current liabilities as they mature, and sufficient also to meet any shrinkage and costs to be incurred in the event of liquidation.

Working Capital. The analyst is cautioned that there are two, or possibly three,[1] definitions for the term "working capital," each arising out of the business practice of a particular group.

1. To many businessmen and economists, working capital means the amount of funds invested in current assets. In other words, it is the total current assets. From their viewpoint, the capital that works currently, from whatever source it may be obtained, is the flow of funds through the cycle of inventories, to receivables, to cash. A summation of this flow at a particular moment in a company's affairs fixes working capital at a definite but arbitrary amount. As the business continues, cash may be used to pay off debt or for current expenses and, either through cash or credit purchases, inventories again may accumulate.

[1] A third concept of working capital being the use of all assets.

Thus the cycle continues. Inasmuch as the total of current assets represents capital funds that are used to produce income, it is called current working capital—a term shortened through usage to working capital.

When working capital means the total of current assets, *net* working capital is the excess of current assets over current liabilities.

2. A second usage of the term working capital is found particularly among accountants and some bankers. They define working capital as the excess of current assets over current liabilities. Thus working capital as here defined is the same net working capital as defined above. The two groups are using the term working capital to define two different financial positions.

Of the two concepts of the term working capital, the author leans to the first definition as being easier to explain, illustrate, and understand. It is quite easy to see that, since net working capital is a balance, working capital is one side of that net position—current assets.

An illustration of the confusion which often results from the loose use of the term working capital is seen in the statement sometimes made that a concern is seeking a short-term bank loan to increase its working capital. The statement can be true only under the first definition of working capital, for this borrowing increases both assets and liabilities. There may, of course, be a Peter and Paul relationship; the concern may borrow from a bank to pay off its merchandise creditors. Here neither gross nor net working capital is affected. To avoid confusion, it is always well to use the more descriptive term in business parlance, net working capital, if that is the subject of conversation. To the credit manager the whole analysis of the working capital relationship is but a consideration of the current assets, the current liabilities, and the relationship between them. In this he is most interested.

Working and Current Assets. A balance sheet will frequently be presented which will contain government or other securities of unquestioned value. These are considered cash equivalents, as they are very liquid. It is customary among many credit men to include such securities among the current assets in considering the current asset–current liabilities relationship. The procedure is justifiable when the analyst is considering the ultimate ability of the concern to liquidate, but the reader should note the distinction between an asset which *may* be readily converted into cash and one which, in the normal course of business, *is* converted into cash. In the one case the management is striving to convert the asset into cash, while in the other, there may be the endeavor to avoid the liquidation of the security. Capital so invested may be misleading because the analyst assumes that it will be negotiated to reduce liabilities, while the management may, for its own reasons, retain its investment in the security even at the expense of a liquid position. However, prime marketable securities reinforce the quick position. They frequently indicate the investment of temporarily idle funds, and they are altogether good to see in the balance sheet.

The Acid Test. Among the relationships mentioned in a preceding section was that of quick current assets to current liabilities. It will be noted that these relationships differ from the current ratio in that a distinction is made among the current assets of those which may be called quick current and slow current. In deriving a "quick ratio" the analyst makes his own choice, but usually cash and cash equivalent and receivables are regarded as quick current, while merchandise is considered as a slow current asset. It is somewhat of an accepted rule with many credit men that $1 of quick assets per $1 of current liabilities indicates a safe position. This is known as the "acid test." The student of credit analysis, however, can no more safely accept this quantity ratio than he can accept the 2 to 1 standard of the current ratio.

Adequacy of Current Position. Some of the measures used for determining the adequacy of the current position are (1) the normal proportion of cash, receivables, inventory, and debt as measured by the industry standard; (2) a sufficient margin in value of current assets to protect creditors in event of asset shrinkage; (3) satisfactory quantities of inventory to take care of usual customers' requirements; (4) an allowance for satisfactory selling terms. Adequacy must be supported by quality analysis. It will be found that the amount of current assets varies widely with the type of business and the period of the business cycle.

Only through experience and comparison is the analyst able to arrive at an approximate conclusion regarding adequacy of current position.

Summary of Current Position Analysis. The aim of the several foregoing sections has been to present the student with a method for examining what is perhaps the most important relationship of all to the bank or mercantile creditor, *viz.*, the current asset–current liability relationship. *That relationship, the student will have gathered, is satisfactory not when the ratio meets any fixed standard, but when the quantity and quality of assets are such that maturing obligations may be met.*

The soundness of a concern's financing, however, is not disclosed solely by its current position. There are a number of other relationships which are of importance and which will be discussed following Income Analysis.

TEXT AND RESEARCH QUESTIONS

1. In what three general classes may all creditors be divided? Explain each class.

2. Why is an analysis of the accounts payable desirable?

3. What types of bills payable are generally looked upon with disfavor by credit men?

4. How should accrued liabilities be regarded in analysis?

5. How will general creditors and those represented by "deposits" share in the assets in the event of liquidation?

6. List in the order of their importance the questions to be raised in analyzing the liability "bonds."

7. What are sinking funds?

8. What are reserves?

9. Why is a consideration of the different classes and amounts of capital stock sometimes desirable?

10. How may failure to pay dividends on preferred stock affect a company?

11. Why is it important to know whether an increase in surplus is due to profits from the business operations or to some other cause?

12. Why is a careful appraisal of the probability of contingent liabilities becoming actual liabilities necessary?

13. How is tangible net worth derived?

14. Why is the current position important?

15. What is working capital?

16. When does a business have sufficient working capital?

PROBLEM

1. The following items comprise the balance sheet of the Farrand Department Stores, Inc., Cleveland, Ohio. Rearrange them according to liquidity in balance-sheet form, showing subtotals for current assets, etc.

First preferred 6 per cent stock	$3,400,000.00
Second preferred 6 per cent stock	None
Real estate	3,801,533.81
Bonds, investments, etc	62,228.63
Cash on hand	32,277.73
Accounts receivable	1,075,425.43
Notes receivable	290,232.30
Cash in banks	200,003.61
Due to lessors	20,193.37
Insurance reserves	136,014.58
Machinery and equipment	571,143.89
Merchandise inventory (physical)	1,455,767.80
Notes payable	720,000.00
Furniture and fixtures	720,355.06
Unearned insurance	13,391.98
Common stock	2,250,000.00
Other reserves (depreciation, etc.)	1,257,496.85
Supplies	6,371.45
Surplus	447,912.62
Automobile equipment	47,078.50
Accounts payable	None
Deposits by employees	44,193.77
Good will	1.00

2. Complete the analysis of the balance sheet of a dress manufacturer for this year (see Fig. 35). Follow the same pattern as indicated in Problem 2, Chapter 19.

CHAPTER 21

INCOME ANALYSIS

Many credit managers are able to remember a time when not only were income statements not available but even the balance sheet was difficult to obtain. Most often, if financial information was obtained at all, it consisted of a balance sheet and sales figures only.

Many companies would not disclose their income account because they feared that it would fall into the hands of a competitor who might be aided by such information. Such a fear is often unwarranted, or at least exaggerated. Indeed, there may sometimes be a suspicion that this imaginary fear may be an excuse rather than a real reason for a refusal to disclose operating details.

The impact of the Great Depression of the thirties, and the financial accounting requirements of the S.E.C., broke through the barrier of incomplete and unaudited financial reports, particularly in the case of large corporations. The smaller businesses thus have no excuse not to give their creditors similar financial reports. Today financial reports, including some details of the operating statement, are generally readily available. Thus the analyst is given better tools for thorough analysis.

Analyzing the Income Report. A single balance sheet discloses the capital employed in a business, by whom that capital is furnished— owners, investors, and creditors—and in what assets and amounts that capital is invested.

The income statement, on the other hand, is the record of the heart beat of a business enterprise. It reflects the way funds have flowed through the accounts over a period of time. Thus it is a schedule which records the various types of income and expenses—in large part estimated—of a business enterprise for a specific period, usually 1 year. There may be statements covering shorter intervals, but rarely is income summarized for longer than 1 year.

The principal difficulties with income reports are that the reports are scanty in detail and are not uniformly presented. Nevertheless, the income statement, however sketchy, is an important adjunct to the balance sheet and is essential to the complete analysis of a concern's financial position.

Form of Income Statement. The fundamental structure of an income or profit and loss statement is extremely simple, since it must in the end conform to the formula that total income, less total expenses, equals net profit.

Such a statement is in fact devoid of details and unenlightening. In addition, it fails to indicate the disposition of the net profit. It should be possible to obtain a definite tie-up between the balance sheet and the Income account. While it is true that the former is in account form, and the latter is usually in report form, nevertheless both are taken from the same books of account. The tie-up between the two lies in the surplus account. Unless the Income account explains the change in the surplus account, it loses considerable of its value to the analyst. Changes in the surplus account may, of course, be due to dividend payments, and other charges and credits not applicable to the period covered by the Income Report.

The profit and loss statement, or Income account, like the balance sheet is the result of facts, accounting conventions, and the personal judgment of the accountant. For instance, one accounting convention is that the income shall be deemed to be, not collections or money actually taken into the business, but sales.

The Income account is, primarily, a report of source of income and of the allocation or use of income. There is, perhaps, less standardization by accountants of the treatment of items that make up the profit and loss statement than in the balance sheet. The analyst should, therefore, be warned to see that there has been no change in accounting procedure when comparing successive profit and loss statements of a single concern, or that accountants of separate businesses have not treated various costs or expenses differently. Cost of sales particularly should be scrutinized. Two accountants working independently to prepare the profit and loss statement of a manufacturer might determine a final net profit not far apart, but the cost of sales might differ materially. This might result from one accountant treating as a general or administrative expense an amount that another accountant might allocate to cost of sales. Two very important items would be affected, the gross profit and the gross profit percentage. Analysts give much weight to the percentage of gross profit to sales. Given a satisfactory gross profit percentage and adequate sales, a business should have sufficient gross profit to cover its operating costs and leave a satisfactory net profit for the owners.

Although earlier financial statement forms call for only a summary of the Profit and Loss or Income account, because the creditor only hoped to get a summary of that account, the new forms are more nearly in line with those suggested by the National Association of Credit Management, as illustrated in Appendix G. This detailed classification aids in analysis. If, in addition, it is supported by schedules, as from a detailed audit, the data would be complete.

The Income account should disclose (1) the gross profit and how it is derived, (2) the operating expenses, and (3) the total income and its disposition. The skeletal form of such a statement follows:

Gross Sales
  less Returns and Allowances
  equals Net Sales
Net Sales
  less Cost of Goods Sold
  equals Gross Profit
Gross Profit
  less Operating Expenses, including Selling and Administrative Expenses
  equals Net Operating Profit
Net Operating Profit
  plus Other Income
  less Other Expenses
  equals Net Profit
Net Profit
  plus and minus Surplus adjustments
  equals Net Balance which added to Opening Surplus
  equals Closing Surplus

Thus the tie-in between the income statement and the balance sheet is completed.

The operating statement of specialized industries naturally will employ different terminology, but the end result is Net Profit.

The Mechanics of Income Account Analysis. The Income or Profit and Loss account reveals the income received, from whatever source, for a given period. The basis of the Income account is Net Sales. That is so because, aside from bad debts, cash discounts, and "other income," net sales represents income available for distribution for the period embraced by the account. The purpose of Income analysis is to determine whether the income is being so managed that the prime object of business, namely, a reasonable profit, is being attained. If the objective is not being attained, a careful consideration of the Income account may reveal the reason. In most instances the failure will be found to be due either to an insufficient income or to bad management of that income.

The analysis of the Income account is greatly facilitated by reducing all items to a percentage of net sales.[1] By this method the analyst simplifies the consideration of the distribution of income. The component parts of the sales dollar are the cost of the goods sold, the expense of doing business, and—let us hope—profit. The detailed Income account further breaks down the cost of goods sold and the expense of doing business into various classifications. The relationship of each of these classifications to total net sales is difficult of comprehension unless the relationship is simplified. Comparison is made easy when all income accounts are reduced to proportions. For instance, the dollar amount of the cost of the goods sold from one period to the next may be unchanged; but if the sales volume were lower, the larger ratio of cost of sales to net sales would highlight this probably reduced profit. A larger proportion of the net sales is charged as cost.

Significance of Income Items. The net sales figure is a necessity in the Income account since it is one of the items from which the gross profit is derived. However, Returns and Allowances—a deduction from gross sales—may materially affect net sales, since it indicates the policy of the concern in selling its merchandise. Furthermore, returns and allowances are expensive and may seriously hamper the management in its attempt to earn a net profit. Returns may be of a particular significance if the company under analysis has recently introduced a new product.

Net sales is the basis of profit and loss analysis. As previously stated, given a satisfactory gross profit percentage and adequate sales, a business should be able to operate at a profit. Whether or not sales are adequate may best be determined through comparing sales with balance-sheet items. If the sales ratios discussed in Chapter 22 are satisfactory, a failure to make a profit should be attributable to some other cause than to inadequate sales.

Cost of Goods Sold. The cost of goods sold in relation to net sales shows the spread between these two important accounts. It is in this area that the efficiency with which a business is conducted is demonstrated. Both fixed and variable costs must be analyzed; usually the latter are more important.

To evaluate the significance of cost of goods sold, the credit and financial analyst must closely watch the changing price levels for goods and labor. The proportion of goods and labor entering in the manufacturing of a given product naturally varies from industry to industry. Thus an increase in a variable cost such as labor (if labor is a small proportion of the cost) would have little effect on the net profit. But

[1] In analysis of the Income statement, R. A. Foulke, in "Practical Financial Statement Analysis," refers to the relationship of Net Sales to the other accounts of the income statement as "internal analysis."

if material cost represented 80 per cent of the cost of sales and raw material price increases, the effect on net profit would be great unless prices were also raised.

The method of valuing inventories is reflected in the cost of goods sold. Thus, if a business enterprise alters its method of valuing inventory from "fifo" to "lifo," income will be affected.

To compare cost of goods sold, the analyst most frequently reduces it to a percentage of net sales, for he is familiar with the industry and will know the gross profit range in that line. It is well to point out that the gross profit percentage of concerns operating in like manner within the same industry is comparable, and the keener the competition, the less divergence will there be among the different concerns. This is so because competition fixes both buying and selling prices. The gross profit percentage therefore is examined to see that it conforms to the normal margin for that industry.

The next main division, Operating Expenses, may be and, for their thorough understanding, must be highly classified. A frequent subdivision is a segregation of selling expense from general and administrative expenses. Since there is a certain inflexibility in the gross profit percentage, it is obvious that there is the necessity to keep the operating expense relatively low if the business is not to show "in the red." The ability to operate within a certain margin of gross profit represents the real test of managerial ability.

There are certain relationships or ratios within the income statement which should be considered. The analyst may choose those which he deems most important, the choice of which may be determined by the nature of the business and the data available. Among these relationships are sales to selling expense, sales to officers' salaries, and sales to net operating profit. Sales in each case is Net. Individual items, too, will be closely scanned to see that they are in proportion to the size of the business conducted.

Sales: Selling Expense. Selling expense is often one of the larger items of expense. Among different industries it varies greatly, but within an industry the variation should range within a few points when expressed on a percentage basis. If, for example, the analyst knows that in a certain industry sales are obtained at an average expense of 9 per cent, a business showing a sales expense of 15 per cent would challenge further inquiry into the reason for such a high cost. Few businesses can stand an additional expense of 6 per cent in sales without bringing the net profit below what might be regarded as a normal return, if not obliterating the net altogether.

Sales: Officers' Salaries. The amount withdrawn by the officers in salaries is often an important question, particularly in a small or closely owned business. The officers instead of limiting their withdrawals to what the business will stand may vote liberal salaries for themselves, thus "eating up the profits." Salaries of executives obviously should be commensurate with the volume of business attained and the net profit produced. Salaries is an item to which the analyst is advised always to give close scrutiny, since not only may it represent an annual drain upon capital, but it carries with it an intimation of the character and managerial ability of those in control. The failure of many an enterprise has been due to the fact that it could not stand the drain made upon it by the officers themselves.

Sales: Net Profit. The net profit per sale is an item which may vary considerably in different industries, but within an industry the range is not very wide. The range in this relationship should be known in a general way or should be ascertained by the analyst. Any deviation would call for a further investigation. It is in a comparative analysis that a consideration of the percentage of net profit to sales percentages may be most indicative. If the percentage gradually or suddenly is getting smaller, it may serve as a serious warning. Sales may be contracting without a decrease in administrative expenses, or the volume of sales perhaps is being maintained by cutting prices. The aim of the management is to produce as large an operating profit as possible. If a satisfactory profit is obtained, it must be the result of a normal net profit per sale or an abnormally high volume of sales compared to net worth, with the result that the high turnover of invested capital offsets the narrow margin of profit.

Analysis of Expense. Whenever the expenses are given in detail, a careful consideration of them may be enlightening. The astute analyst may be able to put his finger upon the weak spot of the entire operation. Poor management may stand revealed through some of the administrative items or operating-expense items.

Certain items should be found to fluctuate with the volume of sales, while others will not. Rent, taxes, and depreciation, for example, may remain quite inflexible in spite of a considerable rise or fall in sales. Other items such as selling expense, freight and cartage, telephone and telegraph have a relationship to sales and should fluctuate with that item. Other expenses may have a wide variation from year to year and, from the analyst's viewpoint, may seem to have been unwisely incurred. Among such fluctuating items are advertising, entertaining, legal and professional expenses, and, perhaps, the expense or cost of borrowed money. This latter item may indicate the subject's credit standing. An exorbitant interest expense may indicate that borrowing cannot be done through banks and may therefore have to be done outside and through more expensive channels. Excessive trading on the equity is sometimes disclosed through relatively large interest costs. The ratio of interest over the amount available for interest indicates earnings protection to creditors.

Net Profit. As a general principle, net profit indicates the return to equity or owners. Only if a business is reasonably profitable will it continue to operate. However, the credit analyst should be careful to see that the net profit is as represented. Particular attention must be paid to unusual income or expense accounts that may materially change the net result. Thus the sale of a building at a $100,000 profit, a non-operating profit, would inflate the net profit, leading the analyst to believe that the firm was highly successful. Unusual profits and losses must be considered as surplus adjustments in order not to distort the figure representing the net profit resulting from the firm's normal operation. This does not mean ignoring such adjustments, but rather considering them in their proper sequence and significance.

Reconciliation of the Surplus Account. Whenever there is an increase in the surplus account from one year to another, some credit men take it for granted that such an increase is the result of profits earned. Likewise, a decrease in surplus is assumed to represent either a loss or, perhaps, dividends paid. These assumptions are in the majority of cases correct but not in all. In a previous chapter, it has been pointed out that surplus may be created or increased in a number of different ways, and the manner of increasing the surplus may have considerable influence upon the credit decision.

The surplus is the connecting link between the Profit and Loss, or the Income account and the Balance Sheet. Hence, a tie-up between these two important statements calls for an explanation of surplus changes or, in accounting terms, a reconciliation of the Surplus account. Where changes in the Surplus account cannot be determined there is an important gap in the analysis which cannot be bridged.

The balance sheet shows the capital employed, the amount of that capital which belongs to the ownership, and the kind of assets in which that capital is invested. Next to a consideration of the amount and the manner of the capital invested, the question which may have the most weight is whether or not the concern is making a profit. Though it may not be possible to examine the operation of the concern in detail, every creditor must be impressed by the fact that his customer is making a profit or, in other words, achieving some measure of success through the operation of the business. An account which discloses the reason for changes in surplus is, therefore, of considerable importance.

Two illustrations are given to show how misleading an unexplained increase in surplus may be. Let it be assumed that in each case the balance sheet disclosed a satisfactory condition, including the increase in surplus as shown.

CONDENSED INCOME STATEMENT, CURRENT YEAR

Net Sales..	$1,327,984
Cost of Sales......................................	1,184,237
Gross Profit.......................................	143,747
Expenses..	171,792
Net Loss from Operations..........................	$ 28,045

Other Income:
Cash Received from Insurance on Life of R. H. Canfield....	$50,000	
Refund on Federal Income Taxes, previous years...........	6,172	$ 56,172
Net Credit to Surplus............................		28,127
Surplus, Beginning of Period.....................		42,629
Surplus before Dividends.........................		70,756
Dividends Paid 6 Per Cent on $150,000............		9,000
Surplus as per Balance Sheet, 12/31..............		$ 61,756

FIG. 33a. Case 1. Surplus adjustments.

In the above illustration, an increase in surplus of over $19,000 would leave a very favorable impression until explained. Assume that Mr. Canfield, the president and treasurer, who died late in the previous year, was regarded as the brains of the business. The two officers next in control were felt to be less competent to manage the business successfully. Without the income statement the creditors might have conceded their error in the judgment of managerial ability, but with the income statement their judgment was strongly confirmed, since the new management, instead of earning a profit of over 18 per cent on the capitalization of $150,000 from operations, lost over 18 per cent of the amount of the issued capital.

CONDENSED PROFIT AND LOSS STATEMENT, PREVIOUS YEAR

Sales, Net..	$326,184
Cost of Sales.....................................	283,275
Gross Profit......................................	42,909
Expenses...	46,316
Net Loss from Operations.........................	3,407
Appreciation of Plant and Equipment Based on Appraisal..	10,000
Net Credit to Surplus............................	6,593
Surplus Beginning of Year........................	5,217
Surplus 12/31....................................	$ 11,810

FIG. 33b. Case 2. Surplus adjustments.

In this case, the balance sheet disclosed the increase in fixed assets, but, as the machinery was known to be somewhat old, the building in need of repairs, it was at first assumed that repairs and new equipment accounted for the increase in valuation. The conservativeness of the credit man asserted itself, and an income account was insisted upon. The loss from operations and the methods of concealing it were thus disclosed.

Thus it is apparent that the details of an income statement should include the reconciliation of surplus for proper analysis and that nonrecurring profits or losses should be segregated as surplus adjustments.

The analysis of assets, liabilities, and income tends to indicate the ability of a business enterprise to liquidate its debts as they mature and to continue as a productive unit in the economic system. However, all these factors may be favorable, yet the business firm might fail through lack of foresight in another direction, namely, insurance protection.

Insurance. Adequate insurance protection of its debtor concerns is of major interest to the thorough credit manager. Its importance has grown to such an extent that business managers consider proper risk handling a prerequisite to productivity and profits and place this responsibility in the hands of risk managers, experts trained by experience and education to handle such work. The job of the risk manager is to prevent his company from suffering a catastrophic uninsured loss of assets and profits. Thus it is the responsibility of the credit man to check carefully the risk-management program of his customer.

In a previous chapter, it was stated that the purpose of capital is to serve as surety for the credit risk, and, in consequence, the extent of that capital and the form in which it is found are thoroughly considered. The purpose of insurance is to protect that capital. Insurance may be likened to the reserve for contingencies, with the important exception that if the contingency becomes a reality, the loss suffered is not a cut into the assets of the company but is, instead, replaced by the insurance company. It may be seen, therefore, that the weaker the capital factor the greater the necessity that it should be bolstered up by full insurance protection, while strong concerns are made stronger by proper and adequate insurance. Then, too, the attitude of the management upon the question of insurance is a measure of its conservatism and foresightedness. A wise insurance program lends confidence to the risk, whether the risk is weak or strong.

While it is now possible to insure against almost every conceivable type of occurrence or accident, a sound risk-management program will not necessarily include all available types. The greater risks, however, should be covered. Foremost among these is the possibility of loss by fire. Other coverages would include liability, life, and mandatory types of insurance.

Fire Insurance. The need for this form of protection, which includes property and inventory coverage, has long been recognized as a fundamental of sound business.

The credit man must consider the fire insurance question from the standpoint of the law of averages. He does not know which of his customers will suffer a fire loss; but he may be assured that, if he is selling a large number of accounts, fires will occur among them. Just as it was desirable to protect the machinery, equipment, or merchandise while in the possession of the creditor, it may be desirable to protect the creditor's interest in such property when the title and possession are with the purchaser. It is important that the credit man guard against a mistake made many times in requiring his customer to furnish proof of fire insurance equal only to the amount of the customer's indebtedness to him. This is a wise precaution, but it does not go far enough. In order to avoid the penalties imposed by the coinsurance clause in the event of underinsurance, it is important that the creditor make certain that the customer owns adequate fire insurance on an over-all basis, not just for the machinery, equipment, or stock in which the creditor has an interest.

The same principle applies to the insurance of real property. If a mortgage is held on a building, it is important that the creditor make certain that there is sufficient fire insurance in force to meet the requirements of coinsurance clauses included in the fire insurance policies. A policy of fire insurance in an amount equal only to the unpaid balance of the mortgage, in most instances, will not be sufficient to repay the mortgage in the event of a total loss.

Adequate Fire Insurance. What is adequate fire insurance? Is it necessary that the property should be insured for its full value, or will a sum less than the full value be adequate? These questions are asked from the credit man's standpoint. If property is fully covered, will that fact lead to carelessness or perhaps worse than carelessness on the part of the insured? The weaker the capital guarantee, the nearer the approach should be to full coverage, while, conversely, the stronger the capital guarantee, the greater the loss that can be absorbed by the capital strength. The credit man will come to his decision on the adequacy of fire insurance according to the conditions of each individual case. In general, however, the creditor will be satisfied if his customer is insured for the amount representing the coinsured percentage.

Coinsurance. Knowing that property in protected areas will rarely suffer a complete loss by fire, businessmen have a tendency to insure only that portion of their properties which they feel they might lose. Thus insurance premiums are lower. To induce the insured to carry more coverage, insurance contracts include a coinsurance clause. In essence, this clause stipulates that in the event of partial loss, in order to collect the full amount of the loss, the insured must own insurance equal to at least the coinsurance percentage of the value of the property insured at the time of the loss.[1] The formula used for determining the amount collectible by the insured in the event of a partial loss is:

$$\frac{\text{Amount of insurance in force}}{\text{Amount of insurance required}^2} \times \frac{\text{amount}}{\text{of loss}} = \frac{\text{amount of}}{\text{loss payment}}$$

The use of this formula in an example demonstrates the principle of coinsurance. If the value of a building, or stock of merchandise, is $125,000 and the fire insurance policy contains an 80 per cent coinsurance clause, the amount of fire insurance required to protect partial losses would be $100,000. Thus if the debtor carries fire insurance of $50,000, and he has a $25,000 fire loss, he would collect only $12,500 from the insurance company. This would be calculated as follows:

$$\frac{\$50,000}{\$100,000} \times \$25,000 = \$12,500$$

Should the same customer suffer a total loss, it is obvious that he can recover no more than the face amount of the policy, which is $50,000. He is a coinsurer for $75,000, the balance of the $125,000 property value. Thus underinsurance could cause heavy losses to debtors, who would in turn be unable to pay their creditors. On the other hand, if the debtor carries adequate fire insurance, he will be fully covered on all partial losses. Thus creditors are fully protected. Even if there is a total fire loss, the debtor's capital factor acts as a margin of protection.

The Moral Hazard and Insurance. While credit men desire that the risk will be protected by adequate fire insurance, they do not overlook the danger that may lurk in fully insured slow-moving or obsolete stock. Suspicious fires are constantly occurring, and convictions for arson are frequent. Credit men do not want to sell the criminal type, nor do insurance companies wish to insure them. Creditors and insurance companies have much the same problems. The factors making the risk a satisfactory one for either are the same.

The risks for both are affected by the condition of business. Statistics have proved that when failures are high fire losses likewise increase, while fires diminish when business is good and failures few. This situation is deplored. The remedy, like the remedy for loose credits, lies in

---

[1] Most territories require an 80 per cent coinsurance clause, but in some instances this may vary. For sprinklered buildings in New York City, the required coinsurance is 90 per cent.

[2] Amount of insurance required is determined by multiplying the value of the property insured by the coinsurance percentage.

a more thorough investigation of the risk and a raising of the general standard required. For this purpose some insurance companies have established departments similar to credit departments, whose function it is to examine and approve the risk before the insurance is placed. Such a selection results in fewer losses for both insurance companies and creditors and in lower premiums for the insured as well.

A full measure of cooperation should exist among the insurance companies, credit men, and good citizens generally to stamp out the crime of arson.

Liability Insurances. Businessmen are becoming more and more aware of the increasing importance of liability protection, and in many organizations such protection for premises, operations, products, and motor vehicles is considered to be equally as important as fire insurance.

Liability insurance is designed primarily to protect an individual or business from claims of third parties arising from bodily injury to persons or damage to property of others occasioned by acts or alleged acts of negligence on the part of the insured. The limits of liability are important considerations of a credit man, who should realize that inadequate liability insurance can greatly jeopardize the assets of a customer. In some instances, inadequate liability limits can be even more damaging than inadequate fire insurance protection, since a successful negligence suit brought by a third party is capable of cutting into the assets and earnings of a customer for years to come. Liability insurance serves to safeguard not only today's assets and profits, but also the future earnings and assets of a business.

Life Insurance. In a previous section dealing with fire insurance, it was brought out that the purpose of insurance is to reinforce the capital protection. Capital, however, is but one of the sources of strength active in a successful business. Of no less importance is managerial ability, which may be summed up in character and capacity. These reside in men; and men die unexpectedly and in many cases leave the business without a successor competent to take the helm. Such a shock to a business may be eased by insurance upon the life of the owner, partner, or individual in the corporation. The death of such a person means at least a temporary money setback. It may or may not be possible to replace him. Insurance would tide over the gap until his successor could get into his full stride and, furthermore, would relieve the minds of creditors. The practice of insuring the key men of a business is becoming constantly more common, and it is a practice to be commended and fostered by credit managers.

Such a policy not only reassures creditors and gives the owners a feeling of security, but it may be and frequently is the collateral which makes possible a loan in time of temporary need. The weaker the organization or the reserve of managerial power, the greater the need for such a security.

The Investigation of Life Insurance. A full investigation of the strength lent to a risk by an insurance policy will naturally include an examination into all the features of the policy. The more important among them are: Whose life is insured? Who is the beneficiary? What are the disability clauses? Is the right to change the beneficiary retained? By whom are the premiums paid? What is the cash surrender value?

In the event of bankruptcy, the life insurance policy has been regarded as an asset of the business when the business is the beneficiary or in some jurisdictions when the bankrupt is the insured and has retained the right to change the beneficiary or when the premiums have been paid from the funds of the business. This is a feature that may well be investigated, since, under the provisions of the Bankruptcy Act, the bankrupt is entitled to the exemption granted him by the laws of the state of his residence. Such a law is found in New York.[1] The remarks above are equally applicable in the event of a forced collection. As a rule, one of the first inquiries made of the judgment debtor in supplementary proceedings is whether or not he carries any life insurance. The purpose of the inquiry is to discover whether, under the policy and the laws of the state, the judgment creditor of the insured may recover the surrender value of the policy.

Mandatory Insurances. Certain types of insurance protection are made mandatory by state or federal laws, such as Old Age and Survivors' Insurance (Social Security), Unemployment Insurance, Workmen's Compensation, Nonoccupational Disability, and Automobile Liability.

---

[1] By Chapter 468 of the Laws of 1927, effective Mar. 31, 1927, the Insurance Law of the State of New York, constituting Chapter 33 of the Laws of 1909, was amended by adding Section 55a providing that "If a policy of insurance, whether heretofore or hereafter issued, is effected by any person on his own life or on another life, in favor of a person other than himself, or, except in cases of transfer with intent to defraud creditors, if a policy of life insurance is assigned or in any way made payable to any such person, the lawful beneficiary or assignee thereof, other than the insured or the person so effecting such insurance or his executors or administrators, shall be entitled to its proceeds and avails against the creditors and representatives of the insured and of the person effecting the same, whether or not the right to change the beneficiary is reserved or permitted and whether or not the policy is made payable to the person whose life is insured if the beneficiary or assignee shall predecease such persons. . . . "

The foregoing amendment now precludes a trustee in bankruptcy of a bankrupt resident in the State of New York from reaching a policy on the life of the bankrupt payable to a designated beneficiary, even though the bankrupt has reserved the right to change the beneficiary.

Social Security. A federal law makes payments for social security mandatory. While, in fact, it is not the employer but the employee who is insured, the employer, under the law must contribute a part of the premium and is responsible for the part contributed by his employees. Since the liability is a prior claim, the analyst needs to be assured that all payments to the government have been made.

Unemployment Insurance. Such protection for employees is subject to state laws. They, too, impose upon the employer the duty of paying the premium, a certain percentage of the employee's wage. In some states the employer is responsible for the entire contribution, while in other states the employee must also contribute a portion of the premium.

Workmen's Compensation. Every state and the District of Columbia have enacted a Workmen's Compensation Law. Under such laws it is mandatory that the employer provide insurance for his employees that will pay certain medical expenses and weekly indemnity in the event the employee is injured while on the job or, in some states, in the course of his employment. Severe penalties can be incurred by the employer if such protection is not in force.

Nonoccupational Disability. In four states[1] at the present time such insurance is required by law. This protection provides for payment of certain benefits to employees who are injured while not on the job, or who may become ill.

Automobile Liability. Massachusetts, New York, and North Carolina make it mandatory under their laws for owners of vehicles to own automobile liability insurance before their vehicles can be registered.

Credit Insurance. This is a form of insurance which may in some instances add some safety to the credit risk, while in other instances the risk is sufficiently strong and no appreciable strength may be added by credit insurance. The purpose of credit insurance is to protect the seller against excessive credit losses.

While the purpose of this section is to consider insurance as a strengthening feature of the credit risk, credit insurance will be found more fully treated in a later chapter as a form of protection for the seller when carried by him, rather than as adding security to the risk when carried by the debtor.

Other Insurance. There are other forms of insurance of varying degrees of importance in different cases, for example, business interruption insurance. Some of them the creditor may regard as desirable or essential for certain risks, and it might be advisable for the credit manager to consult with the risk manager of his own organization for guidance as to what might be considered essential for any one particular credit risk.

[1] Rhode Island, California, New Jersey, and New York.

Summary. Adequate insurance of several types is necessary not only for the survival of a business firm, but also as a protection for its creditors. The credit appraiser, therefore, must consider insurance along with the capital factor in the analysis of the creditworthiness of a business enterprise. He must further ascertain that the debtor has complied with all requirements for mandatory insurance, including the full payment of premiums.

TEXT AND RESEARCH QUESTIONS

1. How does an income statement disclose "where a company is going"?
2. Why do businessmen reluctantly disclose operating figures?
3. How reliable are income statements?
4. Outline a satisfactory income report.
5. What effect does the volume of sales have upon (a) the gross profit percentage and (b) operating expense percentages?
6. Why are all percentages in operating statement analysis computed on the basis of net sales?
7. Why is it desirable to have the gross sales as well as the net sales shown?
8. What items in the operating statement are not affected by increase or decrease in sales?
9. What items, if any, in the operating statement are wholly without the control of the management?
10. Which is the more significant, the percentage of net profit to sales or the percentage of net profit to net worth? Why?
11. In what way other than the payment of dividends can profit be withdrawn from a business?
12. Why is it sometimes impossible to reduce costs as sales decrease?
13. How do changing price levels affect costs?
14. What is the significance of net profit?
15. What are surplus adjustments?
16. What types of insurance should a business carry?
17. What is the 80 per cent coinsurance clause?
18. What do credit men generally regard as adequate fire insurance on a building and its contents?
19. Name three factors in addition to the fire hazard that should be considered by the insurance company when fire insurance is applied for.
20. When is life insurance an asset of the business, and when is it not?

PROBLEMS

1. A comptroller of a certain corporation feels the corporation's current ratio would be safe at 2¼ to 1. The current assets are $625,690, while the current liabilities are $240,650. How much can it expand its current assets by short-term borrowing and not fall below a 2¼ to 1 current ratio?

Show how you derived your answer.

2. The Bradley Manufacturing Co. started the year with the following current assets and current liabilities.

NOTE. For easier calculations the figures have been converted to even thousands of dollars. The student is to convert collections to the nearest thousand dollars. For this problem each month is to be considered as a 30-day period.

Current Assets:

Cash........................	$ 10,000
Accounts Receivable..........	90,000
Inventory....................	100,000
Total Current Assets.......	$200,000

Current Liabilities:

Accounts Payable	
Accruals and Taxes...........	$80,000
Total Current Liabilities.......	$80,000

Assume all its expenses, except for factory labor, are constant throughout the year and are $8,000 monthly. The monthly sales, purchases, and factory labor costs for the first eight months of the year follow:

Month	Sales	Factory labor	Purchases
January.........	$ 30,000	$12,000	$11,000
Feb.............	26,000	11,000	23,000
Mar.............	34,000	14,000	25,000
Apr.............	50,000	32,000	58,000
May.............	90,000	33,000	63,000
June............	120,000	15,000	29,000
July............	70,000	12,000	15,000
Aug.............	30,000	9,000	14,000

Selling terms are net 30 days, but collections average 45 days. Terms of purchase are net 60 days. Collections for the month of January are $60,000. Collections for the month of February will include the balance of the Jan. 1 Receivables, $30,000, plus the sales from Jan. 1 (ignore the holiday) to Jan. 15, since the 45-day period for these sales will fall between the fifteenth and the end of February. This sets forth the method of computing the monthly collections. The minimum cash balance for the entire period is $10,000. Inventory cost comprises purchases and factory labor. Inventory is reduced monthly by 80 per cent of selling price.

Compute the Current Assets, the Current Liabilities, and the Current Ratio at the end of each month for the 8-month period, and draw a graph for the period showing the Sales, Inventory, Purchases, and Current Liabilities. In computing the Current Ratio carry to two decimal points.

3. The Peerless Trading Company carried fire insurance under three different policies with 80 per cent coinsurance, as follows:

Policy 1: Buildings, insurance carried, $30,000
Policy 2: Furniture and fixtures, insurance carried, $6,000
Policy 3: Inventory, insurance carried, $90,000

The company suffered a fire which completely destroyed the inventory and furniture and fixtures and did considerable damage to the building. The following appraisals were made:

	Value	Loss
Building......................	$55,000	$32,000
Inventory.....................	98,000	98,000
Furniture and fixtures...........	5,600	5,600

Calculate the net loss to the company.

CHAPTER 22

RATIOS, THEIR COMPUTATION AND USES
IN FINANCIAL ANALYSIS

The student already has used several ratios, particularly the current ratio, and various internal ratios relating to the income statement. As previously indicated, ratios may be classed as balance sheet, income, and mixed ratios.

The Selection of Ratios. The author uses the term "relationship" freely because he desires to impress upon the student of statement analysis that it is the relationship between certain items which is significant. To simplify this relationship, credit men are accustomed to reduce it to a ratio or to a percentage. The one may be merely the inverse of the other. Thus, where annual net sales are $100,000 and the receivables are $10,000, the ratio of sales to receivables is 10 to 1. This relationship is expressed in many credit departments as the percentage of receivables to sales, 10 per cent in this illustration. While it is the relationship which is important, regardless of how it is expressed, it would simplify and promote the use of relationships if the method of expression became standardized. Although there are as many relationships as there are combinations of items, fortunately only a few need be used. But those selected for consideration may differ according to the analyst's judgment of their significance and according to the type of business being analyzed. The analyst's first requisite is to comprehend fully the significance of the ratios which he uses. He should know whether, in a given relationship or ratio, a higher or lower ratio or percentage would improve the financial position. He should, too, realize that ratios differ among themselves in their bearing upon the credit risk.

How many and what ratios he should use will depend upon the individual company to be analyzed. If the fixed assets are of relatively minor importance, the analyst may decide to dispense with the ratios having fixed assets as a part. In the analysis of many trading concerns the following ratios may be adequate: the current ratio, net worth to debt, sales to receivables, sales to inventory, and sales to net worth.

355

The first two ratios measure the basic financial position, and the three sales ratios disclose the adequacy or inadequacy of sales in relation to the net worth, the inventory carried, and the money tied up in receivables.   Concerns with a larger array of assets and liabilities may call for the use of supplemental ratios determined according to the nature of the concern and its financial statement.   In any event it must be remembered that ratios merely indicate positions which may need further investigation.

A satisfactory ratio does not prove that a business firm is sound.   In using ratios the analyst is cautioned that it is illogical to compare companies unless they are in the same industry.   A collection period ratio for a retailer of dry goods would be quite different from that for an industrial chemical firm.

As a guide to the student, the author presents a comparative table of ratios considered important by three leading financial writers.[1]   Most of these ratios are discussed in this chapter.   The ones suggested by Foulke appear annually as Standard Ratios.

Finally, it must be stressed that any ratios based on poorly prepared statements are practically worthless.

Standard Ratios.   The credit manager or loaning officer who wishes to use ratios as aids in financial interpretation may set up his own standard ratios, or he may adopt published ratios.   Dun & Bradstreet publishes annually ratios for 72 lines of business activity in the manufacturing, wholesaling, and retailing fields.   These ratios for the year 1957 are reproduced in Appendix J through the courtesy of Dun & Bradstreet, Inc.   The Robert Morris Associates publish a series of ratios widely used by loaning officers of banks, and several of the trade associations have compiled ratios for the use of their membership.   The credit manager may prefer to compile from his own files ratios to serve as standards.   While he may have available a far smaller number of statements to use, he has the advantage of knowing whether the businesses used are comparable, a necessary corollary, and their statements are of the same date.

Standard ratios are not necessarily ideal ratios.   They are, rather, average ratios which may be above or below what might be termed an ideal ratio.   But average ratios are necessarily used since there is no way of determining the ideal.   Neither the average nor the ideal ratio would remain constant over a period of years.   For instance, current ratios were lower in 1952 than in former years, owing largely to the drain of cash out of business by increased taxes and more extensive use of creditors' capital.   The credit analyst might regard the point of safety as somewhat below the average on the theory the margin of safety

[1] The following relationships are suggested for use of credit men in "Practical

observed by the majority of businesses would raise the average above a normal point of safety. Obviously it can hardly be true that a business with a ratio one point above the average is safe in so far as that ratio is concerned while if the ratio is one point below average it is unsafe.

Compensating Ratios. A ratio, unacceptable in itself, may be qualified by other ratios that exceed the normal requirement. High ratios of Sales to Receivables and Sales to Inventory, for example, may offset the criticism of a low current ratio. The reasons are set forth in the

---

Credit Analysis," Eugene S. Benjamin, "Behind the Scenes of Business," Roy A. Foulke, and "How to Evaluate Financial Statements," Alexander Wall.

BENJAMIN	FOULKE	WALL
Receivables to Sales	Average Collection Period	Sales to Receivables
Merchandise to Sales	Net Sales to Inventory	Sales to Merchandise
Liabilities to Sales		
Liabilities to Liquid Capital	Current Debt to Tangible Net Worth	
Turnover of Liquid Capital	Turnover of Net Working Capital	
Turnover of Merchandise	Net Sales to Inventory	
Merchandise to Receivables		Merchandise to Receivables
Merchandise to Liquid Capital	Net Working Capital Represented by Inventory	
Debt Reflected in Merchandise	Inventory Covered by Current Debt	
Net Profit on Gross Capital	Net Profit on Tangible Net Worth	Profits to Worth
Plant to Gross Capital	Fixed Assets to Tangible Net Worth	Worth to Fixed Assets
Cash to Bank Loans		
Current Ratio	Current Assets to Current Debt	Current Ratio
	Net Profit on Sales	Profit to Sales
	Net Profits on Net Working Capital	
	Turnover of Tangible Net Worth	Sales to Net Worth
	Total Debt to Tangible Net Worth	Net Worth to Debt
	Net Working Capital Represented by Funded Debts	
		Sales to Fixed Assets

These lists illustrate both the lack of uniformity in expression of relationships and some lack of agreement as to which relationships have the greatest significance. In listing, the author has attempted to place opposite each other those relationships which have practically the same significance.

accompanying illustrations of Company A and Company B. Let it be assumed that these companies are operating in the same industry and have the same percentage of expense to sales.

COMPANY A

Cash........................	$ 25,000	Accounts Payable............	$100,000
Receivables..................	75,000		
Inventory....................	75,000		
	$175,000		$100,000
Annual Sales.................	$750,000		

COMPANY B

Cash........................	$ 25,000	Accounts Payable............	$100,000
Receivables..................	100,000		
Inventory....................	100,000		
	$225,000		$100,000
Annual Sales.................	$750,000		

A comparison of the ratios mentioned might indicate to the casual analyst that Company B is far the better risk.

Ratios	Company A	Company B
Current....................	1.75 to 1	2.25 to 1
Sales-Receivables...........	10 to 1	7.5 to 1
Sales-Inventory.............	10 to 1	7.5 to 1

From the safety standpoint, this conclusion might be correct since Company B has $2.25 of Current Assets for each dollar of Current Liabilities while Company A has only $1.75 of Current Assets for the protection of each dollar of Current Liabilities. But from the operational viewpoint, Company A will have no more difficulty in meeting its obligations as they mature than will Company B. It is noted that for the same volume of sales Company B has $25,000 more invested in each of its Receivables and Inventory than Company A. Since this capital is, in comparative sense, idle capital, it should be furnished by the owners in the form of net working capital. This results in a higher current ratio.

While it will be seen that the higher operating ratios mentioned may compensate for a low current ratio, and, conversely, a high current ratio may compensate for low operating ratios, this is so only within certain limits. Sales, in a given company, will fall within certain limits. If the sales are too low, not enough gross profit is obtained to cover the expenses, with the usual result that a part of the income that should be used to pay mercantile or bank creditors is diverted to meet expenses, thus pyramiding the Current Liabilities. On the other hand, if sales exceed a certain amount, the concern is said to be overtrading. The danger in overtrading is discussed in a subsequent section. Many ratios, both mixed and internal, are based on sales. (Net sales is invariably meant.)

Facts Disclosed by Sales. Sales are undoubtedly the keystone of the whole business structure. Like all keystones, sales must be supported by other satisfactory operating conditions before a sound and profitable business can be developed. The purpose of business is to render a service through sales at a profit. A large capital, a fine plant, and desirable merchandise are useful in a business sense only where sales are obtained with an adequate net profit.

Analysis on the basis of sales will show, therefore, among other things, the activity of the capital, the productivity of the plant, and the freshness of the inventory. A sales analysis should also indicate whether the concern is overtrading or undertrading, the terms taken by customers on purchases, the time necessary to liquidate the inventory, and the time necessary to liquidate current indebtedness. Other important facts may be indicated by the sales analysts. There is no scientific method of applying the measurement. The analyst must use his art of credit appraisal in arriving at his conclusions.

When sales are considered in connection with merchandise, for instance, the relationship is frequently spoken of as the merchandise "turnover." That is, the sales are a certain number of times as large as the inventory, or the money invested in the inventory has been turned over a certain number of times. Thus the "turnover" may be six times, or, as often expressed in ratio form, 6 to 1.

Sales to Receivables. This ratio is computed by taking the figure for net sales and dividing it by all receivables net of reserves that contribute to the sales. Using credit sales would give a better result, but they are not available in most cases. Instalment sales and instalment receivables should be separately analyzed. If a concern's sales are, let us say, $1,000,000 a year, it should receive in the course of the year $1,000,000 in collections, assuming there were no bad-debt losses. Let us assume again that the balance sheet shows receivables of $110,000 and it is known that the terms of sale are net 30 days. If payments are prompt, collection of the $110,000 would be effected in 30 days or at the rate of $1,320,000 per year. Neither of the assumptions made may be quite correct. If the two items, sales of $1,000,000 and receivables of $110,000, are taken together, it is found that the "turnover" of the receivables is approximately nine times per year, or in other words, that the receivables turnover is approximately every 40 days. Let us further assume that the analyst has found, from experience, that the collection turnover in days for the industry represented is approximately

40 days.[1] A ratio of 9 to 1, would, then, be regarded as normal, and any deviation from that ratio might point to the need of a further conclusion, or perhaps a further investigation. A subnormal turnover indicates a longer period to collect a given sum of money, and it may be caused by too liberal credits or laxity of collection methods. This usually means an added expense of financing, because the selling company has to use more capital to carry these accounts, and usually the slower the accounts, the greater the collection cost and bad-debt losses.

On the other hand, while an abnormal relation of sales to receivables would seem to enhance the seller's credit, such a relationship may have a significance which is not so favorable. It may indicate too strict a credit policy, that is, sales sacrificed to a good collection record and low bad-debt losses, accomplished sometimes by bearing down too hard in the collection effort, or it may indicate that the subject, unable to finance itself in the usual manner, has obtained the high ratio by selling some of the receivables.

A closer analysis of an apparently slow turnover of receivables may be found to result from a seasonal condition in the business in which receivables, as appearing in the balance sheet at the particular period taken, may be abnormally high, thus reducing the turnover and leading one to believe that collections were unsatisfactory. Monthly or quarterly statements in which receivables could be fairly averaged over the yearly period would result in the derivation of a more accurate and normal ratio for internal use.

In conclusion, it may be said that the business showing a normal turnover for its industry is effectively meeting trade conditions and maintaining its credit standing because of that relationship. The subnormal relationship may detract from and the abnormal relationship may enhance the desirability of the credit. Whether normal, subnormal, or abnormal it may be necessary to analyze more carefully the cause of the relationship in order correctly to appraise it. The ratio itself is not final, it is merely an indicator. Obviously anyone preparing a false statement will attempt to present normal ratios.

Sales to Inventory. The ideal relationship of sales to inventory would be attained if a concern could at a given price level reduce its inventory to a minimum where any further reduction of stock would necessitate a loss of sales. Such a perfection of inventory is only theoretically possible. Good management requires, however, that the

---

[1] It is quite simple to convert turnover of receivables to collection period. Divide the result obtained into the number of days. (It is most convenient to use the 360-day period for the year.) Comparing the answer with selling terms indicates how closely the company is collecting its receivables. The collection period should approximate the average for the industry.

ideal relationship be attained as nearly as possible. If a business can come as near the ideal as do its competitors, it is competing effectively with them. Errors of judgment, however, are frequently made, and such errors are usually on the side of too large an inventory. This may be due to the fact that too small an inventory is quickly discovered and most easily remedied, while time is required to liquidate the large inventory even after the mistake has become apparent.

The relationship, or ratio, of sales to merchandise will vary with economic conditions. The creditor will place his stamp of approval upon a much smaller ratio in a period of rising prices than he would in a period of falling prices. In other words, a liberal inventory is some protection against rising prices, while the creditor would prefer to see his customer carry an inventory even below normal when prices are falling. As in the case of receivables, money tied up in unnecessary inventory is money not working, and, consequently, the greater the activity and turnover the greater the profit upon the inventory investment.

The point is often raised that the "turnover," obtained by dividing the sales by the inventory taken on a cost basis, does not give a true stock turnover. The statement is, of course, true. The physical turnover of stock would be obtained either by raising the inventory to sales value and then dividing the sales by the result thus obtained, or by dividing the cost of goods sold by the inventory. Both methods are illustrated, as well as the sale to inventory ratio. It is assumed that sales are $84,000, while inventory is $14,000, and the gross profit $33\frac{1}{3}$ per cent, which would call for a markup of 50 per cent.

Sales: Merchandise Turnover:

$$\frac{\text{Sales } \$84,000}{\text{Merchandise } \$14,000} = \text{ratio (6 times)}$$

Physical Turnover Cost Basis:

$$\frac{\text{Cost of goods sold } \$56,000}{\text{Merchandise } \$14,000} = \text{turnover (4 times)}$$

Sales Price Basis:

$$\frac{\text{Sales } \$84,000}{\text{Merchandise at sales price } \$21,000} = \text{turnover (4 times)}$$

While it will be seen from the above that there is considerable difference between the relationship which we are discussing and the physical turnover of the inventory, it is a distinction of little moment so long as the one is not confused with the other. As a matter of fact, it is the comparison of relationships which is desired, and the sales-merchandise relationship is the one most commonly used, owing perhaps to the fact that the sales figure is more often available than is cost of goods sold. Thus, in order to compare companies, sales are used.

The sales-inventory relationship indicates to some degree the efficiency of the management. Rapid turnover indicates good management, liquid stock, fresh and salable merchandise, or merchandise not included. A slow turnover, on the other hand, may reflect too large an investment in inventory, careless buying, an unbalanced inventory (too much of one thing and too little of another, often found in a manufacturing concern), and possibly dead and slow-moving stocks. Again the reader is advised against being too dogmatic in reaching his conclusions from this relationship. Finally, it may be necessary to go back of the ratio itself and obtain a breakdown of the inventory as to raw material, goods in process, and finished goods on both a physical as well as a financial basis in order to determine the true significance of the relationship.

Sales to Net Working Capital. The purpose of this relationship is to consider the efficiency with which net working capital is being utilized. But caution in the acceptance of this ratio must be observed. It can as easily be too high as too low. At first thought the student might assume that the greater the volume of sales attained by net working capital the better. The danger is in failing to realize that mounting sales must usually be accompanied by increased gross working capital, and since gross working capital is the sum of net working capital and current liabilities, as the gross working capital increases so must the liabilities, the net working capital remaining fairly constant. In other words, an increase in the ratio of sales to net working capital is most apt to be accompanied by a decrease in the current ratio.

To be satisfactory the ratio must lie between an upper and lower limit as determined by the judgment of the credit manager.

Sales to Fixed Assets. This is a relationship which the reader will observe can have but little bearing when the fixed assets are, comparatively, very small. Capital invested in furniture and fixtures may be small while sales may be very large. When, however, the fixed assets include the plant, machinery, and equipment of a manufacturer, the relationship assumes considerable importance.[1]

The analyst examines this relationship to discover whether the investment in fixed assets is fully productive and consistent with the current assets. If the subject's competitors are able to obtain $6 of sales to each dollar invested in fixed assets, it is obvious that the concern whose sales are only four times its fixed investment is laboring under a distinct disadvantage. The inference is that the concern is too large for the volume of business done, or a portion of it is idle and unproductive. Such a

[1] Leasing of fixed assets, if in any sizable amount, makes any comparison with other companies impossible.

condition is often due to a lack of foresightedness.   During a period of
rising prices and capacity production the management, striving for
greater volume, proceeds to enlarge its manufacturing facilities.   The
result is a larger capital investment to lie idle during the next depression.
Increased potential volume may have been achieved which has at a later
date only resulted in increased inefficiency and overhead expense.   Many
concerns suffered from this error of management during the boom which
attended the First World War.   In such an expansion capital is usually
diverted, to some extent, from current assets, even though the operation
may be funded.

To summarize, it may be said that capital is invested in plant and
other fixed assets to achieve profitable production or trading.   If a
proportional sales volume is not attained, the justification of the full investment may be doubted.   Such a concern is at a distinct disadvantage
when compared with its competitors.   Unlike some of the other relationships, there is no criticism on the part of the creditor as the relationship
of sales to fixed assets increases.   Such an increasing relationship will
find its limit in the physical capacity of the plant.   It is the decreasing
relationship, or the degree of inefficiency, or idleness, which may give
the creditor concern.

Sales and Net Worth.   This is a relationship which moves within restricted limits.   When outside those limits we have the common
criticism that the concern is "overtrading" or "undertrading," as the case
may be.   Other things being equal, the greater the number of turnovers
of the net worth, the greater the net profit.   Increased volume of business usually requires larger inventories and produces larger receivables.
These call for a larger capital which if not furnished by the ownership
must be supplied by creditors.   Increased sales may, therefore, be accompanied by a decreased relationship of current assets and current
liabilities, and also by a decreased relationship of net worth to borrowed capital.   Both of these conditions reduce the creditors' margin
of safety, and hence may be looked upon by them with disfavor.   An
increased relationship of sales to net worth may, however, be obtained
through velocity.   In this event, the large ratio of sales to net worth
will be accompanied by other high rates of turnover, particularly those
of sales to inventory and sales to receivables.   Thus the relationship of
current assets to current liabilities and net worth to borrowed capital
may not be forced out of a normal limit.   There is danger, however, in
an abnormal velocity.   If it is relying upon a narrow margin of profit,
short terms both in selling and buying, the concern may not be able to
slow up.

Undertrading may be as disastrous to a business as overtrading.   Unless a certain sales volume is produced by the net worth it is, to a degree,

stagnant and unproductive. As the relationship between sales and net worth decreases profits may disappear, capital may be impaired, and the result, if the condition is not corrected, may be the gradual efface-ment of the concern from the business field.

In appraising this relationship some allowance should be made for the general business or particular trade conditions, and, also, for the size of the business unit under analysis. Net worth will remain fairly con-stant from year to year, but sales resistance will vary, particularly in some industries. Thus, a smaller turnover of capital may be general, and while its effects may be as unfavorable as though the smaller turnover were due to less efficiency on the part of the management, some allow-ance should be made for the general business conditions.

Receivables to Merchandise. While both the receivables and the merchandise are classed as current assets, there is some reason for com-paring their relationship to each other. Receivables are regarded as a quick-current asset while merchandise is slow current. Together, they usually form the bulk of the current assets. Their relationship to each other may aid greatly in appraising the liquidity of the current position. In the current ratio they are treated as though they were of equal qual-ity and effect in determining the credit position of a company. This is not the actual fact, however, since they may be of widely differing liquidity. To consider that liquidity and other characteristics of the two items is highly important.

The first point to be drawn to the reader's attention is the difference in the method of appraisal of the two items. Merchandise is carried at the cost of acquisition, or, if the replacement value becomes less than the cost, merchandise is written down to that replacement value. It is never written up, at least never with the accountant's or credit man's approval. Thus losses are taken but not profits. As soon, however, as merchandise is transferred to a buyer, profits are added. If the cost price is advanced, or, according to business parlance, marked up, let us say 50 per cent, an inventory of $10,000 would appear as $15,000 when it reached that receivables stage. When that point is reached the value is pegged. Price changes will not affect it. Of course it may be neces-sary to make some slight allowance for bad debts and collection expenses, but these are minor. In the illustration given it is apparent that the creditor would prefer the value to be in the form of the receivable rather than in the form of merchandise, because receivables are one step nearer cash. By the same reasoning, it may be assumed that the larger the ratio of receivables to merchandise, other things being equal, the stronger the credit position. This, however, may not always be the case. In the illustrations following it would appear that case 1 presented a stronger risk than case 2 although both present the same current ratio.

CASE 1

Cash........................	$ 3,000	Accounts Payable.............	$ 4,000
Receivables..................	15,000	Bills Payable.................	10,000
Merchandise.................	10,000		
	$28,000		$14,000

CASE 2

Cash........................	$ 3,000	Accounts Payable.............	$ 4,000
Receivables..................	10,000	Bills Payable.................	10,000
Merchandise.................	15,000		
	$28,000		$14,000

Let it be assumed, further, that the markup in each case is 50 per cent. It will be seen that merchandise in case 1, were it not for selling and other business expenses, would present a potential value of $15,000 which would increase the current assets to $33,000, while merchandise in case 2 would present a potential value of $22,500 which would raise the current assets in that case to $34,500. But these business expenses often leave very little or, at times, no net gain. The writer does not imply that case 2 is the stronger. Other factors should be considered before such a conclusion is reached. Among those factors are the terms of sale, the economic conditions, that is, whether it may be a rising or falling market, the seasonal position of the business, etc. Let us assume that the terms of sale in case 1 are 60 days, while in case 2 the terms of sale are 30 days. Thus case 2, while the receivables are smaller, is actually receiving more money in a given time than case 1. If it is the end of the active selling season, on a comparative basis, case 1 presents the better position, because it is not left with a large inventory on its hands. If it is a period of rising prices it is apparent that case 2 is the better fortified against any further advance, while the reverse would be true if prices were falling.

Net Worth to Debt. The net worth[1]–debt[2] relationship is of considerable importance because it indicates the amount of owner capital as contrasted to creditor capital used in the business. Since it is the function of owner capital to serve as a guarantee of the liquidation of credit, it follows that the larger the owner capital in comparison with creditor capital the greater the security. Also, the greater the ratio of owner capital to creditor capital the greater the independence of the ownership from the decisions and good will of its creditors. Stated conversely, the greater the debt in comparison to net worth, the greater the dependence of the ownership upon the judgment and attitude of the creditors.

There is an old saying among credit men that the owners of a business should have at least an equal investment with creditors. That is, the

[1] Net Worth = Capital Stock + Surplus = Owner's Capital.
[2] Debt = Total Liabilities.

relationship, or ratio, of net worth to debt should be at least 1 to 1. Like most standards used in financial-statement measurement, this statement can be accepted only in a very general way. Safety may be found with a ratio of less than $1 of investment for each dollar of credit, while on the other hand, danger may be present even if the ratio be greater than 1 to 1.

It would seem that, when long-term debt is present, a ratio of 1 to 1 may not be so dangerous as when all the debt is current. As has been stressed several times, no one test is infallible. All factors must be given due consideration in arriving at a conclusion. However, many analysts consider the debt relationship as indispensable to the analysis.

Net Worth and Fixed Assets. As in the case of sales and fixed assets the relationship of net worth and fixed assets is of little importance when the fixed assets comprise a very minor part of the assets. Where plant and equipment are a necessary part of the business, this relationship may prove to be of considerable value in determining the soundness of a concern's financial structure.[1]

Fixed assets are permanently required in a business, they are being constantly worn out or depreciated, and, if sold, the machinery and equipment portion often will bring but a fraction of their real value. Good business judgment decrees that the ownership should have a very substantial equity in this class of assets. It is sometimes reasonable to expect a concern to use its permanent investment in fixed assets as a means of obtaining current assets.

Since the presumption is that the business is successful, it is able to pledge its fixed assets and earning power to secure a bond issue. In this way, funds for part of the value of the assets are obtained for current purposes. Thus part of the net worth is used to acquire fixed assets and measures debt protection.

The importance of the relationship between the owners' investment and the fixed assets may be illustrated in another way. It indicates the extent of the reliance on borrowed funds for current position. This point may the more easily be seen by illustration.

CASE 1

Current Assets	$ 70,000	Current Liabilities	$ 30,000
Fixed Assets	100,000	Net Worth	140,000
	$170,000		$170,000

CASE 2

Current Assets	$ 70,000	Current Liabilities	$ 30,000
Fixed Assets	100,000	Mortgage	40,000
		Net Worth	100,000
	$170,000		$170,000

[1] This ratio has no significance if the fixed assets are leased.

In case 1, the current assets are supplied for the most part by the ownership and there is no fixed obligation to earn a return on capital, desirable as that end may be to the ownership. In case 2, however, there is the necessity of earning a return upon the $40,000 furnished by the mortgagee, and that necessity becomes a fixed charge. Moreover, in case 2, the general creditors can look to assets of only $130,000 to liquidate their claims, while in case 1, the general creditors have a reliance upon the whole $170,000.

Net Working Capital to Inventory. The student will have noted that one of the relationships suggested by Roy A. Foulke is Net Working Capital Represented by Inventory. To conform to the author's plan of stating a relationship so that an increase in the ratio generally indicates an improved credit position, this relationship is converted to Net Working Capital to Inventory.

In some industries this relationship is of particular importance. This is so because of the variable nature of the inventory. It may be subject to rapid price changes, or to rapid style changes, or to great fluctuation in demand for the product. Danger lurks in an inventory which is too large in comparison to the net working capital. This danger may not be disclosed by the sales-inventory relationship since sales and inventory may expand together, thus not affecting the ratio. Net working capital is less variable, and so provides an excellent gauge of inventory safety.

Overtrading. Overtrading is an expression used in credit circles to signify that the sales of a business concern are abnormal in relation to its net worth. Overtrading is dangerous because debt is usually excessive as measured by net worth.[1] The degree of danger depends upon the degree of overtrading. Obviously, the greater the volume of sales, at a given price and a given margin of profit, in relation to the net worth, the greater the profit. Overtrading is thus a temptation which only a wise management is able to resist.

Increased sales require increased financing. As sales increase, so will it be necessary to increase inventory, although not necessarily in exact proportion to the increase in sales. The increase in the inventory will cause the accounts payable to increase in like amount. The receivables, in turn, will increase in direct ratio to the increase in sales, assuming terms of sale remain stable. The larger inventory is thus financed, somewhat precariously, by the trade creditors, and the added receivables must be financed either by funds borrowed from the bank or by withholding payments from trade creditors.

When a concern is transacting a very heavy volume of business its successful operation depends upon a very close coordination of sales,

[1] Furthermore, interest on debt may be a drain on potential net profit.

purchases, and payments. As long as this coordination can be maintained all is well. Heavy forward commitments for goods may be necessary to provide the inventory for the heavy volume of sales, and conversely, a heavy volume of sales is necessary to provide the funds to meet the heavy commitments. The delicate balance between inflow and outgo of goods is easily disturbed. A drop in the sales for any reason, or, if it be a manufacturing concern, trouble in the production department, will cause the inventory to pile up. Though management may anxiously watch sales, some time may elapse before a definite and prolonged downward trend can be distinguished from a temporary lull in sales. Inventory begins to pile up, and though the management may quickly realize its danger it may be impossible, because of future commitments, suddenly to stop the inflow of goods. The liabilities, already large, continue to expand, while the income necessary to liquidate the expanded liabilities is rapidly dropping. The concern thus using its capital and its credit to the limit in good times has no reserve of either to carry it through a period of adversity. Obligations cannot be met, and the creditors, alerted to the dangerous position, swoop down on the hapless and helpless concern.

Overtrading, its degree, and so its danger, is measured by the relationship of sales to net working capital and sales to tangible net worth. When these ratios are higher than is normal or safe for the line of business, overtrading is indicated, and low ratios of current assets to current liabilities and tangible net worth to debt further confirm it. In the rare cases, through good management a company may appear to be overtrading as measured against the industry. The light debt situation and small interest expense would indicate that good management is the answer.

The ratios not already discussed in this chapter, but included in Foulke's fourteen ratios, are net profits on net sales, net profits on tangible net worth, current debt to inventory, and funded debt to net working capital.

The significance of the net profits ratios is self-evident. Net profits is connected with the three items with which net profits is most concerned. Net profits on tangible net worth reveal whether the management has the ability to earn a return and satisfy investors. The ratios of net profits on net sales and net profits on net working capital are complementary. If net profits are inadequate, these ratios may help to explain the reason.

The current debt to inventory relationship supplies the analyst with another inventory test. Heavy losses due to style changes, perishability, obsolescence, and price declines are hazards of excessive inventories.

Any considerable deviation from the industry average needs justification.

The percentage of funded debt to net working capital is a useful check ratio for comparison purposes. It is generally held that the proprietary investment should exceed the investment in fixed assets, thus supplying a portion at least of the net working capital. Heavy funded debt results in heavy fixed charges. Amortization, debt retirement obligations, interest, and carrying charges *must* be met, while returns on proprietary capital may rise and fall with profits. The student of causes of business failure knows well that the disparity between current and fixed capital often results in reorganization or liquidation. A business with too small current capital in relation to fixed capital is seriously handicapped.

TEXT AND RESEARCH QUESTIONS

1. What ratios would you use in analyzing textile mills? Electrical equipment? Wholesale hardware?

2. What do ratios tend to indicate?

3. What are standard ratios?

4. Why is the volume of sales of particular importance in the analysis of financial position?

5. List five reasons for a slower than average turnover of receivables.

6. Why is it desirable to ascertain the reason for an abnormal or subnormal turnover of receivables?

7. Why do credit men customarily use the relationship of sales to inventory instead of the cost of goods sold to inventory?

8. Discuss the importance of collection period.

9. Why may a comparison of the sales-fixed ratios of different companies or of the same company for different years be misleading?

10. What ratios will be affected by (*a*) an abnormal and (*b*) a subnormal ratio of sales to net worth?

11. List and indicate the significance of the relationship of sales and three other items not mentioned in the text.

12. What is the purpose of the study of the relationships of various balance-sheet items?

13. When is a debt ratio "heavy"?

14. What is meant by overtrading?

PROBLEM

Assume that you are credit manager for one of the large packing houses. Your salesman has been soliciting the Blank Meat Company, who distribute fresh, smoked, and dried meats, etc., to independent meat markets, hotels, and restaurants. The salesman reports that purchases will amount to about $4,000 weekly.

BLANK MEAT MARKET
Jan. 31

Current Assets:

Cash....................	$ 30,670.88
Accounts Receivable.......	30,643.70
Inventory................	55,426.33
Total Current Assets....	$116,740.91

Other Assets:

Investments in Stock......	$ 1,250.00
Paid-in Life Insurance.....	3,375.00
	$ 4,625.00

Fixed Assets:

Land and Buildings........	$103,147.89
Store Fixtures............	54,303.70
	$157,451.59
Less Depreciation.........	31,750.75
	$125,700.84
Automobiles..............	$ 14,195.80
Less Depreciation.........	4,718.24
	$ 9,477.56
Leasehold................	$ 1,000.00
	$136,178.40
	$257,544.31

Current Liabilities:

Accounts Payable.........	$ 32,833.81
Notes Payable—Banks....	56,500.00
Total Current Liabilities.	$ 89,333.81
Mortgage Payable.........	40,000.00

Net Worth:

Capital Stock............	$ 20,000.00
Surplus..................	98,716.01
Gain for year............	9,494.49
Total Net Worth.......	$128,210.50
	$257,544.31

Supplementary Information:

Average sales: per week, $25,000.00

Terms of sale and purchase: net 10 days

Gross profit: 25%

The Blank Meat Company operates one retail meat market in premises that are leased.

(The gross profit is the difference between what the goods cost and the selling price. Out of the gross profit the various expenses, selling, administrative, and financial, must be paid. The average weekly expenses can be derived from the data given. It is suggested, as a conservative measure, that the gross profit and the expenses be regarded as equivalent.)

Make two analyses of the statement.

a. Could payments be expected according to terms? Why?
The following questions are suggested, among others, for consideration:
How much credit will the company require of your concern?
How much, if any, of the cash may be used to retire liabilities?
What is the company's per cent of profit on investment? On sales?
Is inventory reasonable, too large, or too small?
What effect would paying the bank loan have on the company?

b. Could the meat company liquidate as of Jan. 31 and pay all obligations? Itemize the amount estimated to be realized.

c. What one question would you most like answered by the company? By the bank? By the mercantile creditors?

CHAPTER 23

COMPARATIVE STATEMENT ANALYSIS
AND SPECIAL ANALYSES

Thus far our discussion of a financial statement as a source of credit information has been largely confined to the analysis of a single balance sheet, vertical analysis of an income account, and various ratio studies. Valuable as this information may be to the credit analyst, he is greatly aided if he can support his deductions by facts from a definite comparison of two or more financial reports. Comparative analysis is most comprehensive and conclusive only when it is based upon a thorough knowledge of how to examine a single statement internally and in combination with the income statement.

A single statement shows a static condition as of a certain date. Since the credit man is always interested in the future trend of the business, the financial statement is of interest to him only as it may assist in forecasting the future. As has been aptly said, while a single balance sheet may be likened to a still picture, a series of balance sheets presents a moving picture of past performances. The comparison of income statements fills in the action between successive pictures and shows, in part, how the changes occurred. It is true that successive financial statements point out the velocity at which a business is moving and also the direction in which it is headed. The force which is propelling a business at a certain speed and in a certain direction will carry it along, it is assumed, in the same trajectory indicated for some time into the future.

Methods of Comparative Analysis. While all statement analysis is not spoken of as comparative, it is in reality just that. The value of a statement can be appraised only by subjecting it to some sort of comparative measurement. There are, in fact, three general methods of comparative analysis. All statements in analysis are compared (1) with previous statements of the same company, or (2) with statements of the same date of other similar companies, or (3) with a model statement set up in the mind of the analyst. These three methods may be and frequently are used in combination. It is with the first method, or the comparison of a statement with previous statements of the same company, also known as trend analysis, that this section is to deal.

Method of Setting up Statement for Comparison. Having received a customer's latest financial statement, it is desirable to transfer the items to a comparative statement form.

This is generally called "spreading the statement." Samples of spread forms are illustrated in Figs. 34a and 34b. The purpose of spreading is to arrange the accounts on the comparative form in a consistent, logical, and predetermined sequence, in order to facilitate further analysis. Thus there is an evaluation of each account according to the procedures previously discussed in order properly to classify it. A complete comparative form provides adequate space for balance-sheet accounts, income accounts, reconciliation of net income and surplus, and such trend and vertical ratios as may be desired. Consistency in the treatment of accounts from period to period is essential to proper analysis.

In Fig. 34a is illustrated a comparison form for the presentation of balance-sheet analysis, including a study of the current position. On the other hand, Fig. 34b illustrates a detailed comparison of income statements and includes disposition of the net income, surplus adjustments, and ratios.

For comparative purposes, it is not necessary to transfer figures down to the last penny. As a matter of fact, rounding off the transferred account to even hundreds, or to even thousands (*i.e.*, 00 omitted, or 000 omitted), is recommended. This practice permits a greater number of comparisons on each form, saves time in computations, weakens none of the validity of either comparisons or ratios, and altogether simplifies the spreading function.

Vertical analysis involves comparing accounts at the same date; trend or horizontal analysis is from period to period. Thus a comparison form provides for many different kinds of analyses.

Although many small business firms may not spread statements, they do compare the original statements. Among banks, it is general practice to spread most statements. However, there appears to be no such thing as a uniform spread form. Each user works out a form which best suits his purpose.

Some analysts prefer to reduce all statements to a common size for greater ease in the consideration of changes which have taken place, while other analysts, for the same reason, show exact additions to or deductions from individual items. The first method is known as the "common size" or "100 per cent statement." The second method is called the "where got" and "where gone" statement. Both of these methods will be briefly illustrated.

Name				Business		
Corporation	Partnership			Proprietorship		
	000-s omitted			000-s omitted		
Assets-Date						
Cash						
Accounts Rec.-Trade						
Less Reserve						
Inventories						
Marketable Securities						
Current Assets						
Misc. Assets						
Investments						
Plant Account						
Less Res. Deprec.						
Deferred Charges						
Total Assets						
Notes Payable						
Accounts Payable						
Accruals						
Current Liabil.						
Long Term Debt						
Tot. Liabil.						
Capital Stock						
Surplus						
Tot. Net Worth						
Tot. Liabil & N.W.						
Tangible N.W.						
Contingent Liabilities						
Current Assets						
Current Liabilities						
Net Current Assets						
Ratio						
Certified						
Spread by						

FIG. 34a. Balance sheet comparison form.

Name			Business			
		OCO- s omitted		000-s omitted		
Period						
Date Ended						
Cash Sales						
Credit Sales						
Gross Sales						
Returns, etc.						
Net Sales						
Cost of Sales						
Gross Profit						
Selling Expenses						
Admin. Expenses						
Tot. Oper. Expenses						
Operating Profit						
Other Income						
Other Expenses						
Fixed Chgs.						
Fed. Tax						
Net Profit						
Div. or Withdr.						
Surplus Adjust.						
Open. Surplus						
Closing Surplus						
Depreciation Charged						
Ratios						
Oper. Profit Ratio						
Net Profit on Sales						
Inventory Turnover						
Aver.Collect Period						
Tot.Debt to Net Worth						
Net Profit on Net Worth						
Invent. to Net Cur.Assets						
Prepared by						

Fig. 34*b*.   Income statement comparison form.

The Common-size Statement. Those who advocate the 100 per cent or common-size statement, as affording the best means of comparison, claim that size is often mistaken for strength and that size obliterates a sense of proportion. This difficulty is overcome by considering the total assets, and the total liabilities including capital, as each equal to 100. The common-size statement is obtained by dividing each item on

DRESS MANUFACTURER

8/10 E. O. M.

Assets:	Last Year	This Year	Last Year	This Year
Cash.......................... $	88,744.83 $	55,208.18	7.63	3.55
Accounts Receivable, Net.........	306,218.82	579,360.87	26.34	37.27
Merchandise Inventory............	478,937.12	593,293.10	41.19	38.16
Deposit.........................		1,260.00		0.08
Notes Receivable at Real Value....	152,600.00	190,440.87	13.12	12.25
Fixtures........................	21,604.48	28,478.84	1.86	1.83
Investments.....................	76,594.76	76,594.76	6.59	4.93
Officers' Life Insurance...........	9,236.00	12,478.00	0.80	0.80
Sundry Receivables and Advances..	15,493.20	6,890.29	1.33	0.44
Due from Officers................	10,216.00	4,833.54	0.88	0.31
Prepaid Charges.................	3,076.75	5,915.17	0.26	0.38
Total Assets.................	$1,162,721.96	$1,554,753.62	100.00	100.00
Liabilities, Capital, and Surplus:				
Due for Merchandise on Open Account......................... $	561,486.02 $	711,391.76	48.29	45.75
Loan from Bank.................	75,000.00	125,000.00	6.45	8.04
Loan from Others................		65,049.31		4.19
Sundry Accounts Payable.........	14,338.39		1.23	
Corporate Stock Issued...........	300,000.00	300,000.00	25.80	19.30
Surplus in Use as Capital.........	197,709.95	318,027.91	17.87	20.45
Reserve for Taxes................	14,187.00	35,284.64	0.36	2.27
Total Liabilities, Capital, and Surplus...................	$1,162,721.96	$1,554,753.62	100.00	100.00
Sales..........................	$2,487,300.88	$4,792,261.33		

FIG. 35. Illustration of statement comparison. Common-size ratios.

the statement by the total assets (or liabilities), the quotient expressing each item in its percentage of the total.

The statements of a dress manufacturer (Fig. 35) at the close of two different years are used to illustrate this method of setting up a statement for comparison. The statements used also illustrate the desirability of setting up statements received on a standard form, such as that illustrated for the use of banks. By an inspection of the items on the statements of the dress manufacturer the analyst would, no doubt, be impressed by the considerable increase in the Merchandise Inventory and the Receivables. The Accounts Receivable item, it will be noted at a glance, at the end of this year is almost double (189 per cent) the amount of the last year; yet its proportionate increase when compared with the increase of all other items is only 141 per cent. The Merchandise Inventory has increased $114,355.98; yet it has actually been reduced from 41.19 per cent to 38.16 per cent of the total capital employed in the business. This method of setting up a statement for analysis enables one to determine easily the proportion of the capital employed as working capital or, if that term be confusing, the amount of capital invested in the working assets. The two statements show an increase from 88.28 to 91.23 per cent. These totals include the items Cash, Accounts Receivable, Merchandise Inventory, and Notes Receivable. The proportion between current assets and current liabilities is also easily determinable from the common-size statement, though which year presents the larger current ratio the reader probably cannot determine from inspection either of the original statements or the common-size statements.

Another fact plainly brought out by the common-size statement is the relationship between owner capital and creditor capital. Although owner capital has increased from $497,709.95 to $618,027.91, it has decreased from 43.67 to 39.75 per cent of the total capital employed.

From the few comparisons made the reader will have noted that, while this method shows clearly the relation of single items or groups of items to each other and to the total, comparisons of items in different statements cannot be made. In two items mentioned, Receivables and Capital and Surplus, there has been considerable increase. Yet the analyst, relying solely on the common-size statement, would conclude that there has been in each instance a decrease. The reader may form his own opinion as to whether enough is gained by this method of setting up a statement for analysis to compensate for the time involved in making the various necessary computations. There is a further question as to whether financial statements are uniformly prepared.

Comparative Analysis of the Balance Sheet. Tying in with the analysis of a statement at a particular date as to current position, debt position, and various vertical ratios would be a comparison of the changes from period to period, that is, trend analysis. There are at least three possible types of analyses in trends: (1) dollar changes (where-got, where-gone), (2) progressive base-year percentages, (3) base-year percentages.

"Where-got, Where-gone" Statements. It must be evident that an increase in an asset must be accompanied by a decrease in some other asset or by increased capital furnished either by creditors or owners. Conversely, a decrease in any asset means either the increase of some other asset or the withdrawal of capital either by owners or creditors.

The changes that take place in the capital position of a business from year to year are plainly brought out by the "where-got, where-gone" method of comparing a financial statement. The statement shown in Fig. 36 will illustrate the "where-got, where-gone," or it might be called the "what happened," method of comparison.

Assets:	Year B	Year A	Where Got −	Where Gone +
Cash............	$ 228,849.00	$ 156,336.00	$ 72,513.00	
Accounts Receiv-able..........	1,628,294.00	1,936,911.00		$ 308,617.00
Inventory........	5,750,109.00	4,793,144.00	956,965.00	
Real Estate......	3,803,595.00	3,235,323.00	568,272.00	
Treasury Stock...	77,300.00		77,300.00	
Securities........	48,583.00	51,233.00		2,650.00
Unamortized Bond Discount.......	299,396.00	194,989.00	104,407.00	
Sinking Fund.....	495.00	867.00		372.00
Good Will........	590,250.00	590,250.00		
Deferred Assets...	375,279.00	373,390.00	1,889.00	
Total Assets....	$12,802,150.00	$11,332,443.00		

Liabilities, Capital, Surplus:			+	−
Payables.........	$ 3,538,601.00	$ 3,183,088.00		$ 355,513.00
Reserve for Taxes.	47,411.00	77,519.00	$ 30,108.00	
Funded Debt.....	2,179,000.00	2,051,000.00		128,000.00
Real Estate Mort-gage..........	380,500.00	200,500.00		180,000.00
Preferred Stock...	603,015.00	601,200.00		1,815.00
Common Stock...	5,072,800.00	4,911,000.00		161,800.00
Surplus..........	980,823.00	308,136.00		672,687.00
Total..........	$12,802,150.00	$11,332,443.00	$1,811,454.00	$1,811,454.00

FIG. 36. Where-got, where-gone analysis.

NOTE: In order to obtain the balance shown, changes in the amounts of liability, capital, and surplus are reversed from those changes in the assets. Thus the decrease in the payables, a minus item, is added with the plus asset changes. The formula is that increases in assets, plus decreases in liabilities and net worth, equal the decreases in assets plus increases in liabilities and net worth.

The statement illustrated (Fig. 36) is presented just as it was submitted to creditors, without any change as to arrangement, but with the cents omitted. The analyst can see at a glance through the where-got and where-gone setup just what has happened to the individual items, but the significance of the changes is not so easily determined. The author will call attention to only a few of the changes, leaving a more thorough analysis to the reader.

It will be noted that Receivables have increased $308,617 while the Inventory has been reduced $956,965. This may be a change which the creditor is glad to see. The reduction of $720,861 in Current Assets, it will be noted, is accomplished by a reduction of $325,405 in Current Liabilities, which has effected a decrease in the Net Working Capital $395,456 without, however, appreciably changing the current ratio. Real estate has been decreased $568,272. The inference is that a part of the real estate has been sold, or, it may have been more conservatively appraised. If the latter inference is correct, much of the decrease in Surplus, $672,687, is explained. A decrease in the item Unamortized Bond Discount may explain a cut into the Surplus account of $104,407. It will also be noted that while creditor capital has been reduced $633,-405 (the total of Payables, Funded Debt, and Real Estate Mortgage less Reserve for Taxes) the owner capital has been reduced $836,302 (Preferred Stock, Common Stock, and Surplus). Whether these changes, on the whole, have improved the concern's credit position or otherwise, it is left to the reader to determine from a more extended analysis of the changes effective in the year A.

It is apparent that the where-got, where-gone statement, being one of the earliest tools of analysis, pertains only to the balance sheet. To explain changes in surplus or net worth, another analysis tool, the "source and application of funds" statement, was devised.

Comparison by Inspection. While the two methods described may add greatly to the ease with which certain changes in the financial statement are discovered, they are not used except for special situations. The common practice is to compare by an inspection the same items for two or more years with each other. Derivative and supplementary data may also be compared. A form similar to that shown in Fig. 34a aids greatly. Such a form may be necessary when there are a number of accounts to compare. In reaching a conclusion, the analyst is greatly aided by having all items on a comparative basis. Changes in the current position, the importance of which has been previously exemplified, are shown. Supplementary data including contingent liabilities, net sales, net profit, dividends, outside worth of indorsers, and the name of the accountant are called for. It will be noted that the form permits a 6-year comparison. The form illustrated is not presented as a model, but rather as typical of the simpler forms in use by banks.

While a comparison of items will show whether the increase or decrease is favorable or unfavorable, such changes will not of themselves indicate whether the risk is made a desirable or undesirable one. The mere fact that certain items may show improvement will not bring a business within the circle of desirable risks.

Progressive Base Year and Base-year Trend. The percentage change from one period to another, whether it is in the balance sheet or in the income account, may be more significant than large dollar-amount change. In using the progressive base-year trend percentages, a comparison based on the previous year is made for each account. Thus sales may increase from $1,000,000 to $1,250,000, a 25 per cent increase; in the following year $1,250,000 will be the base-year sales.

Base-year Trend. Some analysts prefer to show total growth, or decline, over several time periods. Thus in the example above, $1,000,000 of sales may be selected as the base year and the sales of the successive year will be proportioned to that base year. For limited time periods— say up to 5 years—this form of analysis may prove useful, but in comparing similar companies, the same base year must be used.

Comparative Analysis of Profit and Loss Statement. It has been said that business management pays relatively little attention to its own balance sheet.[1] Business management does, however, give much attention to the profit and loss statement. The internal analyst is both at an advantage and at a disadvantage compared with the external analyst. The advantage lies in the fact that complete information is available to the internal analyst with supporting data, explanations, etc. The credit manager's advantage is in his ability to compare the profit and loss statement with those of similar concerns in the same industry. The credit manager will appraise the efficiency of the management according to the ability of the management to obtain an adequate volume of sales and then to keep the various costs within the normal percentages determined from the industry at large.

In addition to the percentages already described, it is suggested that the analyst compute the percentage horizontally when analyzing the profit and loss statements of a company over a period of years. An illustration of this method of analysis is given in Fig. 37. The vertical percentage relates the item to sales, while the horizontal percentage relates the item to the same item for previous years, showing clearly the trend of expenses in relation to the trend of sales. The profit and loss statements of the Butter and Egg Co., together with its balance sheets (not shown) were submitted by the company to its bank with its application for a loan. The statements cover a period of falling prices and declining sales. The analysis brings out clearly the problem which the management was not able to solve. The vertical percentage figures disclose that the management was able not only to maintain its gross profit percentage but to increase it with the result that while the sales decreased to 46 per cent of the year D in the year A, the most recent year, the gross profit had decreased to only 59.43 per cent for the same

[1] Many businesses would greatly benefit from having the credit manager make a frank and critical analysis of the financial statement from a creditor's viewpoint. Such an analysis should greatly aid the financial management in keeping the business in a sound financial condition.

THE BUTTER & EGG CO.
COMPARATIVE PROFIT AND LOSS STATEMENTS FOR YEARS ENDED DEC. 31, 19—

	(D) 12/31 Three Years Ago	(C) 12/31 Two Years Ago	(B) 12/31 Last Year	(A) 12/31 This Year
Sales (Net)...................	$1,974,103	$1,760,469	$1,348,182	$900,132
Cost Sales				
Gross Profit..................	$ 186,210	$ 177,603	$ 148,259	$110,677
Operating Expense:				
Insurance....................	3,217	5,738	4,492	3,297
Heat, Light, Power...........	1,023	1,198	1,170	1,027
Telephone and Telegraph.....	1,690	2,256	1,938	2,210
Petty Cash...................	3,164	2,888	2,044	1,720
Stationery and Supplies......	1,341	1,988	1,491	1,234
Services, Dues, etc..........	1,856	1,974	1,901	2,458
SAuto Expenses...............	9,605	8,399	7,647	5,951
SCartage.....................	2,796	1,784	2,277	2,688
SCommissions.................	19,857	19,176	16,522	10,992
Payroll......................	92,463	95,337	86,150	72,508
Postage......................	1,390	1,210	1,096	1,196
Brine........................	503	503	503	357
SAdvertising.................	4,172	1,829	1,422	1,693
Sundry Expenses.............	478	782	1,269	707
	$ 143,455	$ 145,062	$ 129,992	$108,038
Officers Salaries.............	11,700			
FRent........................	3,120	4,350	4,350	3,363
FInterest and Discount........	9,611	7,579	7,869	4,289
FFranchise Tax...............	569			
FBad Debts...................	5,521	11,403	6,690	12,071
FDepreciation................	2,099	4,826	2,737	1,933
Total.......................	$ 175,985	$ 173,220	$ 151,568	$129,694
Operating Profit..............	10,225	4,383		
Operating Loss................			3,309	19,017
Life Insurance Division........			329	
Sale Lease....................				5,347
				$ 13,670
Moving Expenses.............				1,495
Net Loss.....................			$ 2,980	$ 15,165

NOTE: The expense items keyed with the letter *S* are treated as Selling expenses and those with the letter *F* as Financial Management expenses, while the remaining items are classified as Administrative expenses. The letters *V* and *H* (below) are abbreviations for vertical and horizontal, respectively.

	V, %	H, %	V, %	H, %	V, %	H, %	V, %	H, %
Net Sales................	100	100	100	89	100	68	100	46
Gross Profit.............	9.44	100	10.09	95.37	11.07	9.62	12.28	59.43
Selling Expenses.........	1.84	100	1.77	85.61	2.07	76.49	2.37	59.53
Administrative Expenses.	6.01	100	6.47	95.91	7.57	85.95	9.36	73.04
Financial Management Expenses.............	1.06	100	1.60	135.18	1.61	103.92	2.41	103.97
Total Operating Expenses	8.92	100	9.84	98.43	11.25	86.13	14.40	73.69
Operating Profit and Loss.	0.52	100	0.25	42.87	*0.25*	......	*3.11*	

FIG. 37. Comparative analysis of the income statement.

year. Had the management been able to cut its operating expenses proportionately to its loss in sales a healthy increase in its operating profit would have resulted through the greater gross profit percentage. This apparently was beyond the power of management. Operating expenses instead of being reduced to 46 per cent of year D, as would have been desirable, or to 59.43 per cent which would have permitted the business to break even for the year, were reduced only to 73.69 per cent. Though the figures do not disclose it, by inference the analyst might conclude that the failure to cut expenses proportionate to the decline in dollar sales was partly due to the fact that volume sales, or tonnage, did not maintain the same rate of decrease. A principal failure of management lay in its inability to effect any decrease in its financial management expenses. These expenses are largely fixed. The percentage figures point clearly to the necessity of a sufficient volume of sales to take care of the fixed expenses.

Other Special Analyses. Over the years the credit analyst has improved his working tools. Out of the where-got, where-gone method of analysis, particularly useful when only balance sheets were available, he developed a method of connecting the income statement with the balance sheet and derived a "source and application of funds" statement. Other tools evolved include trial-balance and break-even point analyses.

Source and Application of Funds. Just as the current analysis is a special source of information relating to liquidity, the source and application of funds statement is used to reconcile the change in net current assets from year to year. It is a record of significant transactions that take place among the slow (noncurrent) assets, slow liabilities, and net worth, balanced out to equal the change in net working capital. The formula is that the sum of the sources of funds, offset by the sum of the uses of funds, equals the change (plus or minus) in net working capital. For example, selling a plant for a profit would be a source of funds; as would be net profit.

It is customary to substitute for the change in surplus all the accounts such as net profit, dividends, etc., either as a source or use of funds. Furthermore, in order to come closer to cash flow, noncash charges to income such as depreciation and depletion are added back to net profit as sources of funds.

The source and application of funds statement is useful in highlighting significant transactions and in correlating the income statement with the balance sheet. As a result, net profit is accounted for. Sometimes confused with the source and application of funds statement is the flow of funds statement. This is used primarily to show that the cash is being received in time and in sufficient amounts to pay debts and expenses as they become due.

Most of the analyses illustrated heretofore have been based on final financial reports, which are often received 3 months or more after the closing date. A fruitful source of current financial data is the trial balance.

The Trial Balance. It is a customary practice for business concerns to draw off a list of the accounts and their balances in the general ledger each month, called "a trial balance." It serves several purposes. If the debits and credits are in balance, there is a strong presumption there are no errors in the accounting procedure; the trial balance at the end of any fiscal period is used as a basis for the preparation of the balance sheet and the profit and loss statement; it furnishes the management with a capitulation of the operations of the business from month to month.

Credit executives, particularly at quarter-annual points or occasionally monthly, seek and obtain trial balances from certain of their accounts and specifically from "workout" cases. It is to be regretted, from the credit executive's viewpoint, that the practice is not much more prevalent, for trial balances, regularly submitted, would keep the creditor informed of progress from one statement date to another. Credit managers are wont to think a customer's financial position remains static, as disclosed by his latest financial statement. Trial balances would disillusion them. Trial balances disclose accurately expansion and contraction of receivables and payables, which may be considerable in a highly seasonable business. The purchases and accounts and notes payable items in consecutive trial balances may indicate the growth and recession of the inventory. The inventory, too, may be more accurately estimated by a method which will be explained later.

Through the estimated inventory the profit and loss for the period may be estimated. Thus trial balances, correctly interpreted, permit the creditor to gauge more accurately his risk from its inception to payment. But perhaps as valuable to the credit executive is the fact that they broaden his knowledge of the field and permit him to see more clearly his customers' operating and financing problems and thus make him a better informed and wiser judge of the risk involved in accepting credit.

Trial Balance Analysis. The correct analysis of a trial balance is based on knowledge of the industry and an analysis of the balance sheets and profit and loss statements of the same company for previous periods. The first step generally taken in analysis is to draw off a balance sheet with a "break-even" inventory. This is done by listing all the asset items exclusive of the inventory usually termed "inventory at beginning." It is the closing inventory of the previous accounting period. A separate listing is made in balance-sheet form of all the liabilities and net worth. Usually the total of the liabilities and net worth (or capital) will exceed the total assets exclusive of the inventory. The excess of net worth and liabilities indicates just how much inventory is needed for the business to "break even" on its operations up to that point. When the break-even figure is obtained, it is inserted in the balance sheet. The balance sheet thus set up may be all the credit executive needs to reassure him, provided the balance sheet is a satisfactory one for that date and provided he is confident the debtor has as much or more inventory than is disclosed by the break-even figure.

The actual inventory may be estimated but full assurance of the accuracy of the estimate is lacking because one element used in the computation is itself a variable. This is the percentage of sales which results in gross profit. The gross profit percentage, which cannot be definitely known, may be approximated by reviewing past operating statements, or a fairly accurate figure may be obtained from friendly businessmen or accountants operating in the same field.

The inventory may be estimated by the following procedure: Let it be assumed that the gross profit percentage in a given case is 18 per cent. The cost of goods sold is, then, 82 per cent of sales. Assuming these percentages are correct for the business whose Trial Balance appears in Fig. 38, the estimated Cost of Goods Sold is $111,394.48 (135,846.93 × 0.82). The cost of goods sold of this business is made up of inventory at the beginning of the period plus purchases, labor, and superintendence, less inventory at the end. In equation form

Cost of goods sold = inventory at beginning + purchases +labor
+ superintendence — inventory at end

Therefore,

Inventory at beginning + purchases + labor + superintendence —
(estimated) cost of goods sold = (estimated) inventory at end

Substituting, we have

$9,470.20 + $114,829.66 + $13,053.12 + $3,132.61 — $111,394.48 =
$29,091.11

The difference between this figure and the break-even inventory represents the estimated net operating profit for the period, subject to deductions for such items as accrued wages and interest, reserves for taxes and for depreciation, and the adjustment of deferred assets.

There are several pitfalls in thus estimating an inventory. There can be no substitute for the accuracy of the physical inventory, but without the means to obtain an actual inventory the credit manager may work with a figure which can be reasonably computed and on which he may reasonably rely. The gross profit percentage which he assumes is all important. A slight variation from actuality will magnify or minify

TRIAL BALANCE
JULY 31, 19—

		Debits	*Credits*
1.	Cash on Hand..................................	$ 165.32 $	
2.	Cash in Bank..................................	8,200.56	
3.	Accounts Receivable...........................	16,151.30	
4.	Notes Receivable..............................		
5.	Trade Acceptances.............................		
6.	U.S. Bonds....................................	1,000.00	
7.	Investments...................................		
8.	Plant and Equipment..........................	12,432.50	
9.	Furn. and Fixtures............................	2,382.25	
10.	Cash Surrender Value Life Insurance.............	200.00	
11.	Due from Employees...........................		
12.	Deferred Charges..............................		
13.	Accounts Payable..............................		23,601.16
14.	Trade Acceptances Payable......................		
15.	Notes Payable—Bank...........................		10,000.00
16.	Contractor Payable............................		
17.	Proprietor's Capital Account Jan. 1, 19—...........		32,378.67
18.	Gross Sales...................................		135,846.93
19.	Returns.......................................		
20.	Discounts Allowed.............................	11,174.81	
21.	Inventory (beginning) Jan. 1, 19—..............	9,470.20	
22.	Purchases.....................................	114,829.66	
23.	Discounts on Purchases........................		7,321.00
24.	Labor...	13,053.12	
25.	Superintendence...............................	3,132.61	
26.	Factory Maintenance...........................	833.50	
27.	Rent..	4,500.00	
28.	Light and Power...............................	209.54	
29.	Sample Making................................	700.00	
30.	Designing.....................................	800.00	
31.	Commissions...................................	420.00	
32.	Traveling.....................................	272.00	
33.	Advertising...................................	75.00	
34.	Entertainment.................................	75.00	
35.	General Expense...............................	803.28	
36.	Packing Supplies..............................	394.43	
37.	Insurance.....................................	395.27	
38.	Stationery....................................	52.12	
39.	Printing......................................	101.50	
40.	Postage.......................................	75.21	

	Debits	Credits
41. Telephone and Telegraph...........................	56.80	
42. Interest Paid......................................	100.00	
43. Auditing...	60.00	
44. Office Salaries....................................	806.00	
45. Stock-room Salaries...............................	402.01	
46. Shipping Salaries.................................	760.04	
47. Proprietor's Drawings.............................	5,063.73	
48. Total..	$209,147.76	$209,147.76

Fig. 38. Sample Trial Balance.

greatly the net profit. Obviously the cost of goods sold must contain the same elements of cost as were included in the profit and loss statement from which the gross profit percentage was derived. This is why the analyst can have assurance of the reliability of his work only when he has before him the concern's balance sheet and operating statement as a guide. Even then other chances of error exist.

Such questions as these may arise in the mind of the analyst. Were there any thefts of inventory? Was any of the inventory a loss through waste in processing? Should we use gross profit percentage, which is an average of the entire year's operations, when we know the trial balance represents a period when the industry usually loses money? Have there been increased labor costs? If several lines are carried which vary in gross profit percentage, are they now in the same proportion as that which determined the percentage used? Have all debits and credits been posted? Was the inventory at beginning an actual or an arbitrary figure? These questions point to the pitfalls of the analyst. Withal, the trial balance is a valuable source of information.

Break-even Point Analyses. In recent years, as terms of sales and loan maturities have lengthened, credit analysts have become more and more interested in break-even point analysis. In the operation of a business enterprise, there is a point at which the income from the sale of its production will almost exactly cover fixed and operating costs. Thus the break-even point is the amount of business volume necessary to cover all costs of operations without profit or loss. It may be translated into number of units or percentage of operating capacity needed to prevent loss.

If the credit analyst knows that 60 per cent of the operation is needed for a profitable business, and his customer is operating at only 40 per cent of capacity, he might question pending orders from that customer.

The credit analyst who knows break-even points for his accounts is in a position to forecast immediately the probable effect of changing inventory or labor costs on the financial accounts of his customers. In

SMITH AND COMPANY, INC.

Assets

		First Year		Second Year		Third Year
Current Assets:						
Cash.............................		$ 56,896		$ 75,448		$ 70,000
Accounts Receivable........	30,884					
Less Reserves.............	3,084	27,800		40,060		40,361
Inventory.........................		33,073		54,906		70,381
Total Current Assets..............		$117,769		$170,414		$180,742
Fixed Assets:						
Land.............................		4,423		4,423		4,423
Building..................	36,117					
Less Reserve..............	3,010	33,107	5,050	31,067	8,076	28,041
Equipment.................	135,145					
Less Reserve.............	5,000	130,145	9,460	125,685	12,234	122,911
Other Assets:						
Good Will........................		80,000		80,000		80,000
Patent............................		17,000		16,000		15,000
Total Assets.....................		$382,444		$427,589		$431,117

Liabilities

	First Year	Second Year	Third Year
Current Liabilities:			
Estimated Income Tax................	$ 32,254	$ 37,673	$ 38,056
Notes Payable.....................	6,000	7,782	8,012
Accounts Payable..................	18,674	20,281	20,696
Total Current Liabilities...........	$ 56,928	$ 65,736	$ 66,764
Total Debentures..................	100,000	135,000	135,000
Capital Stock and Surplus:			
Preferred 5%......................	36,500	36,500	40,000
Common..........................	105,000	105,000	105,000
Reserves			
Contingencies.....................	40,000	40,000	40,000
Surplus Paid......................	20,000	19,000	18,000
Surplus Earned....................	24,016	26,353	26,353
Total Capital..............	$225,516	$226,853	$229,353
Total Liabilities..............	$382,444	$427,589	$431,117

Profit and Loss

	First Year	Second Year	Third Year
Net Sales.........................	$222,500	$215,900	$214,800
Cost of Goods Sold..................	145,737	139,100	143,916
Gross Profit......................	76,763	76,800	70,884
Real Estate Tax....................	6,897	6,900	6,900
Light and Power...................	7,343	5,100	4,940
Selling and Advertising..............	28,035	28,800	25,776
Depreciation......................	8,010	6,500	5,800
Maintenance......................	5,563	3,850	4,296
Interest..........................	3,338	4,725	4,725
Net Profit.......................	19,580	20,925	18,447
Taxes.............................	9,790	10,462	9,224
Dividends			
Preferred.........................	1,825	1,825	2,000
Common.........................	6,300	6,300	7,224
Surplus...........................	1,675	2,337	0

Fig. 39. Comparative figures presented for analysis.

addition, he is in a position to estimate probable profits if he is told the operating level by the customer.

TEXT AND RESEARCH QUESTIONS

1. Why is a comparison of successive balance sheets desirable?
2. How can a concern's financial position be comparatively analyzed?
3. Will all methods of comparative analysis lead to the same conclusion?
4. What are the advantages and disadvantages of the common-size, or 100 per cent, statement?
5. What are the advantages and disadvantages of the "where-got, where-gone" method of analysis?
6. To what extent does comparative analysis of financial position aid in an appraisal of the "capacity" factor?
7. What is the difference between a progressive base-year trend percentage and base-year percentages?
8. Why are businessmen reluctant to issue detailed operating statements?
9. Why is it desirable to be able to account for changes in the surplus account through the income statement?
10. Why are income statement trend percentages useful?
11. Of what use is a Source and Application of Funds statement?
12. How may a trial balance be used in credit analysis?
13. Why is a knowledge of break-even points important to the financial analyst?

PROBLEMS

1. Analyze and criticize the financial statement of Smith and Company, Inc. (see Fig. 39).

What is your criticism of its financial management and policy?

What steps would you suggest be taken to correct the situation as you find it?

2. Refer to the trial balance shown in Fig. 38.

    a. Draw off a "break-even inventory" balance sheet.

    b. Compute the estimated profit or loss for the 7 months' period assuming a gross profit of 16 per cent on sales.

3. Make a complete analysis of the balance sheets and profit and loss statements of Walker-Hartman Company, manufacturers of men's shirts (Appendix I), computing significant ratios from the balance sheets and reducing the classified totals of the profit and loss statements to a common size. State briefly what your analysis discloses.

PART IV

THE PROTECTION AND REDEMPTION
OF CREDIT

CHAPTER 24

COLLECTIONS

With this chapter, the reader embarks upon the final leg of the credit journey. Hitherto attention has been directed, first, to a discussion of the theory of credit and the mechanics with which it is handled, and second, to the solving of the credit problem or, in other words, the measurement and acceptance of the risk, including the third financial statement analysis. Having measured and accepted the credit risk, the credit man must watch the credit until it has been redeemed. He must take such measures as lie open to him to ensure the credit redemption. It is with the redemption of credits, commonly called collections, that we now deal. The collection problem will be discussed in all its stages from the first step—the simple request for payments—to that necessitating the liquidation of a business by voluntary liquidation or by bankruptcy.

Collection Problem Varied. The ease or difficulty of effecting collection varies greatly in different industries, and also among different concerns within the same industry. In many credit departments the collection of accounts is the major problem of the department. This results from the nature of the market. Customers, in general, while ultimately able to pay, may be somewhat slow in paying; merchandise may be widely distributed in rather small units; or the profits may be sufficiently large so that unusual risks may be undertaken. Under such conditions either the risk is not adequately investigated, the creditor relying on the general law of averages to keep losses sufficiently low, or the risk, though recognized as considerable, is accepted. The business house which sells to such a market must expect some trouble in collecting its accounts. On the other hand, if the market is composed of concerns of generally high credit standing, and if customers are further selected with the poorer risks discarded, comparatively little trouble will be experienced with collections. Thus we find one credit manager who, as the result of the credit policy of his house, investigates thoroughly, appraises the risk carefully, and discards all but the highest class of risk.

At the other extreme is the credit manager of the house which is willing to accept almost any risk no matter how great and take its chances upon eventually getting its money. The one needs to give but little attention to collections; the other gives but scant attention to the risk. There is, of course, a wide variation of policies between these two extremes.

A general conclusion regarding collection problems is that they are insignificant in the total operation if sufficient time and acumen are used in the investigation and analysis of a credit risk. To the extent that credit analysis is slighted, collection problems multiply. For example, in many financial institutions and large trade houses where credit analysis is thoroughly applied, there are comparatively few collection problems in proportion to the number of accounts handled.

Credit Manager Logically in Charge. It has been held by some that the credit function differs so greatly from the collection function that there is in reality but little connection between them. Frequently, indeed, the collection department is completely separated from the credit department with the collection manager working under the direct supervision of the comptroller or the treasurer. In most mercantile concerns, however, the credit manager is also the collection manager. This combination or union of both credit and collection work under one head is most logical. The records of each are quite essential to the best work of the other. Furthermore, the credit man is most interested in effecting the collections, since if the collection is not effected, he is charged with the responsibility of the loss. Since, then, the credit department has the customers' records and has a greater interest in collections than any other employees, it is most logical to permit that department to control the account from the time it is opened until the completion of the transaction and the receipt of the final payment.

Importance of the Problem. The collection of accounts forms one of the most important phases of business organization. Business consists of a multitude of individual transactions each of which consists of a series of steps—production, selling, and collection. Collection is the ultimate aim of each transaction. While a good collection record will not alone ensure business success, good collections are one of the essentials of success.

Good business requires that collections shall not only be made but that they shall be made promptly and without any damage resulting to the concern's market. It is this latter requirement, namely, to retain the customer's good will, which makes the collection problem a difficult one and which makes skill and tact essentials of those handling the collections. In the majority of instances collection can be made, and promptly too, if the collector is willing to sacrifice good will, but good will is to be sacrificed only as a last resort. Stated in the order of their importance, the three objectives of the collection department are, first, to collect the debt; second, to collect the debt and retain the customer's good will; and third, to collect the debt promptly, retaining the good will of the customer. If those three objectives cannot all be attained, they are usually abandoned in reverse order. That is, promptness is sacrificed to good will, and, as a last resort, good will is sacrificed to the main objective which is to obtain the payment. It is no easy task to maintain so nice a balance as to result in the collection of the largest number of accounts with the greatest degree of promptness and at the same time lose the fewest possible number of customers.

The amount of profit is affected by the amount of capital unnecessarily invested in accounts receivable. It is the duty of the collection department to see that such capital is freed as promptly as possible for active use in the business. Capital tied up in receivables beyond their maturity not only is a loan of capital without interest but also involves the additional expense of collection. In other words, the customer is trading on your capital at no cost to him. To keep as much capital as free as possible and to collect it with a minimum expense is an added task of the collection department.

Just how much pressure is to be brought to bear to obtain prompt collections and to what extent good will may be jeopardized in the effort are questions of policy to be determined by each individual concern. The arguments which may be presented weigh heavily in favor of a vigorous or "close" collection policy.

Reasons for a "Close" Collection Policy. Along with the improvements in modern business methods there may be noted a general tendency to shorten the terms of financing by the seller. This is apparent not only in the published terms of the seller but it is evident in the greater insistence that the buyer shall comply with those terms. This change is not only noticeable but noteworthy. The seller reaps no advantage from credit terms unnecessarily extended. The shortening of terms, on the contrary, results in a greater turnover of capital with a consequent larger total profit. It enables the seller to take advantage of cash discounts, or to pay promptly, thus enabling him to maintain his own credit standing. Whether wholesaler or retailer, the customer whose buying terms are shortened is influenced to shorten his selling terms. Thus the movement is cumulative, making for greater liquidity of business in general. From the standpoint of the seller, then, the first benefit derived from a close collection policy is the smaller amount of capital necessary, or the greater amount of business achieved with the same capital. There are other advantages each worthy of the seller's careful consideration.

A close collection policy keeps the debtor in a liquid position to buy more goods. If a customer has bought and is owing as much as the seller cares to sell him, subsequent sales to that customer will be delayed so long as his account is unpaid. Even though the creditor might be willing to accept further orders, in spite of the delinquent account, the buyer will often avoid the house where his account is overdue and place his orders with a competitor.

Insistence upon prompt payment may be cheaper in the end. Prompt payment means fewer outstanding accounts and results in reduced book-keeping effort and a fewer number of overdue accounts for the collection department to handle. Customers soon learn which creditors they may ignore and which will insist upon prompt payment with the result that they pay the insistent creditor and allow the lenient one to wait.[1] An account, once impressed with the fact that the creditor will not tolerate long overdue accounts, pays when due, with little or no prompting on the part of the creditor. Prompt collections aid in keeping down losses from bad debts. As an account increases in age, the chances of ever collecting it diminish, consequently the greater the laxity in enforcing terms the greater the bad-debt losses. Several surveys conducted from time to time have proved conclusively that an account that is more than 6 months past due is worth only 67 cents on the dollar, and that one a year past due is worth but 45 cents. The business methods of the house forcing a strict observance of credit terms are respected by customers, and a confidence in the house is inspired which favorably disposes purchasers to it.

Reasons for Slow Payments. Every collection manager will have to deal with apologies of customers for slow payments, and these letters will usually give reasons or excuses for the delinquency. Such communications, by letter or otherwise, are greatly to be desired since they give the collector an insight into the line of attack, or the plan of campaign, which he should follow. The author also wishes, at this point, to call the reader's attention to the difference that may exist between reasons and excuses for delinquency.

While the reasons for slow payment are many, the more common among them may be classified as follows:

The first, and in the author's opinion, the foremost reason for slow payments is the lack of a thorough understanding of terms. Of course the terms are stated upon the seller's order blank and they are again stated upon the invoice. Furthermore, the buyer knows how to interpret the terms. But there is not always a clear understanding between buyer and seller that the terms are just as much a part of the contract as is price. Salesmen can testify to the general care with which the quality of the merchandise is examined and discussed, and also the hag-

---

[1] Cf. BECKMAN and BARTELS, "Credits and Collections in Theory and Practice"; also ETTINGER and GOLIEB, "Credits and Collections."

gling that may take place over the price. Terms, however, may not be mentioned, or, if brought up by the customer, he is given to understand by the salesman that an infringement of terms will not be regarded seriously by his house. If terms as well as price, quality of merchandise, and the service the selling house is able to give were thoroughly discussed and understood by buyer and salesman, much of the difficulty of collections would be removed. In other words, there would be an understanding of terms established, which does not now generally exist. Many houses take pride in saying that theirs is "a one-price house." That is, all customers pay the same price and receive the same terms. Strictly speaking, there are but few such one-price houses. Certainly the house which expects one customer to pay in 30 days and condones the 90-day payment of another can hardly be said to be treating all alike. Concessions in business are sometimes a necessity, but such concessions should be a matter of understanding in advance, and not arbitrarily taken by the purchaser. In a bank loan, for instance, payment dates are fixed at the outset.

A second common reason for delinquency is inadequate capital. Men and women, eager to engage in business for themselves, embark upon the enterprise with insufficient capital, or attempt to do a larger business than their capital warrants. In either case, there is too great a reliance upon creditor capital. Such accounts are frequently short of funds.

The credit investigation, provided it includes a financial statement, should disclose this type of delinquent. The creditor should know full well that the customer is not able to pay according to the terms under which he buys. Yet this fact is frequently ignored, and the collector becomes impatient with a condition which he should have recognized as inevitable when the risk was accepted.

A third reason for slow payments may be attributed to incompetence in management. The incompetence may not extend to purchasing or marketing but there will be found carelessness or incompetence in financing or financial control. The result is the simple neglect of obligations. The debtor should be impressed with the importance of efficient financing, and the cost that may be entailed and loss of credit standing which may follow indifferent or ill-considered financing.

A fourth reason for difficult collections, and one more difficult to deal with than incompetence or indifference, is willful neglect. This class buy with the intent of getting more than they bargain for. They realize that "time is money" and intend to obtain as much as possible. As soon as the debtor's motive is discovered, the creditor should take a firm stand and press hard for immediate payment. Even on future contracts, such a customer will withhold payment as long as he feels he can "get away with it." The obvious action for the creditor to take is, first of all, to have a clear understanding in regard to terms. If payments are delayed thereafter, future transactions based on credit should be denied.

A fifth reason, often encountered in cash-discount terms, is the inability to approve invoices and draw checks on time, because of the pressure of the buyer's office work or the inefficiency of his office and accounting systems. While this is a difficulty which should not prove insurmountable and, indeed, seems more an excuse for slow payments than a cause of them, it is seriously presented by many a debtor as an explanation of his tardiness or in his request for longer terms.

There are, as was intimated in the beginning of this section, many miscellaneous reasons for slow payments, prominent among which are illness, death, fires, floods, and other misfortunes. These often merit the creditor's consideration and sympathetic treatment. It is often good business as well as humanitarian to extend to such a helping hand through continuance of credit. Each case of this nature will naturally be treated according to its own merits.

The debtor's real reasons for slow payment may differ somewhat from his excuses. The debtor would hardly admit some of the reasons set forth in the preceding paragraphs. Instead the excuses most frequently offered are time honored and hackneyed. They set forth that collections have been poor, the weather has been unseasonable, business has not met expectations, or some misfortune has met the debtor in his business.

The good collector will not accept a frail excuse without question. Excuses are subject to verification. Collections may not really be bad, a fact which can be substantiated in several ways; the weather may not differ from what the average records have shown it to be for years; and business in the debtor's locality may be at least normal. The efficient collection manager will have the facts available before him. When a customer is found, however, who is worthy of assistance, aid, when cheerfully given, results in the customer being made to feel that he is dealing with a friendly and considerate house.

Types of Debtors. Any classification of debtors is, of course, an arbitrary one. While a division of debtors into a greater number of classes could be drawn, the author prefers to regard them as composed of only three distinct types.

In the first type will be found those who are classified as prompt pay. Customers in this class habitually discount their invoices, or pay at maturity. Caution must be used if the collector has any occasion to communicate with the customer, because customers of this class are frequently very sensitive where their credit reputation is questioned. To bring the account to the customer's attention is the only requirement for prompt action. Care should be taken therefore that the communication does not impute bad faith or any lack of ability to pay. The customer is so easily affronted that his good will is readily lost.

The second class is composed of those who are regarded as "good but slow." They may be careless about payments, or they may be willing but unable to pay because they are attempting too large a volume of business for their capital. Whatever the cause, they are delinquent but have no dishonest intentions. Sellers, in general, cannot refuse to deal with this class, and yet there is the necessity of obtaining payment as promptly as possible. These are less sensitive than those of the first class. In fact, they may have become somewhat hardened to the collection appeal. A more vigorous and insistent method, consequently, will have to be adopted in order to effect prompt collections with customers of this class.

The third group is composed of the undesirable risk. This class might be further subdivided into the dishonest and the unfortunate, because it is composed of those who could pay if they would, and those who would pay if they could. Creditors, it is clear, sell this class only by mistake. Either the customer is thought to belong among the good but slow when the credit is accepted, or some misfortune may have thrust the customer into this classification during the existence of the credit. In dealing with this class, it is desirable to discover as early as possible in the procedure whether the risk is really undesirable or uncertain, and then to determine whether the undesirability is caused by an unwillingness or an inability to pay. If the former, the creditor will proceed by the shortest method in his attempt to force payment. On the other hand, if convinced of the customer's inability to pay the collector will resort promptly to such remedial or protective measures as are best suited to the situation.

The Marketing Plan and the Collection Policy. The collection problem should be analyzed and the collection policy determined in accordance with the marketing plan of the house. The class of customers sold will affect collection procedure and the collection record. Some houses, because of their size and prestige, are able to attract the best risks, while other houses will have to find their market among customers of second grade, and still a third class will sell risks greater than the second would care to accept. While collections in house number two will be less prompt than in house number one, house number two will have to work a little harder even though the result is inferior. House number three likewise will work harder for results where risks are inferior to those obtained by house number two. Furthermore, the collection policy will be influenced considerably by competition. One house cannot adopt an unduly strict policy of prompt collections, unless it has something of a monopolistic field, especially if its competitors are lax in enforcing terms.   It will be found difficult for one house to overcome what may be a customary condition in the industry.   If, for example, terms of sale call for payment in 30 days and customers in that industry are in the habit of taking 45 or 60 days, one house can hardly enforce its terms without sacrificing some business.   As a matter of fact, the real terms in an industry are not those used in quotations to the trade, but rather those terms used in payments by the trade.   The terms under which a house sells are to be determined not by its quoted terms but rather by it collection turnover.[1]

Collection Competition.   Sales competition is a generally accepted and fully appreciated fact.   The sales department has as potential competitors every other concern selling a product that might fill its market.   The collection department, however, is not thus limited.   It is in competition for the debtor's funds with all the debtor's creditors.   The larger the number of creditors and the greater their aggregate claims in relation to the debtor's available funds, the keener the competition.

It would seem logical to adjust the terms to the customer's ability to pay.   If the analyses of financial condition and ledger experiences both indicate that the buyer requires 60-day terms, creditors cannot expect to enforce 30-day terms.   The present general policy, however, is for a house to adopt fixed terms and then to proceed to accept orders from those who cannot meet these terms as well as from those who can.   This policy is supported by two reasons.   It enables the seller to maintain his claim of one set of terms to all customers, and it enables creditors to prevent the debtor from unduly expanding his business at the creditor's risk.   For, if longer terms were granted, the debtor might soon become delinquent under them, renewing and making more serious the problem that the longer terms were designed to solve.

Necessity of a Systematic Collection System.   To follow up an account most effectively, the attention of the collector to it must be properly timed.   First of all he should know when the account is due and whether or not it is paid at that time.   Attention should be directed to the account and action taken at stated intervals thereafter until the account has been disposed of.   Multiply a single account by several hundreds or thousands and it will be seen at once that collections can be efficiently

---

[1] The collection turnover may be obtained by dividing the average receivables outstanding by the average daily sales, or, by dividing the annual sales by the average receivables to give the number of "turnovers" per year.   Each turnover represents the fractional part of a year that the receivables are outstanding.   Thus with annual sales of $360,000 and average receivables of $40,000 there are $\frac{360,000}{40,000}$ or nine turnovers or one-ninth of the year's business on the books at one time.   One-ninth of 360 equals 40 days.   Such a house is collecting on 40-day terms.

handled only when the work has been thoroughly systematized. There is involved a multiplicity of detail which can be taken care of only by systematic procedure.

An effective collection system will embody prompt action and follow-up at regular intervals, but with sufficient flexibility to meet different conditions as they arise. The aid derived from force of habit is lost to the creditor unless the debtor receives his statements and letters promptly and regularly. The system will require flexibility and will need intelligent direction since, obviously, there are many different reasons and degrees of delinquency. The collection department needs to take particular care that the monotony of its procedure does not in some measure destroy the collection efficiency. It should avoid such a rut. Using the same automatic collection system time and time again on a customer who is habitually slow in payment is a waste of energy and money. The early use of the final collection effort may be warranted for a customer who is calloused to collection efforts.

A good collection system will permit the assistants in the collection department to do much of the routine work without consulting the collection manager. System in the collection department will include some method of following up accounts, sending collection notices, and typing letters covering the early stages of collection. Results will thus be obtained more or less automatically, leaving the collection manager free to direct the action to be taken upon the more difficult cases. No system, it should be emphasized, exists independent of personnel, and no system will run itself. A good system, kept working, will go further than any other one thing to ensure prompt collections. Add to the good system a good personnel and the result is maximum collection efficiency.

Follow-up Systems. It is not possible to outline a system that will fit all businesses. Office procedure is not standardized to that extent. Each business will need to study its own requirements and adapt a system to its needs. It is not always the most elaborate system which is the most efficient. A system that works, that meets the needs of the business at the lowest cost, should be the aim of every office. The nature and number of the accounts, the accounting system, the layout of the offices, the business done, are all factors to be taken into consideration in devising a collection follow-up system.

Having adopted a system for following up collections, there is the necessity of a sufficient and capable personnel to run it. Employing higher priced help may be an economy, or adding an assistant may be more profitable to the house than dropping one.

Whatever the system that may be adopted, it must ensure attention to every overdue account. The oversight or failure to follow up a dangerous risk is unpardonable in the collection department.

The Customers' Ledger. Every follow-up must originate with the account itself; hence the basis of any system is the accounts receivable or customers' ledger. How best to discover those accounts which are daily becoming overdue is the first problem of the credit manager who has to lay out the system to accomplish the desired results. If the accounts are comparatively few in number and the necessity for daily action upon them is not present, it may be found that the simplest and most effective method is for the credit manager to inspect the ledger at regular intervals in order to learn the exact status of each account. As a result of this inspection whatever action is deemed advisable is taken upon the delinquent accounts, and notations made upon the margin of the account of the date and the action taken. The account then rests so far as collection procedure is concerned until the next regular inspection is made. Under this plan, action may be taken upon all delinquent accounts, and, at the same time, the credit manager keeps conversant with the paying habits of all the customers. This method has another distinct advantage in that because of its simplicity there is no duplication of work or records.

Except in the smaller businesses, however, credit men generally feel that the disadvantages outweigh the advantages. Too much of the credit manager's time may be taken in looking through many good accounts for the purpose of discovering a few slow ones. There is, too, the tendency to shirk this part of the credit man's work with the result that collection is conducted at irregular intervals and in a haphazard manner. Still another objection is that not all accounts need following up with the same regularity because of location at different distances, and because of the greater leniency with which some accounts are to be treated. Moreover, some friction may develop between the collection and bookkeeping departments over the use of the ledgers. When the accounts are many in number, only the most rigid adherence to the collection routine could prevent the confusion of the system.

The Collection Tickler. Because of the necessity of relieving the collection department of some of the detail of the follow-up many houses charge the accounting department with the duty of informing the credit department of all accounts which are not paid at maturity. To accomplish this, the ledger clerks look through their respective ledgers at regular intervals, making statements of overdue accounts. For example, a certain house may require that statements be drawn off on the first, the tenth, and the twentieth of each month. Only those accounts are included which have matured since the last previous statement date, since the credit department already had a record of all older bills. A card tickler is used to record the action taken upon these accounts, and to bring them up for attention at the desired intervals.

The collection tickler is nothing more than a card file consisting of individual cards upon which are recorded the name and address of the delinquent together with other pertinent facts including the action taken upon the account. The file consists of 31 divisions, one for each day of the month. The cards bearing the customer's records are filed under the respective date that it is desired to follow them up. Thus the cards filed under a given date present the work for the collection department for that date. When all have had attention, the cards are moved forward to the various dates under which it may be desirable again to take action upon them.

Remittances under this plan are either credited to the individual cards or each morning before the collection procedure is started the cards are checked against the customers' ledger accounts and payments noted.

Under this plan nothing is left to chance. Provided no overdue accounts are overlooked by the ledger clerks and no cards are lost or misfiled, all accounts turn up automatically on the collection desk at the desired time, and overdue accounts are handled systematically and at fixed intervals.

Maturity Lists. A variation of the method described above for bringing delinquent accounts to the credit department's attention is known as the "maturity list." Under this plan the ledger clerks at stated intervals list under their maturity dates the accounts which will mature between the present and the next listing date. Remittances as they are received are checked against the record and daily lists of delinquencies referred to the credit department. While this plan entails more work than the modified ledger plan described in connection with the card tickler, it provides a more prompt notification of all delinquencies to the credit department. Which of the two plans described the collection department will prefer will depend upon how promptly it is desired to start the collection routine after invoices mature.

The Duplicate Invoice System. This method combines some of the features of the card tickler and the maturity list. It is like the former except the invoice is substituted for the card, and like the latter in that it provides a file record of all accounts becoming due from day to day. Where invoicing is done on billing machines it is possible to make an extra carbon copy of invoices to be used as a collection copy with but little additional work. These invoices are placed according to maturities in a vertical file, bill size, equipped with cardboard division cards or folders numbered from 1 to 31. There are two common methods of using such a file: the invoices are withdrawn as remittances are received, or each day, which is a maturity date for a certain number of invoices, the invoices for that day are checked against the ledger accounts and those unpaid referred to the credit department. Often a few days of grace are given before the collection campaign is started. The collection action may be recorded upon the invoices as in the case of the card tickler, or the invoice may form the base of the follow-up letter file which will be presently described.

When customers are making frequent purchases, this plan requires the intelligent cooperation of the ledger department. It would be unwise, for instance, to take practically the same action on two or three consecutive days, although different invoices might mature on those dates. The ledger clerk will inform the credit department of other maturing invoices by noting the amounts and maturity dates of such invoices upon the one in hand. Action might then be deferred, at the discretion of the collection manager, until the other invoices had matured so that all could be grouped under one collection effort.

Before installing any system for discovering and following up delinquent accounts, the credit or collection manager should consider the systems and equipment offered by the office-equipment supply houses. The many excellent filing and follow-up systems for faster availability of records cannot be adequately described in this treatise.

Many larger firms have adopted punched-card systems for their accounts receivable. When such a system is used, it is quite simple to have an aging schedule run off for the close following of delinquent accounts. The usual practice when terms are E.O.M. is to run the schedules off monthly, say after the twelfth. However, an alert credit manager will have a good working arrangement with his bookkeepers, who will inform him of any important delinquencies as they occur.

A Collection Letter Follow-up. A variation of the card tickler or the invoice tickler is provided by a number of plans for following up collection correspondence. A method which has been found practical in many offices may be described as follows. The base of the file on any given name may be the invoice copy, the statement copy, or the carbon copy of the first collection letter. If form letters which require merely the filling in of the name and the address of the customer are used, a carbon copy may be inserted, thus providing a tickler sheet. Whatever the base of the file the person directing the collection procedure indicates the next follow-up date by jotting down that date on the file copy. The correspondence to be filed is then segregated by the file clerk according to follow-up dates. A series of sheets are headed with the working days of the month and the names of the accounts with the follow-up dates corresponding with the heading of the sheet are listed upon these sheets. The correspondence is then filed alphabetically either in the general correspondence file or in a special collection file retained in the collection department. The sheet for each day of the month provides the collection department as the date arrives with a list of the accounts to be followed up on that day. The correspondence is drawn, the accounts investigated, the necessary action taken, new follow-up dates assigned, and the filing procedure repeated.

This system is sometimes reversed by listing the names of the accounts alphabetically with the follow-up date following the name. The correspondence is then filed under the follow-up date in a file with numerical divisions of 1 to 31. The advantage of this method lies in the fact that all the correspondence to be acted upon is in one division and has only to be lifted out in order to work upon it. If necessary to refer to much of the correspondence prior to the follow-up date, it is a more cumbersome method than the former method because it is necessary to refer first to the control sheet to ascertain under which date a given name may be filed. This is a disadvantage. Again it may be said that the conditions within an office will dictate the system which should be adopted.

TEXT AND RESEARCH QUESTIONS

1. Why do some collection departments have a much more difficult task than others?

2. Why is the credit manager most logically also the collection manager?

3. What fourth objective of the collection department might be added to the three listed in the text?

4. What arguments can be advanced to justify an easy or slow collection policy?

5. Why are debtors "slow pay"?

6. What should be the attitude of the creditor toward the debtor willfully delaying or attempting to avoid payment?

7. How does the collection policy of competitors affect a concern's collection problem?

8. If it is recognized that a customer cannot and hence will not meet the creditor's regular terms, what are the reasons for not granting him special terms conforming to his ability to pay?

9. Why should the "mechanics" of collection be fully developed?

10. What factors should be considered in the selection of a follow-up system for collections?

11. Why should collection routine be strictly followed?

12. Devise a method for following up collection correspondence not described in the text.

PROBLEMS

1. You are credit manager of a manufacturer of ladies' silk hosiery. You have before you three delinquent accounts as outlined below. What kind of treatment would you give to each debtor?

> *a.* G has a small store with several departments which he has conducted in the retail section of Buffalo for several years. Payments have always been a little slow. About a year ago a large department store

opened on the corner of G's block. Since that time G's payments have become still slower, and your salesman reports that G has been cutting prices in a vain attempt to meet his new competition. He owes your concern $400 which is 50 days past due and which he has twice promised to remit on a definite date, promises that have not been kept. You fear that he is headed for bankruptcy.

b. H runs a general merchandise store in a small New Hampshire village. His only help is that occasionally given him by his wife. Your salesman reports that he stands well in his community but that he seems to regard the payment of his bills as the least essential of his duties. He does not answer letters. An interchange report indicates that he has no fixed plan of payments; creditors reporting payments say that they range from fairly prompt to very slow.

c. K is the proprietor of a medium-size wearing-apparel store. He has prospered and enjoys a reputation for promptness among his creditors. He usually discounts your bills. He now owes $50 which is about 15 days overdue.

2. Your treasurer has asked you, the credit manager, to submit a report each month which will show the relation of the delinquent accounts to the total receivables. He says that he would like to have a breakdown of the delinquent accounts showing not only dollar amounts but also percentages. He asks also for the average collection period in days. Devise the form for this report.

3. Outline in detail a good collection procedure. Include in your analysis a method of locating past-due accounts, the length of time for the collection effort, and the steps taken within the time limit.

CHAPTER 25

COLLECTION TOOLS

The Invoice. Collection procedure begins with the mailing of the invoice at the time goods are shipped to the customer. The invoice informs the purchaser of the exact amount of the indebtedness and the day it becomes due. To a considerable percentage of customers no other collection instrument is sent because of the large number of accounts which are habitually discounted or paid at maturity. The purchaser generally does not recognize the invoice as a dun, nor does he realize that he is receiving a collection instrument.

The Statement. Usually, the next step in the collection effort consists of mailing a statement of account to the customer. The statement serves two purposes. In the first place, it aids in keeping the records of the seller and the buyer reconciled, and in the second, it acts as a reminder to the buyer of payment dates.

Considerable variation in procedure exists among different houses in the practice of sending statements. One of three plans is usually followed. Under one plan statements are sent to all customers once each month, usually on the first, whether or not there may be any items upon the account which are due. These statements serve as reminders of the maturity dates whether those dates are past or future. A different plan adopted by many concerns calls for statements to be mailed on the first of the month only to those accounts which are already delinquent. Under this plan, the statement serves primarily as a reminder of debts due for payment. A third plan contemplates mailing monthly statements only to those accounts which request that a monthly statement be regularly sent to them. Under this plan, statements are not regularly and systematically sent out except as requested but are rather used at the discretion of the collection department in the collection effort.

To spread the work of the statement group, many businesses, and retail stores in particular, have adopted the cycle billing system: one third of the accounts are billed the tenth of the month, another third the twentieth, and the last group the thirtieth. A cycle system may be used in any of the above plans.

The statement is headed with the name of the creditor sending it out, is addressed to the debtor, and below appears an itemized list of the charges and credits and their dates. As an inducement to act promptly, the terms of payment should be printed prominently on the statement, or if goods are purchased under different terms, such special terms should be stated for each item. This is a strong reminder that the account must be paid according to its terms.

If it is the practice in trade houses to use the statement as a payment reminder, it should be mailed on the first day of each month in order to secure the best results. There are reasons for this procedure which make it important. Not only is there much educative value in the element of promptness in itself, but there is an added reason. Many houses have adopted a certain day of each month when all bills, or as many as can be, are paid. The creditor who fails to have his statement among those considered for payment may have not only to wait for some time but in addition may have to put in further collection effort. Since the task of making out statements usually devolves upon the accounting department, it is often looked upon by that department as outside work, with the result that there may be the tendency to postpone statements until all the regular work is done. While it is, of course, impossible to render statements of accounts when the posting to the customers' ledger is not up to date, the credit man must not allow the collection routine to fall into confusion through the failure of the accounting department to co-ordinate its work with that of the collection department. The importance of collections commands a rigid attention to detail. It is the duty of the credit manager to sell the management on this idea if necessary.

In the use of statements it is quite a common practice to add a collection appeal by means of a rubber stamp. The collection man addicted to the use of rubber stamps usually has at hand a variety such as "Past due," "Please favor," "Please remit," "Kindly send us your check," etc., from which his dunning selection is made. Another plan is to have such reminders printed and gummed, attaching them to outgoing statements. Such stamps or stickers rarely give any offense, unless they are injudiciously used, since it is realized that they are stereotyped and impersonal. For the same reason, they are frequently ineffective. They may, however, be of some little benefit as they indicate the creditor's dissatisfaction with the status of the account, and are, therefore, better than no appeal at all.

Some houses have adopted the practice of mailing a statement just a few days before the account becomes due. When this is done, the usual practice is to stamp the statement "This statement is for comparison only," or "This account is not yet due," or words to that effect. It is hoped that such an advanced reminder will result in payment at the proper time. The reader, no doubt, can see that there might be objections to this practice. Comparatively few accounts fail to pay when due because the maturity date is overlooked. Those accounts which have sufficient funds with which to pay are not aided by the statement. Finally, some customers will be irritated by receiving a statement, which, after all, can hardly be regarded as anything but a premature dun.

The Collection Letter. When the invoice and the statement have failed to bring payment when due, the most widely used method of collection is the letter. The very ease of sending a customer a letter adds to the great number of collection letters, even when some other collection tool might be more effectively used. Letters do form such an important part of the collector's equipment, however, that a more complete treatment of them is reserved for a subsequent chapter.

The Note as a Collection Instrument. The promissory note was formerly a credit instrument in good standing with both buyer and seller. With many credit men it has now largely degenerated into a collection instrument, and as such it is regarded merely as a makeshift. Its use marks merely a step in collection procedure. In some cases the credit man strives to obtain a note, but in almost as many instances it is urged upon him by the debtor. The note has its advantages and disadvantages. If the account is disputed by the debtor, the credit man will be happy to accept a note. While this is, in reality, a compromise, the creditor is willing to forgo the immediate cash if he can thereby avoid litigation over the amount involved. This the note accomplishes. If a suit is necessary, judgment upon a note is almost certain. A compromise settlement is also accepted when the creditor foregoes his right to immediate cash in return for the debtor's formal promise to pay. The creditor feels that payment, though postponed, is much more certain when the debtor is confronted with his own promise to pay, and that no further effort need be expended by the creditor.

Another advantage *may* exist in the fact that the note can be discounted, thus giving the creditor immediate use of the funds. When the note is discounted, it is felt that there is a psychological effect upon the debtor in having the bank as owner present the demand for payment. Thus the bank is brought into the transaction as a collection agent. The psychological effect, however, may not be sufficient to compel the debtor to meet his note when due.

The collector recognizes certain disadvantages in accepting a note from his debtor. In the first place, the collector may have doubts as to whether the note will be paid when due. It is quite common for a debtor to offer a note in order to gain relief from the pressure of an aggressive collector. Having given the note and thus gained temporary relief, he provides no funds to meet it at maturity. The creditor then is under the necessity of accepting a renewal or renewing his collection effort. When the creditor accepts a note, he has extended the period of credit by the duration of the note. No action can be taken against the debtor even though in the meantime a suit or other action should become highly desirable.

Many credit men feel that the acceptance of notes establishes a bad precedent. The debtor, having induced his creditor to accept a note in one instance, is quite inclined to expect that other purchases may be settled in the same way. If the passing of notes becomes the regular practice between debtor and creditor, it means that the customer is buying regularly upon much extended terms.

The credit manager may regard it as advisable to refuse a note when one is offered by the debtor even though he may be willing to extend the time of payment. By refusing the note tactfully and at the same time not binding himself to an extension he is left free to take any action necessary in an emergency. This indication of confidence furthermore makes an appeal to the debtor's pride, which will have a tendency to spur his efforts to pay and which will promote a feeling of good will toward the creditor.

The alert collector will consider the comparative possibilities of obtaining or the advisability of accepting a judgment note, an instalment note, or a plain note or one with the indorsement or guarantee of a responsible party.

Collecting by Draft. Many credit men find the draft to be, like the note, merely a collection instrument. As such the use of the draft differs greatly among different houses. Probably the majority of credit men regard the draft as one of the harsher collection tools and, therefore, delay its use until it is desired to make a final threat. The collection draft, which is almost invariably a sight draft, is logically reserved as one of the final resorts of the creditor because it discloses the relationship between debtor and creditor to a third party, the bank.

The strength of the draft as a collection instrument lies in the imputation that the customer's credit is impugned, and it brings the bank into play as a collection agency. Drafts are less used now than formerly in collection procedure. This may be due in part to the fact that banks are less inclined to handle drafts as a free service and in part to the ineffectiveness of the draft as a collection instrument. When the drawing of drafts was an accepted practice between buyer and seller, the dishonor of a draft was something of a stigma upon the debtor's credit. Under present business practice, drafts are ignored by many businessmen with but little, if any, misgiving as to its effect upon their credit. The majority of creditors who use the draft as a collection instrument draw on the debtor through his own bank though there are some creditors who utilize the services of their banks in the belief that the draft will be given better attention by the collecting agency.

Drafts that are not paid are customarily returned by the bank with a brief notation giving the reason for the debtor's failure to pay. Such notations read "pays no attention," "has sent check," "will send check," "has written," "amount disputed," etc. These notations often give the creditor an insight into the debtor's intentions as to paying the debt, and effectively indicate the next step that should be taken in the collection procedure.

The Use of the Telephone. It would hardly seem necessary to suggest the use of the telephone in collection work because the use of that instrument has become so common that it would be most natural for the creditor to turn to it. Nevertheless, some credit men are so accustomed to make the collection appeal by letter that they are inclined to use such a medium even when the telephone is right at their elbow and their customer in the same town. The telephone, however, is rarely the first medium used even by those who think highly of it. Usually it follows the statement, and sometimes a letter. Whether it would be advisable to dun a customer by telephone before sending him some other reminder will depend somewhat upon custom and usage in the trade, and the particular conditions surrounding the customer at the time.

The telephone has certain distinct advantages as a collection instrument. It saves time. The collector gets his message to the debtor as soon as the connection can be established. It is more definite and certain than the letter because the message brings an answer. A letter can be ignored but the debtor can hardly refuse to promise a check or give his reasons for not doing so. It generally is less expensive than the letter. While it is true that most dictators can dictate more letters than they can make telephone calls in a given period, it should be realized that, when the additional time consumed in typing, signing, enclosing, and mailing the letters is included, the advantage is distinctly in favor of the telephone. The telephone permits a variation of the appeal which is impossible in a letter. The conversation can be made to fit the debtor's state of mind. Less care is necessary in what is said because it is not a matter of written record. Threats can more freely be made, if it is felt necessary to employ such an appeal. It has been found difficult successfully to prosecute one for statements made by telephone, principally because of the difficulty in proving exactly what was said, and who said it. The reader should not gather from the above remarks that the telephone should be made a harsh tool in collections. On the contrary, one of its distinct advantages is the fact that it can be insistently used without offending the debtor. The effective use of the telephone, however, requires superb tact. A blunt approach is never effective. The collector can be insistent and persistent while friendly and with a smile in his voice. It is only slightly less advantageous than a personal interview with the debtor.

The chief disadvantage of the telephone lies in the fact that although the debtor may be in a frame of mind to pay, it is impossible to close the matter then and there. The creditor must rely upon the debtor's sending the check as promised, something which he does not always do. A second disadvantage is the difficulty occasionally experienced of getting into communication with your debtor. If he knows whence the call comes he may have the operator or clerk return the answer "Mr. Debtor is not in at present." A message asking Mr. Debtor to call will bring no result. If it is thought that the debtor is using a ruse to gain time, the creditor can also use a ruse to thwart the debtor's scheme. Let the credit man or some one in his department, telephone giving his personal name. Of course if the debtor refuses to answer any telephone calls, it is high time to proceed with a stronger weapon than the telephone.

The Telephone in Long-distance Collections. The telephone is an agency too infrequently used in making collections from out-of-town customers. This does not mean that the collection manager is unaware of the results that might be achieved by the use of the telephone, but, on the other hand, he does not feel free to incur the expense without the approval of some higher authority, or, if he has that authority, he seeks to avoid the criticism that he might receive for having incurred the expense. The result perhaps is the continual use of letters and a much longer extended debt. The long-distance telephone must be used with discretion. Its use is particularly suggested when letters seem to be nonproductive of results. Before the account is turned over to an attorney or collection agency, or even before good will has been jeopardized by a threat, the long-distance call often can be used to advantage. The creditor at least can learn where he stands with the debtor, and the personal contact may have a psychological influence on the debtor's subsequent behavior in bill paying. If collection is thus accomplished, it is done with much less expense than if given to an attorney.

The Telegram. In the employment of the telegraph for collection more caution is necessary than with the telephone or letter. This is because of the semiprivate nature of the telegram. It may be open to the gaze of many persons before it reaches the recipient who can protect its contents from further inspection. The danger lies in the fact that something may be included in the telegram which may be construed as libelous. Therefore, the creditor should take care to avoid threats of bankruptcy, bad faith on the part of the debtor, criminal prosecution, etc.

The creditor may refer to the account as overdue and say that it will be referred to an attorney, or even threaten a (civil) suit without fear of the consequences. The telegraph companies have from time to time issued suggested wording for collection appeals which they regard as appropriate.

The telegram is regarded as one of the more effective mediums to use. Its power comes largely from the fact that the very use of it suggests the urgency of payment. It also has the advantage of getting the debtor's attention. The same message sent by any other means might not be nearly as effective. It is most often used to prod the debtor into action after a strong letter has been sent. Effectiveness is added by properly timing a telegram, and it can be so worded that its message is not open to any passer-by who may read. For example, "Desire immediate answer our letter twenty-fifth," carries a message to the recipient which anyone else could only surmise. A much more drastic telegram is "Have you remitted? Wire. Otherwise attorney gets account tomorrow." This is about as strong a telegram as can be sent, and it is of course sent only as a last resort. It bears a threat which the creditor will carry out if the telegram is unheeded, for nothing is to be gained by further delay after sending such a message.

The Personal Collector. The personal collector has a place in collection procedure which is hardly filled by any other medium. The personal contact with the debtor allows the give-and-take of conversation that is impossible with letters. It obviates the difficulty of the telephone for the personal collector may bring away with him the check of his customer. While the personal call is often effective, it is usually an expensive method. Its effectiveness often depends upon the personality of the collector, while the costliness depends upon a combination of circumstances such as the territory to be covered, the size of the accounts, the difficulty of the collection, etc.

Personal collectors should be segregated into three general classes for discussion because of the considerable distinction in their types and the use that each is generally put to. First, there is the credit manager or his assistant acting as a personal collector. Under such circumstances it is assumed that he knows all the methods of approach and recognizes his responsibility to collect. He has all the advantages which personal contact gives. With this motive, this ability, and this opportunity to collect, it may be assumed that if the personal call is not productive of results that collection can only be effected by force. A second class of collector is the man who is employed for no other purpose. He is given a certain number of accounts, usually the most difficult, in a certain territory, and he proceeds to call upon them exacting promises or checks, gradually applying more pressure for the purpose, until full collection is made or some other action taken with the account. The personal collector is particularly useful in instalment collections. The telephone has been found cheaper, and often more efficient because the credit manager in telephoning can control the conversation, the pressure applied, and the plan of campaign. To collect in person is a somewhat expensive method since the collector can cover only a certain number of accounts. If his pay is small, the results accomplished will also be small, while if he has the ability to command a good salary or wage, his opportunity as a collector will hardly permit him to earn it. If he is paid upon a commission basis, or even if on a straight salary, he is inclined to work up a clientele for himself by intimating to the debtor that the collector will call monthly for remittances. There is another objection to the use of personal collectors. Customers resent his calls partly because he often lacks the tact to promote good will or solely because he is a collector.

The Salesman. The third type of personal collector is the salesman. The extent to which he should be used, or whether or not he should be used at all, are questions over which credit men have deeply pondered. The salesman, concededly, has not given entire satisfaction as a collector. The decision to use or not to use him as such is generally based upon the particular conditions which obtain within the business, or even within the salesman's own territory. Some salesmen sell a class of customers who are never slow pay. Here there is no problem. Other salesmen sell accounts which are somewhat slow but frequently in such cases the salesman meets only the buyer, who knows nothing about the accounting and financial side of the business. Likewise, the salesman would be a total stranger to the financial department of his customer. Too much of the salesman's time might be consumed in getting an interview with the right person, and then additional time is consumed by clerks in looking up invoices and circumstances to see why payment had not been made or when it would be made. A letter from the collector might save valuable time for both houses and might be just as effective. In reality, a salesman has but a few hours each day which he can devote to calling upon his trade, and he, therefore, wants to devote those few hours to selling, which is likewise desired by his house. The salesman may, however, be used upon occasion as an adjuster. He is in an excellent position to act as such if qualified by training and ability to do so.

The credit man should not hesitate to ask the salesman's aid wherever the give-and-take of conversation is needed to smooth out any misunderstanding. There are many cases where it is almost imperative that the salesman should act as collector. For example, many houses selling to the retail grocery trade place the responsibility of all collections directly upon the sales force. The salesman calls upon the customer once a week. The goods bought one week are paid for the next. If payment is not made, credit is cut off. The plan works well because the buyer is educated to adhere strictly to it. As a matter of fact, wherever the salesman is selling to a small business, or one-man organization, where the man who places the order is the same man who pays the check, the salesman can be made to share effectively the responsibility of making the collections.

There are some disadvantages to making the salesman serve as a collector. It is a distasteful duty to many salesmen and is indifferently performed. Unless the salesman can be made to give conscientious cooperation to the collection department, he may do more harm than good. Sometimes the salesman feels that his chances of selling a customer are lessened if he also plays the role of collector. He feels that he will be less welcome and his customer will constantly have in the back of his mind the debt which he owes. He will be very conservative in buying more goods under those conditions. Whenever both salesman and office are working upon an account, it is very essential that each keep the other informed. The salesman should receive carbon copies of all letters sent, and he should report promptly to the house the result of each interview.

The claim is sometimes made that the habit of paying when the salesman calls slows up collections. The customer, instead of remitting when the bill is due, knows that the salesman follows up payments and therefore he withholds his check until the salesman makes his next call. This is something hard to avoid entirely. Even though the salesman may urge the customer to mail his check and not to hold it, such a habit with some customers is difficult to break.

Some houses employing a large number of salesmen, among whom the turnover is considerable, do not authorize their salesmen either to solicit or to accept remittance. Every credit manager should consider carefully the placing of this responsibility upon a salesman. For protection some houses bond all their salesmen who may collect. To aid the salesman in collection work, he should be given a letter, bearing the corporation seal, authorizing him to accept payment in behalf of his house.

The Collection Agency. After the collection manager has exhausted his own efforts to collect, but before he has abandoned the account as uncollectible, he will probably refer it to a collection agency or attorney. These two mediums follow approximately the same procedure. The difference lies in name rather than in function or method.

The collection agency has no means of collection which are not available to the credit man, nor has it discovered any secret methods of greater effectiveness. Nevertheless, the collection agency is often successful after the creditor has failed.   The advantage is largely psycho-logical.   Debtors know that credit men themselves rarely force collec-tions.   As long as the account remains under the creditor's control, therefore, the debtor has nothing to fear.   The situation is immediately changed, however, when control passes into the hands of a third party. It is known that the collection agency has but one interest in the account, and that is, to get the money and thus earn the commission.   As a general thing, the referring of an account to a collection agency or at-torney is the creditor's ultimatum.   All friendly relations are terminated. It is the relentlessness of the agency which brings results.   Sometimes even the threat of placing the account with an agency is effective.   The average debtor knows the stigma attaching to his credit when his record shows "Collected by attorney"; hence he will make an extreme effort to keep his record clear.   A powerful influence may thus be exerted by large collection agencies which report to their clientele all delinquencies coming under their survey.

The creditor should select the agency to be used with considerable care.   Not all may be found to be morally and financially responsible. Many credit men do not stop to think that they are virtually extending credit to an agency when an account is turned over to it for collection.[1] The laws relating to agency practice do not afford entire protection to creditors.   The agency often receives a free hand, and the creditor, doubting somewhat that the account can be collected, fails to check up all accounts carefully.   The agency temporarily hard pressed for funds and having such an excellent opportunity is tempted to use the creditors' money.   For his own protection, the creditor should make the same careful investigation which he would make of a customer, in addition to considering the efficiency of its collection methods.   It would be well, too, to be sure that the private funds of the agency and moneys collected are carried in separate bank accounts.   It would also be advisable to insist that the agency be covered with a good-size bond for the protection of its patrons.

The reader should not gather the impression that all agencies should be regarded with suspicion.   There are reliable agencies in every section. Some of the larger mercantile agencies also conduct collection bureaus, and collection agencies have been formed by trade associations to serve their own members.   Credit insurance companies also render collection

---

[1] The courts do not seem to be in agreement as to whether the relationship between creditor and collection agency becomes that of creditor and debtor as soon as the agency has collected any money, or whether the relationship remains that of principal and agent.   The distinction is of importance, if action against the agency is contemplated for any breach of relationship on the part of the agency.

service. There is merely a question of selection involved with which the credit manager should be familiar.

The Local Attorney. The local attorney, while he acts as a collection agent, is sufficiently different from the collection agency operating solely as such as to merit brief mention. Often he forms a part of the collection agency's machinery for collection. The usual procedure is for the agency to make an attempt to collect by mailing letters and threats from its home office. If these are unavailing, the account is forwarded to a local attorney who continues the pressure by letter, by telephone, or in person. He has an influence not possessed either by creditor or collection agency because of his proximity to the debtor and because he is in a position to start suit at any time. Thus the debtor senses more keenly the harm which may be done to his credit reputation. The debtor realizes that his position is becoming more serious and a "showdown" nearer. When the account is forwarded to the attorney by a collection agency, often referred to as the forwarding attorney, the creditor has no direct contact with the local attorney. The local attorney, on the other hand, may be used to collect under the direct supervision of the creditor. This is usually done through the use of law lists, a number of which are published and are available to credit departments.

Credit men claim advantages in both methods. By giving all claims to an attorney or collection agency the creditor is dealing with only one party and can hold that party responsible. The forwarding attorney, because of the large number of claims which he handles, can select the most efficient representatives and through the amount of business which he may give them has a better control over the collecting attorney than the creditor could have. One of the complaints frequently heard from credit men is that it is sometimes extremely difficult to get any report from some local attorneys, and the statement is made, probably somewhat exaggerated, that it is about as difficult to get the money from them as from the debtor himself. On the other hand, many credit men prefer to deal direct with the local attorney because they have direct supervision and responsibility for his actions. Then, too, it is felt that the attorney will work harder for collection because he receives the full fee. When a claim is received from a forwarding attorney, the fee is split, one-third going to the forwarder and two-thirds to the local attorney who does the work.[1] The Commercial Law League has adopted uniform rates for the handling of commercial claims and collections. These fees are not

[1] In New York attorneys may not split fees except with other attorneys. A collection agency may, however, employ an attorney when authorized to do so by a client.

obligatory. They may be more or less by arrangement. Members of the bar of certain cities have adopted their own collection rates.

TEXT AND RESEARCH QUESTIONS

1. Why should monthly statements, if used at all, be mailed promptly at the first of the month?

2. Give two objections to mailing statements a few days before an account becomes due.

3. List the arguments against the acceptance of notes on overdue accounts.

4. Through what bank do you believe a draft should be presented to a debtor, and why?

5. List the advantages and the disadvantages of the telephone as a collection aid.

6. What is to be avoided in the use of the telegram in collection work?

7. What are the disadvantages in the use of the personal collector?

8. When should and when should not the salesman be used as a collector?

9. Why is the collection agency more effective than the creditor himself in collection of accounts?

10. What points should be considered in the selection of a collection agency or attorney?

11. What would be the advantage of registering a collection letter?

CHAPTER 26

COLLECTION LETTERS

Why the Collection Letter Is Used. The art of collecting money by mail has developed largely as a result of the widening of business activity. Business has long since ceased to be local. Transportation and communication have permitted the manufacturer and merchant to reach farther and farther for patronage, and advertising—both of goods and credit—has brought distant buyers and seller into a business relationship. Thus many of the conditions that brought about the increased use of credit also made necessary the increased use of correspondence and collection letters. The collection letter is commonly used where it is necessary to round out or complete each business transaction. It is used because the letter and the mail are among the most logical, the most convenient, and the most economical mediums for conveying a message from seller to buyer. Moreover, the letter was the first of several modern means of communication which could be used. The letter thus became a custom or habit which is still firmly intrenched despite the more logical use (in some instances) of the telegram or telephone.

There is another reason for the usefulness of the collection letter. The letter itself is not offensive. Debtors whose accounts are due are accustomed to receive, or at least educated to expect to receive, collection letters. Of course the collection letter badly written may be very offensive, but it is the message and not the fact that a letter is written at which the recipient takes umbrage. The letter may thus be the most desirable medium to use with nearby customers in certain instances, as well as with the more distant ones. Moreover, the letter is a medium which puts the collector in touch with customers all over the world. The collection letter is, without doubt, the most used tool in collection work, and it must therefore be assumed that if it is properly used it is, on the whole, the most economical and satisfactory method of collecting accounts. If it is not properly used, it results in a needless expense.

The Fate of the Collection Letter. Every writer of collection letters wants his letters carefully read and their messages carefully considered.

The good collector will do what he can to ensure such a consideration for his letters by striving to put enough character into the letter so that it will command attention. Not every collection correspondent expects this at all times to be accomplished. Those who have had some experience in collection work know that many a collection letter is doomed to a different fate. The letter may be hastily read and thrown aside for later attention which it never receives. Instead, it is forgotten and time slips by until another collection appeal is received, which in turn may receive the same or a worse fate. Or, in a larger organization the letter may be routed to an employee in the accounting or accounts payable department who for one reason or another side-tracks the letter until more urgent appeals compel attention. This is a rather common result when the account may be in dispute, or in a confused state through lost goods, missing invoices, claims, improper deductions, etc. The partial remedy for this condition is for the seller to insist upon the prompt adjustment of any differences. It is advisable to follow up any such differences persistently. The longer they are permitted to run, the more difficult the adjustment and the greater the confusion of the records.

More serious is the case where the collection letter is not even read. The debtor receives the letter, notes whence it came, correctly infers that it is a collection letter, throws it upon his desk unopened perhaps intending to give it attention when he has greater leisure; or, worse still, it is thrown unopened into the waste basket. Such an action is, of course, an affront to the creditor but he is ignorant of the action. However, the effect of the letter may not be entirely lost even though it is not read. The debtor knows that he is being dunned, and his mind moves, perhaps subconsciously, a little nearer toward payment.

Collection managers long ago tried a "stunt," which advertisers have since copied, to ensure that their messages should be read. This consists in forwarding the letter in a plain envelope. It is thought that the recipient cannot anticipate its contents and that his curiosity will prompt him to examine the letter for its message. The method is sometimes effective where the failure to collect has been due to the failure to get the message across.

Most of the difficulties in getting the message across are traceable to lack of diligence on the part of the correspondent and to the awareness on the part of the recipient that the collection process goes through several steps before he finally must pay. If the creditor is in a position to do so, the author recommends omitting intervening steps in the collection process in those cases where the debtor is regularly indifferent to the preliminary appeals. Thus the collection effort will be easier in the long run. Most firms do what they know they must do if they are able.

The Writer's Mental Attitude. The failure of debtors to respond in so many instances to the collection correspondent's letters tends to discourage and irritate him. Loss of temper or failure completely to master his emotions will creep into his letters and affect their quality. Of all the virtues patience is one of the most important for the collection writer. Impatience results in a tendency to become unduly harsh or sarcastic, or even a "whiney" attitude may be reflected in the letters written. Firmness and confidence—the one begets the other—are two qualities which the successful collection manager will possess. He is constantly applying pressure in different degrees to all delinquent accounts, and he knows that the pressure will be effective. Like the wrestler, sure of his mastery over an opponent, if one hold does not produce a fall, he calmly goes about getting another, constantly boring in, and relentlessly applying pressure until victory is his. With the collector, it is the mental instead of the physical resistance which must be broken down. It cannot be done if the collector "loses his head" or permits himself to get off an even keel. His brain and not his emotion must dominate his actions. Sarcasm, reflected anger, or irritation rarely produce results other than to generate a feeling of hurt in the debtor not at all conducive to the promotion of good will.

The Legal Side of Collection Letters. The collector is sometimes tempted, when good will is no longer a factor to be considered, to resort to threat. This he may do provided he takes care to so frame the threat that it cannot be construed as extortion or blackmail or as attempted extortion or attempted blackmail. Civil suit may be safely threatened but care should be taken never to threaten to invoke a law which calls for a criminal prosecution. Every businessman should be aware of the distinction between a civil and a criminal action. Furthermore, criminal statutes differ in different states so that what may be construed as extortion or attempted extortion in one state will not be so construed in another state.

A second word of warning to the collection manager involves what may appear on the envelope. Anything appearing on the envelope which reflects injuriously upon the character or conduct of another has been declared nonmailable matter. Not only is such matter nonmailable, but such a publication may constitute a libel in which an action will lie. Anything which indicates that the addressee is being dunned for an account *that is past due* should not appear upon the outside of any mailable matter. This obviously excludes the use of post cards in all collection work. Even open-faced or window envelopes must not disclose, by any word which may accidentally show, that the statement or letter constitutes a dun. The reader will not, of course, gather from the above that every recipient of collection letters scans the letter closely to see if any law has been violated. Such laws are commonly violated through ignorance of them, or carelessness, without any harmful consequences to the writers of such letters, but a business house wishes to take no chances. One action brought against a transgressor may be very costly.

Why Letters "Pull." A collection letter "pulls," or induces the debtor to pay, because it strikes in him a responsive chord. A certain collection letter used repeatedly is said to "pull" because it strikes the responsive chord or chords present in the largest number of people. Likewise, a collection letter fails of its purpose because it fails to make the right appeal in the right way. Among the "dead beats" there may be no appeal which could stir them to action, while those who are down and out through misfortune may suffer considerable anguish at not being able to pay.

The good collector studies collection psychology, that is, the science of mental operations—the study of the way the mind of the average person works. The good collector has learned the power of habit, the necessity of securing and holding attention, and the value of the appeal to instincts and emotions to which nearly all men almost automatically respond, and the value of suggestion which sets a man's mind into operation. Certain ideas are established in the minds of debtors by every year, month, and day of their business experience. It is these ideas which are used in collection work. The collection correspondent attempts to develop them or to combat them as the ideas themselves may be pressing for or against payment. Thus an appeal may be directed to a man's sense of fairness, or to his self-interest, or to his shame or fear.

Many a collection is lost or delayed because the collector fails to use the right appeal at the right time. If there could be the happy combination of the most effective appeal, made at the time it would be most effective, which we may call timeliness, and made in the proper "tone," the efficiency of collection departments would be greatly increased. This is a combination hard to hit upon, and the correspondent cannot expect often to strike it. He should, however, strive for it and he will consequently study his problem, which includes the debtor's mental attitude, his financial position, the past relations or experience of creditor and debtor, and the effect of outside or business conditions upon him. These will pass rapidly in review in the mental processes of the experienced collector who has the record of the debtor before him when he makes his appeal. However, only a final-action letter is effective with a habitual offender.

Five Types of Appeal. Analysts of the cause of human behavior tell us we are powerfully influenced by our feeling of pride, our self-interest, our sense of fairness, good will toward others, and fear. Collection letters are built on these various types of appeal; but to know which type of appeal to use and to use it skillfully is not a simple problem. Persons are not all equally moved, for instance, by an appeal to their sense of pride, but all have a self-esteem and are uncomfortable whenever it is lowered. Helen M. Somers says, "pride can be stirred or aroused; it can be pricked; it can be challenged; but it must never be injured."[1] The reaction to injured pride is resentment, ill will, and a lack of cooperation if not an attitude of actual combativeness. Whenever it is necessary to prick pride it should first be fortified to prevent real injury. Skillfully used the appeal to pride is not only effective but it is also a builder of good will. Unskillfully used it may take the form of flattery and result only in a feeling of disdain for the creditor.

When the credit manager appeals to the customer's self-interest, he is appealing to self-protection and selfishness. Most persons react quickly where self-interest is concerned. The difficulty here is to be convincing. "Your failure to pay is hurting your credit standing" is effective only if the debtor believes it to be true. Too often he knows the hurt is so minor he can ignore it. Clearly the force of this appeal varies directly with the extent to which self-interest is affected.

The desire to be fair is not equally developed in all persons. Few, however, would fail to defend themselves from an accusation of unfairness. An appeal to fairness may also contain an appeal to pride. An assertion of your rights or viewpoint evokes fairness since the debtor is called upon to act as a judge. Self-interest or selfishness, however, may be a counterbalancing force. Plainly this appeal is most effective when the sense of fairness is highly developed and the creditor's position is unassailable.

Good will as a force in business is most clearly understood merely by calling attention to its antonym, ill will. Good will is a certain feeling of friendliness and equality and the natural human reaction to it is to reciprocate. One can hardly expect to be the recipient of it unless it is bestowed. To show a genuine, or at least a well-simulated, interest in others will ensure a friendly response.

Fear well may be the strongest of these motivating forces. It may either cause or prevent action and thus may need to be implanted or removed, depending upon whether fear is blocking desired action or whether it is to be used as a motive to stimulate action. Fear and self-interest are closely related though clearly an appeal can be made to self-interest without bringing in the element of fear. In collection work it is sometimes necessary to implant fear, but it should be used sparingly. This is so because it should be saved for final use and also because it is a destroyer of good will.

[1] Somers, H. N., "Psychology in Credit Letters."

The success of the collection correspondent will depend largely upon the choice of appeal to fit the occasion and the skill with which he uses the appeal.

Value of Repetition. While the correspondent may fail to use the most effective argument, or may fail to present it in the most effective manner, or may present it at a time when it is least effective, his effort will not be entirely lost. Though the debtor may not act, he is influenced or impressed. Each repeated suggestion of payment has a tendency to induce agreement that payment is due and must be made. That idea once developed in the mind of the debtor should not be allowed to fade out. If it is, it will be necessary to implant it again at a consequent loss of time. Constant suggestion has a tendency to make the debtor doubt the validity of his objection and then to have some apprehension of trouble. Constant suggestion that he owes a bill is depended upon to bring the debtor to a conviction that it must be paid.

While this constant repetition of a thought makes use of the power of suggestion which tends to culminate in conviction and then action, the process may be too slow to satisfy the creditor. The collector may never lose confidence that the bill will eventually be paid, but he wants the collection effected in the shortest possible time. His reliance therefore is not solely upon the effect that repetition of an idea may give. Instead, he strives to bring the debtor to a conviction that the bill must be paid and to secure action by the debtor by the shortest possible route consistent, of course, with the retention of good will. But the collection correspondent will not fail to make use of this constant repetition. Its aid to the various appeals that may be made will be invoked until the combination of them accomplishes the desired result.

Timing the Appeal. Many an order is taken, a donation obtained, or a bill collected because the person who accomplished it feels that he "struck him at the right time." That a person is more responsive to an idea at certain times than at others is without doubt true. Timeliness of the appeal may involve such factors as the debtor's mental attitude, or let us say his mood, his leisure to consider the appeal when it is received, or whether he may at the time be in funds with which to pay. The writer of a collection letter cannot know just what mood his debtor will be in when the appeal reaches him, nor can he know how engrossed he may be with other features of his business.

Actually the collection correspondent gives these no thought, in practice. He is content to receive the benefit of any such "lucky break." He may, however, give some attention to timing his appeal to the period when his debtor is most likely to be in funds. His collection effort should be most vigorous at that time. Credit men who sell to summer-resort trade know well this necessity. A collection not made by the end of the season may go over until another season, or, indeed, it may not be collected at all. Likewise, the credit man will be most urgent in the collection procedure at the close of the season of any business which is of a seasonal nature to any extent. Obviously, the time to collect is when the customer has the funds. No collection letter, however excellent it may be, can bring in the money when the debtor may not be in funds. It may, perhaps, induce him to get it by borrowing, or by collecting his own accounts. Or the creditor may be successful at the expense of some other creditor whose efforts are less effective. The collection effort will not of course be confined to any one period of the year. It will, however, be stressed when, in the opinion of the collector, success seems most certain. If the effort is not crowned with success at that time, the collector may doubt that his efforts will ever be successful.

Just as there may be a most opportune time to make the collection appeal, so may there be an inopportune time to dun the customer. A strong collection letter received, for example, during the serious illness of the debtor or any member of his family may be resented. The debtor feels that the creditor, even though he might be unaware of trouble, is unjust in adding to the debtor's troubles by pressing for payment while this new trouble is distracting his mind. The credit man, in some instances, may really accomplish more in the way of both sales promotion and collections by writing the customer a friendly and sympathetic letter which will relieve the debtor's mind of any worry he may have had because of the unpaid account.

Dear Mr. Debtor:

I have just learned from Mr. Young, our representative, of your serious illness, and I am, indeed, pleased to know that you are on your way to recovery. It occurs to me that you may be concerned about your account with us. We do not want you to give it a thought until you have completely recovered and are back at your accustomed place in your business. We have asked Mr. Young to learn if we can be of any assistance to your organization during your absence. If we can, it will be a pleasure to render it.

Yours very truly,

Stages in Collection Procedure. As has been said, collection procedure begins with the mailing of the invoice. Thus the steps to follow in collecting are:

1. Mail invoice or include invoice with goods.
2. Establish procedure to find out when account is past due.
3. Have in mind length of time in which the collection is to be effected.
4. Provide for collection efforts within this period at established and progressively smaller intervals of time.

5. If a customer persists in taking the full time to pay for each purchase, and if you are competitively able to do so, omit the intervening efforts and use the final effort. (This type of habitually delinquent customer does not worry about good will.)

Although these steps outline the whole action to be taken once the invoice is mailed, no further moves toward payment can be made by the collector until the invoice is actually due. It is customary then to act on the apparent assumption that payment has been merely overlooked and a mild reminder in the form of a statement or a courteous and brief letter may be written. If the oversight on the part of the debtor is not promptly repaired, the collector must assume that there is some reason for the failure of the debtor to pay. The collector attempts to overcome the debtor's resistance by discussion and persuasion. This is made easier if the collector can learn why payment is being withheld. Consequently, he strives for an explanation as well as for the payment itself. It is during this stage of discussion and persuasion that the collector puts the most thought and effort in his collection correspondence. His letters become more and more insistent. Some collection managers feel that a weak or mild letter following a strong letter will undo much of the effect of the previous correspondence, while, too, the debtor is inclined to resent a harsh letter following close upon a mild appeal.

If the collection manager cannot persuade, he has but one alternative and that is to attempt to coerce. The first step in coercion may be to point out to the debtor the seriousness of his delinquency and the unpleasantness to the debtor which is sure to ensue from his neglect. At some point in the coercion stage, the collector abandons the good-will theme and pursues what he regards as the quickest and most economical means to collect. If the threats of the collector are unproductive of results, and as a matter of fact the credit man can only threaten, the collection may be abandoned or the threats may be carried out. These threats include such measures as turning the account over to a collection agency or collection attorney, or instituting a suit against the debtor in order to enforce payment. These measures will be discussed in subsequent sections.

The reader should not assume that these stages of notification, reminder, persuasion and coercion should invariably be followed. To do so may be to play the debtor's game. His purpose is to delay payment as long as possible, and he knows that he can avoid payment until he is threatened with force. With such a customer, the collection manager will employ different tactics. Satisfied of the debtor's intention, collection will be forced by the quickest process. Each individual case will, in fact, be handled on its own merits. Each will be studied, and it will be found that many different problems will be confronted and will have to be overcome.

Letter Suggestions. It is an accepted fact that much of the collection correspondence which business houses send and receive could be subjected to severe criticism. Letters are not only far from perfect; they are too far from perfection. A few suggestions may serve as an aid to the young collection correspondent and a means of comparison to the more mature collection letter writer.

The first suggestion to be made is to treat your debtor as a man of intelligence. He is intelligent and he is human. Try to avoid the reflection of inanity in letters. The debtor is not only intelligent and human; he has a sense of honor as well. Let the tone of your correspondence be dignified and intelligent. Stress your contractual right and the debtor's obligation. Be insistent in your correspondence. Be neither superior nor patronizing in your attitude.

Collection letters should be forceful and to command attention they should be short. It is well to have only one thought or idea expressed and developed in the letter unless it may be in answer to a complaint, or in the latter stages of persuasion, when several reasons may be presented and the letter made somewhat longer. Not only should collection letters be short as a general thing, but force is attained by the use of short sentences. Avoid long and cumbersome words. Use simple language and choose words of one or two syllables. Force is attained by this studied brevity. Ungrammatical construction detracts from the force of the message. The most important position in the letter is the first sentence. The debtor is impressed or he is not by the first sentence of the letter. What you say in the first sentence and how you say it are of prime importance. The conclusion should be the action you want taken.

What to Avoid in a Letter. To write a superior letter is an art which everyone may not attain to a high degree, but the average individual can *learn* to write a satisfactory collection letter. The writer must remember that "a collection letter is an ambassador on a difficult and delicate mission." It is necessary that the collection letter should be studied and analyzed so that it may overcome the difficulty and yet not fail in the delicacy of its mission, which is to retain the good will of the recipient. Offense to the customer may be largely avoided without the loss of effectiveness.

One of the most difficult things to accomplish is for the letter writer to convey his exact message to a debtor. The letter is a means of conveying thought and often it is an imperfect agent. The tone which the writer wishes to put into the letter may not be the tone received by the reader of the letter.   Someone has truly said that only two masters of a language can exactly transfer thought by words.   Without mastery the one chooses the wrong word or the other incorrectly interprets it.   If this is true in conversation, it is doubly true of the written word where tone, expression, and inflection are absent.   Hence, the average writer, unless he exercises care, is often harsh and sharp in his letters where he intends to be mild and courteous.   The debtor takes a defensive attitude and consequently will seize upon the slightest cause to defend himself or confuse the issue and throw the collection manager on the defensive.   The possible effect of the letter should be carefully studied.   If in doubt of its effect upon the customer's good will, do not send it.

There are some words and phrases best avoided.   A debtor is inclined to resent a "must" attitude upon the part of the creditor.   Likewise, avoid the use of "insist," "demand," "require," "compelled to," etc. Avoid also stereotyped phrases.   This can be largely accomplished by being natural.   Write your letter as you would talk to the debtor.   Strive to avoid monotony of ideas in collection correspondence.   Sometimes a new thought or new mode of approach will occur to a writer or he will write a letter which he considers especially good.   A copy file of such letters should be kept and read over occasionally and criticized.   Such a file will assist the collection correspondent in keeping variety in collection letters.

By all means, avoid all trace of sarcasm in collection correspondence. It is productive only of resentment.   Likewise most writers make a sorry mess of an attempt to be funny.   The recipient cannot see any humor in a collection letter.   It is not intended to convey the impression that humor is never effective but rather that it is most difficult to employ it.   The correspondent unless sure of his ability will wisely not attempt it.

The letters are most effective in which neither the "we" nor "you" attitude is overdone.   A correspondent is inclined too much to the "we" attitude, but he must be careful in attempting to correct this fault that he does not in turn overdo the "you" attitude.   While "we" "us" and "our" may be so plentiful in a letter that they are very noticeable, they at least do not savor of affectation and hypocrisy as does the studied and overdone effect of the word "you."   Let both "we" and "you" be used, the correspondent striving for ease and naturalness in the use of both, and avoiding the overuse of either.

The Use of Form Letters.   Were it not for the speed and possible economy attained by the use of form letters, the author would condemn them out of hand.   These two advantages are so great that it will be found that nearly every collection department handling a *large number* *of accounts receivable* uses form letters to some extent. The superiority of the individually dictated letter lies in the fact that it can be made to fit the occasion and the recipient. Often, however, it does not. A carefully prepared and carefully selected form letter is superior to the poorly written individual letter. It is agreed that the form letter which proves the most effective is the one which carefully simulates a personal letter. Likewise, one of the reasons for the ineffectiveness of the ordinary form letter is because the recipient feels that there is merely a system and not a personality behind it. If the fact that the letter is a form letter is completely disguised, its message will be accepted as a personal one from one man to another. In the early stages of collection, that is, the notification and reminder stages, a large number of identical letters may be sent, because such letters are intentionally less personal than those of the persuasion and coercion stages.

Considerable attention will need to be given to the mechanical appearance of form letters. The most effective is the individually typed and signed, though standardized, letter. Following this are the multigraphed letters simulating the typewritten letter. The effectiveness of such letters depends largely upon whether the name and address and other spaces are carefully filled in with ribbon and type exactly matching the letter. Multigraphed letters should bear a pen-and-ink signature. The least effective form letter is the printed letter which at a glance is recognized as a printed form letter. Such a letter cannot lay claim to be anything except the impersonal appeal which it is. Printed letters should bear printed signatures.

Generally speaking, a form letter should be used but once. Its effectiveness rapidly deteriorates if a customer receives the same letter more than once. Some form letters need rarely if ever to be changed since a creditor will not have occasion to use them with the same customer more than once. An example of such a letter is the treasurer's letter described on page 435. Letters in the early part of the follow-up should be changed every month. Form paragraphs as well as complete form letters may be used. When the letters are to be individually typed they can be built up of form paragraphs chosen to fit the case. Considerable time in dictating can thus be saved, merely by indicating to the typist which paragraphs are to be written.

Specimen Letters. The reader will find at the end of this chapter a number of specimen collection letters. These letters have been selected more or less at random from a file of letters in the author's possession used by credit men in collection work. It is not the author's intention that they shall be regarded as models. They are submitted rather as letters that the reader may study and criticize. It will be noted that these letters do not constitute a series of collection letters, but they cover some of the different occasions which will confront every collection-letter writer in the course of his collection ability.

* * *

A letter apologizing for a blunder. Not all mistakes and oversights are the debtor's.

Gentlemen:

We acknowledge your letter of March 19th in answer to my letter of March 17th. The facts in the case are just as you state and your rebuke is justified. The letters to which you refer were received. They were handed to our claim department; consequently were not seen by any one connected with our credit department. We make this statement in extenuation of our letter, but it is not an excuse, as we should have closer communication between the two departments in our office.

The item has now been credited to your account; so there surely will be no further annoyance to you in this matter. As we have said, the mistake was entirely ours. We acknowledge it. We regret it.

Yours truly,

* * *

A letter aimed at keeping in line a customer not only slow but accustomed to omit invoices and pay on account.

Dear Mr. McKee:

Your attention has been called to invoices of September 4th, $3.33, and September 9th, $33.50, but we have had no acknowledgment to our letters. These invoices are now more than two months past due and frankly we think they ought to be paid without further delay.

You will remember that last summer both your Clyde and Waco store accounts fell into confusion apparently through lack of attention on your part. After a protracted correspondence with you, the accounts were straightened out, and we had great hopes that no more difficulty would be experienced with either of your accounts. We certainly hope that you are not now going to fall into your former casual way of making payments. We have full confidence in your ability and intention to pay, and we ask you to consider the trouble and annoyance to us when there is not a compliance with our terms.

Yours truly,

* * *

A letter hinting more drastic action.

Dear Mr. Blank:

Your November account is so long overdue that you should now give it attention. Prompt action in this matter is urged for the reason that within the next few days we shall have to forward a list of delinquent accounts to our Treasurer and we are anxious not to have your name appear on it. When he receives this list, action on the account is subject to his direction.

Will you not either forward a remittance or write us by return mail? In the meantime, we are going to hold a copy of this letter as a memorandum that a response is expected.

Yours very truly,

*   *   *

A letter holding up an order from a delinquent customer.

Gentlemen:

We regret that we cannot immediately ship the order given our Mr. Wood on Mar. 28.

No provision is made in our costs for carrying accounts beyond our regular terms, and you will readily understand that a point may be reached when a sale becomes a loss. But we want to work with you, for you are important to us. It is only through you that the potential sales of our merchandise to your customers can be realized and we still have confidence in you.

If you will kindly forward a check for your November bill of $76.52, we shall be pleased to give your order our usual prompt service.

Yours very truly,

*   *   *

A letter appealing to the debtor's sense of pride,
with a hint of the urgency of the matter.

Dear Mr. Debtor:

We are being urged in this department to make the collection of invoice of February 1st; $28.66 on your Bridgeton store account.

Under our usual procedure this item would have been referred to a collection agency for adjustment before this time. We do not believe that such action will ever be necessary on your account and we believe that the item remains open at this time through some misunderstanding or through some inability to pass it for payment.

When this letter is received, we wish to request you to investigate this item, and if there is any question about it will you kindly write us directing your reply for the attention of this department so that we may make any investigation or adjustment which may be necessary on our part.

Please give us a reply as early as possible so that we may report to our Treasurer that the item is under investigation by you and will be adjusted shortly.

Yours very truly,

*   *   *

A letter to an old and sensitive customer.

Dear Mr. Brown:

Some unusual circumstance, we feel sure, has prevented your giving your attention to our account.

We are writing you at this time so that you may have a statement of due bills on file, and to express our complete confidence that you will take care of this matter as soon as you have an opportunity to do so.

Yours very truly,

* * *

A letter bordering on the unusual which brought a response when previous letters had failed.

Gentlemen:

There is one task which we dislike to perform, and that is to dun our customers for money. Especially is this unsatisfactory when a request for money due us, courteously made, seems to receive no attention.

Correspondence is much like a quarrel. It cannot be carried on by one party alone.

We have written you several letters, the last one being dated July 29th. We asked for a check or a letter informing us when a check might be expected.

Won't you please be so kind as to give us some response to this letter?

Yours very truly,

A letter to an old and friendly house directed personally to the Treasurer. This account, the credit department knew, was suffering from "dry rot."

Dear Mr. Jenkins:

Because of the very long and very friendly relations which have existed between Smith Brothers Stores and us, we have wished to give you any reasonable extension of time which you might desire on your account with us and have hesitated to take the matter up with you because we have felt that you would not forget us when it was convenient for you to mail a check.

We feel however that we should now call your attention to the enclosed statements for your Scranton and Erie stores. Erie account, while not as large as the Scranton account, you will note goes back to the month of March, and the Scranton account to the month of April. When you receive this letter, we trust that your account will have your careful consideration and that you will either issue instructions that a check be sent us or that you will answer this letter informing us just what we may expect.

If this matter does not come under your immediate supervision, will you kindly hand this letter to the proper person in your organization for attention.

Always glad to be of service to you, we are,

* * *

A customer answers the credit man.

Dear Mr. Roberts:

Reference is made to your letter of Apr. 17, concerning our account and several other letters we have received from you.

First of all, may I suggest that you take an up-to-date modern course in correspondence, with respect to public relations. The very wording of your letter in my opinion would do anything but invite additional business for your company.

When we received our first Xmas order from you, it was so "loaded" with cards for all kinds of relatives and religious cards that we have not been able to sell 20 per cent of the original order. Needless to say, the remaining 80 per cent of the "relatives" are in storage. This is not due to our inability to sell Xmas Cards, since we have made substantial purchases and sales of other Xmas Cards, including the Cards of—. Of course, you can place responsibility where it lies, either with the home office or your salesman, Mr. Reilly.

We have, therefore, a considerable amount of our money tied up in your relative and religious cards, almost all of which were in the high-price bracket, and in which we will have to be unusually optimistic, to realize an even break on the original cost.

It is our feeling that we have been more than fair in a situation where little or no regard was paid to our original order.

We sincerely hope that this clarifies our position and conveys to you our feeling in this matter.

Very truly yours,
(Mrs.) R. A. Peters

✸ ✸ ✸

A letter holding up an order without giving offense.

Dear Madam:

We wish to thank you for the very nice orders you gave our Mr. Sutton under date of July 2nd. We find that the order which you desire shipped immediately amounts to little over $700.00 and the order which you wish held until July 31st amounts to about $985.00. Your order for immediate shipment is already in work and will without doubt go forward within a few days.

On referring to your account we notice a balance of a little over $100.00 which is not due at the present time. The total amount of your open account and your orders is several hundred dollars higher than your account has ever been with us and seems more than is warranted by the very meagre information in the hands of our credit department at the present time. Our Mr. Sutton thinks highly of you and we appreciate very much your business. We have no doubt that you will be pleased to send us a check on account before July 31st, or you may prefer to send us a financial statement for our consideration. We are enclosing a blank for this purpose and we would be very pleased to consider raising your credit limit to the amount required by your orders if we may be favored with your financial statement and it is found satisfactory.

We thank you again for your orders and await with interest your reply indicating the suggestion you prefer to adopt.

Yours truly,

* * *

A letter setting a limit on a discounting customer whose orders have recently increased substantially. First prize letter in a contest conducted by Credit and Financial Management, Granger H. Smith, Buhner Fertilizer Company, Seymour, Ind., author.

For quite some time the management of our company has been noticing the steady growth and progress of your business. It is a source of satisfaction to feel you have permitted us to share in it. The increasing volume of orders we are receiving indicates a close association which we value highly.

A word of appreciation upon your excellent paying record is also in order. We have never had any worries about your account on that score! We know you will continue to meet your responsibilities to the limit of your ability.

I have just finished looking over your current financial statement, however, and must mention several trends which could lead to future difficulty. You may be aware of them. While your gross sales have been growing, your inventory and accounts receivable have increased in greater proportion. Your new store building has attracted new customers, but the cost took a large share of your working capital and higher fixed charges are tending to reduce your margin of profit.

These conditions could cause you a great deal of worry if allowed to get out of hand. In such a case, we would become involved also. It is with our mutual interests in mind, therefore, that I am temporarily suggesting a $10,000 maximum account balance at any one time.

Within the next month, I am planning a trip in the territory and am looking forward to having a visit with you. We can discuss this matter more fully then. I am confident that some arrangements can be made if you feel this credit line is inadequate for the needs of your business.

Sincerely yours,

Jerome King, Credit Mgr.

TEXT AND RESEARCH QUESTIONS

1. *a.* List five reasons why the collection letter is the most used collection tool.

   b. Why do so many letters fail to get results?

2. What part should the collection writer's emotions play in collection correspondence?

3. *a.* How far may a creditor go in threatening a debtor to secure payment?

   b. What should be avoided on the envelope?

4. Why may a letter be effective in some cases and fail to secure action in others?

5. *a.* Why is repetition alone insufficient to bring about satisfactory results?

   b. Name five types of appeal that may be made.

6. *a.* Why is there value in timing the collection appeal?

b. When may a collection letter do harm instead of promoting the collection?

7. *a.* Name four progressive stages in collection procedure.

b. Are these progressive steps to be followed in all cases? Why?

8. List as many letter suggestions as you can and then compare your list with the section Letter Suggestions on pages 425 to 427 of the text.

9. *a.* Why is it difficult for a writer to express his exact thoughts in a letter?

b. Name some of the phrases which should usually be avoided in collection letters.

c. What should be avoided in striving to inject the "you" attitude in collection letters?

10. What are the advantages in the use of form letters? The weaknesses?

PROBLEMS

1. The Whitney Company, a Middle Western wholesaler, does most of its business with retailers whose capital ranges from $2,000 to $10,000. Many of these retailers are insufficiently capitalized and are consequently inclined to be slow paying. The Whitney Company itself has not enough capital to enable it to carry its customers so that its credit manager is under the necessity of keeping its accounts collected in the closest possible manner without at the same time driving away business. Terms of the sale are 2/10 net 30 and 2/10 net 60.

Assume that you are the credit manager for the Whitney Company and that the following problem confronts you for immediate attention: You have written Knowles & Company, Blanktown, Kan., who have a Dun & Bradstreet rating of G 3½, as follows:

Knowles & Company,
Blanktown, Kan.
Gentlemen:

We thank you for the very nice order just received through our Mr. Smith. This order, which is now being filled, has brought our attention to your account. Although there are no invoices on it presently due it is noted that your last payment covered two invoices which, when paid, were 70 and 90 days overdue, and payment was received only after several requests had been made for it.

Your attention is called to the terms of sale which are, of course, as much a part of the contract as is the price. It is felt that we need only to call your attention to this matter and that hereafter you will make your payments in accordance with your terms of purchase.

Thanks again for your order which you should receive about as soon as you receive this letter.

Yours very truly,
Whitney Company
Credit Manager.

* * *

Knowles & Company have answered with the following letter:

Whitney Company,
Des Moines, Iowa.
Gentlemen:

I am sorry to receive your letter in regard to the order given to Mr. Smith. We, like other merchants, sometimes slip up on our expectation to pay our bills at maturity, and we have to use our credit as long as possible without injuring our credit standing.

We have always paid our bills, and in going over our files we cannot see that our payments have deserved a letter before shipment is made.

On thinking this matter over we do not feel so enthusiastic over your goods. Should you feel that ours is not a desirable business, please let us know so that we may line up with some other house. We admit that we are touchy about our credit because we feel that it is the most valuable thing that we have at the present time.

Yours truly,
Knowles & Company.

   a. Criticize your first letter to Knowles & Company.

   b. Write a letter in answer to the above letter.

   2. As credit manager for the Whitney Company construct a series of four form letters to be used in the first stages of collection procedure.

   3. You are a manufacturer in the East and you have a customer in a rural district in the West who is by no means "big business" but who has given you the best coverage in his area for many years. Relations between your company and this account have always been good and his payments have never given any cause for concern. He is one of the best known men in his community and fancies himself as a business leader. He's getting on in years, and as he has grown older has become somewhat gruff and crotchety.

   When his account suddenly shows up 30 days past due, you do not worry particularly but just send out a duplicate statement. However, when he becomes 45 days past due, with no explanation, you check over your credit information to see if there is any clue in it which would explain this slowness. You cannot find any such clue. You order new reports. No clue there either. He is now 60 days past due. Write a letter to the gentleman. Use any approach you think best.

   4. Refer to Mrs. Peters' letter to Mr. Roberts on pages 430 and 431. Write a letter to Mrs. Peters in answer to her letter.

CHAPTER 27

OTHER COLLECTION AIDS AND PROBLEMS

The Treasurer's Letter. Instances will occur where the collection manager after having written several letters has failed to arouse the customer from his lethargy. Just the added "punch" that may be necessary may be produced by a letter written by a higher official, such as the treasurer, general manager, or the president of the company. Such a letter carries added weight from the fact that it comes from a higher authority. When this type of letter is used, it is suggested that the letterhead should bear the imprint of the official's office or title. This aids in securing attention to the letter while the signature gives it weight. The tone of the letter is friendly, dignified, and yet final. It makes no attempt to terrify the delinquent, but it carries a quiet threat which the debtor understands spells action. If such a letter fails to bring at least a response from the debtor there is, of course, no logical course to pursue other than to proceed with a forced collection or abandon the account as a bad debt.

Treasurer's letter:

Mr. John E. Fraser.

Dear Mr. Fraser:

I have just been talking with Mr. Young, our credit manager, in reference to your account. Mr. Young feels that he should adopt drastic action to induce you to forward your check, but I have asked his forbearance a little longer.

The relations between yourself, Mr. Fraser, and us have hitherto been most cordial and pleasant. We have always welcomed your orders, and we have given you our best service. We have had full confidence both in your ability and willingness to take care of your obligations. So far as we know both our service and our merchandise have given you full satisfaction. If we have been amiss in any way, we should be glad to know it so that we may make any amends possible.

There is, we feel sure, some special reason for your failure to take care of your present indebtedness to us amounting to $168.23 running since Sept. 23.

I am, therefore, making this final friendly appeal to you either to mail us your check or to write us why you do not do so.

You, of course, will understand that if you ignore this letter no other recourse will remain to us than to proceed to collect your account by the shortest method possible. Such action, we are confident, you will not impose upon us.

Yours very truly,
Treasurer

A *second illustration of the Treasurer's letter:*

Dear Mr. Goldberg:

The Credit Man in charge of your account in accordance with established rules has asked me to approve the employment of an attorney and the possible litigation in court for the purpose of collecting your account amounting to $32.40.

I cannot bring myself to believe that you will intentionally refuse the payment of a just obligation, nor that you will in the slightest degree jeopardize, for an amount of this size, the excellent credit standing that you now enjoy. Before signing the papers, therefore, I am writing this personal letter to you in all friendliness requesting that you immediately remit in settlement or else that you write me personally and explain exactly why you will not pay.

Of course if you are totally indifferent to the consequence, you will ignore my letter, but I do not believe this to be the case. I am sure that you will aid me in keeping intact the cordial and friendly relations that exist between us and that you will vindicate the faith and confidence which has been reposed in you.

I am enclosing envelope addressed personally for your reply.

Yours very truly,

The Salesman's Letter. Somewhat similar in principle is the salesman's letter. The salesman, however, uses no hint of coercion except as a warning that his house may be considering forcing a payment. His letter is rather the friendly appeal of the intermediary between the customer and the house.

Dear Mr. Blank:

I have not had the pleasure of calling on you for some time owing to the fact that your account with us is considerably past due. I have just received a copy of the letter sent you May 10th, and the credit manager has added a pencil notation to my copy "This account should be paid." I note that you have not answered any of the several letters written you about it. You know how exasperating it is to want some information and not be able to get it. I suspect that that is what has peeved our credit manager.

I believe you will agree with me that our company has extended you more than ordinary business courtesy and that they are now entitled to the $148.20 of your past due account. I feel an unusual interest in this matter because when your account was opened I assured our credit department that it was one account which would never give us any trouble.

I enclose an addressed envelope. Please write me by return mail. I would suggest at the same time that you mail a check direct to the house for the amount stated above, as their letter indicates the matter must be disposed of promptly.

With kindest regards,

Yours sincerely,

Unlike the treasurer's letter the salesman's letter cannot safely be used as a form letter because one letter would not reflect the personalities of several different salesmen. Nor would it be advisable to solicit the aid of every salesman in this manner. Wherever the salesman can be of assistance as a collection correspondent, his aid should be freely sought and cheerfully given.

Collecting Interest on Overdue Accounts. There is every justification for charging interest on overdue accounts. Whenever a purchaser buys goods upon credit, he should realize that he is receiving capital aid for which he must pay. While the financing charge may not be exactly apportioned among all buyers, it is at least distributed over them as a class. This financing charge the seller regards as one of his costs, and it is consequently included in the price as a part of the overhead or as a credit and collection department charge. Thus the expense of carrying the account is taken care of up to the time the account becomes due, but the cost of carrying the account thereafter falls upon the seller unless he collects interest for the overdue period. Without such an interest charge overdue accounts receivable represent money loaned without interest. Not only does the creditor receive no direct recompense but usually there is an expense to the seller to get the use of money which is rightly his. In reality, by withholding the money after the account becomes due, the debtor is borrowing money from the creditor without the creditor's consent. Since he does not pay for the use of the money thus borrowed, he reaps an unfair advantage over his competitor who borrows from his bank in order to pay his merchandise creditors promptly. The slow-paying customer is in reality buying merchandise at a cheaper price than his prompt-paying competitor, and the creditor by condoning slow payments is a party to placing a penalty on prompt pay. The following letter presents an argument difficult to refute even though it will not always bring in a check for interest.

Dear Mr. Walker:

Your letter of Sept. 18 objects to our charge of $8.96 for interest on your overdue account. This charge is in accordance with our terms which are plainly set forth upon our order sheets and invoices, are understood by you, and are just as much a matter of agreement as is the price of the merchandise.

We borrow money ourselves because we must pay our bills promptly, and when our customers do not pay us it means that we have to borrow just that much more, and pay interest on it in order to accommodate our customers. It certainly seems reasonable to pass this charge along to the customers whom we thus accommodate.

If you borrow money from your banker to pay us, he charges you interest. If, instead, you rely upon us for the accommodation, we are entitled to the same consideration you would give your banker, for you are getting the use of our money, while we, in the meantime, are deprived of it.

We want the business of every good customer and you can rest assured that that includes you. You may also rest assured that no customer will get more consideration than will be accorded you. We have but one policy, which is to treat all with equal fairness. Under this policy we cannot consistently exempt you from paying us interest on past due accounts while requiring others to do it. This policy, we feel sure, will appeal to you as just and reasonable.

Yours very truly,

While there can be no question of the reasonableness of an interest charge on overdue accounts but few houses attempt to collect it. The reasons are several. The creditor hopes to buy the good will of the customer by the accommodation and show of generosity, or the creditor fears that good will may be lost if interest is charged. Another creditor may be fainthearted. He doubts his ability to collect interest and hence he does not try. Another may argue that while his terms may be quoted as net 30 or net 60 as a matter of fact his prices include an expectation that customers on the average will be 40 days slow. Another recognizes the overdue account as an expense but since in his business it may be comparatively small he decides to absorb it himself.

As a matter of fact, the expense of overdue accounts is not confined to the cost of the money for the time involved. Slow accounts breed bad-debt losses and collection expenses. One of the most powerful arguments in support of the policy of charging interest on overdue accounts is that it tends to speed up collections, thus lessening both collection costs and bad-debt losses. On the other hand, some debtors feel that because they pay interest they can let the account run as long as they please. This attitude the creditor should strenuously combat because interest merely covers the value of money. The creditor is still carrying the risk and other costs without recompense. The creditor is not in the banking business.

The house which intends to collect interest on overdue accounts should include a statement to that effect on all order blanks, invoices, and statements. Some houses attach a printed sticker to past-due statements and compute the interest charge and add it to the account. Others have found it most effective to render the interest charge upon a regular invoice. It is claimed that payment is more apt to be authorized if the charge is in the form of an invoice. Needless to say, when a creditor renders a charge for interest, he should vigorously follow up the collection of it. To make the charge an empty gesture quickly teaches the debtor to ignore it.

Collecting Unearned Cash Discounts. The nature of the so-called cash discount was fully discussed in Chapter 12. There the true function of it was revealed as a financing charge. The creditor's troubles arise in his attempt to impose this financing charge upon unwilling customers who do not pay cash. Obviously, only the customer who buys for cash is entitled to a cash price. But the customer who does not have the money on the tenth day after the invoice date yet does have it on the fifteenth day cannot see why he should be penalized so heavily because of the few days' delay. Such a debtor is tempted to try to force the discount. Other customers who are always short of funds reason that if they cannot obtain the cash price they will obtain its equivalent, if possible to withhold payment long enough to do so. In some industries the customers have become so aggressive in taking discounts, regardless of the time that payment is made, that the cash discount has all but disappeared among the weaker houses. Resistance to the abuse of the cash price has been weak because the seller has feared that a competitor as weak as or weaker than himself would allow the discount if he did not and thus capture his customer. The financing charge has thus been waived by such weak houses with all except those customers who submit to it. Buyers recognize the unfairness of such a policy and in consequence increase their resistance. In fact the seller as a class has evinced such a weakness in enforcing the discount feature of the contract that certain powerful buyers, emboldened by their success in imposing their will upon weaker sellers, are arrogantly informing their vendors under what terms purchases will in the future be made!

Purpose of Cash Discount. The purpose of the cash discount, as set forth previously, is to divide all purchasers into two classes, cash and credit customers. It seems eminently fair that those who pay cash should have the benefit of the lowest possible price, while those who are financed should pay for the financing. If this is to be done, the line between the two must be sharply drawn, and once drawn no infringements should be permitted. The reader is reminded that cash payment really means payment at once or when delivery is made. By custom a period of grace extends 10 days (or more or less by agreement) which would seem to be ample. Since a division between the cash and credit payment must be drawn at some point, and since 10 days seem to be liberal for cash and, furthermore, and of most importance, since 10 days has been *agreed* upon there seems no logical reason for giving any further days of grace. If all creditor houses would place the same strict construction upon the terms feature of the contract which is placed upon the price, the so-called abuse of the discount would soon disappear. Concerted action is required. One credit man can do much to educate his own customers, but as long as "unearned" discounts are generally permitted they will be generally attempted.

Why Abuse Is Condoned. A condition often exists in the creditor house which tends to promote the abuse of terms. To allow customers to make such short payments is the easiest course to pursue. The decision to accept the payment as made or to attempt to collect the shortage usually falls to the credit man. Not to accept the payment means more work for the credit department, and the danger of antagonizing the customer in the attempt to collect. The easier path for the credit man to pursue is to approve the payment as made. Most concerns are not aware of the amount of discounts thus relinquished in the course of the year. An analysis of discounts allowed might be not only enlightening but even amazing in some concerns. An aggressive, though tactful, credit manager who receives the support of his house may collect the equivalent of his annual salary, which the more easygoing credit manager may give away in the form of cash discounts.

The remedy lies in the severance of terms as a sales factor. The seller should never trade upon his terms either through the sales department or the credit department. If thus removed, terms will become as uniform as price itself. Terms concessions should be unknown. If the seller can truthfully say that no one receives more favorable terms than anybody else, that is his strongest weapon for the enforcement of terms. Trading may be necessary but it should be on price and not on terms. Once a concession on terms has been made, more concessions will follow, and a few special terms soon spread until they become general. A second suggestion is made that the discount be made small, or in other words that the financing charge be made not so large as to be exorbitant. Many houses, dissatisfied with the manner in which their customers pay, increase the discount. This may mean that creditors are competing against each other for what money the debtor possesses using the discount as bait. It may also mean that the debtor is more greedy to receive the benefits of the increased discount, or in other words he refuses to be so heavily penalized, and he deducts it anyway. The debtor who is in an easy credit position does not require a large discount to induce him to pay promptly. He will do so no matter how small the discount may be, provided it exceeds the current rate of interest.

Partial Payments. The collection department is often confronted with the question whether it should encourage or condone a partial payment of an account. Were there not arguments both for and against the partial payment, no problem would be presented. In some instances, partial payments or payments on account should be vigorously resisted, because if permitted to continue the account becomes confused. It is not paid to any definite point. In rendering a statement, all debits and credits must be listed, and unless the debtor confirms the balance as rendered, the books of buyer and seller may become hard to reconcile. The debtor who is proverbially slow should frequently be forced to pay his account up to a certain date. A second and potent reason for opposing a partial payment is the fact that the creditor is entitled to full payment, and he should be satisfied with nothing less. In such a case, the dollar which is not paid is just as much due as the dollar which is paid, and the creditor is fully justified in attempting to collect it. A third reason for opposing the payment on account is that the creditor does not wish to encourage the habit. Collection of the full amount may be much longer delayed if the debtor thinks that the creditor can be satisfied by small payments on account from time to time.

On the other hand, there are cases in which the creditor may feel that it is much preferable to take what he can get, even though it is much less than the whole. The debtor, unable to pay the full account and for that reason withholding any payment, may grasp eagerly at the suggestion of partial payment. Half a loaf is better than none. After all, a creditor cannot complain if he receives his share of the funds which the debtor has to disburse. As a matter of fact, the only fair thing for a debtor to do is to divide his disbursements, after his running expenses have been paid, on a pro rata basis among his creditors. No creditor can seriously object to the action of his debtor if the creditor knows that no other creditor is receiving a preference as to payments. The just creditor will insist upon his share of the debtor's funds, but he will also recognize the right of another creditor to adopt the same attitude.

Delinquent Lists. Many trade associations or trade groups compile what may be termed "delinquent," or "C.O.D.," lists. Such a list usually has two uses. First, it provides a list of those accounts which may be more or less undesirable as credit risks. By means of such a list the seller is forewarned concerning a prospective customer and may, if he sees fit, reject the risk. In some groups, the creditors may go so far as to enter into a "gentlemen's agreement" not to sell the customer except on a cash basis. Such an agreement is usually put in force while one member is having trouble adjusting a disputed account or collecting a delinquent one.

A second use of the delinquent list is as a collection threat. The debtor is informed of the existence of such a list and the creditor's obligation to report all slow and delinquent accounts in order that other members of the association may not suffer loss. The debtor is quick to see the disadvantage of having his name included and pays to avoid it. As a matter of fact, the debtor often has an exaggerated fear of the consequences to him if his name appears upon the list. No debtor except the dead beat can regard such a list as entirely immaterial to him. Threats, however, lose some of their force with some debtors because creditors have used so many meaningless and empty threats that the debtor is inclined to ignore such warnings. Like the boy in the fable they have shouted, "wolf, wolf" too many times and then failed to release the wolf.

Legal Restrictions of Creditor Agreements. Creditors acting in agreement, or appearing to act in agreement, must be careful not to overstep certain legal bounds. Our laws aim to protect businessmen from defamation and from combinations in restraint of trade. The courts have not yet as clearly defined creditors' limitations as might be desired. Cases arising for libel or for defamation of character seem to have set forth a creditor's, or a group of creditors', rights in giving information. But little danger attends the giving of derogatory information, provided it is not deliberately falsified or maliciously published. If so given out, both those who give it and those who distribute it might make themselves liable for misrepresentation or defamation.

That a delinquent list may be kept and circulated within a group is well established. The danger lies in concerted action within the group. The courts have frowned upon the establishment of both "black lists" and "white lists." Agreements, either actual or tacit, to withhold credit have been regarded as in restraint of trade as covered by antitrust laws. In one case,[1] the defendants were enjoined from "agreeing to refuse to make sales to particular customers or from agreeing upon circumstances or conditions which shall exclude customers from extended credit." To attempt to control credit and terms, the courts hold, bears a direct relationship to price fixing and is opposed to public policy.

Another court, however, has injected into a decision the question of whether the methods employed served a useful and necessary purpose.[2] This case has been well summarized in another work.[3]

This association issued monthly to its members a confidential list to all customers whose accounts had been unpaid for a period exceeding fifty days, provided the account exceeded $100, and was undisputed. The rules provide that members shall do business only on a cash basis with concerns so listed. There was no agreement compelling members not to deal, nor other attempt

---

[1] *Cement Manufacturers Protective Association et al. v. United States*, 268 U.S. 588, 604 (1925).

[2] *United States v. Fur Dressers' and Fur Dyers' Association, Inc., et al.*, 5 Fed. (2d) 869 (D. C. S. D. N. Y. 1925).

[3] PRENDERGAST and STEINER, "Credit and Its Uses," p. 204.

made to coerce a debtor into paying, nor were disputed accounts listed. The practice, Judge Bondy decided, "does not go beyond the reasonable requirement, to correct the abuses which have crept into the trade," and hence is not an agreement unreasonably suppressing competition or restraining trade. In arriving at this decision, conditions in the fur trade were cited, such as the fact of 1,090 insolvencies in New York City from 1911 to 1923, with aggregate liabilities of $47,150,000; the small size of bills, which ranged from $20 to $25 each; and the rapid growth of trade abuses. It covered this point and also held that it is not a cause for action to notify a customer that if he does not pay a bill his name will be given to the association as a delinquent debtor. Other state courts have also adopted this view, where the practice may be regarded as one protecting the membership against delinquent or dishonest debtors, rather than as a means of coercion.

These comments are just as valid today as when they were first made.

Offering Delinquent Accounts for Sale. The credit manager is often approached by various collection agencies with unusual schemes for the collection of accounts. The credit man will do well to use caution in employing some of the methods that may be offered. If not actually fraught with danger, they are often at least unethical. Among such schemes may be listed the agency which "guarantees" to collect and includes among its methods advertising the debtor's account for sale. An account receivable is property and as such may be sold. Undoubtedly the owner has the right to advertise such property for sale, *provided* he can do it without libeling the debtor. This is difficult, since the courts are agreed that the listing of one's name as a delinquent and advertising the indebtedness for sale is libelous per se. It is most difficult for the creditor to prove that the real purpose of publication is not to coerce the debtor to pay the delinquent account. If the creditor, called as a defendant in an action, charges that the debtor is the sort of person from whom a just account could not be collected by ordinary means, he must be ready to prove it. "The justification must be as broad as the charge," and advertising delinquent accounts can be justified only by proving, first, that the exact amount indicated is due and unpaid and, second, the debtor is unworthy of trust and credit and is not amenable to the ordinary methods of collection. This twofold burden will prove difficult, if not impossible, to meet in many instances. One justice is quoted as follows:

We are convinced that the whole was a general scheme to force plaintiff to pay money, by threatening to humiliate her by public exposure, and that this was the underlying basis of the system about which this witness testifies. The threat to place the list on the merchants' display windows, and to advertise for sale, etc., could have but one purpose, and that is, through fear, induce the payment of money which could not otherwise be collected.[1]

[1] *Tuyes v. Chambers,* 81 Southern [La.] 265.

The creditor contemplating such a scheme should bear in mind that the responsibility is wholly his. The agency does not share it with him.

The Suit and Judgment. There is no mystery connected with what takes place when an attorney brings a suit against a delinquent debtor, and yet many credit men do not understand the procedure or the different steps that the creditor may take after authorizing suit and before all legal efforts have been exhausted. When the creditor has decided to attempt to force the collection, the first step necessary is the "suit" or, more properly, action-at-law, which, if the creditor proves his case, will culminate in judgment. The action is instituted by the creditor, or plaintiff, filing, usually through his attorney, in the proper court (depending on the jurisdiction and the size of the claim) a formal complaint or declaration of his cause of action to which is attached a petition for judgment. The debtor, through court order, is summoned to appear and answer before the court the complaint of the creditor (usually represented by his attorney). The debtor thus served with a summons has three courses open to him. He may ignore the summons, in which case the plaintiff will obtain judgment by default. He may file with the court a plea, or answer to the complaint. This is a common practice when the bill is disputed, and action along this line is termed "framing an issue" for trial. Or the debtor may appear personally or by attorney when summoned, and defend the action against him. When the court, or jury as the case may be, finds for the plaintiff, judgment is entered accordingly.

A judgment of itself has no force to compel payment. It is merely an official pronouncement, or court decree, that a certain amount is due from a defendant to a plaintiff. When filed, however, the judgment becomes a lien upon whatever real property the debtor may own *within the county in which it was rendered*. In order to place a judgment lien upon real estate located in a county other than the one in which the judgment was taken, it is necessary to get from the clerk of the court a transcript of judgment, which may then be filed in any county in the state, with the same force as though obtained in that county. Furthermore armed with a judgment granted in one state it is usually quite easy to bring an action against a debtor owning property in another state and to obtain judgment. The United States Constitution provides that judgments of the courts of any state shall be entitled to full faith and credit by the courts of any of the United States. A lien thus created is good for a number of years fixed by the statutes of limitations of the various states. In New York, it becomes "outlawed" after 20 years.

Executing the Judgment. By the laws of most states, after the judgment is taken, the defendant is allowed a certain period in which to settle the judgment in court including the court costs. The defendant may also stay the execution of the judgment if he elects to appeal from the judgment to a higher court.

To assist a creditor in collection on a money judgment, the law has provided certain remedial actions. The first action which the lawyer for the creditor will take is to secure a writ of execution directed to a judicial officer, usually a sheriff or marshal, directing that officer to levy on any real or personal property belonging to the debtor. Usually the creditor knows where the sheriff or marshal can locate this property and thus makes the job of executing the writ a simple one. In large cities, such as New York, the judicial officer seldom takes any steps on his own initiative to find the debtor's property but relies entirely on the information given to him by the creditor's attorney. If property is discovered, it is seized and sold, usually at public auction, and the proceeds applied to the judgment. Any excess, after all fees and expenses are paid, would of course be returned to the debtor.

Property Exemptions. Certain properties of the debtor, however, are exempted from seizure. While the state statutes differ, New York[1] is typical in exempting the following:

1. All stoves for use in a dwelling house and 60 days fuel supply; one sewing machine.
2. Family bibles, family pictures, schoolbooks, and $50 worth of other books.
3. A family pew in a church or place of worship.
4. Domestic animals and 60 days food supply (up to $450 for the animals plus the food).
5. All wearing apparel, household furniture, crockery, tableware, and cooking utensils.
6. A wedding ring; a watch not exceeding $35.
7. Working tools of a mechanic or a farmer, professional tools, and farm machinery not exceeding $450.
8. The foregoing do not apply (*a*) where work is performed by a servant or mechanic and (*b*) where the warrant is for the purchase price of these articles.

There are additional exemptions for members of the military service.

Examination in Supplementary Proceedings. Inasmuch as debtors frequently dispose of visible assets before suit, the inadequacy of existing procedure for collecting on a money judgment by levy or sale of property led to the passage of laws providing the judgment creditor with aids supplementary to the writ of execution, for example, the writ of garnishment. A creditor may reach 10 per cent of the debtor's salary (over a certain statutory amount which differs somewhat in the various states). A creditor may also examine the judgment debtor in supplemental proceedings. This device is of inestimable value in ferreting

[1] New York Civil Practice Act, Section 665.

out money or property belonging to, or available to, the debtor. The debtor is brought into court by means of a subpoena served upon him, there to answer, under oath, any questions designed to disclose his present financial status and occupation. Perhaps of no less importance is the chance it affords to trace assets formerly held by the debtor. Thus the debtor may be asked, among others, the following questions:

1. Are you working at present? For whom? At what salary?
2. Do you have a bank account? At present? Or within the last 2 years? In what bank or banks?

(At this point the debtor may be asked to produce his bank statements for a period of at least 6 months before the account was closed out. Any abnormally large withdrawals would invite further examination to discover the circumstances surrounding the withdrawals.)

3. Whether he is the beneficiary of any will or trust fund or whether he has any jewelry and so forth.

For failure or refusal to answer any proper question the debtor may be held in contempt of court. Where a question is objected to by the debtor on the ground that the answer might tend to incriminate him or subject him to a penalty or forfeiture, the judge may direct him nevertheless to answer the question, with the proviso, however, that he may not later be prosecuted or fined on the basis of such answers.

In New York State an additional remedy is afforded the judgment creditor. A section of the Civil Practice Act provides that the court may order payments by the debtor from his income after reasonable allowance for the care of himself and his family. This is in addition to a garnishee. It may be employed to reach the income of a judgment debtor now in federal service (and therefore not subject to garnishee), or it may be applied to a debtor employed by his wife or relatives without a salary or with a salary so inadequate that the court is satisfied that his conduct amounts to a fraud upon the creditors. In the latter event, the court may direct weekly or monthly payments based on the reasonable value of the debtor's service. Should the debtor fail to make these payments, he may be jailed for contempt of court. The attorney for the judgment creditor attempts by questioning the debtor to ascertain precisely what the debtor does in his employment in order to build up the value of his services. He would also question the debtor with respect to his standard of living. Questions such as "How much did you pay for that suit you have on?" "What kind of car do you drive?" "When did you buy it?" "Do you belong to a golf or social club?" "Did you take a vacation recently?" are asked to demonstrate how freely the debtor spends money in contradiction to his statement that he has no income.

Where, as it frequently happens, information necessary to a complete case against the debtor can be secured only from third parties, these too may be subpoenaed in supplementary procedures and questions.

If the examination in supplementary proceedings proves unfruitful, the creditor has exhausted his endeavors to discover the means to satisfy the debt, and, obviously he can go no further (for the time being) with the collection.

Actual executions of judgment by legal process are, as a matter of fact, comparatively rare. Either the debtor has no property which the sheriff can discover upon which to levy, in which case the debtor is said to be "judgment proof," or, having property which could be taken, he defends it by paying the judgment even though necessary to dispose of some of his property to do so. The debtor is, obviously, in a better position to get the true value of his property and at less expense than could be obtained by a forced sale through a sheriff. Even though the debtor may be judgment proof when the judgment is obtained, it may be a mistake to abandon such a claim as worthless. Many a debtor rehabilitates his fortune in after years when the judgment with interest can be collected, subject, of course, to the statute of limitations. An accurate and complete record of accounts which must be temporarily abandoned should be kept. Such a record if checked up periodically might pay many a creditor worth-while dividends.

Charging Off Bad Debts. Considerable difference will be found among concerns in their practice of charging off those receivables which prove to be losses. The question which first arises is the determination of those accounts which are to be considered as lost. Who is to decide that question, and when is the charge to be made? Obviously, the person most competent to decide whether an account is to be regarded as good, doubtful, or bad is the credit manager. He, then, is the most logical person to authorize charges to bad debts, and in many concerns he is the final authority as to whether or not an account shall be retained among the accounts receivable. Sometimes, however, it is felt that the credit manager, because of his interest in keeping the record of bad-debt losses at a minimum, will fail to charge off all accounts which should be so handled. On the other hand, it may be felt that the credit manager may be too ready to abandon accounts as lost which might with more vigorous action be collected. It may be the policy of the house, therefore, to require that all accounts to be charged off be submitted together with a record of their status to the treasurer, who puts the final stamp of approval on the charge to bad debts. The decision of the credit manager, however, is in most cases final, and he will find it to his interest in the long run to follow strictly the policy of the house in charging off bad debts as they occur whether the credit department record may be temporarily improved or hurt by such action. Involved in the policy of the house is of course the question of good accounting practice and what may be permissible under the rules of the income-tax authorities.

That the accounts receivable should be purged of all bad accounts before the books are closed for the period is a statement not subject to controversy. The better policy is to have such entries made as soon as it is known that the expectation of collecting the account must be abandoned. In practice, this means that before the books are closed each month for a trial balance, all transfers from accounts receivable to bad debts, or whatever may be the terminology of the account, are made.

TEXT AND RESEARCH QUESTIONS

1. *a.* Why is a well-worded letter signed by the treasurer often effective after the collection department has failed to secure results?
   b. At what stage in the collection procedure should the treasurer's letter be used?

2. *a.* Why do so few houses attempt to collect interest on overdue accounts?
   b. What preliminary steps should be taken if interest or overdue accounts are to be collected?

3. *a.* Why is the credit man inclined to overlook infractions of cash discount terms?
   b. What are some of the practical questions involved in handling remittances in which the cash discount has been erroneously deducted?
   c. Should a few days of grace be allowed in addition to the regular discount period? Why?

4. Under what circumstances would you suggest that a debtor forward a partial payment?

5. What danger may attend the use of black lists?

6. If accounts receivable are property and can be sold, why is it dangerous to advertise them for sale?

7. *a.* What is a judgment?
   b. Why is the threat of a suit often effective in bringing a payment?

8. *a.* Why are judgments so seldom satisfied through a seizure and sale of personal property?
   b. What different steps can be taken after a suit is begun before the collection effort is finally abandoned as hopeless?

9. Upon whom should the responsibility of charging off bad debts devolve? Why?

10. *a.* What is an examination in supplementary proceedings?
    b. What is its purpose?
    c. When may it be held?

PROBLEMS

1. Your house is trying to enforce its terms of payment. A remittance has just been received with discount of $3.79 deducted by the customer. Payment was mailed on the fifteenth day from the date of invoice. Terms were 2/10 net 60. The customer is rated by Dun & Bradstreet G 3½. This is the customer's second remittance. On his first remittance he deducted discount a few days late. You then wrote him notifying him that you were allowing the discount and asked him to comply with terms in the future.

Construct the letter that you would write the customer upon the receipt of his second remittance.

NOTE. Such questions should be considered as the returning of the check; the retention of payment and request for the balance; and the suggestion that since discount has been lost, the customer may wish to withhold payment until the 60 days have elapsed.

2. Your concern has a claim against Shields' Pharmacy, Thomas O. Shields, proprietor. His business is located in your state. The bill, for $387.63, was dated July 25, last year, and terms of sale were 2/10 net 30. You have incurred the following expenses:

Court fee	$ 7.50
Process server	2.00
Attorney's fee	25.00
Incidental expenses	9.15
Total	$43.65

You have received a judgment dated Apr. 10. What should be its amount?

CHAPTER 28

THE CREDITOR'S LEGAL AIDS

The credit department is charged with a serious responsibility. During the course of a year, funds which may amount to many times the value of the concern's capital pass through the hands of the credit department. Not only must it determine the willingness and the ability of customers to pay, but it should be familiar with its legal rights and remedies as well. Such questions arise as what constitutes a contract between buyer and seller, when does title to merchandise pass, what are the seller's rights when the buyer cancels an order, and what rights are given by law to the seller under certain specific conditions? Only a general knowledge of the law is required, and it is not to be inferred that the credit man ever should pose as the legal adviser of his house. However, he should be familiar enough with the general rights and duties of sellers and buyers to avoid the common pitfalls into which the less informed businessman frequently finds himself plunged.

What Constitutes a Contract? A contract is created when the seller agrees to transfer or effects a transfer of the property either in goods, credit instruments, or services to the buyer for a consideration called the "price." The contract may be unenforcible if either party lacks the legal capacity to contract, and if the transfer or acquisition of property is effected by a minor or mental defective, or one guilty of habitual drunkenness. The seller may, however, collect a reasonable price for necessities thus sold, even in the absence of a contract. The distinction between the agreement to transfer the property in goods and the actual transfer of that property may be important because both the risk to the goods and the right to, or effect of, the cancellation of the contract are involved.

A contract to be enforcible must be in writing if the value of the goods is in excess of specified figures (which varies in different states) unless the buyer accepts part of the goods, and actually receives them, or gives something in earnest to bind the contract, such as partial payment or some note or memorandum, or the contract be in writing signed by the person to be charged or his agent. Mere delivery of goods by the seller and receipt by the buyer do not constitute an acceptance. The buyer, however, accepts by taking some action in relation to the goods which is inconsistent with the ownership of the seller, or when he retains possession for an unreasonable length of time without notice of rejection to the seller. Acceptance is, of course, effected by notification to the seller orally, in writing, or by any other method of intimation.

When Does Title Pass? When disputes arise between buyer and seller the mooted point of the controversy is frequently the passing of title to goods from seller to buyer. This question is of considerable importance because the risk is transferred with the title, as a general thing, though there are certain exceptions. The general rule to follow is that title to goods passes according to the intent of the contracting parties. When that intent is vague or disputed, it is to be ascertained from (1) the terms of the contract, (2) the conduct of the parties, (3) the usages of trade, and (4) the circumstances of the particular case.

The rules for determining intent, unless a different intention can be ascertained from the conditions enumerated above, are summarized as follows:

1. Unconditional contract to sell specific goods in a deliverable state: Property passes when contract is made, even though delivery or payment or both be postponed.

2. Contract to sell specific goods where something remains to be done to put them in a deliverable state: Property passes when that thing is done.

3. Contract where delivery is made "on sale or return" or other similar terms: Property passes on delivery to buyer, but he may revest it in the seller by returning or tendering the goods within the time fixed in the contract, or, if no time has been fixed, within a reasonable time.

4. Contract where delivery is on approval or other similar terms: Property passes:
    a. When the buyer signifies his acceptance or does any other act adopting the transaction.
    b. If the buyer retain the goods without signifying acceptance or giving notice of rejection and a time has been fixed for their return, at expiration of such time; if no time has been fixed, at the expiration of a reasonable time. (What is a reasonable time depends on the circumstances of the case.)

5. Contract to sell by description unascertained goods or "future" goods: Property passes to the buyer when such goods in a deliverable state are unconditionally appropriated to the contract, either by the seller, with the buyer's consent, or by the buyer, with the seller's consent. Such assent may be expressed or implied, and may be given either before or after the appropriation is made.

6. Contract requiring seller to deliver the goods to the buyer, or to prepay transportation charges to a place designated by the buyer: Property does not pass until the goods have been delivered to the buyer or have reached the point of destination designated.

Cancellations and Returns.   Cancellations and returns, particularly the latter, are a source of annoyance and a considerable expense to some businesses.   So common have both become in some industries that the seller is hardly aware of his exact legal rights under the circumstances. In fact, the seller has, in many instances, abrogated his rights by his own action or that of his salesmen.   Cancellations have been so meekly accepted by sellers that both buyers and sellers have come to regard orders as cancelable at the will of the purchaser.   Furthermore, salesmen frequently book orders with the understanding that cancellation is at the option of the buyer, and this is done with the knowledge and consent of employers.   The acceptance of cancellations has become the almost general practice where the goods sold are suitable for sale to others in the regular course of the seller's business.   Indeed, it is probable that the remedy available to the seller in such cases would hardly be worth the attempt to enforce it.   Where the goods are unsuitable for sale to others, or are manufactured to order and are such as cannot be resold for a reasonable price, the seller is less willing to accept a cancellation.

In either event, the seller can hold the buyer liable only for the damages he has sustained up to the time of cancellation, which may include the seller's anticipated profit as a part of the total of his damages.   If a cancellation is received after the goods have been shipped, and the contract is in writing and otherwise legally enforcible, the seller can notify the buyer that the goods belong to him and sue for the price.   If the goods have been manufactured to order and are such as cannot be readily resold for a reasonable price, the seller can always refuse to accept the cancellation and sue for the price, except that he cannot continue to manufacture and add to the expense.   Where the reason for the cancellation is really a fall in price, the seller's damages are computed as the difference between the contract price and the open market price at the time of cancellation, for which amount the buyer can be held legally liable under the contract.

In many industries the returned goods problem presents not only an annoying problem to sellers but it is a serious economic waste.   A refusal to accept goods, or a return of them, is in effect a cancellation of the order.   The seller's rights have been enumerated above.   In many instances, however, the buyer is given the option to return the goods without justifying his reasons for doing so.   Both sellers and buyers share the responsibility for this evil.   Salesmen by high-pressure methods force orders from unwilling purchasers. The buyer, in many cases, places an order to get rid of an importunate salesman. Such unjustified business operation invites cancellations and returns. Again, goods are painted in too glowing terms by the salesman, and the buyer, disappointed with their quality upon their receipt, returns them to the seller with the statement that they do not conform to description, or to sample. A decline in price may be the real reason for a return though some other may be given.

Trade associations and better business bureaus are giving considerable thought to the problem, and are attempting to mitigate the evil. Credit men can assist in the eradication of unwarranted returns by educating their customers to observe their contractual obligations. Unbusinesslike practices on the part of buyers will be resisted by good houses in their relationships with each other, and a general elevation of the standards of doing business among the trade will result.

The Unpaid Seller's Lien. Fortunately for the seller the transfer of title does not always require the actual transfer of goods and their resultant possession. Under certain conditions, the seller can refuse to deliver the goods which he has sold and to which he has lost title. This right is known as the "unpaid seller's lien." Under it the seller holds the goods as security for the fulfillment of the obligation of the purchaser. The right of lien continues while the seller has possession of the goods when:

1. Goods have been sold without any stipulation as to credit.
2. The term of credit under which the goods were sold has expired.
3. The buyer becomes insolvent.

Even though a part delivery of the goods has been made, an unpaid seller may exercise his right of lien as to the goods still in his possession, unless the circumstances under which the delivery was made have shown an intention to waive the lien or right of retention. Furthermore, the seller may retain possession of the goods and sue for the purchase price. If he were obliged to surrender the goods upon obtaining the judgment, he might be exchanging valuable goods for a worthless judgment. The seller should always bear in mind that he cannot hold the goods for any claim except the purchase price, nor after valid tender of the purchase price.

An unpaid seller loses his lien on the goods when:

1. He delivers the goods to a carrier or other bailer for transmission to the buyer, without reserving to himself the title or property in the goods or the right to possession thereof.
2. The buyer or his agent lawfully obtains possession of the goods.
3. He waives the lien.

The technicalities of this law need give the seller but little concern since it will be most natural for him to follow the right course when conditions arise which call for the utilization of this legal aid.

The Right of Stoppage in Transit.   Although the seller loses his lien when he voluntarily loses possession of the goods, there is one circumstance under which the lien may be revived.   When the buyer is, or becomes, insolvent, an unpaid seller, who has parted with the possession of the goods, has the right of stopping them in transit.   This right permits the seller to regain possession (not title) of the goods at any time while they are in transit and such resumption of possession entitles him to the same rights in regard to the goods as he had before parting with their possession.

Two conditions will be noted as essential to the exercise of this right, *viz.*, the insolvency of the buyer and that the goods shall not have reached the possession of the buyer.   These two essentials should be thoroughly understood.   A buyer is deemed insolvent within the meaning of this act who either has ceased to pay his debts in the ordinary course of business or cannot pay his debts as they become due, whether he has committed an act of bankruptcy or not, and whether or not he is insolvent within the meaning of the Federal Bankruptcy law.

Goods are deemed to be in transit:

1. From the time when they are delivered to a common carrier, by land or water, or other bailee, for transmission to the buyer, until the time of delivery to the buyer, or his agent, by such carrier or other bailee.

2. After the time of rejection of the goods by the buyer, even if the seller has refused to receive them back, and they continue in the possession of the carrier or other bailee.

The unpaid seller exercises his right of stoppage in transit by giving reasonable notice to the carrier.   It is then the duty of the carrier to redeliver the goods to the seller, the carrying charges being borne by the seller.   Reasonable notice is to be construed as a notice giving the carrier a reasonable time in which to locate the goods and put the stoppage order into effect.   The carrier is not responsible for the failure to execute the stoppage order if it uses due care and diligence in its attempt to enforce it.   But if the carrier has issued a negotiable bill of lading, this must be surrendered or a sufficient bond given to protect the carrier from any claim arising under it.   If, however, such negotiable document of title has actually been transferred by way of sale to an innocent purchaser for value while the goods are in the hands of the carrier, and before the seller's right has been exercised, his right of stoppage in transit is ended.   A sale of goods, however, by the buyer while the goods are in transit and where there is no negotiable document of title does not affect the seller's right of stoppage.

The seller should be certain in every case before he exercises this right that there are reasonable grounds for it. Actual or technical insolvency is not a requirement; the right may safely be exercised if the buyer gives evidences of insolvency. Failure to pay bills at maturity or permitting a note to go to protest would justify the action. Stoppage in transit merely restores the seller's lien upon the goods. Title still remains in the buyer, but the seller may resell if the buyer does not exercise his right to render the purchase price within a reasonable time. In such a resale the seller may act as agent of the buyer and hold the buyer responsible for any difference between the contract price and the resale price, although it has been held that if the goods are sold at a profit the seller is not accountable to the buyer for such gain.

Right of Rescission. While the right of stoppage in transit, of itself merely restores the seller's lien, the seller may rescind a sale under certain conditions. The effect of the exercise of this right is to restore complete title in the seller, who has previously transferred title but who either has retained or regained possession of the goods. The right of rescission may be exercised when:

1. A right of rescission has been expressly reserved to the seller upon default of the buyer.

2. The buyer has been in default in the payment of the purchase price for an unreasonable time.

3. The buyer has repudiated the contract, or has manifested his inability to perform his obligations thereunder, or has committed a material breach thereof.

If the seller rescinds a sale, he need not account for any profits gained by a later sale but he may on the other hand sue for any damages, including anticipated profit, sustained by the default of the original buyer. When exercising this right of rescission, the seller must make some overt act to manifest to the buyer an intention to rescind. Merely a mental decision to rescind is insufficient. Offering the goods for resale would be sufficient, although notification of such to the buyer might be preferable. It will be noted from the causes for rescission enumerated above that the seller must decide the justification for his action, and then defend it if the buyer brings any action against the seller.

The Right of Replevin. It should be known to every businessman, both buyer and seller, that title to property cannot be obtained by fraud. Where fraud upon the part of the buyer is practiced, therefore, the goods remain the property of the seller and he can take legal measures to recover possession of his property. This action is known as replevin, or the right of recaption. Even though the seller of goods voluntarily delivers them to the buyer, the latter is guilty of a wrongful taking if he obtains them by such fraud as justifies the seller in rescinding or avoiding the sale. Upon its avoidance the owner may insist that no title or right of possession ever passed to the defrauder and retake the goods, provided he executes a bond as security to the purchaser against any injustice he may suffer as the result of such action.[1] If a debtor obtains goods by means of a false financial statement, he has practiced fraud, and the seller can bring an action to replevy the goods. The right remains to the seller even though the buyer may have become a bankrupt and his estate has passed into the hands of the receiver or trustee. It should be borne in mind that in an act of replevin the burden of proof is on the seller to establish his case. The owner of property wrongfully taken may pursue it so long as it may be identified, even though it may have been altered in form, unless it has become annexed to, or become an integral part of, some other commodity. Furthermore, property sold to a third party, who purchases with notice of litigation pending, may be replevied or recaptured notwithstanding the fact that he may have paid full value for it. In the event that a portion of the property may have been concealed, sold, or destroyed, the portion which can be located and identified may be replevied. Such a right extends not only to goods, wares, and merchandise, but to all credit instruments such as notes, checks, bonds, etc., as well.

Legal Procedure. Although this treatise is concerned with the circumstances under which this right may be resorted to, rather than to the method of applying it, a brief explanation of the legal procedure is appropriate at this point. The seller is advised to refer his case at once to a good attorney, who will apply to the proper court for a writ of replevin specifying the property claimed and the grounds upon which the claim is based. The writ, when granted, directs an officer of the court to seize the property and bring it into court. The seller must give a bond of indemnity, with sureties to return the goods, if a return be ordered, or to pay all costs and damages resulting from an action wrongfully brought. The amount of the bond is always at least double the value of the property or goods.[2] The defendant is also given the privilege of "bonding back" the property; that is, the defendant may recover possession by giving security for its return to the seller in the event it is decided the buyer is not in rightful possession of it.

When the defendant elects to do this, he cannot tender the property afterwards in discharge of the action. Thus, while the primary purpose

[1] BREWSTER, S. F., "The Legal Aspects of Credit," p. 53.
[2] *Ibid.*, p. 357.

of replevin is to recover the actual property and not its value, the actual value of the property at the time it was replevined may be obtained together with a judgment covering damages for the injury sustained.

A seller may lose his right of replevin by waiver. For example, a seller, having full knowledge of the fraud committed, brings suit for the purchase price of the goods instead of an action to recover the goods in specie, or if he accepts payment, a note, or security, he waives his right to replevy. Such action on the seller's part constitutes an affirmation of the contract of sale. He may, however, proceed with an action of replevin if any of the actions in the preceding sentence were taken without any knowledge of the fraud that has been committed.

The Right of Attachment. There are times when the creditor would feel much easier if the debtor were not in control of his property. The creditor would like to prevent his debtor from disposing of the property by sale or otherwise for the purpose of avoiding payment. When such an action upon the part of the debtor seems imminent, the creditor may seek to prevent it by placing a lien upon the property in the form of an attachment. This is a harsh legal remedy in that the creditor virtually attempts to execute a judgment before the court has declared the obligation of the debtor to pay.

Under his right of attachment, the creditor seeks to have the debtor's property removed from his control and placed in the custody of a court officer, except where the property is not susceptible of delivery (a *chose in action*), or so heavy and bulky that movement would be attended with great expense. Real estate may be attached by causing a notice of attachment to be filed in the office of the county clerk wherein the property lies. Since the purpose of the attachment is to obtain security for the payment of a debt, it is obvious that the debt must be declared to be in existence. A suit, therefore, always accompanies an attachment action, although the attachment may precede the suit. Jurisdiction over the property attached ceases, however, unless suit is brought within a certain time (usually 30 days) after service of the writ of attachment. Obviously, the rights of the debtor must be carefully protected. Hence the provisional remedy of attachment is highly technical, and varies somewhat according to the laws of the different states relating to attachment.

Grounds for Attachment. The right of attachment is given by statute which specifically enumerates the grounds under which the action may be brought. While there is some variation of the grounds in different states, they are substantially the same in all. The reader will observe that the remedy aims to reach only those cases where collection would be frustrated by the usual methods of collection open to the creditor.

In most states the creditor will be able to resort to this remedy under the following circumstances:[1]

1. When the debtor is a nonresident of the state (not county) where the writ of attachment is sought against the debtor's property located within the state.

2. When the debtor has departed from the state with intent to defraud creditors or to avoid service of legal process.

3. When the debtor with like intent keeps himself concealed within the state.

4. When the debtor has removed property or is about to dispose of property for the purpose of defrauding his creditors.

5. When the debtor has secured property from the creditor by fraudulent representations, such as the making of a false statement in writing regarding his financial condition.

The laws of the state where the property is located will apply, regardless of whether either plaintiff or defendant, or both, may be nonresidents. As the sole object of an attachment is to obtain property as security until a judgment can be obtained and execution levied upon the property thus attached, it follows that only such property should be attached as can lawfully be made subject to execution. In the event that more than one attachment is placed upon the same property they are entitled to satisfaction in the order of their service, unless simultaneously served, in which case the proceeds received from the sale of the property are prorated among the creditors. Insolvency of the debtor will not bar an attachment action, but bankruptcy of the debtor will vacate the creditor's lien unless the lien was taken more than 4 months prior to the filing of the petition in bankruptcy by or against the debtor.

Enforcement of Right. Attachments are hazardous proceedings unless the creditor is sure of his grounds for making the attachment. If the statutory requirements are not exactly complied with, or if the original suit on the debt is not maintained, the debtor may bring an action for damages sustained through the seizure of his property and the injury to his business. The law seeks to protect the creditor from hasty and ill-advised action by requiring him, in most states, to make an affidavit setting forth as fact, among other things, the justness of the claim, the exact indebtedness, how it was incurred, that it is actually due and owing, and the statutory ground for the attachment. Moreover, the plaintiff is required in practically all states to give a bond to the effect that if the defendant recovers judgment, or if the warrant is vacated, the plaintiff will pay all costs which may be awarded to the defendant and all damages which he may sustain by reason of the attachment. In

[1] *Ibid.*, p. 319.

most states the defendant has the privilege of giving a bond for the payment of such judgment as may be levied against him. The acceptance of such a bond releases the lien upon the property.

Garnishment. Garnishment is a remedy whereby the creditor can gain access to the debtor's property in the hands of a third party. Garnishment, like attachment, is a remedy whereby the creditor seeks to impound funds or property as security for the payment of a debt. The essential difference between the two remedies lies in the fact that under garnishment the plaintiff in an action seeks to reach the rights and effects of the defendant which may be in the hands of a third party. The action is known in some states as "third-party proceedings," while in others it is called the "trustee process."[1] The right of garnishment is essentially statutory, and both the grounds for the action and the procedure of it vary greatly in different states.

A garnishee is regarded as an innocent person owing money, or lawfully having in his possession the property of another, and who stands indifferent as to who shall receive the money or property. He is a mere stakeholder or trustee who may not do any voluntary act to the prejudice of either the plaintiff or the defendant in the action. If the third party, having been served with a writ of garnishment, transfers any of the funds or property in his possession belonging to the debtor, he is in no wise relieved of his obligation to the creditor. A bank may be a garnishee, the creditor having the right to impound both the customer's bank account and his safe deposit box, if he has one. Likewise, an employer may be garnished.[2] A writ of garnishment is frequently resorted to as a result of property or property rights disclosed by the examination in supplementary proceedings. As a general rule, a third party is liable as garnishee if the principal debtor has a right of action against the garnishee.

The statutes of the individual states must be consulted to determine under what conditions the remedy of garnishment can be applied. In some states the action can be brought only after an execution against the original debtor has been returned unsatisfied; while in other states it becomes effective by the simple expedient of serving a copy of the writ of attachment on the person in whose hands the plaintiff believes there is money or property belonging to the debtor. In many states garnishment is limited to actions on contract, and not permitted in actions in tort, though in other jurisdictions this distinction is not made.

[1] Garnishment is unknown in South Carolina.

[2] A person's wages can rarely be garnished in full. The various statutes relating to the exemption of property from levy will apply. In the state of New York, for instance, wages of $25 or $30 or more per week, depending on place of residence, are subject to a levy of 10 per cent thereof.

If the property in the possession of the garnishee is an unliquidated or uncertain sum, it usually cannot be garnished.

The Bulk Sales Law.   Were it not for the fact that all the states have enacted laws designed to prevent a secret sale of a stock in trade in bulk, it is easy to conceive that certain unscrupulous and dishonest debtors would take this method of converting their assets into cash and then to disappear.   This, in fact, so often occurred in the past that it was necessary to enact a law to prevent this particular method of perpetrating a fraud.   The creditor, relying upon the visible assets of the business to ensure at least partially the payment of the debt, would find to his chagrin that the title to such assets had been transferred to another, usually for cash and often for an amount considerably less than their true value.   In such instances the purchaser might be a confederate, or at least cognizant of the intended fraud, or even an innocent purchaser acting entirely in good faith.   In any event, the result was the same. The purchaser had acquired a good title to his purchase thus removing beyond reach the assets upon which creditors may have greatly relied. In their stead a creditor could only look to cash, which may be easily concealed and more easily dissipated, even if the debtor had not removed to other parts without notifying his creditors.

The purpose of the Bulk Sales laws enacted by the various states is, then, to prevent the secret sales of goods in bulk.   This is accomplished by requiring the purchaser either to record or to notify personally the creditors of the seller a certain number of days in advance that a sale, transfer, or assignment is to take place.   Failure to comply with the law renders the title of the buyer to such assets defective.   With such a warning the creditors are in a position to take whatever measures lie open to them for the protection of their interests.   No additional rights or remedies are given against the debtor, other than to keep him under surveillance.   Nor does the law make any attempt to prevent the sale, which would be unconstitutional.   Its effect is to place the creditors upon warning, or if not warned by notification of the sale, continues their right to levy upon the assets for the satisfaction of their claims.

Variations in the Laws.   While the general purpose of the laws of various states is the same, the laws vary somewhat in their provisions. The statutes may be roughly classified into three general groups.[1]   There are thirty-two states with statutes which follow the New York form of the Bulk Sales law.   The New York law provides that any sale, transfer, or assignment in bulk of any part or the whole of a stock of merchandise, or of furniture and fixtures, otherwise than in the regular course of busi-

---

[1] The Uniform Commercial Code form may eventually replace these groups.   Pennsylvania, Massachusetts, and Kentucky have adopted this code.

ness, shall be void as against creditors of the seller unless the stipulations of the law are complied with. These stipulations require the purchaser to obtain from the seller prior to the sale a full and detailed inventory showing the quantity and cost price of each article to be included in the sale and also a written list of the names and addresses of the seller's creditors showing the amount owing to each, duly verified. At least 10 days before taking possession of the merchandise or fixtures, or both, and paying therefor, the purchaser must notify personally or by registered mail every creditor listed, or of whom he has knowledge, giving the price, terms, and conditions of the proposed sale. The purchaser must, furthermore, retain the inventory record of the property transferred, furnished by the seller, for 90 days subsequent to the transfer for the inspection of the seller's creditors.

It will be noted from the above that the purchaser who conforms to the requirements enumerated receives a title to the assets taken over which the creditors cannot successfully attack. Furthermore, no responsibility for the payment of the creditors' claims can be imposed on him. By complying with the law the purpose of the law has been fulfilled, *viz.*, to warn the creditors of the impending sale so that they may take any measures deemed necessary for the protection of their interests.

If, however, the purchaser fails to comply with the law he "shall, upon application of any of the creditors of the seller, transferrer or assignor, become a receiver and be held accountable to such creditors for all the goods, wares and merchandise and fixtures that have come into his possession by virtue of such sale, transfer or assignment." This is a penalty which no purchaser, obviously, would incur except through ignorance.

A second group of ten states[1] embrace the general features of the New York law but usually include the following additional stipulations. The purchaser must see that the proceeds of the sale are applied to the claims of the creditors of the seller; noncompliance with the statute is made both fraudulent and void; a false list of creditors knowingly or willfully furnished to the purchaser is a misdemeanor and limits the action of the creditors to 90 days from the consummation of the sale.

A third group of states[2] have enacted a statute which is similar to the statutes already described only in that nonconformity to the statute by the purchaser renders the sale void as against creditors. Other features of the law are that it applies only to persons buying and selling commodities in small quantities, and no personal notice to creditors is required but notice of the proposed sale must be recorded at least 14 days before the sale.

[1] Florida, Georgia, Idaho, Louisiana, Maryland, Montana, Nevada, Oregon, Pennsylvania, Utah, and the District of Columbia.
[2] Arizona, California, and Washington.

Interpretation of the Statutes. For the purpose of clarifying some of the questions that may arise in the reader's mind, some of the more common questions raised will be commented upon. It is not to be assumed, however, that the statements made in this section will apply to the statutes of all the various states. The statute of a particular state together with the decisions of its courts must be consulted in order to construe the rights of creditors and the obligations of seller and purchaser.

A question may arise in the mind of a creditor as to who may be regarded as sellers under this law. It is usually held to apply to those engaged in buying and selling merchandise for profit, whether as wholesalers or as retailers, but not to manufacturers. Nor do the laws usually apply to farmers, bakers, shoemakers, or garage, restaurant, or pool- or billiard-parlor owners. A sale by auction is also exempt from the Bulk Sales law requirements. As to creditors any creditor at the time of the sale, whether a merchandise creditor or not, can bring an action under the Bulk Sales law.

In some states a chattel mortgage has been held to be a sale in bulk. In such states the mortgagee can ensure his claim as against creditors only by complying with the Bulk Sales law. In some states also the incorporation of a business is interpreted as a sale in bulk to the corporation.

The query is often raised as to the right of a creditor whose name may have been omitted from the list of creditors, or the penalty that may be imposed upon the seller for submitting an incorrect list either innocently or willfully. If a creditor's name is omitted he has no redress given by the statute of many of the states. In other states a penalty is provided for sellers who *knowingly* make a false statement or list of creditors. Still other states require that the purchaser shall see to it that the purchase price is distributed ratably among the creditors of the seller.

Creditors' Remedies. The creditor can usually avail himself of any remedy which he might take for a "fraudulent conveyance" where the statute provides for no other exclusive remedy. The courts have held that the following remedies may be used:[1]

1. Execution levied directly against the property transferred in the hands of the purchaser as if no sale had ever taken place.
2. Garnishment proceedings.
3. Attachment on the ground of fraud (contrary New Jersey, New York, and Vermont).
4. Receiver, accounting, and injunction.

[1] See "Credit Manual of Commercial Laws, 1959."

As each of these actions with the exception of receivership has already been described, no further comment is necessary upon them at this time. Receivership, broadly speaking, implies that the goods were received by the purchaser in trust for the creditors. Under the receivership he would be accountable to the creditors for all the merchandise or its proceeds which come into his possession.

The chief practical advantage of the Bulk Sales law is that it provides warning to creditors to watch their interests. A second advantage is that it puts the burden of proof upon the defendant in cases where a creditor seeks to set aside the sale of goods as fraudulent. The creditor must merely show that the sale took place without conforming to the requirements of the Bulk Sales law. Having received notice of an impending sale the creditor may inquire into the adequacy of the consideration. If the consideration is adequate the seller has as much capital as before the sale, although cash is harder to reach for the satisfaction of a debt than is merchandise. If the consideration is revealed by the inquiry to be inadequate, the creditor may move to prevent the sale on the ground that it is a transfer with intent to hinder, delay, and defraud creditors. In the statutes of several of the states, however, protection to the creditor against a misapplication of the proceeds of a sale is automatically provided.

TEXT AND RESEARCH QUESTIONS

1. *a.* Why is it important for a credit man to have some familiarity with the law of contracts?
   b. Name four ways of determining the intent of the contracting parties as to the passing of title to goods.
2. Why is it important to know just when title passes from seller to buyer?
3. *a.* What action may the seller take to enforce the contract if the buyer returns the shipment?
   b. State four causes of the cancellation and returned-goods evils.
4. *a.* When may a seller stop goods which are in transit?
   b. What liability does the seller assume if he wrongly stops goods in transit?
   c. Who has a prior lien, the carrier or the seller?
5. *a.* When may a seller exercise the right of rescission?
   b. May a seller who has exercised such a right retain the goods as his own under American law? Under English law?
6. If a customer obtains the possession of goods by fraudulent representation, what action can be taken and on what ground?
7. *a.* What is the purpose of the right of attachment?
   b. State five grounds for attachment.
8. *a.* If the debtor has property in the hands of a third party or a claim against a third party, how may a creditor recover upon it?

b. What exemptions are allowed to debtors in your state?

c. How many executions may be in operation at one time?

9. a. What is the purpose of the Bulk Sales law?

b. Outline the main provisions of the Bulk Sales law of your state.

10. What action must the purchaser of goods in bulk take in order to secure a good title under the New York law or under the law of your state?

PROBLEM

The Georgia Peach Company of Atlanta, Ga., sold to the X Company of New York a truckload of peaches. After the shipment had been placed in the hands of the trucking company, a common carrier, but before delivery to the X Company, the Georgia Peach Company learned that X was insolvent. The company notified the carrier to stop delivery and subsequently sold the merchandise to A, in Baltimore, at a loss of $200. After the sale, X learned that delivery had been stopped and tendered the purchase price of the peaches to the Georgia Peach Company.

a. Has X any claim against the Georgia Peach Company?

b. Has the Georgia Peach Company any claim against X?

c. Who is entitled to the peaches, A, X, or the Georgia Peach Company? *Answer fully in each instance.*

CHAPTER 29

THE INSOLVENT ACCOUNT

Our discussion of collection protection and credit procedure up to this point has been largely under the assumption that the debtor could pay if he would, and could be made to pay if he would not. Furthermore, our discussion has been conducted from the viewpoint of a single creditor, as though no other creditor had a right, or might be involved in the case. Individual action upon the part of creditors is to be in no sense censured so long as such action does not seriously jeopardize their own or the rights of other creditors, or, in some instances, the business life of the debtor. When such a point is reached, it may not be the best policy for the various creditors to undertake numerous single actions. Obviously the interests of all the creditors, though they may vary in amount, are alike or nearly so. Hence cooperation or concerted action upon the part of creditors is the only logical action to be taken. Such cases are usually found to be to some degree insolvent.

Reasons for Insolvency. Since the creditors willingly, but probably unknowingly, cooperated in permitting the debtor to become insolvent, they should cooperate in working out a plan of debt liquidation. Creditors "took a chance," or were lax in credit analysis, or failed to follow their accounts, an error which, in most cases, led to the present difficulty.

There are three broad groups of potential business insolvencies. Group one consists of a large number of firms who are in business "on a shoestring"; they are too dependent on creditor's capital. A second group of firms consists of those which have losses that are incurred because of style changes, seasonal demand, and similar reasons. Here the creditor takes a loss and permits the business to continue. The third group is made up of those businesses which are poorly managed and are inefficient and wasteful in operation. Creditors losses will be substantial, and the debtor may be liquidated in bankruptcy.

Statistics on the causes of business failure are regularly compiled by Dun & Bradstreet, Inc. Most debtors claim that the cause of their failure was insufficient capital, but the following table (Fig. 40) clearly indicates that the real cause of most failures is poor management.

It is significant that, year in and year out, these ratios are fairly stable. While proper credit analysis will not change the ratios, since they are based on actual failures, it could materially change the number of failures and amount of losses.

Underlying causes	Per cent total all con-cerns	Apparent causes		Per cent total all con-cerns
Neglect..................	3.6	Due to	Bad habits.................	0.8
			Poor health................	2.0
			Marital difficulties..........	0.4
			Other.....................	0.4
Fraud..................	1.7	On the part of the principals, reflected by	Misleading name...........	0.0
			False financial statement.....	0.3
			Premeditated overbuy.......	0.2
			Irregular disposal of assets...	1.0
			Other.....................	0.2
Lack of experience in the line	12.8	Evidenced by inability to avoid conditions which resulted in	Inadequate sales...........	49.0
Lack of managerial experience..................	18.8		Heavy operating expenses....	7.2
			Receivables difficulties.......	9.8
			Inventory difficulties........	7.8
Unbalanced experience*....	19.2		Excessive fixed assets........	6.5
Incompetence.............	41.4		Poor location..............	2.8
			Competitive weakness.......	21.8
			Other.....................	5.1
		Some of these occurrences could have been provided against through insurance	Fire....................	0.5
			Flood.....................	0.1
Disaster.................	1.2		Burglary..................	0.1
			Employee's fraud...........	0.1
			Strike....................	0.1
			Other.....................	0.3
Reason unknown..........	1.3	Total failures..............................		100.0
Total..................	100.0			
Number of failures........	13,739			
Average liabilities per failure.................	$44,784			

a Experience not well rounded in sales, finance, purchasing, and production on the part of an individual in case of a proprietorship, or of two or more partners or officers constituting a management unit.

Source: Based on opinions of informed creditors and information in Dun & Bradstreet's Credit Reports.

Fig. 40.   Classification of causes of business failures in the United States, 1957.

Credit Losses.   Accurate data covering total credit losses are not available.   Nor is any record compiled of the volume of credit transactions. Credit losses have been estimated in some years to exceed $2,000,000,-000 annually.   Huge as this sum is, it is but a small percentage of credit accepted.   Furthermore, this loss is not entirely absorbed by those accepting the credit.   Losses are expected and, in a measure, passed along to purchasers and borrowers in the price of goods and money borrowed and, hence, shared by society as a whole. Undoubtedly, these huge losses could be lessened, but it is also doubtful if they will be materially decreased. Individual concerns prefer to accept losses rather than to restrict sales, which would be the result if only first-class risks were accepted and which, obviously, might mean smaller net profits. Many businesses are doomed to failure from their very inception because of a lack of the right combination of ability, capital, and economic conditions. To curtail losses, it would be necessary for credit men to prevent such businesses, which are made possible only by capital furnished them by creditors, from ever being launched.

A second reason for huge losses is the failure of creditors to salvage much from insolvent concerns. Debtors are allowed too great a degree of insolvency; that is, their liabilities are allowed to become too great in relation to their assets before liquidation is compelled. Then, too, assets at a forced liquidation usually bring but a fraction of their going-concern value; and expenses of liquidation consume a considerable part of the amount realized. Fraud upon creditors, graft, and excessive fees, while they undoubtedly exist and should be vigorously combated, are one of the minor causes of small dividends in insolvency liquidations.

The Meaning of Insolvency. So long as a debtor is able to pay his bills as they mature, no criticism can be leveled at him. He is operating to a certain extent upon his own capital and (probably) credit. His creditors cannot complain since the debtor is adhering strictly to his contractual obligations. If the debtor finds himself unable, or if he is unwilling to pay his debts when they become due, he is operating not solely upon his own capital and credit, but in part upon the capital of others. To illustrate, a debtor may owe, let us say, $12,000 to merchandise creditors, $4,000 of which is past due. The creditors to whom this $4,000 is due may be supplying this capital unwillingly, yet they are unable, at the moment, to collect. Eventually they will be paid, since the debtor has plenty of capital to ensure the payment even though he cannot convert it, or is unwilling to make the necessary sacrifice to convert it into cash. Such a debtor is insolvent in the sense that he is unable to pay his debts as they mature. Let us assume further that the debtor's assets are liquidated at $8,000. Thus there are insufficient assets to cover the $12,000 of liabilities. The debtor is now insolvent in another meaning of the word.

These two conceptions of insolvency are well defined by the Uniform Sales Act and the Bankruptcy Act. Within the meaning of the former, a person is insolvent who either has ceased to pay his debts in the ordinary course of business, or cannot pay his debts as they become due. Under the Bankruptcy Act a person is deemed insolvent "whenever the aggregate of his property . . . shall not, at a fair valuation, be sufficient in amount to pay his debts." There is, therefore, ambiguity in the term "insolvency." The person using it must in some way convey his meaning of the word, whether in the sense of the Uniform Sales Act or within the meaning of the Bankruptcy Act.

It is clear then that a solvent person is one whose aggregate property at a fair value at least equals the amount of his debts and who is able to pay his debts as they mature.

Various Degrees of Insolvency. It is plain that under the broad term of "insolvency," as described in the previous section, there is a wide variation in this general condition applying to different debtors. Sometimes houses of excellent reputation become temporarily insolvent though the debtor would be loath to admit it, and, indeed, creditors rarely think of a debtor as insolvent until the insolvency becomes chronic and serious. Insolvency in its mild form merely calls the collection department into activity. The collection department's activity may be somewhat annoying to the debtor but aside from this fact he is not handicapped except to the extent that he is obliged to forego cash discounts. If his insolvency increases in degree, the collection departments of his various creditors become more insistent; certain of his creditors begin to withhold shipments; legal actions to compel payments may be instituted, with the result that the harassed debtor finds it increasingly hard to conduct his business. Under these conditions some debtors are able to go on for years, while others are slowly driven to the wall. Still others meeting discouragement attempt to preserve their own capital by some fraudulent action. The interests of creditors in all but the milder or temporary cases of insolvency are best conserved by united action.

Rehabilitation and Liquidation. Two courses are open to the creditors in the case of a tottering business, depending largely upon its condition. If the condition is not serious, and the remedy for it can be seen, the business may be assisted in a program of rehabilitation. Under more serious conditions a business may be partially or wholly liquidated. Either procedure, rehabilitation or liquidation, is best effected through the complete cooperation of the creditors. The forms which the creditors' action may take and the agencies through which the action may be taken are: (1) mutual agreement, including such actions as extensions, compositions, assignments, and reorganizations; and (2) through bankruptcy, including liquidation (Chapters X and XI of the Bankruptcy Act).

It is safe to say that, in the majority of instances, both debtor and creditors defer action too long. The trouble if taken in time might be remedied, but the debtor struggles on in the hope that business will improve, and the creditors too often are not aware of the insolvency until it has reached an advanced stage.

Friendly Adjustments. Whenever a debtor finds himself unable to go on or liquidation impending unless drastic action is taken, it is to his interest to preserve the good will of creditors toward him if possible to do so. The creditors, on their part, wish to salvage as much as possible from what is at best a bad situation. In this action the debtor can often be of great assistance. It is, therefore, desirable that both debtor and creditors work together even if from only the purely selfish standpoint of each. Moreover, when credit was approved, the debtor assumed an obligation to protect his creditors from loss—an obligation which he is bound to fulfill to the fullest extent of his powers; while the creditors, on their part, have a humanitarian obligation as well as a selfish interest in adopting an attitude of complete fairness toward a debtor. Debtors scrupulously honest and conscientious may face reversals due to causes entirely beyond their control. Such debtors, at least, are entitled to both the moral support and active assistance of creditors who, over a series of years, have done a profitable business with the now unfortunate debtor.

Friendly arrangement is the most satisfactory method of composing difficulties between debtor and creditors where there is no fraud or serious legal complication. The court is the proper place to settle business difficulties and controversies involving fraud, crime, or complicated questions of law. Court action is necessarily expensive. It is, therefore, good business practice for businessmen to settle, as far as possible, difficulties and controversies involving primarily questions of fact in a friendly manner out of court.

Extensions. The least drastic method of composing the difficulties of a debtor who cannot pay his bills is by means of an extension agreement.[1] By means of extension, the time of payment of accounts is legally postponed to some future date mutually agreed upon by debtor and creditors. This is a method of amicable settlement which is most favorable to the debtor. He receives whatever benefit there may be in the extra time granted him without material sacrifice on his part. The creditors, on their part, surrender their right to proceed at once against the debtor in the hope that by so doing he will be able to acquire sufficient cash to meet his obligations when they mature under the new agreement.

A distinction should be drawn in the reader's mind between an exten-

---

[1] Under Chapter XI of the Bankruptcy Act both extensions and compositions, or compromise settlements, are termed Arrangements. Chapter XI of the Bankruptcy Act greatly facilitates Arrangements with the result that comparatively few extensions and compositions are effected without court control under the Act. The Bankruptcy Act does not deal with the desirability of an Arrangement; it merely provides the machinery by which it is more easily effected.

sion of time which may be granted to a debtor by a single creditor and the extension agreement effected by a debtor with all his creditors. Credit executives acting individually often agree to grant a debtor more time in which to pay his account, but this obviously is not the cooperative action or common agreement of all the creditors to postpone the due date of payment.

When to Support the Extension Agreement. When the financial responsibility of a debtor has not been seriously impaired, and where the causes of the insolvency are temporary and remediable, an extension may prove the proper medium for rehabilitation. The most important consideration on the part of creditors is the honesty of the debtor. If this element of character is lacking, an extension aids the debtor in his dishonest operation. If the creditors are convinced of the dishonesty and unreliability of the debtor, it is folly to temporize with him.

The second main consideration is whether the extension will accomplish its purpose. Has the debtor sufficient financial strength, and is he sufficiently competent to extricate himself from his present difficulties? Unless these questions of honesty, ability, and financial strength can be satisfactorily answered, creditors would be acting contrary to their own interests in giving the debtor more time.

When considering the advisability of an extension, the first point to develop is the cause and the seriousness of the debtor's position. Certain causes of insolvency are to be found which are no reflection on either the character or the ability of the debtor, while others may impugn his ability though not his honesty. Among the former are such causes as storm, flood, tornado, earthquake, and crop failure, while such common causes of embarrassment as lack of capital or too much invested in real estate, merchandise, or receivables may raise the question of sufficient capacity.

Creditors should carefully consider whether the extension agreement is the right action to take before entering into it. Not only must they be willing to extend the time of payment, but it must be remembered that a debtor working under an extension agreement has exposed his financial condition. He will, therefore, find it extremely hard to attract new creditors. It is necessary under these conditions for those creditors who have signed the extension agreement to further support the debtor with new merchandise. Such current credits should be put on a prompt payment basis, and the debtor closely watched to see that he fulfills this requirement.

Credit executives are again cautioned to consider carefully the efficacy of the extension in adjusting the debtor's difficulties before signing such an agreement. Many executives know from experience that extensions are often followed by liquidation. In many instances, the debtor pleads for his chance, and the creditor, acting upon a mere hope instead of his good business judgment, assents to the extension. Unless the debtor has a plan which promises success, or the creditors can point to the cause of his embarrassment and a way out of it, the extension is entered by all parties as not even a good gamble.

Legal Aspects of the Extension. A single creditor may promise a debtor an extension of his indebtedness, which, however, is not legally binding upon the creditor unless he receives some consideration for his promise. When two or more creditors agree among themselves, and with the debtor, to an extension of the debtor's indebtedness, a sufficient consideration is present to make the agreement binding upon all parties to it. Such an agreement may be termed a settlement by contract. It is the substitution of a new contract for an old one. Each creditor who enters the agreement does so in consideration of the forbearance of other creditors. No one creditor, unless released from the agreement by the consent of the other creditors, would have the right to demand payment before the extension had expired. No creditor can be compelled to sign such an agreement, and no creditor who does not sign is bound by it.[1]

The extension agreement is usually consummated by some individual or bureau acting as the adjuster. A trust agreement may be entered into between the debtor and the adjuster acting in behalf of the creditors. Under this method the creditors usually assign their claims to the adjuster, which reduces the creditors to one single creditor. Having assigned their claims, one or two of the creditors are in no danger of jeopardizing the possibility of an agreement by insisting upon prompt payment. The adjuster, if all claims have been assigned to him, is in a position to dictate the action of the debtor or compel him to liquidate. The creditors, acting as a unit through the adjuster, may permit the debtor full control of his business, or it may be continued by the adjuster or under his supervision.

While the majority of creditors are usually willing to cooperate with each other, a few creditors may insist upon an immediate settlement. Such creditors may retard or even prevent the consummation of the settlement, and the difficulty of securing their cooperation is increased if they are located at a distance from the debtor and from each other. Such creditors, if their claims are small, are sometimes paid in full. This is often done by the advice and consent of the larger creditors who are thus in a better position to control the adjustment. In other cases, the agreement may be made binding on the signatory parties only when a certain percentage, 80 per cent both in number and amount of claims, for instance, have signed. In such cases, it will be understood that the creditors refusing to sign may be paid off by the debtor.

[1] Compare Chapter XI, Section 367, of the Bankruptcy Act.

Extension agreements usually call for payments by instalments. The time may be long or short according to the necessities of the case, and the settlement usually takes the form of notes. In the event that a series of notes is given, it is well to have a provision in them to the effect that upon the default of any one of the series the balance becomes due immediately. Otherwise, each note must be sued on separately as it matures. This means, practically, that the later maturing notes will have little or no value. The earlier notes will involve the debtor in litigation which will probably consume whatever equity he may have in the business.

Composition Settlements. There are many cases where the debtor is worthy, but the circumstances are such that an extension would be futile. It would merely postpone more drastic action. If the investigation discloses that the debtor's affairs are badly involved, or where it is evident that an actual deficit exists, it is very improbable that the debtor could regain his feet. It is obvious that if he cannot pay if given time to do so, he never will, or at least it is very improbable that he ever will be able to pay his creditors in full. Under such conditions the debtor is sometimes able to arrange what is termed a "composition settlement" with his creditors, whereby he becomes released of that portion of his indebtedness which he cannot pay.

The composition is a settlement by contract between the debtor and his creditors (not necessarily all) whereby each of the creditors, in consideration of each other's promise to do likewise, agrees to release the debtor from a stated percentage of his indebtedness to each. The new contract may call for cash payment, a note settlement, or a combination of cash and notes. Such a settlement is known as a "common law composition."

Considerable uncertainty exists in the minds of some credit men as to whether the common law composition is binding upon *any* creditors unless *all* creditors enter into the agreement. In theory, all creditors should be a party to the agreement, since the composition is presumed to be a settlement with all creditors. If all creditors do not enter the agreement, one of the signing creditors might seek to set aside the composition on the ground that it was obtained by fraud. The agreement may, however, stipulate the conditions under which it becomes effective, and any creditor signing it is bound by that condition.

The composition settlement may be brought about on the initiative of the debtor, or a creditor who has made some investigation of the debtor's affairs may call a meeting of creditors to consider the action which it is most advisable to take. As in the case of the extension, a settlement may be made more certain if the claims can be assigned to a committee or a single adjuster, who then proceeds to negotiate with the debtor. Overtures, however, are more often made by the debtor who approaches the creditors singly or calls a meeting of creditors for the purpose of laying his affairs before them and submitting his offer. The settlement is often difficult to attain because a few creditors will be found who are not amicably disposed toward the debtor, and this presents an obstacle somewhat difficult to overcome.

When Is a Composition Settlement Justified? In a sense, the composition settlement is a liquidation of the business or a sale of the assets by the creditors. Under this form of liquidation the present proprietor of the business is found to be the most logical purchaser of it. In other words, the assets can be sold to him for the largest amount that could be realized and at the lowest cost. To illustrate, let us assume that a business shows a relation of 80 per cent of assets to liabilities. In theory, these assets belong to the creditors, and a method in fact can be found, by law, for the creditors to take them. Instead of resorting to various legal methods, the creditors, in effect, consider the best means of disposing of the assets. In a forced liquidation, that is, liquidation by law, the assets would realize much less than their book value. If liquidated by bankruptcy, the value of the assets would be considerably dissipated by the various fees and cost of liquidation, so that 25 per cent might be considered the maximum dividend to be obtained. It is plainly to the advantage of the creditor to accept the debtor's offer of, let us say, 40 per cent in such a case. A prompt and satisfactory settlement under the conditions is thus effected, whereas bankruptcy proceedings use up the time of creditors and cause many of them considerable trouble, worry, and expense.

A composition settlement, however, is not always justified by a monetary return. The honest and competent, though perhaps unfortunate, debtor is entitled to the consideration and assistance of his creditors. It is as much the right and duty of businessmen to help such debtors as it would be to subscribe to a fund for the relief of the physical suffering of the masses of a community stricken by a catastrophe. The dishonest debtor deserves no such consideration. It is a principle with good credit men never to bargain with fraud. If the compromiser puts through an advantageous settlement for himself, then he cheats his creditors. If, on the other hand, creditors get the better end of the settlement, they have handicapped the debtor, and it will be only a matter of time before he will be compelled either to put through another even cheaper settlement or retire from business through some other form of liquidation. The composition settlement should not be lightly entered into by creditors. In too many cases, debtor and creditors try to drive as hard a bargain with each other as possible. Too often the question of creditors is "How much will the debtor pay?" instead of "How much can he pay?" A stronger resistance to such compromises would tend to encourage thrift and business efficiency, whereas too free an approval of the principle of the composition settlement is but a cordial invitation for such offers.

Assignments.   The financially involved debtor may be either unwilling or unable to effect an extension or composition settlement with his creditors.   Yet he realizes that he cannot go forward without some drastic action being taken against him.   He may choose to select the form that the liquidation of his business may take rather than to have his creditors force the action through bankruptcy procedure.   Accordingly, he may make an assignment for the benefit of his creditors.   Or, since such an assignment is an act of bankruptcy, this may be the debtor's method of bringing about a petition in bankruptcy without voluntarily filing such a petition himself.   By means of the assignment, a debtor, generally insolvent, transfers to another his property in trust, to apply the property upon the payment of his debts.   The assignment is presumed to give the creditors confidence in the good faith of the debtor and to provide an efficient and economical means of converting the assets into cash and distributing it to creditors.

Advantages and Disadvantages of Assignment.   Assignment provides certain advantages, at least in theory, which are not possessed by any other method of liquidation.   More may be realized from the assets by an efficient assignee who is free to use everyday business methods than is usually realized from the sale of assets through methods prescribed by the bankruptcy law.   Besides the greater sum realized in the sale of the assets, liquidation may be accomplished with greater efficiency and at less cost.   The creditors may at their discretion permit the assignee to continue the business and wait for a favorable market in which to dispose of the assets.

Possessing such possible advantages, it would seem that the assignment would be a favorite method of amicably liquidating a business for the benefit of creditors.   But there are certain disadvantages.   The assignee is the appointee of the debtor, and because of that fact he may not enjoy the confidence of creditors.   It is felt by the latter that the assignee is often merely the tool of the debtor who can control the procedure for his own gain.   A second disadvantage is the uncertainty of the trusteeship.   Since assignment has been made one of the acts of bankruptcy, and since some of the creditors will be suspicious of the debtor's motives, assignment is often promptly followed by a petition of bankruptcy.   Creditors, however, who have assented to the assignment are precluded from filing a petition in bankruptcy.   A disadvantage from the debtor's standpoint is the fact that he is not discharged from his debts except as such discharge may be voluntarily given by creditors.   Some states, however, provide for a discharge of the debtor from his debts, in which case the discharge is effective as against creditors within that state but not effective as against creditors from without.

Practically every state has on its statute books a law dealing with assignments for the benefit of creditors. These laws are far from uniform, but they all place some restrictions upon the assignee and give an insolvency judge practically all the powers vested in a court of equity. The powers of the assignee are usually limited by the express terms of the instrument of assignment and may be further limited by the statute of the state.

The duties of the assignee are to collect, preserve, and distribute the assets assigned, without preferences, except such as may be prescribed by law or by the instrument of assignment. Notice to creditors of the assignment and an invitation to file claims are usual statutory requirements, and, in the absence of statute, it is the duty of the assignee to give notice and a reasonable opportunity to file claims. Either the assignee may be discharged from his trust by a voluntary act of all parties interested in the estate, or he may be compelled to account for his trusteeship in appropriate court proceedings, instituted by interested persons.[1]

Receiverships.[2] A condition may develop in a debtor's business which requires some measure of general protection either for the debtor or for the creditors or for both. An extension may not be regarded as the proper remedy under the circumstances or cannot be effected because of the refusal of some creditors to agree to it; the composition settlement may be unnecessary because the debtor may have sufficient assets, if given time to liquidate them, to meet his liabilities; and for the same reason the debtor is unwilling to make an assignment for the benefit of his creditors. A procedure which combines some of the features of the extension and the assignment and also provides for either the continuation or the liquidation of the business is found in the statutes relating to equity receiverships. An equity receivership, like the extension, defers the date of payment, and at the same time it establishes a moratorium which, instead of ending at a fixed time, remains in force at the discretion of the court. The receiver, like the assignee, is presumed to be a disinterested third party acting with favor toward none but with equal justice toward all.

The general duties of the receiver in equity are to take charge of and safely keep and account for all property over which he is appointed a receiver. He is under the strict control of the court by whom he is appointed, subject at all times to his direction and orders. As a rule, the

[1] See "Credit Manual of Commercial Laws," 1959.

[2] Since 1939, business receiverships have become practically nonexistent.

receiver continues the business, often with the cooperation of creditors, or a creditors' committee. The receivership is terminated by the discharge of the receiver by the court when the need of the receivership is over or the business has been liquidated or successfully reorganized and rehabilitated.

Causes for Equity Receiverships. A receiver in equity may be appointed on the application of either the debtor or one or more creditors. The appointment, however, is not lightly made. The court will not remove the debtor from the conduct of his own business upon the application of a creditor without good cause. Nor will the court lightly deprive the creditor of his right of action at law in enforcing his claim upon the debtor. On the other hand, a creditor need not stand by and see his claim become valueless through litigation brought by others, internal dissension, or for other causes. Insolvency is not a cause for the appointment of a receiver in equity, or more properly stated, the appointment of a receiver when the debtor is insolvent is usually ineffective; since such an appointment is an act of bankruptcy and is usually followed by a petition in bankruptcy.

There are four general classes of cases in which a court will appoint a receiver:[1]

1. Where there is no person competent by reason of interest or otherwise to take the custody and management of the property which constituted the subject matter of litigation.

2. Where, although all the parties may be equally entitled to possession and control of the property, still it is not proper that any of them should have possession or control of it.

3. Where the person holding the property occupies a position of trust relation and is violating his fiduciary duties.

4. Where, after the rendition of a judgment or decree, the ordinary processes of the court cannot carry the judgment or decree into effect.

It will be seen that the object sought by the appointment of an equity receiver is to preserve the estate for the creditors during readjustment, reorganization, or litigation, which is to decide the rights of litigant parties or to establish what is in effect a moratorium in behalf of the debtor.

Duties of the Receiver. The receiver in equity may be appointed either by a state or a federal court of equity. If appointment is by a state court, the receiver can take possession of only the property within the state. Since the jurisdiction of a court ends at the boundaries of the state, for any property of the insolvent located in another state, ap-

---

[1] TARDY, "Smith on Receivers," p. 23.

pointment of an ancillary receiver must be made by a court of that state. The same receiver or different receivers may be appointed by the various states' courts.

A receiver in equity may be appointed by a federal court upon the petition of one or more creditors at least one of whom must be a resident of a state different from the debtor's. To give the federal court jurisdiction the petition must represent claims in excess of $3,000. Any creditor desiring to intervene in the proceeding may do so by filing a notice of intervention, after which he is entitled to notice of all subsequent proceedings.

The receiver is simply an officer of the court, subject to the control of the court and with limited discretionary powers. He is at all times subject to the orders and directions of the court. He must be indifferent to the interests of the parties involved. He operates the business or liquidates it for the benefit of both owner and creditors. He should have some knowledge of the kind of business for which he is receiver. Sometimes the court may appoint more than one receiver, in which case one of the receivers is often the owner of the business, a partner, or a member of the corporation, as the case may be. A principal creditor may be appointed. Frequently, the creditors assist in managing a business or are in close cooperation with the management. A receiver is not personally responsible for his official acts, but he is liable for any fraud or negligence of his own whereby injury accrues to the property intrusted to him.

The fees allowed the receiver and his attorney are set in the discretion of the court, with the result that there appears to be a considerable divergence in fees of different cases. The amount allowed is frequently in excess of the corresponding fees allowed in bankruptcy. Equity courts require receivers to render strict account of the receivership, and the responsibility does not cease until the receiver is discharged by the court.

Creditors' Rights in Equity Receiverships. Receivership does not materially change the nature of the legal rights of creditors. It does, however, suspend those rights. Since the power of possession of the receiver is derived from the court, no unauthorized interference with the receivership will be tolerated by the court. A creditor may not enforce his legal rights except by express permission of the court. A creditor who brings an action in one court against a receiver appointed by another court without the consent of the latter court is guilty of contempt of that court. Even though a creditor may suffer damage by the delay, he may not be permitted to sue on the ground that the greater rights of all are superior to the interests of the individual. Creditors have a right to examine all books, documents, and papers in the hands of the receiver.

Suit may be permitted by the court to determine the validity of a doubtful account.

As business is frequently continued under a receivership, creditors are interested to know where the liabilities for debts contracted under the receivership lie. Any person contracting with a receiver should satisfy himself that there are sufficient assets in the hands of the receiver to satisfy the liabilities which the receiver in his official capacity is assuming. Furthermore, it should be determined that the receiver is acting strictly within the limits of the power granted to him by the court. The liability of a receiver is official and not personal, except where he is personally at fault. A judgment obtained against him in his official capacity creates no personal liability. A receiver will be protected in any act done under the orders of and according to the direction of the court, and the court order under which he acts will be a complete defense to personal liability in any action or proceeding. But if he goes beyond his instructions, he will be personally responsible.

The creditor's right against the debtor continues after the receivership has been terminated. No discharge of the debtor from debts or liabilities is obtainable in either federal or state receivership proceedings.

The Bankruptcy Receivership. The receivership in bankruptcy is referred to in this chapter principally for the purpose of emphasizing the distinction between the equity receivership and the bankruptcy receivership. Both are receivers, and both function under the direct supervision of the court, but the courts are different, and the laws under which they act are different, though the same judge may preside over both. The two receivers do not function at the same time. The equity receiver may be succeeded by a receiver in bankruptcy, the usual result if the debtor is insolvent, while the successor to the receiver in bankruptcy is the trustee. Furthermore, the aim, whether accomplished or not, of the equity receiver is usually to conserve and protect the assets with the view to returning them ultimately to those entitled to them.

The purpose of bankruptcy is the liquidation of the estate. There are two forms of corporations which, though they may be insolvent, are always administered, or liquidated, in a court of equity. They are insurance and banking corporations. The reason for this is that, as stated in the previous section, the equity receivership does not discharge the debtor from his or its liabilities, while bankruptcy, if the provisions of the act are complied with, does provide a discharge of the bankrupt. It is held to be contrary to public policy to absolve the corporations specified from their liabilities. Other distinctions in these two forms of receivership will be made more apparent with a study of the bankruptcy act and bankruptcy procedure.

TEXT AND RESEARCH QUESTIONS

1. Why is it advisable for creditors to act cooperatively in handling cases of insolvency?

2. What is the distinction between the two common conceptions of insolvency?

3. Why are business adjustments of cases of insolvency preferable to adjustments by court action?

4. *a.* What two questions should be answered in the affirmative before the creditor assents to an extension?

   b. Are extensions usually satisfactory remedies?

5. *a.* What is the consideration in an extension agreement that gives it the form of a contract between debtor and creditors?

   b. State two reasons why creditors often refuse to sign an extension agreement. Are these reasons justifiable?

6. *a.* Why is it usually necessary for all the creditors to sign the composition agreement?

   b. Why is it difficult to determine what would be an equitable composition?

7. What caution should be observed in accepting notes under either the extension or composition agreement?

8. Why is assignment for benefit of creditors so frequently followed by bankruptcy proceedings?

9. *a.* What is the distinction between a receivership in equity and a receivership in bankruptcy?

   b. What caution should a seller observe in selling goods to a receivership?

   c. Under what conditions would you approve the continuance of a business by a receiver in bankruptcy?

PROBLEMS

1. The X Company, conducting a department store, has become very slow pay and some creditors have begun to threaten to take drastic action. Suits resulting in judgments would greatly hamper the management in its operations, if they did not precipitate bankruptcy. Your concern is the largest creditor. You, the credit manager, have analyzed the situation and found that the concern has a large amount of overdue accounts, and is heavily stocked with merchandise. To add to the difficulty it is learned that the street where the business is located is being repaved. The concern has been in business 18 years and is well regarded. You have examined the accounts payable ledger and have found there are 29 creditors of less than $100 each whose claims aggregate $1,508 while there are 18 creditors whose claims aggregate $19,420. The bank loan of $10,000 is secured.

Draw up (*a*) a plan for handling the situation and (*b*) present the difficulties likely to be encountered together with (*c*) your arguments in support of the plan.

2. The Peerless Manufacturing Company, Inc., is in financial difficulty.   It called a meeting of creditors who chose a creditors' committee directed to investigate the affairs of the company and report at a subsequent creditors' meeting.   A C.P.A. chosen by the creditors' committee has submitted the following Statement of Affairs:

ASSETS

Current Assets:

Cash in Bank	$ 250.00	
Accounts Receivable—net	8,643.00	
Merchandise Inventory (estimated)	24,000.00	
Total Current Assets		$32,893.00

Other Assets:

Machinery and Equipment	27,048.00	
Furniture and Fixtures	500.00	
Delivery Equipment	1,200.00	
Due from Officers	5,889.55	
Insurance—Unexpired (estimated)	300.00	
Total Other Assets		34,937.55
Total Assets		$67,830.55

LIABILITIES AND CAPITAL

Current Liabilities:

Priority Claims

New York City Excise and Sales Taxes	$ 2,440.67	
Federal Excise and Old Age Benefit Taxes	1,109.54	
New York State Unemployment Insurance Taxes	902.44	
Payroll Accrued and State Insurance Fund	2,619.49	
Total Priority Claims		$ 7,072.14

Unsecured Claims

Accounts Payable	20,589.62	
Loans Payable—		
Mr. X	5,870.00	
Mr. Y	4,000.00	
Rent and Interest Payable	1,388.95	
Total Unsecured Claims		31,848.57
Total Liabilities		$38,920.71

The company wishes to remain in business and has offered an *arrangement* under which all claims of less than $50 (amounting to $4,850) are to be paid in full at once and the remaining claims are to be paid 5 per cent cash and 2½ per cent monthly until fully paid.   The Loans Payable totaling $9,870 are to be subordinated.   The officers of the corporation, who are the owners, have agreed to put in $10,000 cash for which stock will be issued.   Assuming the arrangement offered will be accepted draw up a Giving Effect statement of the corporation.   Comment on the Giving Effect statement from a creditor's viewpoint.

3. A manufacturer of wire novelties is in bankruptcy due largely to incompetence, or a wrong policy, in the management of his business.   He had two

competitors in his field. A large manufacturer of wire is a creditor for $20,000. The debtor has offered an arrangement of 25 per cent, one-half cash and one-half notes. Liquidation by bankruptcy will yield approximately 10 per cent. No question of fraud is involved, and 25 per cent seems to be all the debtor would be justified in offering.

Should the credit manager of the wire company accept the arrangement or should he insist upon liquidation through bankruptcy? What circumstances or conditions would cause him (1) to accept the arrangement or (2) to insist upon bankruptcy?

Make any assumptions you please, and base your answers on your assumptions.

CHAPTER 30

BANKRUPTCY

The Bankruptcy law is a federal law. With its present amendments it provides the creditors of an insolvent estate with the machinery for prompt and efficient realization and pro rata distribution of the debtor's assets. The law also provides, as alternatives to the above, the means to effect either an arrangement[1] or, in the case of a corporation, a reorganization. It also provides that the debtor may, under certain conditions, secure a discharge from his debts.

The law has the threefold purpose of safeguarding the interests of all the creditors, relieving honest debtors from debts which they cannot pay, and benefiting society at large. It safeguards the interests of creditors by preventing preferential payments and by preventing a small minority of creditors from blocking a settlement favored by the majority. It holds in abeyance other legal means of collections which might be resorted to otherwise and which would involve both debtor and creditors in constant litigation. In fact, such a condition existed prior to the enactment of the present law. A suit on a debt, if the debtor was not in the strongest credit position, was a signal for all creditors to rush in and obtain judgments, for judgments had preference in execution according to the order in which they were filed. The first to file judgments, therefore, often received 100 per cent settlement, while creditors filing later judgments received nothing.

The law, mainly through amendments the latest of which became effective Aug. 23, 1958, strives further to safeguard the interest of creditors. A small minority of creditors may be prevented from forcing a liquidation. As an alternative to liquidation, a means to a continuation of the business through an arrangement or reorganization is presented. When

---

[1] The Bankruptcy Act defines an Arrangement as "any plan of a debtor for the settlement, satisfaction, or extension of the time of payment of his unsecured debts, upon any terms." Real Property Arrangements affecting secured creditors are also provided for.

482

a debtor has become insolvent, that is, when his assets are less than his liabilities, he has lost his equity, and the assets really belong to creditors —all creditors. The law as now amended gives fuller recognition to the principle of majority rule.

A second purpose of the Act is to give relief to an honest debtor. A debtor who has turned over all his property as required by law to his creditors has discharged his legal obligation to them. He may go forth with the knowledge that whatever he may subsequently produce is his. Thus, he has an incentive to begin anew. Were the condition otherwise, he would feel that his future was mortgaged, that, strive as he might, the fruit of his labor would go only to enrich others. Only the most courageous would under such circumstances become producers. The weaker debtors would, in many cases, become burdens upon friends and relatives, or even mendicants and public charges.

It is plain to be seen that the public at large benefits by bankruptcy legislation. Credit is approved with greater confidence, and there is less nervousness upon the part of creditors when the weak position of a debtor is recognized. This confidence promotes industry. Society, too, is benefited by the provision of the discharge of the debtor which encourages him to remain a producer rather than to become a burden on society in general. Knowing that such fair treatment will be accorded him, he is less inclined to dishonesty when he realizes that failure is impending. A third purpose of bankruptcy legislation, therefore, is seen in this protection of society in general.

The Credit Executive's Interest in Bankruptcy. There are a number of reasons why the credit executive should make a careful study of both the Bankruptcy law and bankruptcy procedure. To safeguard the creditor's interest is as much the credit executive's duty as is the selection of credit risks. A knowledge of Bankruptcy law is, therefore, as essential as is an analytical ability in the interpretation of financial statements. The Bankruptcy law is complex and technical and therefore challenges the credit executive's interest. Moreover, the bankruptcy courts provide a battleground where interests of debtor and creditors may clash and under whose rules the issue must be finally fought out.

Ideal as the law itself is in purpose, and it must be remembered that it is the result of centuries of laws and experience, in practice it frequently falls far short of the ideal at which it aims. While criticism will be withheld until the main provisions of the law have been discussed, the reader should have in mind the dissatisfaction with any bankruptcy law and proceed with the study of it from a critical point of view. Still another reason for the executive's interest in the Bankruptcy law is that the law is primarily a creditors' law. Throughout the Act it is provided that the creditors shall control the procedure in so far as possible. Naturally, the credit executive should be thoroughly familiar with the tool with which he works.

Bankruptcy Laws of the United States. When our early statesmen prepared and adopted our great Constitution they wisely provided in Section 8, Article I, Clause of the Constitution, that "the Congress shall have power . . . to establish . . . uniform laws on the subject of Bankruptcies throughout the United States."

We have had four Bankruptcy Acts in the life of our nation, with lapses in between when the handling of insolvencies has been left to the various states. The fourth act is still in force, though there have been movements to have it repealed. It was enacted July 1, 1898, and has been amended at average intervals of four years since its enactment. The amendment known as the Chandler Act became effective Sept. 22, 1938. Through this amendment the Act received its most thorough revision in the 40 years of its life.

All the states have enacted insolvency laws, but these laws are inoperative as long as there is a federal act in existence. With a repeal of the federal law the various state laws would control liquidations within their respective jurisdictions. It is the federal law known as the Chandler Act to which the remainder of this chapter will be largely devoted.

The "Depression Amendments." During 1933 and 1934, several amendments of the Bankruptcy law were enacted designed to alleviate the condition of debtors of several classes. While, as has been stated, a main function of the Bankruptcy law was to provide the machinery for the liquidation of the insolvent debtor's assets, the amendments had as their main purpose the prevention of a forced liquidation. This purpose was to be accomplished through extensions, compositions, and reorganizations. While there has long been dissatisfaction with the Bankruptcy law, and many different agencies have been working upon improvements of it, the "depression amendments" were somewhat hurriedly forced through Congress. Ambiguities, contradictions, and uncertainties were the result, not only of the numerous previous amendments of the Act, but also of the hurried tinkering to meet the exigencies of the mid-depression period. It was to correct these recognized faults that the Act was given a thorough overhauling. Undoubtedly the perfect law has not yet been framed. Time and experience, as well as inevitable change in economic conditions, will ever call for frequent revisions. To one interested in the history of bankruptcy legislation, the Chandler Act presents a further and interesting development. Stress has shifted from a law designed to liquidate an insolvent business to one designed to avoid the liquidation of a business. It is an attempt to maintain the production and the employment of the owners and employees of an insolvent business.

Options under the Law. The Chandler Act provides the debtor with several options. The individual debtor may be adjudicated a bankrupt and his estate liquidated, or he may bring about an arrangement of his affairs under Chapter XI of the Act. If the individual debtor is burdened with debts secured by real property, special procedure is provided in Chapter XII, which permits a settlement, satisfaction, or extension of such debts. Partnerships have the same options available to them with a section of the law (Section 5) clarifying questions peculiar to a partnership.

If the debtor be a wage earner, he may voluntarily file a petition in bankruptcy and later secure a discharge from his debts, or he may avail himself of the special provisions of Chapter XII under which he may arrive at an agreement with his creditors both secured and unsecured for a settlement of his debts out of future earnings.

The Chandler Act gives a debtor corporation options depending upon its circumstances. It may be liquidated under regular bankruptcy proceedings or it may effect an arrangement under Chapter XI of the Act. If, because of the complexity of its case, it cannot secure adequate relief under the provision for arrangements it may reorganize under the provisions of Chapter X.

Obviously, any procedure other than liquidation of any type of debtor must have creditor assent as provided by the law. These various options are covered by subsequent sections of this chapter.

Who May Become Bankrupt. Although our laws have never drawn a distinction between traders and nontraders, not every debtor, even though he be insolvent, has the privilege of becoming a bankrupt. The restriction, however, applies to only five classes of corporations, namely, municipal, railroad, insurance, or banking corporations or building and loan associations. These corporations, obviously, may become insolvent, and their assets entirely liquidated, but not by bankruptcy procedure or through the bankruptcy courts. These five classes of corporations are never legally discharged from their obligations. Because of their quasi-public nature it is held contrary to public policy to permit them to seek the certain privileges accorded to a bankrupt. Any person, partnership, corporation (except as noted), etc., may become a voluntary bankrupt.

Anyone who may become a voluntary bankrupt may be made an involuntary bankrupt, with the following exceptions: A wage earner or a farmer cannot be thrown into bankruptcy. Another requirement is that the indebtedness must aggregate at least $1,000. Furthermore, the involuntary bankrupt must have performed one or more of the six definite acts which constitute bankruptcy within 4 months prior to the date on which the petition is filed.

Involuntary bankruptcy originates with the filing of a petition with the federal court by three or more creditors whose claims aggregate $500 or over; or, if all creditors are less than twelve in number, one creditor with a claim of $500 may file the petition. The petition filed by the creditors in an involuntary action alleges the commission of one or more of the acts of bankruptcy, and the petitioners pray that the debtor be adjudged by the court to be a bankrupt within the purview of said acts. While in credit practice a debtor is said to be a bankrupt as soon as a petition is filed, as a matter of fact he is not a bankrupt until so adjudged by the court, but when adjudged, his bankruptcy dates not from the date of his adjudication, but from that of the petition.

The Acts of Bankruptcy. As indicated above, a state of bankruptcy is created by the filing of a petition which alleges the commission of one or more of the six acts of bankruptcy within 4 months of such filing. In a voluntary action, the filing of the petition itself constitutes an act of bankruptcy, namely, act 6. The mere insolvency, no matter how serious, of a debtor does not give creditors the right to have him adjudicated a bankrupt. But it will be seen from the acts that they provide a means whenever insolvency exists to force the debtor to commit an act of bankruptcy and thus to bring the administration of his estate into the bankruptcy court.

Insolvency, as will be seen by the acts themselves, is a prerequisite to most of the acts of bankruptcy. It should, therefore, be clearly defined. According to Section 1, Article 19:

. . . a person shall be deemed insolvent within the provisions of this Act whenever the aggregate of his property, exclusive of any property which he may have conveyed, transferred, concealed, or removed, or permitted to be concealed or removed, with intent to defraud, hinder, or delay his creditors, shall not, at a fair valuation, be sufficient in amount to pay his debts.

The intent and meaning of some of the acts themselves is somewhat obscure. They will, therefore, be briefly commented on when necessary and are as follows:

First:

Concealed, removed, or permitted to be concealed, or removed, any part of his property with intent to hinder, delay, or defraud his creditors, or any of them, or made or suffered a transfer of any of his property, fraudulent under the provisions of Sections 67 or 70 of this Act.[1]

[1] Section 67 covers Liens and Fraudulent Transfers, and Section 70, Title to Property. Transfers fraudulent and voidable under these sections now constitute an act of bankruptcy.

Solvency is a good defense, but the burden of proving it is on the alleged bankrupt. For the 4 months' limitation period, the date of the transfer begins to run when the transferee has perfected his title.[1]

Second:

Made or suffered a preferential transfer, as defined in subdivision A of Section 60 of this Act.

A preference obtains when the debtor, *while insolvent,* transfers any part of his property, within the 4 months' period, to any of his creditors with the result that such creditor, knowing or having reasonable cause to believe the debtor insolvent, receives a greater percentage of his claim than other creditors of the same class. If the debtor claims solvency he has the burden of proving it.

Third:

Suffered or permitted, while insolvent, any creditor to obtain a lien upon any of his property through legal proceedings or distraint and not having vacated or discharged such lien within 30 days from the date thereof or at least 5 days before the date set for any sale or other disposition of such property.

This would result in depleting an insolvent debtor's estate, to the benefit of the creditor obtaining the preference and to the detriment of all other creditors. This act either enables a creditor to collect by means of a judgment or other lien or furnishes a cause for filing a petition in bankruptcy. The insolvent debtor may succeed in staying bankruptcy proceedings for a time, but his principal method of preventing a sale or other disposition of property after a judgment is taken is by an appeal to a higher court. Eventually, the creditors will prevail.

Nor can a creditor obtain a lien and, through no attempt to enforce it, let it ripen after 4 months' time into an unassailable preference. This act effectively deals with the creditor who would obtain an advantage over other creditors.

Fourth:

Made a general assignment for the benefit of his creditors.

Many insolvent debtors though realizing the necessity of liquidation seek to avoid the stigma of the term "bankruptcy." Were it not for the fourth act of bankruptcy, a debtor could manipulate the liquidation of his own estate by making an assignment to one friendly to him although ostensibly for the benefit of creditors. In order to make the Bankruptcy Act supreme over all laws for the liquidation of insolvent estates,

[1] See footnote page 154.

an attempt to circumvent bankruptcy becomes an act of bankruptcy. It is immaterial whether the debtor is solvent or insolvent.

Fifth:

While insolvent or unable to pay his debts as they mature, procured, permitted, or suffered voluntarily or involuntarily the appointment of a receiver or trustee to take charge of his property.

The purpose of this act is largely the same as the purpose of the fourth act. The Bankruptcy law provides the plans for liquidation, reorganization of corporations, or the arrangement of the debts of any type of a debtor. These two acts make it impossible for a debtor to circumvent the will of the creditors who may wish to avail themselves of the machinery thus provided.

Sixth:

Admitted in writing his inability to pay his debts and his willingness to be adjudged a bankrupt.

This act needs no explanation. It is often a means of entering by an involuntary procedure what is virtually voluntary bankruptcy.

Trial. Involuntary bankruptcy is a court action in which the debtor is made the defendant. Accordingly, the alleged bankrupt is served with a copy of the petition in bankruptcy and a summons to appear at court. The debtor may contend that he is solvent, that he has committed no act of bankruptcy, that the court has no jurisdiction, or that the allegation of the petitioning creditors is untrue. He may demand a trial by jury to determine his solvency. Generally, however, he will not appear, and the court will sign the decree upon default. The debtor thus becomes adjudicated a bankrupt by default.

Duties of the Bankrupt. In general, it may be said that the duties of the bankrupt are to render such assistance as he can in the liquidation of his estate, although he has no direct part in the liquidation. His exact duties are eleven in number, as specified in Section 7. Chief among them are to attend the first meeting of creditors; to prepare and file in court within 5 days after adjudication, if an involuntary bankrupt, and with his petition if a voluntary bankrupt, a schedule of his property showing amount, kind, location, and value and a list of his creditors showing addresses and amounts due each;[1] to submit to an examination concerning the conducting of his business at such times as the court may direct; and, finally, to comply with all lawful orders of the court. It is, of course, his duty to turn over to the receiver or the

---

[1] The court may, for cause shown, grant further time for filing schedules of property provided a schedule of creditors is filed as above set forth.

trustee all his property, except that which may be exempt according to state law.

Once the bankrupt has surrendered his property and filed his schedules in bankruptcy, his participation in the affair is over, except as he may be called upon by the court, or by creditors through the court, for information.

Discharge in Bankruptcy. One of the cardinal principles of bankruptcy liquidation is the discharge of the debtor from his legal debts upon surrender of his property. But the privilege had been much abused under the old law. The Chandler Act endeavors not only to speed up discharge, but it takes the initiative away from the debtor, except in the case of a corporation, and gives the right to oppose discharge not only to creditors but to the trustee and to the United States attorney. Furthermore, the court itself may initiate action by directing the United States attorney to examine into the actions of the debtor to see if there are grounds for refusing discharge. A corporation may apply for a discharge within 6 months after its adjudication and adjudication itself operates as an application for discharge (unless the right is waived) of any other debtor. The law recognizes the debtor's wish to emerge from his unsuccessful venture financially a free man. The creditors, on their part, can interpose no objections if the debtor's conduct has been beyond reproach.

Reasons for Denial of Discharge. The lethargy of creditors, whose duty it was under the old Act to oppose discharge, had become notorious. Thus it was comparatively easy for the unscrupulous as well as the honest debtor to become discharged of his obligations and re-enter business. Now he must evade not only the watchfulness of his creditors but that of the trustee, the prosecuting attorney, and the court, which includes the referee. All, including the debtor, are notified when a hearing upon the subject of discharge is to be held. If any objector shows that there are reasonable grounds for believing the debtor has committed any of the acts which would prevent his discharge in bankruptcy, the burden of proving he has not committed any of such acts falls upon the bankrupt.

The seven reasons for refusing a discharge are of sufficient importance to be given in detail. They are as follows: (1) committed an offense punishable by imprisonment as herein provided; (2) destroyed, mutilated, falsified, concealed, or failed to keep books of account or records from which his financial condition and business transactions might be ascertained, unless the court deem such failure or acts to have been justified, under all the circumstances of the case; (3) obtained money or property on credit or obtained an extension or renewal of credit, by making or publishing or causing to be made or published, in any manner whatsoever, a materially false statement in writing respecting his financial condition; (4) at any time, subsequent to the first day of the 12 months immediately preceding the filing of the petition transferred, removed, destroyed, or concealed, or permitted to be removed, destroyed, or concealed, any of his property, with intent to hinder, delay, or defraud his creditors; (5) has, within 6 years prior to bankruptcy, been granted a discharge, or had a composition or an agreement by way of composition or a wage earner's plan by way of composition confirmed under this Act; (6) in the course of the proceedings under this Act refused to obey any lawful order of, or to answer any material question approved by, the court; or (7) has failed to explain, satisfactorily, any losses of assets or deficiency of assets to meet his liabilities.

Officers and Their Duties. While the administration of the Bankruptcy Act is highly technical and is the more involved because of the almost numberless situations that can arise under it and with which the courts must deal, it is, nevertheless, simple in its general plan and purpose. The legal questions which may arise are to be solved by legal experts, but the credit man should be thoroughly familiar with the general procedure and with the various officers and their duties in the liquidation of a bankrupt's estate. The officials are usually only four in number: the court (judge), the referee, the receiver, and the trustee.

The Court. The administration as well as the interpretation of the law is under the jurisdiction of the court. The district courts of the several states and possessions, which are presided over by federal judges, constitute courts of bankruptcy. The court takes no part in the detailed administration of a case in bankruptcy, but the entire administration of a case by referee and trustee is subject always to a review by the judge.

The Referee. The referee is the court's officer created for the purpose of relieving the court of the ordinary details which arise in the conduct of every case. Such a number of referees as may be necessary are appointed by a concurrence of judges of a bankruptcy court, or by the senior judge of the court. Appointment is for a period of six years. Referees may be full-time or part-time appointees. Among the qualifications for the office the referee must be a resident of the district, not a relative of any of the judges of the courts of bankruptcy or of the judges of the Appellate Courts of the districts for which he is appointed, and a member of the bar of the district in which he is to function.

Referees may, under the jurisdiction given them, adjudicate or dismiss petitions referred to them, examine witnesses and compel the production of documents; in the absence of the judge, exercise his powers for taking possession or releasing the property of the bankrupt; grant, deny, or revoke discharges; and, in fact, perform the duties of courts of bankruptcy except as limited by the Act.

Among the more important of the referee's duties are the following:

1. Give notice to creditors and other parties in interest.
2. Prepare and file schedules of property and lists of creditors required to be filed by bankrupts or cause the same to be done.
3. Examine all schedules of property, lists of creditors, and statements of affairs, and, if defective, cause them to be amended.
4. Furnish information as requested by parties in interest.
5. Declare dividends and cause to be prepared dividend sheets.
6. Keep all the records incident to the administration of the Act.

Referees shall not act in cases in which they are in any way interested, practice as attorneys in any bankruptcy proceedings, nor purchase any property of an estate in bankruptcy.

Full-time referees receive as full compensation for their services not more than $12,500, and part-time referees not more than $6,000, per annum. Funds for referees' salaries and expenses are raised through filing fees collected by the clerk of the court. Upon the filing of a petition the clerk collects $17 for the referee's salary account and $15 for the referee's expense account. In cases of voluntary bankruptcy these fees may be paid in instalments. Additional fees for these funds are charged in accordance with the schedule of fees fixed by the conference of senior circuit judges. These fees are fixed so that the funds collected will, as near as may be, fit the amount paid out as salaries and expenses. All fees collected are paid into the U.S. Treasury and salaries and expenses are paid out of such funds by the United States.

The Receiver. It is the duty of the trustee to liquidate the bankrupt's assets, but, since he is elected by the creditors, some time must necessarily elapse between the filing of the petition and the qualification of the trustee to act. In the meantime the debtor might abandon the property. Certainly, in some instances, it would not be to the creditors' interest to permit him to remain in possession of his assets. The court, therefore, is empowered[1] to

. . . appoint, upon application of parties in interest, receivers or the marshals to take charge of the property of bankrupts and to protect the interests of creditors after the filing of the petition and until it is dismissed or the trustee is qualified . . . . Provided, however, that the court shall be satisfied that such appointment or authorization is necessary to preserve the estate or to prevent loss thereto.

Authorize the business of bankrupts to be conducted for limited periods by receivers, the marshals, or trustees, if necessary in the best interests of the estates, . . .

[1] Section 2 (3) (5).

One of the greatest abuses under the former statute was the maladministration of the estate by receivers who had obtained authority to conduct or sell the business. It was common practice for receivers to ask for this authority under such pretexts as the necessity for speedy liquidation because of high rents and other charges or because of the decline in value of the estate if liquidation must await the appointment of a trustee. A period of at least 20 days between the filing of an involuntary petition in bankruptcy must elapse according to the statute, and the time may be lengthened to 40 or more days, before the trustee is elected. Consequently, when the trustee was appointed to liquidate the estate there was often nothing for him to do.

The Fees of the Receiver as Prescribed by Law. These fees are based on sums turned over by the receiver for the estate and, if the receiver acts with full powers, are as follows:

10 per cent on the first $500 or less
6 per cent on sums in excess of $500 but less than $1,500
3 per cent on sums of $1,500 but less than $10,000
2 per cent on sums of $10,000 but not more than $25,000
1 per cent on sums in excess of $25,000

If the receiver acts merely as custodian, his maximum fees are:

2 per cent on the first $1,000 or less
½ per cent on all above $1,000 disbursed by him or turned over to lienholders or trustee

The court may allow a lesser fee in either case.

The Trustee. In theory, at least, the trustee is the most important officer to the creditors of all the bankruptcy officers. It was plainly the intent of the framers of the Act that the creditors should control the liquidation of the estate, subject, of course, to the rules of the Act. This was to be accomplished by their appointment of the trustee. To the trustee was delegated the task of converting the assets into cash and, as his title indicates, to act generally in the interests of creditors. It is obvious that the size of dividends depends first upon getting possession of all the debtor's property and then getting the most possible for it and with the least expense. As the creditors' representative, that is what the trustee is expected to accomplish. Hence, no more important duty devolves upon a credit man in a bankruptcy case than to participate in the election of a competent trustee. Participation by the creditor includes the active use of his influence with his fellow creditors as well as a mere registering of his vote.

The trustee is elected at the first meeting of creditors by a majority vote in number and amount of claims of all creditors whose claims have been allowed and are represented in person or by proxy. Fights for control of the liquidation of estates occur at the first meeting of creditors. But little can be done by creditors after they have permitted a sharp and dishonest attorney to get control of the estate, beyond keeping his actions and fees within reasonable bounds. On the other hand, if a trustee of the right type is elected, little need be done by creditors. The trustee will protect their interests. Before the trustee can serve, he must qualify by furnishing a bond as stipulated by the court. The trustee is discharged by the court after he has wound up the affairs of the estate.

Like the fees of the other officers, those of the trustee are fixed by statute. The trustee receives a fee of $5 which is a part of the fee paid by the petitioning creditors, except when such a fee is not required. He also receives a commission on what is paid to creditors. These fees are at the same rate as for receivers. If the above commissions should total less than $100 the court may allow the trustee an additional sum which, with his commission, shall not exceed $100.

If the trustee is authorized to conduct the business he may be paid such sums as are allowed by the court but not to exceed the amount allowed for "normal administration."

Creditors' Committees. While it is the function of the trustee to serve the interests of the creditors, in practice there had been no effective method of creditor cooperation with him. The 1938 amendment provides:

creditors may, at their first meeting, also appoint a committee of not less than three creditors, which committee may consult and advise with the trustee in connection with the administration of the estate, make recommendations to the trustee in the performance of his duties and submit to the court any question affecting the administration of the estate.

Thus creditors' committees have, for the first time, an official standing in court. The beneficial results of this provision will depend in any given case upon the committee selected by the creditors and upon the court.

Provable and Allowable Claims. One of the purposes of the Bankruptcy law is the promotion of business. Therefore any business debt incurred by the borrowing of money, the purchase of goods, and the hiring of services which was owing at the time the petition was filed may be proved. A creditor may prove such claims even though they are unliquidated; that is, the claim or its amount is uncertain or in dispute, provided the creditor proceeds with liquidation as directed by the court.

Unliquidated claims based upon a mere tort, such as libel and slander or assault and battery or the violation of any personal right, are not provable. If the claim is of such a nature as to permit the waiver of the tort, however, and recover upon an implied contract, it is provable in bankruptcy. If, prior to the filing of the petition, the liability was fixed by being reduced to judgment it is provable.

When a person is contingently liable with the bankrupt, such as the endorser of a note or the giver of a guarantee, such endorser or guarantor is entitled to share in the bankrupt's estate as a creditor. He may, therefore, prove his claim in the name of a creditor to whom he is liable or, if the creditor's name is unknown, in his own name. If the creditor elects to prove the claim, it cannot be proved also by the person contingently liable, such as the guarantor or endorser.

If a creditor holds security, such security must be converted into cash according to the terms of agreement or as the court may direct. If the security brings less than the claim, the creditor is entitled to dividends as a general or unsecured creditor upon the unpaid balance.

A distinction should be drawn between provable claims and allowable claims. Not all claims which are provable may be allowable or, if allowed, may be allowed in full. To be allowable a claim must be, first of all, provable and filed in proper form. For instance, a creditor who has received a voidable preference, though he may have a provable claim, will not have preference or preferences. And when a creditor holds security, his claim is allowable only after the value of the security has been determined and deducted from his claim.

Filing Proof of Claims. The filing of the creditor's proof of claim is his most important duty in a bankruptcy action. Unless the claim is filed, the creditor can neither share in the dividends paid nor participate in the election of a trustee. Yet creditors often neglect this important and simple act for the protection of their own interests. Unless the claim is an unliquidated one or complicated for some other reason, the filing of it is a simple matter. A creditor should supply himself with the necessary forms which may be obtained at any law stationers. The filing is accomplished by filling out the form, attaching to it an itemized statement and whatever instruments in writing it may be founded upon, if any, and forwarding it to the referee. In order to ensure its receipt with the referee, either registered mail should be used or the creditor may enclose an addressed and stamped envelope and ask for a receipt. When the claim is filed, provided it be an allowable one, the creditor is ensured his share of any dividends that may be paid. He has, however, an implied obligation to participate in any activity of the creditors undertaken to protect their interests.

Creditors are warned against giving their claims to unknown attorneys to file. It is a very common practice for attorneys wishing to control a bankruptcy liquidation to offer to file a creditor's claim without charge. The forms submitted by such attorneys invariably contain a power of attorney authorizing the attorney to act for the creditor. The attorney files the proof of claim and then votes the claim, not as the creditor probably would vote if present in person, but to accomplish his own not always honorable design. Liquidation under the control of such an attorney frequently is expensive and inefficient. Less is therefore available for creditors, and, furthermore, dividends are paid through the attorney, who deducts a fee for collection before remitting to the creditor. Occasionally, a creditor having given such a power of attorney discovers his error and regrets his action. It should be remembered that the creditor may revoke the power of attorney at any time.

The warning given in the preceding paragraph naturally would not apply to claims which might be referred to the creditor's regular counsel. However, the services of counsel are in the majority of cases unnecessary. The creditor or his credit man should have sufficient knowledge of bankruptcy procedure to see that his rights are protected. Nor does the warning apply to reputable creditor's committees or to recognized adjustment bureaus fostered by creditors. Such bureaus or committees have no ulterior motive in the solicitation of claims. Indeed, their solicitation is frequently for the express purpose of preventing control getting into the hands of one or more attorneys. To cooperate with such a bureau or committee is usually to ensure the election of a more competent trustee and to ensure a more businesslike administration of the bankrupt's estate.

Claims must be proved within 6 months after the first date set for the first meeting of creditors. The court may, however, for cause shown, grant a reasonable extension of time for filing claims.

Order of Priority. Creditors may be divided into two general classes: secured and unsecured. The secured creditors have a lien upon specific assets. If the security is not sufficient to cover the claim, the creditor becomes a general creditor for the balance. The unsecured creditors may be further subdivided into the two classes of preferred and general creditors. The general creditors will share in the estate only after the secured and preferred creditors have been paid in full. Nor does the law recognize equality among the preferred creditors. It stipulates that certain debts shall be paid in full in advance of the payments of dividends to creditors and in the following order: (1) the actual and necessary cost of preserving the estate subsequent to filing the petition; the fees for the referee's salary and expense funds; the filing fees paid by creditors in involuntary cases, and where property of the bankrupt, transferred or concealed by him either before or after the filing of the petition, shall have been recovered for the benefit of the estate or the bankrupt by the efforts and at the expense of one or more creditors, the reasonable expense of such recovery; the cost of administration, including the trustee's expenses in opposing the bankrupt's discharge, the fees and mileage payable to witnesses as now or hereafter provided by the laws of the United States, and one reasonable attorney's fee, for the professional services actually rendered, irrespective of the number of attorneys employed, to the petitioning creditors in involuntary cases, while performing the duties herein prescribed, and to the bankrupt in voluntary and involuntary cases, as the court may allow. (2) Wages due workmen, clerks, traveling or city salesmen, or servants which have been earned within 3 months before the date of the commencement of proceedings, not to exceed $600 to each claimant. (3) Reasonable costs of creditors who have prevented discharge or caused its revocation, or produced evidence resulting in the bankrupt's conviction for a criminal offense under the Act. (4) Taxes due and owing, the amount and legality of which is determined by the court. (5) Debts entitled to priority under the laws of the United States, but not debts entitled to priority under State Law, except that where a landlord may have priority by State Law for rent, priority is recognized for rent owing for use and occupancy within three months prior to the bankruptcy.

In the event of the confirmation of an arrangement being set aside, or a discharge revoked, debts contracted subsequent to the arrangement or the debtor's discharge have priority and are to be paid in full in advance of the debts in the bankruptcy or arrangement proceeding.

Dischargeable Debts. Even though a bankrupt secures a discharge from bankruptcy, there may be some debts for which he is still liable. As a matter of fact, a discharge from bankruptcy does not remove any indebtedness or obligation. Such a discharge merely removes any legal method of enforcing payment. The indebtedness itself still remains, a fact that has been recognized by many bankrupts, who, although discharged, have at some later time voluntarily met the obligation in full and with interest.

As we have seen, a claim may be a just one and yet not a provable one. Such claims are outside bankruptcy jurisdiction. In other words, neither are they provable, nor is the bankrupt discharged from them. In addition to the nonprovable debts, a bankrupt is not discharged from the following provable debts: (1) amounts due as a tax levied by the United States, the state, county, district, or municipality; (2) liabilities for obtaining property by false pretenses or false representations or willful and malicious injuries to the person or property of another; or for alimony due or to become due or for maintenance or support of wife or child or for seduction of an unmarried female or for criminal conversation; (3) liabilities which have not been duly scheduled in time for proof and allowance, with the name of the creditor if known to the bankrupt, unless such creditor had notice or actual knowledge of the proceedings in bankruptcy; or (4) obligations created by his fraud, embezzlement, misappropriation, or defalcation while acting as an officer or in any fiduciary capacity; or (5) wages due to workmen, clerks, traveling or city salesmen, or servants, which have been earned within 3 months before the date of commencement of the proceedings in bankruptcy; (6) monies due to an employee received or retained by his employer to secure the faithful performance by such employee under the terms of a contract of employment.

Arrangements. The discussion of the Act thus far, the student has noted, deals with the liquidation of an insolvent debtor's estate and his discharge from his obligations. Liquidation is not always to the best interests of creditors or of society. Under the chapter on arrangements the Act provides the debtor and his creditors the medium through which any plan for the settlement, satisfaction, or extension of his unsecured debts may become effective. Since the broad purpose of the plan is to have debtor and creditors compose their difficulties by mutual agreement it would seem that the wisest procedure would be to eschew the restrictions which the law is bound to impose. The difficulty here has been the ease with which a dissenting minority could defeat an out-of-court proceeding by filing a petition in bankruptcy. Under a plan of arrangement a majority in number and amount of creditors can make the plan binding on all if it is found by the court to be fair and equitable, and the debtor has not been guilty of any of the acts which would be a bar to his discharge.

Petition for Arrangement. A debtor may file an original petition for an arrangement or he may file a petition in a pending proceeding either before or after his adjudication. The provisions of the arrangement may be filed with the petition or may be filed later within such time as fixed by the court, and action is restricted to the debtor. Modification of the plan may be made in writing by the debtor with leave of the court before or after the arrangement is confirmed. These provisions limit the creditors to working through the debtor. He must be "sold" on the plan of arrangement. Creditors cannot impose a plan upon him against his will.

Subsequent to the filing of a petition the judge may refer the proceeding to a referee, and may appoint a receiver unless a trustee is already serving in which case the trustee continues to function. The court, within ten days, calls a meeting of creditors which must be held not less than 15 days nor more than 30 days after the giving of notice. The judge or referee presides at the meeting, allows or disallows proofs of claim, examines the debtor or has him examined, and receives the written acceptances of creditors on the proposed arrangement.

The law also provides for the appointment of a receiver or trustee to distribute the consideration and fixes the time and place for the deposit of the consideration by the debtor.

The creditors may appoint a committee and nominate a trustee who will be appointed by the court if it becomes necessary to administer the estate in bankruptcy.[1]

Provisions of Arrangement. An arrangement affects only the unsecured creditors. But their rights generally, or the rights of some class of them, may be altered through the plan upon any terms or for any consideration. This is sufficiently broad to include all the forms of settlement with which creditors are familiar or which they could be induced to accept.

The unsecured debts may be treated on a parity or they may be divided into classes and treated in different ways; executory contracts may be rejected; the debtor may be allowed to continue his business with or without supervision by a receiver or committee of creditors; payments may be made on account and debts incurred after the filing of the petition may be given priority over debts affected by the arrangement; and, in fact, any provisions may be incorporated which are not inconsistent with the Act.

Confirmation of Arrangement. To become effective the arrangement must be accepted in writing by a majority in number and amount of all creditors or of each class of creditors who are affected by the plan. The arrangement does not become effective until confirmed by the court who must be satisfied that:

1. The provisions of the law have been complied with.
2. It is for the best interests of the creditors and is feasible.
3. The debtor has not been guilty of any acts which would bar a bankrupt from discharge.
4. The proposal and acceptance are in good faith.

The Act provides that the court may, under certain conditions, retain jurisdiction after the confirmation; if an arrangement is withdrawn or abandoned before acceptance the court may proceed with liquidation under bankruptcy or dismiss the proceedings, whichever may be in the interests of creditors; or, under certain conditions, set aside or modify

---

[1] By amendment effective Oct. 7, 1952, expenses of a creditors' committee, legally constituted, which were incurred either before or after the filing of the petition may be recovered provided that the services were found to have been beneficial to the estate. Prior to this amendment the only expenses allowable were those incurred *after* the official appointment of a committee, when much of the work might necessarily already have been done.

the arrangement. The 1952 amendment clarifies one point by stating that confirmation shall not be refused because the debtor retains an interest.[1] Another is clarified by the provision that if the arrangement fails and is followed by bankruptcy proceedings, the creditors' claims as affected by the arrangement shall rank on a parity with debts incurred after confirmation, unless the arrangement as confirmed provides otherwise.

Effect of Law on Arrangement. Aside from introducing court supervision the chapter on arrangements (Chapter XI) in its broad effects does not restrict creditors in their attempt to arrive at a common-sense settlement with the debtor. In fact, creditors can now negotiate with a debtor openly and unhurriedly before any action is instituted for they need not fear a nuisance-minority which, prior to the Act, could always disrupt negotiations by throwing the debtor into bankruptcy. The Act should, indeed, have the opposite effect. Since there would be no gain in throwing a debtor into bankruptcy, for negotiations could not be halted, there should be possible the effectuation of many an honest adjustment without resorting to court procedure at all.

Corporate Reorganizations. The chapter of the Bankruptcy law covering corporate reorganizations (Chapter X) proves of much less interest to unsecured, short-term creditors than did Section 77*b* of the previous act which it displaced. This is so because any corporation in difficulty could file under Section 77*b* while under the Chandler Act corporations with unsecured debts only seek relief through the chapter on arrangements (Chapter XI). An added reason is that many corporations reorganizing under Chapter X have as their main purpose a modification

---

[1] A decision which restricted the scope of arrangements by corporations was that of the United States Supreme Court in *Case v. Los Angeles Lumber Products Co.* (308 U.S. 106). The Los Angeles Lumber Products Company, an insolvent corporation, in 1937 elected to attempt to effect a reorganization under Section 77B then in force. The plan, accepted by 92.81 per cent of the bondholders, 99.75 per cent of the Class A shareholders, and 90 per cent of the Class B shareholders, was approved by the U.S. District Court of the Southern District of California, and the decision below was affirmed by the Circuit Court of Appeals for the Ninth Circuit. On appeal by a dissenting bondholder the United States Supreme Court reversed the decisions of the lower courts on the ground that the plan of reorganization was not "fair and equitable" in that the corporation was insolvent and the plan permitted the stockholders an equity in the business in violation of the doctrine of the Boyd case (*Northern Pacific Ry. v. Boyd*, 228 U.S. 482). The court held that the words "fair and equitable" import the requirement that the plan observe priority, and that no junior interest in the debtor's property may be recognized or provided for unless the net value of the assets of the debtor is greater than the total amount of the senior interests, or unless new consideration is paid for participation by the junior interest. The law, as amended, does not include the phrase "fair and equitable."

of their capital structure, and so may not include any modification of current liabilities in the reorganization plan. Since bondholders and stockholders are likely to be those chiefly affected, this chapter of the law has, however, a wide public interest.

Petitions under Chapter X. Any corporation, except a municipal corporation, which may file a petition in bankruptcy may file under Chapter X as an original action or after a petition has been filed or adjudication rendered in regular bankruptcy proceedings. Three or more creditors with claims aggregating $5,000 or over may institute an involuntary proceeding, or an indenture trustee may file under the same conditions as in a voluntary proceeding.

The petition must make a broad statement of facts including the debtor's financial condition, why relief cannot be obtained by virtue of an arrangement, and that the corporation is insolvent or unable to pay its debts as they mature. The filing fee is $100 if no bankruptcy proceeding is pending, otherwise $70. If a controverting answer is filed, the issues raised are determined by the court without jury, after which the court either approves or dismisses the petition.

Trustee or Debtor in Possession. If the indebtedness is less than $250,000, the debtor may be left in possession or a trustee may be appointed, but if the indebtedness exceeds that sum the judge must appoint one or more trustees. If more than one trustee is appointed one of them may be a director, officer, or employee of the debtor. Removal, as well as appointment of trustees, is within the jurisdiction of the judge. Among his duties the trustee must report to the judge any facts ascertained by him relating to fraud, misconduct, mismanagement, etc., and he must prepare a brief statement of the results of his investigation which he submits to creditors, stockholders, indenture trustees, and the Securities and Exchange Commission. Where a trustee has been appointed he must prepare a plan of reorganization or report why a plan cannot be effected.

Reorganization Plans. Within a time fixed by the judge, where a debtor is continued in possession, plans may be proposed by the debtor, any creditor or indenture trustee, any stockholder, provided the debtor is solvent, or the examiner if so directed by the judge. Where a trustee has been appointed it is his duty to prepare a plan. He may, of course, accept suggestions and advice of creditors and stockholders and employ experts. After the trustee's plan has been submitted, or after he has reported he is unable to prepare a plan, amendments or new plans may be proposed by the debtor, any creditor, or stockholder.

Because of the wide public interest attendant upon the reorganization of many large corporations, the Securities and Exchange Commission must have the plan, before its approval, referred to it if the indebtedness exceeds $3,000,000. If the indebtedness is less than that sum, submission to that Commission is optional. When submitted the plan cannot be approved until the Commission has filed a report or has notified the judge that it will not do so. The Commission's report is advisory only. The Commission's report will, however, carry considerable weight because of the Commission's prestige.

The judge must approve the plan or plans before submission to stockholders and creditors for acceptance, and no advance solicitation of acceptances may be made except with the consent of the court.

Before a plan can be confirmed by the judge, it must be accepted:

1. By creditors holding two-thirds in amount of the claims filed and allowed in each class.

2. If the debtor is solvent, by a majority of the stockholders of each class.

3. Provided in each instance that acceptance is not necessary by any class whose interests are not materially and adversely affected by the plan.

Provision of Plan. The plan itself has mandatory and permissive provisions. There are fourteen provisions in all, divided into nine "shall" and five "may" stipulations. They are briefly summarized as follows:

A. Mandatory provisions:
1. Modification or alteration of the rights of creditors generally, or any class of them.
2. Payment of costs and expenses.
3. Specification of claims, if any, to be paid in cash, in full.
4. Specification of the creditors or stockholders, or any class of them, not affected by the plan.
5. Adequate protection of the claims of any class of creditors affected by, but which does not accept, the plan (a) by sale or retention by the debtor of such property subject to such claims, (b) by sale of such property at not less than a fair upset price, and the transfer of such claims to the proceeds of such sale, (c) by appraisal and payment in cash of the value of such claims, or (d) by such methods as will fairly and equitably provide such protection.
6. If the debtor is solvent, protection of any class of stockholders affected by the plan but which does not accept the plan (a) by the sale of such property at not less than a fair upset price, (b) by payment in cash of the appraised value of their stock, or (c) by such method as will equitably and fairly provide such protection.
7. Provision for execution of the plan which may include (a) retention of the property by the debtor, (b) transfer of its property to one or more corporations, (c) merger or consolidation with another corporation, (d) sale of its property, at not less than a fair price to be fixed by the court and distribution of all or any proceeds of the sale among those having an interest therein, (e) the satisfaction or modification of liens, (f) the can-

cellation or modification of indentures, (*g*) the curing or waiving of defaults, (*h*) the extention of maturities and changing of interest rates or other terms of securities, (*i*) the amendment of the debtor's charter, and (*j*) the issuance of securities for any appropriate purpose.

8. Provisions covering the manner of selection of directors, officers, or voting trustees, and their successors.

9. Provision for the inclusion in the debtor's charter or corporation organized to carry out the plan of provisions (*a*) prohibiting the issuance of nonvoting stock, and for the fair and equitable distribution of voting power among the several classes of securities, (*b*) defining the terms, position, rights, and privileges of the several classes of securities including the issuance, acquisition, retirement, or redemption of such securities, and the payment of dividends thereon; and, if the debtor's indebtedness is $250,000 or over, the issuance, not less than once annually, of balance sheet and profit and loss statement.

B. Permissive provisions:

1. The plan may deal with all or any part of the debtor's property.
2. May provide for the rejection of any executory contract except contracts in the public authority.
3. Where any indebtedness under the plan is for a period of more than 5 years provisions for its retirement out of a sinking fund or otherwise, (*a*) if secured, within the useful life of the security therefor; or (*b*) if unsecured, within a specified reasonable time, not to exceed 4 years.
4. Provision for the settlement or adjustment of claims belonging to the debtor; and, for claims not provided for in the plan, shall provide for their retention and enforcement.
5. Any other provisions not inconsistent with the Act.

Confirmation of Plan. The judge shall confirm the plan if satisfied:

1. That the plan contains the mandatory provisions.
2. It is fair, equitable, and feasible.
3. The proposal and acceptance of the plan were made in good faith.
4. All payments for services, costs, and expenses have been disclosed, are reasonable, and subject to the judge's approval.
5. That the identity, qualifications, and affiliations of directors, officers, or voting trustees under the plan are fully disclosed, and that their functioning is equitable, compatible with the interests of stockholders and creditors, and consistent with public policy.

Upon confirmation all provisions become binding and enforcible whether affecting existing contracts or those to be effected under the plan.

If reorganization is not effected, the case reverts to a bankruptcy proceeding if a prior bankruptcy proceeding was pending. If, however, the reorganization proceeding was an original proceeding, the judge, after hearing and upon notice to the debtor and all parties in interest, may, in his discretion, adjudicate the debtor a bankrupt or dismiss the proceeding.

Among the provisions of the Act are the suspension of the statute of limitations, special provision for approval of plans of public utilities, permission, at the judge's discretion, of representation of the debtor's employees to be heard on the economic soundness of the plan affecting the interests of the employees, and a stipulation that the right of employees to join unions shall not be interfered with.

Wage Earners' Plans. A special voluntary proceeding is provided by Chapter XIII whereby wage earners may attempt to effect a settlement of their debts out of future earnings. Under these plans the wage earner must submit his future earnings to the supervision and control of the court which is vested with power to modify the time and amount of payments if a change in the wage earner's circumstances make such a modification necessary. Before a plan can be confirmed it must be accepted by a majority in number and amount of unsecured creditors and by all secured creditors whose interests are affected by the plan. In general, this chapter follows the procedure and theory underlying the Act.

Agricultural Compositions and Extensions. Farmers in financial distress are accorded relief under a special procedure provided under Section 75 of the Act. Relief under this section is in the form of an extension or composition. The Act permits the court to stay actions for the collection of debts whether unsecured or secured, and provides for the retention by the farmer of his property and its repurchase over an extended period of time. Conciliation Commissioners vested with many of the functions of referees may be appointed for each county having an agricultural population of 500 or more farmers. Action is voluntary only and acceptance of any plan is by a majority in number and amount of all creditors, including secured creditors whose claims are affected by the plan.

Other Provisions of the Act. Reorganization of railroads engaged in interstate commerce and the supervision of such reorganization by the Interstate Commerce Commission are provided for under Section 77 of the Bankruptcy Act. The provisions of this section, in view of their length, are not regarded as of sufficient interest to the reader to warrant their summation here.

Real Property Arrangements. The chapter of the Bankruptcy Act on arrangements (Chapter XI) excluded from its provisions secured creditors. Where interests of the secured creditors of corporations are to be modified it can be accomplished under the Corporate Reorganization Chapter (Chapter X). Debtors other than corporations may effect arrangements covering debts secured by real property under the special procedure provided by the chapter on Real Property Arrangements (Chapter XII). Thus the purpose of the chapter is to provide individual debtors owning real property encumbered by mortgages the same relief available to corporations through Chapter X.

Action may be brought under Chapter XII only by the debtor but he may petition for a real property arrangement after a petition in bankruptcy has been filed or after foreclosure proceedings have been instituted. A trustee may be appointed or the debtor may be left in possession and operation of his property. Creditors are to be classified and an arrangement may not be confirmed unless accepted by the creditors of each class holding two-thirds in amount of the debts of such class if their interests are affected. When confirmed, the arrangement becomes binding upon all creditors, the debtor, or any corporation or trust organized for the purpose of carrying out the arrangement.

Other provisions dealing with such features as the powers of the court, the stay of prior bankruptcy proceedings, the appraisal of property, meetings of creditors, discharge of debtor, rejection of executory contracts, and other provisions follow the general tenor of the Bankruptcy Act.

Protecting the Creditors' Interest. While the action necessary upon the part of the creditor has been brought out in the preceding sections, it will be well for the reader to consider chronologically the duties of the creditor. They may be divided into six separate actions.

Upon receiving notice that a petition in bankruptcy has been filed by or against a debtor, the credit executive's first thought is to prevent any further shipments reaching the debtor. To accomplish this he will immediately issue "stoppage-in-transit" orders on any recent shipments, cancel all orders that may be in process, and change all necessary office records. These precautions being taken, he proceeds to the second action, which is to prepare and file the proof of debt, as explained previously.

His third duty is to attend the meeting of creditors and participate in the election of a trustee and a creditors' committee. His fourth is to maintain a general supervision over the proceedings and an interest in the conduct of the case. This includes, of course, cooperation with the trustee, the creditors' committee, and other creditors in any way that it may be required.

It is a fifth duty of the credit executive to oppose the discharge if there are grounds for so doing. The credit man fails in his duty to the credit fraternity if he permits a bankrupt to evade his obligations and become free to engage again in business when not entitled to such freedom.

The final duty is to attend the final meeting of creditors. At this meeting, the trustee presents his final account, and the trustee's attorney files his request for allowances which are passed upon by the referee. At this meeting, the creditors have an opportunity to oppose any unjust or exorbitant claims for fees that may be presented. Unfortunately, these meetings are not frequently attended. Hence, there is no one to protect the creditors' interests but the referee, who often is not in a position to judge the merits of the various claims presented.

Examination of Debtor. The bankrupt is required to attend the first meeting of creditors and submit to examination. At that meeting "the judge or referee shall preside . . . and shall publicly examine the debtor or cause him to be examined, and may permit creditors to examine him" (Section 55*b*). It is the mandatory duty of the trustee to examine the debtor unless he has already been fully examined by the referee, receiver, or creditors. It is also the trustee's mandatory duty to examine the bankrupt at the hearing upon objections to his discharge (Section 47*a*). Examination of the debtor may also be obtained through application of any officer or creditor to the court to order any designated person to be examined concerning the acts, conduct, or property of the bankrupt (Section 21*a*). Also, a bankrupt's spouse now may be examined relative to the financial affairs of the bankrupt and the spouse's connection with them, despite any state law to the contrary.

With these provisions it should prove difficult for a bankrupt to conceal his past illegal actions from a competent trustee and a vigilant creditor body.

Reclamation Proceedings. Many creditors are under the impression that it is possible under certain conditions to reclaim goods which are in the hands of the bankrupt, receiver, or trustee. Creditors are inclined to think that shipments made just prior to the petition in bankruptcy can be retaken by the shipper. This is possible, if the shipment has not reached the possession of the bankrupt or his representative, through the right of stoppage in transit. If, however, the goods have arrived and have been received, the right to reclaim rests upon two conditions. The first is the question of title. If the bankrupt has not title, then neither has the receiver or trustee, since their title is derived from the bankrupt himself. The creditor, for instance, may hold and prove that title did not pass because of the fraudulent representations of the debtor. If the credit was the result of a materially false financial statement, and this fact can be proved, the goods may be reclaimed, provided the second condition can be fulfilled.

This second condition is the positive identification of the goods to be reclaimed. The identification must be to the satisfaction of the court and not to the satisfaction of the creditor himself. It should be borne in mind that in a reclamation proceeding, the burden of proof is on the creditor to establish his case, and his success in such an action rests upon his proof of title and identification.

Turnover Proceedings.   One of the provisions of bankruptcy proceedings is intended to force the bankrupt to give up any assets which it is thought that he may be concealing.   This is known as the institution of turnover proceedings.   When property has been traced to the recent possession or control of a bankrupt, it is presumed to remain there until he satisfactorily accounts to the court for its disappearance or its disposition.   When convinced of such possession, the court will grant what is called a "turnover order" which directs the bankrupt to turn over to the trustee the property described.

The bankrupt may be required to give an accounting of his property, or of its disposition.   If his books of account fail to disclose the cost to him of property sold by him during the period under consideration, the burden of proof is upon the bankrupt to establish his loss by showing the property was sold at a price less than the cost to him.

Turnover proceedings also cover property belonging to the bankrupt but in the possession of third parties.   Third parties include receivers or trustees appointed in prior proceedings, or assignees or agents appointed to take charge of and liquidate the debtor's assets.

Punishment for failure to obey an order for the turnover of property is under contempt of court.

Dividends.   The law provides for both the method of liquidating the estate and distribution of the proceeds among the creditors.   The trustee cannot proceed to sell the property wherever and for whatever he pleases.   He must first have it appraised, and then he is required to obtain at least 75 per cent of the appraised valuation.   The above is a general statement subject to certain exceptions.   The act also stipulates how and when the dividends, if any, shall be disbursed.

The first dividend is declared within 30 days of the date set for the first meeting of creditors if the proceeds of the estate exceed the amount necessary to pay the debts of priority and claims which have not been, but probably will be, presented and, in addition, amounts to 5 per cent or more of the allowed claims.   Subsequent dividends must be declared as often as the money on hand reaches 10 per cent of the allowed claims.   When the estate is closed, a final dividend is paid.

Dividends unclaimed for a year or more are to be distributed to creditors, whose claims have been allowed, up to 100 per cent and any excess is payable to the bankrupt.   But unclaimed dividends belonging to minors must be retained by the Clerk of the Court for one year after the minor attains his majority.

A Few Interesting Facts.   One who makes a careful study of the Bankruptcy Act cannot fail to be impressed with the excellence of it.

The best minds of the country have been devoted to its perfection. Congress has had the benefit of the advice and counsel of credit men resulting from their experience. In fact, much of the credit for the Act of 1898 and its various amendments can be given to the National Association of Credit Management. Excellent as the law itself may be, much is left to be desired in the administration of it. Although intended as a creditors' law, the creditors have not seemed to fare so well from it.

The extent of losses through bankruptcy over a period of years is somewhat appalling. In the 19 years ended June 30, 1938, there were 908,467 bankruptcies in the United States. The number increased almost every year from approximately 15,000 in 1920 to 67,031 in 1933. Since 1933, a considerable drop has occurred due, perhaps, to the fact that the weak concerns were largely eradicated by the depression and the further fact that less than the usual number of new enterprises came into existence. It is interesting to note that the number of bankruptcies steadily increased during the so-called prosperity years of the 1920's.

The decade of the 'forties were years of feverish activity for the most part. Failures are few when business conditions are so favorable. In the year 1940 there were 13,619 business failures reported by Dun & Bradstreet, Inc. Business failures decreased steadily during the years of the Second World War.

Although only 809 business failures were reported for the year 1945, the lowest number on record, the average liability per failure, $37,361, was the highest since 1920. This trend of higher average liability has persisted, averaging greater than $40,000 for the years 1945 through 1958.

The amount recovered by creditors through bankruptcy proceedings is small. The gross amount received for the assets is far below the total of the liabilities and the expenses of liquidation consume a considerable part of the gross. Creditors receive, on the average, a very small fraction of their claims against concerns liquidated by bankruptcy.

TEXT AND RESEARCH QUESTIONS

1. *a.* What are the purposes of the Federal Bankruptcy Act?
   b. May the various states in the United States pass insolvency laws?
   c. How would cases of insolvency be handled if the Federal Act were repealed?
2. *a.* Why is it necessary for the credit man to make a thorough study of the Bankruptcy Act and bankruptcy court procedure?
   b. Who may go into voluntary bankruptcy? Into involuntary bankruptcy?
   c. What conditions must exist before creditors can throw a debtor into bankruptcy?

3. State in brief the six acts of bankruptcy.

4. *a.* How is a claim in bankruptcy proved and before whom?
   b. When may claims be filed?
   c. What is a provable debt?
   d. What advantage if any is to be gained by having an attorney file the creditor's proof of claim?

5. *a.* When is the first meeting of creditors called?   By whom?
   b. What business is transacted at this meeting?
   c. When is the final meeting called?
   d. What is the purpose of the final meeting of creditors?

6. *a.* When, by whom, and how is the trustee elected?
   b. What are the duties of the trustee?

7. *a.* How is the referee appointed, and for what term?
   b. List his main duties.

8. *a.* From what debts is it impossible for a bankrupt to be discharged?
   b. Why is an exception made of these debts?

9. *a.* When may a debtor apply for a discharge from bankruptcy?
   b. What conditions may prevent his receiving a discharge?
   c. Why should a creditor oppose the discharge of a bankrupt if there are grounds for doing so?

10. Under what conditions can a creditor reclaim goods which he has shipped to a customer against whom a petition in bankruptcy has been filed?

11. What are the five essential duties of a creditor in the administration of a case in bankruptcy?

12. What reversal of purpose of the Bankruptcy law is revealed in the Chandler Act?

13. Outline the main provisions for a corporate reorganization under Chapter X.

14. Give two main reasons for the huge credit losses through bad debts.

PROBLEM

Herbert A. MacAvoy, 8793 Fifth Ave., New York, N.Y., has been petitioned into bankruptcy. He owes your corporation, of which you are treasurer, $268.43 for goods sold to him. Zenas H. Garrand, an attorney unknown to you, has offered to file your claim without charge to you. The debtor is located in the southern district of New York.

Prepare a proof of claim to be filed with the referee in this case. The name of your corporation is the Acme Products Co., Inc., and Chas. E. Nichols your chief clerk is a notary.

CHAPTER 31

ADJUSTMENT BUREAUS

Inception of Adjustment Bureaus. Adjusters and adjustment bureaus, to serve creditors in different capacities, have long existed. But these agencies for the most part were privately owned and operated for the private gain of the owner. Although termed adjusters, or operating under the name of an adjustment bureau, the functions of these enterprises were largely confined to collections. The proprietors were, in other words, merely operating a collection agency under a name which it was hoped would remove some of the stigma so often attached to the word "collections." Dissatisfied with the services of such agencies, different organizations of businessmen, or trade associations, have attempted to provide an intermediary between a debtor and his creditors. The object was to secure for creditors either a prompt settlement of their claims in full, or the most advantageous adjustment of the case that could be effected.

Early National Bankruptcy acts seemed to favor the debtor. Under all such bankruptcy legislation, creditors were (and still are) required to cooperate; consequently they decided that voluntary cooperation, possibly to avoid debtor's bankruptcy and its attendant administrative costs and delays, would yield greater dividends. "The first organized effort on the part of creditors to deal with the problem seems to be recorded in the Proclamation of 1868 by the wholesale merchants and bankers of San Francisco, in which they agreed to take joint action against bankruptcy frauds."[1]

Out of this cooperative effort there was organized an agency which would make available to creditors the advantages to be derived from the concerted efforts of the creditors themselves. As reorganized in 1877, this group of businessmen became known as the Board of Trade of San Francisco. Its usefulness was quickly evidenced, and its success

[1] Credit Association Adjustment Bureau Procedure, compiled by Robert Peal, edited by George Brainard.

may be attested by the fact that it exists today. Following the success of the first venture, similar associations were formed.

It is with the adjustment bureau sponsored and recommended by the National Association of Credit Management that this chapter will deal. The subject is thus restricted in treatment because credit men themselves through their own association have taken the lead in adjustment-bureau practice and organization.

This has been a natural development. Dissatisfied with the inefficiency of an outside or privately conducted agency, or suspicious of its integrity, credit men naturally turned to an organization which could have no interests other than the interests of creditors themselves. Furthermore, here was an organization which the credit men themselves controlled. The remedy for dissatisfaction with a bureau lay within the body of creditors themselves. The development of this service to business has continued until there are today bureaus placed in the principal key markets of the United States. Their operation is not limited purely to local territory but expands as occasion may require to include adjacent markets. In this way, the organization is equipped to function for almost the entire country.

Functions of the Adjustment Bureau. The approved adjustment bureaus have been established to give members of the National Association of Credit Management and other creditors well-regulated, efficient, and economical organizations for cooperation in handling the affairs of embarrassed or insolvent debtors.

The first step in bureau operation is the devising of rules of conduct for creditors' meetings. Under these rules the principal function of an adjustment bureau is to bring together creditors and debtor to discuss the latter's affairs. If possible, both publicity and litigation are avoided. As a consequence, the affairs of an ailing debtor may be prevented from worsening and his debts settled amicably, without recourse to bankruptcy. Also, because of the relatively quicker settlement, costs may be less and dividends greater, or the business may be saved as a continuing economic unit. Thus it is apparent that the problems in the administration of an adjustment bureau vary widely and involve all areas of business activities.[1]

Membership Responsibility. To assist the bureau in the performance of its duties, creditors are asked to agree to cooperative action, based upon the majority opinion. They agree to disclose any private interest they may have and to hold in confidence the actions of the committees' or creditors' meetings.

---

[1] Interestingly, about 80 per cent of the adjustment cases involve new businesses organized for less than 6 years.

The following example of instructions to creditors' committees indicates the exacting responsibility of members:

Instructions to Creditors' Committees Operating Through the
San Francisco Board of Trade

The Committee of which you are a member is the sole governing body in the case now before us. The Board of Trade can only handle it according to your direction. The Board's facilities are at your command.

The Secretary will keep minutes of your proceedings and maintain a complete record in the case. He will carry out your instructions. The Board's Attorney will advise you on questions of law and prepare all needed legal paper. Please observe the following rules for the efficient handling of your case:

1. Organize your first meeting by appointing a permanent chairman.
2. Be regular and prompt in attendance at meetings.
3. Avoid discussions with the debtor or others outside of your committee room.
4. Refrain from individual discussion with the debtor, thereby avoiding possible serious embarrassment and difficulty to yourselves and the entire committee.
5. When calling the debtor before you, have him addressed by the chairman or secretary or by some delegated member of the committee in such manner as to make clear that the communication comes from the committee as a whole and not from any individual member thereof.
6. Keep in strict confidence all that passes in the committee room so that there may be freedom of discussion and sound decision. Any member who does not adhere strictly to the code of secrecy loses the confidence of the other members, impedes the proper considerations of the case and should therefore immediately disqualify himself and resign from the committee.

Provisions of by-laws of Board of Trade of San Francisco relating to creditors' committees:

At creditors' meetings, committees shall be chosen to direct and control whatever action is agreed upon by creditors or to take such action as may seem advisable when the creditors refer the cases to the committees for consideration and decision.

All creditors' and committee meetings shall be held at the Rooms of the Association and a record kept of the same.

If any member of a Creditors' Committee intends to give to a filing debtor or prospective purchaser of, or bidder for, the assets any financial or other aid, he must immediately disclose the fact to the Secretary and to the other members of the Committee and resign from the Committee.[1]

Creditors should make it a point to attend all meetings where they have an interest of sufficient amount. Failure to do so creates in the

---

[1] Credit Association Adjustment Bureau Procedure.

mind of the debtor the impression that his creditors are not much concerned, and he in turn adopts the same attitude.

Origin of Estates. The adjustment bureau must not originate business. Such business as it does handle is brought to its attention at the suggestion of members. The usual procedure is that a member, or a group of creditors, requests a meeting with the debtor to discuss delinquencies in payment. Prior to the meeting with the debtor, the creditors may—as a group—go over the situation to clarify objectives and present a unified front. Other cases are brought to the bureau by a debtor who may visit the bureau to discuss affairs, by attorneys representing embarrassed debtors, by creditors because of customers' fire losses, by partners who may be in disagreement, or in dissolution, or upon the death of one of the partners. Occasionally a trade group discussion involving comparison of notes around the conference table may reveal the serious plight of a debtor.

Conduct of Creditors' Meetings. In these meetings acrimonious debate should be avoided. Naturally the debtor does not wish to lose a business derived from many years work; yet the creditors want to be paid. Of course the possibility of fraud is always present as affecting unsecured creditors, particularly those cases in which the assets of the debtor are pledged elsewhere. However, statistics show that there are few outright cases of fraud. As a general rule the meeting begins with statutory questions regarding organization, ownership, and condition of the assets.

The debtor should be given the opportunity to answer all questions properly and he may even be permitted to put forward a plan of solution to his problems.

When the discussion is complete, the debtor may temporarily be excused while the creditors attempt to decide on the proper course of action. Usually the bureau's representative, as chairman, or secretary of an appointed creditors' committee, handles the case.

The solution usually calls for one of the following courses of action to be taken:

1. Outright liquidation
2. Extension of time
3. Compromise plan
4. Bankruptcy

Forms of Control. When the course to be followed has been decided upon, the adjustment bureau proceeds to gain control of the debtor estate. The forms usually resorted to in gaining control include the assignment for benefit of creditors, the trust deed, the trust mortgage, and the stock transfer. The form used depends upon the circumstances in the case and the means of adjustment which the creditors have adopted.

By means of the assignment for the benefit of creditors, the debtor assigns or transfers all of his assets to one or more trustees, officials of the bureau. This method of control is effective only when the assent of the creditors to it is obtained, as the making of an assignment for the benefit of creditors is an act of bankruptcy. If three or more creditors refuse to assent to the assignment, they may, in the event that their claims aggregate $500, prevent the administration by the bureau by filing a petition in bankruptcy.

The trust deed accomplishes a purpose similar to the assignment. All the debtor's property is transferred to the bureau in trust for creditors. When the adjustment has been completed and the terms of settlement fulfilled, the business is turned back to the debtor.

A trust mortgage grants a trustee (the bureau) the power to foreclose an estate when, in the trustee's opinion, the business is not being properly conducted. Under this form of control the business may be continued by the debtor as the mortgagor. Under proper supervision the debtor is often able to conduct his business to greater advantage than if the business were placed in the hands of another. Personal contact of the debtor with his customers is an essential asset. If, in spite of these factors, there is no apparent progress, the trust mortgage enables the trustee to secure control of the debtor and his business without delay. It is apparent that the trustee maintains at all times a controlling influence over the business.

If the debtor concern is a corporation, control of the business may be granted the bureau by a transfer of stock; an agreement is entered into whereby the bureau gains ownership until the debtor's affairs have been put on a sound and normal basis. This transfer is easily accomplished by the endorsement of the stock certificates and the surrender of them to the possession of the bureau.

Regardless of the method through which the bureau takes over an embarrassed estate, compliance with the Bulk Sales laws is essential. Each state has its own law for the sale, transfer, or conveyance of any property. These laws are made for the protection of creditors. It devolves upon the bureau to unearth violations of the Bulk Sales law, but it must be careful not to break the same law in its activities. Once the assets are reduced to the possession of the adjustment bureau, they are amply protected by adequate insurance, and wherever necessary a custodian is engaged to guard against any possible misdirection of the assets. Prompt coverage of insurance is essential in cases of assignment, since the debtor by that act automatically cancels all fire insurance policies.

The minutes of all meetings are recorded, and reports of the progress of the case are made regularly to all creditors.

Friendly Liquidations. When a debtor's affairs are hopelessly involved, and neither extension nor compromise settlement is practicable, in many cases the most advantageous procedure is liquidation of the debtor's assets on a friendly basis. Litigation in the courts should usually be avoided, not alone because of the expenditures which may accrue, but also because of the unpleasantness which may arise. The adjustment bureau is fully equipped with a skilled personnel to perform properly this phase of administration.

Extensions. In the event that the debtor's business is solvent, but the assets are frozen, a definite plan to adjust the situation is advanced by the committee. Systems are devised, if possible, which will remedy the difficulty. If it appears that too much capital is tied up in accounts receivable, proper collection methods are recommended. When the amount of merchandise is too great for the volume of business transacted, the committee will offer a plan that will eventually establish an inventory proportionate to the sales. When the remedy has been decided upon, the bureau sends one of its men to supervise or carry out the plans of rehabilitation.

Rarely is a definite period of time for an extension determinable. Whenever a substantial sum has been collected, the administrator, which may be the adjustment bureau, distributes a pro rata share to the creditors. These distributions are continued until 100 per cent of the indebtedness is paid. The adjustment bureau thus may act in both an advisory and a supervisory capacity. A genuine service is rendered to both creditors and debtor which could not be otherwise so effectively performed without considerable inconvenience and expense.

Compromise Settlements. The investigation of the bureau may reveal an insolvent condition. Insolvency, however, may not exist to a very marked degree. When the honest debtor is found to be in such a predicament, and if he expresses the desire to continue his business, in the hope that he can some day make a successful enterprise out of it, the adjustment bureau will aid him if such assistance is thought to be justified. The details of his affairs are considered from every angle. It is realized that business assets are of greater value to the going concern than if the assets are hurriedly sold under the hammer. An immediate settlement, equally fair to debtor and creditors, is preferable to both.

Receiverships. Some types of business organizations may be in financial distress, but no adjustment can be made through the methods already mentioned. In such instances, resort must be had to legal methods of conducting the case. Receiverships, either in bankruptcy or in equity, may be the means adopted. In such instances, the adjustment bureau, acting through an individual within the bureau, strives to secure the appointment as receiver and thus to serve the creditors.

Bankruptcies. Many cases of embarrassment are so far involved that they cannot be kept out of the bankruptcy courts. Should a debtor concern file a petition in bankruptcy or cause creditors to file a petition against it, the adjustment bureau may be of service in various ways. The bureau may act as the representative of creditors, or an individual of the bureau with approval of the court may secure election as the trustee. Approved bureaus can operate very effectively in this capacity.

Protection against Unapproved Practices. The approved adjustment bureaus of the National Association of Credit Management provide creditors with protection against unapproved practices. Although many independent concerns exist and function capably as the representatives of creditors in some channels of adjustment, there are others whose activities are uncertain and not beyond question. It is recommended, therefore, that complete confidence be had that the private adjustment bureau is acting in good faith and on sound principles before a creditor forwards a claim for collection or adjustment.

In an endeavor to secure business, some attorneys occasionally resort to practices which do not benefit anyone but themselves. At the first evidence of the financial difficulties of a merchant, which comes to the attention of such an attorney through the claims forwarded to him by creditors, from reliable information received from sources close to the merchant or sometimes from the merchant himself, he attempts to secure the names of all creditors and the exact amounts due them. The unscrupulous attorney may then institute bankruptcy proceedings as soon as he has a sufficient number of claims.

Field Men. The field representative is a very important factor in bureau operations, and his conduct and method of operation must be above reproach. So-called "strong-arm methods" are a thing of the past. It is usually part of his work to interview local creditors, bankers, or lawyers. He must avoid making promises that cannot be fulfilled. He should give the assignor every possible consideration, bearing in mind, however, that he represents primarily the interests of creditors. He must be firm, tactful, and discreet. The reputation of the bureau depends in large measure on the field representative's conduct.

An Investigation Exemplified. The thoroughness with which an investigation is conducted by the bureau is best illustrated by quoting a portion of a report on an actual case. Names and places are, of course, fictitious. The investigator, it will be noted, has covered twenty-seven subjects in his investigation. These are enumerated, and his detailed report on the first five subjects follows. While the report cannot be quoted in full, it may be stated that all subjects are covered in the same thorough and detailed way.

SUBJECTS INVESTIGATED

1. Possession
2. Cash on Hand and in Bank
3. Insurance
4. Perishables
5. Inventory
6. Real Estate
7. Report on Merchandise and Fixtures
8. Sale of Assets
9. Conditional Sales Contracts, Judgments, and Liens
10. Taxes Accrued—State and City, Federal Income, Withholdings, Social Security
11. Accounts and Bills Receivable
12. Collateral
13. Merchandise at Depot or in Transit
14. Commission Goods, Containers, Seeds, etc.
15. Preferences
16. Labor Claims
17. Creditors' List
18. Rent
19. Suits
20. Local Claims
21. Custodian and Caretaker
22. Exemptions
23. Books and Records
24. Labor for Invoicing
25. Relatives' Claims
26. Antecedents and Family History
27. Trust Deed

Report for Office:

In Re: Martin Green and Henry Brown, father and son-in-law, co-partners as The Golden Rule, Blank, Ariz.

I received your telegram at Aberdeen on Dec. 10, 19—, with instructions to go to Claremont, take possession of the assets, invoice, and investigate. I immediately wired you that I would leave on the first train.

Possession:

The next morning I called at the store and found Martin Green in charge. I introduced myself and obtained from him two keys to the storeroom, that is, to the front door of the storeroom. Martin Green said that these were all the keys that there were, that he and his son-in-law Henry Brown were the only ones that had keys. There was an inside entrance to the second floor, and I barred this door and securely bolted it and instructed the debtor that he and his son-in-law and families would have to use the outside stairway.

Cash on Hand and in Bank:

I found in the cash drawer $7.10, which I took. I also found cash in the Claremont State Bank for which I obtained a check and bought a draft for the sum total of cash on hand and in the bank. This has been remitted to the office. I notified A. M. Black, cashier of the Claremont State Bank, to return but not to protest any checks which might be presented later.

Insurance:

I asked Mr. Green to get his insurance policies, and he told me that they did not have any insurance, that their insurance had all been canceled about a month ago. I then found out from A. M. Black, cashier of the bank, legal description of this property, and I wired the office as follows: "In re Golden Rule Claremont place six thousand on merchandise one thousand on fixtures contained in two story frame building shingle roof located on lot one block two original town of Claremont."

Perishables:

Before starting to take the inventory, I disposed of certain merchandise which would deteriorate or perhaps spoil if the store was closed for any length of time. From this source I realized $22.31, which I am remitting herewith.

Inventory:

After I had properly arranged the stock, I proceeded to take an inventory of the assets. My inventory shows as follows:

Assets:

Merchandise at today's market	$ 6,678.23
Furniture and fixtures at original cost	1,224.10
Bills receivable pledged as collateral to Hartman Shoe Co., Pershing, given 6/19/—	242.10
Bills receivable pledged as collateral to Marshall Co., Pershing, given 8/5/—	409.40
Cash on hand and in bank	31.90
Cash for sale of perishables	22.31
	$ 8,608.04

Liabilities:

Merchandise creditors	$14,290.10
Henry Smith, Orient, Me., a brother of Mrs. Martin Green	1,400.00
Sarah Green, daughter, labor claim	462.10
Sam Green, son, labor claim	300.00
State and city taxes past due	184.10
State and city taxes accrued	166.47
Federal income taxes	956.00
Withholding—for employees	xxx
Social security	xxx
Total	$17,758.77

Real Estate:

In addition to the above-mentioned assets, the debtor owns a store building, in which the stock and fixtures were located. This building is described as Lot 1 Block 2 Original Town of Claremont. It is a good frame store building, 20 × 80; rear end of the building is partitioned off into a wareroom. The building is plastered upstairs and down, it has a good plate-glass front, and the debtors and their families live on the second floor, and for this reason the property is exempt. This property under present condition is worth probably $3,500 to $4,000.

Achievements of the Adjustment Bureau. The results achieved by adjustment bureaus cannot be entirely appraised by an analysis of the costs of administration and the dividends paid to creditors. Some of the good work of the bureaus yields its return to creditors in the form of debtors with renewed courage in themselves and renewed faith in their creditor partners. Another benefit is the deterrent effect which such an organization of credit men may have upon a debtor who might be contemplating a fraudulent failure. The results achieved, however, are by no means entirely intangible. Both the costs of administration and the dividends paid to creditors will bear the closest scrutiny. Perfection, or maximum results, are by no means claimed, but the accomplishments of the adjustment bureaus are instilling further confidence in this medium for handling embarrassed accounts.

Because the bureau maintains paid, experienced personnel, it has advantages over a trustee in Bankruptcy proceedings, in which the trustee may or may not be experienced. Further, a trustee may know little about liquidating accounts receivable. In addition, the bureau is in touch with wholesalers and merchandisers and thus is in a position to obtain better prices in the liquidation of inventories and other assets.

The Future of Adjustment Bureaus. Organizations do not live long upon past reputations, but they receive support according to their present daily achievements. Adjustment bureaus have met an urgent need of creditors. As creditors better understand the purpose and achievements of the adjustment bureaus, the bureaus should receive greater support. Creditors, however, must not forget that the bureau is merely their agency and that they may control it and should feel a responsibility for it. It is for the creditors themselves to keep their bureaus in the highest state of efficiency and honesty.

The reasons why the bureaus should receive the support of creditors can be summed up in three statements. (1) Adjustment bureaus are trained and skilled in investigating and liquidating embarrassed estates. (2) They are organized to handle such cases efficiently. (3) They are organizations in which creditors can have confidence, since they are organized to operate without profit and are under the direct control of creditors themselves.

TEXT AND RESEARCH QUESTIONS

1. For what purpose are adjustment bureaus formed?
2. *a.* What difficulty must the adjustment bureau first surmount when called to handle an embarrassed concern?
   b. Why does the adjustment bureau always conduct its own investigation?
3. *a.* What different forms of settlement may be arranged by the adjustment bureau?
   b. Name two advantages of the adjustment bureau's collection department as a collection medium.
4. How does the general body of credit men retain control and supervision over the various local adjustment bureaus?
5. What is the first action taken by the bureau upon being called into a case?
6. In what different ways may the bureau secure control of the debtor estate?
7. What precaution must a creditor observe if an independent agency or attorney is attempting to make an adjustment?
8. *a.* How do attorneys sometimes proceed to secure control of an embarrassed debtor's estate?
   b. Why should the activities of bankruptcy rings be combated vigorously?
9. Upon what should the creditor always insist before agreeing to an extension or composition offered by a debtor?
10. What are the factors to be considered in measuring the efficiency of the adjustment bureau?

PROBLEM

Your concern has a customer in Staunton, Va., who owes it $168.27 which is now 40 days past due. You have written several collection letters without response from the debtor, but you are just in receipt of a letter from an attorney who states that the customer has placed his affairs in the attorney's hands. After a thorough investigation (according to the letter) the attorney has found debts totaling $8,264.90 and assets with an estimated value of $6,274. Mr. Debtor has a relative who has offered to loan him $2,500, provided the creditors are willing to accept 30 per cent in full settlement of their claims. The attorney advises acceptance of this offer and urges quick action lest the relative withdraw his offer of assistance. The attorney calls attention to the fact that the alternative is bankruptcy, which probably would not yield more than a 10 per cent dividend.

Describe fully what action you would take upon the receipt of the attorney's letter.

CHAPTER 32

CREDIT INSURANCE AND GUARANTIES

Credit Insurance. Credit insurance is a contract under which the insurer, in consideration of a stipulated premium, undertakes to indemnify the manufacturer, jobber, or wholesaler against excessive credit losses. The principle of credit insurance is extended over all business conducted on a credit basis. Credit losses in the aggregate are enormous. Every business conducted on a credit basis expects losses to occur through the inability of some customers to pay. Businessmen, therefore, endeavor to include in their sales price a sum which, when averaged over all sales, will compensate them for any credit losses that may be sustained. Similarly credit insurance companies include in their premiums a sum which, when averaged over all their contracts, will meet the losses the companies will have to pay.

This passing along of risks for a fixed compensation is held as justifiable in that it represents the substitution of a certain specific loss for an uncertain general loss. It means theoretically that the risk has been almost completely removed, as the premium for security may be estimated definitely in advance and added to other costs which in turn are finally passed along to the ultimate consumer. It should, however, be stated that an exception to the above statement occurs when the credit losses of a business exceed the amount for which it is insured.

Enormous as credit losses are in the aggregate, the percentage of credit losses to sales is remarkably small.[1] The Analytical Department of Dun & Bradstreet, Inc., has compiled information concerning credit losses in numerous lines of business. In most cases the percentage of loss applied to sales was rather low. In certain lines, however, the loss percentage is above 1 per cent of annual sales. These figures vary from year to year, and from a study of the figures, the need for establishing a fixed level of losses will be readily seen.

---

[1] A distinction should be made between different types of losses. Credit losses, unlike fire losses, are not social losses. Assets are not destroyed; they are still available for utilization.

In essence, credit insurance is a guaranty of the value of working capital represented by accounts receivable. A company's assets are almost always protected by insurance while they are in the possession of the company. The various forms of casualty insurance, such as fire, theft, water damage, flood damage, etc., are automatically adopted. At the moment of delivering the merchandise to a customer, however, all such protection ceases. It is at this point that credit insurance begins to function by continuing the guaranty of value until the account receivable is collected.

Development of Credit Insurance Companies. As early as 1885 and 1886, laws were enacted in New York, New Jersey, and Louisiana permitting the incorporation of companies to issue policies, contracts, or bonds of indemnity against losses to those engaged in accepting credit.

The early efforts of credit insurance companies were not attended with much success. It was not until 1889 that a company, The United States Credit System Company of New Jersey, was organized which was destined to operate for any length of time. Credit insurance companies took on added stability as a result of the National Bankruptcy Act of 1898, which gave them the opportunity of broadening the definition of insolvency. At the present writing only two companies are writing domestic credit insurance in the United States.[1] Nevertheless, credit insurance is further developed in this country than in any other.

Credit Insurance Policies. The basis of credit insurance is statistical. Through the many years of business, credit insurance companies have created a business mortality table, based on the experience of those companies insuring their receivables in that period. This establishes the basis for primary loss to apply to the individual company making application for credit insurance. The mortality table represents an average. Those companies whose individual experience is less than the average are able to obtain a primary loss lower than average. Those companies whose experience is higher than the average must use their own experience for primary loss purposes. The deductible amount usually represents a small fraction of 1 per cent of annual sales.

Classification of Business Lines.[2] In establishing the mortality table, referred to above, the insuring companies have divided all lines of business into five classes. At the same time they have followed the coding of business known as Standard Industrial Classification (S.I.C.) estab-

---

[1] These companies are The American Credit Indemnity Company and the London Guarantee and Accident Company, Ltd. The American Credit Indemnity Company is the only one to write credit insurance exclusively.

[2] Insurers are classifying risks in three groups; namely, wholesalers, manufacturers, and retailers. However, in each group hazardous classes continue to pay higher premiums.

lished by the United States government. These five groupings are an average of losses on an experience basis, and serve as a guide for what in future years might be expected by companies in those same lines. Class 1 would contain the least hazardous type of risk. Class 5 represents the other extreme. A few examples of classification are as follows:

Class 1. Advertising, steel, barrels, coffee, foundry products, macaroni, spaghetti and noodles, industrial machinery, photographic equipment, cold-rolled steel, and woven labels

Class 2. Cotton batts, braids and dress trimmings, candy and confectionery, cereals, manufacturers of girdles, lithographing

Class 3. Bedding, childrens' clothing, concrete products, fertilizers, furniture, scrap iron, lumber, store and office fixtures, wool or cotton waste

Class 4. Nonalcoholic beverages, broad woven nylon fabrics, clocks, men's and women's clothing (except furs), knit goods, millinery, piano actions, radio and television supplies (manufacturing and wholesale), work clothing

Class 5. Beer, women's shoes (jobbers), costume jewelry, furs, gold, silver, and platinum refiners, spirituous liquors, precious metals, straw hats

Coinsurance. The insured should always bear a part of the loss. This is a sound insurance principle. The coinsurance clause is usually 10 per cent and may be higher in covering more hazardous risks. The term "coinsurance," as used in connection with credit insurance, more closely corresponds to deductible average as used in marine insurance than it does to coinsurance as generally understood in other branches of insurance. The policyholder is thus required to share a small part of the loss which may include his profits. The purpose of the insurance is not to insure the policyholder's profit but to indemnify him against his extraordinary losses and to protect the actual working capital which is invested in accounts receivable. It is possible under some forms of credit insurance policies to have a rider attached eliminating coinsurance on certain first and second grades of credit.

Coverage. The term "coverage" in credit insurance refers to the maximum insurance on any single customer. The maximum aggregate loss to be borne by the insurance company is referred to as the "policy amount." The policy amount is net after all deductions and is in large part determined by the premium required for coverage applying to individual debtors, but the figure is quite flexible and is frequently increased over the basic amount. This is the rule followed under General Coverage policies.

The insuring companies also insure single accounts. The standard for this type of coverage is quite high and as a natural consequence the premiums are low. There is no middle ground.

Both the cost of insurance and the amount of coverage on single risks are based upon the capital and credit ratings of the various agencies. Where an agency does not assign ratings, accounts can be covered by name by special riders attached to the policy. The insured stipulates the agency he intends or wishes to use, and both the coverage and the premium are computed from a table established for that agency. It is permissible to buy coverage on certain groups of ratings and omit coverage of other ratings if they are not needed. This is determined by the needs of the insured. Agencies in use at the present time are:

Dun & Bradstreet, Inc.
Jewelers Board of Trade
Lyon Furniture Mercantile Agency
Lumberman's Credit Association, Inc.
The Feakes Mercantile Agency, Inc.
Produce Reporter Company
Packer Produce Mercantile Agency
Motor and Equipment Manufacturers Association
Smith Mercantile Agency

The ratings employed by Dun & Bradstreet are shown below;

TABLE OF RATINGS AND COVERAGE

Column One			Column Two			Column Three		
Rating		Gross amount covered	Rating		Gross amount covered	Rating		Gross amount covered
AA	A1	$	AA	1	$	AA	1½	$
A+	A1	$	A+	1	$	A+	1½	$
A	A1	$	A	1	$	A	1½	$
B+	1	$	B+	1½	$	B+	2	$
B	1	$	B	1½	$	B	2	$
C+	1	$	C+	1½	$	C+	2	$
(Blank)	1	$	(Blank)	2	$	C	2½	$
C	1½	$	C	2	$	D+	2½	$
D+	1½	$	D+	2	$	D	2½	$
D	1½	$	D	2	$	E	3	$
E	2	$	E	2½	$	F	3½	$
F	2½	$	F	3	$	(Blank)	3	$
G	3	$	G	3½	$			
H	3	$	H	3½	$			
J	3	$	J	3½	$			
K	3	$						

FIG. 41. Ratings used in credit insurance.

Figure 42 shows a copy of the American Credit Indemnity Company's premium rates applying to the regular ratings shown in the table in Fig. 41. In this rate sheet, the maximum limits of coverage applying to each rating are shown.

Page 2

COLUMN ONE

Group	Rating		Maximum Open Limits	Policy Limits	Group Totals	Prem. per M.	Premium
1	Aa	A1	$108,000	$			
	A+	A1	$ 50,000	$			
	A	A1	$ 50,000	$	$	$ 3.00	$
2	B+	1	$ 50,000	$			
	B	1	$ 50,000	$			
	C+	1	$ 50,000	$	$	$ 4.00	$
	Blank	1	$ 50,000	$	$	$ 5.00	$
3	C	1½	$ 30,000	$			
	D+	1½	$ 25,000	$			
	D	1½	$ 20,000	$	$	$ 6.00	$
4	E	2	$ 10,000	$			
	F	2½	$ 5,000	$	$	$ 7.00	$
5	G	3	$ 2,500	$			
	H	3	$ 1,500	$			
	J	3	$ 1,000	$			
	K	3	$ 500	$	$	$10.00	$
			Non Selective Coverage TOTAL	$	$	$ 5.00	$
			TOTAL (Carry to Page 3 Line 1)				$

COLUMN TWO

Group	Rating		Maximum Open Limits	Policy Limits	Group Totals	Prem. per M.	Premium
6	Aa	1	$ 25,000	$			
	A+	1	$ 25,000	$			
	A	1	$ 25,000	$	$	$14.00	$
7	B+	1½	$ 25,000	$			
	B	1½	$ 25,000	$			
	C+	1½	$ 25,000	$	$	$15.00	$
	Blank	2	$ 15,000	$	$	$15.00	$
8	C	2	$ 15,000	$			
	D+	2	$ 12,500	$			
	D	2	$ 10,000	$	$	$20.00	$
9	E	2½	$ 5,000	$			
	F	3	$ 3,000	$	$	$30.00	$
10	G	3½	$ 1,500	$			
	H	3½	$ 750	$			
	J	3½	$ 500	$	$	$30.00	$
			Non Selective Coverage TOTAL	$	$	$12.50	$
			TOTAL (Carry to Page 3 Line 2)				$

COLUMN THREE

Group	Rating		Maximum Open Limits	Policy Limits	Group Totals	Prem. per M.	Premium
11	Aa	1½	$ 10,000	$		$28.00*	$
	A+	1½	$ 10,000	$		$28.00*	
	A	1½	$ 10,000	$		$28.00*	
12	B+	2	$ 10,000	$		$30.00*	
	B	2	$ 10,000	$		$30.00*	
	C+	2	$ 10,000	$		$30.00*	
15	Blank	3	$ 1,500	$		$30.00*	
13	C	2½	$ 7,500	$		$35.00*	
	D+	2½	$ 6,250	$		$35.00*	
	D	2½	$ 5,000	$		$35.00*	
14	E	3	$ 2,500	$		$40.00*	
	F	3½	$ 1,500	$		$40.00*	
			Non Selective Coverage TOTAL	$		$20.00*	$
			TOTAL (Carry to Page 3 Line 3)				$

*If the coverage on a rating under Column Three be not more than 50% of the coverage on the corresponding Capital Rating under Column Two, then the coverage on such rating under Column Three may be charged for at the following rates per M; Group 11—$14.00; Group 12—$15.00; Group 13—$20.00; Group 14—$30.00; Group 15—$30.00.

FIG. 42.　Schedule for premium computation.

The insured may stipulate how much coverage he wishes on each of the various ratings, but usually he may not stipulate more than is shown as maximum limits in the form shown in Fig. 42. If it is necessary to sell certain customers amounts higher than ordinarily allowed against their rating, this can be done by naming the accounts for the higher than average coverage and limiting the higher coverage to these specified accounts. It will be noted that the coverage on accounts with second and third credit ratings is less than on accounts with like capital but with a first rating. Thus the insured may ask for $50,000 at the regular premium rate on an account with a rating of C + 1. If the nature of the insured's business is such that he would be very unlikely to extend as high a credit, a lesser amount will be satisfactory which will reduce the premium. A customer with the same capital rating but with a second credit rating or C + 1½ is limited to $25,000, and C + 2 or third credit rating to $10,000, but, if desired, second credit ratings may be covered for more than first credits.

If the agency revises a rating by report and the policyholder has been notified of such revision, the revised rating governs all subsequent shipments. If a customer's name is not listed in the latest rating book, then a report published within 4 months prior to date of shipment, or, if no such report has been published, then the report published within 4 months after shipment, is accepted to ascertain the rating to be covered.

It is also possible to obtain a policy providing coverage without reference to mercantile agencies. Where this is done, there is a single limit of coverage applying to any customer to whom the policyholder may ship. These policies provide 75 per cent coverage on each account shipped. This type of policy is not limited to any one class but can be applied generally. The more frequent application of this type is with those lines of business not normally rated by the mercantile agency. Thus complete coverage may be obtained.

If an account is not covered in full by a policy and a loss occurs, the insured may collect up to the amount of the coverage as determined by the policy. The fact that the account has been "oversold" does not affect his insurance. It merely means that the insured has voluntarily assumed the risk in excess of the coverage. Should there be any salvage on the account, it is prorated between the insurance company and the insured as their interests appear. Thus a customer with a rating of E 2 may be covered by the policy to the extent of $10,000, while the insured may have extended a credit of $12,000. In the event of loss, the policyholder will collect on the basis of a $10,000 loss. If any dividends are subsequently paid, the insurance company and the policyholder will share them on the basis of 10/12 and 2/12, respectively.

Credit insurance coverage is no longer limited to any class of ratings. It is now possible to insure all the accounts shipped by a company. The rates for insuring the more hazardous portion of a business are naturally higher because the risk is greater. At the same time, the primary loss to be borne would be higher because the loss expectancy is greater. Most important, however, is the fact that complete coverage can be obtained.

There is a recent development in General Coverage policies of permitting the policyholder to report at the end of each month the amount of coverage used and additional premium is charged for that month only. This coverage is known as "available coverage" and is designed for those businesses whose shipments are of a seasonal nature. It is usual that a prepaid amount of coverage is created in the policy. The policyholder then reports to the insuring company the amount owing by each account at the end of the month, which amount is in excess of the prepaid limit. The net result of this type of coverage is a reduction in premium, because in the months when the coverage is not used, there is no additional premium charged.

Primary Loss. This term refers to the loss which the insured must bear before any payment will be made under the policy. The policy is predicated upon the insured's bearing the primary loss for his business; thus the cash premium for insurance is of necessity much less than would be the case if the insurance company undertook to make good all credit losses. Primary loss is the amount that years of experience have indicated should be expected each year. It is pointed out by credit insurance authorities that, while the primary loss is calculable for a typical business, the skillful handling of credits may, in a particular instance, show losses for a given year to be less than normal. In such cases this difference represents a saving to the insured if he bears the primary loss himself, since he pays no premium to cover it. In determining the primary loss for any specific policy, the experience tables in that line are consulted, and the experience of the applicant under consideration is used to vary the primary loss for that particular policy. For instance, if the experience for the line as a whole is 4/10 of 1 per cent, and the risk under consideration through skillful credit analysis has maintained an average of 2/10 of 1 per cent, the experience table for the line will be merited so that the insured will receive a reduction because of his favorable experience.

The primary loss of a policyholder is not increased because of any abnormal losses should the policyholder demonstrate careful credit judgment. In determining the primary loss, consideration is given to the line of industry to which the insured belongs; the class of customers he sells, whether they be regular or inferior rated; the amount of the single limit; the terms of sale; the volume of business and his experience for the past 5 years, or the length of time in business, if that be shorter. In arriving at the loss experience, such portions of the losses sustained by the insured as would not have been covered by the policy contemplated may be disregarded.

Premium. The premium is calculated on (1) the coverage applying to the various ratings of the mercantile agency selected, (2) the sales volume, and (3) additional charges for special riders or conditions attached to the policy. The policy is regularly written on a 1-year basis.

In Fig. 42 you will find the basic charge for the various regular ratings covered. This is the basis for arriving at the premium to insure any business.

For the purpose of computing the premium, the ratings of the mercantile agency selected are divided into groups, and the premium is usually calculated on the single limits used for first, second, or third credit ratings. The rates as applied to Dun & Bradstreet, Inc., are illustrated for one type of policy. Thus in groups 3 and 8 the applicant may specify coverage as follows:

FIRST CREDITS		SECOND CREDITS	
C1½	$10,000	C2	$ 7,500
D + 1½	10,000	D + 2	7,500
D1½	7,500	D2	7,000
	$27,500		$22,000

The cost of the coverage would be ascertained by first multiplying the limits of coverage by the premium rated ($27,500 at $6 per M and $22,000 at $20 per M or a total of $605). Having thus ascertained the premium for each group according to coverage, we should make further charges for sales volume, inferior rating coverage, the policy amount, and any special riders attached. Computation of the premium, as has been shown, is somewhat technical and fails to give the reader, in the absence of an actual illustration, an idea of the cost of the premium of credit insurance. Probably a much simpler statement is the fact the premiums as a whole average about $\frac{1}{12}$ of 1 per cent of the sales volume covered. To this general statement there are many exceptions where the cost will be either more or less depending on the amount of coverage, the volume, and the risk the insurance company assumes.

An applicant for credit insurance may be willing to bear more than the average primary loss, while he may be unwilling to take the entire risk to which he may be subjected. This can be accomplished by increasing the primary loss as originally calculated and lowering the premium to be paid. This is known as division of premium and primary loss, and is frequently employed where the applicant thinks in terms of reinsurance.

Insolvency. The applicant for credit insurance should know the conditions under which an account will be accepted as a loss. The policy defines "insolvency" with sufficient exactness and with a broad interpretation of the word. Most policies carry the same definitions of insolvency. To give the reader an illustration of this broad interpretation, the definitions of insolvency of one type of policy are given.

Condition 2—Past Due Accounts. When the Policyholder, during the term of this Policy, shall have filed with the Company for collection an account against a debtor not insolvent as defined in Condition 3, at the time the account was so filed, then so much of such account that was due and payable at the date of filing, but not more than ninety (90) days past due under the original terms of sale, shall be treated in any adjustment under this Policy as though the debtor had become insolvent as defined in Condition 3. Every such account so filed shall include all indebtedness then due and payable and shall be accompanied with a Notification of Claim as prescribed in Condition 4.

Condition 3—Insolvency Defined. The Insolvency of a debtor for the purposes of this Policy shall be deemed to have occurred only when:

1. A debtor shall have absconded.
2. A sole debtor shall have died.
3. A sole debtor shall have been adjudged insane.
4. A receiver shall have been appointed for a debtor.
5. A debtor shall have transferred or sold his stock in trade in bulk.
6. A writ of attachment or execution shall have been levied on a debtor's stock in trade and said stock sold thereunder, or the writ returned unsatisfied.
7. A debtor shall have made a general offer of compromise to his creditors for less than his indebtedness.
8. Possession shall have been taken under a chattel mortgage given by a debtor on his stock in trade.
9. A debtor's business shall have been assigned to or taken over by a committee, appointed by a majority in number and amount of his creditors.
10. There shall have been a recording of or taking possession under an assignment or a deed of trust made by a debtor for the benefit of his creditors.
11. A voluntary or involuntary proceeding shall have been instituted to adjudge a debtor bankrupt.
12. A proceeding for the relief of a debtor shall have been instituted in a Court of Bankruptcy.

Filing the Claim. Within twenty (20) days after acquiring knowledge of a debtor's insolvency under Condition 3 (Insolvency Defined), the indemnified must file notification of claim with the company. The purpose of such prompt action is to give the insurance company the right to represent the policyholder properly in the estate of the debtor and to take such actions as are necessary to prove the claim against the debtor's estate. When the claims, either insolvency or past due items, are filed, the company attempts to effect collection or salvage the account. As collections are made, they are remitted immediately to the policyholder. When the aggregate of the uncollected claims, after deducting coinsurance, exceeds the primary loss, payment for excess loss is made by the insurance company.

Claim Settlement. The policy also defines how losses are to be computed. From each gross covered and proved loss, the following are deducted:

1. All amounts collected from the debtor or obtained from any other source.

2. The invoiced price of goods returned, reclaimed or replevined, when such goods are in the undisputed possession of the Policyholder.

3. Any discount to which the debtor would be entitled at the time of adjustment.

4. Any legally sustainable setoff that the debtor may have against the Policyholder.

5. Any amount mutually agreed upon as thereafter obtainable.

This illustration will indicate that credit is given the policyholder for the net amount realized.

After making the deductions provided for above for each gross loss covered and proved under this policy, the result shall be the net loss. From the aggregate amount of net loss there shall be deducted the coinsurance, usually 10 per cent; and from the remainder the agreed primary loss; and the remainder, not exceeding the amount of the policy, shall be the amount due and then payable to the insured.

If the indebtedness of the debtor to the insured at the date of the insolvency is not covered in full by this policy, then said deductions are made pro rata, that is, in the ratio which the amount covered bears to the whole of such indebtedness. In that event, such assigned accounts shall be handled by the company for the joint benefit of the insured and the company as their interests may appear.

If any covered and filed account of the insured is disputed, in whole or in part, the same shall not be allowed in any adjustment under the policy until such disputed account has been finally determined to be a valid and legally sustainable claim against the debtor or the debtor's estate, at which time the account, so far as covered, shall be adjusted under the policy and the amount then due the insured by the company shall be paid.

The following illustrates the method of adjustment as outlined above:

Name of customer	Loss amount	Collected by company	Net returned	Excess over single account limit	Amount admitted as loss
James Hallman...	$ 8,000	$2,000	....	......	$ 6,000
Louis Gardner....	5,000	......	$200	......	4,800
Henry Burton....	12,000	......	....	......	12,000
George Fisher....	14,000	......	....	$4,000	10,000
					$32,800
			Coinsurance 10 per cent...		3,280
					$29,520
			Primary loss.............		1,800
					$27,720

Fig. 43.   Illustration of claim adjustment.

According to the above illustration, the insured will recover $27,720. If the company should subsequently succeed in collecting, let us say, the account of Henry Burton, there would be returned to the policyholder $1,200. If the account were insolvent at the date of adjustment, there would be no fee charge. If, however, the Burton account were a past due item filed within ninety (90) days of the due date, there would be deducted from the $1,200 the policyholder's pro rata share of collection costs. The remaining $10,800, less the cost of collection, would be credited to the salvage.

Application for Policy. The formal application for a policy contains representations and warranties signed by the applicant in which he notes the line of business and how long in it; whether he is a jobber or manufacturer; terms of sale; the territory covered by such sales; whether any change is contemplated in the method of doing business; whether the applicant has ever carried credit insurance; and a statement of his sales and losses due to insolvency during the past 5 years.

Credit Insurance Discussed. While the previous description of credit insurance is far from complete, since no attempt has been made to acquaint the reader with the provisions of all the policies, enough has been given to inform one as to the general conditions under which credit insurance policies are written. The average businessman considers the method of determining the three important factors of coverage, normal loss, and premiums very complicated. Hence, but few make any serious attempt to understand the basic principles under which a policy is written. Nor is it necessary. Credit insurance, as all other forms of insurance, should be considered only with these factors in mind:

1. The value of the property to be insured
2. The risk involved
3. The cost of insurance

The usual procedure is to leave the technical aspects of the problem to the insurance company. It is not necessary for the insured to understand how the policy is written. He does not know how the premiums are determined in either fire or life insurance. He knows the protection which he receives and the cost of it, the two all-important features.

The fundamental purpose of credit insurance is protection of working capital invested in accounts receivable. Follow, if you will, the cycle of working capital. Dollars are exchanged, through credit, for inventory which, if the subject is a manufacturer, is first raw material, then work in process, and finally finished goods. In all these three periods, the value of the dollar is surrounded with insurance protection of various types. From the point of view of protection against fire, theft, and other obvious risks a manufacturer employs many safeguards. Sprinkler systems are installed, watchmen are employed, and in addition taxes are paid to support fire departments and police protection. At the moment of shipping, that manufacturer by his own act cancels all protection. At the same time, he passes title to someone else with sublime trust in the ability of that customer to pay 30, 60, or more days later. At the moment the product has its greatest value, it is transferred to someone else. The function of credit insurance is the protection of working capital while it is in the hands of the customer. To assist further in the certainty of recapturing this capital, the credit insurance company maintains service departments to bring whatever pressure may be necessary to secure prompt payment of the accounts receivable.

Credit insurance companies today are being asked to assume credit risks for huge amounts of money—some as great as $1,500,000. Before the insuring company will assume such a risk, it not only scrutinizes the accounts very closely but insists on using reinsurance facilities to spread the risk still further. In this respect the insuring company practices what it preaches—diversification of risk. The employment of reinsurance facilities makes it possible for the company to assume such risks and in like manner this facility makes it possible for the manufacturing company to accept the larger orders with their consequent larger profits.

The advocates of credit insurance state that it is a guaranty that a wholesaler or manufacturer shall not suffer from bad-debt losses which are in excess of the normal amount incident to the volume of his annual business. This statement is true when the insured confines his sales to insurable risks and limits the credit to the coverage established by the policy. If this plan is followed, it may mean a restriction of sales, for it is quite probable that prior to taking credit insurance some accounts were sold which would not come within the protection of the policy, or insurable accounts were sold beyond the limit of a coverage. Assuming that risks are accepted without regard to the restrictions of the policy, sales of $1,000,000, for example, may contain $200,000 of sales to accounts in part of inferior rating and in part in excess of the coverage limits. Losses on such sales are not insured. If bad-debt losses are 1½ per cent on these inferior rated accounts, it is evident that $3,000 of bad-debt losses are not covered.

The Increase of Sales through Credit Insurance. It is advanced that under credit insurance a business may expand safely through the acceptance of credit of good, insured accounts. Without credit insurance such expansion might be hazardous. The insurance company contends that it can take a larger risk because the law of averages is working for them to a greater extent than it will for any single company. Their risk is not confined to any single business, to any line of business, or to any one territory. The average manufacturer cannot have all these factors in his favor. Under credit insurance through a general coverage policy the insured can "level off" his credit risk.

The credit man, knowing that his house is protected against excessive losses, can authorize shipments with more confidence. This statement is true in so far as insurable risks are concerned. Uninsurable risks must receive just as careful scrutiny as though no insurance were carried, for the credit manager is placing the risk with his house. When an order is received from an insurable risk, the temptation may be to fill it. Either the credit man will not make the same careful investigation that he otherwise would or, granting that a thorough investigation is made and the account found doubtful, the risk to the insured is much reduced. For example, an order for $500 is received. The account, though a questionable risk, is insurable. Let us assume the net profit on the order to be $25. For this sum the credit man would not take this particular risk. Under his policy he would collect $450 ($500 less coinsurance of 10 per cent). The risk therefore becomes the possibility of $25 profit against $25 actual loss. It would be no more than natural for the credit man to be influenced in his action by the insurance policy.

The proponents of credit insurance will claim that this attitude toward the policy is a perversion of the whole theory of credit insurance. Undoubtedly it is. The theory of credit insurance is that it is for the protection of a business operating in a normal manner against excessive losses which are largely occasioned by conditions and circumstances which arise after deliveries are made. Attention will also be called to the fact that the attitude described above may result in excessive losses which would raise the normal loss for the ensuing year and, consequently, raise the cost of insurance, a fact which should militate strongly against such an attitude. If a shipper is to be guided solely by the insurance policy, the question arises whether the insured needs a capable and efficient credit man. The insurance companies emphatically say "yes."

It is dangerous, however, to contemplate the use of credit insurance as taking the place of sound credit checking, and if a policy is bought for that purpose, eventually the policyholder will come to grief. Collections will get out of hand and working capital very soon becomes tied up in past due accounts. This is a costly operation, and credit insurance is not designed for this purpose. In fact, where a company does not maintain a credit department, the credit insurance company hesitates to write a policy. It prefers to back the judgment of the credit manager, who can then operate with a great deal more confidence, knowing that judgment cannot long be misplaced because the insurance company stands by to give protection where mistakes are made.

Fire and Credit Insurance. Credit insurance has been likened to fire insurance. The two are hardly comparable. In the majority of cases, all property which might be destroyed by fire is in one location or building. A fire could encompass its complete destruction. All the eggs are in one basket. Such a risk is too great a hazard to be carried alone. On the other hand, sales are spread over a wide territory and among many customers. It is inconceivable that all or even a large part should fail in any one year. Of course a panic or severe depression or business calamity might occur, but in the event of wholesale insolvencies, the capital of credit insurance companies would, perhaps, be insufficient to indemnify all policyholders. In such an event, not only might the insurance companies be unable to make good, but in the event that they could, the insured would probably find that the face of his policy was not large enough. Furthermore, in writing fire insurance, each risk is more or less carefully considered before being insured, while credit insurance companies classify their risks solely according to mercantile agency ratings which are not guaranteed and which credit men often do not accept without verification.

Losses Passed on to the Insured. The normal loss is assumed to be one of the normal expenses of the business which is distributed in the price of the goods sold. Assume that a businessman who carries no insurance has abnormal losses one year. Why could he not recoup the next year by adding a little more to the selling price? Every businessman knows that increasing the selling price of his merchandise is not so simply accomplished. If he cannot pass the loss along to his trade, however, it must come out of his own profit. The same condition will prevail even if he carries credit insurance. If abnormal loss is experienced, the normal loss amount of the policy for the ensuing year will be thereby increased, so that the loss would probably be borne eventually by the insured. It is obvious that the creditor, speaking of him in his generic sense, must stand his own losses. The insurance company can pay back to him only what he has paid to it after the insurance company's expenses and profits have been deducted. This is, of course, true of all forms of casualty insurance.

From this discussion it is apparent that credit insurance, as at present conducted, protects the insured to a considerable degree against unanticipated losses. The businessman will carefully consider the protection afforded and the cost of the protection. He will also consider the need for protection. In the case of a house selling relatively few accounts, and when the risk is, therefore, inadequately distributed, it may be particularly advisable to have such risks underwritten. The need for such underwriting is doubly great if the creditor concern is not firmly established. The concern with limited capital might find its foundation severely shaken by abnormal losses. Such a concern would prefer to pay a fixed loss than to have its very existence threatened. The strong concern, however, with diversified risks may prefer to set up a contingent reserve equivalent to the insurance premium that it would have to pay. Such a reserve might be sufficient to offset abnormal losses over a period of years in the concern where credits are handled by an efficient credit department in the care of a well-qualified credit manager. Indeed, many a business principal regards his credit department as sufficient credit insurance.

It is true that any insurance company is really the custodian of the funds of its policyholders. It collects from many to reimburse the unfortunate few. This is the principle of insurance and the purpose of all insurance funds. Insurance should never attempt to insure against a certainty. Its purpose is the protection against the unforeseen—the uncontrollable. In credits, very often, the risk was present when the credit was accepted, but, as all available credit information is incomplete, it may not disclose the true condition.

In many instances banks insist on their clients carrying credit insurance because it places another endorsement on the accounts receivable. It strengthens the credit position of the carrier.

Another step forward is the adoption of the bank rider. This compares in part to the former collateral benefit rider, by which a third party is assigned an interest in a policy. It has been broadened to give the same powers of filing accounts, etc., to a bank or lending institution that are possessed by the policyholder himself. In this manner the accounts receivable assigned to a bank as collateral for loan purposes assume a more positive value to that bank because they can police the collections of the accounts assigned as collateral, if that be necessary.

This enlargement of the collateral benefit privileges has led to departments being set up by certain banks handling accounts receivable loans. This use of credit insurance for security purposes in reality provides an endorsement to the obligation of the debtor. Two-name paper is always better than the single promise to pay.

GUARANTIES

A creditor may sometimes attempt to ensure the redemption of a credit by securing the promise of another to be answerable for the debtor's obligation. This is termed "a contract of guaranty" or "surety," as the case may be. The words guarantor and surety are sometimes used interchangeably. But, strictly, a surety is one who is bound with the principal upon the original contract and in the same terms, while a guarantor is bound upon a collateral contract to make good in case the principal fails. The distinction as to whether a contract is one of guaranty or of surety is unimportant for our discussion.

A consideration of the protection of credit by means of guaranties involves three points: (1) who may become guarantors, (2) the credit of the guarantor, and (3) the form of the contract of guaranty. The second, the credit of the guarantor, may be dismissed as having been adequately covered in Part II of this book. The first and third points will receive further discussion.

Who May Become Guarantors. It is much more important that the credit man should know who may *not* be held as guarantors than to know who may be so held. Obviously, only those who may legally contract can enter into this form of contract. There is no other restriction which applies to individuals except in the case of married women. A partnership may guarantee in the regular course of business, that is, in the furtherance of its own business, and the signature of a partner will bind the firm. A partner, however, cannot bind the firm in an accommodation guaranty, though such a guaranty can become binding if signed by each partner.

A corporation, according to the general rule of law, cannot guarantee the liability of others, except in so far as it becomes a guarantor in the ordinary course of its business or unless it receives the proceeds of the paper which it guarantees. This statement will hold even though the implied power to guarantee seems to be given by its charter. A corporation has, however, implied power to enter into a contract of guaranty or suretyship *whenever the transaction can reasonaly be said to be incidental to the conduct of the business authorized by its charter*. But authority to lend credit to another is not to be implied simply from the fact it may be beneficial to the corporation. A fine legal distinction may be drawn between such contracts of guaranty. The credit man is advised, therefore, not to accept a corporation guaranty unless certain that it can be enforced.

Unless there is specific authority contained in its charter, a bank has no implied power to lend its credit and cannot become an accommodation endorser or a guarantor. If, however, a guaranty is necessary to protect the bank's own rights, or where the guaranty relates to commercial paper and is incidental to the purchase and sale thereof, or if such guaranty is specially authorized by law, there is an exception to the general rule. A bank's endorsement is of course binding in favor of the bona fide holder of the instruments so endorsed, for the reason that there is no obligation on the holder to inquire whether the bank owned the paper at the time of its endorsement.

In the absence of an enabling statute, a married woman cannot make contracts of guaranty. In many states where she may otherwise guaranty, she is prohibited from guaranteeing the account of her husband, except in a special way. A guaranty of a married woman, either for her

GUARANTY OF PAST AND FUTURE INDEBTEDNESS

(The following form specifically limits the liability of the guarantor and has the advantage of specifically permitting the creditor to extend the time of payment to the principal debtor without notice to the guarantor and without releasing the guarantor's liability.)

To...

Gentlemen:

For and in consideration of (*recite actual consideration*), the receipt of which is hereby acknowledged, I hereby guarantee, absolutely and unconditionally, at all times, unto you, the payment of any indebtedness or balance of indebtedness of .... of .... State of .... hereinafter called debtor, to you, to an amount not exceeding .... dollars, whether such indebtedness now exists, or is incurred hereafter, and in whatever form it may be evidenced.

I hereby waive notice of acceptance of the guaranty, and all notice of the goods and merchandise sold by you to said debtor, and all notice of defaults by said debtor, and I consent to any extension or extensions of the time or times of payment of said indebtedness, or any portion thereof, and to any change in form, or renewal at any time, of such indebtedness, or any part thereof, or to any evidence thereof taken at any time by you.

This is to be a continuing guaranty, and the extension of the time of payment or the acceptance of any sum or sums on account, or the acceptance of notes, drafts or any security from said debtor, shall in no way weaken or impair the validity of this guaranty. Should any purchase heretofore or hereafter made by the said debtor, of you, be not paid at maturity, you shall have the right to proceed against me therefor at any time, without any notice whatsoever and without any proceeding or action against the said debtor, and I hereby waive any demand whatsoever for payment.

This guaranty shall continue at all times to the amount of .... dollars regardless of the amounts received from or paid by the said debtor and shall not be revoked by the death of the guarantor but shall remain in full force and effect until the undersigned or the executor or administrator of the undersigned shall have given notice in writing to make no further advances on the security of this guaranty and until such written notice shall be received

FIG. 44. A form of guaranty.

husband or for anyone else, should not be accepted unless it is determined that such a guaranty is legally binding in the state where made.

The Form of the Contract of Guaranty. Only a few fundamental rules with respect to guaranties can be here given, as the subject varies too much in the different states. This section will point out a few essential principles of general application.

Writing. The old English statute of Frauds, which is substantially reenacted in all the states, provides that a guaranty cannot be enforced unless it be in writing.

by you from the undersigned or his executor or administrator. A registry return receipt for said letter shall be conclusive evidence of receipt of notice or revocation.

This guaranty shall not be abrogated or affected in any manner by any change in the firm or status of the debtor, whether caused by death, by the admission of any new member or members or by the withdrawal of any member or members, or by any change from any cause whatsoever.

It is further understood that nothing herein contained shall prevent you from extending credit to the said debtor, to an amount exceeding the sum above stated, being the amount guaranteed hereunder, at any time, and such action on your part shall not abrogate or affect this guaranty.

Should you extend credit to the said debtor, in a sum or sums exceeding the amount of this guaranty, then in that event, you shall have the right to make such application of any payment or payments on account, as you may see fit.

Should the said debtor, at any time, become bankrupt or insolvent, then in that event, you shall have the right, at your option, without demand or notice whatsoever, to prove and file your entire claim in any court of competent jurisdiction, whether such claim exceeds the amount of this guaranty or not, and to collect any dividends that may be realized on said entire claims; and in that event, you shall have the right, at your option, without any notice or demand whatsoever, to proceed against me at any time, for the difference between the amount of said entire claim due you by the said debtor, and the amount of such dividend or dividends thereon, up to and including the sum above stated, being the amount guaranteed hereunder; if such difference should exceed the sum above stated, being the amount guaranteed hereunder, I shall not be liable for such excess, but for any difference between said entire indebtedness and said dividends thereon, up to and including said sum above stated, being the amount guaranteed hereunder, you shall have the right, at your option, to proceed against me, at any time, without any demand or notice whatsoever.

The guarantor hereby waives the benefit of all Homestead Exemption laws.

In witness hereof, I have hereunto set my hand and seal at . . . .
State of . . . . this . . . . day of . . . . 19. . . . .
. . . .

FIG. 44. (Concluded).

Strict Construction. Guaranties are always construed by the courts strictly in favor of the guarantor. He cannot be held beyond the precise terms of his contract.

Consideration. Guaranties, like other contracts, are not good unless there be a consideration. Though ordinarily a consideration may be proved when not so stated or be disproved when stated, it is preferable to state a consideration, as this raises a prima facie presumption of one.

Date. Guaranties should always be dated, as the date is often an important element. For example, after an order is received and filled, a guaranty of its payment without other consideration would not be good.

Variance of Contract Releases Guarantor. Any agreement between the creditor and debtor to vary the terms of the sale or contract guaranteed without the consent of the guarantor releases the guarantor.

Extension of Time. An agreement with the debtor to extend the time of a guaranteed account or note, without the consent of the guarantor, is such a variance and discharges the guarantor. Whether the creditor must notify the guarantor that the principal has defaulted in the payment or other obligation covered by the guaranty is a disputed question. Unless the creditor knows of the requirement by the state under which the contract will be interpreted, it will be safer either to notify or to have the contract waive the requirement.

Death of Guarantor. The death of the guarantor has the same effect as an express revocation, though some states require that the holder of the guaranty should have actual notice of the death in order that it should operate as a revocation.

With these principles in mind it is suggested that the reader make a careful study of the guaranty shown in Fig. 44. It will be noted that this form attempts to overcome the strict construction in favor of the guarantor by getting him to waive a number of his rights. If he cannot be induced to sign such a guaranty, the creditor must be much more alert to see that he does not release the guarantor by acts either of commission or omission.

TEXT AND RESEARCH QUESTIONS

1. *a.* How does business in general endeavor to protect itself against losses through bad debts?
   b. What is the purpose of credit insurance?
   c. What is the purpose of the classification of business by credit insurance companies?
2. *a.* Why is a coinsurance clause always inserted in a credit insurance policy?
   b. What is the usual amount of coinsurance carried by the insured?
3. *a.* What is the meaning of coverage?
   b. How is the normal loss of the insured determined?
4. *a.* What three factors are considered in the computation of the premium?
   b. How can the insured decrease the amount of premium which he will have to pay?
5. If the average business pursues its normal selling policy, why does not credit insurance insure it against all abnormal loss (except, of course, coinsurance)?

6. *a.* In what way does credit insurance invite the acceptance of risks which the credit manager may judge to be subnormal credit risks?

b. Why cannot credit insurance be likened to fire insurance?

7. You are the credit manager of the General Merchandise Wholesaling Co., and your concern has been considering taking out credit insurance. The president of your company has asked you to submit a brief outlining the advantages and the disadvantages of credit insurance to your concern. Prepare such a brief.

8. *a.* What is the distinction between a guarantor and a surety?

b. What three points must always be considered before a guaranty is accepted by the seller?

9. *a.* Under what circumstances can a corporation become a guarantor?

b. How would you proceed to determine whether a guaranty given by a married woman could be enforced?

10. *a.* Why is it necessary to study very carefully the form of the guaranty?

b. May a guarantor revoke his guaranty?

c. Does a release of the debtor discharge the guarantor?

d. May a guarantor avail himself of defenses to the contract between the debtor and the creditor?

PROBLEMS

1. Jones, an automobile dealer, sold a sport roadster to Brown, whom he knew to be somewhat reckless and wild, on a small payment plan. A few days later he met Smith, a friend of Brown's, and expressed to Smith his fear that he had made a poor sale. Smith said to Jones in the presence of a mutual acquaintance, "Don't worry, Jones. If he does not pay you, I'll guarantee that you will get your money."

a. Should Jones have asked for this statement in writing?

b. Can Jones hold Smith if the statement can be proved?

c. Could Jones hold Smith if the statement were in writing?

d. Rewrite the statement so that Smith could unquestionably be held.

2. The X Corporation's sales are $1,000,000, and bad-debt normal loss has been determined as ½ per cent. The credit insurance premium is ⅙ per cent of annual sales. By what percentage will bad debts have to increase in order to recover the premium? (In this problem, ignore such relevant items as coinsurance, noninsurable risks, costs of collection, etc.)

3. X, a contractor, wishes to buy material from Y, who refuses to check X's credit. X suggests Y ask A, who is acceptable to Y as a risk, for a guaranty. Y sends A a guaranty form, including all sorts of waivers, which A refuses to sign. But he states in his letter "If you will deliver the material to X, I will pay the bill." Does this protect Y? Why or why not?

APPENDIXES

A.   Illustration of Part of an Acceptance Agreement............... 543
B.   Guide for Exchange of Credit Information................... 544
C 1. Regular Report of Dun & Bradstreet, Inc.................... 547
C 2. Revised Report of Dun & Bradstreet, Inc.................... 548
D.   Complete N.C.O. Report, Including Financial Statement and
      Accountant's Supplementary Information.................. 550
E.   Comparative Interchange Reports........................... 557
F.   Credit Bureau of Greater New York, Inc., Reports............. 561
G.   Financial Statement Form................................ 563
H.   Continuing Statement Agreement.......................... 565
I.   Problem for Comparative Analysis......................... 566
J.   Foulke's Ratios... 569
K.   Credit Application Form................................. 574

ILLUSTRATION OF PART OF AN ACCEPTANCE AGREEMENT

ACCEPTANCE AGREEMENT

MANUFACTURERS TRUST COMPANY
55 Broad Street
New York 15, N. Y.

New York,..19........

Dear Sirs:

For and in consideration of your accepting from time to time drafts drawn on you by the undersigned or by persons designated in writing by the undersigned, the undersigned hereby agree(s) as follows:

1. To pay to you, in New York Clearing House Funds, not later than one business day before the maturity of each draft accepted by you, an amount sufficient to cover such acceptance(s), the amount of your commission at such rate as you may determine to be proper interest at the prevailing rate, where chargeable, and all pertinent expenses.

2. That as security for prompt and unconditional payment of the obligations of the undersigned hereunder, and every obligation of the undersigned to you and your claims of every nature and description against the undersigned, whether now existing or hereafter owing, originally contracted with you and/or another or others and acquired in any manner by you, whether contracted by the undersigned alone or jointly or severally with others, direct or indirect, absolute or contingent, secured and not secured, matured or not matured (all of which are hereinafter called "Obligations"), you are hereby given the right to the possession and disposition of any and all property shipped in connection with each draft, accepted by you hereunder and in any way relative thereto and any and all shipping documents, warehouse receipts, policies or certificates of insurance or other documents covering such property or relative thereto or to such drafts, whether or not such documents, goods or other property be released to or upon the order of any of the undersigned on trust or bailee receipts, and in and to the proceeds of each and all of the. foregoing, all of which to be held by you, subject to all the terms of this agreement.

3. In order to further secure the payment of Obligations, you are hereby given a continuing lien for the amount of all Obligations upon any and all property of the undersigned in your actual or constructive possession or in transit to you, or your correspondents from or for the undersigned, whether for safekeeping, custody, pledge, transmission, collection or otherwise. You are also given a continuing lien and/or right of set-off for the amount of Obligations upon the deposits (general or special) and credits of the undersigned with, and all claims of the undersigned against, you.

4. The property enumerated in paragraphs 2 and 3 hereof and any property now or hereafter pledged, or deposited with you or your agent to secure Obligations are hereinafter collectively called "Collateral". That without the necessity for any reservation of rights against the undersigned and without notice to or further assent by the undersigned, the liability of any party for or upon Obligations or Collateral may from time to time, in whole or in part, be renewed, extended, premature, modified, compromised, settled for cash, credit or otherwise and upon any terms and conditions you may deem advisable, and you may discharge or release said other person(s) from such liabilities and any Collateral may from time to time, in whole or in part, be exchanged, sold or surrendered by you. You shall not be liable for any failure to collect or demand payment of or to protest or give any notice of nonpayment of Collateral or any part therof or for any delay in so doing nor shall you be under any obligation to take any action whatsoever with respect to Collateral. You may endorse the undersigned's name on all notes, checks, drafts, bills of exchange, money orders or commercial paper included in Collateral or representing the proceeds thereof. The undersigned hereby waives protest of any negotiable instrument to which the undersigned may be a secondary party. All Collateral may be registered in the name of your nominee.

5. In the event that any property is released by you to or upon the undersigned in trust, the undersigned will sign and deliver to you trust receipts and/or statement of trust receipt financing and will pay all the required filing fees, and upon the undersigned's failure to do so you are authorized as the agent of the undersigned, to sign any such receipt or statement. Upon any transfer, delivery, surrender or indorsement to undersigned or upon the undersigned's request, of any bill of lading, warehouse receipt or other documents, relative to any drafts drawn hereunder, at any time held by you or by any of your correspondents, the undersigned will indemnify and hold you harmless from all claims, demands, or actions which may arise against you or any correspondent by reason thereof.

6. To procure promptly any necessary import, export or other license for the importing, exporting, shipping or warehousing property covered by any documents held by you or the undersigned's correspondents relative to any draft(s) accepted by you hereunder or included in the Collateral, and to comply with all foreign and domestic laws and governmental regulations in regards to the shipment and/or warehousing and/or the financing thereof and to furnish all certificates in that respect as you may require; to keep the property adequately covered by insurance satisfactory to you and to make the loss or adjustment, if any, payable to you; to pay all taxes, shipping, warehousing, cartage or other charges or expenses, upon, or with respect to the said property and to reimburse you therefor upon demand in the event that you or your correspondents pay for or incur any liability in connection with any of the aforementioned charges or any above mentioned licenses.

7. You and any of your correspondents may receive and accept as "a bill of lading" in connection with any transaction hereunder, any document issued or purporting to be issued on behalf of any carrier which acknowledges receipt of property for transportation, whatever the specific provision of such document and the date of each such document shall be deemed the date of shipment of the property mentioned therein. You may receive and accept as insurance documents either policies or certificates.

8. Neither you nor any of your correspondents shall be responsible for (a) the existence, character, quality, quantity, condition, packing, value or delivery of the property purporting to be represented by the documents; (b) any difference in character, quality, quantity, condition or value of the property from that expressed in the documents; (c) the validity, sufficiency or genuineness of documents or of any indorsements thereon, even if such documents should in effect prove to be in any and all respects, invalid, insufficient, fraudulent or forged; (d) the time, place, manner or order in which shipment is made; (e) the character, adequacy, validity or genuineness of any insurance; or any other risk connected with insurance; (f) any deviation from instructions, delay, default or fraud by the shipper and/or any one else in connection with the property or the shipping thereof; (g) the solvency, responsibility or relationship to the property, of any party issuing any documents in connection with the prop-

(Over)

280 2.58

SOURCE: Manufacturers Trust Company.

543

APPENDIX B

GUIDE FOR EXCHANGE OF CREDIT INFORMATION

Because of conflicts in exchange of credit information, the National Association of Credit Management and Robert Morris Associates designed the following:

STATEMENT OF PRINCIPLES IN THE EXCHANGE OF CREDIT INFORMATION BETWEEN BANKS AND MERCANTILE CREDITORS

The first and cardinal principle in the exchange of information is absolute respect for the confidential nature of inquiries and replies and of the identities of inquirers and sources.

WRITTEN inquiries should be by direct communication, manually and responsibly signed, and should correctly give name and address of the subject of inquiry. When an inquiry is made in person or by telephone, the inquirer should satisfactorily identify himself.

EVERY inquiry should indicate specifically: amount involved, reason, terms, availability of background information and whether source was given as reference. If inquirer's bank is used, the subject's bank of account should be named if known. When multiple bank inquiries are made, it should be so stated, and if to banks in the same locality their names are given.

FILE revisions should be undertaken only when necessary, and such inquiries should contain an expression of experience if appropriate.

WHEN inquiries are made on behalf of third parties it should be clearly stated but the identity of the other party must not be disclosed without permission.

REPLIES should be prompt. If written they should be manually and responsibly signed and as complete as possible, consistent, however, with the amount and nature of the inquiry. Specific questions should be answered if practicable.

IF confidential nature of relationship with subject prevents disclosure of desired information, answers should so state.

THIS statement rests upon two fundamentals:
CONFIDENCE
CONSIDERATENESS

The principles that it embraces relate to one or the other of these fundamentals, and they are therefore grouped under those two headings.

CONFIDENCE

Credit information is confidential. It is intended solely to assist an actual or bona fide prospective creditor to reach a decision in a genuine credit problem. Any other use of it is a breach of confidence and of this Statement of Principles. Credit information is not for competitive use.

The source of credit information is confidential. The identity of the source of information deserves the same confidence as the information itself, and should not be revealed to anyone including the subject of the inquiry.

The identity of a credit inquirer is confidential. By the very fact of an inquiry, and to the extent that experience is stated, an inquirer has in a sense revealed credit information which deserves the protection of confidence. This applies equally to inquiries for one's own use and to those made on behalf of others.

Exceptions should be only by permission. If it is necessary to use credit information for a purpose other than stated, or the identity of an inquirer or source is to be revealed it should only occur with the permission of the parties who would ordinarily be entitled to the protection of confidence.

A betrayal of confidence invites a denial of future consideration. Otherwise the entire voluntary structure of cooperation supporting the exchange of confidential business details is in danger.

CONSIDERATENESS

An inquiry should clearly describe the subject, state its object and scope, and show that it is made responsibly. Name and address of the subject should be completely and correctly stated. The reason and amount involved are essential. The identity of the inquirer should be established in letter inquiries—including firms—by manual, not fascimile, signature. It is an acknowledged basic courtesy to enclose a stamped addressed return envelope.

Sharing experience is helpful. When seeking information, it imparts a sense of confidence in the source of information and may well result in a more complete reply.

Unnecessary file revisions and duplicate bank inquiries should be avoided. File revisions should relate to seasonal requirements, and usually from several months to a year is deemed adequate except in cases of adverse experience. Unless addressing the customer's banks of account only for the experience of each, inquiries should be confined to one bank to avoid duplicate checking.

Inconsiderate inquiries invite inconsiderate replies. Thus unsigned form letters without reason or amount cannot inspire full sharing of credit information.

A reply should be made promptly and be adequate for the inquiry. The identity of the inquirer, the relationship to the subject, and the object and scope of the inquiry should govern the completeness of the reply, which should be as full as circumstances deserve. If information is withheld as being in confidence, the fact should be stated. A letter of reply should be signed in the same manner as a letter of inquiry.

APPENDIX C 1

REGULAR REPORT OF DUN & BRADSTREET, INC.

Dun & Bradstreet, Inc.   *Report*   **RATING UNCHANGED**

5912
PENN PINES PHARMACY

CD JUNE 26 195—

BROOKLYN 19 N Y
1246 HAZEL ROAD

RATING: E 2

STARTED: 1950   **PAYMENTS:** Discounted
NET WORTH: $26,865   SALES: $89,232 (Annual)

SUMMARY
THIS BUSINESS IS IN A GROWING NEIGHBORHOOD. SALES ARE INCREASING AND OPERATIONS ARE PROFITABLE.

HISTORY
The style was registered by the owner on April 30, 1950.

Starting capital consisted of $10,500 in savings, a $3,500 bank loan, and a $3,000 loan from members of the owner's family, making a total of $17,000. All loans since repaid.

Miles Gross is 41, single, and native born. A registered pharmacist, he graduated from Columbia College of Pharmacy in 1937. Employed as a pharmacist by Liggett Drug Co. between 1937 and 1950. and by Ray Drug Co. until this business was started.

OPERATION—LOCATION
Operates a pharmacy with a soda fountain. Drugs and prescriptions afford 50% of sales; balance divided between fountain, sundries, and confectionery. Fixtures are new with a twenty-foot soda fountain. Two clerks employed.

Rents the first floor of a two-story building in good condition. Store measures 20 x 50 feet. Location is in a recently developed residential section.

FINANCIAL INFORMATION
A fiscal year-end statement at April 30, 195— cents omitted:

ASSETS		LIABILITIES	
Cash on Hand	$ 304	Accts Pay	$ 3,724
Cash in Bank	1,872		
Merchandise	14,950		
Total Current	17,126	Total Current	3,724
Fixts & Equip	10,913		
Station Wagon	2,464		
Deposits	86	NET WORTH	26,865
Total Assets	30,589	Total	30,589

Net sales from May 1, 195— to April 30, 195— $89,232; gross profit $26,181; net profit $10,199; withdrawals $3,732. Monthly rent $150. Fire insurance on merchandise and fixtures, $25,000.

Signed: June 26, 195— PENN PINES PHARMACY by Miles Gross, Owner Received by Mail. No accountant indicated.

————o————

After the war, residential construction stopped up in this section with the result that both sales and profits of this business have mounted steadily. Part of earnings have been re-invested in the business to finance its steady expansion.

PAYMENTS

HC	OWE	P DUE	TERMS	May 20, 195—	
2431	2146		2—10	Dis.	Sold 3 yrs. to date
340	230		2—10—N30	Disc	Sold 1948 to 5—5—
250			2—10	Disc	Sold 3 yrs.
136	136		2—10 Prox	Disc	Sold yrs. to date
75			2—10—EOM	Disc	
15			30	Ppt	Sold 1—49 to 5—5—

6—26—5— (241 29)

APPENDIX C 2

REVISED REPORT OF DUN & BRADSTREET, INC.

5072-5251   CD 8 AUGUST 14
ADAMSON HARDWARE CO.   WHOL & RET   LITCHFIELD, ILL.
                                                                 MONTGOMERY COUNTY
                                                                 294-300 MAIN STREET

Miss Joan M. Adamson, Partner   Miss Carol T. Adamson, Partner

RATING: —

    STARTED: 1895 (present control 1947)   PAYMENTS: Slow Generally
    NET WORTH: $249,540   SALES: $889,650

SUMMARY

SALES EXPANSION AND LARGE PARTNERSHIP WITHDRAWALS HAVE BROUGHT ABOUT AN UNBALANCED CONDITION REFLECTED IN HEAVY DEBT AND SLOW MOVING INVENTORY. TRADE PAYMENTS ARE SLOW NOTWITHSTANDING STEADY BANK LOANS.

HISTORY

    The business name was registered by the partners on March 15, 1947.
    This enterprise was started in 1895 as a retail hardware business by the late Carl H. Adamson, who subsequently expanded to include both wholesale and retail sales. On February 13, 1945, Adamson died, and his will bequeathed all his real estate, personal and business assets to his two daughters, Joan M. Adamson and Carol T. Adamson. The Estate continued the business until 1947, when the present partners assumed equal ownership. The partners, born in 1891 and 1893 respectively, are single, and are not active in the management of the business.
    The active management has been left in the hands of Robert Casey, born 1900, married. He was formerly employed as Sales Manager by Thomas Hardware & Supply Co. St. Louis, Mo., for twenty years until becoming employed here in 1946.

OPERATION-LOCATION

PRODUCTS: Wholesales (80% of sales) and retails (20%) hardware, paints, sporting goods, electrical appliances, linoleum, fire arms, cement and roofing materials. (U.S.Standard Industrial Classifications: # 5072 and #5251). Sales of hardware alone represent about 65% of the total volume.

DISTRIBUTION: At wholesale to dealers (50%), lumber yards (30%), factories (10%), and contractors (10%). Retail distribution is to local residents and farmers.
Number of Accounts: About 400 active wholesale accounts are sold.
Territory: Within radius of about 80 miles.
Terms: 2%-10th Prox and cash
Salesmen: Four salaried salesmen.
Seasons: Peak sales in March, with low points during January and February and again in July and August.
Employees: In addition to the salesmen, there are fifteen store and office employees

FACILITIES: Store occupies the combined ground floor space of three adjoining buildings, with warehouse space being utilized in buildings to the rear. Four trucks are used for delivery purposes, and a siding connects the property which is owned by the firm, with tracks of the Illinois Central Railroad.

FINANCIAL INFORMATION

	Dec 31	Dec 31	Dec 31
Current Assets	$ 236,967	$ 538,884	$ 494,611
Current Liabilities	31,521	292,808	283,080
Net Working Capital	205,446	246,076	211,531
Net Worth	206,340	272,629	249,540
Net Sales	250,622	523,408	889,650

(CONTINUED)

Dun & Bradstreet, Inc.   *Report*   **RATING UNCHANGED**

ADAMSON HARDWARE CO.

CD 8 AUGUST 14
WHOL. & RET.

LITCHFIELD, ILL.
(PAGE #2)

FINANCIAL INFORMATION (Continued)
A financial statement at December 31, — cents omitted:—

ASSETS		LIABILITIES	
Cash on Hand & in Banks	$ 8,519	Accts. Pay.	$148,949
Accts. Rec. (Whol) (A)	46,622	Notes Pay.Bank	125,000
Accts. Rec. (Ret.) (B)	14,206	Notes Pay. Trucks	3,365
Merchandise	425,264	Accrued Wages & Taxes	5,766

Total Current	494,611	Total Current	283,080
Fixed Assets	36,723		
Prepaid	1,286	Net Worth	249,540
	---------		---------
Total Assets	$532,620	Total	$532,620

Net Sales 1954 $889,650, gross profit $179,604; net profit before withdrawals $28,615, withdrawals $51,704.
Accounts Receivable less bad debt reserves (A) $8,516 (B) $368. Fixed assets are net. Inventory valued at lower of cost or market. No contingent debt reported. Merchandise covered by reporting form fire insurance policy.
Signed: April 20,1955 Adamson Hardware Co., Joan M. Adamson, partner
Received by mail.
Public Accountant: William Kearns, CPA, Litchfield, Ill.

------O------

For a number of years, annual sales were fairly steady, but increased materially in 1953, and again last year through intensive promotional effort following the increase in post-war residential development. In expanding sales,however, inventories were considerably increased, a portion of which increase was financed through bank loans. The larger inventories also brought about increases in Accounts Payable, and the partnership became generally slow in meeting trade obligations.

It was stated on August 11,1955 by Robert Casey, General Manager, that steps are being taken to reduce inventories and to put trade payments on a current basis. Purchasing has been curtailed, prices have been reduced, particularly on items subject to reduced customer demand, and several employees have been released. He added that sales continue to hold even with last year, and that operations have been profitable. Partnership drawings, which last year greatly exceeded net profit, have been curtailed according to Robert Casey and are being kept in line with the earnings of the business.

Accounts are maintained at two local banks where balances average in high four to low five figures. Loans have been granted on own paper and borrowings have been steady since early in 1953.

HC	OWE	P DUE	TERMS	PAYMENTS AUG. 12,	
4850			1-10-30	Disc.	Sold 1945 to 1955
2492			2-10-30	Disc.	Sold 1925 to date
7740	2185		2-10-30	Prompt to Slow	Sold years to 1955
14803	10070	5875	1-10-30	Slow 6-7 Mos.	Sold years to date
7550	2650		2-10-60	Slow 30	Sold years
7550	2900	1900	2-10-30	Slow 60-90	Sold years to date
5000	5000	5000	1-10-30	Slow 120	Sold years to date
5000	1588	1588	2-10-30	Slow 150	Sold years to date
5000	1000	1000		Slow 60	Sold years
4475	1642	1642	2-15-30	Slow 18	Sold 1944 to date
4134	2090	525	2-10-30	Slow 60	Sold years
3839			2-10-30	Slow 30-40	Sold years
2258	330		1-10-30	Slow 30-40	Sold years to date
1738	708	708	1-10 EOM	Slow 120	Sold years to date
1663	596	558	1-10-30	Slow 120	Sold years

8-14   (744   129)

APPENDIX D

COMPLETE N.C.O. REPORT, INCLUDING FINANCIAL STATEMENT AND ACCOUNTANT'S SUPPLEMENTARY INFORMATION

NCO *Specialized Service*

CURRENT
INFORMATION

TAILORED APPAREL CO.   MFRS. MEN'S SUITS
FZ:HL-111-A   SPORT COATS & SLACKS   PHILADELPHIA 47, PA.
                           APRIL 18,   245 N. Spring St.

ANTECEDENT COMMENT - Records clear. Established 1940. Various
changes since. John Phillips dominant factor. Amply experienced
and well regarded personally. Successful. Also an officer of
affiliated contracting unit Vance Clothing Co. Inc. and Vice-
Pres. of Summer Wear Co. Inc. (separately reported by NCO) since
inception in 1950. Subject specializes in woolen and worsted
clothing while Summer Wear Co. Inc. manufacture suits of
synthetic fabrics only. Subject manufacturers medium price line.

CONDITION AND TREND -	11/30	11/30	11/30
Cash	$ 32,000	$ 29,000	$ 49,000
Receivables	210,000	313,000	480,000
Merchandise	59,000	348,000	240,000
Due from Affil.	-	59,000	6,000
Current Assets	301,000	749,000	775,000
Current Debts	130,000	580,000	540,000
Working Capital	171,000	169,000	235,000
Net Worth	208,000	293,000	357,000
Sales	1,802,000	2,310,000	3,016,000

Auditor: Dennis & Kaufman, C.P.A.

TRADE - GOOD

	HIGH CREDIT	OWING	PAST DUE	.TERMS	PAYMENTS
	$33,000	33,000	0	60/60	ppt
	30,000	25,000	0	60	ppt
Over	25,000	15,000	0	60/60	ppt-ant
	29,000	19,000	0	60	ppt-ant
	25,000	2,000	0	60	ppt
	23,000	23,000	0	60	ppt
Over	10,000	1,200	0	60	ppt
	10,000	1,800	0	60/60	ppt

Since inception in 1940 payments usually prompt or better with purchases generally in 60 or 70 days. Occasionally extended 60 plus
60 terms.   -continued-

NCO *Specialized Service* **ANTECEDENTS**
& Method of Operation

TAILORED APPAREL CO.   MFGRS. MEN'S SUITS   PHILADELPHIA 47, PA.
FZ:HL-111-A   SPORT COATS & SLACKS   245 N. Spring St.
                       APRIL 18,

REFERENCES
J.P. Stevens Co. Inc.   Meinhard & Co. Inc.
John P. Maguire & Co. Inc.   Virginia Woolens
Cleveland Worsted Co. Inc.   Burlington Mills

ANALYSIS - Started 1941 with $25,000. Since then operations, con-
sistently profitable on an active volumn. Sales with the exception
of fiscal year ending Nov. 30, 1956, have steadily increased. Only
summarized operating data made available in connection with the
Nov. 19, 1957 statement. Retained earnings of $60,000 and in
addition invested $25,000 capital. For current year made $67,000
before withdrawals of $3,300.

A comparison of gross profit and expenses of the last two years
percentagewise, showed gross profit dropped but expenses were
also cut. Consequently despite a narrower margin of profit, expanded volume permitted earnings to remain about the same.

During 1956 invested 25,000 in affiliated contracting unit Vance
Clothing Co. Inc. and during 1957 invested $75,000 in the then newly
organized Summer Wear Co. Inc., which as previously stated manufacture men's suits, sport coats and slacks of synthetic fabrics in
contrast to subject which confines its activities to woolen and
worsted garments.

Prior to Nov. 1957 statement, statements were quite liquid although,
because of the active volume, occasionally unbalanced. Nov. 1957
statement was topheavy as the result of forward buying because of
prevailing conditions at that time. In addition to general trend
of the industry of forward purchasing subject was enjoying steadily
increased demand for its products. While the Nov. 1957 statement
showed inventory in excess of business equity and liabilities four
times working capital condition was considered generally satisfactory.
Current exhibit considerably improved as the result of reduction in
both previously mentioned items. However, still unbalanced
primarily as the result of the active turnover. Financing assisted
by sizable unsecured bank accommodation. Of the indebtedness about
about 15% was owing to affiliate. Creditors quite well protected.
FINANCIAL - SATISFACTORY.

CREDIT SUGGESTION - LINE OF $10,000, OUTSIDE OF PRINCIPAL
SUPPLIERS, SUGGESTED

NCO *Specialized Service*  ANTECEDENTS
& Method of Operation

TAILORED APPAREL CO.   MFGRS. MEN'S SUITS   PHILADELPHIA 47, PA.
JOW:HL-111-   SPORT COATS & SLACKS   245 N. Spring St.
                             APRIL 18,

John Phillips   Jane (Mrs. Phillips) Gordon
                        Ann (Phillips) Cane

HISTORY - Established 1940 as a partner of John Phillips and George
Lang trading as Tailored Apparel Co. 1942 they admitted Samuel Phillips,
father of John, without change in style. 1945 George Lang withdrew and
the two remaining partners continued without change in style. 1948
Samuel Phillips died. Subsequently his widow Jane Gordon and their
daughter Anna (Phillips) Cane became partners without change in style.

PERSONNEL - John Phillips, born 1908, married. For six years he was
employed by Tremor Co., mfrs. clothing,Philadelphia. Then for three
years employed by Albert Barton Co., Inc., mfrs. clothing, N.Y.C.
1937 he succeeded his father, the late Samuel Phillips, as Vice-Pres.
and Secy. of Albert Barton Co. Inc. but he had no financial interest.
Liquidated 1936. Then became employed by Burke Clothing Co., NYC.
1940 gave up that connection and helped to establish subject. Since
connected as outlined under History except that from 1943 until 1945
he was in the U.S. Army. In addition during 1949 he helped organize
and became Secy-Treas. of the affiliated Vance Clothing Co., Inc.
which is discussed under affiliate. In addition during Sept. 1950 he
helped organize and became Vice-Pres. of the Summer Wear Co., Inc.,
mfrs. of clothing, 4950 Bond St., Philadelphia, Pa., which concern
specializes in using synthetic fabrics.

Jane (Mrs. Phillips) Gordon, is the widow of the late Samuel Phillips
and is the mother of the other two partners. Not active in the day
to day management.

Anna (Phillips) Cane has been a partner in this business since the
death of her father in 1948. Not active in the day to day management.

METHOD OF OPERATION - LINE - Manufacture medium priced men's woolen
and worsted suits, sport costs and slacks.
DISTRIBUTION - Sell retailers throughout the United States on 1/10 net
30 days. A branch selling office is maintained at 150 Fifth Ave., N.Y.C.
EQUIPMENT - Lease approximately 30,000 square feet at caption address.
Cut on premises. Garments completed by the affiliated contracting unit,
Vance Clothing Co. Inc. and also other contractors.

AFFILIATE - Vance Clothing Co. Inc., contractors of coats and
trousers, 1291 Concord Ave., also known as 1481 S. Main St., Philadelphia, was chartered under Pennsylvania laws during Sept. 1948 with
an authorized capital of $50,000 in 100 shares. Corporation works

-continued-

NCO *Specialized Service*

ANTECEDENTS
& Method of Operation

TAILORED APPAREL CO.   MFRS. MEN'S SUITS   PHILADELPHIA 47, PA.
JOW:HL-111-   SPORT COATS & SLACKS   245 N. Spring St.
                                  APRIL 18,

John Phillips   Anna (Phillips) Cane   Jane (Mrs.Phillips) Gordon

exclusively for Tailored Apparel Co. Its officers are Abraham Cohen,
Pres. and John Phillips, Secy. and Treas.

BANKS -   Liberty National Bank   Philadelphia, Pa.
           Central Trust Co.   "   "

FINANCIAL STATEMENT SUBMITTED TO NATIONAL CREDIT OFFICE, INC.

Name.......... Tailored Apparel Co. .... Business. mfrs. Young men's clothing

Street and No.. 245 N. Spring St. .... City. Philadelphia Zone.... State.... Pa..

Owner—Partners—Officers and Directors	Title	% Ownership	In charge of
John Phillips	Partner		
Jane Gordon	"		
Anna Cane	"		

⇨ STATEMENT OF (DATE)   11/30/ 1958 ⇦

ASSETS			LIABILITIES		
ASSETS Century	$12,468.82				
CASH IN BANK........$ Liberty	35,891.16		ACCOUNTS PAYABLE		$301,216.40
ON HAND......$		$ 268.30	DUE TO CONTRACTORS (without		
U. S. GOVERNMENT SECURITIES...........			offset)		80,612.95
RECEIVABLES for Mdse. Sold to Customers (Age on opposite page) ACCOUNTS............$485,611.67			UNSECURED LOANS PAYABLE To Banks.....................		90,000.00
			To Partners or Officers...............		
Less Res. for Discounts........$ 4,012.30			To Others..............		
Less Res. for Doubtful........$ 1,303.90		480,295.47	SECURED LOANS PAYABLE Owing to..............		
NOTES & TRADE ACCEPTANCES (Less $_____ discounted)		5,618.20	ACCRUED WAGES & EXPENSES...........		32,690.28
DUE from FACTOR or FINANCE CO.			TAXES—Accrued and Payable: a. Withholding & Payroll...............		
			b. Federal & State Income.............		35,000.00
PHYSICAL INVENTORY OF MDSE. (Valued at lower of Cost or Market) Raw Materials........$158,270.63			c. All Other.............		
			RESERVE for Income Taxes since last closing		
In Process........$ 39,681.20			MORTGAGE—DEFERRED DEBT— Due within 12 mos...........		
Finished Mdse......$ 42,008.31		239,960.14	CURRENT LIABILITIES		539,519.63
			MORTGAGE—DEFERRED DEBT— Due after 12 mos...............		
CURRENT ASSETS		774,502.09			
Due from Partners, Officers, or Employees			LOANS Subordinated until...........(date)		
Due from Affiliated or Assoc. Companies					
LAND & BUILDINGS $			TOTAL LIABILITIES		
Less Depreciation..$			IF CORPORATION Capital Stock Pfd. $		
MCHY., EQUIP., FURN., & FIXT........$		8,500.00	Capital Stock Common..........$		
Less Depreciation..$			Capital Surplus...$		
INVESTMENTS (Describe on opp. page)		112,000.00	Earned Surplus...$		
PREPAID & DEFERRED...............		1,429.63	Deficit (red)......$		
			CORPORATE, PARTNERSHIP, or INDIVIDUAL............NET WORTH		356,912.59
TOTAL ASSETS		$896,432.22	TOTAL LIABILITIES & CAPITAL		$896,432.22

DEPOSITORY BANKS.................................

ACCOUNTANT — Was above statement prepared by an outside accountant? Yes☐ No☐ Is he C.P.A.?☐ Registered?☐ Licensed?☐

INSURANCE—Fire: Mdse. $_____; Bldg. & Fixt. $_____

Accountant's Name.................................

Use & Occup. $_____; Burglary $_____; Life, Benefit

Address ....

Business $_____ on._____

On what date are your books closed?.................................

LIST PRINCIPAL SUPPLIERS ON REVERSE SIDE

PROFIT AND LOSS STATEMENT

FOR PERIOD FROM.... 12/1 TO.... 11/30

GROSS SALES .... $ 3016485.30

Less RETURNS $120,814.25

Less DISCOUNTS $30,420.16 $ 151234.41

NET INCOME FROM SALES.......... $ 2865250.89

Inventory—begin'g 328,620.80

Purchases—Net 1,290,867.90

Labor 1,096,140.13

Factory Overhead ....$ 75,612.26

Total $2,791,241.09

Inventory at end... $48,960.14

Cost of Goods Sold .... $ 2542280.95

GROSS PROFIT ON SALES.................. $ 322969.94

Selling & Ship. Exp. $ 70,180.29

Salaries—Officers or Principals 148,514.60

Adm. & Gen. Exp. ....$ 4,820.67

Bad Debts .... $ 2,140.80

Depreciation ....$ — $ 225656.36

INCOME or (LOSS) ON SALES............... $ 97313.58

Other Income (exclude discount earned).. $

Total $

Deductions from Income .... $

NET PROFIT or (LOSS) before Income Taxes .... $ 97313.58

Provision for Fed. & State Income Taxes.. $ 30111.20

NET PROFIT or (LOSS) .... $ 67202.38

RECONCILIATION OF SURPLUS OR NET WORTH

Beginning (date) ....12/1.................. $ 293018.40

ADD:

Profit for Period ....$

Other Credits to Surplus ....$ $ 67202.38

Total $ 360220.78. —

DEDUCT:

Loss for Period ....$

Div. & Withdr'ls ....$

Other Charges to Surplus ....$ $ 3310.19

NET WORTH or SURPLUS at end.............. $ 356910.59

TO NATIONAL CREDIT OFFICE, INC.
Two Park Avenue
New York 16, N. Y.

The undersigned warrants that the foregoing figures and answers are true and accurate in every respect and orders this statement mailed to you with the intention that it shall be relied upon in the extension of credit or insurance by such concerns, including factors or agents, who may subscribe to your service now or hereafter. My (Our) accountants are authorized to supply you with any supplementary information that may be required.

Dated at................this................day of..........................19.......

Signed in the presence of:

Name..

Address.....................................

EXPLANATION OF ASSETS AND LIABILITIES

RECEIVABLES

For goods shipped during months of:

a.............................. $

b.............................. $

c.............................. $

d. Prior, Months.............. $

Do these include any consigned goods, uncredited returns, or unshipped merchandise?..........

Have all bad accounts been charged off or reserved?..........

During the past year have you sold, pledged, or assigned any receivables?.............. If so, name financing concern and describe transaction: ....

....

Unfilled orders on hand.............. $ (date)

MERCHANDISE

If not valued at Lower of Cost or Market, state basis used

....

Is original inventory record retained by you ☐ or outside auditor ☐

Is any merchandise pledged as security for any debt?

If so, state amount so pledged. $

Merchandise Purchase Commitments as of .... $ (date)

INVESTMENTS — Describe

a. .... $

b. .... $

(If in subsidiary or affiliated concerns state % owned)

LIABILITIES

Merchandise received or charged to you but not included in Assets or Liabilities.............. $

Amount of Contingent Liabilities.... $

Are any liabilities secured in any way?.............. If so, state amount, creditor, and nature of security:..............

....

Annual Rent $................ Lease Expires................

NET WORTH

Has this been decreased since statement date by withdrawal, retirement of capital, payment of dividends, bonuses, or personal Income Taxes?..............

If so, by what amount? $

TAXES

Have all Federal, State, and Local tax assessments been paid or shown accrued on statement?..............

Tax Closing date?.............. Date of latest return examined by Internal Revenue Service?..............

....
(Name of Corporation, Partnership or Proprietorship)

By..............

....
(Signature of Officer, Partner or Owner) (Title)

NATIONAL CREDIT OFFICE, INC. • **TWO PARK AVE., NEW YORK 16, N. Y.**

ACCOUNTANT'S SUPPLEMENTARY INFORMATION

Relating to the attached financial statement as of_____ 11/30 _____(date)

Issued by __Tailored Apparel Co._____ Address __Philadelphia, Pa._____

A. Do the figures on this statement agree with the figures in your report: Yes **X** No____
   Exceptions_____

B. Did you confirm the following items by direct correspondence:
   1. Cash _____Yes **X** No____   4. Due from Contractors___Yes___ No___   7. Due to Contractors___Yes___ No___
   2. Accounts Receivable _____Yes___ No**X**   5. Accounts Payable ____Yes___ No___   8. Others (describe) ___Yes___ No___
   3. Customers Notes and Acceptances___Yes___ No___   6. Notes Payable _____Yes___ No___
   Describe any other method used and relate to the item affected:_____

C. ACCOUNTS RECEIVABLE
   1. Does aging agree with your report? Yes **X** No____   If not, give aging below for merchandise shipped to customers:

Months	_____	$_____
of	_____	$_____
shipment:	_____	$_____
	Prior Months_____	$_____
	Total	$_____

   2. In your opinion, is provision for bad debts adequate: Yes **X** No____ If no opinion, explain:_____
   3. In your opinion, is reserve for discounts adequate: Yes___ No___ If no opinion, explain:_____
   4. To your knowledge, have any receivables been sold, pledged or assigned during the year immediately preceding the statement date: Yes___ No**X**
     If yes, explain:_____
   5. To your knowledge, do Accounts Receivable include any amounts due from subsidiary or affiliated concerns: Yes___ No___
     Do Accounts Receivable include any individual accounts owing in excess of 25% of the net worth shown on attached financial statement: Yes___ No___
     If yes, state amount $_____ and number_____

D. MERCHANDISE INVENTORY
   1. Did you observe and test the count of the physical inventory quantities: Yes___ No**X**
     If no, state how verified __accepted as submitted_____
   2. If not verified, was detailed listing of inventory submitted to you: Yes___ No___ Is copy of original inventory listing in your possession: Yes___ No___
   3. How was the inventory priced?___ __lower of cost or market_____
   4. Did you test the inventory as to prices: Yes___ No___; Arithmetical Accuracy: Yes___ No___
   5. To your knowledge, has any merchandise been pledged as collateral during the year immediately preceding statement date: Yes___ No___
     If yes, explain:_____

E. INVESTMENTS — Describe_____

F. GENERAL
   1. Are you a Certified Public Accountant: Yes___ No___ What State_____ How often do you audit the books?_____
   2. Have all expenses and tax liabilities known to you been accrued: Yes___ No___
   3. Does the statement include all assets and liabilities known to you: Yes___ No___ Exceptions:_____
     Explain_____
   4. Do you know of any material contingent liabilities: Yes___ No___ Explain:_____
   5. Tax closing date:_____ Last taxable year examined by Internal Revenue Service:_____
   6. If client is not incorporated, state amount you believe will be withdrawn for personal income taxes of principal or partners on income earned to statement date and not shown in statement: $_____
   7. Other comments, if any_____

TO NATIONAL CREDIT OFFICE, INC.

   The above information is in answer to your inquiry regarding the attached financial statement of my/our client as of the date shown.

   ┌   **Dennis & Kaufman**   ┐   _____
          Marlow Building   (Firm Name of Accountant)
          Philadelphia, Pa.   _____
                                        (Signature of Individual Authorized to Sign)
   └   ┘   Dated_____

APPENDIX E

COMPARATIVE INTERCHANGE REPORTS

FORM 6

NATIONAL ASSOCIATION of CREDIT MEN

Credit Interchange Report

Guarding the Nation's Profits

OFFICES IN PRINCIPAL CITIES

------- --------- COMPANY ---------, ILLINOIS   OCTOBER 11
-------- COUNTY

The accuracy of this Report is not guaranteed. Its contents are gathered in good faith from members and sent to you by this Bureau without liability for negligence in procuring, collecting, communicating or failing to communicate the information so gathered.

BUSINESS CLASSIFICATION	HOW LONG SOLD	DATE OF LAST SALE	HIGHEST RECENT CREDIT	NOW OWING INCLUDING NOTES	PAST DUE	TERMS OF SALE	DIS-COUNTS	PAYS WHEN DUE	DAYS SLOW	COMMENTS
CHICAGO 927-16										
Hdwe										Order $798
Hdwe	yrs	9-57	371	122		1-10-30		x		
Elec	yrs	7-57	246			1-10	x			
Ind S	yrs	8-57	1841	536	128	2-10-30			10	
Hdwe	yrs	8-57	439			1-10-30		x		
CENTRAL IOWA 930-434										
Ind S	yrs	8-57	318	247		1-10-30		x		
Hdwe	yrs	7-57	1341	318	242	1-10-30			15	Slower
MINNESOTA 930-637										
Farm S	1945	7-57	438	108	108	2-10-70			10	Was disc
ST. LOUIS 930-649										
Elec	yrs	8-57	2142	914		1-10-30		x		
Ind S	1943	7-57	829			30		x		
LOUISVILLE 930-584										
Hdwe	yrs	8-57	1314	424		1-10-30		x		
P&H	yrs	6-57	493			1-10-30	x			
INDIANAPOLIS 930-418										
Hdwe	yrs	8-57	936	494		1-10-30		x		
Bu 3 MC										

FORM 6

NATIONAL ASSOCIATION of CREDIT MEN
Credit Interchange Report

OFFICES IN PRINCIPAL CITIES

-------- --------- COMPANY   ---------, ILLINOIS   FEBRUARY 7,
                                    ----- COUNTY

The accuracy of this Report is not guaranteed. Its contents are gathered in good faith from members and sent to you by this Bureau without liability for negligence in procuring, collecting, communicating or failing to communicate the information so gathered.

BUSINESS CLASSIFICATION	HOW LONG SOLD	DATE OF LAST SALE	HIGHEST RECENT CREDIT	NOW OWING INCLUDING NOTES	PAST DUE	TERMS OF SALE	DIS-COUNTS	PAYS WHEN DUE	DAYS SLOW	COMMENTS
CHICAGO 127-29										
Hdwe	1951	1-58	805	218	143	1-10-30	x		15	Slower
Elec	yrs	1-58	250			1-10				
Ind S	yrs	1-58	1825	932	572	2-10-30			30	
Hdwe	yrs	1-58	522	498	318	1-10-30			25	
Hdwe	yrs	1-58	409			1-10-30		x		
MINNESOTA 128-628										
Farm S	yrs	1-58	419	98	75	2-10-70			30	Slower
CENTRAL IOWA 128-612										
Hdwe	yrs	1-58	1339	629	417	1-10-30			30	
Ind S	yrs	1-58	319	119		1-10-30		x		
LOUISVILLE 128-607										
Hdwe	yrs	1-58	1320	246		1-10-30		x		
P & H	1948	1-58	487			30		x		
ST. LOUIS 128-516										
Elec	yrs	1-58	2100	843	619	1-10-30			30	Slower
Ind S	yrs	1-58	825	622		30		x		
INDIANAPOLIS 128-707										
Hdwe	yrs	1-58	942	374	229	1-10-30			15	Slower

Bu 3 MB

FORM 6

NATIONAL ASSOCIATION of CREDIT MEN

Credit Interchange Report

Guarding the Nation's Profits

OFFICES IN PRINCIPAL CITIES

•

---------- --------- COMPANY   ---------, ILLINOIS   JUNE 6,
                                       ------ COUNTY

The accuracy of this Report is not guaranteed. Its contents are gathered in good faith from members and sent to you by this Bureau without liability for negligence in procuring, collecting, communicating or failing to communicate the information so gathered.

BUSINESS CLASSIFICATION	HOW LONG SOLD	DATE OF LAST SALE	HIGHEST RECENT CREDIT	NOW OWING INCLUDING NOTES	PAST DUE	TERMS OF SALE	DIS- COUNTS	PAID WHEN DUE	DAYS SLOW	COMMENTS
CHICAGO 526-32										
Hdwe	1951	5-58	805	38	27	1-10-30			15-45	
Hdwe	yrs	5-58	410			COD				Too slow
Hdwe	yrs	5-58	521	217	217	1-10-30			60	COD now
Elec	yrs	5-58	248			2-10-30			30	
Ind S	yrs	5-58	1825	418	229	2-10-30			60	Slower
INDIANAPOLIS 527-642										
Hdwe	yrs	4-58	925	130	130	1-10-30			60	Slower
ST. LOUIS 527-518										
Ind S	yrs	5-58	815	218		30			30	
Elec	yrs	5-58	2136	624	597	1-10-30			45	Slower
CENTRAL IOWA 527-533										
Ind S	yrs	5-58	310			1-10-30				Too slow
Hdwe	yrs	5-58	1285	436	392	1-10-30			45	
LOUISVILLE 527-634										
Hdwe	yrs	5-58	1300	288	109	1-10-30			30	
P&H	1948	5-58	475	211	211	30			60	Too slow
MINNESOTA 527-509										
Farm S	yrs	5-58	410	75	68	2-10-70			90	Cash now

Bu 3 MB

FORM 6

NATIONAL ASSOCIATION of CREDIT MEN

Credit Interchange Report

Guarding the Nation's Profits

OFFICES IN PRINCIPAL CITIES

-------- --------- COMPANY   ----------, ILLINOIS   OCTOBER 10,
                           ------ COUNTY

The accuracy of this Report is not guaranteed. Its contents are gathered in good faith from members and sent to you by this Bureau without liability for negligence in procuring, collecting, communicating or failing to communicate the information so gathered.

BUSINESS CLASSIFICATION	HOW LONG SOLD	DATE OF LAST SALE	HIGHEST RECENT CREDIT	NOW OWING	PAST DUE	TERMS OF SALE	DIS-COUNTS	PAYS WHEN DUE	DAYS SLOW	COMMENTS
CHICAGO 926-13										
Hdwe	1951	9-58	800	17	17	COD				Too slow
Elec	yrs	7-58	250							Account
						closed. Too slow.				
Ind S	yrs	12-57	1825	198	198					CACM for
						collection				
Hdwe	yrs	8-58	240			1-10-30				Very slow
Hdwe	yrs	9-58	411			COD				Too slow
MINNESOTA 929-633										
Farm S	yrs	8-58				Cash past year				
INDIANAPOLIS 929-436										
Hdwe	yrs	8-58	920			1-10-30				Closed - Too
						slow.				
CENTRAL IOWA 929-342										
Ind S	yrs	1957								Too slow
Hdwe	yrs	6-58	1275	392	392	1-10-30			90	NSF checks
LOUISVILLE 929-618										
Hdwe	yrs	8-58	639	214	198	1-10-30			60	
P & H	1948	9-58	450			30				
ST. LOUIS 929-629										
Elec	yrs	9-58	2136	413	389	1-10-30			90	
Ind S	yrs	9-58				COD				Was slow
Bu 3 MC										

APPENDIX F

CREDIT BUREAU OF GREATER NEW YORK, INC., REPORTS

<u>EMPLOYMENT CHECK</u>

BROWN, JOHN J.

Res: 32-24 99th Street
    Corona, L.I.

Bus: U. S. Government
    U. S. Customs
    Customs House, N.Y.C.

REC: 10/21
WRN: 10/22

fmly: 111-11 Northern Road, Corona, L.I.

Subject is described as about 55 years of age, and a widower.

He is employed by the United States Customs, Custom House, New York City. He has been connected here for over 25 years, and is Principal Clerk. Income is reported to be $2800. per annum, plus a bonus of $450. a year.

He is very highly regarded according to Mr. Skippe, Chief Clerk of the Survey Office, consultant.

We have favorable trade in file.

FOR: #9000
BY: K-111

SPECIAL

REPORT

DEPT.

CREDIT BUREAU OF GREATER NEW YORK, Inc.
853 BROADWAY, NEW YORK 3, N. Y.

The information given on this form is in answer to an inquiry, and is communicated subject to the following conditions. That the information furnished by this Bureau shall be held in strict confidence and shall not at any time be revealed to the subject of the inquiry or to any one else that the facts upon which this report is based were obtained by the Bureau from sources deemed reliable, the accuracy of which information is, however, in no way guaranteed.

TELEPHONES:

SERVICE: SPring 7-3900
EXECUTIVE: SPring 7-9500

S 3

561

PUBLIC, JOHN Q.	(MARY A.)	REC'D: 10/20	WRITTEN: 10/22	

PUBLIC,   JOHN Q.   (MARY A.)   REC'D: 10/20   WRITTEN: 10/22

SURNAME   GIVEN NAMES   WIFE OR HUSBAND   OCCUPATION   SALES REPRESENTATIVE
7500 Parkway, Forest Hills, L.I.   FIRM NAME   Never-Rip Shirt Corp.
RESIDENCE   CITY   STATE   ADDRESS   8000 Broadway
                                                                         New York City
FORMER
RESIDENCES } 729 W. 57th Street, N.Y.C.   OCCUPATION

                                                             FIRM NAME

                                                             ADDRESS

IDENTITY: Mr. Public is married, approximately 45 years of age, two dependent children
           of school age - 10 and 14 years old.

RESIDENTIAL HISTORY: He and his family are residents at 7500 Parkway, a good class
     elevator apartment house in favorable surroundings. Have been tenants here since
     1950 and are leasing apartment 3-A, 4 rooms, at a rental of $130. monthly. Live
     under good circumstances, and the building management reports them to be prompt pay
     and satisfactory tenants. They formerly lived for 6 years at 729 W. 57th Street
     under similar conditions.

BUSINESS AND RESOURCES: Mr. Public is in the employ of the Never-Rip Shirt Corp., 8000
     Broadway, New York City. This is a large well established concern, manufacturers of
     men's shirts. Firm has a mercantile rating of $500,000/750,000. Mr. Jones, Secretary
     of the firm, advises Mr. Public has been with them since 1949 as a sales representative.
     He covers both local and out-of-town territory. Works on salary and commission basis
     and his earnings are reported to be about $8500. annually. Highly regarded by his
     employers.

BANK: Local bank reports joint account since 6/47. Medium 3-figure balances, non-
       borrowing, satisfactory. Came well introduced; impressions favorable.

LITIGATION: CLEAR

TRADE INFORMATION

DATE CLEARED	MEMBER	SELLING SINCE	HIGH CREDIT	PAYS	REMARKS
10/20/58	7	old	$24.	30-60	
	8	1944	17.	30	
8/10/58	2	inq.			
2/25/58	3	1940			inactive
	104	1947	24.	30-90	
	204	1946	13.	30	
11/23/57	330	old	55.	30	
7/21/57	146	1939	57.	30	
	418	old			inactive
	Special report dated 1/13/58				

FOR: #9000 (J-1:FF)

APPENDIX G

FINANCIAL STATEMENT FORM

Form No. 10   This Form Approved and Published by THE NATIONAL ASSOCIATION OF CREDIT MANAGEMENT

FINANCIAL STATEMENT OF   DATE_____19____

FIRM NAME_____

Address_____ City_____

At close of business on_____19____ State_____

ISSUED TO_____ `<— { NAME OF FIRM / Requesting Statement`

[PLEASE ANSWER ALL QUESTIONS. WHEN NO FIGURES ARE INSERTED, WRITE WORD "NONE"]

ASSETS	Dollars	Cents	LIABILITIES	Dollars	Cents
Cash in Bank	$		Accounts Payable	$	
Cash on Hand			(For Merchandise)		
			Notes and Acceptances Payable		
Accounts Receivable			(For Merchandise)		
(Amounts Pledged $_____)			For Borrowed Money:		
Notes and Trade Acceptances Receivable			Notes Payable—Unsecured		
(Amounts Pledged $_____)					
Merchandise Inventory.			Notes Payable—Secured		
(Not on Consignment or Conditional Sale)					
			Income Taxes Payable or Owing		
(Amounts Pledged $_____)					
Other Current Assets: (Describe)			Other Taxes, including Sales Tax, Owing		
			Rental, Payrolls, Etc., Owing		
			Other Current Liabilities: (Describe)		
TOTAL CURRENT ASSETS			TOTAL CURRENT LIABILITIES		
Land and Buildings (Depreciated Value)			Mortgage on Land and Buildings		
Leasehold Improvements (Amortized Value)			Chattel Mortgage on Merchandise or Equipment		
Machinery, Fixtures and Equipment (Depreciated Value)			Other Liabilities, Unsecured		
			Other Liabilities, Secured (Describe)		
Due From Others — Not Customers					
Other Assets: (Describe)			TOTAL LIABILITIES		
			Net Worth or { Capital Stock $_____ / Surplus $_____ }		
	$			$	
TOTAL ASSETS			TOTAL LIABILITIES AND NET WORTH		

BUY PRINCIPALLY FROM THE FOLLOWING FIRMS:

NAMES	ADDRESSES	AMOUNT OWING
		$

THE REVERSE SIDE OF THIS FORM MUST BE COMPLETED ➤➤

STATEMENT OF PROFIT AND LOSS FOR PERIOD FROM_____TO_____

NET SALES FOR PERIOD	$		DETAILS OF OPERATING EXPENSES:	$	
Cash $_____			Salaries - Officers (or owners) _____		
Credit $_____					
			Salaries - Employees _____		
Inventory at start of Period $_____			Rent, Heat, Light		
			[Include Amortization of Leasehold] __		
Purchases for Period $_____			Advertising _____		
TOTAL $_____			Delivery _____		
Less: Inventory at					
Close of Period $_____			Insurance _____		
COST OF GOODS SOLD_____			Taxes, Including Sales Taxes _____		
GROSS PROFIT _____			Depreciation (Fixtures, Trucks, etc.)· ___		
Less: Operating Expense _____			Miscellaneous (Other Operating Expenses) __		
NET OPERATING PROFIT _____			TOTAL OPERATING EXPENSE _____	$	
Other Additions and Deductions (net) __					
			SUPPLEMENTAL INFORMATION (DETAILED)	$	
NET PROFIT BEFORE FEDERAL INCOME TAXES___			If Incorporated, Amount of Dividends Paid __		
				$	
Less: Federal Income Taxes _____			Interest Paid (Expense) _____		
	$			$	
NET PROFIT AFTER TAXES _____			Cash Discount Earned (Income) _____		

Fire Insurance Carried: On Merchandise $_____ On Furniture and Fixtures $_____ On Buildings $_____

Liability Insurance Carried On Premises $_____ On Auto and Truck $_____Other Insurance (Type and Am't)_____

Name of Bank_____

Title to Business Premises is in the name of_____

If Premises leased state Annual Rental $_____Lease Expires_____

   The foregoing statement (both sides) has been carefully read by the undersigned (both the printed and written material) and is, to my knowledge, in all respects complete, accurate, and truthful. It discloses to you the true state of (our) (my) financial condition on the date indicated. Since that time there has been no material unfavorable change in (our) (my) financial condition other than indicated below under "Remarks." The figures submitted are not estimated. They have been taken from (our) (my) books.
   (We) (I) make the foregoing financial statement in writing intending that you should rely upon it for the purpose of our obtaining merchandise from you on credit.

Name of Individual or Firm_____

If Partnership, name partners_____

If Corporation, name officers_____

How long established_____Previous business experience_____
_____where_____

Date of signing Statement_____ Street_____ City._____ State_____

Witness _____ Signed by_____

Residence Address
of Witness _____ Title _____

REMARKS: (Attach separate sheet if necessary)

APPENDIX H

CONTINUING STATEMENT AGREEMENT

CORPORATION FINANCIAL STATEMENT AND AGREEMENT

NAME..ADDRESS..

The undersigned (called "Borrower") to induce Manufacturers Trust Company (called "Bank") from time to time to advance credit, or make loans, renewals, or extensions to Borrower or to have Borrower become obligated to Bank in any manner, directly or contingently, alone or jointly and/or severally with another and/or others, hereby furnishes BANK with the following and true financial statement AS OF THE................DAY OF................, 19..... knowing that Bank relies hereon and (unless written notice of change is given as hereinafter set forth) will continue to rely hereon in advancing such credits and in making such loans, renewals or extensions, and in having Borrower become obligated to Bank in any manner. In consideration thereof the undersigned agrees: This statement shall be considered continuing as true unless written notice of change is given; written notice of any material change will be given immediately to Bank; proper, accurate and up-to-date books of account will be kept by Borrower and upon request all or any thereof will be produced for examination with the right to copy them by representatives of Bank; Borrower and/or Borrower's accountant shall promptly comply with all of Bank's requests from time to time for information concerning Borrower's affairs and for the inspection of statements, papers and records of Borrower (whether same be confidential or not). If Borrower shall fail to notify Bank of any material change, fail to produce on request any books or records called for or to permit the examination thereof, or if Borrower's accountant shall fail or refuse to comply with Bank's request for information, or inspection as above provided, or if any statement herein is or shall become untrue, or if Borrower shall fail to pay, withhold, collect or remit any tax or tax deficiency when assessed or due or fail to pay any obligations, whether in writing or not, or if at any time, in the sole opinion of the Bank the financial responsibility of Borrower shall become impaired or unsatisfactory to the Bank, or if any of the following events occur with respect to Borrower, or any indorser, acceptor, surety or guarantor of, or any other party, to Borrower's obligations to Bank and claims of every nature and description of Bank against Borrower, whether or not represented by negotiable instruments or other writings, whether now existing or hereafter incurred, originally contracted with Bank and/or another or others and now or hereafter owing to Bank or acquired in any manner by Bank, whether contracted by Borrower alone and/or jointly or severally with another or others direct or indirect, absolute or contingent, primary or secondary, secured or unsecured, matured or not matured (all of which are hereafter collectively called "Liabilities"), to wit: default in the punctual payment of said Liabilities, or any part thereof, failure to perform any agreement contained herein or contained in any security document or any other instrument, or any other obligation of every nature and description made or indorsed or delivered by any of them to Bank or to another and acquired in any manner by Bank, whether such agreements or obligations are now or hereafter in existence; death, (or if Borrower or any of said parties to said Liabilities be a partnership, the death or suspension of the usual business activities of any member thereof), dissolution, insolvency, or if insolvency be imminent or threatened, commission of an act of bankruptcy, assignment for the benefit of creditors, calling of a meeting of any creditors, appointment of a committee of any creditors or liquidating agent, offer of a composition or extension to any creditors, making, or sending a notice of an intended, bulk sale; assignment, pledge or mortgage, of any account receivable or other property; suspension of payment; the whole or partial suspension or liquidation of their usual business; commencement of any proceeding, suit, or action (at law, or in equity, or under any of the provisions of the Bankruptcy Act, as amended) for reorganization, composition, extension, arrangement, receivership, liquidation or dissolution, by or against Borrower, or any of said parties; appointment of or application for a receiver, conservator, rehabilitator or similar officer or committee of, or any property of, Borrower or any of said parties; the making of any tax assessment by the United States or any state, entry of a judgment or issuance of a warrant of attachment or an injunction against, or against any property of, Borrower, or any of said parties; commencement against Borrower or any of said parties of any proceeding under Article 45 of the New York Civil Practice Act or amendments thereto; then, and in any such event, said Liabilities shall become immediately due and payable without notice or demand. Borrower hereby waives protest of any and all negotiable instruments now or hereafter held by the Bank to which Borrower is or may be a party. In addition to any other security, Bank is hereby given a continuing lien for the amount of said Liabilities upon any and all moneys, securities and other property of Borrower and the proceeds thereof, now or hereafter actually or constructively held or received by or in transit in any manner to Bank, its correspondents or its agents from or for Borrower, whether for safe keeping, custody, pledge, transmission, collection or otherwise coming into possession of Bank in any way or placed in any safe deposit box leased by Bank to Borrower. Bank is also hereby given a continuing lien and/or right of set-off for the amount of said Liabilities upon or with respect to any and all deposits (general or special) and credits of Borrower with, and any and all claims of Borrower against, Bank at any time existing, hereby authorizing Bank at any time or times, without prior notice, to apply such deposits or credits, or any part thereof, to such Liabilities and in such amounts as it may select, although contingent and although unmatured and whether any collateral security therefor is deemed adequate or not, and Bank shall have at all times and for any reason the right to withhold payment of the balance of any deposit account (whether general or special) of Borrower with Bank. Upon the happening of any of the events hereinabove set forth, Bank may appropriate and apply to the payment of any and all said Liabilities, any and all security therefor and any and all of said moneys, deposit accounts, claims, securities or other property or proceeds thereof and/or may sell, assign, give option or options to purchase, and deliver the whole or any part thereof, in one or more parcels, at public or private sale or sales (at Bank's office or elsewhere) or at any exchange or broker's board, for cash, upon credit or for future delivery, without demand, advertisement, or notice, which are hereby expressly waived, and upon any such sale the Bank may become the purchaser of any such property free from any right of redemption, which is hereby waived and released. Until Borrower shall give Bank a new statement or notice in writing to the contrary, this statement shall be regarded as a representation and warranty on each occasion that Borrower shall become obligated to Bank in any manner, or that Bank shall extend credit or make, renew or extend a loan to Borrower, or shall discount any paper made or indorsed by Borrower, that the following statement is, on each such occasion, true and specifically made and repeated for the purpose of inducing Bank on the faith thereof to advance credit, make a loan, or grant a renewal or extension to Borrower, or have Borrower become obligated to Bank in any manner, and that on each such occasion the actual net worth of Borrower is no less than that shown in the following statement, and notwithstanding the receipt of such notice or of a new statement (except a statement on Bank's form) on each such occasion, the foregoing agreements, rights and remedies of Bank shall be read into and become part of the said obligations of Borrower. If an attorney is used to collect or enforce said Liabilities or to enforce, declare or adjudicate any rights or obligations under this agreement, whether by suit or by any other means whatsoever, an attorney's fee of 15% of the principal and interest then due by Borrower to Bank shall be payable by Borrower. In any litigation (whether or not arising out of or relating to such Liabilities, this statement or any transaction hereunder) in which Borrower and Bank shall be adverse parties, Borrower waives trial by jury and the right to interpose any defense, set-off or counterclaim of any nature or description.

APPENDIX I

PROBLEM FOR COMPARATIVE ANALYSIS

WALKER-HARTMAN COMPANY
MANUFACTURERS OF MEN'S SHIRTS
COMPARATIVE BALANCE SHEETS AS OF DEC. 31

Assets

	Last Year		This Year	
Current Assets:				
Cash in Hand and in Bank		$ 2,701.41		$ 965.22
Accounts Receivable	$57,872.12		$113,145.51	
Less Reserve Bad Debts	2,178.21		3,512.93	
Reserve Trade Discount	861.22		3,284.12	
	$ 3,039.43	54,832.69	$ 6,797.05	106,348.46
Accounts Receivable—Sundry		211.90		528.49
Merchandise Inventory		51,673.09		69,307.35
Total Current Assets		$109,419.09		$177,149.52
Investments—at cost—Stock		1,400.00		1,400.00
Fixed Assets:				
Machinery and Equipment	15,350.40		17,914.58	
Less Reserve for Depreciation	2,413.84	12,936.56	4,076.34	13,838.24
Furniture and Fixtures	$ 917.54		$ 1,323.21	
Less Reserve for Depreciation	167.15	750.39	259.92	1,063.29
Building Improvements	$ 428.79		$ 428.79	
Less Reserve for Depreciation	214.40	214.39	345.42	83.37
Automobiles	$ 2,012.06		$ 2,012.06	
Less Reserve for Depreciation	1,341.38	670.68	1,648.78	363.28
Total Fixed Assets		$ 14,572.02		$ 15,348.18
Deferred Charges:				
Unexpired Insurance		1,144.04		1,042.41
Advances to Salesmen		1,520.55		4,169.79
Supplies		718.27		811.49
Prepaid Interest		846.44		185.74
Total Deferred Charges		$ 4,229.30		$ 6,209.43
		$129,620.41		$200,107.13

Liabilities

	Last Year	This Year
Current Liabilities:		
Accounts Payable—Trade	$ 24,715.03	$ 85,392.43
Accounts Payable—Sundry	3,169.92	886.89
Notes Payable—Bank	22,000.00	24,000.00
Loans Payable—Individual		1,000.00
Accrued Salaries, etc.	766.82	880.05
Accrued Taxes	1,720.68	1,646.14
Total Current Liabilities	$ 52,372.45	$113,805.51
Net Worth	77,247.96	86,301.62
	$129,620.41	$200,107.13

WALKER-HARTMAN COMPANY
MANUFACTURERS OF MEN'S SHIRTS
COMPARATIVE STATEMENTS OF PROFIT AND LOSS
FOR THE YEARS ENDING DEC. 31

	Last Year	This Year
Sales...............................	$270,765.86	$335,598.94
Less Discounts and Allowances.........	9,133.31	11,061.25
Net Sales...........................	$261,632.55	$324,537.69
Cost of Sales........................		
Inventory Raw Materials		
Jan. 1...................	$ 18,286.13	$ 23,834.11
Purchases.................	142,617.62	185,550.27
Freight, Express, and		
Drayage................	5,730.75	6,159.83
Buying Expense............	559.70	609.30
	$167,194.20	$216,153.51
Less Inventory Raw		
Materials, Dec. 31.....	23,834.11	26,764.95
Materials and Supplies Consumed..................	$143,360.09	$189,388.56
Labor and Supervision.......	48,430.49	76,696.66
Rent.....................	2,735.00	2,475.00
Power and Light...........	1,371.79	1,637.85
Insurance.................	883.98	991.68
Factory Supplies and Expense	1,294.35	1,027.27
Burglar Alarm.............	270.00	247.50
Taxes....................	1,937.22	2,887.64
Machinery Maintenance.....	709.03	1,227.86
Royalties..................	350.07	279.74
Depreciation—Machinery and		
Equipment..............	1,448.56	1,662.50
Amortization—Building		
Improvements...........	142.93	131.02
	$202,933.51	$278,653.28
Less Goods in Process,		
Dec. 31...............	576.81	10,722.96
Cost of Goods Manufactured.	$202,356.70	$267,930.32
Add Inventory Finished		
Goods, Jan. 1............	42,062.68	27,262.17
	$244,419.38	$295,192.49
Less Inventory Finished		
Goods, Dec. 31.........	27,262.17	31,819.44
Cost of Goods Sold.....................	217,157.21	263,373.05
Gross Profit.........................	$ 44,475.34	$ 61,164.64

	Last Year	This Year
Expenses:		
Selling		
Advertising and Selling......	$ 2,052.48	$ 1,297.50
Shipping Supplies...........	971.79	1,543.30
Shipping Salaries............	1,509.51	2,605.25
Delivery Expense...........	217.65	226.45
New York Office............	272.50	
Commissions and Traveling..	15,684.17	24,754.89
Salesmen's Accounts Charged		
Off.....................	2,524.01	1,655.63
Taxes......................	372.27	
Depreciation—Automobiles..	670.69	307.40
Total Selling Expense......	$ 24,275.07	$ 32,390.42
General Administration		
Office Salaries..............	3,075.16	4,087.03
Credit and Collection Expense	1,099.88	728.21
Stationery and Office Supplies	365.63	697.00
Postage....................	857.85	874.81
Legal and Auditing..........	450.00	410.50
Telephone and Telegraph....	414.99	418.16
Bank Charges..............	174.80	218.25
Miscellaneous Expense.......	173.19	97.01
Taxes......................	434.65	1,053.86
Donations..................	181.45	247.45
Bad Accounts Charged Off...	3,384.57	4,194.99
Depreciation—Furniture and		
Fixtures..................	85.61	92.77
Total General and Administrative...............	$ 10,697.78	$ 13,120.04
Total Expense........................	34,972.85	45,510.46
Net Operating Profit.................	$ 9,502.49	$ 15,654.18
Additions		
Sundry Income.........................		1,370.33
Discounts Taken.......................	1,606.27	992.75
Gross Income........................	$ 11,108.76	$ 18,017.26
Deductions		
Interest Paid.........................	1,674.65	2,008.29
Net Income...........................	$ 9,434.11	$ 16,008.97
Analysis of Net Worth Account		
Balance Jan. 1........................	$ 74,795.88	$ 77,247.96
Add Net Income Jan. 1 to Dec. 31........	9,434.11	16,008.97
	$ 84,229.99	$ 93,256.93
Less Withdrawals, Jan. 1 to Dec. 31.......	6,982.03	6,955.31
Total...............................	$ 77,247.96	$ 86,301.62

APPENDIX J

FOULKE'S RATIOS

THE RATIOS

In 1931 Roy A. Foulke, Vice President of Dun & Bradstreet, Inc., first compiled these ratios. Since their first appearance, the number of lines covered by these surveys has gradually increased. Today the ratios are compiled annually for 72 lines — 12 retail, 24 wholesale, and 36 manufacturing. They offer a useful, though by no means absolute, yardstick for financial self-appraisal by management.

The data used are based upon a sampling of business enterprises with a tangible net worth which only occasionally is below $75,000. . . . The center figure for each of the lines of business is the median. The other two figures in each line are quartiles; for each ratio they indicate the upper and lower limits of the experiences of that half of the concerns whose ratios are nearest to the median. When any figures are listed in order according to their size, the median is the middle figure (same number of items from the top and the bottom) and the quartiles are the figures that are located one-quarter and three-quarters down the list.

DEFINITION OF TERMS

AVERAGE COLLECTION PERIOD: The number of days that the total of trade accounts and notes receivable (including assigned accounts and discounted notes, if any), less reserves for bad debts, represents when compared with the annual net credit sales. Formula — divide the annual net credit sales by 365 days to obtain the average credit sales per day. Then divide the total of accounts and notes receivable (plus any discounted notes receivable) by the average credit sales per day to obtain the average collection period.

CURRENT ASSETS: Total of cash, accounts and notes receivable for the sale of merchandise in regular trade quarters less any reserves for bad debts, advances on merchandise, inventory less any reserves, listed securities when not in excess of market, state and municipal bonds not in excess of market, and United States Government securities.

CURRENT DEBT: Total of all liabilities due within one year from statement date including current payments on serial notes, mortgages, debentures or other funded debts. This item also includes current reserves such as gross reserves for Federal income and excess profits taxes, reserves for contingencies set up for specific purposes, but does not include reserves for depreciation.

FIXED ASSETS: The sum of the cost value of land and the depreciated book values of buildings, leasehold improvements, fixtures, furniture, machinery, tools, and equipment.

FUNDED DEBT: Mortgages, bonds, debentures, gold notes, serial notes or other obligations with a maturity of more than one year from the statement date.

DEFINITION OF TERMS

INVENTORY: The sum of raw material, material in process, and finished merchandise. It does not include supplies.

NET PROFITS: Profit after full depreciation on buildings, machinery, equipment, furniture, and other assets of a fixed nature; after reserves for Federal income and excess profits taxes; after reduction in the value of inventory to cost or market, whichever is lower; after chargeoffs for bad debts; after miscellaneous reserves and adjustments; but before dividends or withdrawals.

NET SALES: The dollar volume of business transacted for 365 days net after deductions for returns, allowances, and discounts from gross sales.

NET SALES TO INVENTORY: The quotient obtained by dividing the annual net sales by the statement inventory. This quotient does not represent the actual physical turnover which would be determined by reducing the annual net sales to the cost of goods sold, and then dividing the resulting figure by the statement inventory.

NET WORKING CAPITAL: The excess of the current assets over the current debt.

TANGIBLE NET WORTH: The sum of all outstanding preferred or preference stocks (if any) and outstanding common stocks, surplus, and undivided profits, less any intangible items in the assets, such as good-will, trademarks, patents, copyrights, leaseholds, mailing lists, treasury stock, organization expenses, and underwriting discounts and expenses.

TURNOVER OF TANGIBLE NET WORTH: The quotient obtained by dividing annual net sales by tangible net worth.

TURNOVER OF NET WORKING CAPITAL: The quotient obtained by dividing annual net sales by net working capital.

RETAIL

14 IMPORTANT RATIOS IN 12 RETAIL LINES—1957

Line of Business (and Number of businesses reporting)	Current assets to current debt Times	Net profits on net sales Per cent	Net profits on tangible net worth Per cent	Net profits on net working capital Per cent	Net sales to tangible net worth Times	Net sales to net working capital Times	Collection period Days	Net sales to inventory Times	Fixed assets to tangible net worth Per cent	Current debt to tangible net worth Per cent	Total debt to tangible net worth Per cent	Inventory to net working capital Per cent	Current debt to inventory Per cent	Funded debts to net working capital Per cent
FOR 12 RETAIL LINES—1957 MEDIANS AND QUARTILES														
Clothing, Men's and Boys' (162)	5.10	4.69	10.15	15.17	3.39	4.43	**	4.2	5.9	19.0	56.4	69.4	32.3	15.4
	2.88	2.07	3.78	4.92	2.54	3.14	**	3.3	14.0	41.6	98.9	97.1	55.2	36.5
	2.00	0.21	0.51	0.56	1.72	2.35	**	2.6	31.9	78.9	168.9	133.3	80.4	66.4
Clothing, Men's and Women's (91)	8.97	8.47	16.99	25.19	2.97	3.95	**	5.2	8.7	11.2	34.0	44.9	28.6	8.6
	3.62	4.06	8.96	11.94	2.33	2.98	**	3.5	17.0	25.4	52.3	67.3	55.2	23.2
	2.33	1.83	5.30	6.63	1.27	1.95	**	2.7	32.1	52.5	91.4	112.3	78.8	33.7
Department Stores (447)	5.80	3.01	8.31	11.81	4.00	5.30	**	7.9	13.8	14.5	43.6	51.0	34.8	15.6
	3.57	1.83	5.05	6.98	2.83	3.95	**	5.7	25.0	27.4	61.5	67.1	59.2	32.7
	2.24	0.65	2.13	2.69	2.24	3.05	**	4.5	45.4	49.5	92.6	96.1	91.6	53.6
Dry Goods (77)	14.65	11.10	23.74	28.43	3.95	4.84	**	6.2	5.7	5.7	34.9	57.4	12.7	11.9
	5.17	3.53	8.81	10.55	2.46	3.08	**	3.8	15.4	17.5	58.3	81.8	32.9	25.6
	2.59	0.27	0.82	0.95	1.45	2.45	**	3.0	26.6	48.7	103.7	118.4	62.2	52.6
Furnishings, Men's (43)	6.41	5.44	13.67	28.82	2.97	3.77	**	4.3	4.4	12.7	56.7	72.5	23.8	21.3
	2.68	3.03	4.64	6.58	1.94	2.44	**	3.0	13.2	30.2	101.3	95.8	48.5	32.0
	1.85	0.39	0.67	0.81	1.49	1.79	**	2.4	34.6	79.0	220.7	158.5	81.9	66.8
Furniture, 50 per cent or more, installment (147)	7.27	3.19	7.28	8.21	3.41	3.72	83	6.0	5.2	14.2	40.4	28.8	55.6	10.7
	3.46	1.49	4.37	4.44	2.03	2.38	153	4.9	14.2	37.7	81.9	42.6	93.9	23.2
	2.11	0.09†	0.17†	0.27†	1.63	1.73	199	3.3	28.9	79.6	127.5	72.0	148.6	40.7
Groceries and Meats, Chain (53)	2.56	1.59	17.08	37.99	14.90	26.91	**	15.6	42.3	39.0	56.0	112.9	56.4	22.8
	1.71	1.40	14.42	26.41	11.18	18.42	**	14.1	66.1	58.7	96.9	155.1	82.6	53.1
	1.43	1.15	10.00	11.60	7.88	14.19	**	11.7	39.4	83.0	129.4	250.1	111.3	111.5
Groceries and Meats, Independent (48)	3.36	1.38	16.53	36.86	14.20	39.48	**	22.1	20.2	21.0	60.7	85.6	48.3	18.4
	1.79	1.01	12.66	22.78	9.89	18.73	**	17.5	51.4	46.5	96.8	132.8	85.3	60.2
	1.27	0.54	3.74	7.74	5.87	10.02	**	12.4	70.9	73.6	123.6	236.3	111.7	147.7
Hardware (42)	7.18	2.56	9.02	17.40	3.94	6.38	**	5.4	6.5	13.7	43.6	70.2	23.9	17.7
	3.35	1.12	3.27	5.51	2.48	4.00	**	3.2	19.6	28.9	77.0	83.4	49.6	32.6
	1.73	0.07†	0.16†	0.26†	1.75	2.59	**	2.6	40.2	74.4	130.8	161.9	89.7	91.5
Lumber and Building Materials (130)	8.89	4.56	9.83	17.42	3.95	5.93	43	7.4	12.6	11.9	34.4	49.3	28.2	9.9
	4.21	1.66	4.80	6.26	2.47	3.35	67	5.5	25.1	25.4	71.7	66.3	56.6	25.2
	2.33	0.58	1.35	1.87	1.62	2.21	92	3.9	42.2	57.7	113.9	86.5	102.2	53.7
Shoes (80)	4.23	6.12	11.76	23.25	4.54	9.18	**	6.6	4.3	22.4	39.3	88.4	30.2	9.2
	2.70	2.44	7.75	11.32	3.48	5.01	**	3.9	15.2	38.9	66.1	117.9	47.7	21.1
	1.98	0.34	2.34	3.04	2.30	2.89	**	2.5	37.0	61.6	108.3	153.2	73.2	63.9
Women's Specialty Shops (203)	4.33	3.74	10.70	15.11	4.72	6.95	**	9.0	9.7	23.8	57.4	41.8	65.5	11.1
	2.52	1.90	6.12	10.20	3.29	4.92	**	6.6	22.3	46.9	85.6	68.2	100.9	32.0
	1.81	0.27	0.85	1.28	1.92	3.45	**	5.0	36.1	80.4	132.6	105.1	155.7	58.1

**Not computed; necessary information as to the division between cash sales and credit sales was available in too few cases to obtain an average collection period usable as a broad guide. †Loss.

WHOLESALE

14 — IMPORTANT RATIOS IN 24 WHOLESALE LINES—1957

FOR 24 WHOLESALE LINES—1957 MEDIANS AND QUARTILES

Line of Business (and Number of Businesses)	Current assets to current debt (Times)	Net profits on net sales (Per cent)	Net profits on tangible net worth (Per cent)	Net profits on net working capital (Per cent)	Net sales to tangible net worth (Times)	Net sales to net working capital (Times)	Collection period (Days)	Net sales to inventory (Times)	Fixed assets to tangible net worth (Per cent)	Current debt to tangible net worth (Per cent)	Total debt to tangible net worth (Per cent)	Inventory to net working capital (Per cent)	Current debt to inventory (Per cent)	Funded debts to net working capital (Per cent)
Automobile Parts & Accessories (175)	4.94	3.27	9.81	14.40	4.89	6.33	27	5.9	6.1	19.5	41.6	69.9	34.3	7.9
	3.15	2.05	6.35	9.49	3.19	4.63	34	4.5	13.1	36.2	64.9	88.6	55.8	18.9
	2.19	1.03	3.96	5.08	2.16	3.00	42	3.6	28.2	62.1	94.5	114.6	79.6	32.0
Baked Goods (49)	2.59	3.26	13.83	84.81	7.88	44.66	9	35.5	54.0	17.8	35.5	49.0	100.3	55.2
	1.89	2.01	9.49	33.64	5.00	18.57	12	25.5	69.4	27.4	57.9	73.6	144.1	106.8
	1.45	0.73	8.46	8.34	3.15	9.28	23	18.8	87.0	41.9	117.4	123.6	203.7	211.0
Cigars, Cigarettes & Tobacco (85)	3.35	0.72	9.83	15.27	20.00	33.42	14	43.4	5.2	32.1	41.3	51.5	65.9	4.6
	2.21	0.33	4.81	6.47	13.27	17.55	17	27.0	11.8	63.5	77.5	74.0	114.5	19.6
	1.63	0.15	1.92	2.60	8.70	12.73	24	16.8	22.8	100.2	122.3	108.1	161.1	36.9
Confectionery (22)	4.96	1.72	14.01	27.48	11.29	12.43	11	22.1	4.0	16.1	11.3	52.8	38.3	3.4
	2.93	0.95	7.22	7.79	7.99	9.64	25	16.3	8.1	39.1	27.5	79.9	72.7	14.1
	2.24	0.39	2.14	2.25	4.48	6.74	37	8.4	29.5	67.6	64.9	96.6	105.2	36.5
Drugs & Drug Sundries (69)	3.17	3.11	14.52	19.39	7.75	9.31	20	9.0	5.1	39.4	52.1	70.6	58.0	5.3
	2.42	2.36	10.65	11.41	5.57	6.83	31	6.6	13.0	64.0	79.5	89.2	75.6	18.6
	1.92	1.04	6.30	8.14	4.48	5.08	45	5.8	29.0	88.2	118.5	107.8	104.5	30.8
Dry Goods (156)	6.09	2.11	9.17	10.58	6.08	7.42	35	8.0	2.0	15.3	36.0	47.5	34.7	7.7
	3.17	1.07	3.96	4.54	4.17	4.71	49	6.2	4.8	38.2	61.8	68.6	65.8	17.4
	2.08	0.40	1.38	1.48	2.85	3.41	62	5.0	9.6	88.6	112.5	96.3	112.1	36.1
Electrical Parts & Supplies (129)	4.20	2.43	10.82	13.25	6.81	8.97	33	8.0	5.7	25.1	50.7	60.3	53.7	6.5
	2.79	1.29	4.85	6.26	4.60	5.86	42	6.2	10.4	43.4	66.6	75.7	82.5	12.8
	1.84	0.48	1.66	1.61	3.13	3.72	53	4.7	19.2	90.8	111.6	96.9	118.4	23.8
Fruits & Produce, Fresh (50)	5.15	2.90	21.89	55.55	13.73	27.26	11	86.8	9.3	14.1	47.2	15.6	95.3	16.9
	2.77	0.60	6.67	9.02	10.25	15.80	15	66.7	18.5	34.9	122.5	28.9	201.9	50.9
	1.89	0.15	1.11	2.18	5.91	12.07	27	29.8	37.0	81.2	182.5	65.7	331.7	161.3
Furnishings, Men's (31)	5.00	6.20	20.24	25.00	4.38	5.65	25	8.3	2.2	17.5	37.1	49.8	50.1	10.0
	2.76	2.18	6.70	8.52	2.65	3.38	43	5.1	4.0	50.8	74.1	69.9	74.0	14.9
	2.26	0.16	0.64	0.69	1.53	2.46	69	3.1	19.0	70.5	111.4	99.7	119.3	24.9
Gasoline, Fuel Oil, & Lubricating Oil (42)	3.63	1.69	13.04	31.10	13.41	22.49	23	54.2	26.4	22.1	45.9	31.7	78.8	12.1
	1.98	1.03	8.62	14.00	6.23	14.07	36	18.2	40.2	41.8	71.2	55.0	151.5	36.0
	1.44	0.56	4.24	8.70	3.63	6.98	46	13.7	67.6	114.6	151.6	77.8	268.3	101.2
Groceries (255)	5.06	1.34	12.49	16.97	14.65	17.29	11	14.3	7.7	21.3	61.5	74.1	34.8	10.2
	2.81	0.72	6.79	8.51	8.57	10.71	15	10.9	14.4	47.6	88.1	98.2	55.8	22.8
	2.07	0.32	2.94	3.88	6.39	7.75	23	8.1	28.9	77.0	136.2	131.7	79.5	46.5
Hardware (200)	6.23	2.64	7.83	9.66	4.30	5.17	26	5.8	6.9	16.2	33.4	67.5	26.2	8.3
	3.92	1.47	4.39	5.43	3.02	3.62	33	4.1	14.0	29.5	54.2	83.9	40.5	20.5
	2.39	0.62	2.74	2.95	2.21	2.64	48	3.2	25.3	56.9	101.1	104.9	70.4	29.9
Hosiery & Underwear (39)	5.81	4.11	17.35	17.67	5.62	6.16	28	8.3	1.1	18.5	....	42.1	38.6	....
	3.58	0.64	2.64	2.71	4.62	4.90	43	5.2	3.7	38.2	....	76.0	65.1	....
	2.12	0.28	0.74	1.37	2.57	3.61	61	4.2	15.0	60.9	....	100.8	89.7	....
Household Appliances, Electrical (100)	3.60	1.61	8.08	9.49	7.71	8.80	31	11.2	4.5	29.3	82.3	63.4	62.4	11.4
	2.18	0.82	5.02	5.67	5.91	-6.32	40	6.5	9.5	74.6	103.9	91.5	89.6	22.3
	1.67	0.26	1.87	2.61	3.62	4.47	52	5.2	21.3	114.3	164.6	125.6	115.5	39.7
Iron & Steel Sheets, Strips, Bars & Plates (60)	5.88	4.46	19.19	26.71	5.25	7.89	24	11.1	10.2	14.2	41.8	58.4	33.1	15.8
	3.55	2.68	7.75	12.78	3.27	4.38	32	5.7	23.1	29.0	71.3	82.1	50.9	23.8
	2.41	0.80	3.91	5.53	2.36	2.75	40	3.2	38.6	60.4	114.0	110.1	81.5	40.5
Lumber (91)	7.35	2.95	12.01	13.47	6.90	23.43	37	18.4	3.3	10.7	46.8	27.3	38.0	13.7
	3.49	1.39	6.93	8.87	4.98	7.25	42	7.6	10.8	28.9	91.5	66.6	75.9	34.7
	1.90	0.23	1.22	1.29	3.21	4.12	56	3.9	21.6	85.8	134.3	95.8	179.4	83.9
Lumber & Building Materials (87)	6.16	3.04	6.92	7.99	4.80	6.33	29	8.6	10.2	13.9	35.8	55.2	30.1	7.8
	3.36	1.30	3.46	4.57	3.37	4.92	43	5.2	20.4	30.8	63.1	70.2	63.2	23.7
	2.21	0.19	0.73	0.81	2.22	2.69	58	3.6	34.1	62.9	104.7	93.1	98.6	39.4
Meat and Poultry (39)	4.01	1.60	14.13	25.25	14.96	34.37	10	75.2	9.8	19.2	23.6	27.6	94.7	11.6
	2.29	0.77	7.36	15.25	9.51	19.77	17	38.1	22.8	57.7	58.1	54.3	131.4	33.8
	1.70	0.17	1.61	2.74	4.85	7.41	26	19.3	48.4	96.7	111.0	82.8	204.1	50.2
Paints, Varnishes & Lacquers (32)	5.01	4.04	17.96	25.27	4.61	5.10	34	8.7	7.6	18.7	30.2	63.6	33.7	5.6
	3.44	2.32	6.72	7.61	3.30	3.69	42	5.8	17.9	33.6	45.3	76.8	60.1	26.2
	2.44	1.13	4.81	3.11	2.26	2.84	57	3.7	32.9	61.8	61.3	90.3	89.8	34.1
Paper (133)	4.21	1.85	9.25	12.55	7.82	10.21	25	11.6	4.4	23.9	45.5	56.8	43.9	11.5
	2.99	1.19	6.21	7.51	5.04	6.37	32	7.8	10.9	42.9	68.6	79.5	75.8	18.7
	1.97	0.51	3.18	4.81	3.99	5.09	42	6.4	24.7	85.4	103.1	95.3	114.3	33.3
Plumbing & Heating Supplies (156)	6.07	1.91	7.15	9.54	4.87	5.80	33	8.7	6.9	15.8	29.5	59.1	31.0	5.1
	3.45	1.09	3.86	4.43	3.72	4.38	45	5.9	14.7	30.6	59.2	77.2	47.9	16.7
	2.36	0.45	1.84	2.42	2.70	3.28	57	4.1	25.0	57.3	96.6	103.1	75.3	32.8
Shoes, Men's, Women's & Children's (54)	3.81	1.64	7.64	10.31	6.89	7.65	48	9.0	1.3	30.6	42.7	53.2	60.0	12.5
	2.15	0.64	1.94	4.27	4.07	4.61	53	7.6	4.6	72.4	101.8	69.3	105.9	17.6
	1.75	0.13	0.62	0.75	2.72	3.18	68	4.0	8.3	105.0	197.9	101.8	141.6	26.9
Wines & Liquors (44)	3.71	1.96	10.55	15.00	7.69	11.25	13	15.2	4.9	27.2	72.9	70.0	48.0	6.0
	2.12	1.05	7.02	9.26	5.74	8.51	28	6.9	14.6	62.4	130.9	88.2	90.6	13.7
	1.64	0.57	3.43	5.40	3.83	5.47	51	4.9	32.5	125.6	141.4	130.1	145.7	29.6
Womenswear, Coats, Suits & Dresses (32)	3.62	4.12	13.84	20.74	6.56	7.63	33	15.2	1.6	21.4	44.3	23.7	80.8	15.2
	2.57	0.35	1.44	1.67	4.12	5.67	58	7.4	7.1	51.9	113.8	43.9	155.7	41.5
	1.88	0.97†	6.11†	7.37†	2.12	3.05	68	5.1	16.4	79.3	244.9	92.8	221.6	66.9

MANUFACTURING

14. IMPORTANT RATIOS IN 36 MANUFACTURING LINES—1957

Line of Business (and Number of Businesses)

Line of Business (and Number of Businesses)	Current assets to current Debt (Times)	Net profits on net sales (Per cent)	Net profits on tangible net worth (Per cent)	Net profits on net working capital (Per cent)	Net sales to tangible net worth (Times)	Net sales to net working capital (Times)	Average collection period (Days)	Net sales to inventory (Times)	Fixed assets to tangible net worth (Per cent)	Current debt to tangible net worth (Per cent)	Total debt to tangible net worth (Per cent)	Inventory to net working capital (Per cent)	Current debt to inventory (Per cent)	Funded debts to net working capital (Per cent)

FOR 36 MANUFACTURING LINES—1957 MEDIANS AND QUARTILES

Line of Business	Curr. assets to curr. Debt	Net prof. on net sales	Net prof. on tang. net worth	Net prof. on net wkg. cap.	Net sales to tang. net worth	Net sales to net wkg. cap.	Avg. coll. period	Net sales to invty.	Fixed assets to tang. net worth	Curr. debt to tang. net worth	Total debt to tang. net worth	Invty. to net wkg. cap.	Curr. debt to invty.	Funded debts to net wkg. cap.
Airplane parts and Accessories (38)	2.45	5.09	19.71	31.14	5.68	10.53	26	11.0	29.9	31.1	51.1	80.2	77.8	11.8
	1.97	3.14	12.05	21.73	3.83	6.67	40	6.0	49.8	75.4	95.5	105.1	110.8	36.6
	1.35	1.98	5.37	8.58	2.51	4.92	56	3.9	67.8	137.2	180.8	172.2	167.9	53.0
Automobile Parts and Accessories (70)	4.16	5.91	14.21	26.02	3.20	6.01	25	8.1	21.2	18.3	35.9	56.7	46.1	13.4
	3.01	3.75	10.24	17.22	2.45	3.69	32	5.8	35.8	29.2	52.5	79.0	72.6	26.8
	2.20	2.11	4.96	9.26	1.88	3.10	40	4.1	51.9	48.3	81.0	105.3	92.0	47.0
Bedsprings and Mattresses (65)	6.79	4.63	15.07	15.34	3.14	5.56	24	10.1	19.4	12.0	32.2	45.8	32.5	11.9
	3.71	2.61	6.27	10.11	2.71	4.51	44	7.2	26.9	24.4	47.6	59.4	61.1	21.9
	2.37	1.44	4.98	7.34	1.87	3.23	63	5.3	44.3	33.7	71.2	91.2	97.5	44.9
Bolts, Screws, Nuts, and Nails (55)	5.09	5.97	16.78	29.94	3.38	7.50	20	8.2	34.9	15.3	42.7	55.6	44.0	38.2
	3.10	5.10	10.11	19.74	2.80	4.38	24	5.1	45.7	22.5	79.6	75.7	66.4	54.2
	2.20	1.19	3.62	8.72	1.86	3.30	31	4.2	64.5	41.3	118.7	100.5	102.5	88.3
Breweries (40)	4.06	4.38	13.03	39.69	2.83	10.93	8	26.8	55.9	14.0	22.0	32.7	72.1	22.5
	2.71	2.52	5.58	15.37	2.36	8.26	18	19.5	68.5	18.5	33.4	46.8	129.0	44.2
	1.96	0.72†	1.66†	2.21†	1.96	5.17	30	13.2	85.1	30.0	50.8	65.1	200.7	90.6
Chemicals, Industrial (67)	3.64	8.20	13.24	32.67	2.76	6.33	31	7.9	34.8	18.8	41.4	48.1	60.7	19.8
	2.87	5.27	10.04	22.31	1.94	4.35	37	6.7	56.6	26.3	53.6	65.3	89.1	43.4
	2.09	2.80	7.21	12.54	1.46	3.25	42	5.3	81.7	39.8	73.2	95.6	133.9	64.3
Coats and Suits, Men's and Boy's (194)	4.12	1.77	7.96	9.68	6.29	7.42	26	7.7	2.7	26.7	57.9	50.3	51.6	9.2
	2.48	0.59	2.64	3.46	4.39	5.24	46	5.4	6.1	57.8	108.0	81.9	82.7	25.6
	1.76	0.11	0.46	0.56	2.85	3.27	75	4.1	15.8	118.8	222.6	120.7	131.7	44.0
Coats and Suits Women's (79)	3.32	2.08	9.82	12.11	11.78	15.86	26	20.6	4.0	33.1	101.3	46.3	84.7	12.5
	2.15	0.54	4.70	6.28	6.53	8.70	30	14.0	7.6	71.3	114.7	72.7	121.1	32.9
	1.60	0.05	0.33	0.43	4.29	5.16	43	9.1	14.6	129.9	186.2	123.1	174.8	80.0
Confectionery (42)	4.64	2.89	9.33	23.13	4.82	11.67	15	10.7	32.7	15.0	43.4	54.5	48.1	13.6
	2.72	1.74	6.93	11.16	3.02	6.70	18	6.8	42.4	26.0	52.9	74.8	72.8	27.1
	2.16	0.14	0.35	0.54	2.53	4.01	27	5.7	61.6	47.5	69.6	104.9	105.8	39.8
Contractors, Building Construction (179)	2.71	3.08	15.79	33.45	11.53	18.81	**	**	10.4	37.1	59.1	**	**	10.3
	1.73	1.56	10.68	17.33	5.98	9.90	**	**	22.8	81.1	148.4	**	**	18.6
	1.35	0.81	6.09	10.69	3.47	4.53	**	**	42.9	167.2	230.5	**	**	38.7
Contractors, Electrical (51)	3.10	6.53	27.33	34.85	6.22	8.66	**	**	5.9	41.4	58.4	**	**	15.4
	2.43	3.69	17.70	22.99	5.05	7.48	**	**	13.8	53.9	116.3	**	**	29.2
	1.73	1.58	12.58	14.71	3.65	3.92	**	**	25.7	96.7	167.0	**	**	45.1
Cotton Cloth Mills (47)	7.41	3.46	7.32	13.51	2.08	6.32	9	5.1	37.4	9.1	27.4	64.4	22.8	15.2
	4.62	1.21	2.17	7.35	1.63	3.58	37	4.2	50.0	16.9	39.7	81.0	38.7	24.1
	2.55	0.13	0.15	0.76	1.30	2.39	46	3.1	63.3	33.1	90.0	119.5	70.2	44.4
Cotton Goods, Converters, Non-Factored (43)	7.54	1.40	5.51	6.38	5.14	4.98	17	7.4	0.6	14.3	....	50.7	26.0	....
	2.74	1.02	2.62	2.65	2.99	2.71	38	5.0	1.1	45.2	....	77.4	66.3	....
	1.73	0.13	0.54	0.64	1.98	2.07	50	3.4	3.5	134.0	....	92.8	133.3	....
Dresses, Rayon, Silk, and Acetate (99)	2.75	1.35	16.38	23.20	15.71	19.35	24	34.5	4.2	43.3	102.3	30.2	113.9	20.4
	1.92	0.63	7.17	11.06	11.47	14.67	32	19.7	7.7	89.2	144.6	61.6	195.8	44.1
	1.49	0.23	1.48	1.72	8.35	10.16	39	15.2	13.8	169.3	231.5	117.9	294.9	70.8
Drugs (43)	3.82	12.80	25.00	37.40	2.73	4.53	33	7.9	15.6	15.6	32.9	46.5	53.1	15.5
	2.85	9.45	18.87	31.48	2.08	3.35	38	5.5	34.3	34.1	52.7	62.8	90.0	26.4
	2.19	3.30	9.82	11.48	1.58	2.39	51	4.4	38.8	44.8	68.0	83.6	118.0	45.6
Electrical Parts and Supplies (74)	4.14	6.31	16.70	33.48	3.75	5.75	20	7.4	24.3	21.2	37.1	62.5	62.9	13.6
	3.00	4.13	11.35	16.75	2.75	4.58	32	5.2	35.9	30.1	62.7	75.2	62.6	26.9
	2.36	2.43	7.55	10.28	2.16	3.22	39	4.0	52.4	46.3	87.1	100.3	89.4	46.1
Foundries (108)	4.86	5.12	13.98	25.03	3.28	6.35	24	13.6	36.2	14.5	31.9	33.6	48.9	15.8
	3.41	3.70	9.72	17.25	2.68	4.50	30	7.5	48.4	23.1	47.3	56.3	81.6	34.4
	2.16	2.33	6.27	9.80	2.09	3.30	40	5.4	63.3	35.7	63.2	80.4	134.8	50.6
Furniture (146)	4.62	4.57	12.84	22.01	4.43	6.90	27	9.1	20.7	17.2	38.5	49.8	98.4	9.9
	3.17	2.22	7.70	12.90	2.97	4.90	41	5.9	31.5	29.8	59.7	68.7	72.2	23.0
	2.15	0.44	2.83	2.76	2.20	3.27	48	4.5	50.9	50.8	91.2	101.7	104.6	47.6
Hardware and Tools (102)	5.21	5.65	15.25	25.17	3.47	6.70	25	9.7	24.3	16.0	26.9	55.6	36.6	10.7
	3.57	3.69	10.25	15.44	2.30	3.36	34	4.8	36.8	24.9	43.5	75.7	50.4	24.8
	2.54	1.74	3.82	4.96	1.91	2.73	41	3.4	50.4	34.7	71.0	95.5	86.5	43.4
Hosiery (75)	7.32	2.95	9.14	15.47	4.50	7.52	19	10.9	29.6	9.5	26.8	51.2	26.4	14.5
	3.47	1.67	3.89	7.32	2.58	4.49	31	5.8	42.1	19.6	52.2	72.3	55.9	27.5
	2.19	0.59	1.71	2.10	1.54	2.78	39	4.5	59.1	34.6	90.6	107.1	84.5	77.6
Lumber (72)	6.15	7.29	11.18	21.44	3.23	5.72	22	7.1	18.0	9.4	19.8	47.9	29.1	15.0
	3.63	3.54	5.32	9.56	1.66	3.72	32	5.5	31.1	17.3	49.5	77.8	55.5	38.8
	2.04	0.18	0.56	0.68	0.73	1.91	53	3.0	48.5	37.0	97.2	125.0	85.0	91.5
Machine Shops (151)	4.18	5.99	16.30	32.25	3.45	6.95	22	18.0	32.2	17.2	30.2	36.9	49.2	16.2
	2.88	3.99	10.90	17.97	2.28	4.50	33	8.5	45.2	28.2	49.8	69.2	91.9	31.8
	1.94	1.70	4.05	7.70	1.74	3.34	42	4.2	62.4	42.7	86.1	97.1	171.8	52.9
Machinery, Industrial (364)	4.42	5.97	14.47	21.63	3.62	5.03	32	7.0	22.5	20.2	40.6	55.1	45.9	9.8
	3.09	3.76	10.16	15.14	2.50	3.69	44	4.6	32.6	31.2	60.3	74.6	69.7	25.6
	2.23	2.36	5.83	8.63	1.91	2.60	57	3.4	45.2	52.5	90.2	97.7	106.7	51.5

MANUFACTURING Cont.

14

Line of Business (and Number of Businesses)

IMPORTANT RATIOS IN 36 MANUFACTURING LINES—1957

	Current assets to current debt	Net profits on net sales	Net profits on tangible net worth	Net profits on net working capital	Net sales to tangible net worth	Net sales to net working capital	Average collection period	Net sales to inventory	Fixed assets to tangible net worth	Current debt to tangible net worth	Total debt to tangible net worth	Inventory to net working capital	Current debt to inventory	Funded debts to net working capital
	Times	Per cent	Per cent	Per cent	Times	Times	Days	Times	Per cent	Per cent	Per cent	Per cent	Per cent	Per cent
FOR 36 MANUFACTURING LINES—1957 MEDIANS AND QUARTILES														
Meats and Provisions, Packers (72)	3.63	1.84	12.83	33.98	11.23	24.89	10	32.0	44.2	19.1	39.3	49.4	69.6	28.8
	2.42	0.78	6.04	15.66	7.36	16.88	11	24.7	58.4	31.7	66.7	64.4	98.1	50.2
	1.80	0.44	2.95	7.67	5.66	12.75	14	17.5	78.7	48.4	92.5	98.3	149.6	80.6
Metal Stampings (85)	4.83	5.98	15.83	29.41	4.11	9.18	25	10.3	30.8	13.9	26.8	46.0	44.5	15.6
	3.04	4.14	10.09	17.33	2.49	5.01	35	6.2	43.7	25.6	54.5	71.8	74.5	32.1
	2.07	1.80	4.20	9.07	1.77	3.37	42	4.6	62.5	45.2	82.2	101.7	108.3	57.4
Outerwear, Knitted (68)	3.47	2.22	8.85	11.54	6.53	9.76	21	12.7	3.4	30.0	66.7	38.8	72.3	4.5
	2.18	1.15	4.02	5.62	3.98	7.61	36	6.2	11.4	61.2	86.7	76.1	105.7	14.9
	1.67	0.15	0.92	1.40	2.80	4.28	48	4.7	29.5	96.7	178.2	142.2	139.6	39.6
Overalls and Work Clothing (58)	5.07	2.47	8.21	13.48	5.31	8.58	20	5.6	8.7	21.5	41.8	67.1	33.6	7.6
	3.10	1.49	4.67	5.59	3.61	4.30	33	4.4	16.6	35.4	86.0	92.0	52.1	22.2
	2.10	0.55	1.88	2.16	2.13	2.79	44	3.5	29.7	68.2	126.1	123.3	76.6	35.5
Paints, Varnishes, and Lacquers (138)	5.54	3.39	10.62	18.28	4.06	6.32	25	9.8	22.0	15.4	27.7	50.6	39.6	11.2
	3.40	2.03	6.14	9.39	2.64	4.78	36	6.9	34.9	24.2	44.0	67.7	66.1	23.6
	2.50	1.02	2.68	3.24	2.18	3.74	45	5.0	50.8	39.4	68.5	91.3	95.0	37.7
Paper (65)	3.64	7.98	10.90	41.21	1.90	6.27	21	9.7	56.3	14.1	26.3	50.3	60.0	27.4
	2.79	5.30	8.48	27.44	1.64	4.86	26	7.0	71.3	17.6	35.6	69.6	83.3	50.4
	2.12	3.68	5.28	18.29	1.14	3.81	31	5.5	92.4	24.9	52.9	91.7	115.9	101.0
Paper Boxes (69)	4.96	5.38	12.10	40.00	3.20	8.92	20	15.0	37.8	15.1	46.5	43.9	55.3	39.2
	2.52	3.51	9.49	23.20	2.54	6.15	29	10.0	58.3	24.5	62.8	55.7	81.7	67.3
	1.81	1.34	5.96	8.81	1.89	4.88	33	7.1	82.3	45.3	92.0	75.6	128.3	128.8
Petroleum, Integrated Operators (37)	2.92	13.88	15.01	64.04	1.56	7.03	30	9.2	72.0	13.7	27.2	52.1	77.7	65.8
	2.41	7.61	11.32	42.67	1.18	5.40	38	7.6	89.0	18.4	51.5	71.2	109.5	109.7
	1.78	5.99	7.86	28.37	0.95	4.03	45	6.7	104.5	26.5	73.4	86.2	146.7	171.0
Printers, Job (64)	3.26	4.28	10.22	37.11	3.83	12.37	28		42.1	21.9	31.9			16.1
	2.38	2.13	7.44	19.57	2.65	6.58	37	‡‡	60.0	31.3	41.9	‡‡	‡‡	27.9
	1.67	1.34	3.04	10.79	2.36	5.18	46		75.2	43.4	68.8			81.2
Shirts, Underwear, and Pajamas, Men's (58)	3.41	1.29	7.25	9.53	6.67	9.46	26	7.4	2.7	38.3	61.4	69.4	50.0	11.9
	2.20	0.77	3.18	3.92	5.40	5.78	50	5.4	5.9	66.8	81.3	102.2	83.5	19.6
	1.57	1.14†	3.59†	4.50†	3.06	3.72	58	3.8	15.7	141.7	139.7	146.1	107.8	28.7
Shoes, Men's, Women's, and Children's (107)	3.65	3.34	10.20	13.34	5.15	7.04	31	7.9	11.9	30.5	56.7	59.8	51.7	13.7
	2.55	1.82	7.44	8.23	3.54	4.13	49	5.2	17.9	49.5	74.0	84.4	68.0	24.6
	1.90	1.11	3.43	4.30	2.43	2.80	60	3.5	28.4	78.6	102.3	109.2	125.9	43.0
Steel, Structural Fabricators (sell on short terms) (101)	3.93	6.42	21.64	43.98	5.21	8.75	34	8.5	24.0	23.8	64.9	50.1	51.3	16.6
	2.60	3.84	14.93	25.90	3.24	4.73	47	6.2	32.9	36.0	82.1	81.3	84.9	31.2
	1.95	1.76	6.62	11.60	2.31	3.75	60	4.2	50.6	63.6	147.2	99.4	119.9	68.7
Stoves, Ranges, and Ovens (56)	6.98	5.55	12.10	20.61	3.92	6.29	29	7.2	17.7	14.5	30.7	57.7	33.8	7.2
	3.74	1.81	5.25	12.68	3.09	4.64	41	5.2	29.4	28.9	56.7	72.6	54.9	27.8
	2.56	0.61	1.70	3.06	2.21	3.49	51	4.6	40.0	43.6	80.9	95.4	75.6	45.4

†Loss.
**Building and construction contractors and electrical contractors do not have inventories in the credit sense of the term. They carry only such materials as lumber, bricks, tile, cement, structural steel, and build-ing equipment to complete jobs on which they are working. Electrical contractors carry electrical equipment and supplies to complete particular jobs on which they are working. Concerns operating in these lines generally have no customary selling terms, each contract being a special job for which individual term are arranged.
–Job printers do not have inventories in the credit sense of the term. They carry only current supplies such as paper, ink, binding materials, and lead for type-setting.

APPENDIX K

CREDIT APPLICATION FORM

The estate of the Borrower, and any Co-makers, have the protection afforded by the insurance placed by the Bank on the life of the Borrower, by the terms of which the insurer has agreed, in event of the death of the Borrower during the period for which the loan is made, to pay to the Bank an amount sufficient to discharge the loan to the extent not theretofore repaid.

Application for Personal Loan

To THE FIRST NATIONAL CITY BANK OF NEW YORK, NEW YORK, N. Y.

I hereby make application for a personal loan of → $

Date_____

Amount of Note	No. of Months	MONTHLY PAYMENTS

Beginning one month from date loan is made. ☐   Beginning on ☐ , 195

(Please Print)

Name of Applicant _____

| First Name | Middle name | Last name | City of Birth | Date of Birth |

Filed

Send Mail to — **Res.**

Residence Address _____

| No. & Street | Apt. No. | Post Office, City or Borough | Zone No. | State | Years There |

Last Previous Address _____

| No. & Street | | Post Office, City or Borough | Zone No. | State | Years There |

CHECK ONE ↕

Single ☐
Married ☐ Name of wife (or husband), if married   Is your wife (husband) employed?   How many dependents?   Residence Telephone Number

Send Mail to — **Bus.**

Carded

Name of Applicant's Employer or Business _____   Kind of Business _____

(Corp. or Trade Style)

Business Address _____   Tel. No._____   Ext._____

| No. & Street | Post Office, City or Borough | Zone No. | State |

Position _____   Badge or Employment No._____   Length of Service With Present Employer_____   Yearly Salary or Wages → $_____

Dept._____   Name and Title of Superior_____   Other Income, if any give source_____ $_____

If not with present Employer two years or more _____

| Previous Employer | Address | City | State | No. of Years |

Do you or wife (husband) own a Motor Car? _____ Yes or No   Owned by you or wife husband   Make_____   Year_____

Are you at present a Borrower on a Personal Loan Note at this Bank? _____   Are you a Co-maker?_____

Have you any judgments, garnishments, suits or legal proceedings against you? (Yes or No) _____ If so give particulars_____

Real Estate owned by You and/or Wife (Husband) (If none state "None")._____

	Address	City	State	Purchase Price	Mortgage Balance
				$	$

BANK ACCOUNTS (If none state "None")

Personal Checking a/c: Regular ☐   Special ☐ _____   BRANCH

Business Checking a/c: Regular ☐   Special ☐ _____

Savings a/c: _____   A/C NO._____

I list below all my applications, loans and installment accounts (including CHATTEL MORTGAGES AND CONDITIONAL SALE CONTRACTS) outstanding, **WITH THIS BANK OR ELSEWHERE. IF NONE STATE "NONE".**

Name of Bank, Company or Individual	Address	Date Made	Account Number	Original Amount	Balance Unpaid	Amount Due Each Month	Arrears If Any
				$	$	$	$
				$	$	$	$
				$	$	$	$

I hereby affirm that each of the answers in the foregoing Application is true and correct, and authorize you: (a) to obtain information from any source(s) to which you may apply relative to this Application—each such source being hereby authorized to provide you with such information, and (b) in event of a loan not being granted, to return the promissory note and assignment form, if any, relative hereto, to me by ordinary mail at my sole risk. This Application in any event shall be and remain your property.

The proceeds of the loan, which will be evidenced by a promissory note, shall be the face amount thereof less a charge computed on that amount for the period from the date of the note to and including the date when the last amount payable thereunder is to become due, at a rate not exceeding four dollars and twenty-five cents per annum discount per one hundred dollars face amount of loan. You are hereby authorized to: (1) insure my life during the term of the loan and for the amount owing at any time on account thereof; (2) remit by ordinary mail the net proceeds of the loan to me, by your check, for the risk of the receipt of which I hereby assume full responsibility, and (3) release the said note (as and when paid) to any of the signers thereof.

PLEASE COMPLETE INFORMATION ON REVERSE SIDE

Signature of Applicant (sign full name) _____

Loan No.

App. No.

SC ☐	Date_____
OE ☐	By_____
COM ☐	Branch_____
	Co. No._____

Deduct Unpaid Balance PL No

| Last Pay't. Rec'd. | Date | Amount | Interviewer |

Amount of Note....$_____

Discount Charge (includes cost of Life Insurance) $_____

Proceeds ....$_____

Amount of Monthly Payment...$_____

| WA ☐ | A P P |

| C O M |

4.25 P.A.   PL-3285 Rev. 5/58 PFD. The First National City Bank of New York, Personal Credit Department

BIBLIOGRAPHY

BECKMAN, T. N., and R. BARTELS: "Credit and Collections in Theory and Practice," 6th ed., New York, McGraw-Hill Book Company, Inc., 1955.

BENJAMIN, EUGENE S.: "Credit Analysis," New York, Mimeographed, 1933.

BOARD OF GOVERNORS OF THE FEDERAL RESERVE SYSTEM: "Consumer Instalment Credit," Washington, D.C., Government Printing Office, 1957.

BOGEN, J. I., editor: "Financial Handbook," 3d ed., New York, The Ronald Press Company, 1952.

BONNEVILLE, J. H., L. E. DEWEY, and H. M. KELLEY: "Organizing and Financing Business," 6th ed., Englewood Cliffs, N.J., Prentice-Hall, Inc., 1959.

BREWSTER, S. F.: "Legal Aspects of Credit," New York, The Ronald Press Company, 1923.

BURTON, T. E.: "Crises and Depressions," New York, D. Appleton & Company, 1902.

CREDIT UNION NATIONAL ASSOCIATION: "The Credit Union Year Book," Madison, Wis., 1958.

DAUTEN, C. A.: "Financing the American Consumer," St. Louis, Mo., American Investment Company of Illinois, 1956.

ETTINGER, R. P., and D. E. GOLIEB: "Credits and Collections," 4th ed., Englewood Cliffs, N.J., Prentice-Hall, Inc., 1956.

FOSTER, M. B., J. I. BOGEN, R. ROGERS, and M. NADLER: "Money and Banking," 4th ed., Englewood Cliffs, N.J., Prentice-Hall, Inc., 1953.

FOULKE, R. A.: "An Inquiry into the Purpose of the Production of Wealth," New York, Dun & Bradstreet, Inc., 1954.

FOULKE, R. A.: "Behind the Scenes of Business," rev. ed., New York, Dun & Bradstreet, Inc., 1956.

FOULKE, R. A.: "Practical Financial Statement Analysis," 4th ed., New York, McGraw-Hill Book Company, Inc., 1957.

FOULKE, R. A., and R. V. PROCHNOW: "Practical Bank Credit," Englewood Cliffs, N.J., Prentice-Hall, Inc., 1939.

GALLOT, F. PASCHAL: Why Compensating Balances? *Credit Executive*, August–September, 1958.

JOHNSON, J. F.: "Money and Currency," Boston, Ginn & Company, 1921.

KEMMERER, E. W.: "High Prices and Deflation," Princeton, N.J., Princeton University Press, 1920.

KING, W. I.: "The Causes of Economic Fluctuations," New York, The Ronald Press Company, 1936.

KING, W. I.: "The Keys to Prosperity," New York, Constitution and Free Enterprise Foundation, 1948.

575

MILL, JOHN STUART: "Principles of Political Economy," New York, D. Appleton & Company, 1884.

MITCHELL, W. C.: "What Happens during Business Cycles," National Bureau of Economic Research, Inc., New York, The Riverside Press, 1951.

MUNN, G. G.: "Bank Credit," New York, McGraw-Hill Book Company, Inc., 1925.

NATIONAL ASSOCIATION OF CREDIT MANAGEMENT—Studies Released by Credit Research Foundation: "Training for Credit Management," 1952; "Measurement of Credit Department Effectiveness," 1954; "Credit Orientation and Training for Salesmen," 1958; "Reserve for Bad Debts," 1958.

NATIONAL ASSOCIATION OF CREDIT MANAGEMENT: "Credit Manual of Commercial Laws, New York, 1959.

NATIONAL ASSOCIATION OF MUTUAL SAVINGS BANKS: "Mutual Savings Banking Today," New York, 1958.

NEIFELD, M. R.: "Personal Finance Comes of Age," New York, Harper & Brothers, 1939.

PHELPS, C. W.: "Retail Credit Fundamentals," St. Louis, Mo., National Retail Credit Association, rev. ed., New York, McGraw-Hill Book Company, Inc., 1947.

PHELPS, C. W.: "Using Installment Credit," Studies in Consumer Credit No. 4, Baltimore, Md., Commercial Credit Company, 1955.

PRENDERGAST, W. A., and W. H. STEINER: "Credit and Its Uses," New York, Appleton-Century-Crofts, Inc., 1931.

SANZO, R.: "Ratio Analysis for Small Business," Small Business Administration, Washington, D.C., Government Printing Office, 1957.

SOMERS, H. N.: "Psychology in Credit Letters," New York, National Association of Credit Men, 1947.

STEINER, W. H.: "The Mechanism of Commercial Credit," New York, Appleton-Century-Crofts, Inc., 1931.

WALL, A., and R. W. DUNING: "Ratio Analysis of Financial Statements," Appendix, New York, Harper & Brothers, 1928.

INDEX

Acceleration clause, 296
Acceptance Agreement, 543
Acceptances, bank, 80
  trade (*see* Trade acceptance)
Accommodation paper, 134, 135
Accountant, certifications, 306–307
  versus credit manager, 308
  ethical standard of, 306
  liability of, to creditors, 307
  as source of information, 282
Accountant's report, 306
  competency of, 305
  supplementary information, 294
  verification of financial statement, 306
Accounts payable, classification of, 325
Accounts receivable, trade, aging, 314
  analysis of, 314
  assignment to banks, 157
  pledged, 314
Accrued liabilities, 326
Acid test, 336
Adjustment bureaus, 509
  achievement of, 518
  administration procedure, 512
  cases, origin of, 512
  compositions under, 514
  debtors, control, 512
  extensions under, 514
  functions of, 510
  future of, 518
  inception of, 509
  instructions to creditors' committee, 511
  investigation exemplified, 515
  membership responsibility, 510
  organization of, 509
  personal investigation by, 516–518

Adjustment bureaus, unapproved
  practices, protection against, 515
Adjustments, friendly, 469
Age as credit factor, 53
  (*See also* Capacity)
Agencies (*see* Mercantile agencies)
Agricultural compositions and extensions
  in bankruptcy, 503
American Credit Indemnity Company, 523
Antecedents, facts covered by, 104, 219, 241
  importance of, 104
  record of, complete, 56
  type of business, 104
A.O.G. terms, 173
Arrangements, confirmation of, 498
  definition of, 482*n*.
  effect of law on, 498
  meaning of, 497
  petition for, 497
  provisions of, 498, 499
  purpose of, 497
  real property, 503
  (*See also* Bankruptcy)
Assets, classification of, 310
  current, 311
  deferred, 321–322
  fixed, 321
  intangible, 322
  miscellaneous, 311, 321
  other, 321
  prepaid, 322
Assignee, duties of, 475
Assignments, 474
  advantages and disadvantages of, 474
  (*See also* Hypothecation)

Attachment, grounds for, 457
  requirements in, 458
  right of, 457
  and suit, 457
Attorney, as collection agent, 415
  cost of service, 280
  how to use, 279
  as source of information, 125, 277
  type of report of, 278
Authority to purchase, 86
Average collection period, 359
Ayres, Milan V., 207

Bad Check law, 73
  application of, 73
  of New York, 74
  penalties under, 75
  preexisting debt, 73
  provisions of, 73
Bad debt losses, 466, 507
  (*See also* Bankruptcies; Credit losses)
Bad debts, charging off, 447
  reserve for, 316
Balance sheet, 287
  (*See also* Financial reports)
Balance sheet relationships, 333
  (*See also* Ratios)
Bank acceptances, 80
Bank credit, compared with mercantile
    credit, 129
  effect of, 129
  lines of, 143–145
  standard of, 130
Bank credit department, analysis by,
    137–145
  branch, credit control, 43
  credit folder, 41
  efficiency measurement of, 43
  establishing credit lines, 143
  functions of, 40, 137
    filing, 40
  growth of, 39
  investigations by, 140
  loaning committee, 144
  reasons for, 39
  structure of, 41
  type of work in, 40, 137
Bank credit manager, 41
  (*See also* Credit executive; Credit
    manager)

Bank investigators, information from, 140
Bank loans, classification of, 133
Bank service charges, 131, 132
Bank stories, 120
Bankrupt, duties of, 488
  who may become, 485
  (*See also* Bankruptcy)
Bankruptcies, number of, 11, 507
  (*See also* Business failures)
Bankruptcy, 482
  acts of, 486–488
  adjustment bureau, services of, 509
    (*See also* Collection agency)
  agricultural extensions, 503
  arrangements (*see* Arrangements)
  claims, filing proof, 494
    order of priority, 495
    provable and allowable, 493
  corporate reorganization, 499
  court of, 490
  credit executive's interest in, 483
  credit losses through, 507
  creditors' meetings, 493
  "depression amendments," 484
  discharge in, 489
    reasons for denial, 489
  dischargeable debts, 496
  dividends in, 506
  examination of debtor in, 505
  liquidation, 468
  officers and their duties, 490
  options under law, 485
  protecting creditor's interest in, 504
  reclamation proceedings, 505
  turnover proceedings, 506
  wage earners' plans, 503
  (*See also* Insolvency)
Bankruptcy laws, purposes of, 482
  in United States, 484
Banks, classifications, 128
  client relationships, 131
  credit process in, 137
  definition of, 128
  how to use, 145
  information from, 147
    interpretation of, 141, 148
    reasons for withholding, 146
  as inquirers, 149
  investment, 127
  as source of information, 145
  (*See also* Consumer credit; Retail
    credit)

Beckman, T. N., 191
Benjamin, Eugene S., 356
Bertcher, Samuel, 317
Bill of exchange (drafts), 76
Bills of lading, in C.O.D. shipments, 82
  as collateral, 81
  definition of, 81
  forms of, 81
Bills payable, classification of, 325
Bishop's Service, Inc., 280
Bonds, appraisal of, 328
  classification of, 66
  definition of, 65
  as liability, 328
Book account, 59
  advantages and disadvantages, 60
Borrower, average bank balance of, 131
Branch bank credit control, 43
Branch office credit control, 42
Break-even inventory, 383
Break-even point analysis, 385
Brewster, S. F., 456
Bulk Sales laws, 460, 513
  creditors' remedies in, 460
  interpretation of, 462
  purpose of, 460
  variations in, 460, 461
Burton, T. E., 211
Business conditions, indices of, 18
  as risk factor, 54
Business cycles, 13, 17
  causes of, 15
    interest in, 13
  elimination of, 13
  four phases of, 13, 19
  three types of, 13
Business failures, 11, 507
  causes of, 466
Business profits, 12
Business record as credit factor, 111
  (*See also* Four C's of Credit)
Business units, corporations, 107
  partnerships, 106
  single proprietorships, 105
  trusts, 109
Butter & Egg Co., analysis of, 380

Cancellations and returns, 452
Capacity, appraisal of, 52

Capacity, definition of, 53
  factors of, 53
  importance of, 55, 220
Capital, 53
  versus credit, 6
  definition of, 53
  function of, in credit risk as guarantee, 54
  as net worth, 331
Capital goods, 6
Capital stock, 330
Case v. Los Angeles Lumber Products Co., 499n.
Cash, analysis of, 313
Cash discount, 174
  abuse of, 440
  analysis of, 175
  annual interest rate, 178
  factors influencing, 177
  as financing charge, 177
  history of, 174
  purpose of, 439
  unearned, collection of, 439
Cash discount terms, options under, 176
Cashiers' checks, 73
C.B.D. terms, 172
Certificate of protest, form of, 63
Certified checks, effect of certification, 72
  illustrated, 72
Chandler Act, 484, 485
  Chapter X of (*see* Corporate reorganizations)
Character, appraisal of, 52
  bank stories, 120, 148
  definition of, 51
  and reputation, 50
  trade stories, 120, 185
Checks, acceptability of, 70
  cashiers', 73
  certification of, 72
  in full of account, 71
  as medium of transfer, 70
  postdated, 74
  presentation of, 74
  stopping payment of, 71
  travelers, 80
Classification of risks, trade, 182
Clearance reports, 557, 560
C.O.D. shipment by freight, 82
  terms, 172
  (*See also* Terms of sale)

Coinsurance, 347, 348, 522
Collateral security, 134
Collection agency, 413
 fees, 415, 416
 relationship to creditor, 414
 selection of, 414
 (*See also* Mercantile agencies)
Collection letters, 417
 appeals in, 420–422
 effectiveness of, 420
 fate of, 417
 legal side of, 419
 mental attitude of writer, 419
 plans for following up, 402
 of salesman, 436
 specimens, 427–432
 suggestions for, 425
 of treasurer, 435
 use of, 407, 417
 value of repetition in, 422
 what to avoid in, 425
Collection policy, close, reasons for, 393
 and marketing plan, 397
Collection problem, importance of, 392
 variations of, 391
Collection procedure, stages in, 423
Collection system, necessity for, 398
Collection tickler, 400
Collection turnover, derivation of, 398
Collections, competition in, 398
 follow-up systems, 399
 maturity lists, 401
 slow payments, 394
 telegram in, 410
 telephone in, 409
 timing of appeal, 422
 types of appeal, 422
 value of repetition, 422
 (*See also* Collection letters; Mercantile agencies)
Commensurate balance, 131
Commercial bank credit defined, 129
Commercial banks, 128
 as credit transfer agency, 129
 influence of, 129
 personal loan departments, 197
 (*See also* Consumer credit)
Commercial Law League, fees, 415
Commercial letter of credit, definitions
   of, 83
 function of, 83

Commercial paper, 135
 classification by National Credit
   Office, 239
 reasons for popularity, 136
 trend in, 136
Commercial paper broker, function of,
   135
 origin of, 136
Commission houses (*see* Factors)
"Common size" statements, 372
Comparative statement analysis, 371,
   376
 problems for, 567–568
Compensating balance, 131
Compensating ratios, 357
Competitive datings, 171
Composition settlements, 472, 514
 justification of, 473
Consumer credit, 190
 justification of, 192
 personal loans, 194, 197
 statistics, 193, 204
Consumer credit institutions, 190
Consumer instalment loans, statistics,
   193, 204
Consumer loans by licensed lenders, 195
Contingent liabilities, 332
 shown on balance sheet, 332
Continuing clause in financial statement,
   296, 565
Contract, elements of, 450
Cooperative societies, 109
Corn Exchange Bank v. Klauder, 154n.
Corporate reorganization, 499
 petition, filing of, 500
 plan, confirmation of, 502
 presentation of, 500
 provisions of, 501
 trustee, duties of, 500
  how appointed, 500
 (*See also* Arrangements; Bankruptcy;
   Composition settlements)
Corporations, 107
 advantages of, 108
 definition of, 107
 foreign, 108
 as guarantors, 535
 limitations of, 108
 powers of, 108
 profits of, 12
Cost of goods sold, 341
Costs in small loans, 196

Court of bankruptcy, 490
Credit, abuse of, 10
  attitude toward, 166
  bank (*see* Bank credit)
  classification of, 3, 127
  as confidence, 5
  consumer (*see* Consumer credit)
  definitions of, new positive, 4
  derivation of word, 3
  documents of, 58
  as field of occupation, 23
  instalment (*see* Instalment credit)
  limit of credit economy, 8
  losses, 466
  meaning of, 3–8
  as means of exchange, 9
  of persons and property, 134
  phases of, 6
  potential, 3, 5
  as power, 6
  process in banks, 137
  redemption of, 11
  retail (*see* Retail credit)
  study of, phases, 6
  trade (*see* Trade credit)
  in use, 3, 5
    (*See also* Credit limits)
  use of, 9
    liability, 7
  value of, 178
  and wealth, 6
Credit application form, 574
Credit Bureau of Greater New York, 262
  membership, 262
  method of operation, 262
  speed of service, 265
  types of credit reports, 262, 561–562
Credit department, efficiency of, measurement, 43
  function of, 32
  independence of, 35
  mechanical aids to, 39
  personnel of trade, 36
  place in business organization, 33, 41
  relation to sales department, 34
    (*See also* Bank credit department)
Credit department files, 37
  correspondence, 38
  credit folder, 41
  customers' ledger, 38
  duplicate invoice, 38

Credit department files, filing function, 40
  handling of orders, 180
  importance of system in, 36
Credit ethics, 143, 544
Credit executive, in banks, 23
  future of, 24
  interest in bankruptcy, 483
  position of, 23
  qualifications of, 24–27
    education, 27
  work of, 22
    (*See also* Credit manager)
Credit factors, age of business, 104
  comparative weight of, 55
  in credit decisions, 103
  location, 110
  record of owners, 111
  regrouped, 104
    (*See also* Antecedents)
Credit and Financial Management, 98
Credit forms, 98, 294, 298, 373–374, 543, 563–564, 574
Credit information, agencies (*see* Mercantile agencies)
  confidential nature of, 143
  as fact or opinion, 115
  general classification of, 116
  interpretation of, 141
  legal aspects of, 142
  sources of, banks, 145
    retail, 199
    trade, 149
Credit information file, 38, 41
Credit instruments, acceptability of, 59–61
Credit insurance, 351, 520–521
  adjustment methods, 529
  agencies in use, 523
  businesses, classification of, 521–522
  coinsurance, 522
  definition of, 520
  discussion of, 530–532
  filing of claim, 528
  and fire insurance, 532
  insolvency, definition of, 527
  normal loss, 533
  policies, 521
  premium computation, 524–525, 527
  primary loss, 526
  ratings and coverage, 522
  sales increase through, 531

Credit interchange bureaus, 250
  advantages and disadvantages of, 267
  functions of, 250
  as means of avoiding duplication, 251
  methods of operation, 252
  reports, analysis and comparison of,
    254, 260
  (*See also* Mercantile agencies)
Credit interchange service, inception of,
    250
  (*See also* Interchange service; Mer-
    cantile agencies)
Credit investigator, information secured
    by, 140
  qualification, 139
Credit limits, in banks, 143, 145
    factors influencing, 144
  formulas, 187
  in instalment, 207
  in retail, 198
  in trade, 183
    factors influencing, 183–184
    methods used in fixing, 185
    revision of, 187
Credit lines (*see* Credit limits)
Credit losses, 466
  (*See also* Bad debts)
Credit manager, as business builder, 280
  in charge of collections, 392
  cooperation, 33
  importance, 23
  interest in bankruptcy, 483
  mercantile and retail credit, 191
  (*See also* Credit executive)
Credit Manual of Commercial Laws, 98
Credit policies, effect on acceptability of
    risk, 48
  liberal, reasons for, 48
  and merchandising attitude, 49
  varying, reasons for, 48
Credit Research Foundation, 92
  published products of, 93
Credit risks, acceptability of, 47
  basis of judgment in, 115
  classification of, 182
  factors of, 47
  four C's of credit, 47
Credit unions, 196
  membership reported, 197
  object of, 196
  reasons for success, 197

Credit unions, resources of, 197
  where found, 197
Creditor agreements, legal restrictions
    of, 442
Creditors, classifications of, 324
Creditors' committees, 511
Creditors' meetings, 493
Current assets, analysis of, 335
  definition of, 311
Current liabilities, analysis of, 324–327
  definition of, 312, 324
Current position, 333
  adequacy of, 336
  ratio fallacy, 334
  summary of, 336
  (*See also* Working capital)
Customers' ledger as source of collec-
    tion information, 400
  (*See also* Interchange service)

Dating, definition of, 169
  for distant territory, 171
  season, 170
  types of, 170
Debtors, examination in bankruptcy,
    505
  types, in collections, 396
Debts (*see* Bad debts)
Deferred assets, 311, 322
Deferred charges, 311, 322
Delinquent accounts, sale of, 441, 443
Deposit insurance, 130*n.*
Deposits, analysis of, 327
  bank, how created, 128
  insurance of, 130*n.*
Discount companies (*see* Finance com-
    panies)
Discount terms, classification of, 174
  trade, 174
  (*See also* Cash discount)
Discounted receivables, 315
Dishonesty as cause of failure, 56
Double-name paper, 135
Drafts, classes, 76
  as collection instruments, 408
  how accepted, 76
  use of, 76
Dun & Bradstreet, Inc., Analytical Re-
    ports, 217, 220
  correspondents of, 215

Dun & Bradstreet, Cost Plus Reports, 218
    Credit Clearing House, 227
    departments of, 213
    discussion of service, 231
    Dun's Review and Modern Industry,
        229
    international division, 228
    interpretation of reports, 218
    Key Accounts Reports, 218
    library, 230
    limitations of, 232
    Marketing Services Company, 229
    Mercantile Claims Division, 228
    Municipal Service Department, 222
    offices of, 213
    organization of, 213
    origin of, 211
    other services, 229
    priority service, 232
    ratings, 224
        interpretation of, 225
        key to, 225
        purpose of, 225
    Reference Book, 222
        illustration from, 224
        statistics, 227
        use of, 226
    reporters, 214
        city, 214
        consulting, 230
        resident, 214
        traveling, 215
    reports, 217, 218, 547–549
        analytical, 214
    sources of information used by, 214
    Special Purpose Reports, 218
    Trade Reports, 216
    types of reports, 217
    (*See also* Mercantile agencies)

Endorsement, effect of, 62
E.O.M. terms, 173
Equity receivership (*see* Receivership)
Estate ownership, 109
Examination in supplementary proceed-
        ings, 445
Exchange of credit information, guide
        for, 544–546
Exemptions, legal, 459
    property, 445

Expense analysis, 343
Extensions, 469, 514
    consummation of, 471
    legal aspects of, 471
    when to support, 470

Factoring, advantages and disadvan-
        tages to client, 159
    legal aspects of, 160
Factors, 157
    capital funds of, 158
    charges of, 158
    and commission houses, 157
    and finance companies compared, 161
    functions of, 157
    invoices, 158
    loans by, 158
    margins retained, 158
Factors' credit department, 159
Factors' lien laws, 161
Factors' liens, establishment of, 160–161
Factors' posting requirement, 161
False financial statements, 294
    federal law on, 297
    how proven, 295
    issuance as crime, 295
    material falsity, 295–296
    New York law on, 297–301
        Section 442, 301
    (*See also* Financial reports)
Field warehousing, 162
    financing through, 162
    method of, 162
Finance companies, 152
    capital funds of, 158
    classification of loans, 153
    growth of, 152
    (*See also* Hypothecation)
Financial position, investigation of, 112
Financial reports, acceleration clause,
        296
    analysis methods, 309
    authority for facts of, 305
    balance sheet, definition, 287
    classification, of assets, and liabilities
        by groups, 310
        by Securities and Exchange Com-
            mission, 312
    of income statement, 340
    continuing clause in, form, 565
    purpose of, 296

Financial reports, false (*see* **False** financial statements)
  forms of, 293, 563, 564
    envelope, 298, 299
  how received, 119
  importance of date, 309
  income reports, 287, 338–349
  procuring, by direct method, 289
    by indirect method, 288
  purpose of, 304, 312
  as source of information, 287, 288
  submission of, objections to, 290, 293
    reasons for, 289
Financial statement (*see* Financial reports)
Fire insurance, 347
  adequate, analysis of, 347
  coinsurance clause, 347
  and credit insurance, 351, 532
  and moral hazard, 348
Fixed assets, 311, 321
Foreign Credit Interchange Bureau, 96
Form letters in collections, 426
Foulke, Roy A., 356, 569
Four C's of Credit, 47, 218–219, 248
Fraud, convictions for, 91
Fraud Prevention Department, National Association of Credit Management, 91
Friendly adjustments, 469, 514
Friendly liquidations, 474, 514
Furniture and fixtures, 321

Garnishee, definition of, 459
Garnishment, 459
Graduate School of Credit and Financial Management, 93
Gross profit, importance of, 339, 340
  percentage significance, 341, 383
Group exchanges, 266
  advantages and disadvantages of, 267
  operation of, 266
Guaranties, 534
  form of, 536, 537
Guarantor, effect of death of, 538
  who may become, 535

Handling of orders, 180
Hypothecation, advances under, 154

Hypothecation, advantages to borrower, 155
  to banks, 157
  and cash discount, 155
  cost of, 155
  notification and nonnotification plans, 153
  objections to, 156
  of receivables, 153, 156
  recording statutes, 156

Income report, analysis of, 338
  comparative, 379
  mechanics, 340
  definition of, 338
  form of, 293, 339, 340
  ratios (*see* Ratios)
  significance of items, 341
  (*See also* Financial reports)
Income Statement (*see* Income report)
Indirect datings, 169
Industrial banks, 190, 197
Industrial loan companies, 190
Industry, knowledge of, 113
Insolvency, 467
  analysis of, 465
  definitions of, 467, 528
  degrees of, 468
Instalment credit, in business field, 190, 203
  financing of, 205
  interest rates, 207
  limits, 207
  origin of, 203
  safety principles in, 207
  sales, extent of, 203
  statistics, 193, 204
  terms, 203
  use and abuse of, 208
Instalment sale contract, form, 206
  provisions, 206
Instalment sales financing, 205
Insurance, 346
  credit, 520
  fire, 347
  liability and compensation, 349
  life, 349
  mandatory, 350
  of profits, 520
  purpose of, 346, 520
Intangible assets, 322

Interchange service, credit, 250
  discussion of, 267
  reports, 557, 560
  (*See also* Mercantile agencies)
Interest, on anticipations, 180
  on delinquent accounts, 180, 437
Inventory, 316
  accuracy of, 317
  analysis, 319
  estimation of, 383
  financing, 152–153
    by field warehousing, 162
  valuation of, 317
  (*See also* Ratios)
Investigations, personal, 138
  reasons for, 103
  by telephone, 140
Investigator, qualifications of, 139
Investment banks, function of, 128
Investment credit, 59, 127
  bonds, 65
  shares of stock, 66
Investments, analysis of, 320
Invoice file, use in collections, 401

Joint stock companies, 109
Judgment, definition of, 444
  effect of, 444
  execution of, 444
Judgment note, legality of, 65

King, Willford I., 16

Last in–first out inventory method, 318
Legal aspects of credit information, 142
Legal composition of business as credit
    factor, 105
Letter of indication, 82
Letters, collection (*see* Collection let-
    ters)
  of credit, 82
    application for, 84
    commercial, 83
    illustration, 83, 85
    travelers', 82
    variations of, 84
Liabilities, 312
  accrued, 326

Liabilities, classification of, 312
  current, 312–327
  long-term, 328–329
  contingent, 332
Libel in collection letters, defenses
    against, 419
Licensed lenders, 195
Life insurance, 349
  investigation of, 350
Limits (*see* Credit limits)
Liquidation (*see* Bankruptcy)
Loan sharks, 195
  borrowers defrauded by, 195
  interest rates of, 195
Loans and discounts, classification of,
    133
  secured by accounts receivable, 157
Location as credit factor, 110
Long-term liabilities, 312, 328, 329
Long-term reserves, 329
Los Angeles Lumber Products Co.,
    Case v., 499n.
Lyon Furniture Mercantile Agency, 244
  collection department, 245
  Lyon-Red Book, 244
    key to, 245
  method of operation, 244
  "result" sheet, 247

Machinery, 311
Management as credit factor, 112, 185
Marketable securities, 320
Massachusetts Trust, 110
Maximum sales and minimum losses,
    181
Mercantile agencies, advantages of co-
    operation, 122
  Bishop's Agency, Inc., 280
  classification of, 120
  Collection Services, 228, 245, 413
  Credit Bureau of Greater New York,
    262
  Credit Interchange Bureau, 250
  derivation of name, 120
  discussion of service, 231, 235, 247,
    267
  Dun & Bradstreet, Inc. (*see* Dun &
    Bradstreet, Inc.)
  influence on business, 122, 125
  interchange service, 222, 248, 250,
    262

Mercantile agencies, and law, 121, 123
  liability for gross negligence, 123
  listing of, 121
  Lyon Furniture Mercantile Agency,
    244, 245
  National Credit Office, Inc., 236
  National Retail Credit Association,
    250, 261
  origin and growth of, 211, 235
  prejudice against, 121
  Proudfoot's Commercial Agency, Inc.,
    280
  reports, trade investigation section,
    219
      analysis of, 219
  special, 235
  use of, by banks, 124
Mercantile credit (*see* Trade credit)
Merchandise (*see* Inventory)
Mill, John Stuart, 8
Miscellaneous assets, 321
Mitchell, W. C., 15, 18
Morris Plan banks, 197
Mortgages, effect on risk, 328

National Association of Credit Manage-
    ment, 23, 90
  achievements of, 98
  collection departments, 97
  Credit Research Foundation, 92
  Foreign Credit Interchange Bureau,
    96
  Fraud Prevention Department, 91
  industry credit groups, 97
  local association of, 91
  organization of, 90
  publications of, 98
  Washington Service Bureau, 98
National Business Year Council, 310n.
National Credit Interchange Service
    System, 252
  analysis of reports, 254
  operation of, 252
  organization of, 252
  (*See also* Interchange service)
National Credit Office, Inc., 236
  Bank Service Department, 238
    commercial paper reports, 239
  C.I.A. reports, 242
  Credit News, 242

National Credit Office, Inc., credit reports,
    240, 550, 556
  group meetings, 242
  industries covered, 237
  Market Planning Service, 239
  suggested credit lines, how deter-
    mined, 240, 242
  textile department subscribers, extent
    of, 240
  textiles, major divisions of, 239
National Institute of Credit, 94
  awards, 95
  courses of study, 95
  Director of Education, 96
  organization of, 94
National Retail Credit Association,
    organization, 261
  services, 262
  (*See also* Mercantile agencies)
Natural business year, 310
Negotiable instruments, 60
  characteristics of, 61
  essentials of, 61
  negotiation of, 62
  presentation of, 62
  protection to holder of, 61
  protest of, 63
    form, 63
Net income, how estimated, 383
  as return to equity, 344
Net working capital related to inven-
    tory, 367
Net worth, 312
  question of amount, 331
  relation of, to debt, 365
    to fixed assets, 366
  tangible, 331
New York Institute of Credit, 96
Northern Pacific Ry. v. Boyd, 499n.
Notes (*see* Promissory notes)
Notes payable, analysis of, 325
Notes receivable, analysis of, 315

Office mechanism, importance of, 39
Opinions as basis of judgment, 115
Orders, handling of, 180
Overdue accounts, collecting interest on,
    180
Overtrading, 367
  danger of, 368

Paper (*see* Commercial paper)
Par payment of checks, 133
Par payment and nonpar payment banks, 133
Partial payments, 440
Partnership, advantages of, 107
  creditors' claim against, 106
  disadvantages of, 107
  ideal combination in, 107
  termination of, 107
  types of, 106
Pawnbrokers, 195
Personal collector, 411
Personal credit (*see* Consumer credit)
Personal finance companies, 195
Personal interview, 117
  how to conduct, 118
  plant visits, 119
  as source of credit information, 117
Personal investigations, 138
  by adjustment bureau, 515
  advantages, 138
  by banks, 138
  information secured by, 138
  by manufacturers, 138
Personal investigator, qualifications of, 139
Plant, machinery, and tools, 321
  visits as source of information on, 119
  (*See also* Fixed assets)
Privileged communication, 142
Profit and loss (*see* Financial reports; Income report)
Promissory notes, 63–65
  advantages of, 64
  as collection instruments, 407
  definition of, 63
  special forms, 65
  use in business, 64
Proof of claim, filing, 494
  order of priority, 495
Protest for nonpayment, form, 63
  notice of, 63
Proudfoot's Commercial Agency, Inc., 280
Proximo terms, 173
Public credit, 127
Public records as source of credit information, 125

Quick assets, 311

Rating book (*Reference Book*), 222
Ratios, 355
  business failures, 466, 507
  choice of, 355
  compensating, 357
  Foulke's, 569–573
    14 important, table of, 569–573
  horizontal, 380
  net working capital to inventory, 367
  net worth, to debt, 365
    to fixed assets, 366
  others, 356
  receivables to merchandise, 364
  sales, to fixed assets, 362
    to inventory, 360
    to net profit, 343
    to net working capital, 362
    to net worth, 363
    to receivables, 359
    to selling expense, 342
  standard, 357
  trend of, 379
  2 to 1 current, fallacy of, 334
  vertical, 380
  (*See also* Statement analysis)
Receivables, hypothecation of, and merchandise, 153, 156
Receiver, in bankruptcy, appointment of, 491
  fees of, 492
  in equity, 476
Receiverships, 475, 514
  bankruptcy, 478
  and equity, compared, 478
  equity, causes for, 476
    creditors' rights in, 477
Recission, right of, 455
Referee in bankruptcy, 490
  duties and compensation of, 491
Reference Book, Dun & Bradstreet, Inc., 222
Reorganizations (*see* Corporate reorganization)
Replevin, legal procedure in, 456
  right of, 455
Reserves, definition of, 329
  for doubtful accounts, 316
  interpretation of, 329
  for taxes, 327
  types of, 329
Retail credit, application, 198, 574

Retail credit, basis of, 198
  and competition, 192, 200
  financing instalment sales, 205
  justification of, 192
  proper basis for, 192
  sources of information, 199
  terms, 201
  and trade credit, 190
  trends in, 201
  (*See also* Consumer credit; Instalment credit)
Retailer, small, problems of, 202
Returns and cancellations, 452
Risk, acceptability of, 48
Robert Morris Associates, 23, 99
Robinson-Patman Act, 174*n.*
Rubber stamps, use in collections, 406

Sale terms (*see* Terms of sale)
Sales, adequacy of, 341, 359
  analysis of, facts disclosed by, 359
    (*See also* Statement analysis)
  ratio of, to fixed assets, 362
    to inventory, 360
    to net profit, 343
    to net working capital, 362
    to net worth, 363
    to receivables, 359
    to selling expense, 342
Sales finance companies (*see* Finance companies)
Salesman, attitude of, to credit department, 272
  as collector, 412, 436
  as credit assistant, 271
  credit information of, 273
  education of, 276
  reliability of information, 276
  report forms, 274
Season datings, 170
Seasonal cycle, 13
Securities Exchange Commission, 501
Shares of stock, classification of, 67
  as credit instruments, 66
Single-name paper, 134
Single proprietorship, 105
Slow payments, reasons for, 394–396
Small-loan companies, 195
Small-loan institutions, loans of, 194, 196, 197

Small-loan laws, 195
Small loans, bad-debt losses in, 196
  costs of making, 196
  rates, 195, 196
Solvency, 468
Somers, Helen M., 421
Source and application of funds, 378, 381
Sources of information, classification of, 116
  direct, 116
  indirect, 116
  judgment in selecting, 115
  personal investigators, 140
  (*See also* Banks; Mercantile agencies; Trade credit)
Special mercantile agencies, advantages and disadvantages, 235
Spreading statements, 372
Standard ratios, 357
State Street Trust Co. v. Ernst et al., 308*n.*
Statement, monthly, use in collections, 405
Statement analysis, comparative, methods, 371, 376
  break-even point, 385
  common size statements, 372, 375
  comparison by inspection, 378
  forms for, 373, 374
  source and application of funds, 378, 381
  spreading statements, 372
  trial balance, 382
  (*See also* Financial reports)
Steiner, W. H., 168–169
Stock, 66, 67
Stoppage in transit, right of, 454
Subordinated debt, 328, 329
Suit and judgment, 444
Supplementary proceedings, 445
Surplus, definition of, 330
  how acquired, 331
Surplus account, reconciliation of, 344

Taxes, reserve for, 327
Telegram as collection instrument, 410
Telephone, in collections, 409
  in investigations, 140

Terms of sale, 167
  cash, 172
  C.B.D., 172
  C.O.D., 172
  credit period, 167
  dating, 169
  discount, 174
  E.O.M., 173
  factors influencing, 167
  instalment, 203
  interpretation of, 179
  M.O.M., 173
  proximo, 173
  regular, 168
  retail, 201
  R.O.G., 173
  special, 172
  (*See also* Cash discount)
Third-party proceedings, 459
Title, passage of, 451
Trade acceptance, abuse of, 78
  advantages of, 78
  as asset, analysis of, 316
  definition of, 76
  form, 77
  procedure under, 77
  proper use of, 78
  reasons for nonuse of, 79
Trade credit, classification of risks, 182
  compared, with banks, 165
    with retail credit, 191
  definition of, 165
  department files of, 37
  efficiency of, measurement, 44
  function of, 32
  measure of risk, 181
  as source of credit information, 120
  trends in, 166
Trade discount, 174
Trade investigators, information secured
    by, 140

Trade stories, 120
Trading assets (*see* Current assets)
Travelers' checks, 80
Travelers' letters of credit, 82
Treasurer's letter in collections, 435
Trial balance, 382
  analysis of, 382
  illustration, 383–385
Trust receipt, definition of, 86
  in domestic trade, 86
  form, 87
  function of, 86
  weakness of, 86
Trust Receipts Act (Uniform), 88
Trustee in bankruptcy, fees, 493
  how elected, 492
  importance of, 492
Trusts, 109
Turnover, merchandise, 360
Type of business as credit factor, 104

Ultramares Corp. v. Touch Niven, 308n.
Uniform Commercial Code, 61n.
Uniform Trust Receipts Act, 88
Unpaid seller's lien, 453

Vertical ratios, 380

Wall, Alexander, 356
Warehouse receipts, as collateral, 81
  definition of, 81
Warehousing, field, 81, 162
Wealth defined, 6
"Where got, where gone" statement, 376
Working capital, 324, 334
  definitions, 334
  net, 335
  (*See also* Current position)
Working and current assets, 335